SAS Publishing

D1872224

SAS/GRAPH® 9.1 Reference
Volume 2

The Power to Know®

The correct bibliographic citation for this manual is as follows: SAS Institute Inc. 2004. *SAS/GRAPH® 9.1 Reference, Volumes 1, 2, and 3*. Cary, NC: SAS Institute Inc.

SAS/GRAPH® 9.1 Reference, Volumes 1, 2, and 3

ISBN 1-59047-195-4

SAS Institute Inc., SAS Campus Drive, Cary, North Carolina 27513.

1st printing, January 2004

Contents

CHAPTER

17

Generating Web Output with the Annotate Facility

Overview of Generating Web Output with the Annotate Facility

You can use the Annotate facility to enhance your Web presentation, or you can generate an entire Web presentation using Annotate and the GANNO procedure. In either case you can use the Annotate facility to generate drill-down presentations with the GIF, JPEG, or PNG device driver.

Note that your graph may conceal your annotations unless your annotations are specified with the option WHEN=AFTER. Specifying this option causes the annotations to be displayed after the graph, so that they will not be occluded. This is particularly important for interactive presentations, where the back wall of the graph may be made visible by default.

Note also that annotations disappear when the Web user selects another graph type. The annotations reappear when the Web user selects the Refresh button in the Web browser.

To learn how to use Annotate data sets to generate drill-down Web presentations, see "Generating Web Output with the Annotate Facility" on page 499.

Reference information on generating and applying Annotate data sets is provided in Chapter 25, "Annotate Dictionary," on page 613. Usage information is provided in Chapter 24, "Using Annotate Data Sets," on page 587. For information on the GANNO procedure, see Chapter 26, "The GANNO Procedure," on page 707.

Generating Web Output with the Annotate Facility

You can use the Annotate facility to generate drill-down Web presentations in two ways: you can use PROC GANNO and an Annotate data set as the sole basis of a drill-down presentation, or you can apply an Annotate data set to add drill-down functionality to a Web presentation that is generated with the GIF, JPEG, or PNG device driver.

When to Use PROC GANNO to Generate Web Output

You can use ODS, the GANNO procedure, an Annotate data set, and a device driver to generate a Web presentation with drill-down links. This method of generating a drill-down presentation is preferred if you do not need to use an image from another SAS/GRAPH procedure in your Web presentation. For example, you could use PROC GANNO to generate an HTML output file that showed a JPEG image, with accompanying text, and a selectable label containing the text "Click Here". Larger presentations with multiple drill-down links are also entirely feasible.

To generate a drill-down graph with PROC GANNO, see "Generating Web Links with the Annotate Facility" on page 500.

When to Apply Annotate Data Sets to Web Output

You can use Annotate data sets to add drill-down links to Web presentations generated by any procedure that uses the ANNOTATE= option. The Web presentation must be generated with the GIF, JPEG, or PNG device driver.

Using an Annotate data set to add drill-down links is preferable in the following circumstances:

- When you cannot add drill-down functionality by other means. Some SAS/GRAPH statements do not support the HTML= option, which SAS/GRAPH needs to generate an image map in the HTML output file. If the procedure does support the ANNOTATE= option, then you can use that procedure as the basis of a drill-down Web presentation.
- When you do not want Web users to drill down by selecting graph elements. For example, if you did not want your Web users to drill down by selecting the bars in a bar chart, you could define graphics elements with drill-down links using the Annotate facility.

To use the Annotate facility to add drill-down links to a Web presentation, see "Generating Web Links with the Annotate Facility" on page 500.

Generating Web Links with the Annotate Facility

Follow these steps if you are adding drill-down links to a Web presentation or if you are generating an entire Web presentations with PROC GANNO:

1. Plan your Web presentation so that you know how and where you want to apply Annotate graphical elements with drill-down links. Also determine your drill-down URLs.
2. Generate an Annotate data set. Elements that can be defined as drill-down hot zones are generated by Annotate functions that use the HTML variable. To see which functions use the HTML variable, refer to Figure 24.4 on page 593. To generate the Annotate data set, see Chapter 24, "Using Annotate Data Sets," on page 587.
3. Specify the GIF, JPEG, or PNG device driver using the DEVICE= option in a GOPTIONS statement.
4. Close the listing destination and open an HTML output file in ODS.

```
ods listing close;
ods html file="annodril.htm"
    style=science;
```

5 Generate a GIF, JPEG, or PNG image and identify the Annotate data set. Use the GANNO procedure or another SAS/GRAPH procedure that uses the ANNOTATE= option.

6 Close the HTML output file.

7 Generate any additional HTML files or images as needed to provide files that are named in drill-down URLs.

Examples

For an example of creating web output with the GANNO procedure, see Example 4 on page 719.

For examples of applying Annotate data sets to web output, see "Examples" on page 604.

CHAPTER 18

Creating Interactive Treeview Diagrams

Creating Treeview Diagrams

The Treeview applet generates node/link diagrams for hierarchical data, with optional fish-eye distortion that highlights the central area of interest, as shown in the following figure:

Display 18.1 A Treeview Applet Web Link Diagram

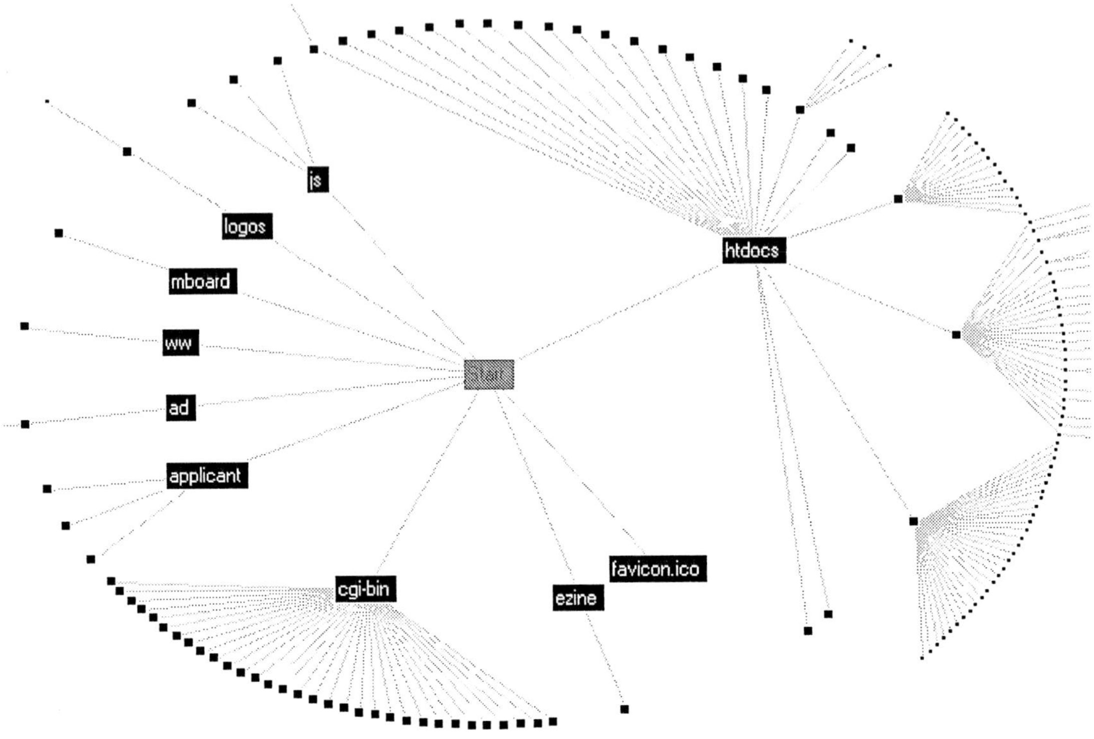

You can scroll across the diagram by selecting off-center nodes or by searching for nodes. Positioning the cursor over a node can display optional data tips. If you then right-click, you access a pop-up menu. The menu enables you to highlight or hide subtrees or drill-down to an optional URL. The menu also enables you to select all nodes, display all previously hidden nodes, reset the view, display applet help, and search for nodes using various search parameters.

SAS/GRAPH programming for the Treeview applet differs from some of the other applets in that it does not use ODS, a device driver specification, or a SAS/GRAPH procedure. Instead, the DS2TREE macro references data sets to generate and configure an HTML output file that runs the Treeview applet.

When to Use the Treeview Applet

The Treeview applet is well-suited for the illustration of hierarchical data sets. The fish-eye distortion factor, coupled with extensive node selection features, means that a single node/link diagram can accommodate large data sets. Applet parameters can be set to specify the layout of the diagram. You specify a starting node, and then you specify how the other nodes are to be drawn in relation to that node. The resulting diagram can be as complex as the Web link diagram in Display 18.1 on page 504, or as simple as an organizational tree for a department in a corporation.

If you need a higher degree of configurability to illustrate weighted relationships between the nodes and links in your diagram, then the Constellation applet might be a better choice than the Treeview applet, as described in "Creating Constellation Diagrams" on page 513.

Interactivity Enabled by the Treeview Applet

The following picture shows the pop-up menu that a user can invoke by right-clicking a Treeview diagram in a browser. The picture shows all the options that are available for interacting with the diagram. For a description of these options, right-click on any Treeview diagram and select **`Treeview Applet Help`** from the pop-up menu.

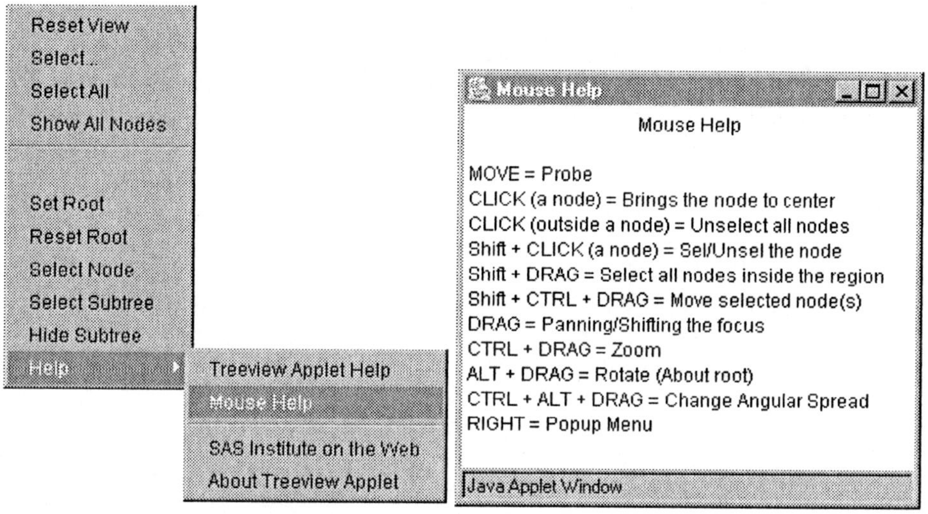

Programming with the DS2TREE Macro for the Treeview Applet

The DS2TREE macro generates HTML output files for the Treeview applet. Macro arguments enable you to generate and format an HTML file and to customize the appearance of your node/link diagram.

Follow the steps shown in the following code to generate a Web presentation that runs the Treeview applet.

```
/* 1. Define the name and storage location of the HTML output file */
/*    and the location of the jar files.                            */
%let htmlfile = your_path_and_filename.htm;
%let jarfiles = http://your_path_to_archive;

/* 2. Define a data set that contains parent-child relationships. */
data myorg;
input name $ empno mgrno deptname $22. deptcode $;
cards;
Peter      2620   1420   Documentation            DOC
Linda      6915   1420   Research & Development   R&D
Maria      1320   1420   Legal                    LGL
Vince      1420   1750   Executive                EXE
Jim        6710   6915   Quality Assurance        QA
Nancy     22560   6915   Quality Assurance        QA
Patrick   28470   6915   Quality Assurance        QA
Elsa      33075   6915   Development              DEV
Clement   22010   6915   Development              DEV
Murielle   3020   6915   Development              DEV
```

```
David     11610   6915   Research                RES
;
run;

/* 3. Specify titles and footnotes: (optional). */
title1 'Organizational Chart';
footnote1 'To display the department name, place the cursor over a node.';
footnote2 'To rotate the chart, click and drag a node.';

/* 4. Run the DS2TREE macro. */
/* You must change the CODEBASE= argument (using either http://      */
/* or a directory path such as C:/) to specify the location of your  */
/* sas.graph.treeview.jar file and its associated jar files          */
/* (sas.graph.nld.jar, sas.graph.j2d.jar). See the CODEBASE= argument in:   */
/* ''Arguments for the APPLET Tag'' on page 536.*/
/* (Make sure that ods listing is open when running macro.) */
ods listing;
%ds2tree(ndata=myorg,          /* data sets and files */
         codebase=&jarfiles,
         xmltype=inline,
         htmlfile=&htmlfile,
         nid=empno,            /* roles of variables */
         nparent=mgrno,
         ntip=deptname,
         nlabel=name,
         height=500,           /* appearance */
         width=600,
         tcolor=navy,
         fcolor=black);
```

Display the resulting HTML file in a Web browser to run the Treeview applet and display the node/link diagram.

The preceding example shows how the arguments of the DS2TREE macro identify a data set and specify how the variables in that data set are to be interpreted to generate the diagram. Appearance arguments define the size of the diagram and the color of the text in the title and footnotes.

For information on generating more complex diagrams for the Treeview applet, see "Enhancing Presentations for the Treeview Applet" on page 506.

For definitions of all DS2TREE macro arguments, see "DS2TREE Macro Arguments" on page 507.

Enhancing Presentations for the Treeview Applet

The Treeview applet displays interactive node/link diagrams. The diagrams are generated in SAS using a hierarchical data set and the DS2TREE macro, as described in "Programming with the DS2TREE Macro for the Treeview Applet" on page 505.

To enhance Treeview applet presentations, specify additional arguments for the DS2TREE macro. The following table describes some of the available enhancements and identifies the DS2TREE arguments that implement them. For a complete list of macro arguments, see "Macro Arguments" on page 535.

Table 18.1 Treeview Applet Enhancements

Enhancement	DS2TREE Argument
Specify a stylesheet to format your HTML output file.	SSFILE, SSFREF, SSHREF, SSMEDIA, SSREL, SSREV, SSTITLE, SSTYPE
Specify dash patterns for link lines.	LSTIP, LSTIPFAC
Specify a background color, image, or drill-down URL.	IBACKPOS, IBACKLOC, IBACKURL
Add pop-up data tips to nodes.	NTIP, TIPS
Add drill-down URLs to nodes.	NURL
Specify an action for the pull-down menu.	ACTION, NACTION
Change the amount of fisheye distortion.	FACTOR, FISHEYE
Specify a JavaScript response to node selection.	SELIFUNC, SELLFUNC, SELUFUNC
Determine layout of diagram.	SPREAD, TREEDIR, TREESPAN

DS2TREE Macro Arguments

The arguments of the DS2TREE macro specify the configuration of the HTML output file, the location of the data that is used to generate the diagram, and the configuration of the applet's interactive features.

The DS2TREE macro uses the following syntax:

%DS2TREE(*argument1=value1*, *argument2=value2*, ...);

The arguments of the DS2TREE macro can be divided into the following categories:

- "Arguments for the APPLET Tag" on page 536. The CODEBASE argument is required.
- "DS2TREE and DS2CONST Arguments for Data Definition" on page 537. For DS2TREE the arguments NDATA and NID are required.
- "Arguments for Generating HTML and XML Files" on page 544.
- "DS2TREE and DS2CONST Arguments for Diagram Appearance" on page 545.
- "Arguments for Page Formatting" on page 552.
- "Arguments for Stylesheets" on page 554.
- "Arguments for the SAS TITLE and FOOTNOTE Tags" on page 556.
- "Arguments for Character Transcoding" on page 561.

Sample Programs: Treeview Macro

The following sample programs generate Treeview diagrams:

- "Sample Treeview with XML Embedded in the HTML File" on page 507
- "Sample Treeview with XML Written to an External File" on page 509
- "Treeview with Hotspots" on page 510.

Sample Treeview with XML Embedded in the HTML File

This sample program generates a very simple Treeview diagram.

Results Shown in a Browser

The following is the Treeview diagram that is generated by the sample code. Notice the pop-up menu. Because the diagram is displayed by the Treeview applet, it is not just a static picture. A user can manipulate the diagram, for example, by bringing selected nodes to the center, spreading out the nodes, and searching for nodes.

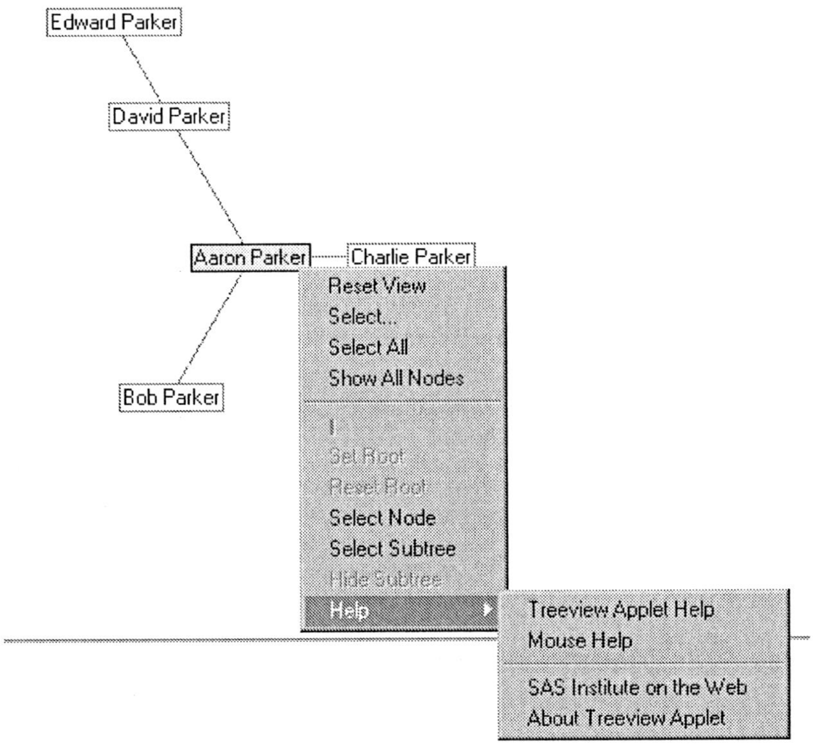

SAS Code

The following is the complete SAS code used to generate the Treeview diagram from a SAS data set. Note the following:

- The parameter HTMLFILE= specifies the complete path and name of the HTML file to be created by the DS2TREE macro. If you want to run this sample, then change the values of HTMLFILE and CODEBASE to the locations that you want to use.
- The parameter XMLTYPE=INLINE tells the DS2TREE macro that the XML it generates from the SAS data set should be included inline in the HTML file.
- The parameter CUTOFF=1 specifies that every node on the graph be labeled. Use this parameter to suppress node labels for diagrams with numerous nodes.

```
data father_and_sons;
input id $8. name $15. father $8.;
cards;
aaron   Aaron Parker
bob     Bob Parker     aaron
charlie Charlie Parker aaron
david   David Parker   aaron
edward  Edward Parker  david
```

```
;
run;

/* make sure ods listing is open when running macro */
ods listing;
 /* run the macro */
%ds2tree(ndata=father_and_sons,  /* data set */
        /* specify complete url if jar files are not in same directory as html file */
        codebase=http://your_path_to_archive,
        xmltype=inline,
        htmlfile=your_path_and_filename.htm,
        nid=id,          /* use this variable as the id */
        cutoff=1,        /* display the name on every node */
        nparent=father,/* this identifies the parent of each node */
        nlabel=name,     /* display this on each node */
        height=400,
        width=400,
        tcolor=navy,
        fcolor=black);
```

Sample Treeview with XML Written to an External File

This sample program generates the same Treeview as the previous example, "Sample Treeview with XML Embedded in the HTML File" on page 507, with the difference that the XML is written to an external file instead of being embedded in the HTML file.

SAS Code

The following is the complete SAS code to generate the Treeview diagram from a SAS data set. Note the following:

- The parameter HTMLFILE= specifies the complete path and name of the HTML file to be created by the DS2TREE macro. If you want to run this sample, then change the value of HTMLFILE to something that makes sense for you.
- The parameter XMLTYPE=EXTERNAL tells the DS2TREE that the XML it generates from the SAS data set should be written to an external file.
- The parameter XMLFILE= specifies the path and file name of the XML file to be created.
- The parameter XMLURL= specifies how the XML file is to be addressed from within the HTML file.
- The parameter CUTOFF=1 specifies that every node on the graph be labeled. Use this parameter with a value between 0 and 1 to suppress node labels for diagrams with numerous nodes.

```
data father_and_sons;
input id $8. name $15. father $8.;
cards;
aaron   Aaron Parker
bob     Bob Parker     aaron
charlie Charlie Parker aaron
david   David Parker   aaron
edward  Edward Parker  david
;
```

```
run;
goptions reset=all;
/* make sure ods listing is open when running macro */
ods listing;
 /* run the macro */
%ds2tree(ndata=father_and_sons,  /* data set */
         codebase=http://your_path_to_archive,
         htmlfile=your_path_and_filename.htm,
         xmltype=external,
         makexml=y,
         xmlurl=http://www.xtz.com/weboutput_treeview2_sample.xml,
         xmlfile=u:/public/weboutput_treeview2_sample.xml,
         nid=id,         /* as the id, use this variable specified here */
         cutoff=1,       /* display the name on every node */
         nparent=father,/* this identifies the parent of each node */
         nlabel=name,    /* display the value of this variable on each node */
         height=400,
         width=400,
         tcolor=navy,
         fcolor=black);
```

Treeview with Hotspots

This sample program generates the same Treeview as the previous example, "Sample Treeview with XML Embedded in the HTML File" on page 507, with the difference that a node is associated with a URL and can be activated by a user double-clicking the node.

SAS Code

The following is the complete SAS code to generate the Treeview diagram from a SAS data set. Note the following:

- The parameter NURL= specifies that the URL to be opened when the corresponding node is double-clicked.
- The parameter DRILTARG=_TOP specifies that the HTML file is to be opened in the same window as the Treeview diagram instead of in a new window, as is the default.

```
data father_and_sons;
input id $8. name $15. father $8. url $30.;
cards;
aaron   Aaron Parker           http://www.xyz.com/index.html
bob     Bob Parker     aaron   http://www.xyz.com/index.html
charlie Charlie Parker aaron   http://www.xyz.com/index.html
david   David Parker   aaron   http://www.xyz.com/index.html
edward  Edward Parker  david   http://www.xyz.com/index.html
;
run;
/* make sure ods listing is open when running macro */
ods listing;
/* run the macro */
%ds2tree(ndata=father_and_sons,  /* data set */
         /* specify complete url if jar files are not in same directory as html file */
         codebase=http://your_path_to_archive,
         xmltype=inline,
```

```
htmlfile=your_path_and_filename.htm,
nid=id,         /* as the id, use the variable specified here  */
cutoff=1,       /* display the name on every node */
nparent=father,/* this identifies the parent of each node */
nlabel=name,    /* display the value of this variable on each node */
height=400,
width=400,
tcolor=navy,
fcolor=black,
nurl=url,
driltarg=_top );
```

CHAPTER 19

Creating Interactive Constellation Diagrams

Creating Constellation Diagrams

The Constellation Applet provides interactivity for node/link diagrams that illustrate data that is associative, hierarchical, or requires an arc list. Node and link color and size can be associated with specified data values.

Display 19.1 A Constellation Applet Affinity Diagram

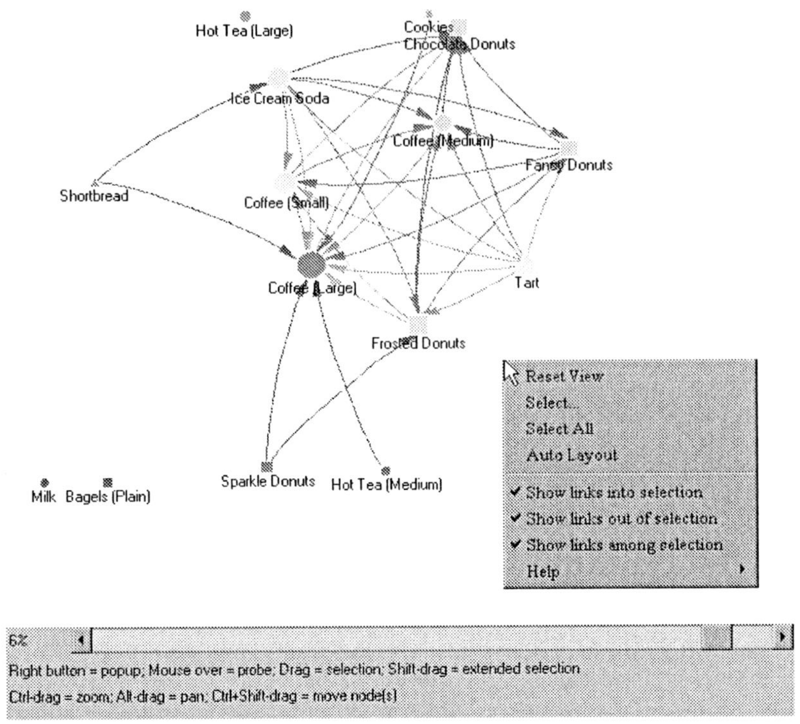

Interactive features of the Constellation Applet include pop-up data tips for links and nodes, subsetting of links via an embedded scroll bar, pan and zoom, fish-eye distortion of a central image area, and several node and link selection modes. You can define drill-down URLs for nodes, specify menu text for the drill-down action, insert a background image, and specify a drill-down URL for the background image, among other enhancements. You can also specify your own JavaScript methods to define responses to drill-down actions.

The Constellation Applet, like the Treeview and Rangeview applets, differ from the other applets in that the diagrams that they display are not generated by SAS/GRAPH procedures. The DS2CONST macro generates and formats an HTML output file, and specifies the appearance and behavior of the node/link diagram based on values in a data set.

When to Use the Constellation Applet

The Constellation Applet is best used to illustrate relationships between links and nodes, which can be shown in affinity, sequence, and Web-click path diagrams, for example. Colors, link line widths, and link directional indicators can be specified to illustrate relationships. Pop-up data tips can be specified for nodes and links, along with drill-down URLs for nodes and for an optional background image. For diagrams that illustrate associative data, an embedded scroll bar subsets the data in the diagram dynamically.

The Constellation Applet can be used to display hierarchical data, but so can the Treeview Applet, which should also be considered for hierarchical diagrams such as organizational trees, because of its unique layout capabilities. For information on the Treeview Applet, see "Creating Treeview Diagrams" on page 503.

Programming with the DS2CONST Macro for the Constellation Applet

The DS2CONST macro enables you to generate complete Web presentations for the Constellation Applet. The macro has a large number of arguments that you can use to generate and format an HTML output file, configure the diagram, and describe how data sets and variables are to be applied to the diagram.

The macro arguments are structured so that you can associate a variable with an aspect of the diagram. The values of the variable are then used for that part of the diagram. For example, the NLABEL argument specifies the name of the variable whose values define the text labels that are to be applied to the nodes. Other arguments provide default values that are used when no variable value is provided.

Descriptions of all of the arguments of the DS2CONST macro are provided in "DS2CONST Macro Arguments" on page 518.

Follow the steps outlined in the following code to use the DS2CONST macro to generate a Web presentation for the Constellation Applet.

```
/* 1. Define the name and storage location of the HTML output file, */
/*    and the location of the jar files.                             */
%let htmlfile = your_path_and_filename.htm;
%let jarfiles = http://your_path_to_archive;

/* 2. Define a nodes data set */
data nodedata;
length nodeLabel $8 nodeId xLoc yLoc 8;
input nodeLabel nodeID xLoc yLoc;
cards;
Snacks    5  375   25
SftDrink  3   25   25
Books     2  200   25
BeerWine  4  200  300
Dairy     1   25  300
Bakery    0  375  300
;
run;

/* 3. Define a links data set */
data linkdata;
length from to value 8 tip $45;
input from to value @13 tip $char45.;
cards;
0  0  0      Bakery => Bakery #0
0  1  0.7    Bakery => Dairy #0.7
0  2  0.1    Bakery => Books #0.1
0  3  0.3    Bakery => SftDrink #0.3
0  4  0.1    Bakery => BeerWine #0.1
0  5  0.2    Bakery => Snacks #0.2
1  0  0.5    Dairy => Bakery #0.5
1  1  0      Dairy => Dairy #0
1  2  0.1    Dairy => Books #0.1
1  3  0.2    Dairy => SftDrink #0.2
1  4  0.3    Dairy => BeerWine #0.3
1  5  0.4    Dairy => Snacks #0.4
2  0  0.1    Books => Bakery #0.1
2  1  0.2    Books => Dairy #0.2
```

```
2  2  0      Books => Books #0
2  3  0.3    Books => SftDrink #0.3
2  4  0.3    Books => BeerWine #0.3
2  5  0.3    Books => Snacks #0.3
3  0  0.2    SftDrink => Bakery #0.2
3  1  0.3    SftDrink => Dairy #0.3
3  2  0.2    SftDrink => Books #0.2
3  3  0      SftDrink => SftDrink #0
3  4  0.6    SftDrink => BeerWine #0.6
3  5  0.8    SftDrink => Snacks #0.8
4  0  0.2    BeerWine => Bakery #0.2
4  1  0.4    BeerWine => Dairy #0.4
4  2  0.1    BeerWine => Books #0.1
4  3  0.5    BeerWine => SftDrink #0.5
4  4  0      BeerWine => BeerWine #0
4  5  0.9    BeerWine => Snacks #0.9
5  0  0.3    Snacks => Bakery #0.3
5  1  0.4    Snacks => Dairy #0.4
5  2  0.1    Snacks => Books #0.1
5  3  0.5    Snacks => SftDrink #0.5
5  4  0.5    Snacks => BeerWine #0.5
5  5  0      Snacks => Snacks #0
run;

/* 4. Define a title  */
title1 'Grocery Affinity Diagram.';

/* make sure ods listing is open when running macro */
ods listing;
/* 5. Run the DS2CONST macro  */
%ds2const(ndata=nodedata,
          ldata=linkdata,
          datatype=arcs,
          cnode=red,
          colormap=y,
          height=650,
          width=600,
          codebase=&jarfiles,
          htmlfile=&htmlfile,
          nid=nodeID,
          nlabel=nodelabel,
          nx=xLoc,
          ny=yLoc,
          lfrom=from,
          lto=to,
          lvalue=value,
          ltip=tip);
```

Note: You must change the CODEBASE= argument (using either *http://* or a directory path such as *C:/*) to specify the location of your sas.graph.constapp.jar file and its associated jar files (sas.graph.nld.jar, sas.graph.j2d.jar). See the CODEBASE= argument in "Arguments for the APPLET Tag" on page 536. △

Display the resulting HTML file in a Web browser to run the applet and generate the diagram.

Arguments in the DS2CONST macro identify the name of the nodes and links data sets. In the nodes data set, arguments identify a node ID variable and a node label variable. Other arguments identify the links data set and the variables that define the nodes at the start and end of each link line.

For information on more complex presentations for the Constellation Applet, see "Enhancing Presentations for the Constellation Applet" on page 517.

Enhancing Presentations for the Constellation Applet

The Constellation Applet displays interactive node/link diagrams. These diagrams can show relationships between nodes and links. The Constellation Applet displays affinity, sequence, and ring diagrams that are generated out of arc, associative, or hierarchical data sets. The Constellation Applet provides a number of interactive features by default, as described in "Creating Constellation Diagrams" on page 513.

Enhancements to Constellation Applet presentations are configured in your SAS/GRAPH program by specifying arguments in the DS2CONST macro. The following table lists some of the available enhancements and the DS2CONST arguments that implement them. These enhancements enable you to provide data tips and drill-down URLs for nodes and links, and to increase the visible distinctions between the data values that are associated with the nodes and links.

Table 19.1 Constellation Applet Enhancements

Enhancements	DS2CONST Arguments
Specify link weights and configure a scroll bar that controls the display of links based on weight.	LVALUE, MINLNKWT, SCLNKWT
Configure a fish-eye lens for large diagrams.	FACTOR, FISHEYE
Lay out the diagram automatically or as specified in a data set.	LAYOUT
Specify a stylesheet to format the HTML output file.	BDCLASS, SEPCLASS, SPCLASS, SSFILE, SSHREF See "Arguments for Stylesheets" on page 554.
Add pop-up data tips to nodes and links.	LTIP, NTIP
Define responses to node selection by defining JavaScript methods	SELIFUNC, SELNFUND, SELUFUNC
Define drill-down URLs for nodes and links.	LURL, NURL
Specify menu option text for a drill-down action.	ACTION, NACTION
Specify a browser window or frame that displays drill-down URLs.	DRILTARG
Add a background color, image, or drill-down URL.	IBACKLOC, IBACKPOS, IBACKURL,
Specify text colors, fonts, styles, and sizes.	NFNTNAME, NSFNTNAM, CTEXT, CATEXT See "DS2TREE and DS2CONST Arguments for Diagram Appearance" on page 545.

Enhancements	DS2CONST Arguments
Specify colors for nodes and links.	NCOLVAL, NCOLOR, CNODE, LCOLVAL, LCOLOR, CLINK
Specify dashed link lines.	LSTIP and LSTIPFAC

Note that a number of enhancements apply only to associative data sets when you specify the macro argument DATATYPE=ASSOC. The macro argument definitions identify which features apply only to associative data.

The DS2CONST macro requires you to specify node and link data sets. As an enhancement, you can define a node styles data set that contains style information only. You can use the node styles data set to standardize the appearance of a series of diagrams, among other uses.

Reference information on the arguments of the DS2CONST macro is provided in "DS2CONST Macro Arguments" on page 518.

DS2CONST Macro Arguments

The arguments of the DS2CONST macro specify the configuration of the HTML output file, the location of the data that is used to generate the diagram, and the configuration of the applet's interactive features.

The DS2CONST macro uses the following syntax:

%DS2CONST(*argument1=value1*, *argument2=value2*, ...);

The arguments of the DS2CONST macro can be divided into the following categories:

- "Arguments for the APPLET Tag" on page 536. The CODEBASE argument is required.
- "DS2TREE and DS2CONST Arguments for Data Definition" on page 537. For DS2CONST the arguments NDATA, NID, LDATA, and LTO are required.
- "Arguments for Generating HTML and XML Files" on page 544.
- "DS2TREE and DS2CONST Arguments for Diagram Appearance" on page 545.
- "Arguments for Page Formatting" on page 552.
- "Arguments for Stylesheets" on page 554.
- "Arguments for the SAS TITLE and FOOTNOTE Tags" on page 556.
- "Arguments for Character Transcoding" on page 561.

Sample Programs: Constellation Macro

The following sample programs generate these kinds of Constellation diagrams:

- "Constellation Chart with DATATYPE=ARCS" on page 518
- "Constellation Chart with DATATYPE=ASSOC" on page 520
- "Constellation Chart with XML Written to an External File" on page 522
- "Constellation Chart with Hotspots" on page 524.

Constellation Chart with DATATYPE=ARCS

This sample program generates a very simple Constellation diagram. It displays a number of countries and the languages spoken in those countries.

Results Shown in a Browser

The following is the Constellation diagram that is generated by the sample code shown below. Notice the help window. Because the diagram is displayed by the Constellation applet, it is not just a static picture. A user can manipulate the diagram, for example, by moving nodes and searching for nodes. The Mouse Help window in the following diagram documents for the user what interactivity is available (right-click a diagram to invoke the window).

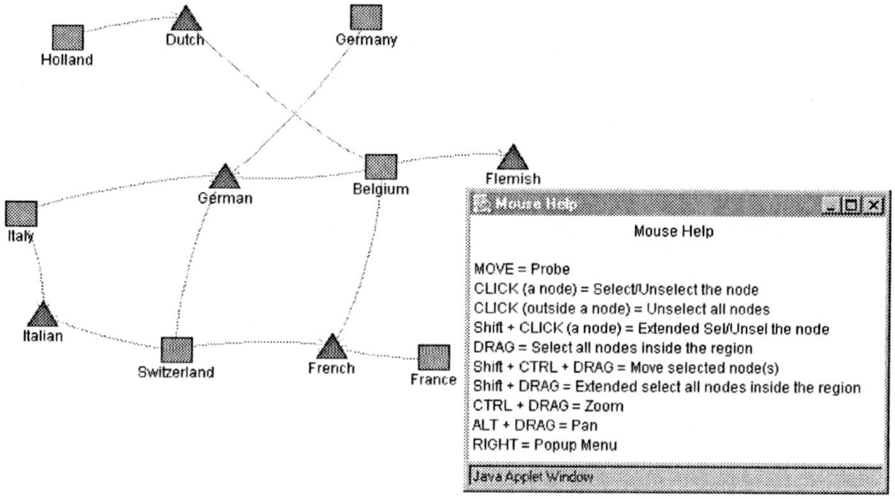

SAS Code

The following is the complete SAS code used to generate a Constellation diagram from a SAS data set. Notice the following:

- The parameter HTMLFILE= specifies the complete path and name of the HTML file to be created by the DS2CONST macro. If you want to run this sample, then change the value of HTMLFILE to the location where you want the HTML file stored.
- The parameter NSHAPE= specifies the variable in the SAS data set that encodes the shape of each node.
- The parameter NCOLOR= specifies the variable in the SAS data set that encodes the color of each node.

```
/*Define a nodes data set of countries and languages  */
data nodedata;
input nodeLabel $15. shape $10. color $8. size;
cards;
France         square    red       .1
Germany        square    red       .1
Italy          square    red       .1
Belgium        square    red       .1
Switzerland    square    red       .1
Holland        square    red       .1
German         triangle  blue      .1
French         triangle  blue      .1
Italian        triangle  blue      .1
Flemish        triangle  blue      .1
```

```
Dutch         triangle  blue      .1
;
run;

/*Define a links data set */
data linkdata;
input from $15. to $15.;
cards;
France         French
Germany        German
Belgium        French
Belgium        German
Belgium        Flemish
Belgium        Dutch
Switzerland    French
Switzerland    German
Switzerland    Italian
Italy          Italian
Italy          German
Holland        Dutch
;
run;
goptions reset=all;
/* make sure ods listing is open when running macro */
ods listing;
 /*Run the DS2CONST macro*/
%ds2const(ndata=nodedata,
          ldata=linkdata,
          datatype=arcs,
          cnode=red,
          colormap=y,
          height=400,
          width=500,
          code=ConstChart,
          codebase=http://your_path_to_archive,
          htmlfile=your_path_and_filename.htm,
          nid=nodelabel,
          nlabel=nodelabel,
          lfrom=from,
          lto=to,
          fntsize=12,
          nshape=shape,
          ncolor=color,
          nsize=size);
```

Constellation Chart with DATATYPE=ASSOC

This sample program generates a very simple Constellation diagram with DATATYPE=ASSOC.

Results Shown in a Browser

The following is the Constellation diagram that is generated by the sample code. A Constellation diagram with DATATYPE=ASSOC depicts the strength of the relationships among variables. Variables in the SAS data set determine the size and color of nodes, as well as the width and color of the lines between nodes. At the bottom of the picture, notice the slider bar which allows a user to choose how many of the links on the diagram are displayed. Move the slider to the left, and only the most important links are displayed. Move the slider to the right, and all of the links are displayed.

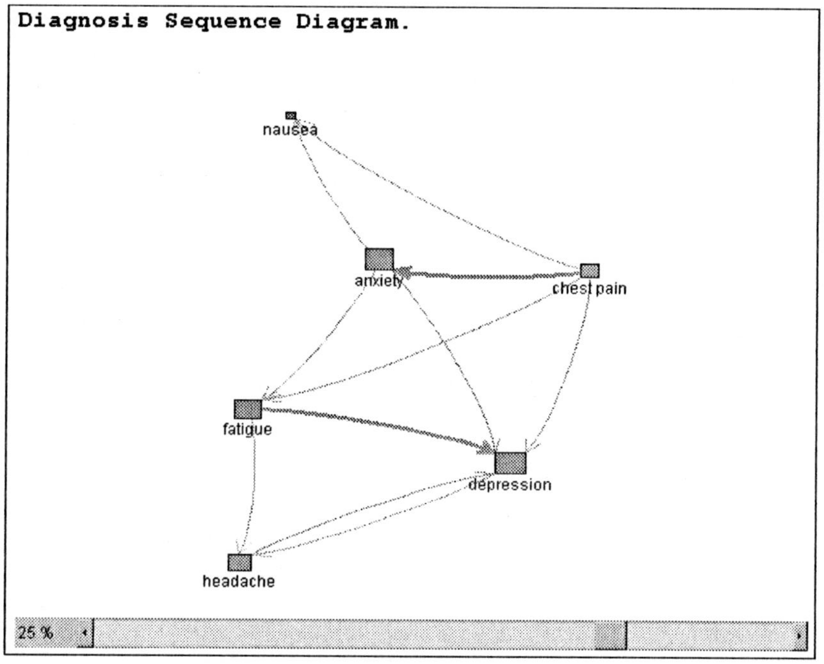

SAS Code

The following is the complete SAS code to generate a Constellation diagram from a SAS data set. Notice the following:

- The parameter HTMLFILE= specifies the complete path and name of the HTML file to be created by DS2CONST. If you want to run this sample, then change the value of HTMLFILE to something that makes sense for you.
- The parameter NVALUE= specifies the data set variable that is used to determine the size and color of each node.
- The parameter LVALUE= specifies the data set variable that is used to determine the width and color of each line between nodes.

```
data nodedata;
length nodeID value 8 label $11 tip $25;
input nodeID value @11 label $char11. @25 tip $char25.;
cards;
0   6556  depression    depression: #6556
1   6322  anxiety       anxiety: #6322
2   5980  fatigue       fatigue: #5980
3   5286  headache      headache: #5286
4   4621  chest pain    chest pain: #4621
6   3149  nausea        nausea: #3149
;
run;

data linkdata;
```

```
length from to linkvalue 8 tip $40;
input from to linkvalue @13 tip $char40.;
cards;
2  0  5978  #5978, Support:63.0790, Conf:99.9833
4  1  4621  #4621, Support:48.7602, Conf:100.0000
1  0  4307  #4307, Support:45.4469, Conf:68.1272
1  2  3964  #3964, Support:41.8276, Conf:62.7017
2  3  3010  #3010, Support:31.7611, Conf:50.3429
0  3  3009  #3009, Support:31.7506, Conf:47.5957
1  6  2772  #2772, Support:29.2498, Conf:43.8469
4  6  2609  #2609, Support:27.5298, Conf:56.4596
4  0  2606  #2606, Support:27.4982, Conf:56.3947
4  2  2263  #2263, Support:23.8789, Conf:48.9721
3  0  1980  #1980, Support:20.8927, Conf:40.6821
3  1  1701  #1701, Support:17.9487, Conf:34.9497
3  2  1701  #1701, Support:17.9487, Conf:34.9497
1  3  1593  #1593, Support:16.8091, Conf:25.1977
4  3  1152  #1152, Support:12.1557, Conf:24.9297
0  6  623   #623, Support:6.5738, Conf:9.8545
2  6  623   #623, Support:6.5738, Conf:10.4198
6  3  597   #597, Support:6.2995, Conf:20.0268
3  6  372   #372, Support:3.9253, Conf:7.6433
6  0  344   #344, Support:3.6298, Conf:11.5398
run;

/* make sure ods listing is open when running macro */
ods listing;

title1 'Diagnosis Sequence Diagram.';
%ds2const(ndata=nodedata,
          ldata=linkdata,
          datatype=assoc,
          minlnkwt=30,
          height=450,
          width=600,
          codebase=http://your_path_to_archive,
          htmlfile=your_path_and_filename.htm,
          colormap=y,
          nid=nodeID,
          nlabel=label,
          nvalue=value,
          fntsize=12,
          ntip=tip,
          lfrom=from,
          lto=to,
          lvalue=linkvalue,
          ltip=tip,
          linktype=arrow);
```

Constellation Chart with XML Written to an External File

This sample program generates the same Constellation diagram as the previous example, "Constellation Chart with DATATYPE=ASSOC" on page 520, with the difference that the XML is written to an external file instead of being embedded in the HTML file.

SAS Code

The following is the complete SAS code to generate the Constellation diagram from a SAS data set. You can notice the following:

- The parameter HTMLFILE= specifies the complete path and name of the HTML file to be created by DS2CONST. If you want to run this sample, then change the value of HTMLFILE to something that makes sense for you.
- The parameter XMLTYPE=EXTERNAL tells the DS2CONST macro that the XML that it generates from the SAS data set should be written to an external file.
- The parameter XMLFILE= specifies the path and file name of the XML file to be created.
- The parameter XMLURL= specifies how the XML file is to be addressed from within the HTML file.

```
data nodedata;
length nodeID value 8 label $11 tip $25;
input nodeID value @11 label $char11. @25 tip $char25.;
cards;
0    6556   depression     depression: #6556
1    6322   anxiety        anxiety: #6322
2    5980   fatigue        fatigue: #5980
3    5286   headache       headache: #5286
4    4621   chest pain     chest pain: #4621
6    3149   nausea         nausea: #3149
;
run;

data linkdata;
length from to linkvalue 8 tip $40;
input from to linkvalue @13 tip $char40.;
cards;
2  0   5978   #5978, Support:63.0790, Conf:99.9833
4  1   4621   #4621, Support:48.7602, Conf:100.0000
1  0   4307   #4307, Support:45.4469, Conf:68.1272
1  2   3964   #3964, Support:41.8276, Conf:62.7017
2  3   3010   #3010, Support:31.7611, Conf:50.3429
0  3   3009   #3009, Support:31.7506, Conf:47.5957
1  6   2772   #2772, Support:29.2498, Conf:43.8469
4  6   2609   #2609, Support:27.5298, Conf:56.4596
4  0   2606   #2606, Support:27.4982, Conf:56.3947
4  2   2263   #2263, Support:23.8789, Conf:48.9721
3  0   1980   #1980, Support:20.8927, Conf:40.6821
3  1   1701   #1701, Support:17.9487, Conf:34.9497
3  2   1701   #1701, Support:17.9487, Conf:34.9497
1  3   1593   #1593, Support:16.8091, Conf:25.1977
4  3   1152   #1152, Support:12.1557, Conf:24.9297
0  6   623    #623, Support:6.5738, Conf:9.8545
2  6   623    #623, Support:6.5738, Conf:10.4198
6  3   597    #597, Support:6.2995, Conf:20.0268
3  6   372    #372, Support:3.9253, Conf:7.6433
```

```
6  0  344    #344, Support:3.6298, Conf:11.5398
run;
title1 'Diagnosis Sequence Diagram.';

/* make sure ods listing is open when running macro */
ods listing;

%ds2const(ndata=nodedata,
          ldata=linkdata,
          datatype=assoc,
          minlnkwt=30,
          height=450,
          width=600,
          codebase=http://your_path_to_archive,
          htmlfile=your_path_and_filename.htm,
          xmltype=external,
          makexml=y,
          xmlurl=http://www.xyz.com/Web_output/const_assoc_external.xml,
          xmlfile=u://Web_output/const_assoc_external.xml,
          colormap=y,
          nid=nodeID,
          nlabel=label,
          nvalue=value,
          fntsize=12,
          ntip=tip,
          lfrom=from,
          lto=to,
          lvalue=linkvalue,
          ltip=tip,
          linktype=arrow);
```

Constellation Chart with Hotspots

This sample program generates the same Constellation diagram as in "Constellation Chart with DATATYPE=ARCS" on page 518 and adds hotspots to the nodes of the diagram.

SAS Code

The following is the complete SAS code to generate the Constellation diagram from a SAS data set. Notice the following:

- The parameter NURL= specifies the variable in the SAS data set that contains the URL to be linked to when a user double-clicks the node.

```
/*Define a nodes data set of countries and languages  */
data nodedata;
input nodeLabel $15. shape $10. color $8. size url $40.;
cards;
France          square    red       .1 http://www.xyz.com
Germany         square    red       .1 http://www.xyz.com/rnd/webgraphs/
Italy           square    red       .1 http://www.xyz.com
```

```
Belgium        square    red      .1 http://www.xyz.com/rnd/webgraphs/
Switzerland    square    red      .1 http://www.xyz.com
Holland        square    red      .1 http://www.xyz.com
German         triangle  blue     .1 http://www.xyz.com
French         triangle  blue     .1 http://www.xyz.com/rnd/webgraphs/odssyntax.htm
Italian        triangle  blue     .1 http://www.xyz.com
Flemish        triangle  blue     .1 http://www.xyz.com
Dutch          triangle  blue     .1 http://www.xyz.com
;
run;

/*Define a links data set: */
data linkdata;
input from $15. to $15.;
cards;
France         French
Germany        German
Belgium        French
Belgium        German
Belgium        Flemish
Belgium        Dutch
Switzerland    French
Switzerland    German
Switzerland    Italian
Italy          Italian
Italy          German
Holland        Dutch
;
run;
goptions reset=all;
 /* make sure ods listing is open when running macro */
ods listing;
 /*Run the DS2CONST macro:*/
%ds2const(ndata=nodedata,
          ldata=linkdata,
                nurl=url,
                datatype=arcs,
          cnode=red,
          colormap=y,
          height=400,
          width=500,
          code=ConstChart,
          codebase=http://your_path_to_archive,
          htmlfile=your_path_and_filename.htm,
          nid=nodelabel,
          nlabel=nodelabel,
          lfrom=from,
          lto=to,
          fntsize=12,
          nshape=shape,
          ncolor=color,
          nsize=size);
```

CHAPTER

20

Creating Critical Success Factor Diagrams

Using the DS2CSF Macro

The Rangeview Applet generates a critical success factor (CSF) diagram, as shown in the following figure.

Display 20.1 Critical Success Factor Diagram

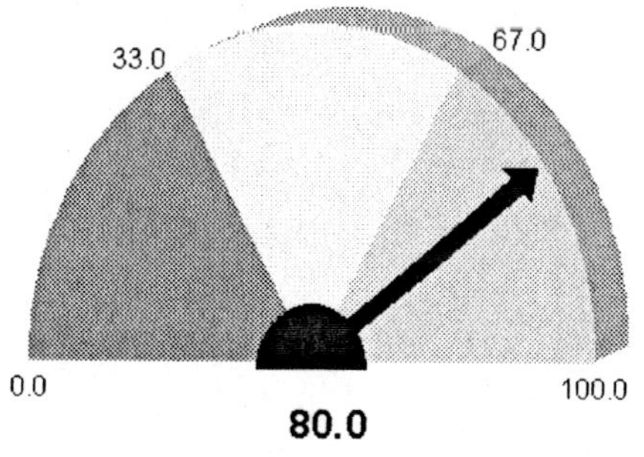

The critical success factor diagram is fully configurable, based on either the classical style (shown above) or a style that resembles a digital gauge, as shown in the following figure.

Display 20.2 Digital Display

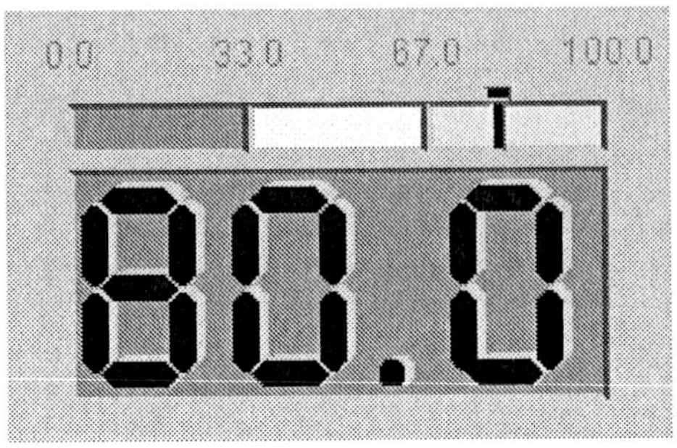

Ranges of values, colors, text sizes, and text fonts are all specified in the SAS/GRAPH program. You can also specify a drill-down URL that will be displayed in a specified browser window when the Web user selects any part of the diagram.

When to Use the Rangeview Applet

The Rangeview Applet provides a simple means of displaying a significant value within a range of values. The drill-down functionality enables you to provide additional information that is related to that critical success factor. While the level of interactivity is not high, the applet can generate CSF diagrams quickly, and uses your own style sheets to standardize the appearance of the diagram.

Programming with the DS2CSF Macro for the Rangeview Applet

The DS2CSF macro generates Web output for the Rangeview Applet. This macro generates and formats an HTML output file, identifies the location of the Rangeview Applet's Java archive, configures the diagram, and provides the data that the applet uses to display the diagram.

Follow the steps shown within this code to generate an HTML output file that will display a critical success factor diagram.

```
/* Define the name and storage location of the HTML output file */
/*    and the location of the jar file                           */
%let htmlfile = your_path_and_filename.htm;
%let jarfile = http://your_path_to_archive;

/* Run a DATA step */
data test;
  myvar=80;
run;

/* Specify an optional title */
title1 'Test Results Indicate Readiness';

/* Run the DS2CSF macro */
%ds2csf(htmlfile=&htmlfile,  /* files and data sets */
        archive=rvapplet.jar,
        codebase=&jarfile,
        openmode=replace,
        data=test,
        var=myvar,               /* CSF variable */
```

```
csftyp=digital,        /* Specify appearance */
bgtype=color,
bg="#E0E0E0",
tcolor="#002288",
tsize=5,
tface="Arial",
fcolor="#002288",
fsize=3,
clabval=red,
clabtxt=fuchsia,
depth=Two_And_A_Half_Dimension,
valuepos=Bottom_Center,
labelpos=Top_Center);
```

Display the HTML output file in a Web browser to run the Rangeview Applet and display a critical success factor diagram.

In the preceding example, the arguments of the DS2CSF macro specify the path to the HTML output file and the Java archive of the Rangeview Applet. The VAR argument identifies the variable in the data set that is to be illustrated in the diagram. The value that is to be indicated as the critical success factor is the value for this variable in the first observation in the data set. A digital-style diagram is specified by the CSFTYP= argument.

For more information on usages of the Rangeview Applet, see "Enhancing Presentations for the Rangeview Applet" on page 529.

For definitions of all of the arguments of the DS2CSF macro, see "DS2CSF Macro Arguments" on page 530.

Enhancing Presentations for the Rangeview Applet

While the Rangeview Applet does not provide interactivity other than a drill-down URL, a number of enhancements enable you to control the appearance of the diagram, as described in the following table.

Table 20.1

Enhancement	DS2CSF Argument
Specify a stylesheet to format your HTML output file.	SSFILE, SSHREF, etc. See "Arguments for Stylesheets" on page 554.
Specify a color for the background, hub, and outline.	CBACK, CHUB, COUTLINE
Specify a drill-down URL and display target.	DRILURL, DRILTARG

Specify an analog or digital gauge.	CSFTYPE
Set the indicator shape, height, width, and color.	INDICTYP, HINDIC, WINDIC, CINDIC

DS2CSF Macro Arguments

The DS2CSF macro generates HTML output for the Rangeview Applet. The last three letters, CSF, stand for critical success factor, which is the type of diagram that is generated by this applet.

Macro arguments specify the configuration of the HTML output file, the location of the data used to generate the diagram, and the customizations, such as a drill-down URL, that you can add to your presentation.

The DS2CSF macro uses the following syntax:

%DS2CSF(*argument1=value1*, *argument2=value2*, ...);

The arguments of the DS2CSF macro can be divided into the following categories:

- "Arguments for the APPLET Tag" on page 536

  The ARCHIVE and CODEBASE arguments are required.
- "DS2CSF Arguments for Data Definition" on page 561
- "Arguments for Generating HTML and XML Files" on page 544
- "DS2CSF Arguments for Diagram Appearance" on page 562
- "Arguments for Page Formatting" on page 552
- "Arguments for Stylesheets" on page 554
- "Arguments for the SAS TITLE and FOOTNOTE Tags" on page 556
- "Arguments for Character Transcoding" on page 561.

Sample Programs: DS2CSF Macro

The following sample programs generate diagrams using the DS2CSF macro:

- "Sample Diagrams Using DS2CSF" on page 530
- "Adding a Link to a Critical Success Factor Diagram" on page 532.

Sample Diagrams Using DS2CSF

A CSF (Critical Success Factor) diagram represents a value in a range of data. This value can be obtained from a SAS data set variable or an SCL variable. The range of data used by the CSF is depicted by segments, with each segment containing a beginning and ending value, and possibly a different color. The number of segments and their corresponding colors are defined in a RANGE entry that is associated with the CSF.

Results Shown in a Browser

The sample program displays two forms of CSF—one an analog dial, and the other a digital display.

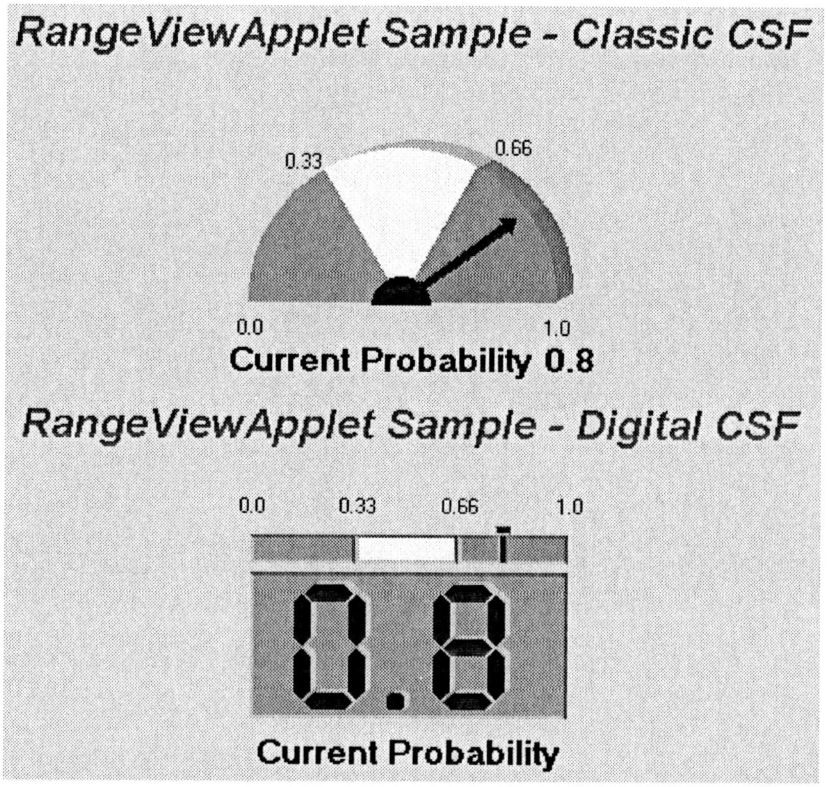

SAS Code

The following is the complete SAS code to generate a web presentation. Note the following:

- The HTMLFILE= parameter specifies the name of the HTML file to be produced by DS2CSF. If you want to run this sample, then change the value of HTMLFILE= to something that makes sense for you.
- The data set variable X specifies the value to be displayed on the CSF diagram. In this case, the critical value equals 0.8.
- The parameter

  ```
  range=sashelp.javagrt.sample1.range
  ```

  specifies a range entry that defines the range segments and their corresponding color. In this case, the range entry defines three segments: 0–0.33, 0.33–0.66, and 0.66 to 1.
- The data set variable X specifies the value to be displayed on the CSF diagram. In this case, the critical value equals 0.8.

```
data test; x=0.8; label x='Current Probability'; run;

title 'RangeViewApplet Sample - Classic CSF';

%ds2csf(data=test,
        var=x,
        htmlfile=your_path_and_filename.htm,
        openmode=replace, pagepart=head,
        center=y,
```

```
it is not in the same directory as the html file */
        archive=http://your_path_to_archive,
        csftyp=classic, septype=none, cback=#e0e0e0,
        bgtype=color, bg="#e0e0e0",
        ttag=bold + italicized, tcolor="#002288", tsize=5,
        tface="Arial, Helvetica",
        range=sashelp.javagrf.sample1.range);

title 'RangeViewApplet Sample - Digital CSF';

%ds2csf(data=test,
        var=x,
        htmlfile=your_path_and_filename.htm,
        openmode=append, pagepart=foot,
        center=y,
        archive=rvapplet.jar,
        /* specify complete url if not in same directory as the html file */
        archive=http://your_path_to_archive,
        csftyp=digital, labelpos=Bottom_Center, cback=#e0e0e0,
        bgtype=color, bg="#e0e0e0",
        ttag=bold + italicized, tcolor="#002288", tsize=5,
        tface="Arial, Helvetica",
        range=sashelp.javagrf.sample1.range);
```

Adding a Link to a Critical Success Factor Diagram

You can add a hotspot to a diagram created with the DS2CSF macro. However, unlike the Treeview and Constellation macros, you can add only a single hotspot to a diagram, that is, to the diagram as a whole. You can not add hotspots to different portions of the diagram.

SAS Code

The SAS code creates a diagram and links to the specified URL when a user clicks anywhere on the diagram. DRILURL= specifies the URL to link to, while DRILTARG=_self specifies that the new Web page is to be displayed in the same window as the diagram.

```
data test; x=0.8; label x='Current Probability'; run;

title 'RangeViewApplet Sample - Classic CSF';

%ds2csf(data=test,
        var=x,
        htmlfile=your_path_and_filename.htm,
        openmode=replace, pagepart=head,
        center=y,
      drilurl=http://www.xyz.com,
        archive=rvapplet.jar,
        /* specify complete url if not in same directory as the html file */
        archive=http://your_path_to_archive,
        csftyp=classic, septype=none, cback=#e0e0e0,
        bgtype=color, bg="#e0e0e0",
        ttag=bold + italicized, tcolor="#002288", tsize=5,
```

```
tface="Arial, Helvetica",
range=sashelp.javagrf.sample1.range);
```

CHAPTER 21

Macro Arguments for the DS2CONST, DS2TREE, DS2CSF, and META2HTM Macros

Macro Arguments

Macro arguments specify the configuration of the HTML output file, the location of the data that is used to generate the diagram, and the configuration of the applet's interactive features.

The macros use the following syntax:

%macroname(argument1=value1, argument2=value2, ...);

The macro arguments can be divided into arguments used by all macros, arguments used by the DS2CSF macro, and arguments used by the META2HTM macro. The following arguments apply to all macros:

- "Arguments for the APPLET Tag" on page 536. The CODEBASE argument is required.
- "DS2TREE and DS2CONST Arguments for Data Definition" on page 537. For DS2TREE the arguments NDATA and NID are required. For DS2CONST the arguments NDATA, NID, LDATA, and LTO are required.
- "Arguments for Generating HTML and XML Files" on page 544.
- "DS2TREE and DS2CONST Arguments for Diagram Appearance" on page 545.
- "Arguments for Page Formatting" on page 552.
- "Arguments for Stylesheets" on page 554.
- "Arguments for the SAS TITLE and FOOTNOTE Tags" on page 556.
- "Arguments for Character Transcoding" on page 561.

The following arguments apply only to the DS2CSF macro:

- "DS2CSF Arguments for Data Definition" on page 561.
- "DS2CSF Arguments for Diagram Appearance" on page 562.

The following arguments apply only to the META2HTM macro:

- "META2HTM Arguments for Saving the HTML File" on page 564. All these arguments are required for saving the HTML file.
- "META2HTM Arguments for Applet Behavior" on page 565.

Arguments for the APPLET Tag

The following arguments configure the APPLET tag in the HTML output file. The CODEBASE argument is required.

AHUNITS=PIXELS | PERCENT
: specifies the units of the HEIGHT= argument. The default value is PIXELS. See also the AWUNITS= argument.

Used by: DS2TREE, DS2CONST

ALIGN=*position*
: specifies the alignment of the applet window in the browser window or frame. Values can be LEFT, RIGHT, TOP, BOTTOM, TEXTTOP, MIDDLE, ABSMIDDLE, BASELINE, or ABSBOTTOM.

Used by: DS2TREE, DS2CONST, DS2CSF, META2HTM

ALT=*text*
: specifies the text that will be displayed on mouseover by browsers that understand the tag but cannot run Java applets. The default value is **`SAS Institute Inc. applet_name`**.

Used by: DS2TREE, DS2CONST, DS2CSF, META2HTM

ARCHIVE=*filename*
: specifies the name of the Java archive file(s). This argument is required for DS2CSF and META2HTM.

Note: The path to the Java archive is specified in the CODEBASE argument. △

The following table shows what archive files to use with each of the macros. For DS2TREE and DS2CONST, you do not have to specify a value for ARCHIVE= because the values shown are generated by default.

DS2TREE	archive=%str(sas.graph.treeview.jar, sas.graph.nld.jar, sas.graph.j2d.jar)
DS2CONST	archive=%str(sas.graph.constapp.jar, sas.graph.nld.jar, sas.graph.j2d.jar)
DS2CSF	archive=rvapplet.jar
META2HTM	archive=metafile.zip

Note: Before SAS 9.1, treeview.jar and constapp.jar also contained the classes that are now included in the auxiliary JAR files (sas.graph.nld.jar and sas.graph.j2d.jar). Although you can continue to use the older JAR files by specifying ARCHIVE=treeview.jar or ARCHIVE=constapp.jar, future versions may not support these older JAR files. △

Used by: DS2TREE, DS2CONST, DS2CSF, META2HTM

AWUNITS=PIXELS | PERCENT
specifies the units of the WIDTH= argument. The default value is PIXELS. See also the HEIGHT= and AHUNITS= arguments.

Used by: DS2TREE, DS2CONST

CODEBASE=*path-or-URL*
specifies the path of the SAS Java archives specified in the ARCHIVE= argument.
The CODEBASE argument is required. You can specify CODEBASE="." if the HTML file and Java archive files are in the same directory.

Note: You can specify the location pointed to by the SAS system option APPLETLOC=, or you can specify a different location. To display the current value of APPLETLOC, run the following code:

```
proc options option=appletloc;
run;
```

The value of the APPLETLOC system option is not used as the default value. △

Used by: DS2TREE, DS2CONST, DS2CSF, META2HTM

HEIGHT=*applet-height*
specifies the height of the applet window. The unit of measure is pixels unless changed by the AHUNITS= argument. The default value is 600 for all macros except the DS2CSF macro. The default for the DS2CSF macro is 175.

Used by: DS2TREE, DS2CONST, DS2CSF, META2HTM

HSPACE=*pixels*
specifies the amount of horizontal space, in pixels, to the left and right of the graph or diagram.

Used by: DS2TREE, DS2CONST, DS2CSF, META2HTM

NAME=*applet-name*
specifies the name for this instance of the applet. You need to use this argument only if you have more than one instance of the APPLET tag in your HTML file, and if you have included your own scripts or DHTML that communicates with or acts on a particular instance of the applet.

Used by: DS2TREE, DS2CONST, DS2CSF, META2HTM

VSPACE=*pixels*
specifies the amount of vertical space, in pixels, to the top and bottom of the graph or diagram.

Used by: DS2TREE, DS2CONST, DS2CSF, META2HTM

WIDTH=*applet-width*
specifies the width of the applet window. The unit of measure defaults to pixels unless specified by the AWUNITS= argument. The default value is 800 for all macros except the DS2CSF macro. The default for the DS2CSF macro is 225.

Used by: DS2TREE, DS2CONST, DS2CSF, META2HTM

DS2TREE and DS2CONST Arguments for Data Definition

The following arguments for the DS2TREE and DS2CONST macros define how the applet will use the data set to generate the node/link diagram.

For DS2TREE the arguments NDATA and NID are required.

For DS2CONST the arguments NDATA, NID, LDATA, and LTO are required.

DATATYPE=ARCS | ASSOC | HIER
: specifies the type of the XML data. Valid values are defined as follows:

ARCS
: indicates that the data set is in the form of an arc list. This is the default value.

ASSOC
: indicates that the data set is associative. The links can be displayed based on their weighted values, and node size and link width can represent the relative size of the node and link values.

HIER
: indicates that the data set is hierarchical.

Used by: DS2CONST

LABELS=Y | N
: indicates whether or not node labels are displayed in the diagram. The default value is Y.

Used by: DS2CONST, DS2TREE

LAYOUT=AUTO | USER
: when the value is AUTO (default), specifies that the Constellation Applet lays out the diagram using stress and strain equations. Specifying the value USER indicates that the node positions are specified in the NX and NY arguments.

Used by: DS2CONST

LCOLOR=*variable-name*
: specifies the name of the variable that determines the color of the link lines. The values of this variable must be HTML 3.2 color names, or you must use the LCOLFMT= argument to convert those values to valid color names. The default color is provided by the CLINK= argument (see "DS2TREE and DS2CONST Arguments for Diagram Appearance" on page 545).

In the DS2CONST macro, the LCOLOR= argument is overridden by the LCOLVAL= argument.

Used by: DS2CONST, DS2TREE

LCOLFMT=*user-defined-format-name*
: specifies the name of a user-defined SAS format that converts the values in the variable named in the LCOLOR= argument to valid HTML color names. Note that the SAS format does not change any values in the data set. The formatted values are applied to the diagram only.

Used by: DS2CONST, DS2TREE

LCOLVAL=*variable-name*
: specifies the name of the variable that determines the color mapping of link lines. This argument is valid only when the value of the DATATYPE= argument is ASSOC, and only when the value of the COLORMAP= argument is Y. If the LCOLVAL= argument is not specified, the link colors are determined by the following arguments in the following order: LCOLOR= (see above) and CLINK= (see "DS2TREE and DS2CONST Arguments for Diagram Appearance" on page 545).

Used by: DS2CONST

LDATA=*data-set-name*
: specifies the name of the SAS data set that contains the link data that is used to generate the diagram.

This argument is required.

Used by: DS2CONST

LFROM=*variable-name*
specifies the name of the variable whose values define the nodes at the start of link lines. The LFROM variable values must be coordinated with the values of the variables that are named in the NID= and LTO= arguments.
This argument is required.

Used by: DS2CONST

LINKTYPE=LINE | ARROW
when the value is ARROW (default), indicates that link lines are to be drawn with arrowheads that indicate the direction of flow.

Used by: DS2CONST

LPT=*password*
specifies the password that is needed for accessing a password-protected link data set (specified with the LDATA= argument). The LPT= argument is required if the data set has a READ or PW password. You do not need to specify this argument if the data set has a WRITE or ALTER password.

Used by: DS2CONST

LSTIP=*variable-name*
specifies the name of the variable in the data set that determines the stipple mask. The stipple mask generates dashed or dotted link lines. The value of the variable must be an integer, which is then converted into a binary value. In the binary value, a "1" bit means that a pixel is to be drawn and a "0" bit means that no pixel is to be drawn. For example, if the variable has a value of 61680, the binary conversion of that value will be 1111000011110000. This stipple mask generates a dashed link line with dashes and spaces that are four pixels wide. See also the LSTIPFAC= argument.

Used by: DS2CONST, DS2TREE

LSTIPFAC=*variable-name*
specifies the name of the variable in the data set whose value specifies a multiplier for the binary stipple mask (see the LSTIP= argument). The multiplier lengthens the dashes in the base mask. For example, if the multiplier is 2, a stipple mask that specifies 4-pixel dashes and 4-pixel spaces will generate link lines with 8-pixel dashes and spaces.

Used by: DS2CONST, DS2TREE

LTIP=*variable-name*
specifies the name of the variable in the data set that provides the text that is displayed in the pop-up data tips windows for links.

Used by: DS2CONST, DS2TREE

LTIPFMT=*user-defined-format-name*
specifies the name of a user-defined SAS format that is applied to the values in the variable specified in the LTIP= argument to configure those values for display in the pop-up data tips window. Note that the SAS format does not change any values in the data set. The formatted values are applied to the diagram only.

Used by: DS2CONST, DS2TREE

LTO=*variable-name*
specifies the name of the variable whose values identify the nodes at the ends of link lines. The LTO variable values must be coordinated with the values of the variables that are named in the LFROM and NID arguments.

This argument is required.

Used by: DS2CONST

LVALUE=*variable-name*
specifies the name of the variable whose values determine the weights of the link lines, which determines the color and relative thickness of link lines. The variable values must be real numbers. The link weights are used with the MINLNKWT= argument (see below) and the SCLNKWT= argument (see "DS2TREE and DS2CONST Arguments for Diagram Appearance" on page 545) to control the display of link lines. The LVALUE= argument is valid only when the value of the DATATYPE= argument is ASSOC.

Used by: DS2CONST

LWHERE=*subset-expression*
specifies a WHERE clause that subsets the link data for display in the diagram. If the expression contains any special characters (for example, % or &), include %NRBQUOTE in the expression to process those characters correctly. The following example shows how to correctly specify INT%:

```
LWHERE=%NRBQUOTE(value="Int%")
```

See also the NWHERE argument.

Used by: DS2CONST

LWIDTH=*variable-name*
specifies the name of the variable in the data set that determines the width of the link lines.

For DS2CONST: When this argument is not specified, the width is determined by the LVALUE argument. This argument is valid for DS2CONST only when the value of the DATATYPE argument is ASSOC.

Used by: DS2CONST, DS2TREE

MINLNKWT=*minimum-link-weight*
specifies the initial minimum link weight, which determines which links are initially displayed. The initial diagram show only those links that have weights that are greater than or equal to the minimum weight. In the Constellation Applet, a scroll bar allows the Web user to change the minimum link weight to change the number of links that are displayed. Selecting the brower's Refresh option restores the intial minimum link weight that is specified in the MINLNKWT argument. Link weights are determined by the LVALUE argument. This argument is valid only when the value of the DATATYPE argument is ASSOC.

Used by: DS2CONST

NACTION=*variable-name*
specifies the name of the variable in the nodes data set that provides the menu text that is displayed when the Web user selects a node with the right mouse button. Selecting this menu option text displays the URL that is associated with that node in the NURL= argument. This argument overrides the ACTION= argument (see "DS2TREE and DS2CONST Arguments for Diagram Appearance" on page 545). The default menu option text is `Open URL`.

Used by: DS2CONST, DS2TREE

NCOLFMT=*SAS-format-name*
specifies the name of a user-defined SAS format that converts the values in the variable named in the NCOLOR= argument to valid HTML color names. Note that the data in the data set is not altered; the formatted value is used in the hierarchical tree rather than the data value.

Used by: DS2CONST, DS2TREE

NCOLOR=*variable-name*
specifies the variable in the nodes data set that determines the background color of the nodes, using HTML 3.2 color names or 6-digit hexadecimal RGB values . If the variable does not contain valid HTML color names, then you can use the NCOLFMT=argument to convert those values to the HTML color names. See also the NCOLVAL= and NVALUE=arguments.

Used by: DS2CONST, DS2TREE

NCOLVAL=*variable-name*
specifies the name of the variable in the nodes data set that determines the color mapping for the nodes. This argument is valid only when the DATASET= argument is set to ASSOC, and only when the value of the COLORMAP= argument is Y. If this argument is not specified, then the node color is determined by the LVALUE= argument.

Used by: DS2CONST

NDATA=*SAS-data-set-name*
specifies the SAS data set that contains the node data.
This argument is required.

Used by: DS2CONST, DS2TREE

NFNTNAME=*node-font-variable-name*
specifies the name of the variable that determines the text font for the node labels. The variable value can be SERIF, SANSSERIF, DIALOG, DIALOGINPUT, or MONOSPACED. The default node font is specified by the FNTNAME= argument (see "DS2TREE and DS2CONST Arguments for Diagram Appearance" on page 545).

Used by: DS2CONST, DS2TREE

NFNTSIZE=*variable-name*
specifies the name of the variable in the nodes data set that determines the size of the text font used for node labels. This font size is expressed in points. This argument overrides the FNTSIZE= argument.

Used by: DS2CONST, DS2TREE

NFNTSTYL=*node-font-style-variable-name*
specifies the name of the variable that determines the font style for the node label. The valid values that can be assigned to the variable are BOLD, ITALIC, and PLAIN.

Used by: DS2CONST, DS2TREE

NID=*variable-name*
specifies the name of the variable in the nodes data set whose values are to illustrated as the nodes in the diagram. The node ID variable type can be either numeric or character. For the DS2CONST macro, the values of the NID variable must be coordinated with the values of the LFROM and LTO variables.
This argument is required.

Used by: DS2CONST, DS2TREE

NLABEL=*node-label-variable-name*
specifies the name of the variable that represents the node labels. This variable type can be either numeric or character.

Used by: DS2CONST, DS2TREE

NPARENT=*node-parent-variable-name*
specifies the name of the variable that represents the parent nodes. This variable type can be either numeric or character.

Used by: DS2TREE

NPW=*password*
specifies the password that is needed for accessing a password-protected data set. This argument is required if the data set has a READ or PW password. You do not need to specify this argument if the data set has only WRITE or ALTER passwords.

Used by: DS2CONST, DS2TREE

NSCBACK=*variable-name*
specifies the name of the variable in the node styles data set that determines the background color of the nodes. The variable values must be HTML 3.2 color names. The default value is determined by the CNODE= argument (see "DS2TREE and DS2CONST Arguments for Diagram Appearance" on page 545).

Used by: DS2CONST, DS2TREE

NSCTEXT=*variable-name*
specifies the name of the variable in the node styles data set that provides the colors for the node label text. Valid variable values must be HTML 3.2 color names. The default color is provided by the CATEXT= argument.

Used by: DS2CONST, DS2TREE

NSDATA=*SAS-data-set-name*
specifies the name of the node styles data set.

Used by: DS2CONST, DS2TREE

NSFNTNAM=*variable-name*
specifies the name of the variable in the node styles data set that determines the text font that is to be used for node labels. Valid variable values can be SERIF, SANSSERIF, DIALOG, DIALOGINPUT, or MONOSPACED. This argument overrides the FNTNAME= argument.

Used by: DS2CONST, DS2TREE

NSFNTSIZ=*variable-name*
specifies the name of the variable in the node styles data set that determines the size of the node label text, in points. This argument overrides the FNTSIZE= argument.

Used by: DS2CONST, DS2TREE

NSFNTSTY=*variable-name*
specifies the name of the variable in the node styles data set that determines the style of the node label text. Valid variable values can be BOLD, ITALIC, or the default value, PLAIN. This argument overrides the FNTSTYL= argument.

Used by: DS2CONST, DS2TREE

NSHAPE=*variable-name*
specifies the name of the variable that determines the shape of the nodes. Valid variable values can be CIRCLE, DIAMOND, NONE, SQUARE, or TRIANGLE. The default value is SQUARE. This argument overrides the NODESHAPE= argument.

Used by: DS2CONST

NSID=*variable-name*
specifies the name of the variable in the node styles data set that represents the nodes.

Used by: DS2CONST, DS2TREE

NSIZE=*variable-name*

specifies the name of the variable that determines the size of the nodes. The values of this variable can be real numbers. Node sizes are determined based on the value of the LAYOUT= argument. When LAYOUT=USER, the values of the NSIZE variable are interpreted as literal pixel measurements. When LAYOUT=AUTO, the values of the NSIZE variable determine the size of the nodes based on the relative size of individual values. The values of the NSIZE variable can be scaled with the SCLNSIZE= argument (see "DS2TREE and DS2CONST Arguments for Diagram Appearance" on page 545). This argument is valid only when the value of the DATATYPE= argument is ASSOC.

Used by: DS2CONST

NSPW=*password*

specifies the password that is needed to access a password-protected node styles data set. This argument is required if the data set has a READ or PW password. You do not need to specify this argument if the data set has only WRITE or ALTER passwords.

Used by: DS2CONST, DS2TREE

NSTYLE=*variable-name*

specifies the name of the variable that determines the style of the nodes. This variable type can be either numeric or character, and the values must correspond to the node identifiers specified in the NSID= argument.

Used by: DS2CONST, DS2TREE

NSWHERE=*subset-expression*

specifies a WHERE clause that subsets the node styles data set for display in the diagram. If the expression contains any special characters (for example, % or &), then include %NRBQUOTE in the expression to process those characters correctly. The following example shows how to correctly specify INT%:

```
NSWHERE=%NRBQUOTE(value="Int%")
```

Used by: DS2CONST, DS2TREE

NTEXTCOL=*variable-name*

specifies the name of the variable that determines the color of the text for the node labels. Valid variable values must be HTML 3.2 color names.

Used by: DS2CONST, DS2TREE

NTIP=*variable-name*

specifies the name of the variable that provides the data or text that is displayed in the pop-up data tips window.

Used by: DS2CONST, DS2TREE

NTIPFMT=*user-defined-format-name*

specifies the name of a user-defined SAS format that is applied to the data tips variable that is named in the NTIP= argument. Note that the data set is not altered; the formatted value is used only in the diagram.

Used by: DS2CONST, DS2TREE

NURL=*drill-down-URL*

specifies the name of the variable that provides the drill-down URLs for the nodes. These URLs are displayed when the Web user double-clicks on a node or selects the node with the right mouse button and chooses an option from the pop-up menu. Menu text is determined by the NACTION= argument above and by the ACTION= argument in "DS2TREE and DS2CONST Arguments for Diagram Appearance" on page 545. The default menu option text is **`Open URL`**.

Used by: DS2CONST, DS2TREE

NVALUE=*variable-name*
specifies the name of the variable that determines the relative node size. This argument is valid only when DATATYPE=ASSOC.

If you do not specify a particular node color using either the NCOLOR or NCOLVAL argument (and if COLORMAP=Y), then this argument also determines a default node color. By default, the largest value of NVALUE is mapped to red, the median value to green, and the lowest value to blue. Values in between result in interpolated colors.

Used by: DS2CONST

NWHERE=*subset-expression*
specifies a WHERE clause that subsets the nodes data set for display in the diagram. If the expression contains any special characters (for example, % or &), then include %NRBQUOTE in the expression to process those characters correctly. The following example shows how to correctly specify INT%:

```
NWHERE=%NRBQUOTE(value="Int%")
```

See also the LWHERE= argument.

Used by: DS2CONST, DS2TREE

NX=*variable-name*
NY=*variable-name*
specify the variables that determine the locations of the centers of the nodes. These arguments are valid only when the LAYOUT= argument is set to USER. The values are expressed in pixels. Positive values are measured from the top-left corner of the screen. Negative values are measured from the bottom-right corner of the screen.

Used by: DS2CONST

Arguments for Generating HTML and XML Files

The following arguments determine the name, storage location, and file makeup of Web presentations that run in the Constellation Applet or the Treeview Applet.

HTMLFILE=*external-filename*
specifies the name and storage location of the HTML output file. If the external file does not exist, then it is created for you. Either this argument, or HTMLFREF=, is required if you specify MAKEHTML=Y. Note: Do not use the HTMLFILE= argument if you use the HTMLFREF= argument.

Used by: DS2TREE, DS2CONST, DS2CSF

HTMLFREF=*fileref*
specifies the SAS fileref that identifies the name and storage location of the HTML output file. If the external file does not exist, then it is created for you. Either this argument, or HTMLFILE=filename, is required if you specify MAKEHTML=Y. Note: Do not use the HTMLFREF= argument if you use the HTMLFILE= argument, and do not use a reserved name (see "Reserved Names" on page 566).

Used by: DS2TREE, DS2CONST, DS2CSF

MAKEHTML=Y | N
specifies whether or not an HTML file is to be generated. The default value is Y, which generates the HTML output file. If you specify MAKEHTML=N and MAKEXML=Y, then only an XML file is generated.

Used by: DS2TREE, DS2CONST

MAKEXML=Y | N
: specifies whether or not an XML file is to be generated. The default value is Y, which generates the XML output file. If you specify MAKEXML=N and MAKEHTML=Y, then only an HTML file will be generated. Note that under these circumstances, you must specify a value for the XMLURL= argument.

Used by: DS2TREE, DS2CONST

OPENMODE=REPLACE | APPEND
: indicates whether the new HTML or XML output or both overwrites the information that is currently in the specified file(s), or if the new output is appended to the end of the existing file(s). The default value is REPLACE. Specify APPEND to add your new HTML-enhanced output to the end of an existing file. Note: OPENMODE=APPEND is not valid if you are writing your resulting HTML to a partitioned data set (PDS) on z/OS.

Used by: DS2TREE, DS2CONST, DS2CSF

RUNMODE=B | S
: specifies whether you are running the DS2TREE macro in batch or server mode. Batch mode (RUNMODE=B, the default) means that you are submitting the DS2TREE macro in the SAS Program Editor or you have included it in a SAS program. Server mode (RUNMODE=S) generates the HTTP header that is required by Application Dispatcher in the SAS/INTRNET software.

Used by: DS2TREE, DS2CONST, DS2CSF

XMLFILE=*external-filename*
: specifies the name and storage location of the XML output file. If the external file does not exist, then it is created for you. This argument, or XMLFREF=, is required if you specify MAKEXML=Y and XMLTYPE=EXTERNAL. Note: Do not use the XMLFILE= argument if you use the XMLFREF= argument.

Used by: DS2TREE, DS2CONST

XMLFREF=*fileref*
: specifies the SAS fileref that identifies the name and storage location of the XML output file. If the external file does not exist, then it is created for you. This argument, or XMLFILE=, is required if you specify MAKEXML=Y and XMLTYPE=EXTERNAL. Note: Do not use the XMLFREF= argument if you use the XMLFILE= argument, and do not use a reserved name (see "Reserved Names" on page 566).

Used by: DS2TREE, DS2CONST

XMLTYPE=INLINE | EXTERNAL
: specifies whether the XML output file is to be written to an external file or included inline with the HTML. The default value is INLINE. If you specify EXTERNAL you must also specify a value for either the XMLFILE= or XMLFREF= arguments. This argument is required if you specify MAKEXML=Y.

Used by: DS2TREE, DS2CONST

XMLURL=*URL*
: specifies the URL of the existing file that contains the XML tags that define the node/link diagram. This argument is required if specified XMLTYPE=EXTERNAL.

Used by: DS2TREE, DS2CONST

DS2TREE and DS2CONST Arguments for Diagram Appearance

The following arguments for the DS2TREE and DS2CONST macros specify non-default behavior and appearance of the node/link diagram in the respective applet.

None of the following arguments are required.

ACTION=*text*
: specifies the default text that is displayed in a pop-up menu when the Web user selects a node with the right mouse button. Selecting this menu option displays the URL that is associated with that node in the NURL= argument. This argument is overridden by the NACTION= argument (see "DS2TREE and DS2CONST Arguments for Data Definition" on page 537). The ACTION= argument is useful when you want to use a single menu text string for most of the nodes in your diagram. The default menu option text is `Open URL`.

Used by: DS2CONST, DS2TREE

ANGLE=*link-angle*
: works with the TREESPAN= argument to determine the direction of growth for the diagram. The ANGLE= argument is valid only when you do not specify the TREEDIR= argument. The TREESPAN= argument defines the angular width of the tree (narrow or wide layout). The TREESPAN angle can be visualized as a V shape, with the starting node positioned at the base of the V. The rest of the nodes are laid out between the spreading arms of the V. The ANGLE= argument specifies the angle of the V shape. By default, the value of the ANGLE= argument is zero (0) and the V shape opens to the right, as if the letter V was rotated 90 degrees clockwise, to the three-o'clock position. Values of the ANGLE= argument that are greater than zero rotate the V shape counterclockwise away from the three-o'clock position. Valid values for the ANGLE= argument range from zero (0) to 360 degrees.

Used by: DS2TREE

BORDER=Y | N
: specifies whether or not a border is drawn around the background area. The default value is N.

Used by: DS2CONST, DS2TREE

CATEXT=*default-text-color*
: specifies a default color for the text in the diagram, using an HTML 3.2 color name or a 6-digit hexadecimal RGB value. For DS2CONST, this argument is overridden by the FNTNAME= argument (see below) and the NTEXTCOL argument (see "DS2TREE and DS2CONST Arguments for Data Definition" on page 537).

Used by: DS2CONST, DS2TREE

CBACK=*color*
: specifies a background color for the Treeview Applet. The value must be a valid HTML 3.2 color name.

Used by: DS2TREE

CHANDLE=*color*
: specifies the color of the Collapse/Expand handle on the nodes. The handle is represented by a small plus sign (+) that is prefixed to the label of the node when its subtree is collapsed. The value must be a valid HTML color name.

Used by: DS2TREE

CLINK=*default-link-color*
: specifies a default color for the links in the diagram, using an HTML 3.2 color name or a 6-digit RGB value. For DS2CONST, this argument is overridden by the LCOLOR= and LCOLVAL= arguments (see "DS2TREE and DS2CONST Arguments for Data Definition" on page 537).

Used by: DS2CONST, DS2TREE

CNODE=*color*
specifies the node background color. The value must be a valid HTML color name. The value specified here can be overridden by specifying a value of TRUE for the NCOLOR= argument.

Used by: DS2TREE

CNODE=*default-node-color*
specifies a default background color for the nodes, using an HTML 3.2 color name or a 6-digit RGB value. This argument is overridden by the NCOLOR=, NCOLVAL=, NVALUE=, or NSCBACK= arguments (see "DS2TREE and DS2CONST Arguments for Data Definition" on page 537).

Used by: DS2CONST

COLORMAP=N | Y
when the value is N (default), specifies that the Constellation Applet is to use the NCOLOR= and LCOLOR= arguments (see "DS2TREE and DS2CONST Arguments for Data Definition" on page 537) to determine node and link colors rather than using the color map.

Used by: DS2CONST

CSELECT=*color*
specifies a color for nodes that are selected by the mouse or as the result of a node search. The value must be a valid HTML 3.2 color name.

Used by: DS2CONST, DS2TREE

CUTOFF=*detail-percentage*
specifies the percentage of the nodes that will be displayed with node labels. After the percentage has been reached, nodes are drawn as rectangles. The size of those rectangles decreases as the distance from the starting node increases. Valid values range from 0.0 to 1.0 (The decimal value is mapped to a percentage from 0% to 100%). The default value is 1.0. See also the DEPTH argument.

Used by: DS2CONST, DS2TREE

DEPTH=*max-path-length*
specifies a whole number greater than zero that determines the maximum number of links that are to be displayed in the node/link diagram. Paths whose lengths exceed the limit are truncated. This argument affects only the initial display of the diagram. Nodes that are initially hidden can become visible as a user selects nodes and navigates around the diagram.

Note that this value is ignored if the value of the CUTOFF= argument is 1.0. There is no default value for this argument.

Used by: DS2TREE

DRILTARG=*target-window-or-frame*
specifies the HTML target or the name of the browser window or frame where drill-down URLs are displayed. The default behavior is to open a new browser window and reuse it for subsequent drill-down requests. Specifically, the default value is _BLANK, which is one of several reserved names for targets in HTML. The value can also be the name of a window or frame in the Web presentation.

Used by: DS2CONST, DS2TREE

DUPCHECK=TRUE | FALSE
specifies whether or not the applet will check for duplicate node IDs. The default value is FALSE. When set to TRUE, this argument will cause the applet to update an ID if a duplicate ID is found, instead of creating a new node with the same ID. This enables you to collect node information from different locations in the data set.

Used by: DS2TREE

FACTOR=*fish-eye-distortion-factor*
specifies the distortion factor for the fish-eye lens. The distortion factor determines the amount that the central region of the display is to be expanded (or zoomed). The value specified must be greater than or equal to 1.0. The default value is 1.0, which represents the lowest amount of distortion. This argument is valid only when the value of the FISHEYE= argument is Y. The maximum effective value (beyond which no further distortion is visible) is variable depending upon the number of nodes in the diagram.

Used by: DS2CONST, DS2TREE

FISHEYE=Y | N
indicates whether or not the diagram is to be displayed with the fish-eye distortion, which displays the central region of the diagram at a specified size and displays the rest of the diagram as if it were mapped onto a ball, with the nodes and links disappearing over a curved horizon. The Web user can move the diagram past the central region by scrolling or searching for nodes. The amount of distortion used in the fish-eye lens is determined by the FACTOR= argument. The default value is Y.

Used by: DS2CONST, DS2TREE

FNTNAME=*default-node-label-font*
specifies the default text font for node labels. Valid values can be SERIF, SANSSERIF, DIALOG, DIALOGINPUT, or MONOSPACED. This argument is overridden by the NFNTNAME or NSFNTNAM= arguments (see "DS2TREE and DS2CONST Arguments for Data Definition" on page 537).

Used by: DS2CONST, DS2TREE

FNTSIZE=*node-font-size*
specifies the size of the node label text font, in points. This argument is overridden by the NFNTSIZE= argument.

Used by: DS2CONST, DS2TREE

FNTSTYL=*node-font-style*
specifies the text font style for node labels. Valid values are BOLD, ITALIC, and PLAIN. PLAIN is the default value. This argument is overridden by the NFNTSTYL= argument.

Used by: DS2CONST, DS2TREE

IBACKLOC=*image-URL*
specifies a URL for the image that you want to use in the background of the diagram. See also the IBACKPOS= argument.

Used by: DS2CONST, DS2TREE

IBACKPOS=CENTER | SCALE | TILE | POSITION
specifies how to display the background image in the IBACKLOC= argument. Specify one of the following options:

CENTER
centers the image in the browser window without resizing the image.

SCALE
resizes the image to fit the browser window.

TILE
fills the browser window by replicating the image at its original size.

POSITION
positions the image without resizing at the values specified by the IBACKX= and IBACKY= arguments.

Used by: DS2CONST, DS2TREE

IBACKURL=*background-drilldown-URL*
specifies the URL that is displayed when you click on the background image. This argument is valid only when the value of the IBACKPOS= argument is POSITION. If you are including the Powered by SAS logo, then you must use this argument to link the image to the SAS Web site.

Used by: DS2CONST, DS2TREE

IBACKX=*corner-coordinate*
IBACKY=*corner-coordinate*
specifies the x (horizontal) and y (vertical) pixel coordinates of the upper left-hand corner of the background image. Positive values are measured from the upper-left corner of the background area. Negative values are measured from the lower-right corner of the background area. These values are valid only if the value of the IBACKPOS= argument is POSITION. Always specify both the IBACKX= and IBACKY= arguments.

Used by: DS2CONST, DS2TREE

NODEBDR=LINE | NONE | FILL | OUTLINE
specifies the appearance of the node border line, using one of the following values:

LINE
show solid border lines around the nodes.

NONE
show no border lines or background.

FILL
show background but no border lines.

OUTLINE
show a border line and background. This is the default value.

Used by: DS2TREE

NODESEP=*character(s)*
specifies which character(s) should be used to separate the selected nodes in the return value for the various getSelectedNodes methods. The default separator is a semicolon (;). If the getSelectedNodesIds method is called, and a JavaScript method is not specified with the SELIFUNC= argument, then the selected node IDs are returned as a single string separated by the NODESEP= character(s).

Used by: DS2CONST, DS2TREE

NODESHAP=*shape*
specifies the shape of the nodes. Valid values can be CIRCLE, DIAMOND, NONE, SQUARE, or TRIANGLE. The default value is SQUARE. This argument is overridden by the NSHAPE= argument (see "DS2TREE and DS2CONST Arguments for Data Definition" on page 537).

Used by: DS2CONST

RBSIZING=Y | N
the default value N indicates that size information from the resource bundle is not to be used for sizing the two dialog boxes that can be invoked from the pop-up menu that appears when a user right-mouse-clicks on a diagram. The two dialog boxes are the About dialog box and the Mouse Help dialog box.

Specify Y for this argument for languages other than English.If you specify Y, then the height and the width of the dialog box frames are read in from the resource bundle. This allows translators to set appropriate heights and widths for the frames in the resource bundle, based on the length of the message strings in each language.

Used by: DS2CONST, DS2TREE

SCLNKWT=Y | N
when the value is Y (default), specifies that the link weight values are to be scaled into the range of 0–1, which corresponds to 0–100%. When SCLNKWT=Y, the scroll bar in Constellation Applet displays a percentage of the range of the link weights. When SCLNKWT=N, the link weights are not scaled and the scroll bar reflects the actual link weight data values. These values are real numbers that are specified in the LVALUE= argument (see "DS2TREE and DS2CONST Arguments for Data Definition" on page 537). The SCLNKWT= argument is valid only when the value of the DATATYPE= argument is ASSOC. Note that the range of link weights (maximum minus minimum) must be greater than 2 when SCLNKWT=N. Otherwise, the scroll bar will not correctly map the link weights.

Used by: DS2CONST

SCLWIDTH=Y | N
when the value is Y (default), indicates that the link width values are to be scaled into the range of 0–1. Specifying N indicates that the link widths are already scaled into that range. This argument is valid only when the value of the DATATYPE= argument is ASSOC.

Used by: DS2CONST

SCNSIZE=Y | N
when the value is Y (default), indicates that the node size values are to be scaled into the range of 0–1. Specifying N indicates that the node sizes are already scaled into that range. This argument is valid only when the value of the DATATYPE= argument is ASSOC. Node sizes are specified with the NSIZE= argument (see "DS2TREE and DS2CONST Arguments for Data Definition" on page 537).

Used by: DS2CONST

SELIFUNC=*JavaScript-method-name*
specifies the name of the JavaScript method that will be used by the getSelectedNodesIds method. The getSelectedNodesIds method first collects all the IDs for the selected nodes. Then, if a method is specified with the SELIFUNC= argument, the getSelectedNodesIds method calls that method and passes to that method all of the selected node IDs as arguments. If there is no method specified with the SELIFUNC= argument, then the getSelectedNodesIds method concatenates all of the IDs into a single string, separates the individual IDs with the value that is specified by the NODESEP= argument, and returns the string. The value for this argument is case-sensitive.

Used by: DS2CONST, DS2TREE

SELLFUNC=*JavaScript-method-name*
specifies the JavaScript method that will be used by the getSelectedNodesLabels method. The getSelectedNodesLabels method first collects all the labels for the selected nodes. Then, if a method is specified with the SELLFUNC= argument, the getSelectedNodesLabels method calls that method and passes to that method all of the selected node labels as arguments. If there is no method specified with the SELLFUNC= argument, then the getSelectedNodesLabels method concatenates all of the labels into a single string, separates the individual labels with the value that is specified by the NODESEP= argument, and returns the string. The value for this argument is case-sensitive.

Used by: DS2CONST, DS2TREE

SELUFUNC=*JavaScript-method-name*

specifies the JavaScript method that will be used by the getSelectedNodesURLs method. The getSelectedNodesURLs method first collects all the URLs for the selected nodes. Then, if a method is specified with the SELUFUNC= argument, the getSelectedNodesURLs method calls that method and passes to that method all of the selected node URLs as arguments. If there is no method specified with the SELUFUNC= argument, then the getSelectedNodesURLs method concatenates all of the URLs into a single string, separates the individual URLs with the value specified by the NODESEP= argument, and returns the string. The value for this argument is case-sensitive.

Used by: DS2CONST, DS2TREE

SHOWLINKS=Y | N

specifies whether initially to display all arc lines between nodes. Specifying N suppresses all arc lines. The default value is Y.

Note: This argument affects only the *initial* display. A viewer can subsequently control which arc lines are displayed by right-mouse clicking and selecting a `Show links` option from the pop-up menu. △

Used by: DS2CONST

SPREAD=*angular-factor*

specifies the angular spreading factor for the layout of the diagram. The value specified must be greater than or equal to 1.0. The default value is 1.25.

Used by: DS2TREE

TIPS=Y | N

indicates whether or not pop-up data tips are displayed when the cursor is positioned over nodes or links or both. The default value is Y.

Used by: DS2CONST, DS2TREE

TIPTYPE=TRACKING | STATIONARY

when the value is TRACKING (default), indicates that the pop-up data tips windows are to move with the cursor while the cursor moves within the area of a single node or link.

Used by: DS2CONST

TREEDIR=C | D | L | R | U

determines the growth direction of the node/link diagram using the following values.

C | CIRCULAR
: grows the tree in a circular pattern. This is the default value.

D | DOWN
: grows the tree from top to bottom using center alignment.

L | LEFT
: grows the tree from left to right and top to bottom.

R | RIGHT
: grows the tree from right to left and top to bottom.

U | UP
: grows the tree from the bottom up using center alignment.

If the value of the TREEDIR= argument is UP or DOWN, then the value of the TREESPAN= argument is used to set the angular width of the diagram. The starting node is aligned horizontally in the center of the applet. The diagram grows out of the starting node based on the angular width specified in the TREESPAN= argument. The wider the angle, the wider the layout of the diagram.

The TREEDIR= argument overrides the ANGLE= argument.

Used by: DS2TREE

TREESPAN=*angular-diagram-width*

specifies the angular width of the diagram in degrees. Valid values must be greater than zero and less than 360. The default value is 60. For details, see the TREEDIR= and ANGLE= arguments.

Used by: DS2TREE

ZOOM=*starting-percentage*

specifies the zoom value that is used for the initial display of the diagram. After the initial display, the Web user can change the zoom percentage using the slider-bar beneath the diagram on the Web page. Selecting the Refresh button on the browser runs the applet and restores the initial zoom setting. The default value is 100 percent. The initial diagram can be scaled up with a value greater than 100 or scaled down with a value less than 100.

Used by: DS2CONST

Arguments for Page Formatting

The following arguments format the HTML output file. The rendering of some of these arguments may vary in certain browsers. Several of the following arguments apply only to certain macros, as noted in the descriptions of the arguments.

The BGTYPE=, BRTITLE=, CENTER=, CTEXT=, and DOCTYPE= arguments apply to the entire page for the current invocation of the macro. If you append data to an existing HTML page, then the HTML formatting will not change. You may want to use these arguments only when you replace, rather than append, HTML files.

BDCLASS=*body-stylesheet-name*

specifies the name of the stylesheet that is to be applied to the body of the HTML output file.

Used by: DS2TREE, DS2CONST, DS2CSF.

BG=*color-or-image*

specifies the background color or image, based on the value of the BGTYPE= argument. The color can be specified as an HTML 3.2 color name or as a 6-digit hexadecimal RGB value. When BGTYPE=IMAGE, this argument specifies a background image, using a path or a URL, relative or absolute.

Used by: DS2TREE, DS2CONST, DS2CSF, META2HTM.

BGTYPE=NONE | COLOR | IMAGE

specifies the background type, using one of the following values:

NONE

causes the applet to display its default background color. This is the default value.

COLOR

specifies that the value of the BG= argument must be an HTML 3.2 color name or hexadecimal RGB value.

IMAGE

specifies that the value of the BG= argument must be the path or URL pointing to an image file that will be displayed in the background of the applet window.

Used by: DS2TREE, DS2CONST, DS2CSF, META2HTM.

BRTITLE=*browser-window-title*

specifies the text that appears in the title bar of the browser window. By default, no title is displayed.

Used by: DS2TREE, DS2CONST, DS2CSF, META2HTM.

CENTER= Y | N

specifies whether or not the graph or diagram is centered in the browser window. The default value is N.

Used by: DS2TREE, DS2CONST, DS2CSF, META2HTM.

CTEXT=*default-text-color*

specifies a default text color that replaces the default text color in the browser. Other color arguments can be used to override this new default. The color can be specified as an HTML 3.2 color name or as a six-digit hexadecimal RGB value.

Used by: DS2TREE, DS2CONST, DS2CSF.

DOCTYPE=*DOCTYPE-tag*

generates the following DOCTYPE tag by default, which specifies HTML version 3.2:

```
<!DOCTYPE HTML PUBLIC "-//W3C//DTD HTML 3.2 Final//EN">
```

To use a different DOCTYPE tag, specify the entire contents of the tag as the value of the DOCTYPE= argument, including the angle brackets.

If you specify DOCTYPE="", then no DOCTYPE tag is generated in the HTML output file.

Used by: DS2TREE, DS2CONST, DS2CSF, META2HTM.

ENCODE=Y | N

when the value is Y (default), replaces the angle bracket characters (< and >) in SAS TITLE and FOOTNOTE lines with the HTML character entities (> and <) respectively. Specifying ENCODE=N causes the browser to interpret the angle brackets as parts of HTML tags. For example, you would use ENCODE=N if you wanted to use the following TITLE statement:

```
title '<FONT COLOR="red">Out of Range Data</FONT>';
```

This argument is supported by the DS2CONST, DS2TREE, and DS2CSF macros.

Used by: DS2TREE, DS2CONST, DS2CSF.

PAGEPART=ALL | HEAD | BODY | FOOT

specifies which part or parts of the HTML page are to be written into the HTML output file. This argument is helpful when are appending HTML output to the end of an existing HTML file, or when you are using separate files for the head, body, and foot of your Web page.

ALL

writes the entire HTML file, including metagraphics codes for the META2HTM macro or the XML tags for the DS2CONST, DS2TREE, and DS2CSF macros. This is the default value. Do not use this value if you are appending an existing HTML file.

HEAD

writes the HTML header information and metagraphics codes (for META2HTM) or XML (for DS2CONST and DS2TREE) into the HTML file. The header information consists of the HEAD and BODY tags. HTML footer information is not included.

BODY
: writes only the metagraphics codes (for META2HTM) or XML tags (for DS2CONST, DS2TREE, and DS2CSF) into the HTML output file. No head or foot information is generated in the HTML output file.

FOOT
: writes metagraphics codes or XML tags and the </BODY> and </HTML> tags to conclude the HTML file.

Used by: DS2TREE, DS2CONST, DS2CSF, META2HTM.

SASPOWER=*logo-image-file*
: specifies the path or URL, relative or absolute, to the image file of the SAS Powered logo. In the HTML file, the image appears at the bottom of the page. Selecting the image displays the SAS home page. By default, the logo is omitted. To obtain the logo image file, see http://www2.sas.com/dispatcher/index.html. See also the SPCLASS= argument.

Used by: DS2TREE, DS2CONST, DS2CSF, META2HTM.

SEPCLASS=*page-separator-stylesheet*
: specifies the path or URL, relative or absolute, to the style sheet that is used for the page separator. If the value of the SEPTYPE= argument is RULE, then the value of the SEPCLASS= argument is used on the CLASS attribute of the HTML tag <HR>. If the value of the SEPTYPE= argument is IMAGE, then the value of SEPCLASS= argument is used on the CLASS attribute of the HTML tag <IMG>.

Used by: DS2TREE, DS2CONST, DS2CSF.

SEPLOC=*separator-image*
: specifies the path or URL, relative or absolute, to the image that you want to use as the separator between the graphs in your presentation. This argument is valid only if the value of the SEPTYPE= argument is IMAGE.

Used by: DS2TREE, DS2CONST, DS2CSF, META2HTM.

SEPTYPE= IMAGE | NONE | RULE
: specifies the type of separator that is used between multiple applets in your presentation. The valid values are defined as follows:

IMAGE
: specifies separate graphs using the image specified in the SEPLOC= argument.

NONE
: specifies not to use a separator between applets.

RULE
: inserts a line between applets. This is the default.

Used by: DS2TREE, DS2CONST, DS2CSF, META2HTM.

SPCLASS=*logo-stylesheet-name*
: specifies the name of the style sheet class that is to be used for the Powered by SAS logo.

Used by: DS2TREE, DS2CONST, DS2CSF.

Arguments for Stylesheets

DS2CONT, DS2TREE, DS2CSF, and META2HTM enable the following arguments for style sheet specifications in the HTML output file. See also the BDCLASS=, SEPCLASS=, and SPCLASS= arguments in "Arguments for Page Formatting" on page 552.

Style sheet arguments reference style information in one of two ways. Most of the arguments specify parameters in the HTML LINK tag:

```
<LINK HREF="1qtr98.css" TYPE="text/css" REL="stylesheet">
```

Use these arguments when you do not want to enter your style information directly into your HTML file when you create that file.

Other arguments embed the style information into the header of the HTML file. Use these arguments when you want to collect style information from multiple style sheets. The end result must create a complete STYLE tag in your HTML file.

You can combine LINK tag arguments with arguments that embed style information, but you cannot use the same ordinal number in two arguments. For example, you can specify the arguments SSHREF1= and SSFILE2=, but you cannot specify SSHREF1= and SSFILE1=.

The following arguments link to two different style sheets and include text comments for each stylesheet.

```
ssfile1=comments1.txt,      /* embeds text               */
sshref2=/style/style1.css, /* links to stylesheet        */
sstype2=text/css,           /* parameters for style sheets */
ssrel2=stylesheet,
ssfile3=comments2.txt,      /* embeds text               */
sshref4=/style/style2.css, /* link to stylesheets        */
sstype4=text/css,
ssrel4=stylesheet,
```

SSFILE1–SSFILE5=*file-specification*
: embeds in the HTML file the entire contents of the specified file.

Used by: DS2TREE, DS2CONST, DS2CSF, META2HTM

SSFREF1–SSFREF5=*fileref*
: embeds in the HTML file the entire contents of the file that is referenced by the SAS fileref.

Used by: DS2TREE, DS2CONST, DS2CSF, META2HTM

SSHREF1–SSHREF5=*style-sheet-URL*
: specifies the URL of the stylesheet in the HREF= attribute of the LINK tag. If you specify a relative URL, it must be relative to the location of the HTML output file.

Used by: DS2TREE, DS2CONST, DS2CSF, META2HTM

SSMEDIA1–5=*media*
: specifies the media for which the style sheet was designed. The value is applied to the MEDIA= attribute of the LINK tag. The default value is SCREEN. Examples of other valid MEDIA values include BRAILLE for tactile feedback devices, and HANDHELD for small-screen devices.

Used by: DS2TREE, DS2CONST, DS2CSF, META2HTM

SSREL1–5=*relationship*
: specifies the REL= attribute of the LINK tag, which describes the relationship from the linked file to the HTML file. The value of this tag is generally STYLESHEET. The arguments SSREL1–5= can also be used with the arguments SSREV1–5 to link HTML pages in a series. For example, the SSREL1= argument can specify the next document in the series, and the SSREV2= argument can specify the reverse relationship, which would be the previous document in the series. Both arguments, SSRELn= and SSREVn=, can appear in the same LINK tag.

Used by: DS2TREE, DS2CONST, DS2CSF, META2HTM

SSREV1–5=*relationship*
specifies the REV= attribute of the LINK tag, which describes the relationship from the HTML file to the linked file. See the SSREL1–5= argument for details.

Used by: DS2TREE, DS2CONST, DS2CSF, META2HTM

SSTITLE1–5=*title-of-linked-page*
specifies the TITLE= attribute of the LINK tag. The TITLE= attribute provides a title for the referenced page. Use this argument when you are using the SSRELn= and SSREVn= arguments to specify next and previous links in a series of Web pages.

Used by: DS2TREE, DS2CONST, DS2CSF, META2HTM

SSTYPE1–5=*stylesheet-type*
specifies the TYPE= attribute of the LINK tag. For cascading style sheets, this value usually is TEXT/CSS. For JavaScript style sheets, this value is generally TEXT/JAVASCRIPT.

Used by: DS2TREE, DS2CONST, DS2CSF, META2HTM

Arguments for the SAS TITLE and FOOTNOTE Tags

The following arguments determine the content and appearance of the SAS TITLE and FOOTNOTE tags in the HTML output file.

FCLASS=*footnote-style-sheet-name*
TCLASS=*title-style-sheet-name*
specify the name of the style sheet class that is to be used for the SAS TITLE or FOOTNOTE.

Used by: DS2TREE, DS2CONST, DS2CSF.

FCOLOR=*footnote-text-color*
TCOLOR=*title-text-color*
specify the color of the text in the SAS TITLE or FOOTNOTE, using an HTML 3.2 color name or a six-digit hexadecimal RGB value.

Used by: DS2TREE, DS2CONST, DS2CSF.

FFACE=*footnote-text-font*
TFACE=*title-text-font*
specify a text font for the SAS TITLE or FOOTNOTE. Valid values are browser-specific.

Used by: DS2TREE, DS2CONST, DS2CSF.

FSIZE=*n* | +*n* | –*n*
TSIZE=*n* | +*n* | –*n*
specify the size of the text font that is to be used for the SAS TITLE or FOOTNOTE, where *n* is an integer. Valid values are browser-specific depending on how the browser handles the SIZE attribute on the FONT tag.

Used by: DS2TREE, DS2CONST, DS2CSF.

FTAG=*tag-string*
TTAG=*tag-string*
specify a text string that the macro translates into one or more tags that will enclose the SAS TITLE or FOOTNOTE.

The default value is as follows:

```
PREFORMATTED + HEADER 3
```

Used by: DS2TREE, DS2CONST, DS2CSF.

For each possible value of the TTAG= and FTAG= arguments, the following table shows the HTML tags that are generated by the macro for the SAS TITLE and FOOTNOTE lines (the corresponding end tags are generated automatically):

TTAG or FTAG Value	HTML Tag or Tags Enclosing the SAS TITLE or SAS FOOTNOTE
NO FORMATTING	(none)
STRONG	<STRONG>
EMPHASIS	<EM>
HEADER 1	<H1>
HEADER 2	<H2>
HEADER 3	<H3>
HEADER 4	<H4>
HEADER 5	<H5>
HEADER 6	<H6>
PREFORMATTED TEXT	<PRE>
CITATION TEXT	<CITE>
COMPUTER CODE TEXT	<CODE>
KEYBOARD INPUT TEXT	<KBD>
LITERAL TEXT	<SAMP>
VARIABLE TEXT	<VAR>
BOLD	<B>
ITALICIZED TEXT	<I>
UNDERLINE TEXT	<U>
TYPEWRITER	<TT>
BIG TEXT	<BIG>
SMALL TEXT	<SMALL>
STRIKE OUT TEXT	<STRIKE>
DEFINING INSTANCE TEXT	<DFN>
PREFORMATTED + STRONG	<PRE><STRONG>
PREFORMATTED + EMPHASIS	<PRE><EM>
PREFORMATTED + HEADER 1	<PRE><H1>
PREFORMATTED + HEADER 2	<PRE><H2>
PREFORMATTED + HEADER 3	<PRE><H3>
PREFORMATTED + HEADER 4	<PRE><H4>
PREFORMATTED + HEADER 5	<PRE><H5>
PREFORMATTED + HEADER 6	<PRE><H6>
PREFORMATTED + CITATION	<PRE><CITE>

TTAG or FTAG Value	HTML Tag or Tags Enclosing the SAS TITLE or SAS FOOTNOTE
PREFORMATTED + COMPUTER CODE	<PRE><CODE>
PREFORMATTED + KEYBOARD INPUT	<PRE><KBD>
PREFORMATTED + LITERAL	<PRE><SAMP>
PREFORMATTED + VARIABLE	<PRE><VAR>
PREFORMATTED + BOLD	<PRE><B>
PREFORMATTED + ITALICIZED	<PRE><I>
PREFORMATTED + TYPEWRITER	<PRE><TT>
PREFORMATTED + UNDERLINE	<PRE><U>
PREFORMATTED + BIG	<PRE><BIG>
PREFORMATTED + SMALL	<PRE><SMALL>
PREFORMATTED + STRIKE OUT	<PRE><STRIKE>
PREFORMATTED + DEFINING INSTANCE	<PRE><DFN>
STRONG + EMPHASIS	<STRONG><EM>
STRONG + ITALICIZED	<STRONG><I>
STRONG + CITATION	<STRONG><CITE>
STRONG + COMPUTER CODE	<STRONG><CODE>
STRONG + KEYBOARD INPUT	<STRONG><KBD>
STRONG + LITERAL	<STRONG><SAMP>
STRONG + VARIABLE	<STRONG><VAR>
STRONG + TYPEWRITER	<STRONG><TT>
STRONG + BIG	<STRONG><BIG>
STRONG + SMALL	<STRONG><SMALL>
EMPHASIS + CITATION	<EM><CITE>
EMPHASIS + COMPUTER CODE	<EM><CODE>
EMPHASIS + KEYBOARD INPUT	<EM><KBD>
EMPHASIS + LITERAL	<EM><SAMP>
EMPHASIS + VARIABLE	<EM><VAR>
EMPHASIS + TYPEWRITER	<EM><TT>
EMPHASIS + BIG	<EM><BIG>
EMPHASIS + SMALL	<EM><SMALL>
BOLD + EMPHASIS	<B><EM>
BOLD + ITALICIZED	<B><I>
BOLD + CITATION	<B><CITE>
BOLD + COMPUTER CODE	<B><CODE>

TTAG or FTAG Value	HTML Tag or Tags Enclosing the SAS TITLE or SAS FOOTNOTE
BOLD + KEYBOARD INPUT	<B><KBD>
BOLD + LITERAL	<B><SAMP>
BOLD + VARIABLE	<B><VAR>
BOLD + TYPEWRITER	<B><TT>
BOLD + BIG	<B><BIG>
BOLD + SMALL	<B><SMALL>
ITALICIZED + CITATION	<I><CITE>
ITALICIZED + COMPUTER CODE	<I><CODE>
ITALICIZED + KEYBOARD INPUT	<I><KBD>
ITALICIZED + LITERAL	<I><SAMP>
ITALICIZED + VARIABLE	<I><VAR>
ITALICIZED + TYPEWRITER	<I><TT>
ITALICIZED + BIG	<I><BIG>
ITALICIZED + SMALL	<I><SMALL>
STRONG + EMPHASIS + BIG	<STRONG><EM><BIG>
STRONG + CITATION + BIG	<STRONG><CITE><BIG>
STRONG + COMPUTER CODE + BIG	<STRONG><CODE><BIG>
STRONG + KEYBOARD INPUT + BIG	<STRONG><KBD><BIG>
STRONG + LITERAL + BIG	<STRONG><SAMP><BIG>
STRONG + VARIABLE + BIG	<STRONG><VAR><BIG>
STRONG + TYPEWRITER + BIG	<STRONG><TT><BIG>
EMPHASIS + CITATION + BIG	<EM><CITE><BIG>
EMPHASIS + COMPUTER CODE + BIG	<EM><CODE><BIG>
EMPHASIS + KEYBOARD INPUT + BIG	<EM><KBD><BIG>
EMPHASIS + LITERAL + BIG	<EM><SAMP><BIG>
EMPHASIS + VARIABLE + BIG	<EM><VAR><BIG>
EMPHASIS + TYPEWRITER + BIG	<EM><TT><BIG>
BOLD + EMPHASIS + BIG	<BOLD><EM><BIG>
BOLD + ITALICIZED + BIG	<BOLD><I><BIG>
BOLD + CITATION + BIG	<BOLD><CITE><BIG>
BOLD + COMPUTER CODE + BIG	<BOLD><CODE><BIG>
BOLD + KEYBOARD INPUT + BIG	<BOLD><KBD><BIG>
BOLD + LITERAL + BIG	<BOLD><SAMP><BIG>
BOLD + VARIABLE + BIG	<BOLD><VAR><BIG>
BOLD + TYPEWRITER + BIG	<BOLD><TT><BIG>

TTAG or FTAG Value	HTML Tag or Tags Enclosing the SAS TITLE or SAS FOOTNOTE
ITALICIZED + CITATION + BIG	<I><CITE><BIG>
ITALICIZED + COMPUTER CODE + BIG	<I><CODE><BIG>
ITALICIZED + KEYBOARD INPUT + BIG	<I><KBD><BIG>
ITALICIZED + LITERAL + BIG	<I><SAMP><BIG>
ITALICIZED + VARIABLE + BIG	<I><VAR><BIG>
ITALICIZED + TYPEWRITER + BIG	<I><TT><BIG>
STRONG + EMPHASIS + SMALL	<STRONG><EM><SMALL>
STRONG + ITALICIZED + SMALL	<STRONG><I><SMALL>
STRONG + CITATION + SMALL	<STRONG><CITE><SMALL>
STRONG + COMPUTER CODE + SMALL	<STRONG><CODE><SMALL>
STRONG + LITERAL + SMALL	<STRONG><SAMP><SMALL>
STRONG + VARIABLE + SMALL	<STRONG><VAR><SMALL>
STRONG + TYPEWRITER + SMALL	<STRONG><TT><SMALL>
EMPHASIS + CITATION + SMALL	<EM><CITE><SMALL>
EMPHASIS + COMPUTER CODE + SMALL	<EM><CODE><SMALL>
EMPHASIS + KEYBOARD INPUT + SMALL	<EM><KBD><SMALL>
EMPHASIS + LITERAL + SMALL	<EM><SAMP><SMALL>
EMPHASIS + TYPEWRITER + SMALL	<EM><TT><SMALL>
BOLD + EMPHASIS + SMALL	<BOLD><EM><SMALL>
BOLD + ITALICIZED + SMALL	<BOLD><I><SMALL>
BOLD + CITATION + SMALL	<BOLD><CITE><SMALL>
BOLD + COMPUTER CODE + SMALL	<BOLD><CODE><SMALL>
BOLD + KEYBOARD INPUT + SMALL	<BOLD><KBD><SMALL>
BOLD + LITERAL + SMALL	<BOLD><SAMP><SMALL>
BOLD + VARIABLE + SMALL	<BOLD><VAR><SMALL>
BOLD + TYPEWRITER + SMALL	<BOLD><TT><SMALL>
ITALICIZED + CITATION + SMALL	<I><CITE><SMALL>
ITALICIZED + COMPUTER CODE + SMALL	<I><CODE><SMALL>
ITALICIZED + KEYBOARD INPUT + SMALL	<I><KBD><SMALL>

TTAG or FTAG Value	HTML Tag or Tags Enclosing the SAS TITLE or SAS FOOTNOTE
ITALICIZED + LITERAL + SMALL	<I><SAMP><SMALL>
ITALICIZED + VARIABLE + SMALL	<I><VAR><SMALL>
ITALICIZED + TYPEWRITER + SMALL	<I><TT><SMALL>

Arguments for Character Transcoding

The following arguments allow you to specify a character set or convert character data to the corresponding Unicode Numeric Character Reference (NCR).

CHARSET=*char-set-name*
: specifies the character set name that will be written into the META tag of the HTML output file. For information on available character set names, see http://www.iana.org/assignments/character-sets.

Used by: DS2TREE, DS2CONST, DS2CSF, META2HTM

TRANLIST=*transcoding-list-name*
: specifies the name and location of an existing transcoding list, either user-defined or from SAS. The transcoding list name must be a four-level name, and the fourth level must be SLIST, as in the following example:

```
TRANLIST=SASHELP.HTMLGEN.IDENTITY.SLIST
```

This argument is required if you are implementing character transcoding.

SAS provides a number of transcoding lists in the SASHELP.HTMLNLS catalog. For a description of these transcoding lists, and for information on generating your own transcoding lists, see the SAS Web site at http://support.sas.com/rnd/web/intrnet/format/lang2.html.

Used by: DS2TREE, DS2CONST, DS2CSF, META2HTM

DS2CSF Arguments for Data Definition

These arguments for the DS2CSF macro define how the data set is to be interpreted by the Rangeview Applet as it generates the critical success factor graph.

DATA=*SAS-data-set-name*
: specifies the name of the data set that is to be used to generate the graph. The default data set is the one that was most recently created.

Used by: DS2CSF

LABELS=Y | N
: when the value is Y (default), indicates that the graph label and critical success value are displayed beneath the gauge. Specifying LABELS=N suppresses the display of the diagram label and critical success value.

Used by: DS2CSF

PW=*password*
specifies the password that is needed to access a password-protected data set. This argument is required if the data set has a READ or PW password. It is not required if the data set has a WRITE or ALTER password.

Used by: DS2CSF

VAR=*variable-name*
specifies the name of the variable in the SAS data set that is to be represented in the graph. The indicated value is the value of this variable in the first observation in the data set.

Used by: DS2CSF

DS2CSF Arguments for Diagram Appearance

The following arguments allow you to configure your range view diagram to suit the needs of your Web presentation.

CBACK=*color*
specifies a background color for the graph. The value must be a valid HTML 3.2 color name or a six-digit hexadecimal RGB value.

Used by: DS2CSF

CHUB=*color*
specifies a color for the half-circle area in the bottom middle of the classic diagram. The value must be a valid HTML 3.2 color name or a six-digit hexadecimal RGB value.

Used by: DS2CSF

CINDIC=*color*
specifies the color of the indicator in both the classic and the digital styles of the diagram. The value must be a valid HTML 3.2 color name or a six-digit hexadecimal RGB value.

Used by: DS2CSF

CLABTXT=*color*
specifies the color of the text label (and value, in the classic graph) that appear in a bold text font. The value must be a valid HTML 3.2 color name or a six-digit hexadecimal RGB value.

Used by: DS2CSF

CLABVAL=*color*
specifies the color of the data value labels that appear above the gauge. The value must be a valid HTML 3.2 color name or a six-digit hexadecimal RGB value.

Used by: DS2CSF

COUTLINE=*color*
specifies the color of the outline that is drawn around the classic or digital gauge. The value must be a valid HTML 3.2 color name or a six-digit hexadecimal RGB value.

Used by: DS2CSF

CSFTYPE=CLASSIC | DIGITAL
when the value is CLASSIC (default), specifies that the graph is to be rendered as an analog gauge with a needle that points to the critical success factor. Specifying a value of DIGITAL displays a diagram that resembles a liquid-crystal display.

Used by: DS2CSF

CVALUE=*color*
specifies the color of the critical success value. This value is shown in a bold text font along with the text label value in the classic graph. In the digital graph, the value appears in a digital font. The value must be a valid HTML 3.2 color name or a six-digit hexadecimal RGB value.

Used by: DS2CSF

DEPTH=TWO_DIMENSION | TWO_AND_A_HALF_DIMENSION
when the value is TWO_AND_A_HALF_DIMENSION (default), specifies a diagram that appears to have a degree of depth.

Used by: DS2CSF

DRILURL=*URL*
specifies the URL, relative or absolute, that is to be displayed when the user selects any part of the diagram.

Used by: DS2CSF

DRILTARG=*target-window-or-frame*
specifies the HTML target or the name of the browser window or frame where drill-down URLs are to be displayed. The default behavior is to open a new browser window and reuse it for subsequent drill-down requests. Specifically, the default value is _BLANK, which is one of several reserved names for targets in HTML. The DRILTARG value can also be the name of a window or frame in the Web presentation.

Used by: DS2CSF

HINDIC=*indicator-height-percentage*
specifies the height of the indicator for the classic diagram (see the CSFTYPE= argument). Valid values must be greater than zero and less than 100.

Used by: DS2CSF

INDICTYP=*indicator-shape*
specifies the shape of the indicator for the classic diagram (see CSFTYPE). Valid values can be ARROW, HARPOON, LINE, NEEDLE, or SPEAR.

Used by: DS2CSF

LABELPOS=*text-label-location*
specifies the location of the text label that identifies the critical success factor. Valid values can be TOP_LEFT, TOP_CENTER, TOP_RIGHT, BOTTOM_LEFT, BOTTOM_CENTER, or BOTTOM_RIGHT.

Used by: DS2CSF

RANGE=*range-name*
specifies the four-level name of the RANGE entry that defines range values and colors. For example:

```
range=sashelp.javagrf.sample1.range
```

To define a range entry, you can use the BUILD command:

```
build libname.catname.entryname.RANGE
```

This opens a window that you use to define the range. Use the scrollbar on the window to navigate between segments of the range.

Used by: DS2CSF

VALUEPOS=*CSF-value-location*
specifies the location of the critical success value. Valid values can be TOP_LEFT, TOP_CENTER, TOP_RIGHT, BOTTOM_LEFT, BOTTOM_CENTER, or BOTTOM_RIGHT.

Used by: DS2CSF

WINDIC=*indicator-width*
specifies the width of the critical success indicator, in pixels. The default value is 8.

Used by: DS2CSF

META2HTM Arguments for Saving the HTML File

The META2HTM macro enables the following arguments for generating and saving an HTML file.

Note: All of the following macro arguments are required. △

CAPTURE=ON | OFF
CAPTURE=ON enables the capture of metagraphics output. Set CAPTURE=ON above the SAS/GRAPH procedure that will generate metagraphics for the HTML output file. Set CAPTURE=OFF after you run and quit the SAS/GRAPH procedure.

The following arguments are enabled when CAPTURE=ON or when CAPTURE=OFF: CENTER=, HTMLFILE=, HTMLFREF=, OPENMODE=, and PAGEPART=.

The following arguments are enabled only when CAPTURE=OFF: SASPOWER=, SEPLOC=, SEPCLASS=, and SPCLASS=.

Any other arguments are valid only when CAPTURE=ON.

This argument is required.

Used by: META2HTM

HTMLFILE=*external-filename*
specifies the name and path of the HTML file where the output will be written. If the file you specify does not exist, it is created for you.

This argument is *required* if HTMLFREF is omitted. HTMLFILE= and HTMLFREF= are mutually exclusive arguments.

Used by: META2HTM

HTMLFREF=*fileref*
specifies the fileref that points to the location of the HTML file where the output will be written. If the file you specify does not exist, then it is created for you. Do not use a reserved name. See "Reserved Names" on page 566 for more information.

This argument is *required* if HTMLFILE is omitted. HTMLFREF= and HTMLFILE= are mutually exclusive arguments.

Used by: META2HTM

OPENMODE=APPEND | REPLACE
indicates whether the new HTML output overwrites the information currently in the specified file or if the new output is appended to the end of the existing file. The default value is REPLACE. If you do not want to replace the current contents,then supply APPEND to add your output to the end of an existing HTML file.

Always use OPENMODE=APPEND with the CAPTURE=OFF argument.

OPENMODE=APPEND is not valid if you are writing in the z/OS operating environment.

This argument is required.

Used by: META2HTM

RUNMODE=B | S

specifies whether you are running the macro in batch or server mode. Batch mode (the default) means that you are submitting the META2HTM macro in the Program Editor or you have included it in a SAS program. Server mode is used with Dispatcher Applications in the SAS/INTRNET software. Specifying server mode generates an HTTP header that is required by Application Dispatcher.

This argument is required.

Used by: META2HTM

META2HTM Arguments for Applet Behavior

The META2HTM macro enables the following arguments, which are used to control the behavior of the applet. Many of these arguments specify applet parameters.

CBACK=*hex-color*

specifies the color of the applet control area, using a six-digit hexadecimal RGB value.

Used by: META2HTM

CTIPHILT=*hex-color*

specifies a six-digit hexadecimal RGB value for the color of the graph element that has been selected to display its pop-up data tips window. The default highlight color is red. See also the TIPTYPE= argument.

Used by: META2HTM

PAGECTL=Y | N

when the value is N (default), prevents the display of the page-selection control. For further information, see "Metaview Applet Parameters" on page 475.

Used by: META2HTM

SLIDECTL=Y | N

the default value of N prevents the display of the graph-selection control. For further information, see "Metaview Applet Parameters" on page 475.

Used by: META2HTM

TIPTYPE=HIGHLIGHT | STICK | FIXED_STICK

specifies the appearance of data tips.

HIGHLIGHT

specifies that the text tip is to appear as a disconnected pop-up window. The outline of the selected graph element is highlighted in the color specified in the CTIPHILT= argument. This is the default value.

STICK

specifies that a line will connect the cursor and the selected graph element. The pop-up text tip window appears above the cursor and follows the cursor as it moves within the selected graph element.

FIXED_STICK

specifies that a line will be drawn between the text tip pop-up window and the center of the selected graph element. The text tip window does not move with the cursor.

See also "Metaview Applet Parameters" on page 475.

Used by: META2HTM

ZOOMCTL=Y | N
: specifies whether or not the zoom control appears in the applet control area. By default, the control is displayed.

Used by: META2HTM

Reserved Names

Do not use the following names as the value of a macro variable:

Libnames and Filerefs
- HTML
- CATENT
- HTMSS

Global Macro Variables
- _htmovp
- _htmcap
- _htmtitl
- _htmwher

Data Sets or Views
- WORK._BYGRP

Catalogs
- WORK._HTMLG_
- SASHELP.HTMLNLS

Catalog Entries
- SASHELP.HTMLGEN.DSPROP.SLIST
- SASHELP.HTMLGEN.IDENTITY.SLIST
- SASHELP.HTMLGEN.OUTPROP.SLIST
- SASHELP.HTMLGEN.TABPROP.SLIST
- SASHELP.HTMLGEN.TAGS.SLIST

CHAPTER 22

Enhancing Web Output

Enhancing Web Output

When you enhance a Web presentation, you specify additional options, arguments, or parameters to configure and add to the Web presentation that is generated by default. The number and type of enhancements that are available depend on the type of the Web presentation. Presentations that run with Web executables (ActiveX Control or Java applets) enable the largest number of enhancements. Depending upon the type of Web presentation, enhancements include:

- Using ODS styles to enhance the appearance of graphical output. See "Using ODS Styles" on page 488.
- Displaying pop-up text when the cursor is over a portion of the diagram. See "Adding Data Tips to Web Presentations" on page 568.
- Adding hotspots that link to other Web pages. See "Adding Drill-Down Links to Web Presentations" on page 571.

- Adding annotations to Web presentations. See Chapter 17, "Generating Web Output with the Annotate Facility," on page 499.
- Modifying colors in the presentations. See "Specifying Colors in SAS/GRAPH Programs" on page 92.
- Displaying images as part of a graph. See "Specifying Images in SAS/GRAPH Programs" on page 106.
- Changing text fonts. See "Specifying Fonts in SAS/GRAPH Programs" on page 75.

Adding Data Tips to Web Presentations

You can add pop-up data tips to most SAS/GRAPH Web presentations. The text is displayed when the user's cursor is over a specified area of a graph. See the following sections for basic information on adding data tips to Web presentations:

- "Data Tips in GIF, JPEG, and PNG Files" on page 568
- "Data Tips in ACTXIMG and JAVAIMG Images" on page 568
- "Data Tips in Java and ActiveX Web Presentations" on page 568
- "Data Tips in Metaview Applet Presentations" on page 569
- "Data Tips in Treeview Diagrams" on page 569
- "Data Tips in Constellation Charts" on page 569
- "Data Tips in Critical Success Factor Diagrams" on page 569
- "Data Tips in Animated GIFs" on page 570.

Data Tips in GIF, JPEG, and PNG Files

For Web output that is generated with ODS and the GIF, JPEG, and PNG device drivers, SAS adds default data tips using the values of fields in the SAS data set. Also, if you specify DESCRIPTION= as an option on the SAS/GRAPH procedure, then SAS adds the text of that description as a data tip for the entire graphic. Specify DESCRIPTION="" to suppress this default data tip.

You can also add custom data tips to the output of any SAS/GRAPH procedure that supports the HTML= option. For this technique, see "Adding Data Tips with the HTML= Option" on page 570.

Data Tips in ACTXIMG and JAVAIMG Images

When you specify DEVICE=ACTIXIMG or JAVAIMG, and use ODS HTML, SAS adds default data tips using the values of fields in the SAS data set. Also, if you specify DESCRIPTION= as an option on the SAS/GRAPH procedure, then SAS adds the text of that description as a data tip for the entire graphic. Specify DESCRIPTION="" to suppress this default data tip.

By using the HTML= option of a GBARLINE, GCHART, GPLOT (except for high-low), or GRADAR procedure, you can add custom data tips to graphs created with the ACTXIMG device driver. For information, see "Adding Data Tips with the HTML= Option" on page 570. SAS/GRAPH does not directly support adding custom data tips to Web presentations created with DEVICE=JAVAIMG. You can, however, use any image-map tool available to you to create an image map for the resulting PNG file.

Data Tips in Java and ActiveX Web Presentations

By default, Web presentations created by the ACTIVEX control or JAVA applets automatically include data tips using the values of fields in the SAS data set. Use the

TIPS=NONE parameter to suppress data tips. See "Parameter Reference for Java and ActiveX" on page 424.

You can provide your own custom data tips to the output of any SAS/GRAPH procedure that supports the HTML= option. (This feature is supported by the Map applet but is not currently supported by the Graph applet.) For information on this technique, see "Adding Data Tips with the HTML= Option" on page 570.

Note: When you provide data-tip text using HTML='ALT="*variable_name*"' the Java applets automatically suppress the display of the default data tips. The ActiveX Control, however, adds your custom text to the default text. To suppress the default text in ActiveX presentations, use the TipMode=HTML parameter in an ODS statement. See "Parameter Reference for Java and ActiveX" on page 424 .

For example:

```
ODS HTML parameters=("TipMode"="HTML")
```

△

Data Tips in Metaview Applet Presentations

For graphs displayed by the Metaview applet, you can add data tips to the output of any SAS/GRAPH procedure that supports the HTML= option. For more information, see "Adding Data Tips with the HTML= Option" on page 570.

Data Tips in Treeview Diagrams

You can add data tip text to a Treeview diagram by including the text in the SAS data set from which the Treeview is generated. For example, the following data set specifies a different data-tip for each observation:

```
data father_and_sons;
input id $8. name $15. father $8. datatip $30.;
cards;
aaron   Aaron Parker           Data tip for Aaron Parker...
bob     Bob Parker     aaron   Data tip for Bob Parker...
charlie Charlie Parker aaron   Data tip for Charlie Parker...
david   David Parker   aaron   Data tip for David Parker...
edward  Edward Parker  david   Data tip for Edward Parker...
;
run;
```

Use the TIPS, NTIP, and NTIPFMT parameters of DS2TREE (see "DS2TREE and DS2CONST Arguments for Data Definition" on page 537) to control data tip text.

Data Tips in Constellation Charts

You can add data tips to a Constellation diagram by including the text in the SAS data set from which the diagram is generated, as is done for Treeview diagrams as shown in "Data Tips in Treeview Diagrams" on page 569. Use the TIPS, NTIP, and NTIPFMT parameters of DS2CONT (see "DS2TREE and DS2CONST Arguments for Data Definition" on page 537) to control data-tip text.

Data Tips in Critical Success Factor Diagrams

The Critical Success Factor macro DS2CSF does not support adding data tips.

Data Tips in Animated GIFs

SAS/GRAPH does not directly support inserting data tips into animated GIFs.

Adding Data Tips with the HTML= Option

You can add custom data tips to the output of any SAS/GRAPH procedure that supports the HTML= option. Use the HTML option in the following form:

HTML='ALT="*variable_name*"'

The following code fragment illustrates the basic technique of adding data tips with the HTML= option.

```
/* initialize a data tip variable in the data set */
   length rpt $40;

/* assign values to the link variable */
if Region='Central' then
     rpt='alt="Central region"';
   else if Region='South' then
     rpt='alt="Southern region"';
   else if Region='West' then
     rpt='alt="Western region"';

/* create a chart that uses the data tip variable */
proc gchart data=regsales;
   vbar3d region / sumvar=sales
   patternid=midpoint
   html=rpt;
run;
```

In this case, the HTML= option identifies the variable RPT as containing ALT= plus the text of data tip to be displayed. The value of RPT, in turn, is set by an IF statement according to the contents of a SAS data set. The maximum length for the value of the variable is 1024 characters, including the characters "ALT=".

The following code uses a variable inside the HTML= variable to substitute the appropriate text for a data tip. It also uses the concatentation operator || to concatenate the string "region" to the name of the region, and the newline character '0D'x to create a second output line.

```
/* initialize a data tip variable in the data set */
   length rpt $40;

/* assign values to the link variable */
rpt='ALT="Region: ' || trim(left(Region)) || '0D'x ||
    'Second line of text ' || '"';
/* create a chart that uses the data tip variable */
proc gchart data=regsales;
   vbar3d region / sumvar=sales
   patternid=midpoint
   html=rpt;
run;
```

For more on the HTML option, see "Adding Links with the HTML= and HTML_LEGEND= Options" on page 574.

Adding Drill-Down Links to Web Presentations

You can add hotspots to most SAS/GRAPH Web presentations. The hotspots enable a user to select an element of a graph to open a Web page showing either another graph or related information. See the following sections for basic information on adding links to Web presentations:

- "Links in GIF, JPEG, and PNG Files" on page 571
- "Links in ACTXIMG and JAVAIMG Images" on page 571
- "Links in Java and ActiveX Web Presentations" on page 571
- "Links in Metaview Applet Presentations" on page 572
- "Links in Treeview Diagrams" on page 572
- "Links in Constellation Charts" on page 573
- "Links in Critical Success Factor Diagrams" on page 573
- "Links in Animated GIFs" on page 573.

Links in GIF, JPEG, and PNG Files

To add a hotspot link to static images generated with the GIF, JPEG, and PNG device drivers, use the HTML= option or HTML_LEGEND= option or both, with a SAS/GRAPH procedure as described in "Adding Links with the HTML= and HTML_LEGEND= Options" on page 574. The links are implemented in an HTML image map. The elements in the graph, such as bars or pie slices, become selectable hot spots in the Web presentation. In your SAS program, drill-down URLs are defined in a data set variable. SAS generates the image map for you in the HTML output file.

A complete example of hotspots created in this way is shown in "GIF Output with Hotspot Links" on page 452.

Links in ACTXIMG and JAVAIMG Images

To add a hotspot link to an image created with the ACTXIMG device driver and a GBARLINE, GCHART, GPLOT (except for high-low), or GRADAR procedure, use the HTML= option as described in "Adding Links with the HTML= and HTML_LEGEND= Options" on page 574.

SAS/GRAPH does not directly support hotspots for Web presentations created with DEVICE=JAVAIMG. You can, however, create an image map for the resulting PNG file using any image-map tool available to you.

Links in Java and ActiveX Web Presentations

The ActiveX Control and two of the SAS Java applets (Graph and Map) support four implementations of links in Web presentations. Hotspots are not supported for contour diagrams in either the ActiveX Control or the Contour applet.

To specify the drill-down mode, use the DRILLDOWNMODE parameter as follows (for more information, see "Configuring Drill-Down Links with ACTIVEX" on page 392):

ODS HTML PARAMETERS=
("DRILLDOWNMODE"="LOCAL" | "SCRIPT" | "URL" | "HTML");

Local mode (Graph applet only)
: responds to drill-down actions by dynamically generating and displaying new graphs based on a subset of the data in the selected graph element. In this mode, the graphic to be displayed is generated by the applet from data it already has (rather than being a pre-existing HTML page that you have created yourself). At each drill-down level, the user can configure the graph type, data subset, variable roles, and colors.

Script mode
: calls a JavaScript method that you specify in your SAS/GRAPH program, and passes to that method information on the selected graph element or map region. It is up to you to write the JavaScript to respond to the mouse-click. You can use the data passed to the JavaScript function to determine what part of the diagram was clicked on and, therefore, what URL is appropriate to link to. This is the default drill-down mode for the Map applet.

URL mode
: displays URLs that are provided by link variables. The link variables are identified to the graphics procedure with the HTML= option. The URLs identify pre-existing HTML files that you will have created yourself. The drill-down functionality of the URL mode is similar to the drill-down functionality that is provided by the GIF, JPEG, and PNG device drivers.

HTML mode
: generates drill-down URLs based on a substitution pattern that you specify in your SAS/GRAPH program. The Graph applet and Map applet complete the URL by inserting the specified data from the graph element that was selected in the drill-down action. An example link specified in HTML mode is the following:

```
ods html file=statepop.htm
   parameters=("DRILLDOWNMODE"="HTML"
      "DRILLPATTERN"='http://www.state.{&statename}.us');
```

In this example, the value of the data set variable STATENAME completes the drill-down URL.

Note: The variable must be used in the chart. It is not sufficient that it simply be in the data set. △

Any mode (Graph applet and ActiveX control)
: attempts to implement each of the four drill-down modes in succession until a valid Web destination is found. The order of the attempts is Local (Graph applet only), Script, URL, and HTML.

Links in Metaview Applet Presentations

To generate drill-down presentations for the Metaview applet, use either the HTML= or HTML_LEGEND= options or both and an enhancement variable, as introduced in "Adding Links with the HTML= and HTML_LEGEND= Options" on page 574.

Links in Treeview Diagrams

You can add hotspots to Treeview diagrams so that when a user selects a node another Web page is opened. The easiest way to add hotspots is to include the URL to be linked to in the SAS data set from which the Treeview is generated. For example, the following data set specifies a different URL for each observation:

```
data father_and_sons;
input id $8. name $15. father $8. url $30.;
cards;
aaron   Aaron Parker           http://www.yourdomain.com/aaronparker.html
bob     Bob Parker     aaron   http://www.yourdomain.com/bobparker.html
charlie Charlie Parker aaron   http://www.yourdomain.com/charlieparker.html
david   David Parker   aaron   http://www.yourdomain.com/davidparker.html
edward  Edward Parker  david   http://www.yourdomain.com/edwardparker.html
;
run;
```

A simple, but complete example is shown in "Treeview with Hotspots" on page 510.

Links in Constellation Charts

You can add hotspots to Constellation diagrams so that when a user selects a node another Web page is opened. The easiest way to add hotspots is to include the URL to be linked to in the SAS data set from which the diagram is generated, as is done for Treeview diagrams as shown in "Links in Treeview Diagrams" on page 572. A simple example of a Constellation diagram with hotspots is shown in "Constellation Chart with Hotspots" on page 524.

Links in Critical Success Factor Diagrams

You can add a hotspot to a critical success factor diagram created with the DS2CSF macro. However, unlike the Treeview and Constellation macros, you can add only a single hotspot to the diagram, i.e., the diagram as a whole. The following code fragment links to the specified URL when a user clicks anywhere on the diagram. The DRILURL= option specifies the URL to link to, while DRILTARG=_self specifies that the new Web page is to be displayed in the same window as the dial.

```
%ds2csf(data=test,
        var=x,
        htmlfile=u:/public_html/Web_output/csf.html,
        openmode=replace, pagepart=head,
        center=y,
      drilurl=http://www.sas.com,
        archive=rvapplet.jar,
        /* specify the complete url for the jar file                */
        /* if it is not in same directory as the html file          */
        /* archive=http://sww.sas.com/avd/codebase/rvapplet.jar,    */
        csftyp=classic, septype=none, cback=#e0e0e0,
        bgtype=color, bg="#e0e0e0",
        ttag=bold + italicized, tcolor="#002288", tsize=5,
        tface="Arial, Helvetica",
        range=sashelp.javagrf.sample1.range)
```

Links in Animated GIFs

SAS/GRAPH does not directly support inserting hotspots into animated GIFs. If you want to enable linking from an animated GIF, you must use whatever third-party tools are available to you. You can also make the entire image a hotspot by including the <IMG> tag inside an <A HREF=> tag.

Adding Links with the HTML= and HTML_LEGEND= Options

The HTML= and HTML_LEGEND= options can be used in a number of statements that generate graphs. These options are be used to add drill-down links to Web presentations that are generated with the following device drivers:

- GIF, JPEG, or PNG
- JAVA and ACTIVEX
- JAVAMETA

In these Web presentations, the HTML= and HTML_LEGEND= options identify a variable that provides drill-down URLs. This variable is referred to as a *link variable* because of its use in establishing links.

The HTML= and HTML_LEGEND= options are also used to implement a number of different enhancements to Web presentations that run in the Metaview applet. In this case, the variables that are identified by the HTML= and HTML_LEGEND options are referred to as *enhancement variables* because of their broader use than just establishing links.

Working with Link and Enhancement Variables

To use link or enhancement variables in a Web presentation, you need to define those variables, add data to those variables, and then identify those variables in the HTML= option or HTML_LEGEND option or both.

The following code fragment defines a link variable named RPT and assigns that variable a length of 40 characters:

```
data regsales;
  input Region State Sales;
  length rpt $40
```

Be sure to define your link variable with a length that will be sufficient to contain your URLs (plus the HREF= option). The maximum length is 1024 characters.

The values of the link variable use the following syntax:

'HREF=*URL*<*"anchor-name"*>'

This syntax is used in the following example:

```
RPT='href="reports.html#west"';
```

The following table lists the valid values of the link variable:

Table 22.1 Valid Values of the Link Variable

Value Assigned to a Link Destination Variable	Implications
'HREF="<*path*>reports.html"' 'HREF="<*path*>reports.html#west"'	Tells the browser to look in the file reports.html. If <*path*> is not provided, the file must be in the same location as the HTML file that initiates the link. For the value that has #west, go to the output with the anchor name west. Users must have access to your file system in order to access the link target.
'HREF="http://www.company.com/web/reports.html"'	Tells the browser to go to the Web site address http://www.company.com/web and look in the file reports.html.
'HREF="http://www.company.com/web/reports.html#west"'	For the value that has #west, go to the output with the anchor name west. Users must have access to the Web to follow the links.
'HREF="#west"'	Go to the target with the anchor name west. The target must be referenced or contained in the same HTML file as the drill-down graph that contains the link. For example, if the drill-down graph is in the file sales.html, then the target output must be referenced or contained in sales.html. Because this target is in the same file as the drill-down graph, this link will work whether the output is viewed within your file system or across the Web.

Assigning Values to Link and Enhancement Variables

The most obvious method of adding these variables to your data set is to manually add them to the desired observations in your data set. This method is not practical or feasible in many cases, in which case you can use IF/THEN statements or variable substitution.

The following picture shows how link variables are assigned to a bar chart. The three bars represent regional sales for a company's central, southern, and western regions.

Figure 22.1 Links in Drill-Down Graphs

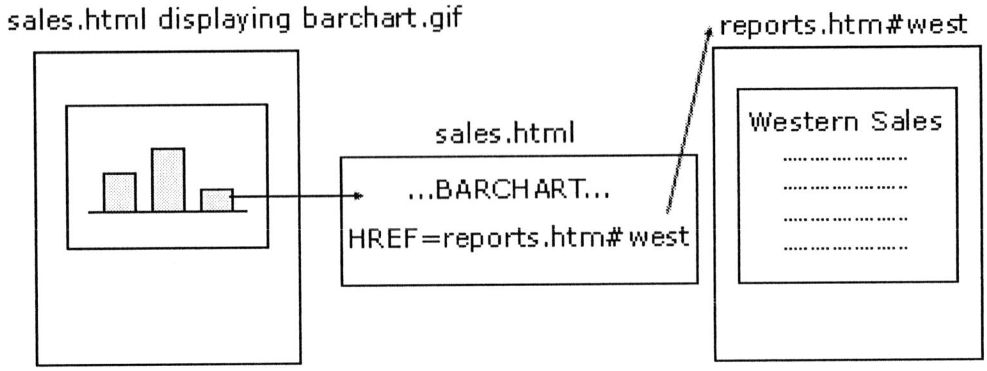

Each bar in the chart needs to link to a different anchor tag in an HTML file named reports.html. The anchor names in the linked file are "central," "south," and "west." The following DATA step uses an IF/THEN statement to assign values to the link variable.

```
/* create data set REGSALES */
data regsales;
   length Region State $ 8;
   format Sales dollar8.;
   input Region State Sales;
   length rpt $40; /* the link dest. variable */

/* assign HREF values to link dest. variable */
if Region='Central' then
     rpt='HREF="reports.html#central"';
  else if Region='South' then
     rpt='HREF="reports.html#south"';
  else if Region='West' then
     rpt='HREF="reports.html#west"';

/* create a chart that uses the data tip variable */
proc gchart data=regsales;
   vbar3d region / sumvar=sales
   patternid=midpoint
   html=rpt;
run;
  datalines;
West CA 13636
West OR 18988
West WA 14523
Central IL 18038
Central IN 13611
Central OH 11084
Central MI 19660
South FL 14541
South GA 19022
;
```

The following table shows the values in the data set REGSALES.

Display 22.1 Values in the REGSALES Data Set

Region	State	Sales	rpt
West	CA	$13,636	href="reports.html#west"
West	OR	$18,988	href="reports.html#west"
West	WA	$14,523	href="reports.html#west"
Central	IL	$18,038	href="reports.html#central"
Central	IN	$13,611	href="reports.html#central"
Central	OH	$11,084	href="reports.html#central"
Central	MI	$19,660	href="reports.html#central"
South	FL	$14,541	href="reports.html#south"
South	GA	$19,022	href="reports.html#south"

To illustrate the use of variable substitution, assume that you are developing for the Metaview applet a presentation that uses the HREF drill-down mode of linking. You need to add an enhancement variable to each observation in the data set. The value of that variable is a URL that has a common base and a filename that is derived from a variable in the data set. The following example defines the base URL, defines an enhancement variable, and uses variable substitution to assign values to the enhancement variable.

```
%let htmlpath=http://webServer1/graph/javameta;
data yearsonly;
   set prdsummary(where=(_type_ eq 2));
   length htmlvar $200;
   htmlvar='href='||quote("&htmlpath/y"||put(year,4.)||'.htm');
run;
```

In the preceding example, the values of the enhancement variable HTMLVAR are URLs. Each URL combines the base address in HTMLPATH with the value of the YEAR variable and a filetype of HTM.

CHAPTER 23

Troubleshooting Web Output

Troubleshooting Web Output

This chapter contains information that you can use to resolve rendering problems on client workstations.

If you or a member of your audience cannot display your presentation, then refer to the following table for solutions.

NOTE: to ensure that software requirements have been met, see "What does your audience need to view the presentation?" on page 380.

Table 23.1 Web Troubleshooting

Symptom	Cause	Remedy
Can't access the HTML file.	Incorrect URL.	Check the URL in the browser.
	Network access denied.	Check operating environment permissions for the HTML file.
		Check firewall access permissions for Internet clients.
Browser can't display the file.	Browser or Java plug—in may not meet requirements.	Check the requirements. See "What does your audience need to view the presentation?" on page 380.

	ActiveX control may not have been installed or may be out of date.	Install the ActiveX control manually (see "Manually Installing the ActiveX Control" on page 389). Consider updating the presentation to prompt users to install the control (see "Prompting for Installation of the ActiveX Control" on page 390).
	User attempting to run the ActiveX control in a browser other than Internet Explorer.	Switch to the required version of the Internet Explorer Web browser.
	User has not been authenticated for that browser and that Web page.	Check to see if authentication is needed, and then authenticate. See "Connecting to Web Servers that Require Authentication" on page 583.
	Browser doesn't recognize the file as HTML.	Ensure that the type of the HTML file is correctly specified.
		Ensure that the DOCTYPE and MIME tags are correctly formatted.
	Browser permissions too restrictive.	Check browser permissions. See "Checking Browser Permissions" on page 582.
Browser displays blank page.	Browser cannot access the referenced image file.	If *not* running an applet or control, check the image file at the location specified in the HTML file.
	Browser cannot run the applet or control.	For Java, ensure that the HTML file is correctly referencing the Java plug-in and SAS Java archive. See "Specifying the Location of Control and Applet Files (CODEBASE= and ARCHIVE= Options)" on page 422.
		Check browser permissions for running Java scripts. See "Checking Browser Permissions" on page 582.
		In the UNIX operating environment, remove any CLASSPATH environment variables. See "Removing CLASSPATH Environment Variables" on page 583.
		Open the browser's Java Console and trace the source of the error.

Graph is distorted.	NOGTITLE or NOGFOOTNOTE option on the ODS statement is not properly reclaiming space.	Use the HPOS= or ASPECT= GOPTION to restore the correct aspect. Use hardware fonts.
Browser displays popup message `Error: Not enough virtual memory to produce plot.`	Client RAM is insufficient for rendering.	Generate a new graph using a smaller data set or a simpler graph. If using PROC GMAP, consider using PROC GREDUCE.
Graph is not rendering as specified by the ODS graph style.	A style attribute may not be enabled for your ODS destination.	Ensure that the attribute is enabled for your ODS destination. For example, the URL attribute is not enabled for the PS destination. Refer to the table of style attributes for the STYLE statement of the TEMPLATE procedure in *SAS Output Delivery System: User's Guide.*
	A style attribute may be overridden by a global option, global statement option, procedure option, or statement option.	Specify the minimum options needed for your graph, for example:**`goptions reset=all device=activex;`**
In ActiveX, the user gets the message `There is a pending reboot for this machine...`	1 Virus-scanning software may be interfering with the installation of the control. 2 Other instances of the control might be running.	1 Turn off any virus-scanning software before installing the control. 2 Be sure to close all instances of Internet Explorer before installing the control.
Text font is incorrect.	Java font is defined differently.	Change browser fonts or change the SAS/GRAPH program. See "Correcting Text Fonts" on page 583.
Text in browser shows incorrect characters.	Browser misinterpreting special characters.	Replace special characters with character entities. See "Using HTML Character Entities" on page 582.
Graph in browser differs from graph in SAS.	A graphics option or global statement may be unsupported or partially supported for that applet or control. See also "Resolving Differences Between Client and Server Graphs" on page 584.	Refer to the descriptions for the options you are using and to Appendix 1, "Summary of ActiveX and Java Support," on page 1507 for information on whether a statement or option is supported.

	A default value in the applet or control is overriding a default option value.	Specify a value for the option rather than relying on the default. See "Resolving Differences Between Client and Server Graphs" on page 584.
	GPLOT lines drawn in reverse order on the client.	This change was made intentionally to maintain the integrity of plots drawn with the AREAS= option.
In ActiveX, black-and-white image is not displayed	ActiveX does not enable 8-bit grayscales images.	Convert the image to 24-bit monochrome.
Graph loses attributes after graph type is changed in the Web browser.	Some attribute loss is inherent in graph type changes.	Select the Refresh button in the Web browser to restore the original graph.
Changes made through the Data Options dialog cause the graph to revert to its original view.	The graph discards subsetting information if you make changes through the Data Options dialog.	Make any changes needed through the Data Options dialog before subsetting the graph.
Colors wrong in Netscape.	Netscape is running without its own color map.	Run Netscape with the install option. See "Resolving Colors in Netscape" on page 583.

Checking Browser Permissions

Access permissions vary from browser to browser, but some form of access control is enforced in most browsers. To check your permissions, open the browser's Preferences or Internet Options window. Then look for the advanced options. Use your browser's help system and contact your system support representative as needed to ensure that the browser permissions allow the following:

- Stylesheets
- Java
- JavaScripts
- Java Console

In the Security tab of the Internet Explorer's Internet Options window, make sure that the selected Web content zone enables access to the Web presentation.

Using HTML Character Entities

If a special character in your Web presentation does not resolve in the browser, that character may need to be changed to a character entity in the source file or in the SAS program. A character entity is a standardized string of characters that represents a special character. The browser recognizes the string and replaces it with the special character when it is formatting the display. One common character entity is > . This entity represents the greater-than symbol (<).

Lists of standard character entities are provided in HTML reference books and in HTML references on the Worldwide Web.

For presentations that run in the Constellation, Treeview, and Rangeview applets, the macros DS2CONST, DS2TREE, and DS2CSF enable the ENCODE argument, which you can use to automatically replace or not replace angle brackets (“<” and “>”) in TITLE and FOOTNOTE statements.

Connecting to Web Servers that Require Authentication

If you are unable to run a Java applet or install the ActiveX control, then you may be trying to access a Web server that requires authentication. To resolve this problem, access a different file on that server and enter your user ID and password. Redisplaying your Web presentation should now allow you to access that Web server.

Removing CLASSPATH Environment Variables

In the UNIX operating environment, if the Java applet does not run after you have verified that your Java archive is correctly specified, then you should remove any CLASSPATH environment variables that have been set. The Java archive files contain all the required classes to run the applets. Your CLASSPATH may point to old versions of the required classes (for example, for use with the webAF software). This can cause the applets to fail to load. Most applications allow you to specify a CLASSPATH at startup, by using a startup option. This is often safer for running multiple clients than using the environment variables.

Correcting Text Fonts

If your presentation displays an incorrect text font on a given client computer, then the cause may be that the client computer maps a Java logical font name such as Courier to a different physical font set. If the logical font is not mapped to any physical font, Java uses a default font. To correct the problem, edit your HTML file or your SAS/GRAPH program to specify a different logical font name.

For programs that use the JAVA or JAVAMETA device drivers, or that use the macros DS2CONST, DS2TREE, or DS2CSF, specify one of these logical font names: Courier, Dialog, DialogInput, Helvetica, Monospaced, Serif, SansSerif, or TimesRoman. These names are case-sensitive. If you specified them in uppercase letters in your SAS program, this could be the source of your problem.

The JAVA device driver can use the physical font set Lucida, which is provided in the Java plug-in. If your Java presentation shows unexpected fonts, switching to the Lucida font should clear up the problem. For further information on font specifications, see “Specifying Fonts in SAS/GRAPH Programs” on page 75.

Resolving Colors in Netscape

In the UNIX operating environment, the Netscape browser can run out of available screen colors and begin using default colors such as black. To alleviate this problem, run the Netscape program with the INSTALL option, as follows:

```
netscape -install
```

Running the Netscape program with the INSTALL option generates a separate color map for that browser.

Resolving Differences Between Client and Server Graphs

A *client* graph is rendered on the client's (recipient's) system using data sent from the server. The user may be able to manipulate and interact with the graph. Client graphs are intended for display on the Web. Graphs generated with the JAVA and ACTIVEX device drivers, for example, are client graphs.

A *server* graph is rendered on the server (the machine where the SAS session is running). Interaction with server graphs is limited to features defined by the server such as drill-down links and pop-up data tips. A server graph may or may not be intended for display on the web. Graphs generated with the GIF, JPEG, and PNG device drivers, for example, are server graphs.

Because of technological differences between SAS, Java, and ActiveX, client graphs may differ from server graphs even if the graphs are generated with the same SAS procedure code. In addition, graphs generated with Java may differ from graphs generated with ActiveX. The graphs may differ in appearance, in the default values used for certain options, or in the availability of certain features.

For example, differences between client and server graphs may occur if you are using a global statement or procedure option that is not enabled for that applet or control. Most global statement and procedure options are fully supported by the client device drivers. Exceptions are identified in the procedure and statement documentation and summarized in Appendix 1, "Summary of ActiveX and Java Support," on page 1507.

In certain cases, differences between client and server graphs can occur when an applet or control overrides the default value of a procedure option. To resolve this issue, specify a value for the option rather than relying on the default. For example, consider a bubble plot that is being displayed in the Graph applet. The default bubble size is 5. The Graph applet overrides that default with a larger bubble size. To apply a bubble size of 5, specify BSIZE=5 in the BUBBLE statement, rather than relying on the default value of the BSIZE= option.

PART 3

The Annotate Facility

CHAPTER
24

Using Annotate Data Sets

Overview

The Annotate facility enables you to generate a special data set of graphics commands from which you can produce graphics output. This data set is referred to as an *Annotate data set*. You can use it to generate custom graphics or to enhance graphics output from many SAS/GRAPH procedures, including GCHART, GCONTOUR, GMAP, GPLOT, GPRINT, GRADAR, GSLIDE, and G3D.

Enhancing Existing Graphs

The Annotate facility enhances output from SAS/GRAPH procedures by adding graphics elements to the output. For example, you can

- label points on a map using map coordinates
- label bars on horizontal and vertical bar charts
- label points on a plot
- create a legend for a three-dimensional graph.

Figure 24.1 on page 588 shows GMAP procedure output annotated with stars and labels at selected cities.

Figure 24.1 Annotate Graphics Applied to a Map

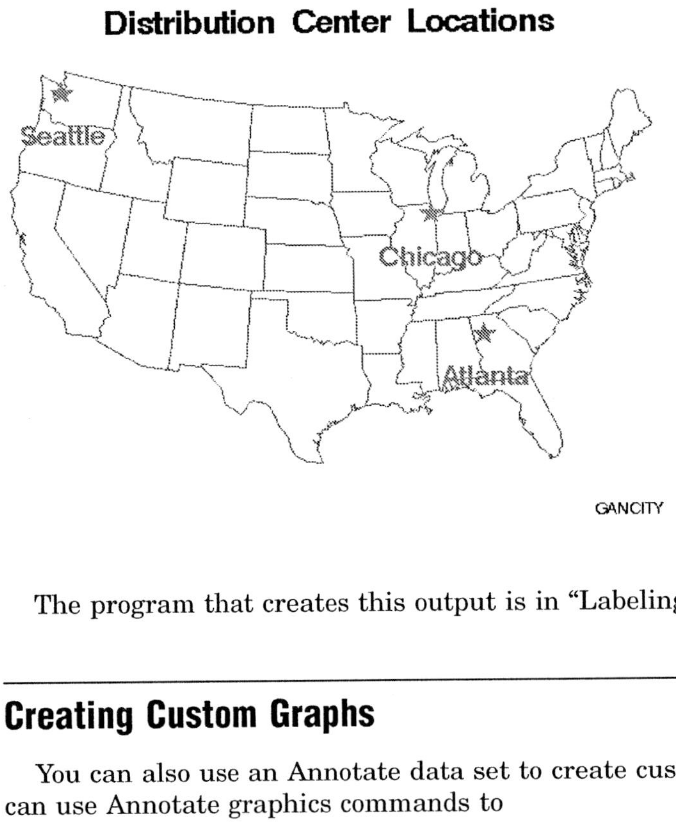

The program that creates this output is in "Labeling Cities on a Map" on page 604.

Creating Custom Graphs

You can also use an Annotate data set to create custom graphics. For example, you can use Annotate graphics commands to

- create various types of graphs (including pie charts, bar charts, and plots)
- draw graphics elements such as lines, polygons, arcs, symbols, and text.

Figure 24.2 on page 589 is an example of a custom graph that uses Annotate commands to draw the graphic elements.

Figure 24.2 Custom Graphics Using Only Annotate Commands

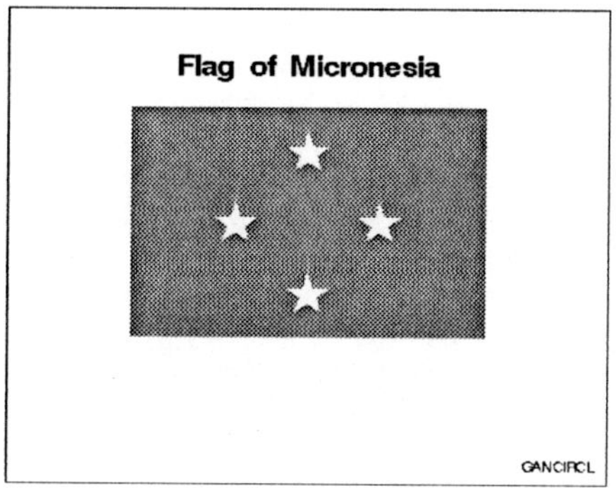

The program that creates this output is in "Drawing a Circle of Stars" on page 609.

Creating Annotate Graphics

In order to create and use Annotate graphics, you must first understand the structure and functioning of the Annotate data set. For this information see "About the Annotate Data Set" on page 589. Once you understand the way the data set works, you can follow these three steps to create Annotate graphics:

1 Determine what you want to draw, and where (location) and how (coordinate system) you want to position it on the graphics output. (See "About Annotate Graphics" on page 595.)

2 Build an Annotate data set of graphics commands using the Annotate variables and functions. (See "Creating an Annotate Data Set" on page 599.)

3 Submit a SAS/GRAPH procedure to produce the graphics output. (See "Producing Graphics Output from Annotate Data Sets" on page 601.)

About the Annotate Data Set

In an Annotate data set, each observation represents a command to draw a graphics element or to perform an action. The graphic elements drawn by these commands can be added to SAS/GRAPH output or displayed with the GANNO or GSLIDE procedure as a custom graphic.

The observations in an Annotate data set use a set of predefined Annotate variables. The values of the variables in the observation determine what is done and how it is done. To create these observations, you assign values to the variables either explicitly with a DATA step or implicitly with Annotate macros. See "Creating an Annotate Data Set" on page 599.

The following sections describe the items in an Annotate data set and explain how SAS/GRAPH software uses the commands in an Annotate data set to create graphics elements.

Structure of An Annotate Data Set

Output 24.1 is an example of an Annotate data set called TRIANGLE. The observations in this data set contain the commands that create a text label, move to a point in the output, and draw a triangle. (The DATA step that creates TRIANGLE is shown in “Using the DATA Step” on page 600.)

Output 24.1 Listing of the Annotate Data Set TRIANGLE

OBS	FUNCTION	X	Y	HSYS	XSYS	YSYS	STYLE	COLOR	POSITION	SIZE	LINE	TEXT
1	label	20	85	3	3	3	swissb	green	6	6.0	.	Sample Annotate Graphics
2	move	28	30	3	3	3	swissb	green	6	6.0	.	Sample Annotate Graphics
3	draw	68	30	3	3	3	swissb	red	6	0.8	1	Sample Annotate Graphics
4	draw	48	70	3	3	3	swissb	red	6	0.8	1	Sample Annotate Graphics
5	draw	28	30	3	3	3	swissb	red	6	0.8	1	Sample Annotate Graphics

Note: A blank denotes a missing value for a character variable. A '.' denotes a missing value for a numeric variable. △

Each observation in this data set contains complete instructions for drawing a graphic or moving to a position to draw a graphic. The value of the FUNCTION variable determines what the observation does. Other variables control how the function is performed. This list describes each observation in the TRIANGLE and the task it performs:

1 Create a label. This instruction draws a green label at position 20,85 (in X,Y coordinates). The value of the FUNCTION variable (LABEL) tells the program *what* to do. The values of the coordinate variables X and Y combined with the values of the coordinate system variables HSYS, XSYS, and YSYS tell *where* to do it. The values of the attribute variables STYLE, COLOR, TEXT, POSITION, and SIZE tell *how* to do it. These variables specify the font (SWISSB), the color and text of the label, the position of the label in relation to X and Y (centered on the point), and the size of the text.

2 Go to the starting point for the triangle. The value of the FUNCTION variable (MOVE) tells the program to go to the point specified by X and Y. This is the only instruction in the observation. Notice that the values of the variables specified for the first observation persist but are not used because they have no effect on the MOVE function.

3 Draw the first line of the triangle. The value of the FUNCTION variable (DRAW) tells the program to draw a line from the current point (the one specified by MOVE in the second observation to the new point specified by X and Y. The value of the COLOR variable changes to red.

4 Draw the second line of the triangle.

5 Draw the third line of the triangle.

Figure 24.3 on page 591 shows the green title and the red triangle produced by the TRIANGLE data set and displayed with the GANNOChapter 26, “The GANNO Procedure,” on page 707 procedure. Notes on the figure in black contain the X and Y coordinates of the graphics elements.

Figure 24.3 Annotate Output from the TRIANGLE Data Set

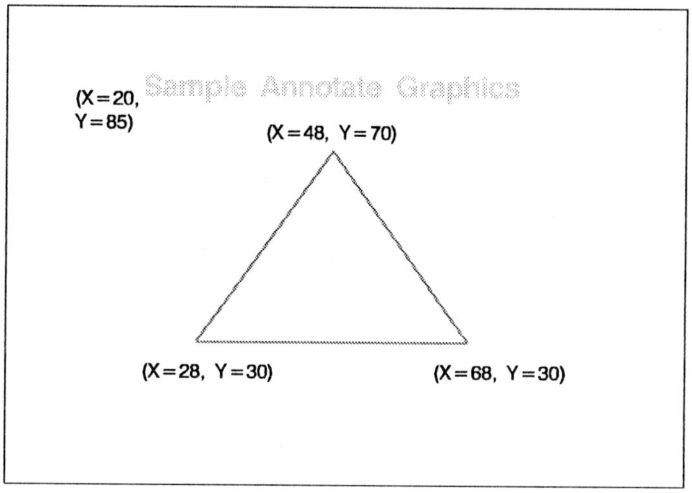

Annotate Variables

Annotate variables have predefined names. In each observation, the Annotate facility looks only for variables with those names. Other variables can be present, but they are ignored. Conceptually, there are three types of variables:

an action variable
: tells *what* to do. The only action variable is FUNCTION, which specifies what graphics element to draw (graphics primitive) or what action to take (programming function).

positioning variables
: tell *where* to do it. The positioning variables specify the point at which to draw the graphics element.

attribute variables
: tell *how* to do it. The attribute variables specify the characteristics of the graphics element (for example, color, size, line style, text font).

There is also an HTML variable, which provides linking information when you want to use the annotate data set to generate a drill-down graph that can be viewed in a Web browser.

Table 24.1 on page 591 lists all Annotate variables, grouped by task, and briefly describes each one. See "Annotate Variables" on page 642 for a complete description of each variable.

Table 24.1 Summary of Annotate Variables

Task Group	Variable	Description
Variable that defines an action	FUNCTION	specifies a drawing or programming action; Table 24.2 on page 594 describes these actions.
Positioning variables that determine coordinate values	GROUP	uses the value of the GCHART GROUP= option in place of X or Y
	MIDPOINT	uses the value of the GCHART MIDPOINT= option in place of X or Y

Task Group	Variable	Description
	SUBGROUP	uses the value of the GCHART SUBGROUP= option in place of X or Y
	X	specifies a numeric horizontal coordinate
	Y	specifies a numeric vertical coordinate
	Z	specifies a numeric third dimensional coordinate; used with G3D procedure only
	XC	specifies a horizontal character coordinate; only used with data coordinate systems 1, 2, 7, 8
	YC	specifies a vertical character coordinate; only used with data coordinate systems 1, 2, 7, 8
Positioning variables that contain internal coordinates	XLAST, YLAST	contain the X and Y coordinates of the last nontext function
	XLSTT, YLSTT	contain the X and Y coordinates of the last text function
Positioning variables that specify coordinate systems	HSYS	specifies type of units for the SIZE variable
	XSYS	specifies coordinate system for X or XC coordinates
	YSYS	specifies coordinate system for Y or YC coordinates
	ZSYS	specifies coordinate system for Z coordinate (G3D procedure only)
Attribute variables	ANGLE	angle of text label or starting angle of a pie slice
	CBORDER	colored border around text or symbol
	CBOX	colored box behind text or symbol
	COLOR	color of a graphics primitive
	LINE	line type to use in drawing or special control over pies and bars
	POSITION	placement and alignment for text strings
	ROTATE	angle at which to place individual characters in a text string or the delta angle (sweep) of a pie slice
	SIZE	size of an aspect of a graphics primitive; depends on FUNCTION variable (for TEXT, height of characters; for PIE, pie slice radius; for DRAW, line thickness; and so on)
	STYLE	font or pattern for a graphics element, depends on the FUNCTION variable
	TEXT	text to use in a label, symbol, or comment
	WHEN	whether a graphics element is drawn before or after procedure graphics output
Web variable	HTML	specifies link information for a drill-down graph

See Figure 24.4 on page 593 for a table that shows you which Annotate functions are used with which Annotate variables.

Figure 24.4 Annotate Variables used with Annotate Functions

Variables \ Functions	BAR	CNTL2TXT	COMMENT	DEBUG	DRAW	DRAW2TXT	FRAME	IMAGE	LABEL	MOVE	PIE	PIECNTR	PIEXY	POINT	POLY	POLYCONT	POP	PUSH	SWAP	SYMBOL	TXT2CNTL
ANGLE									x		x		x								
CBORDER									x											x	
CBOX									x											x	
COLOR	x				x	x	x		x		x			x	x	x				x	
FUNCTION	x	x	x	x	x	x	x	x	x	x	x	x	x	x	x	x	x	x	x	x	x
GROUP	x				x				x	x	x	x		x	x	x				x	
HSYS					x	x	x		x		x	x								x	
HTML	x						x	x	x		x				x					x	
IMGPATH								x													
LINE	x				x	x	x				x				x						
MIDPOINT	x				x				x	x	x	x		x	x	x				x	
POSITION									x												
ROTATE									x		x										
SIZE	x				x	x	x		x		x	x	x		x					x	
STYLE (fonts)									x											x	
STYLE (images)								x													
STYLE (patterns)	x						x				x				x						
SUBGROUP	x				x				x	x	x	x		x	x	x				x	
TEXT			x						x											x	
WHEN	x				x	x	x		x	x	x	x	x	x	x	x				x	
X	x				x			x	x	x	x	x		x	x	x				x	
XC	x				x				x	x	x	x		x	x	x				x	
XSYS	x				x		x		x	x	x	x		x	x	x				x	
Y	x				x			x	x	x	x	x		x	x	x				x	
YC	x				x				x	x	x	x		x	x	x				x	
YSYS	x				x		x		x	x	x	x		x	x	x				x	
Z	x				x			x	x	x	x	x		x	x	x				x	
ZSYS	x				x			x	x	x	x	x		x	x	x				x	
XLAST YLAST	x	x			x			x		x	x	x	x	x			x	x	x		x
XLSTT YLSTT		x							x								x	x	x	x	x

Annotate Functions

The FUNCTION variable accepts a set of predefined values (functions) that perform both graphics tasks and programming tasks.

The graphics functions draw the graphics elements that are illustrated in "Graphics Elements" on page 595.

The programming functions control the internal coordinates, manipulate the LIFO stack, and help you debug an Annotate data set. These programming functions are discussed in "Internal Coordinates" on page 598, "Using the LIFO Stack" on page 603, and "Debugging" on page 604.

Table 24.2 on page 594 summarizes the tasks that are performed by the Annotate functions. See "Annotate Functions" on page 615 for a complete description of the FUNCTION variable and its values.

Table 24.2 Summary of Graphics Tasks Performed by Annotate Functions

Task Group	If you want to...	Use this function...
Graphics tasks	begin to draw a polygon (starting point) and, optionally, specify a fill color and pattern	POLY
	continue drawing a polygon (additional vertex) and, optionally, specify an outline color of the polygon	POLYCONT
	draw a line from the current (X,Y) position (see MOVE and TXT2CNTL)	DRAW
	draw a point	POINT
	draw a rectangle from the current (X,Y) position (see MOVE and TXT2CNTL); optionally, fill with a pattern	BAR
	draw a symbol	SYMBOL
	draw line from (XLAST, YLAST) coordinates to (XLSTT, YLSTT) coordinates	DRAW2TXT
	draw pie slice, circle, or arc	PIE
	draw text	LABEL
	move to the specified point (X,Y)	MOVE
	put a frame around the area defined by XSYS and YSYS, optionally, fill with a pattern	FRAME
Programming tasks	insert a comment in the data set (no action); documentation aid	COMMENT
	copy (XLAST, YLAST) coordinates to (XLSTT, YLSTT) coordinates	CNTL2TXT
	copy (XLSTT, YLSTT) coordinates to (XLAST, YLAST) coordinates	TXT2CNTL
	exchange LSTT and LAST coordinates	SWAP
	get coordinates of a point on a pie slice outline	PIEXY
	get values for LAST and LSTT coordinates from LIFO stack	POP
	put current values of LAST and LSTT coordinates onto LIFO stack	PUSH

Task Group	If you want to...	Use this function...
	set pie radius and coordinates for center; does not draw a pie	PIECNTR
	turn on trace of previous values and LIFO stack	DEBUG

See Figure 24.4 on page 593 for a table that shows you which Annotate functions work with which Annotate variables.

About Annotate Graphics

When you create Annotate graphics, you specify these things:

- what to draw (graphics elements)
- where to draw those elements (the coordinates of the position on the output)
- how to draw (characteristics of the element such as size or color).

The following sections describe the components of the graphics output that are produced by an Annotate data set.

Graphics Elements

In an Annotate data set, the FUNCTION variable determines the graphics element that is drawn.

The particular graphics elements that you can draw are shown in Figure 24.5 on page 595 along with the value of the FUNCTION variable or Annotate macro that draws them.

Figure 24.5 Annotate Graphics Elements

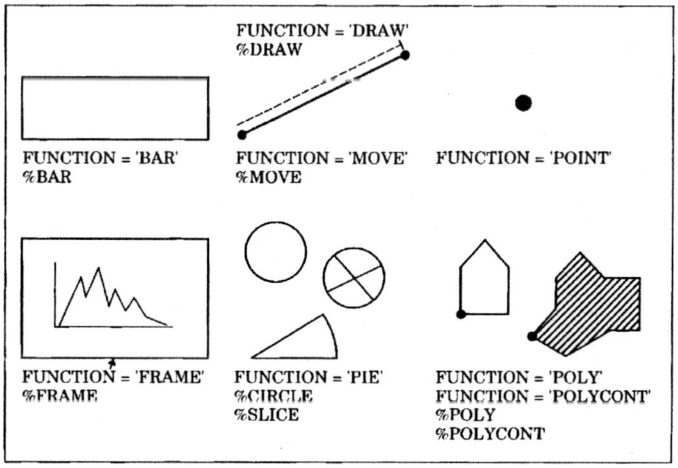

You can control the position of graphics elements in the following ways:

- explicitly, using coordinates that you supply.
- dependently, based on the location of features in the SAS/GRAPH output. For example, when you use the GCHART procedure, you can label the parts of a

subgrouped vertical bar chart by using the SUBGROUP variable in your Annotate data set. The Annotate facility enables you to label subgroups without having to specify the actual coordinates of the subgroup bar.

- dependently, based on values that are supplied from other data sets. For example, you can label the ending point of a plot line in the GPLOT procedure by extracting the value of the last point in the sorted input data set.

Coordinates

Coordinates specify where to put graphics elements. These variables can contain coordinate values:

- X, Y, and sometimes Z are used for numeric coordinates.
- XC and YC are used for character coordinates.
- GROUP, MIDPOINT, and SUBGROUP can be used when you annotate output from procedures such as GCHART. Use these variables to specify coordinates for horizontal or vertical bar charts.

Coordinates are interpreted in terms of a coordinate system in order to identify a precise location in the graphics output.

Coordinate Systems

A coordinate system determines how coordinates are interpreted. You specify a coordinate system to use for each dimension, using the XSYS, YSYS, and ZSYS variables (for X, Y, and Z, respectively). Use ZSYS to annotate graphics output only from the G3D procedure.

You also specify a coordinate system for the SIZE variable using the HSYS variable. HSYS takes the same kinds of values as XSYS, YSYS, and ZSYS. The SIZE variable specifies the size of a graphics element, such as the width of lines (for example, FRAME), the radius of pie slices (for example, PIE, PIECNTR, and PIEXY), or the height of text (for example, LABEL and SYMBOL).

These are the important components of the Annotate coordinate systems:

- *Area:* Each coordinate system refers to one of three drawing areas: data area, procedure output area, and graphics output area. Coordinates are measured from a different origin for each area; they also have different limits. Figure 24.6 on page 597 shows the areas on the graphics output and the coordinate systems that use them.

Figure 24.6 Areas and Their Coordinate Systems

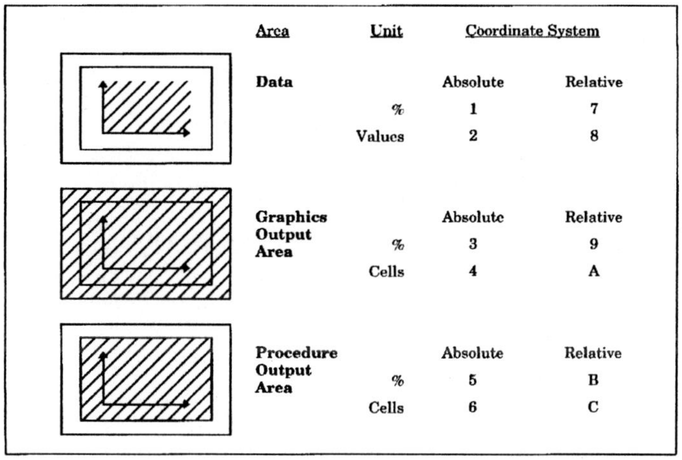

- *Units:* The units for a coordinate system are based on one of the following:
  - data values (for data coordinate systems). The range of values depends on the range of data expressed along the axes of the graph.
  - cells (for coordinate systems for the procedure output area or graphics output area). The range of values depends on the type of area. See "Ranges for Cells" on page 598.
  - percentages of the total area available, that is, percent of the data area, or percent of the procedure output area, or percent of the graphics output area.
- *Placement:* The placement of a coordinate can be absolute or relative. Absolute coordinates name the exact location for a graphics element in the graphics output. Relative coordinates name the location with respect to another graphics element in the output.

Table 24.3 on page 597 describes the coordinate system values for the XSYS, YSYS, ZSYS, and HSYS variables.

Table 24.3 Coordinate System Values for XSYS, YSYS, ZSYS, and HSYS Variables

Type of Coordinates	Area	Units	Range	Value for XSYS, YSYS, ZSYS, HSYS
Absolute	data	%	0-100% of axis	1' *
	data	values	minimum to maximum of axis	2' *
	graphics output area	%	0-100% of graphics output area	3'
	graphics output area	cells	0 to limit of graphics output area	4'
	procedure output area	%	0-100% of procedure output area	5'
	procedure output area	cells	0 to limit of procedure output area	6'
Relative	data	%	0-100% of axis	7' *

Type of Coordinates	Area	Units	Range	Value for XSYS, YSYS, ZSYS, HSYS
	data	values	minimum to maximum of axis	8' *
	graphics output area	%	0-100% of graphics output area	9'
	graphics output area	cells	0 to limit of graphics output area	A'
	procedure output area	%	0–100% of procedure output area	B'
	procedure output area	cells	0 to limit of procedure output area	C'

*Coordinate systems 1, 2, 7, and 8 are not valid with block, pie or star charts in the GCHART procedure or surface, prism or block maps with the GMAP procedure.

Ranges for Cells

The available range for coordinate systems that are measured in cells differs by area:

graphics output area
: The range of cells that are available for the graphics output area depends on the device and the number of rows and columns that are set by the HPOS= and VPOS= graphics options or by the PCOLS and LCOLS device parameters.

procedure output area
: As with the graphics output area, the range of cells available for the procedure output area depends on the device and the number of rows and columns set by the HPOS= and VPOS= graphics options or by the PCOLS and LCOLS device parameters. However, the procedure output area is sized *after* areas for titles and footnotes are allocated and is reduced accordingly. If you specify that the legend appear outside of the axis area, the procedure output area also decreases by the size of the legend.

See "Procedure Output and the Graphics Output Area" on page 34 for descriptions of the procedure output area and the graphics output area.

Internal Coordinates

The Annotate facility maintains two pairs of internal coordinates that are stored in internal variables:

- coordinates of the last graphics element drawn or the coordinates from the last move are stored in the variables XLAST and YLAST
- coordinates of the last text drawn are stored in the variables XLSTT and YLSTT.

Many functions use these internal coordinates as a starting point, relying on the coordinates that are specified with the function as an ending point. For example, in the BAR function, the (XLAST, YLAST) coordinate pair is used for the lower left corner; the position defined by the X and Y variables is used for the upper-right corner. (For details, see "BAR Function" on page 615.) These internal variables can also provide default coordinates if X, XC, Y, or YC contains a missing value.

The internal coordinates are automatically updated by some of the Annotate functions. The text functions, LABEL and SYMBOL, update the (XLSTT,YLSTT) variables. The BAR, DRAW, MOVE, PIE, and POINT functions update the (XLAST,YLAST) variables.

You cannot explicitly assign a value to XLAST, YLAST, XLSTT, or YLSTT because they are internal variables. For example, you cannot make this assignment:

```
xlast=50;
```

However, you can use several functions to directly manipulate the values of the internal coordinates. The functions are shown in Figure 24.7 on page 599.

Figure 24.7 Programming Functions That Manipulate System Variables

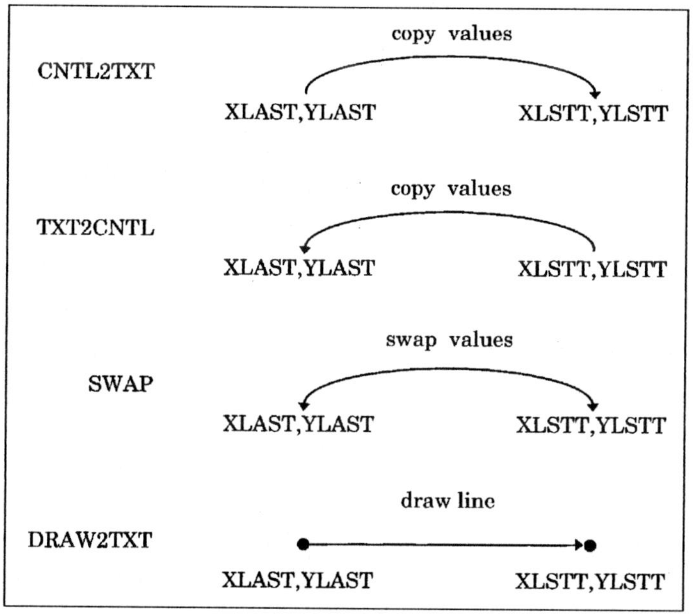

For a complete description, see "Annotate Internal Coordinates" on page 678.

Attribute Variables

Attribute variables control the appearance of the graphics elements. Each function uses only a subset of these variables. See Table 24.1 on page 591 for a list of attribute variables.

What an attribute variable controls often depends on the graphics element to which it applies. For example, the SIZE variable controls the width of a line when it is used with FUNCTION='DRAW', but it controls the text height when it is used with FUNCTION='LABEL'.

For a complete description of the attribute variables and the aspect of the graphics elements that they control, see "Annotate Variables" on page 642.

Creating an Annotate Data Set

Once you have determined what you are going to draw and how you want it to appear in the output, you need to build an Annotate data set. Although there are many ways to create SAS data sets, the most commonly used method for creating Annotate data sets is with a DATA step that uses either

- assignment statements that you explicitly output as separate observations
- Annotate macros, which implicitly assign values to Annotate variables.

Most of the examples in this documentation use a DATA step with assignment statements. For more information on creating SAS data sets, see *SAS Language Reference: Concepts*.

Using the DATA Step

When you use the SAS DATA step with assignment statements, each statement provides a value for an Annotate variable. After you have assigned all of the variable values for an observation, you must use an OUTPUT statement to write the observation to the data set. For example, the following statements create the TRIANGLE data set shown in Output 24.1:

```
data triangle;

      /* declare variables */
   length function style color $ 8 text $ 25;
   retain hsys xsys ysys '3';

      /* create observation to draw the title */
   function='label'; x=20; y=85; position='6';
      text='Sample Annotate Graphics';
      style='swissb'; color='green'; size=6;
      output;

      /* create observations to draw the triangle */
   function='move'; x=28; y=30; output;
   function='draw'; x=68; y=30; size=.8; line=1;
      color='red'; output;
   function='draw'; x=48; y=70; output;
   function='draw'; x=28; y=30; output;
run;

proc ganno annotation=triangle;
run;
quit;
```

Notice that a RETAIN statement sets the values of the HSYS, XSYS, and YSYS variables. RETAIN statements are useful when you want to select the values for variables that are required for many functions and the value is the same for all of them.

The SIZE, LINE, and COLOR variables are included with only the first DRAW function. Using this method to create the data set, the values set in the first DRAW function carry over to subsequent DRAW functions.

The PROC GANNO takes as input the annotate data set “triangle” created by the previous DATA step and creates the output shown in Figure 24.3 on page 591.

Using Annotate Macros in the DATA Step

A set of Annotate macros is provided in the SAS sample library. You can use macro calls in a DATA step to create observations in an Annotate data set. You can also use Annotate macros and explicit variable assignments together in the same DATA step. For complete information, see “Annotate Macros” on page 679 and “Using Annotate Macros” on page 697.

Effect of Missing Values

Annotate data sets follow the same rules for missing values as any other SAS data set. (See *SAS Language Reference: Concepts* for information on the effect of missing values in a data set.)

Variables that have a missing value use a default value. For example, if the COLOR variable has a missing value, then the first color in either the colors list that is defined by the COLORS= graphics option, if specified, or the device's default colors list is used. If the FUNCTION variable has a missing value, LABEL is used. If the X variable is missing, the value of the XLSTT internal coordinate is used for text functions and the XLAST internal coordinate is used for nontext functions. See "Annotate Variables" on page 642 for the default value of each Annotate variable.

You probably should not depend on this effect when you create an Annotate data set. If the data set is structured so that observations depend on prior observations setting attributes for them, then you may have extra work to do if you change the order of observations later.

Sometimes missing values are required to produce the desired results. If you have calculated the coordinates of a point and have the values stored in (XLAST,YLAST) or (XLSTT,YLSTT), you can force Annotate to use the internal coordinates by supplying missing values for the X and Y variables. See "Annotate Internal Coordinates" on page 678 for details on using the (XLAST,YLAST) and (XLSTT,YLSTT) internal coordinates.

Producing Graphics Output from Annotate Data Sets

You can display Annotate graphics in two ways:

- annotate output from a SAS/GRAPH procedure by assigning the Annotate data set to the PROC statement or the action statement, or both.
- display only the Annotate graphics by assigning the Annotate data set to either the GANNO or GSLIDE procedure.

Including Annotate Graphics with Procedure Output

To annotate SAS/GRAPH procedure output, you must include the ANNOTATE= option in the appropriate statement in the procedure. ANNOTATE= must name the Annotate data set that you have already created. If you want the Annotate graphics to apply to all graphs produced by a procedure, you should include ANNOTATE= in the PROC statement. If you want the Annotate graphics to apply only to the graph produced by an action statement within the procedure, include ANNOTATE= in the action statement. You can specify Annotate data sets in both places.

When you annotate a SAS/GRAPH procedure, the Annotate graphics are displayed and stored as part of the graphics output that the procedure produces.

Producing Only Annotate Graphics Output

To produce Annotate graphics without other procedure output, use the GANNO procedure or the GSLIDE procedure:

- The GANNO procedure produces graphics output consisting only of Annotate graphics. See Chapter 26, "The GANNO Procedure," on page 707Chapter 26, "The GANNO Procedure," on page 707 for information on displaying or storing Annotate graphics.

- The GSLIDE procedure can also produce graphics output consisting only of Annotate graphics. In addition, you can enhance the graphics output with TITLE, NOTE, and FOOTNOTE statements. See Chapter 44, “The GSLIDE Procedure,” on page 1277 for details.

Using the Annotate Variables for Web Output

Most of the annotate variables can be used in programs that generate output for the Web. For more information on the annotate functions and variables, see the Chapter 25, “Annotate Dictionary,” on page 613. For information on using annotate data sets in Web output, see Chapter 17, “Generating Web Output with the Annotate Facility,” on page 499.

Annotate Processing Details

Order in Which Graphics Elements Are Drawn

When a procedure uses an Annotate data set, it reads and interprets the observations one at a time, starting with the first observation and proceeding to the last. The order of the observations in the data set determines the order in which the graphics elements are generated. If the coordinates of two graphics elements overlap, the graphics element produced by an earlier observation can be overwritten by any graphics elements that are produced by subsequent observations. As a result, graphics elements can overlay each other and they can also overlay or be overlaid by procedure output.

CAUTION:

Overlay behavior is device-dependent. Most terminals, cameras, and some printers demonstrate overlay behavior because the process of drawing updates pixels as each graphics element is drawn. Plotters do not overlay the graphics elements internally before plotting; they draw graphics elements on top of each other on the paper. The area where graphics elements overlap shows one color bleeding through the color that overlays it. To ensure that one graphics element overlays another, use the WHEN variable. △

Controlling the Processing with the WHEN Variable

The WHEN variable determines the order in which observations in an Annotate data set are processed. It determines if observations are processed *before* or *after* output that is produced by a SAS/GRAPH procedure. This means that Annotate graphics can be overlaid by procedure output or can overlay procedure output. By default, Annotate graphics are drawn before the procedure output.

In effect, you can have two sets of Annotate graphics elements that are generated for the same output:

- Annotate graphics drawn before procedure output (the default, WHEN='B').
- Annotate graphics drawn after procedure output (WHEN='A').

Within each set, graphics elements are drawn in the order that they appear in the Annotate data set and overlay each other as appropriate (on devices that demonstrate overlay behavior). For details, see the description of the WHEN variable on “WHEN Variable” on page 666.

Using BY-Group Processing with the Annotate Facility

You can use the Annotate facility with procedures that use BY statements to annotate each graph that is generated with a BY statement. The Annotate graphics for each graph are generated depending on the value of the BY variable. To use BY-group processing with the Annotate facility, your program must meet the following conditions:

- □ Both the input data set for the procedure and the Annotate data set must contain the same BY variable.
- □ The BY variable must be defined as the same type (character or numeric) and length in both data sets.
- □ If a label or format is associated with a BY variable in one data set, the same label or format has to be associated with it in the other data set.
- □ Both data sets must be sorted by the BY variable.
- □ The ANNOTATE= option must be specified in an action statement in the procedure. If you specify the ANNOTATE= option in the PROC statement, the Annotate graphics are used for all graphs that are generated by the procedure rather than for unique values of the BY variable.

See “BY Statement” on page 141 for details.

Using the LIFO Stack

The FUNCTION variable supports several programming functions that manipulate the internal coordinates and provide other utility operations. Several of these functions use the LIFO stack to track and set variable values.

The *LIFO* (last-in-first-out) *stack* is a storage area where you can keep internal coordinate values for later use. It is useful when you want to save the current values of (XLAST,YLAST) and (XLSTT,YLSTT) and use them with functions later in the DATA step.

You store and retrieve values from the stack using the PUSH and POP functions. The PUSH function copies the current values of XLAST, YLAST, XLSTT, and YLSTT onto the stack. The POP function copies values from the stack into XLAST, YLAST, XLSTT, and YLSTT.

LIFO stacks manage the stored data so that the last data stored in the stack is the first data removed from the stack. This means that a POP function retrieves the values most recently stored with a PUSH function. Figure 24.8 on page 603 illustrates how PUSH and POP functions work together.

Figure 24.8 Using PUSH and POP to Store and Retrieve Coordinate Values

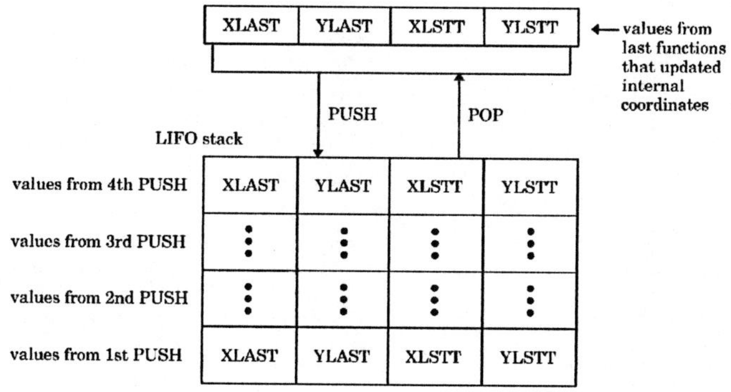

See also "Internal Coordinates" on page 598.

Debugging

You can print your Annotate data set with the PRINT procedure. This is an easy way to examine the Annotation that you have specified or to debug your program. For example, a listing such as the one in Output 24.1 provides complete information about the value that you specify for each variable in every observation.

For more complex problems, the DEBUG function enables you to display the values of Annotate variables and internal coordinates before and after a function is submitted. The values are written to the SAS log.

If there is an error in your Annotate data set, one or more diagnostic messages are printed in the SAS log:

- If an error is found in preprocessing, this message appears:

```
NOTE: ERROR DETECTED IN ANNOTATE= libref.dataset
```

- If an error is found as an observation is being read, this message appears:

```
PROBLEM IN OBSERVATION number-message
```

  where *message* is the text of the error message.

- If the error limit of 20 errors is reached at any point during processing of the data set, a termination message similar to this one appears:

```
ERROR LIMIT REACHED IN ANNOTATE PROCESS

                20 TOTAL ERRORS
```

For an explanation of common diagnostic messages, refer to the Help facility.

Examples

The following examples show how to annotate graphics that are created with SAS/GRAPH procedures and how to build custom graphics:

- "Labeling Cities on a Map" on page 604
- "Labeling Subgroups in a Vertical Bar Chart" on page 607
- "Drawing a Circle of Stars" on page 609

Other examples that use Annotate data sets are as follows:

- Example 1 on page 710 (and others in that chapter
- Chapter 44, "The GSLIDE Procedure," on page 1277
- "Drawing a Circle of Stars" on page 609

Labeling Cities on a Map

Features:

Annotate function:	LABEL SYMBOL
Annotate variables:	HSYS
	POSITION

SIZE

TEXT

WHEN

X and Y

XSYS

YSYS

Sample library member: GANCITY

Figure 24.9 Map with Labeled Cities

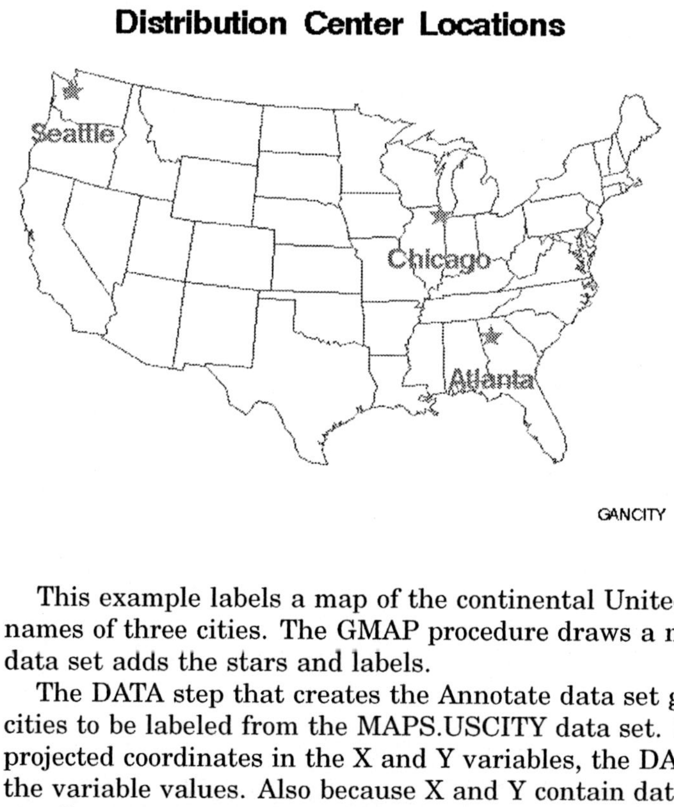

This example labels a map of the continental United States with the location and names of three cities. The GMAP procedure draws a map of the U.S. and an Annotate data set adds the stars and labels.

The DATA step that creates the Annotate data set gets the *x* and *y* coordinates of the cities to be labeled from the MAPS.USCITY data set. Because MAPS.USCITY stores projected coordinates in the X and Y variables, the DATA step does not need to reassign the variable values. Also because X and Y contain data values (the map data set coordinates), the XSYS and YSYS variables specify coordinate system 2, absolute data values. However, the HSYS variable that controls text height uses coordinate system 3, percent of the graphics output area.

See Example 4 on page 1180 for an example of labeling a map using map coordinates in units of latitude and longitude.

See Chapter 35, "The GMAP Procedure," on page 995 for more information on using map data sets

.

Note: If the libref MAPS is automatically assigned at your site to the SAS data library containing the Institute-supplied map data sets, you can omit the LIBNAME statement. △

Assign the libref MAPS, if necessary, and set the graphics environment.

```
libname maps 'SAS-data-library';
goptions reset=global gunit=pct border cback=white
         colors=(black blue green red)
         ftext=swissb htitle=6 htext=3;
```

Subset the U.S. map data set by omitting Alaska and Hawaii.

```
data lower48;
   set maps.us;
   if state ne stfips('AK');
   if state ne stfips('HI');
run;
```

Create the Annotate data set, CITYSTAR. CITYSTAR contains the commands that draw a star and a label at each of the three cities. Setting WHEN to A draws the annotation after the map.

```
data citystar;
   length function style color $ 8 position $ 1
          text $ 20;
   retain xsys ysys '2' hsys '3'
          when 'a';
```

Include the values of selected variables from MAPS.USCITY. X and Y contain projected coordinates; CITY contains names; STATE contains FIPS codes. Because there are several Atlantas, a STATE value is necessary.

```
   set maps.uscity(keep=x y city state);
   if (city='Atlanta' and state=13)
      or city='Chicago'
      or city='Seattle';
```

Create the observation that draws the star. The text string V is the character code for the star figure in the MARKER font assigned by the STYLE variable.

```
   function='symbol'; style='marker'; text='V'; color='red'; size=5;
      output;
```

Create the observation that labels the city. TEXT is assigned the value of CITY. The font is SWISSB. SIZE uses the units assigned by HSYS so text height is 5 percent of the height of the graphics output area. POSITION 8 places the label directly below the city location.

```
   function='label'; style='swissb'; text=city; color='green';
      size=5; position='8'; output;
run;
```

Define the title and footnote for the map.

```
title 'Distribution Center Locations';
footnote font=swiss j=r 'GANCITY';
```

Define patterns for the map areas. MEMPTY colors only the state borders.

```
pattern value=mempty color=blue repeat=49;
```

Generate the map and assign the annotate data set to the CHORO statement.

```
proc gmap data=lower48 map=lower48;
   id state;
   choro state / annotate=citystar discrete nolegend;
run;
quit;
```

Labeling Subgroups in a Vertical Bar Chart

Features:

Annotate function:	LABEL (default)
Annotate variables:	MIDPOINT
	POSITION
	SUBGROUP
Sample library member:	GANVBAR

Figure 24.10 Bar Chart with Labeled Subgroups

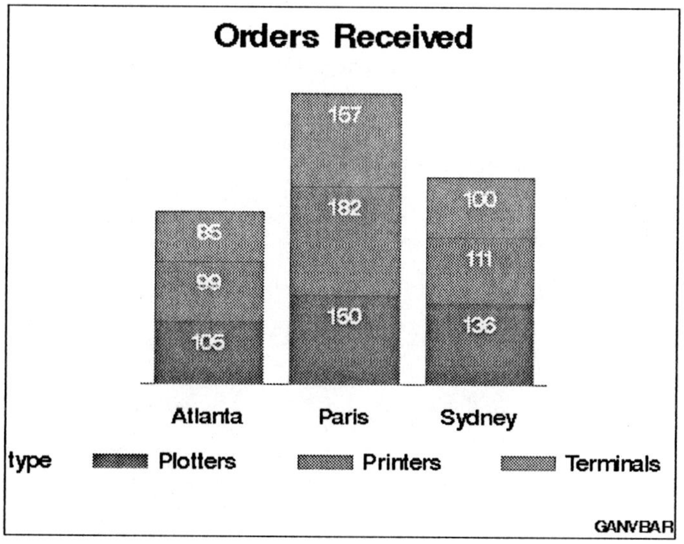

This example shows how to label subgroups in a vertical bar chart that is generated by the GCHART procedure. Each bar represents total orders for a city and is subgrouped by the type of order. The Annotate facility labels each subgroup with the number of orders for that category. The coordinates that position the subgroup labels are derived from the values of the GCHART procedure variables CITY (the chart (or midpoint) variable) and TYPE (the subgroup variable). These variables are assigned to the corresponding Annotate variable.

See Chapter 29, "The GCHART Procedure," on page 773 for more information on creating bar charts.

Assign the libref and set the graphics environment.

```
libname reflib 'SAS-data-library';
goptions reset=global gunit=pct border cback=white
         colors=(blue green red) ctext=black htitle=6
         ftitle=swissb htext=4 ftext=swiss;
```

Create the data set SOLD.

```
data sold;
   length type $ 10;
   input city $ units type $ ;
   datalines;
Atlanta   99 Printers
Atlanta 105 Plotters
Atlanta   85 Terminals
Paris    182 Printers
Paris    150 Plotters
Paris    157 Terminals
Sydney   111 Printers
Sydney   136 Plotters
Sydney   100 Terminals
;
run;
```

Create the Annotate data set, BARLABEL. The MIDPOINT variable uses the values of the chart variable CITY to provide the X coordinate for the subgroup labels. The SUBGROUP variable uses the values of the variable TYPE to provide the Y coordinate that vertically positions the labels in the bar. Because no function is specified, the data set uses the default function, LABEL. The POSITION value **E** places the labels just below the top of each subgroup bar.

```
data barlabel;
   length color style $ 8;
   retain color 'white' when 'a' style 'swissb'
      xsys ysys '2' position 'E' size 4 hsys '3';
   set sold;
   midpoint=city;
   subgroup=type;
   text=left(put(units,5.));
run;
```

Define the title and footnote.

```
title 'Orders Received';
footnote h=3 j=r 'GANVBAR';
```

Define axis characteristics. AXIS1 suppresses the vertical axis. AXIS2 drops the midpoint axis label.

```
axis1 label=none major=none minor=none style=0
      value=none;
axis2 label=none;
```

Generate a vertical bar chart and assign the Annotate data set to the VBAR statement.

```
proc gchart data=sold;
   vbar city / type=sum
               sumvar=units
               subgroup=type
               width=17
               raxis=axis1
               maxis=axis2
               annotate=barlabel;
run;
quit;
```

Drawing a Circle of Stars

Features:

Annotate function:	BAR
	CNTL2TXT
	FRAME
	LABEL
	MOVE
	PIECNTR
	PIEXY
	SYMBOL
Annotate variables:	COLOR
	HSYS, XSYS, YSYS
	LINE
	STYLE
	TEXT
	XLAST and YLAST
	XLSTT and YLSTT
Sample library member:	GANCIRCL

Figure 24.11 Stars Positioned in a Circle with GANNO

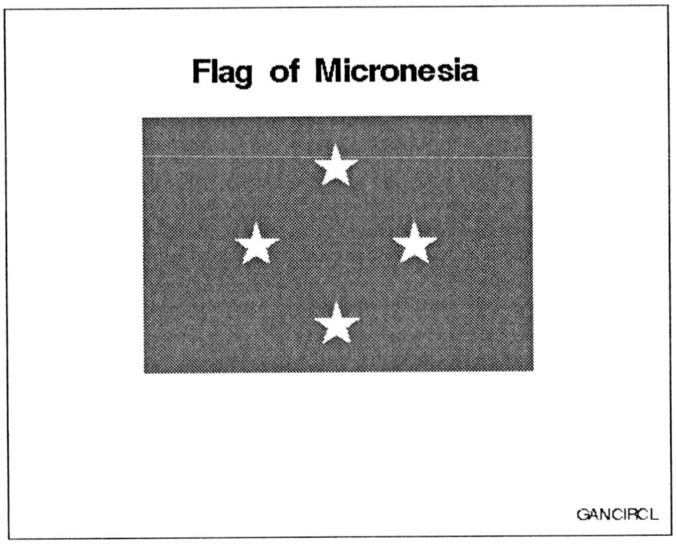

This example shows how to use an Annotate data set to draw a flag that is composed of a rectangle and four stars. The stars are positioned by placing them on an imaginary circle. The program uses the PIECNTR and PIEXY functions to find the points on the circle and the CNTL2TXT programming function to transfer coordinate values. It also processes Annotate assignment statements in a DO loop. The GANNO procedure displays the Annotate graphics.

Set the graphics environment.

```
goptions reset=global cback=white colors=(black);
```

Create the Annotate data set, FLAG. XSYS, YSYS, and HSYS specify coordinate system 3, absolute size of the graphics output area.

```
data flag;
   length function style color $ 8 text $ 30;
   retain xsys ysys hsys '3';
```

Draw a frame. The FRAME function uses the default color BLACK to draw a frame around the graphics output area specified by the XSYS and YSYS variables.

```
   function='frame'; output;
```

Draw the footnote. The LABEL function draws the text specified in the TEXT variable. X and Y explicitly position the footnote on the graphics output area.

```
   function='label'; x=92; y=5; text='GANCIRCL';
      style='swiss'; size=3; position='5'; output;
```

Draw the title. The values of FUNCTION, POSITION, and COLOR remain the same because no new values are assigned.

```
    x=50; y=90; text='Flag of Micronesia';
       style='swissb'; size=6; output;
```

Draw the background. MOVE specifies the lower left corner of the rectangle that forms the flag. BAR draws the rectangle using the values of X and Y for the upper right corner. The LINE value of 3 fills the figure with the specified color.

```
    function='move'; x=20; y=30; output;
    function='bar'; x=80; y=80; color='blue';
       line=3; style='solid'; output;
```

Draw the circle of stars. The DO loop repeats the processing instructions defined by the nested assignment statements, placing a star every 90 degrees around the circle. To increase the number of stars, reduce the size of the angle between them and adjust the ending angle.

```
 do star_ang=0 to 270 by 90;
```

The PIECNTR function is set to the center of the rectangle. PIEXY calculates a point on the arc based on the value of STAR_ANG and updates the internal coordinates XLAST and YLAST.

```
    function='piecntr'; x=50; y=55; size=15; output;
    function='piexy'; size=1; angle=star_ang; output;
```

The programming function CNTL2TXT copies the values of XLAST and YLAST to the text-handling coordinates XLSTT and YLSTT. Assigning missing values to X and Y forces the SYMBOL function to use the values of XLSTT and YLSTT to position the star. The text string V is the character code for the star figure in the MARKER font assigned by the STYLE variable.

```
    function='cntl2txt'; output;
    function='symbol'; style='marker'; text='V';
       angle=0; color='white'; size=10; x=.; y=.;
       output;
    end;
 run;
```

Use the GANNO procedure to process the Annotate data set and generate the graphics output.

```
 proc ganno annotate=flag;
 run;
 quit;
```

CHAPTER 25

Annotate Dictionary

Annotate Dictionary Overview

The Annotate facility enables you to generate a special data set of graphics commands from which you can produce graphics output. This data set is referred to as an Annotate data set. You can generate a complete graph using an Annotate data set in conjunction with the Chapter 26, "The GANNO Procedure," on page 707 or Chapter 44, "The GSLIDE Procedure," on page 1277 procedures, or you can apply an Annotate data set to graphics that were generated with procedures such as Chapter 29, "The GCHART Procedure," on page 773, Chapter 30, "The GCONTOUR Procedure," on page 885, and Chapter 35, "The GMAP Procedure," on page 995, among others.

In addition, SAS/GRAPH supports the following procedures on the client using Java or ActiveX:GCHART, GCONTOUR, GMAP, GPLOT, GRADAR, and G3D.

In an Annotate data set, each observation represents a command to draw a graphics element or perform an action. The observations use a set of predefined "Annotate Variables" on page 642. "Annotate Functions" on page 615 determine what is to be done with each observation. "Annotate Macros" on page 679 simplify the process of drawing a graphics element. "Annotate Error Messages" on page 699 are sent to the SAS log.

For usage information and example programs , refer to "Using Annotate Macros" on page 697 and Chapter 24, "Using Annotate Data Sets," on page 587.

Annotate Functions

In an Annotate data set, the value of the FUNCTION variable specifies what action the observation performs. Annotate functions act in conjunction with Annotate variables that determine where and how to perform the action. Many of these variables are function-dependent, that is, what they do depends on the function they are used with. For example, with the LABEL function the STYLE variable specifies a font; with the BAR function, STYLE specifies a pattern.

This section describes all of the values of the FUNCTION variable. For each function it

- □ describes the function's action.
- □ notes whether the function updates the internal coordinate variables XLAST, YLAST and XLSTT, YLSTT.
- □ describes how other Annotate variables behave with the function. For a complete description of each variable, see "Annotate Variables" on page 642.

For a summary of drawing and programming tasks performed by the FUNCTION variable, see Table 24.2 on page 594 .

The variables that are available for use with each function are listed in Figure 24.4 on page 593.

BAR Function

Draws a rectangle whose lower-left corner is defined by the internal variables (XLAST, YLAST) and whose upper-right corner is defined by the specified X, Y variable pair. You can define the color of the fill, the fill pattern, and the edge lines to be drawn.

Updates: XLAST, YLAST

Syntax

FUNCTION='BAR';

Associated Variables

COLOR=*'color'*
: specifies the color of either the interior of the bar or the outline of the bar. *Color* can be any SAS/GRAPH color name. The part of the bar affected depends on the value of the STYLE variable. If STYLE specifies a pattern or fill, the COLOR variable determines the color of the interior. If STYLE specifies an empty pattern, the COLOR variable determines the color of the outline of the bar.

GROUP=*group-value*
MIDPOINT=*midpoint-value*
SUBGROUP=*subgroup-value*
: specify coordinates for HBAR and VBAR charts from the GCHART procedure. Use these variables only with the data coordinate systems 1, 2, 7, and 8.

HTML=*'link-string'*
: specifies the text that defines the link for drill-down.

LINE=0...3
: specifies the direction in which to adjust the outline of the bar. Use LINE values 1 and 2 to offset a particular bar from an axis or adjoining area. The following figure illustrates LINE values.

Figure 25.1 LINE Values for Bars

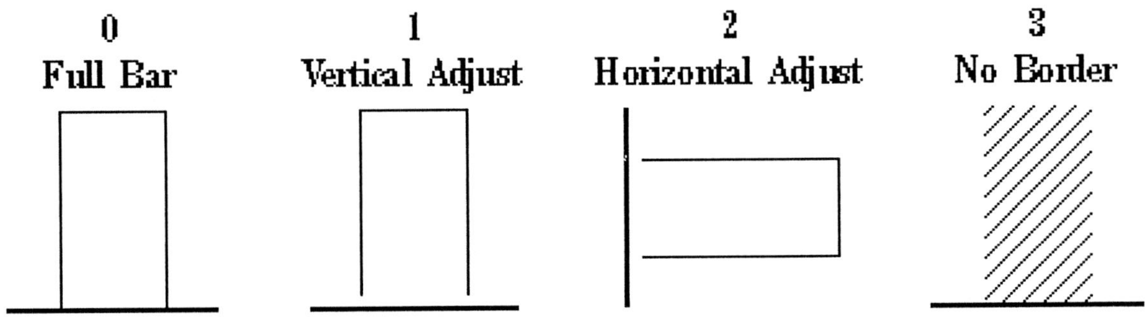

SIZE=*thickness*
: specifies a line thickness for the rectangle

STYLE=*'fill-pattern'*
: specifies the pattern that fills the bar. *Fill-pattern* can be the following bar and block patterns:

SOLID S	a solid fill.
EMPTY E	an empty fill.
style<density>	a shaded pattern: *style* can be R | X | L *density* can be 1...5

WHEN='B' | 'A'
: specifies when to draw the bar in relation to other procedure output. See “WHEN Variable” on page 666.

X=*horizontal-coordinate*
Y=*vertical-coordinate*
Z=*depth-coordinate*
XC='*character-type-horizontal-coordinate*'
YC='*character-type-vertical-coordinate*'
: define the upper-right corner of a bar (rectangle) whose lower-left corner is (XLAST,YLAST). Use the Z variable only when you are annotating output from the G3D procedure. Figure 25.2 on page 617 illustrates the use of these coordinates.

XSYS='*coordinate-system*'
: specifies the coordinate system for the X or XC variable. The XC variable can be used only with XSYS='2'. See “XSYS Variable” on page 670 for an explanation of *coordinate-system*.

YSYS='*coordinate-system*'
: specifies the coordinate system for Y or YC variable. The YC variable can only be used with YSYS='2'. See “YSYS Variable” on page 674 for an explanation of *coordinate-system*.

ZSYS='*coordinate-system*'
: specifies the coordinate system for the Z variable. See “ZSYS Variable” on page 676 for an explanation of *coordinate-system*.

Details

Figure 25.2 on page 617 shows how the XLAST, YLAST, and X, Y variables define the diagonal corners of the bar. With character data, the XC and YC variables are used in place of the X and Y variables. The values of the XLAST and YLAST variables are usually initialized with a MOVE function or another function that updates the XLAST and YLAST pair. When the XC variable is used, set XSYS='2'. When the YC variable is used, set YSYS='2'.

Figure 25.2 Points Used to Construct a Bar

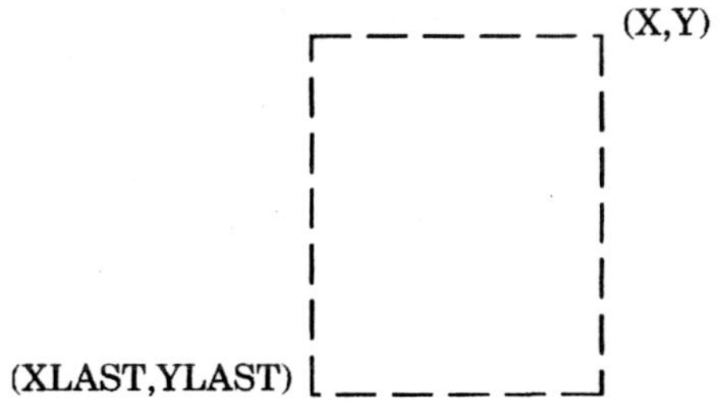

CNTL2TXT Function

Copies the values of the internal coordinates stored in the variable pairs (XLAST, YLAST) to (XLSTT, YLSTT).

Updates: XLSTT, YLSTT

Syntax

FUNCTION='CNTL2TXT';

Details

You can use CNTL2TXT to calculate the position of labels on a graph. For example, the following DATA step uses CNTL2TXT to position a pie slice label in the center of the arc and just beyond the arc itself, as shown in Figure 25.5 on page 619.

First, use the PIE function to draw the pie slice:

```
data pielabel;
   retain xsys ysys '3';
   length function style $ 8;
   function='pie'; size=20; x=30; y=30;
      style='empty'; rotate=45; output;
```

Then use the PIEXY function to calculate a point outside of the arc as shown in Figure 25.3 on page 618.

```
/* find a point that is half of the arc (rotate*.5) */
      /* and is 4 units beyond the radius (size=1.1) */
   function='piexy'; angle=rotate*.5; size=1.1; output;
```

Figure 25.3 Position Calculated with the PIEXY Function

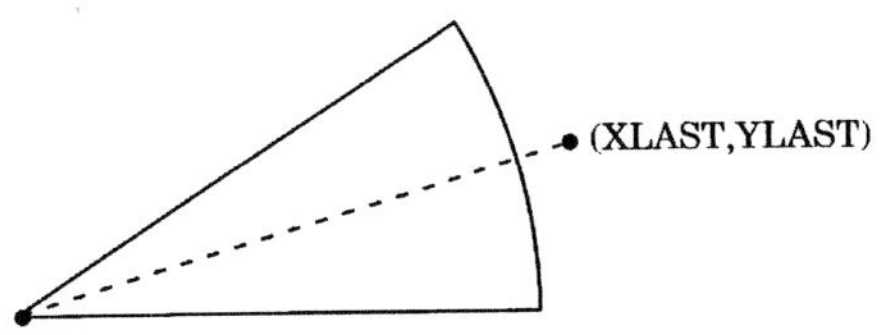

At this point, the XLAST and YLAST variables contain the coordinates of the point that is calculated by PIEXY. However, (XLAST, YLAST) cannot be used directly by text functions. Use CNTL2TXT to copy the coordinates in (XLAST, YLAST) to the XLSTT and YLSTT variables, which text functions can use. Figure 25.4 on page 618 shows the results.

```
function='cntl2txt'; output;
```

Figure 25.4 Coordinates after Using the CNTL2TXT Function

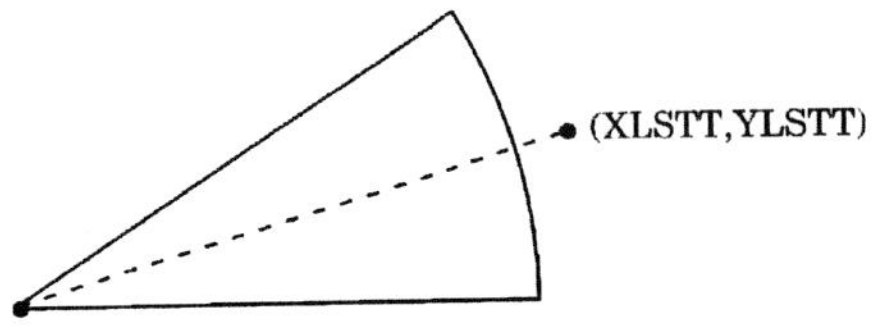

Now you can use the LABEL function to write the label as shown in Figure 25.5 on page 619. Specify missing values for the X and Y variables to force LABEL to use the XLSTT and YLSTT variables instead of the X and Y variables.

```
/* write the label 'Slice 1' and position it to      */
      /* the right of the point stored in XLSTT and YLSTT */
   function='label'; text='Slice 1'; angle=0; rotate=0;
      position='6'; style='swissb'; size=4; x=.; y=.;
      output;
run;

   /* draw the Annotate graphics */
proc ganno anno=pielabel;
run;
quit;
```

Figure 25.5 Labeled Pie Slice

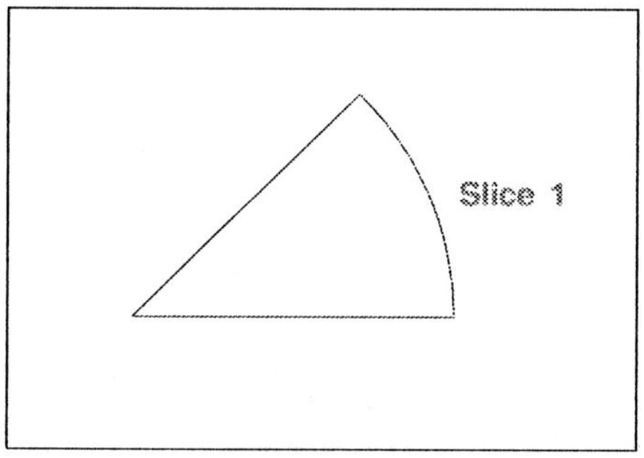

COMMENT Function

Inserts comments within the Annotate data set. The observations generated by the COMMENT function are ignored when the data set is processed.

Syntax

FUNCTION='COMMENT';

Associated Variables

TEXT='*text-string*'
: specifies the comment to write to the data set.

DEBUG Function

Writes the values of internal coordinates and Annotate variables to the SAS log before and after processing the next command (unless it is DEBUG) in the Annotate DATA step.

Syntax

FUNCTION='DEBUG';

DRAW Function

Draws a line in the graphics output from the (XLAST, YLAST) coordinates to the (X, Y) coordinates specified in the function.

Updates: XLAST, YLAST

Syntax

FUNCTION='DRAW';

Associated Variables

COLOR='*color*'
: specifies the color of the line that is being drawn. *Color* can be any SAS/GRAPH color name.

GROUP=*group-value*
MIDPOINT=*midpoint-value*
SUBGROUP=*subgroup-value*
: specify coordinates for HBAR and VBAR charts from the GCHART procedure. Use these variables only with the data coordinate systems 1, 2, 7, and 8.

HSYS='*coordinate-system*'
: specifies the coordinate system for the SIZE variable. See "HSYS Variable" on page 649 for an explanation of *coordinate-system*.

LINE=1...46
: specifies the line type of the line that is being drawn. See "Specifying Line Types" on page 207 for an illustration of the line types.

SIZE=*line-thickness*
: specifies the thickness of the line that is being drawn. The units depend on the value of the HSYS variable. For example, if HSYS='3', the SIZE variable is in units of percent of the graphics output area. If HSYS='4', the SIZE variable is in units of cells of the graphics output area.

As the thickness of the line increases, it may be impossible to center around a given coordinate. For example, if you specify a thickness of value 2 and HSYS='4', the first line is drawn at the (X, Y) coordinates. The second is drawn slightly above the first. The exact amount varies by device, but it is always one pixel in width. A thickness of value 3 produces one line above, one line at, and one line below the (X, Y) coordinate position. See Figure 25.6 on page 621 for examples of line thicknesses.

Figure 25.6 Sample Line Thicknesses Used with the SIZE Variable

WHEN='B' | 'A'
: specifies when to draw the line in relation to other procedure output. See "WHEN Variable" on page 666.

X=*horizontal-coordinate*
Y=*vertical-coordinate*
Z=*depth-coordinate* (PROC G3D only)
XC='*character-type-horizontal-coordinate*'
YC='*character-type-vertical-coordinate*'
: specify the endpoint of a line drawn from (XLAST, YLAST) to (X,Y).

XSYS='*coordinate-system*'
: specifies the coordinate system for the X or XC variable. The XC variable can be used only with XSYS='2'. See "XSYS Variable" on page 670 for an explanation of *coordinate-system*.

YSYS='*coordinate-system*'
: specifies the coordinate system for the Y or YC variable. The YC variable can be used only with YSYS='2'. See "YSYS Variable" on page 674 for an explanation of *coordinate-system*.

ZSYS='*coordinate-system*'
: specifies the coordinate system for the Z variable (PROC G3D only). See "ZSYS Variable" on page 676 for an explanation of *coordinate-system*.

DRAW2TXT Function

Draws a line from (XLAST, YLAST) to (XLSTT, YLSTT) without updating any of those variables.

Syntax

FUNCTION='DRAW2TXT';

Associated Variables

COLOR=*'color'*
specifies the line color. *Color* can be any SAS/GRAPH color name.

HSYS=*'coordinate-system'*
specifies the coordinate system for the SIZE variable. See "HSYS Variable" on page 649 for an explanation of *coordinate-system*.

LINE=1...46
specifies the line type of the line that is being drawn. See "Specifying Line Types" on page 207 for an illustration of the line types.

SIZE=*line-thickness*
specifies the thickness of the line that is being drawn. See "DRAW Function" on page 620 for details.

WHEN='B' | 'A'
specifies when to draw the line in relation to generation of the procedure output. See "WHEN Variable" on page 666.

Details

DRAW2TXT is useful for underlining text.

DRAW2TXT does not update the (XLAST, YLAST) or (XLSTT, YLSTT) coordinates; neither can it interrupt a POLYCONT sequence.

FRAME Function

Draws a border around the portion of the display area defined by the XSYS and YSYS variables. Optionally specifies a background color for the framed area.

Syntax

FUNCTION='FRAME';

Note: The FRAME function is not supported for client-side annotate with Java. △

Associated Variables

COLOR=*'color'*
specifies the frame color and, if the STYLE variable is specified, fills the interior of the frame. *Color* can be any SAS/GRAPH color name.

HSYS=*'coordinate-system'*
specifies the coordinate system for the SIZE variable. See "HSYS Variable" on page 649 for an explanation of *coordinate-system*.

Note: The HSYS variable is not supported for client-side output with ActiveX. △

HTML=*'link-string'*
specifies the text that defines the link for drill-down.

LINE=1...46
specifies the line type with which to draw the frame. See "Specifying Line Types" on page 207for an illustration of the line types.

SIZE=*line-thickness*
specifies the thickness of the line with which to draw the frame. See "DRAW Function" on page 620 for details.

Note: The SIZE variable is not supported for client-side output with ActiveX. △

STYLE='*fill-pattern*'
specifies the pattern that fills the area that is bounded by the frame. *Fill-pattern* can be the following bar and block patterns:

SOLID
S — a solid fill.

EMPTY
E — an empty fill.

style<density> — a shaded pattern:
style can be R | X | L
density can be 1...5

See also the discussion of fill patterns for bars and blocks in VALUE= on page 171.

WHEN='B' | 'A'
specifies when to draw the frame in relation to other procedure output. See "WHEN Variable" on page 666

XSYS='*coordinate-system*'
YSYS='*coordinate-system*'
define the area to be enclosed by the frame. For example, if XSYS='1' and YSYS='1', the frame encloses the axis area as shown in Figure 25.7 on page 623. See "XSYS Variable" on page 670 and the YSYS variable on "YSYS Variable" on page 674 for an explanation of *coordinate-system*.

Figure 25.7 Frame Created When XSYS='1' and YSYS='1'

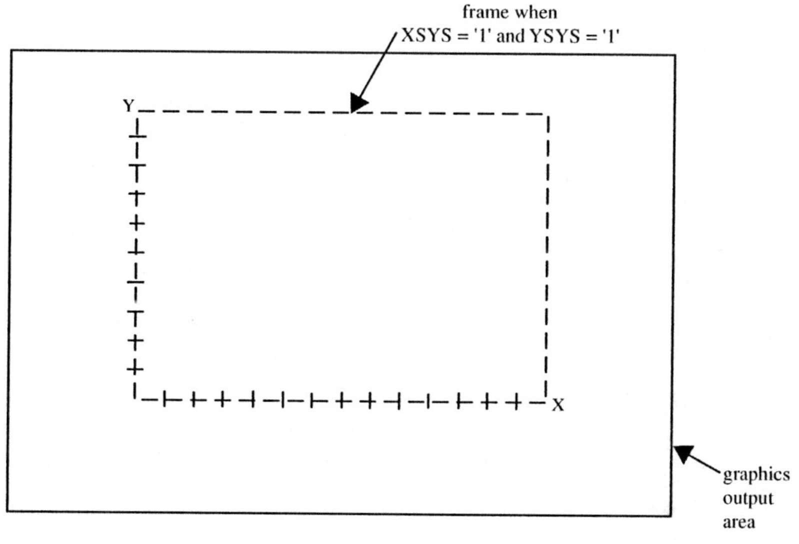

If XSYS='3' and YSYS='3', the frame encloses the entire graphics output area, as shown in Figure 25.8 on page 624.

Figure 25.8 Frame Created When XSYS='3' and YSYS='3'

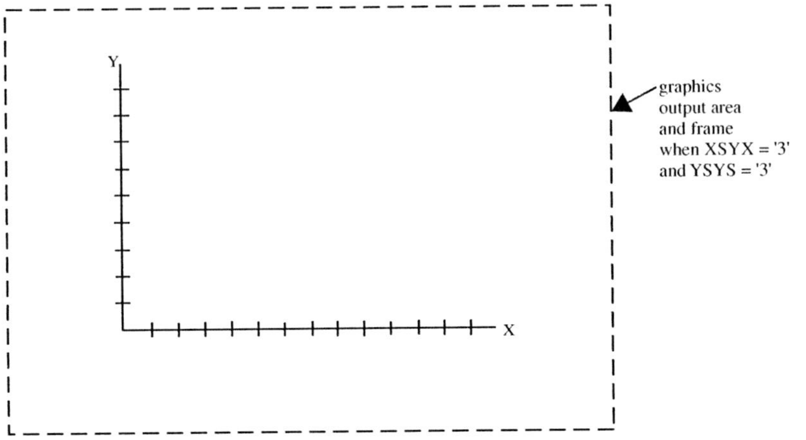

The values for XSYS and YSYS do not have to be the same. If XSYS='3' and YSYS='5', the frame encloses the entire width of the graphics output area; however, vertically, the frame only encloses the procedure output area as shown in Figure 25.9 on page 624.

Figure 25.9 Frame Created When XSYS='3' and YSYS='5'

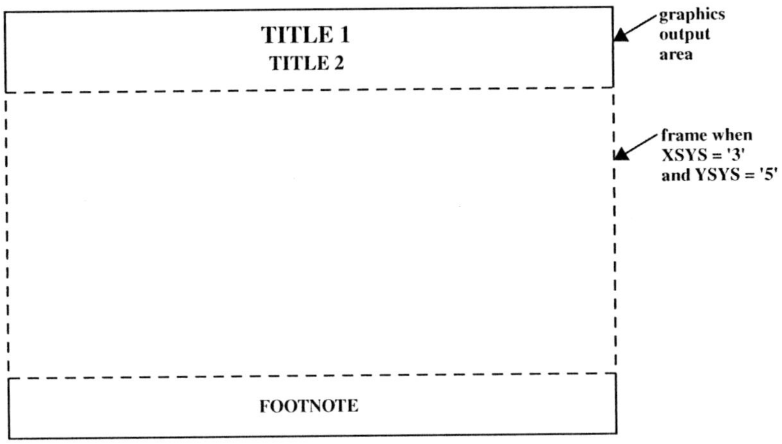

See "XSYS Variable" on page 670 and "YSYS Variable" on page 674 for an explanation of these variables and the areas that they affect.

Details

Use FRAME to simulate the CBACK= graphics option on devices (such as plotters) that do not support that option. For devices that do support the CBACK= graphics option, FRAME works in addition to that option. FRAME does not alter the (XLAST, YLAST) coordinates. See "CBACK" on page 266 for more information on CBACK=.

IMAGE Function

Displays an image in the graphics output from the current (X,Y) coordinates to the (X, Y) coordinates that are associated with the IMGPATH variable.

Updates: XLAST, YLAST

Syntax

FUNCTION='IMAGE';

Associated Variables

HTML='*link-string*'
specifies the text that defines the link for drill-down.

IMGPATH=*fileref* | '*external-file*'
specifies the image file to be displayed in the graphics output. The syntax of external file specifications varies across operating environments.

STYLE = 'TILE' | 'FIT';
specifies how the image is to be applied to fill the specified area of the graphics output. The default value of TILE replicates the image to fill the area. The FIT value stretches a single instance of the image to fill the area.

X=*horizontal-coordinate*;
specifies the horizontal coordinate that determines the size of the image displayed in the graphics output.

Y=*vertical-coordinate*;
specifies the vertical coordinate that determines the size of the image displayed in the graphics output.

Z=*depth-coordinate*;
specifies the depth coordinate for 3D output.

ZSYS='*coordinate-system*'
specifies the coordinate system for the Z variable. See "ZSYS Variable" on page 676 for an explanation of *coordinate-system*.

Details

The following example shows how the IMAGE function adds a single stretched instance of an image to the graphics output, beginning at the current coordinates and ending at the specified coordinates:

```
x=10; y=5; function='move' output;
x=35; y=15; imgpath='/images/gifs/picture.gif';
style='fit';
function='image'; output;
```

LABEL Function

Places text in the graphics output. Associated variables can control the color, size, font, base angle, and rotation of the characters displayed.

Updates: XLSTT, YLSTT

Syntax

FUNCTION='LABEL';

Associated Variables

ANGLE=0...360
: specifies the baseline angle of the character string with respect to the horizontal. The pivot point is at (X, Y), and the rotation is in a counterclockwise direction.

CBORDER='*color*' | 'CTEXT'
: draws a colored border around the text. *Color* can be any SAS/GRAPH color name.

CBOX='*color*' | 'CBACK
: draws a solid, colored box behind the text. *Color* can be any SAS/GRAPH color name.

COLOR='*color*'
: specifies the color of the text. *Color* can be any SAS/GRAPH color name.

GROUP=*group-value*
MIDPOINT=*midpoint-value*
SUBGROUP=*subgroup-value*
: specify coordinates for HBAR and VBAR charts from the GCHART procedure. Use these variables only with the data coordinate systems 1, 2, 7, and 8.

HSYS='*coordinate-system*'
: specifies the coordinate system for the SIZE variable. See “HSYS Variable” on page 649 for an explanation of *coordinate-system*.

HTML='*link-string*'
: specifies the text that defines the link for drill-down.

POSITION='*text-position*' | '0'
: controls the text string placement and alignment. *Text-position* can be one of the characters 1 through 9, A through F, <, +, or >. Invalid or missing values default to POSITION='5'. POSITION should always be a character variable of length 1. For details, see “POSITION Variable” on page 656.

ROTATE=*rotation-angle*
: specifies the rotation angle of each character in the string. It is equivalent to the ROTATE= option in the FOOTNOTE, NOTE, and TITLE statements.

SIZE=*height*
: specifies the height of the text string. The SIZE variable units are based on the value of the HSYS variable.

STYLE=*'font'* | *'"hardware-font-name"'* | 'NONE'
: specifies the font with which to draw the text that is specified by the TEXT variable. See "STYLE Variable (Fonts)" on page 661 for a description of the various font specifications.

TEXT=*'text-string'*
: specifies the text to be written. *Text-string* can be up to 200 characters. Define the TEXT variable with sufficient length to contain all of the characters in your text string. If you need longer strings, use separate observations and POSITION='0' to continue the text.

WHEN='B' | 'A'
: specifies when to draw the text strings in relation to other procedure output. See "WHEN Variable" on page 666

X=*horizontal-coordinate*
Y=*vertical-coordinate*
Z=*depth-coordinate* (PROC G3D only)
XC=*'character-type-horizontal-coordinate'*
YC=*'character-type-vertical-coordinate'*
: specify the start point of the text string. The Z variable can be used only with the G3D procedure. Optionally, you can modify the placement of the text string with the POSITION variable.

XSYS=*'coordinate-system'*
: specifies the coordinate system for the X or XC variable. Use the XC variable only with XSYS='2'. See "XSYS Variable" on page 670 for an explanation of *coordinate-system*.

YSYS=*'coordinate-system'*
: specifies the coordinate system for the Y or YC variable. Use the YC variable only with YSYS='2'. See "YSYS Variable" on page 674 for an explanation of *coordinate-system*.

ZSYS=*'coordinate-system'*
: specifies the coordinate system for the Z variable. See "ZSYS Variable" on page 676 for an explanation of *coordinate-system*.

MOVE Function

Moves the drawing pointer to a specific location without drawing a line.

Updates: XLAST, YLAST

Syntax

FUNCTION='MOVE';

Associated Variables

GROUP=*group-value*
MIDPOINT=*midpoint-value*
SUBGROUP=*subgroup-value*

specify coordinates for HBAR and VBAR charts from the GCHART procedure. Use these variables only with the data coordinate systems 1, 2, 7, and 8.

WHEN='B' | 'A'
specifies when to perform the move in relation to other procedure output. See also "WHEN Variable" on page 666.

X=*horizontal-coordinate*
Y=*vertical-coordinate*
Z=*depth-coordinate* (PROC G3D only)
XC='*character-type-horizontal-coordinate*'
YC='*character-type-vertical-coordinate*'
specify the coordinates to which the pen is to be moved. The Z variable can only be used with the G3D procedure.

XSYS='*coordinate-system*'
specifies the coordinate system for the X or XC variable. Use the XC variable only with XSYS='2'. See "XSYS Variable" on page 670 for an explanation of *coordinate-system*.

YSYS='*coordinate-system*'
specifies the coordinate system for the Y or YC variable. Use the YC variable only with YSYS='2'. See "YSYS Variable" on page 674 for an explanation of *coordinate-system*.

ZSYS='*coordinate-system*'
specifies the coordinate system for the Z variable. See "ZSYS Variable" on page 676 for an explanation of *coordinate-system*.

Details

Use MOVE to prepare for a DRAW command, a BAR command, or programming functions.

PIE Function

Draws pie slices in the graphics output.

Updates: XLAST, YLAST to coordinates for center of the slice.

Syntax

FUNCTION='PIE';

Associated Variables

ANGLE=*starting-angle*
specifies the starting angle of the slice arc. The default is 0.00 (horizontal) if the ANGLE variable is not specified for the first slice. After the first slice, the default is the ending angle of the slice arc just drawn if ANGLE=. (missing). Therefore, you can specify consecutive pie slices more easily by omitting the start and end calculations that are otherwise required. If you want the next slice to start at an

angle that is different from the ending angle of the previous slice, you must specify a value for the ANGLE variable.

COLOR=*'color'*
: specifies the color of the pie slice, if a pattern is specified in the STYLE variable. If you specify STYLE='EMPTY', the COLOR variable also specifies the outline color of the pie slices. *Color* can be any SAS/GRAPH color name.

GROUP=*group-value*
MIDPOINT=*midpoint-value*
SUBGROUP=*subgroup-value*
: specify coordinates for HBAR and VBAR charts from the GCHART procedure. Use these variables only with the data coordinate systems 1, 2, 7, and 8.

HSYS=*'coordinate-system'*
: specifies the coordinate system for the SIZE variable. See "HSYS Variable" on page 649 for an explanation of *coordinate-system*.

HTML=*'link-string'*
: specifies the text that defines the link for drill-down.

LINE=0...3
: specifies which slice line (or lines) to draw. See Figure 25.10 on page 629 for line values and their actions. LINE=0 draws only the outside of the arc and enables you to draw a circle.

Figure 25.10 LINE Values Used with the PIE Function

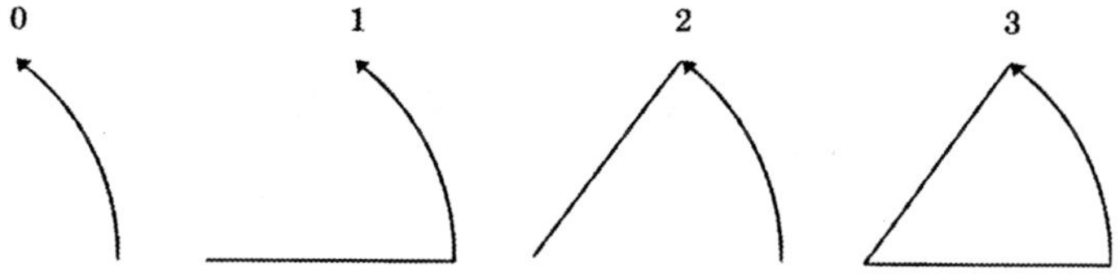

ROTATE=*rotation-angle*
: specifies the angle of rotation or the delta angle of the slice arc. The default is 0.00.

For example, if you specify these statements, the slice arc that is drawn begins at 90 degrees (vertical) and ends at 135 degrees (90+45):

```
function='pie'; angle=90; rotate=45; output;
```

The ANGLE variable is internally updated to the end value, 135 degrees. The value is modified only internally. If a second PIE is used and the ANGLE variable contains a missing value, the start angle is assumed to be the previous end, or 135 degrees. The arc continues from that point.

If you specify the previous statements and then specify these statements, the slice begins at 135 degrees (the end angle from the previous slice) and extends another 45 degrees to the end point, 180 degrees.

```
function='pie'; angle=.; rotate=45; output;
```

This action repeats for every missing angle in the sequence.

SIZE=*radius*
: specifies the radius of the circle being drawn. The SIZE variable uses units that are determined by the HSYS variable.

STYLE='*fill-pattern*'
specifies the value of the pattern that fills the pie slices. *Fill-pattern* can be the following pie patterns:

PSOLID
PS — a solid fill.

PEMPTY
PE — an empty fill.

P*density<style<angle>>* — a shaded pattern:
density can be 1...5
style can be X | N
angle can be 0...360

For example, if STYLE='P5N15', a pie slice with a fill of parallel lines is produced. The fill uses the heaviest density to draw the lines, and the parallel lines are drawn at a 15-degree angle from perpendicular to the radius of the pie slice. See also the discussion of fill patterns for pie and star charts in VALUE= on page 174.

WHEN='B' | 'A'
specifies when to draw the pie slice in relation to other procedure output. See "WHEN Variable" on page 666.

X=*horizontal-coordinate*
Y=*vertical-coordinate*
Z=*depth-coordinate* (PROC G3D only)
XC='*character-type-horizontal-coordinate*'
YC='*character-type-vertical-coordinate*'
define the center of the slice. The pivot point for all slices is the point referenced by X, Y, and Z (with PROC G3D only). The first PIE command that is issued sets the center at the (X,Y) value. If subsequent values for X and Y are missing, the coordinates of the center point are used.

XSYS='*coordinate-system*'
specifies the coordinate system for the X or XC variable. Use the XC variable only with XSYS='2'. See "XSYS Variable" on page 670 for an explanation of *coordinate-system*.

YSYS='*coordinate-system*'
specifies the coordinate system for the Y or YC variable. Use the YC variable only with YSYS='2'. See "YSYS Variable" on page 674 for an explanation of *coordinate-system*.

ZSYS='*coordinate-system*'
specifies the coordinate system for the Z variable. See "ZSYS Variable" on page 676 for an explanation of *coordinate-system*.

See Also

"CNTL2TXT Function" on page 617

PIECNTR Function

Sets new center and radius values for later use by the PIEXY function but does not draw an arc.

Updates: XLAST, YLAST

Syntax

FUNCTION='PIECNTR';

Associated Variables

GROUP=*group-value*
MIDPOINT=*midpoint-value*
SUBGROUP=*subgroup-value*
: specify coordinates for HBAR and VBAR charts from the GCHART procedure. Use these variables only with the data coordinate systems 1, 2, 7, and 8.

HSYS='*coordinate-system*'
: specifies the coordinate system for the SIZE variable. See "HSYS Variable" on page 649 for an explanation of *coordinate-system.*

SIZE=*radius*
: specifies the new radius of the pie slice. The new radius is used by a subsequent PIEXY function. The HSYS variable determines the SIZE variable units.

WHEN='B' | 'A'
: specifies when to draw the pie slice in relation to other procedure output. See "WHEN Variable" on page 666

X=*horizontal-coordinate*
Y=*vertical-coordinate*
Z=*depth-coordinate* (PROC G3D only)
XC='*character-type-horizontal-coordinate*'
YC='*character-type-vertical-coordinate*'
: define the center and radius of the slice. All slices are referenced from that center. Use the Z variable only with the G3D procedure.

XSYS='*coordinate-system*'
: specifies the coordinate system for the X or XC variable. Use the XC variable only with XSYS='2'. See "XSYS Variable" on page 670 for an explanation of *coordinate-system.*

YSYS='*coordinate-system*'
: specifies the coordinate system for the Y or YC variable. Use the YC variable only with YSYS='2'. See "YSYS Variable" on page 674 for an explanation of *coordinate-system.*

ZSYS='*coordinate-system*'
: specifies the coordinate system for the Z variable. See "ZSYS Variable" on page 676 for an explanation of *coordinate-system.*

PIEXY Function

Calculates a point on the outline of the slice arc.

Updates: XLAST, YLAST

Syntax

FUNCTION='PIEXY';

Associated Variables

ANGLE=*rotation-angle*
: specifies the angle of rotation when moving around the perimeter of a pie. The ANGLE variable determines the angle at which the point is located relative to 0 (the three o'clock position). The default is 0.00.

SIZE=*radius-multiplier*
: determines the distance from the center of the slice to the point that is being calculated. The point's distance is the current value of the SIZE variable multiplied by the radius (that is, the SIZE variable) of the previously drawn slice. To position a graphics element inside the pie slice, set the SIZE variable to less than 1; to position it outside of the pie slice, set the SIZE variable to greater than 1. For example, if you specify these statements, the point calculated is 1.1 times the radius (where the radius is taken from the SIZE variable that is used with the previous FUNCTION='PIE' or FUNCTION='PIECNTR' observation).

```
function='piexy'; size=1.1; output;
```

WHEN='B' | 'A'
: specifies when to update the internal coordinate pair (XLAST, YLAST) in relation to other procedure output. See"WHEN Variable" on page 666.

Details

PIEXY does not draw anything but places the calculated coordinates of the point in the internal coordinate pair (XLAST, YLAST). Then you can use XLAST and YLAST with other functions to perform other graphics actions, such as labeling pie slices. If you need to use the calculated position for a text function, use the SWAP or CNTL2TXT to put (XLAST, YLAST) into (XLSTT, YLSTT).

PIEXY assumes that a pie slice has been drawn or that FUNCTION='PIECNTR' has been used. Erroneous results can occur if a slice has not been drawn and PIEXY is invoked.

Figure 25.11 on page 632 shows a pie slice that is drawn with the PIE function. Figure 25.12 on page 633 shows a point beyond the arc that was calculated using the PIEXY function.

Figure 25.11 Pie Slice Drawn with the PIE Function

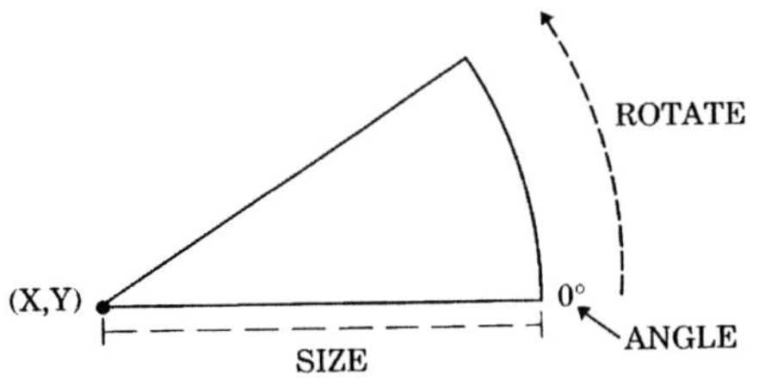

Figure 25.12 Point Calculated with the PIEXY Function

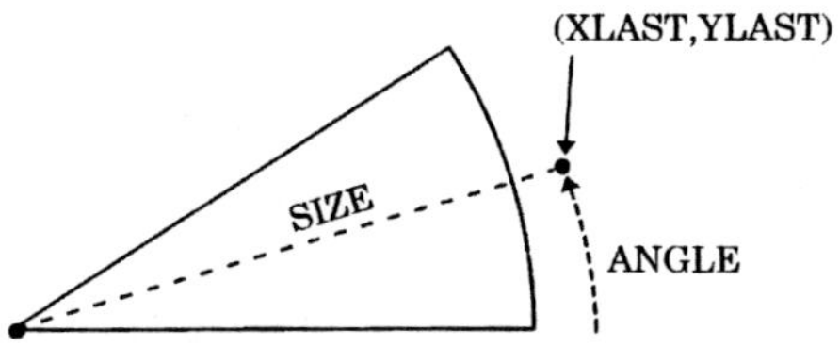

See Also

"CNTL2TXT Function" on page 617

POINT Function

Places a single point at the (X, Y) coordinates in the color you specify. The point is one visible pixel in size.

Updates: XLAST, YLAST

Syntax

FUNCTION='POINT';

Associated Variables

COLOR='*color*'
: specifies the color of the point to be drawn. *Color* can be any SAS/GRAPH color name.

GROUP=*group-value*
MIDPOINT=*midpoint-value*
SUBGROUP=*subgroup-value*
: specify coordinates when used with HBAR and VBAR charts from the GCHART procedure. Use these variables only with the data coordinate systems 1, 2, 7, and 8.

WHEN='B' | 'A'
: specifies when to draw the point in relation to other procedure output. See "WHEN Variable" on page 666

X=*horizontal-coordinate*
Y=*vertical-coordinate*
Z=*depth-coordinate* (PROC G3D only)
XC='*character-type-horizontal-coordinate*'
YC='*character-type-vertical-coordinate*'
: specify the coordinates of the point that is to be drawn. Use the Z variable only with the G3D procedure.

XSYS='*coordinate-system*'
specifies the coordinate system for the X or XC variable. Use the XC variable only with XSYS='2'. See "XSYS Variable" on page 670 for an explanation of *coordinate-system*.

YSYS='*coordinate-system*'
specifies the coordinate system for the Y or YC variable. Use the YC variable only with YSYS='2'. See "YSYS Variable" on page 674 for an explanation of *coordinate-system*.

ZSYS='*coordinate-system*'
specifies the coordinate system for the Z variable. See "ZSYS Variable" on page 676 for an explanation of *coordinate-system*.

POLY Function

Specifies the beginning point of a polygon. Associated variables can define the fill pattern and color, as well as the line type that outlines the polygon.

Syntax

FUNCTION='POLY';

Associated Variables

COLOR='*color*'
specifies the color of the interior of the polygon, if a pattern is specified for the STYLE variable. The outline color is specified with the POLYCONT function. *Color* can be any SAS/GRAPH color name.

GROUP=*group-value*
MIDPOINT=*midpoint-value*
SUBGROUP=*subgroup-value*
specify coordinates for HBAR and VBAR charts from the GCHART procedure. Use these variables only with data coordinate systems 1, 2, 7, and 8.

HTML='*link-string*'
specifies the text that defines the link for drill-down.

LINE=1...46
specifies the line type that outlines the polygon. See "Specifying Line Types" on page 207 for an illustration of the line types.

SIZE=*thickness*
specifies a line thickness for the polygon

STYLE='*fill-pattern*'
specifies the value of the pattern that fills the polygon. *Fill-pattern* can be the following map patterns:

MSOLID MS	a solid pattern
MEMPTY ME	an empty pattern

M*density*<*style*<*angle*>> a shaded pattern:

density can be 1...5

style can be X | N

angle can be 0...360.

For example, if STYLE='MSOLID' for the POLY function, the fill area that is drawn by the POLYCONT sequence uses a solid fill. If STYLE='M5N15', the fill area uses a shaded fill of parallel lines. The *fill-pattern* value M5N15 specifies that the lines use the heaviest density, are parallel, and are drawn at a 15-degree angle from the horizontal. See also the discussion of fill patterns for maps in VALUE= on page 173.

WHEN='B' | 'A'
specifies when to begin the polygon in relation to other procedure output. See "WHEN Variable" on page 666

X=*horizontal-coordinate*
Y=*vertical-coordinate*
Z=*depth-coordinate* (PROC G3D only)
XC='*character-type-horizontal-coordinate*'
YC='*character-type-vertical-coordinate*'
specify the initial point of the polygon that is being created. Use the Z variable only with the G3D procedure.

XSYS='*coordinate-system*'
specifies the coordinate system for the X or XC variable. Use the XC variable only with XSYS='2'. See "XSYS Variable" on page 670 for an explanation of *coordinate-system*.

YSYS='*coordinate-system*'
specifies the coordinate system for the Y or YC variable. Use the YC variable only with YSYS='2'. See "YSYS Variable" on page 674 for an explanation of *coordinate-system*.

ZSYS='*coordinate-system*'
specifies the coordinate system for the Z variable. See "ZSYS Variable" on page 676 for an explanation of *coordinate-system*.

Details

Use POLY with POLYCONT to define and fill areas in the graphics output. POLY and POLYCONT do not update the (XLAST, YLAST) coordinates.

See Also

"POLYCONT Function" on page 635

POLYCONT Function

Continues drawing a polygon begun with the POLY function. POLYCONT specifies each successive point in the polygon definition.

Syntax

FUNCTION='POLYCONT';

Associated Variables

COLOR='*color*'
: specifies the polygon outline color. *Color* can be any SAS/GRAPH color name. You can specify an outline color only with the first POLYCONT command in the sequence; all subsequent POLYCONT commands ignore the COLOR variable. If you do not specify a color, the POLYCONT function uses the interior color that was specified with the POLY function.

GROUP=*group-value*
MIDPOINT=*midpoint-value*
SUBGROUP=*subgroup-value*
: specify coordinates for HBAR and VBAR charts from the GCHART procedure. Use these variables only with the data coordinate systems 1, 2, 7, and 8.

WHEN='B' | 'A'
: specifies when to draw the polygon in relation to other procedure output. See "WHEN Variable" on page 666

X=*horizontal-coordinate*
Y=*vertical-coordinate*
Z=*depth-coordinate* (PROC G3D only)
XC='*character-type-horizontal-coordinate*'
YC='*character-type-vertical-coordinate*'
: specify a point on the outline of the polygon that is being created. Use the Z variable only with the G3D procedure.

XSYS='*coordinate-system*'
: specifies the coordinate system for the X and XC variable. Use the XC variable only with XSYS='2'. See "XSYS Variable" on page 670 for an explanation of *coordinate-system*.

YSYS='*coordinate-system*'
: specifies the coordinate system for the Y and YC variable. Use the YC variable only with YSYS='2'. See "YSYS Variable" on page 674 for an explanation of *coordinate-system*.

ZSYS='*coordinate-system*'
: specifies the coordinate system for the Z variable. See "ZSYS Variable" on page 676 for an explanation of *coordinate-system*.

Details

The polygon definition is terminated by a new POLY command or by any of these functions:

BAR

DRAW

DRAW2TXT

FRAME

LABEL

MOVE

PIE

PIECNTR

PIEXY

POINT

SYMBOL

Use POLY and POLYCONT together to draw a polygon. The (X, Y) observation from the POLY function and the last (X, Y) observation from POLYCONT are assumed to connect. Thus, you are not required to respecify the first point. For example, these statements draw a pentagon like the one in Figure 25.13 on page 638:

```
data house;
   retain xsys ysys '3';
   length function $ 8;
      /* start at the lower left corner */
   function='poly'; x=35; y=25; output;
      /* move to the lower right corner */
   function='polycont'; x=65; y=25; output;
      /* move to the upper right corner */
   function='polycont'; x=65; y=65; output;
      /* move to the center top*/
   function='polycont'; x=50; y=80; output;
      /* move to the upper left corner and complete the figure */
   function='polycont'; x=35; y=65; output;
run;

proc ganno anno=house;
run;
quit;
```

Figure 25.13 Pentagon Produced with the POLY and POLYCONT Functions

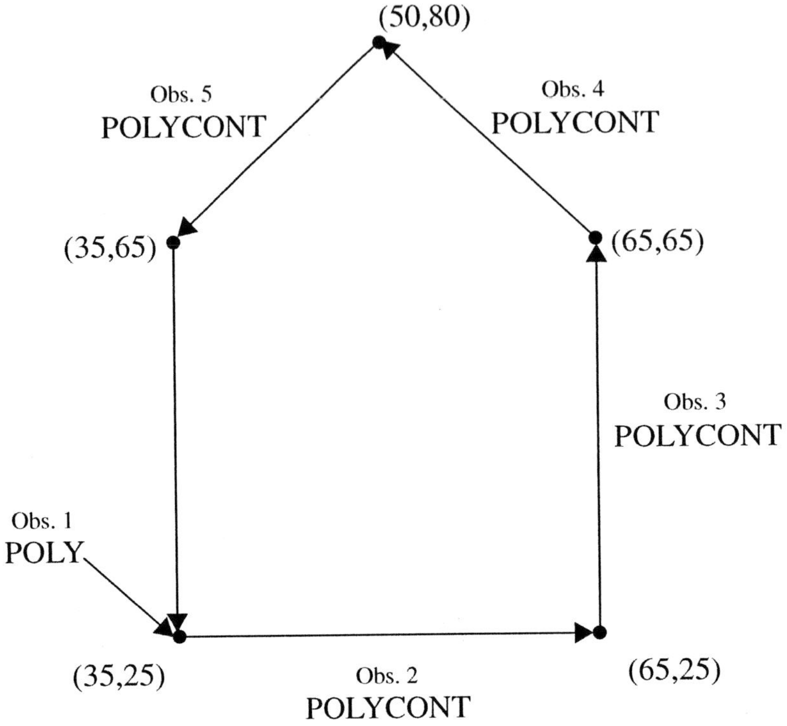

Missing values for the X and Y variables that are specified with POLYCONT are interpreted differently from the way that they are interpreted with the other functions. Other functions use the missing values to request a default value. POLYCONT interprets a missing value as a discontinuity (that is, a hole) in the polygon. If you are not using the data coordinate system and you specify an X or Y value of –999 in a POLYCONT observation, the default of (XLAST, YLAST) is used. Missing values indicate holes and are handled identically in the Annotate facility and the GMAP procedure. See "Displaying Map Areas and Response Data" on page 1005 for more information on handling missing values.

POP Function

Removes the (XLAST, YLAST) and (XLSTT, YLSTT) values from the LIFO stack and updates the internal coordinate pairs with the retrieved values.

Updates: (XLAST, YLAST) and (XLSTT, YLSTT)

Syntax

FUNCTION='POP';

Details

Use POP when you want to access the values of (XLAST, YLAST) and (XLSTT, YLSTT) that you most recently stored with the PUSH function. See the PUSH function for a description of the LIFO stack.

PUSH Function

Adds current (XLAST, YLAST) and (XLSTT, YLSTT) values to the LIFO stack.

Syntax

FUNCTION='PUSH';

Details

The LIFO (last-in-first-out) stack is a storage area where you can keep internal coordinate values for later use by utility functions without recalculating those values. LIFO stacks manage the stored data so that the last data stored in the stack is the first data removed from the stack.

Use the stack to save the current values of (XLAST, YLAST) and (XLSTT, YLSTT) and use them with functions later in the DATA step. You store and retrieve these values from the stack with the PUSH and POP functions. The PUSH function copies the current values of XLAST, YLAST, XLSTT, and YLSTT onto the stack. The POP function copies values from the stack into XLAST, YLAST. XLSTT, and YLSTT.

SWAP Function

Exchanges values of (XLAST, YLAST) with (XLSTT, YLSTT) and vice versa.

Updates: (XLAST, YLAST) and (XLSTT, YLSTT)

Syntax

FUNCTION='SWAP';

Details

Use SWAP when you want to use both the (XLAST, YLAST) and (XLSTT, YLSTT) coordinates for text and nontext functions, respectively.

SYMBOL Function

Places symbols in the graphics output. Associated variables can specify the color, font, and height of the symbols displayed.

Updates: XLSTT, YLSTT

Syntax

FUNCTION='SYMBOL';

Associated Variables

CBORDER='*color*' | 'CTEXT'
draws a colored border around the text. *Color* can be any SAS/GRAPH color name.

CBOX='*color*' | 'CBACK'
draws a solid, colored box behind the text. *Color* can be any SAS/GRAPH color name.

COLOR='*color*'
specifies the symbol color. *Color* can be any SAS/GRAPH color name. The COLOR variable behaves in the same way as the COLOR= option in the SYMBOL statement. See COLOR= on page 185 for details

GROUP=*group-value*
MIDPOINT=*midpoint-value*
SUBGROUP=*subgroup-value*
specify coordinates for HBAR and VBAR charts from the GCHART procedure. Use these variables only with the data coordinate systems 1, 2, 7, and 8.

HSYS='*coordinate-system*'
specifies the coordinate system for the SIZE variable. See "HSYS Variable" on page 649 for an explanation of *coordinate-system*.

HTML='*link-string*'
specifies the text that defines the link for drill-down.

SIZE=*height*
specifies the height of the symbol that is being drawn, using units determined by the HSYS variable. The SIZE variable is equivalent to the HEIGHT= option in the SYMBOL statement. See HEIGHT= on page 187 for details.

STYLE='*font*' | "'*hardware-font-name*'" | 'NONE';
specifies the font that is used to draw the symbol that is specified by the TEXT variable. See "STYLE Variable (Fonts)" on page 661 for a description of the various font specifications.

When the STYLE variable is used with the SYMBOL function, it behaves the same as the FONT= option in the SYMBOL statement. By default, no font is specified and the symbol that is specified by the TEXT variable is taken from the special symbol table. If you use STYLE to specify a symbol font, such as Marker, the string that is assigned by the TEXT variable is the character code for a symbol. If you use STYLE to specify a text font, such as Swiss, the string assigned by the TEXT variable is displayed as text. See FONT= on page 186 for details.

TEXT=*'special-symbol'* | *'text-string'*;

specifies the symbol to be displayed. *Special-symbol* can be up to eight characters long. Values for *special-symbol* are those described in the VALUE= option of the SYMBOL statement and are illustrated in VALUE= on page 199.

For client-side rendering using ActiveX, the following values are supported: plus, X, star, square, diamond, triangle, dot, circle, ", #, $, %, =. If a symbol is not supported, a plus sign (+) is drawn instead.

For client-side rendering using Java, the following values are supported: plus, X, star, square, diamond, triangle, dot (draws a circle), circle, *, +, >. If a symbol is not supported, a plus sign (+) is drawn instead.

If you also specify a text font with the STYLE variable, you can specify a text string that is displayed as the symbol. The maximum length for *text-string* is 200 characters.

When the TEXT variable is used with the SYMBOL function, it behaves the same as the VALUE= option in the SYMBOL statement. See VALUE= on page 199 for details.

WHEN='B' | 'A'

specifies when to draw the symbols in relation to other procedure output. See "WHEN Variable" on page 666

Y=*vertical-coordinate*
Z=*depth-coordinate* (PROC G3D only)
XC=*'character-type-horizontal-coordinate'*
YC=*'character-type-vertical-coordinate'*

specify the point at which the symbol is placed. Use the Z variable only with the G3D procedure.

XSYS=*'coordinate-system'*

specifies the coordinate system for the X or XC variable. Use the XC variable only with XSYS='2'. See "XSYS Variable" on page 670 for an explanation of *coordinate-system*.

YSYS=*'coordinate-system'*

specifies the coordinate system for the Y or YC variable. Use the YC variable only with YSYS='2'. See "YSYS Variable" on page 674 for an explanation of *coordinate-system*.

ZSYS=*'coordinate-system'*

specifies the coordinate system for the Z variable. See "ZSYS Variable" on page 676 for an explanation of *coordinate-system*.

Details

SYMBOL is similar to the LABEL function with these exceptions:

- SYMBOL draws symbols. If you do not specify a font, SYMBOL can use the symbols found in Figure 7.21 on page 202.
- The text cannot be rotated or angled.
- The text string cannot be longer than eight characters.
- The text string is always centered with respect to *x* and *y*.

TXT2CNTL Function

Copies the values (XLSTT, YLSTT) to (XLAST, YLAST), replacing previous values of (XLAST, YLAST).

Syntax

FUNCTION='TXT2CNTL';

Details

TXT2CNTL allows nontext functions to use the ending position of a text string as a starting or ending point.

Annotate Variables

When an Annotate data set is processed, the Annotate facility looks at the values of specific variables in order to draw graphics. This section describes all of the Annotate variables in alphabetical order. Not all variables are used with all functions. Refer to the description of the individual functions in "Annotate Functions" on page 615 for more information about how each variable is used with each function. For a summary of Annotate variables and their uses, see Table 24.1 on page 591.

ANGLE Variable

Specifies the angle at which the graphics output is drawn.

Type: numeric

Default: function dependent

Syntax

ANGLE=0...360;

Functions

The ANGLE variable is function dependent.

If function is...	then the ANGLE variable specifies...
LABEL	the baseline angle of the character string with respect to the horizontal. With the LABEL function, the pivot point is at (X,Y) and the direction of rotation is counterclockwise. The default value is 0.
PIE	the starting angle of the slice arc, measured counterclockwise. The default for the first PIE function is ANGLE=0 (horizontal, or 3:00 postion), or is the ending point of the arc of the previous slice. Specify a value for the ANGLE variable if you want the next slice to start at an angle that is different from the edge of the previous slice, or if you want the first slice to start at an angle other than horizontal.
PIEXY	the angle that works with the SIZE variable to establish the new XLAST, YLAST point relative to the last pie element established with the PIE or PIECNTR functions. The angle is measured counterclockwise starting at the 3:00 position. The default value is 0.

CBORDER Variable

Draws a colored border around text or symbols.

Type: character

Length: 8 for color codes and up to 64 for color names

See also: CBOX

Syntax

CBORDER='*color*' | 'CTEXT';

color

specifies the color that fills the box. The *color* value can be any SAS/GRAPH color name. See Chapter 6, "SAS/GRAPH Colors and Images," on page 91 for more information about specifying colors.

Specifying a null value for the *color* value (CBOX=' ')cancels the CBOX variable.

CTEXT

draws the border in the same coloras the text or symbol. The text color is determined by (1) the COLOR variable or (2) the CTEXT=graphics option or (3) the first color in the colors list.

Functions

You can use the CBORDER variable with these functions:

LABEL

SYMBOL

Details

Once you have specified CBORDER, it remains in effect for all subsequent observations that use the LABEL or SYMBOL function and draws a border around all text or symbols. To turn off the border for subsequent text or symbols, specify CBORDER=' '.

To fill the area defined by CBORDER, use the CBOX variable in conjunction with CBORDER.

CBOX Variable

Draws a solid box behind the text or symbol and fills the box with the specified color.

Type: character

Length: 8 for color codes and up to 64 for color names

See also: CBORDER

Syntax

CBOX='*color*' | 'CBACK';

color
specifies the color that fills the box. *Color* is any SAS/GRAPH color name. See Chapter 6, "SAS/GRAPH Colors and Images," on page 91 for more information about specifying colors.

Specifying a null value for *color* (CBOX=' ')cancels the CBOX variable.

CBACK
fills the box with the same color as the background color of the graph. The background color is either (1) the color specified by the CBACK= graphics option or (2) the default background color for the device.

Functions

You can use the CBOX variable with these functions:

LABEL

SYMBOL

Details

Once you have specified CBOX, it remains in effect for all subsequent observations that use the LABEL or SYMBOL function.

The color of the text or symbol within the box is controlled by the COLOR variable.

By default, the solid box has no border. To add a colored border to the box, use the CBORDER variable in conjunction with CBOX.

COLOR Variable

Specifies the color used by the function.

Type: character

Length: 8 for color codes and up to 64 for color names

Default:

1 first color in colors list of the COLORS= graphics option

2 first color in device's default colors list.

Syntax

COLOR='*color*';

color
specifies any SAS/GRAPH color name. See Chapter 6, "SAS/GRAPH Colors and Images," on page 91 for more information about specifying colors.

Functions

The COLOR variable is function dependent.

If function is...	then the COLOR variable specifies...
BAR	the color that outlines and, optionally, fills the bar if a pattern is specified in the STYLE (patterns)"STYLE Variable (Patterns)" on page 662 variable. If no pattern is specified, the *color* value is applied only to the outline of the bar.
DRAW, DRAW2TXT	the color of the line.
FRAME	the color of the outline of the frame. If a fill pattern is specified, *color* also determines the color of the inside of the frame.
LABEL	the color of the text.
PIE	the color for the pie slice if a pattern is specified with the STYLE (patterns)"STYLE Variable (Patterns)" on page 662 variable. If no pattern is specified, *color* determines the color of the outline of the pie slice.
POINT	the color of the point.
POLY	the fill color for the interior of the polygon if a pattern is specified with the STYLE variable. If the STYLE variable is missing or EMPTY, *color* is ignored. Use the POLYCONT function to specify the outline color.
POLYCONT	the color that outlines the polygon when used with the first POLYCONT function. COLOR is ignored for subsequent POLYCONT functions in the POLYCONT sequence.
SYMBOL	the color that draws the symbol.

FUNCTION Variable

Specifies a graphics command or programming function for the Annotate facility to perform.

Type: character

Length: 8

Default: LABEL

Syntax

FUNCTION='*function-name*';

function-name
specifies the name of an Annotate function. The *function-name* value can be any of the following.

BAR	draws and, optionally, fills a rectangle.
CNTL2TXT, DRAW2TXT	copies (XLAST, YLAST) to (XLSTT, YLSTT), overwriting the previous values of (XLSTT, YLSTT).
COMMENT	places comments in your data set. The observation is ignored when the data set is processed.
DEBUG	writes the values of all Annotate variables to the SAS log before and after the next observation.
DRAW	draws a line in the graphics output.
FRAME	draws a border around the area defined by XSYS and YSYS and specifies a background color for the framed area .
IMAGE	displays an image in the graphics output from the current (X,Y) coordinates to the coordinates that are associated with the IMGPATH variable.
LABEL	draws text and is the default for the FUNCTION variable.
MOVE	moves to the specified point (does not draw a line).
PIE	draws a pie slice, arc, or circle that can be filled.
PIECNTR	sets new center and radius values. The PIEXY function can use this information in a later observation.
PIEXY	returns the coordinates of a point on a pie slice. Other functions can use this information in a later observation.
POINT	draws a point.
POLY	begins drawing a polygon (first vertex). Use the POLYCONT function in successive observations to supply the remaining vertices.
POLYCONT	continues drawing a polygon.
POP	gets values from the LIFO stack and changes the current value of (XLAST, YLAST) and (XLSTT, YLSTT) to those values.

PUSH	puts the current values for (XLAST, YLAST) and (XLSTT, YLSTT) in the LIFO stack.
SWAP	exchanges the values of (XLAST, YLAST) and (XLSTT, YLSTT).
SYMBOL	draws a symbol. See Figure 7.21 on page 202 for a list of the symbols.
TXT2CNTL	copies the values (XLSTT, YLSTT) to (XLAST, YLAST), overwriting the previous values of (XLAST, YLAST).

All other variables in the observation that contain the function act as parameters for the action. For a detailed description of each function and the Annotate variables that can be used in conjunction with it, see "Annotate Functions" on page 615.

GROUP Variable

Positions graphics elements on the bars of a vertical or horizontal bar chart drawn using the GROUP= option in the GCHART procedure.

Type: Numeric or character; must match the type of the GROUP= variable used in the GCHART procedure.

Length: Should match the length of GROUP= variable in the GCHART procedure.

Default: none

Restriction: Used only with vertical or horizontal bar charts produced by the GCHART procedure.

Syntax

GROUP=*group-value*;

group-value
references value(s) of the variable that is identified by the GROUP= option in the GCHART procedure either as a variable name or as an explicit data value. *Group-value* can be one of the following:

group-variable	the name of a group variable.
group-data-value	a specific numeric data value.
'group-data-value'	a specific character data value.

To annotate all the bars in a horizontal or vertical bar chart, specify a variable name. To annotate a bar chart for a specific value of the GROUP variable, specify a specific value.

Functions

You can use the GROUP variable only with the data coordinate systems 1, 2, 7, and 8, and with these functions:

BAR

DRAW

LABEL

MOVE

PIE

PIECNTR

POINT

POLY

POLYCONT

SYMBOL

Details

Using the GROUP variable is similar to using the X and Y variables with data system coordinates to position graphics elements in a vertical or horizontal bar chart.

Figure 25.14 on page 649 shows how the GROUP variable works with the SUBGROUP and MIDPOINT variables to label the bars of a vertical bar chart.

Figure 25.14 Using the GROUP Variable to Position a Label in a Bar Chart

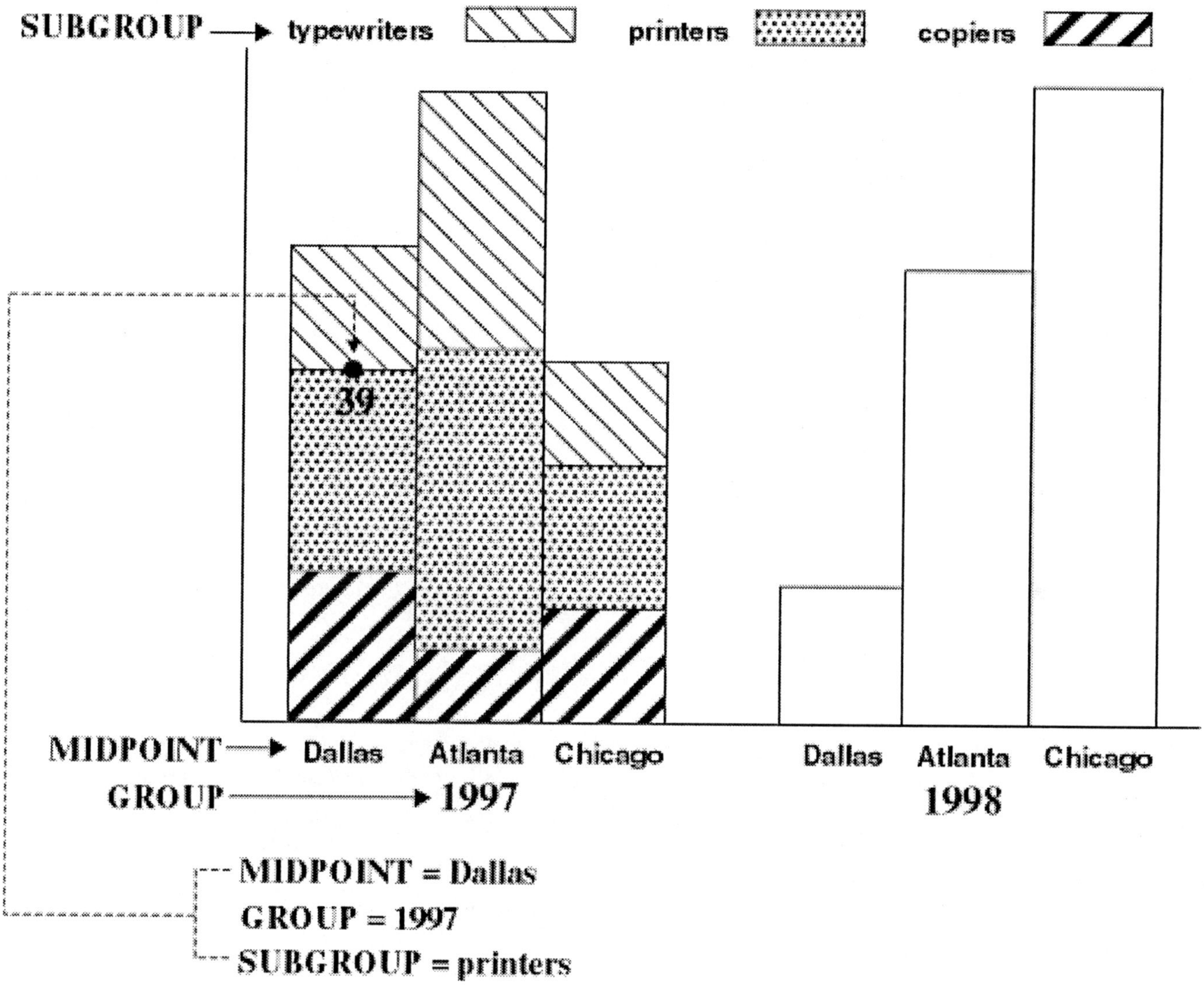

The label showing the number of units that were sold in Dallas in the year 1997 is positioned by the values that are assigned to these Annotate variables:

- GROUP=YEAR (where YEAR is a variable in the GCHART data set)
- MIDPOINT=CITY (where CITY is a variable in the GCHART data set)
- SUBGROUP=ITEM (where ITEM is a variable in the GCHART data set).

HSYS Variable

Defines the coordinate system and area of the output used by the SIZE variable to display the Annotate graphics. Additionally, you can use the HSYS variable with client-side annotation with Java or ActiveX to control the markersize and linesize for the BAR, DRAW, DRAW2TXT, POLY, and SYMBOL functions.

Type: character

Length: 1

Default: 4

Syntax

HSYS='*coordinate-system*';

coordinate-system
specifies a value that represents a coordinate system. Values can be 1 through 9 and A through C as shown in the following table:

Absolute Systems	Relative Systems	Coordinate System Units
1	7	percentage of data area
2	8	data values
3	9	percentage of graphics output area
4	A	cell in graphics output area
5	B	percentage of procedure output area
6	C	cell in procedure output area

These values are also used by the XSYS and YSYS variables. See "Coordinate Systems" on page 596 for a description of the areas and coordinate systems.

Functions

You can use HSYS with these functions, all of which also use the SIZE variable:

DRAW

DRAW2TXT

FRAME

LABEL

PIE

PIECNTR

SYMBOL

Details

The coordinate system that you specify with the HSYS variable affects how the function interprets the value of the SIZE variable. For example, if you use HSYS='3' and SIZE=10 with the DRAW function, the thickness of the line is 10 percent of the graphics output area. If you use HSYS='1' and SIZE=10 with DRAW, the thickness of the line is 10 percent of the data area.

HTML Variable

Defines a link in the HTML file created for a drill-down graph. This link is associated with an area of the graph and contains valid HTML syntax that can point to a report or another graph that you want to display when the user drills down on the area.

Type: character

Length: up to 1024

Default: none

Syntax

HTML='*link-string*';

link-string
specifies the text that defines the link for drill-down. For more information about drill-down graphs and how to specify the link string, see "Adding Links with the HTML= and HTML_LEGEND= Options" on page 574.

Functions

You can use the HTML variable with these functions:

BAR

FRAME

IMAGE

LABEL

PIE

POLY

SYMBOL

Details

Use a LENGTH statement to set the length of the HTML variable to the longest string you need for the link string. Be sure to set the HTML value to a null if you continue writing observations to the annotate data set after you are done assigning links. For example, the following code defines link information for two squares, but then sets the HTML variable to null when drawing a frame; otherwise the backgound area within the frame will use the link information from the last defined HTML value and become a hot zone in the graph.

```
data squares;
     length function style color $ 8
            html text $ 15;
     xsys='3'; ysys='3';

        /* draw a green square */
     color='green';
     function='move'; x=10; y=65; output;
     function='bar';  x=30; y=95; style='solid';
```

```
          html='href=green.gif'; output;

          /* draw a red square */
       color='red';
       function='move'; x=60; y=65; output;
       function='bar';  x=80; y=95;
          html='href=red.gif'; output;

          /* draw a blue frame */
       function='frame'; color='blue'; style='empty';
          /* set null link for background area in frame */
          html=''; output;
run;
```

IMGPATH Variable

Specifies an image to be displayed from the current (X,Y) coordinates to the (X,Y) coordinates that are associated with this variable.

Type: character

Length: 255

Syntax

IMGPATH = *fileref* | '*external-file*';

fileref
specifies an existing fileref that points to an external image file.

external-file
specifies the full path or full file name of an external image file. The format of the external file specification varies between operating envirionments.

Details

The IMGPATH variable can be used only with the "IMAGE Function" on page 625.

The manner in which the specified image is to be displayed is determined by the "STYLE Variable (Images)" on page 662.

LINE Variable

Controls the drawing of a line by determining either the type of line to draw or the relative position of the line.

Type: numeric

Default for all functions: 1

Syntax

LINE=*line-type*;

Functions

The behavior and syntax of the LINE variable is function-dependent.

BAR
: In the BAR function, valid values for the LINE variable can be 0, 1, 2, or 3. These values determine how the outline of the bar is to be drawn, as shown in the following figure.A value of 0 draws the outline all the way around the bar. A value of 1 draws the outline only on the vertical sides of the bar. A value of 2 draws the outline only on the horizontal sides of the bar. A value of 3 draws no outline.

Figure 25.15 LINE Values for Bars

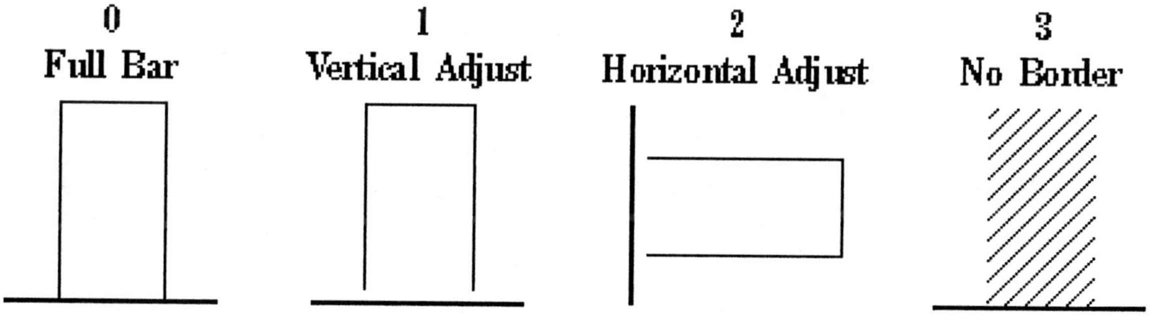

DRAW, DRAW2TXT, FRAME, POLY
: Valid values are whole numbers from 0 to 46. A value of 0 specifies that the line not be drawn. A value of 1 specifies a solid line. The remaining values specify different segmented lines, as illustrated in Figure 7.22 on page 208.

PIE
: Valid values are 0, 1, 2, or 3. The value specifies which lines of a pie slice are to be drawn for the current arc, as shown in Figure 25.16 on page 653.

Figure 25.16 LINE Values Used with the PIE Function

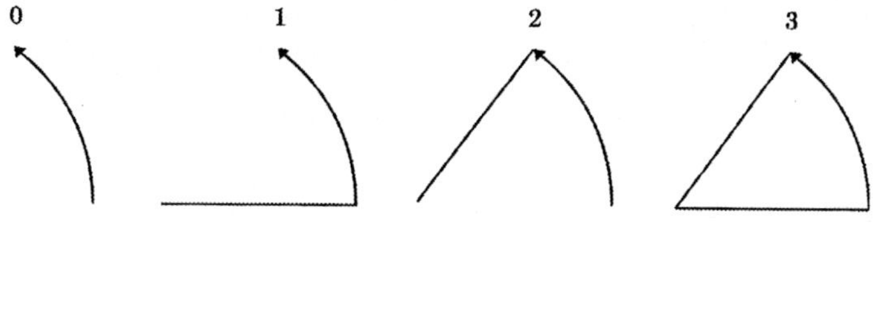

MIDPOINT Variable

Positions graphics elements on the bars of a vertical or horizontal bar chart drawn by the GCHART procedure.

Type: Numeric or character; must match the type of the MIDPOINT= variable in the GCHART procedure.

Length: Should match the length of the MIDPOINT= variable in the GCHART procedure.

Default: none

Restriction: Used only with vertical or horizontal bar charts produced by the GCHART procedure.

Syntax

MIDPOINT=*midpoint-value*;

midpoint-value
references midpoint data value(s) in the GCHART procedure either as a variable name or as an explicit data value. *Midpoint-value* can have one of the following forms:

midpoint-variable	the name of a midpoint variable.
midpoint-data-value	a specific numeric data value.
'midpoint-data-value'	a specific character data value.

Generally, specify a variable name if you want to annotate all of the bars in a horizontal or vertical bar chart. To annotate a bar chart for a specific value of the MIDPOINT variable, specify a specific value.

Functions

You can use the MIDPOINT variable only with the data coordinate systems 1, 2, 7, and 8, and with these functions:

BAR

DRAW

LABEL

MOVE

PIE

PIECNTR

POINT

POLY

POLYCONT

SYMBOL

Details

Using the MIDPOINT variable is similar to using the X and Y variables to position graphics elements in a vertical or horizontal bar chart when using data system coordinates. For example, suppose you produce a vertical bar chart in which the chart variable CITY produces a bar for each city in a data set. The height of each bar is determined by the value of the SUMVAR= variable, UNITS.

You can label these bars by assigning the chart variable CITY to the Annotate MIDPOINT variable. The MIDPOINT variable provides the *x* coordinate for the label. By default, Annotate assigns the statistic variable, in this case the SUMVAR= variable, UNITS, to the Annotate Y variable, which provides the *y* coordinate for the label.

Figure 25.17 on page 655 shows how the values of the MIDPOINT and Y variables position the label that shows the number of units sold in Atlanta. The value, which is calculated and printed by the LABEL function, is 56.

Figure 25.17 Using the MIDPOINT Variable to Position a Label in a Bar Chart

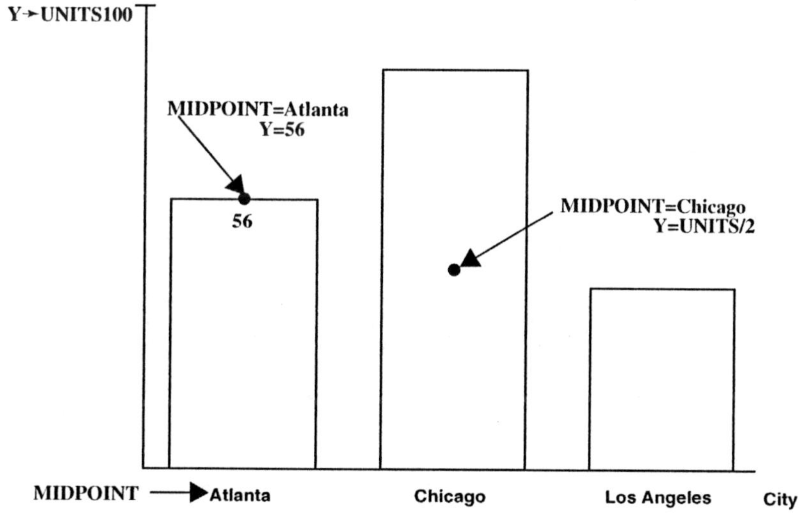

The labels in this figure are positioned by the values that are assigned to these Annotate variables:

- MIDPOINT=CITY (where CITY is the chart variable); the MIDPOINT variable provides the horizontal coordinate in the vertical bar chart.
- Y=UNITS (where UNITS is the SUMVAR= variable); the Y variable provides the vertical coordinate. By specifying Y=units/2, you can vertically center the label in the bar.

Note: In a horizontal bar chart, the MIDPOINT variable controls the *y* coordinate and the statistic variable controls the *x* coordinate. △

CAUTION:

Be careful when using MIDPOINT and X and Y variables in the same data set. Using the MIDPOINT and X variables in an Annotate data set that is used to annotate a VBAR chart or the MIDPOINT and Y variables in the same data set used to annotate an HBAR chart can cause unexpected results. When annotating a VBAR chart, the

Annotate facility uses the MIDPOINT variable as the horizontal coordinate if it exists in the Annotate data set and ignores the X variable. Consequently, you should use the MIDPOINT variable as the horizontal coordinate for all observations in an Annotate data set if you use it for one.

A similar behavior occurs if you use both the MIDPOINT and Y variables in an Annotate data set that is used to annotate HBAR charts. The MIDPOINT variable is always used, regardless of whether it has a missing value, and the Annotate facility ignores the Y variable. In this case, as well, use the MIDPOINT variable for the vertical coordinate for all observations in an Annotate data set if you use it for one. △

POSITION Variable

Controls placement and alignment of a text string specified by the LABEL function.

Type: character

Length: 1

Default: 5

Syntax

POSITION='*text-position*' | '0';

text-position

specifies the placement of the text string in relation to the position that is defined by the X and Y variables. *Text-position* can be one of the characters 1 through 9, A through F, <, +, or >. These characters represent the positions that are described in the following table:

Position	Right Aligned	Centered	Left Aligned
One cell above	1	2	3
Centered	4 | <	5 | +	6 | >
One cell below	7	8	9
Half cell above	A	B	C
Half cell below	D	E	F

These positions are illustrated in Figure 25.19 on page 658.

'0'

specifies a pause in the string in order to change an attribute, such as the color of the text.

Details

Stacking text strings To stack text strings, specify a different position value of each string. Figure 25.18 on page 657 shows two ways to stack text.

Figure 25.18 Combining POSITION Values to Stack Text

Positioning numeric labels The <, +, and > positions perform the same function as 4, 5, and 6, respectively, but are recommended only for labels that are numbers. The <, +, and > positions are especially useful when you are labeling a horizontal bar chart. You can use <, +, or > if the numbers in your font are significantly smaller than the text and you are having trouble centering labels. If the numbers in your font are the same height or close to the same height as the text, you can use positions 4, 5, and 6 to center the labels.

Note: You cannot stack <, +, and > positions as you can 4, 5, and 6 positions. △

Figure 25.19 Effect of POSITION Values on Text Strings

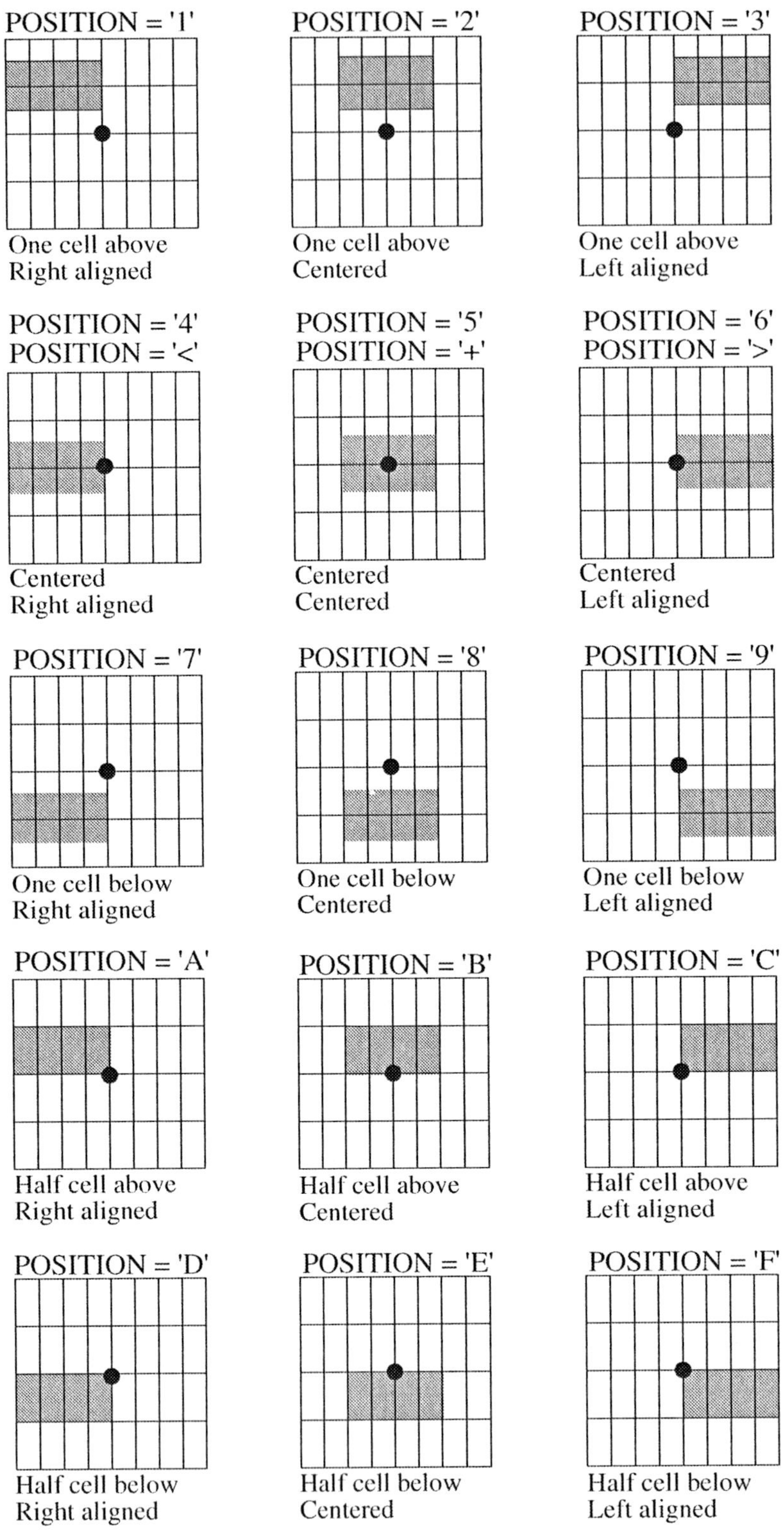

Changing attributes in the middle of a text string 0 is a special value to use when you want to pause and then continue a text string. With this value you can change colors, fonts, and so on in the middle of a line, while retaining the exact position of the text at the pause. When POSITION='0', the combined text string is left-justified beginning at the point that is defined by the X and Y variables. However, you must define missing values for X for the continuation string. The following Annotate data set changes the font in the middle of the string. The result is shown in Figure 25.20 on page 659.

```
data anno;
   length style $ 8 text $ 12;
   xsys='3'; ysys='3'; hsys='3'; x=5; y=50;
      style='swissb'; size=10; text='This is the';
      position='0'; output;
   x=.; style='swissbi'; text=' ITALIC font';
       output;
run;
```

Figure 25.20 Using POSITION='0' to Change the Attributes of a Text String

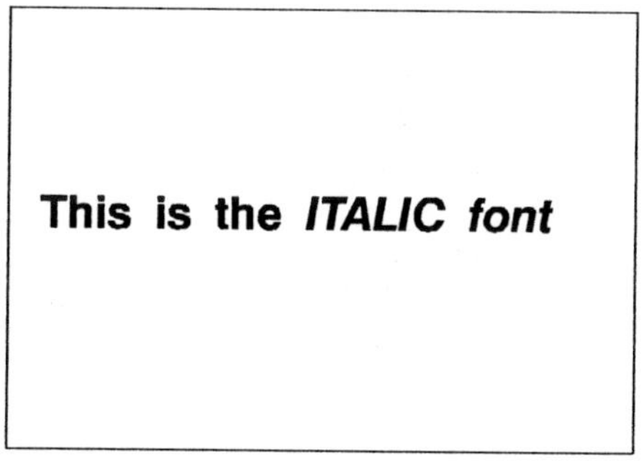

ROTATE Variable

Specifies the angle at which to rotate the graphics element.

Type: numeric

Default: 0.00

Syntax

ROTATE=*rotation-angle*;

Functions

The ROTATE variable is function dependent.

If function is...	then the variable...
PIE	specifies the sweep of the generated arc that begins at the angle that is specified by the ANGLE variable that is used with the PIE function.
LABEL	rotates the individual text characters with respect to the baseline.

SIZE Variable

Determines the size of the graphics element with which it is used.

Type: numeric

Length: 8

Default: 1.00 (2 when HSYS=3)

Syntax

SIZE=*size-factor*;

Functions

The SIZE variable is function dependent.

If function is...	then the variable...
DRAW, DRAW2TXT, FRAME, POLY, or POLYCONT	determines the thickness of the line being drawn.
LABEL	specifies the height of the text.
PIE or PIECNTR	determines the radius of the pie.
PIEXY	sets the radius multiplier.
SYMBOL	selects the height of the symbol.

Details

The SIZE variable uses the coordinate system that is specified by the "HSYS Variable" on page 649, which specifies the type of coordinate system used to generate the graph.

As the thickness of the line increases, it may be impossible to center around a given coordinate. For example, if you specify a thickness of value 2 and HSYS='4', the first line is drawn at the (X, Y) coordinates. The second is drawn slightly above the first. The exact amount varies by device, but it is always one pixel in width. A thickness of value 3 produces one line above, one line at, and one line below the (X, Y) coordinate position.

The SIZE variable is equivalent to the HEIGHT= option in the SYMBOL statement. See HEIGHT= on page 187 for details.

See Figure 25.6 on page 621 for examples of line thicknesses.

Figure 25.21 Sample Line Thicknesses Used with the SIZE Variable

STYLE Variable (Fonts)

Specifies a font for text or symbols produced by the LABEL or SYMBOL functions.

Type: character

Length: Depends on specification.

Default: default hardware font

Not supported by: ActiveX (Partial), Java

Syntax

STYLE='*font*' | "'*hardware-font-name*'" | 'NONE';

font
specifies a font. *Font* can be either the name of a software font that is stored in a catalog or a hardware font specification of the form HW*xxxnnn*. For example, STYLE='CENTB' specifies a software font that is stored in the catalog SASHELP.FONTS. The maximum length for *font* is 8 characters.

hardware-font-name
specifies the name of a hardware font as shown in the Chartype window of the device entry. The maximum length for *hardware-font-name* is 256 characters. *Hardware-font-name* must be enclosed in both double and single quotation marks, for example, STYLE="'Palatino-Italic'".

NONE
specifies the default hardware font.

See Chapter 5, "SAS/GRAPH Fonts," on page 75 for more information about specifying fonts.

If the value of the STYLE variable is missing, SAS/GRAPH software searches for a font specification in this order:

1 the font specified by the FTEXT= graphics option
2 the hardware font, if the device supports one
3 the SIMULATE font.

Details

When the STYLE variable is used with the SYMBOL function, it behaves the same as the FONT= option in the SYMBOL statement. By default, no font is specified and the symbol that is specified by the TEXT variable is taken from the special symbol table. If you use STYLE to specify a symbol font, such as Marker, the string that is assigned by the TEXT variable is the character code for a symbol. If you use STYLE to specify a text font, such as Swiss, the string assigned by the TEXT variable is displayed as text. See the FONT= option of the SYMBOL statement for details.

Note: Java does not support the STYLE variable. However, you can use special symbols from the MARKER font by using the SYMBOL function. △

STYLE Variable (Images)

Determines the appearance of images specified with the IMGPATH variable and the IMAGE function.

Type: character

Default: 'TILE'

Syntax

STYLE='TILE' | 'FIT';

'TILE'
Uses copies of the image to fill the image area.

'FIT'
Stretches one instance of the image to fill the image area.

Details

This version of the STYLE variable can be used only with the "IMAGE Function" on page 625.

STYLE Variable (Patterns)

Specifies a pattern for bars, pies, frames, and rectangles

Type: character

Length: 8

Default: EMPTY | PEMPTY | MEMPTY

Not supported by: Java (partial), ActiveX (partial)

Syntax

STYLE='*fill-pattern*';

fill-pattern

specifies a pattern to use with the graphics element. The value for *fill-pattern* is function-dependent:

Function

Valid Fill Pattern Values

BAR,FRAME

SOLID | S	Fill with a solid color.	
EMPTY | E	No fill.	
style<density>	*style*	R for right-slanted fill lines, L for left-slanted fill lines, or X for crossing fill lines
	density	Whole numbers 1 through 5 specify increasing thickness for the fill lines.

Note: Client-side rendering using Java or ActiveX supports only SOLID and EMPTY and defaults to EMPTY if any other value is used. △

An illustration of these pattern styles is provided in the definition of the VALUE= option of the PATTERN statement.

PIE

PSOLID | PS	Solid fill.	
PEMPTY | PE	No fill, the default.	
P*density<style<angle>>*	*density*	Whole numbers 1 through 5 specify increasing thickness for the fill lines.
	style	N, the default, optionally specifies parallel fill lines; X optionally specifies crossed fill lines.
	angle	Optionally specifies the angle of the fill lines. Values range from 0 to 360. The angle is measured counterclockwise from the horizontal. The default is 0°, which draws horizontal lines.

Note: Client-side rendering using Java or ActiveX supports only PSOLID and PEMPTY and defaults to PEMPTY if any other value is used. △

An illustration of these pattern styles is provided in the definition of the VALUE= option of the PATTERN statement.

POLY

MSOLID | MS	Fill with a solid color.	
MEMPTY | ME	No fill, the default.	
M*density<style<angle>>*	*density*	Whole numbers 1 through 5 specify increasing thickness for the fill lines.
	style	N, the default, optionally specifies parallel fill lines; X optionally specifies crossed fill lines.
	angle	Optionally specifies the angle of the fill lines. Values range from 0 to 360. The angle is measured counterclockwise from

the vertical. The default is 0°, which draws vertical lines.

Note: Client-side rendering using Java or ActiveX supports only MSOLID and MEMPTY and defaults to MEMPTY is any other value is used. △

An illustration of these pattern styles is provided in the definition of the VALUE= option of the PATTERN statement.

SUBGROUP Variable

Positions graphics elements within subgrouped bars of a vertical or horizontal bar chart produced by the GCHART procedure.

Type: Numeric or character; must match the type of the SUBGROUP variable used in the GCHART procedure.

Length: Should match the length of the SUBGROUP= variable in the GCHART procedure.

Default: none

Restriction: The bar charts must have been produced using the SUBGROUP= option.

Syntax

SUBGROUP=*subgroup-value*;

subgroup-value
references value(s) of the SUBGROUP= variable in the GCHART procedure either as a variable name or as an explicit data value. *Subgroup-value* can have one of the following forms:

subgroup-variable	the name of a subgroup variable.
subgroup-data-value	a specific numeric data value.
subgroup-data-value	a specific character data value.

Generally, specify a variable name if you want to annotate all of the bars in a horizontal or vertical bar chart. To annotate a bar chart for a specific value of the SUBGROUP variable, specify a specific value.

Functions

You can use the SUBGROUP variable only with the data coordinate system 1, 2, 7, or 8, and with these functions:

BAR

DRAW

LABEL

MOVE

PIE

PIECNTR

POINT

POLY

POLYCONT

SYMBOL

Details

Using the SUBGROUP variable is similar to using the X and Y variables with data system coordinates to position the graphics elements in subgroup segments in vertical and horizontal bar charts.For example, in a vertical bar chart that produces a bar for each city in a data set, you can easily label the subgroups in each bar by setting *subgroup-variable* to the GCHART variable by which the bar is being subgrouped. This variable provides the *y* coordinate of the label (so don't specify a competing value for y, but instead specify *y*=. or *y*=*y*).

The MIDPOINT variable works well with the SUBGROUP variable to provide the *x* coordinate. In this example, if you set the MIDPOINT variable to the GCHART variable that contains the names of the cities, the MIDPOINT variable provides your *x* coordinate. Rather than providing the X and Y variables, you would use the SUBGROUP and MIDPOINT variables. Figure 25.22 on page 665 shows how the SUBGROUP variable works with the MIDPOINT variable to label the bars of a vertical bar chart.

Figure 25.22 Using the SUBGROUP Variable to Position a Label in a Bar Chart

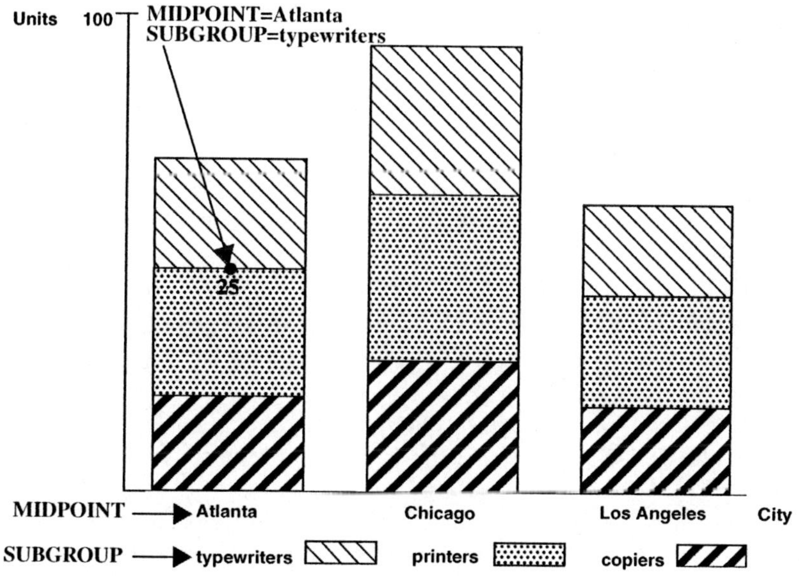

The label showing the number of printers sold in Atlanta is positioned by the values that are assigned to these Annotate variables:

- MIDPOINT=CITY (where CITY is a variable in the GCHART data set)

□ SUBGROUP=ITEM (where ITEM is a variable in the GCHART data set).

TEXT Variable

Specifies the text or symbol to be placed on the graphics output.

Type: character

Length: up to 200

Default: blank string

Syntax

TEXT=*'text-string'* | *'special-symbol'*;

text-string
specifies the text that is used as a label (LABEL or COMMENT function) or symbol (SYMBOL function). The maximum length for *text-string* is 200 characters.

special-symbol
specifies the name of a symbol from the special symbol table that is illustrated in Figure 7.21 on page 202. The maximum length for *special-symbol* is eight characters.

Functions

You can use the TEXT variable with these functions:

COMMENT

LABEL

SYMBOL

Details

Define the TEXT variable with sufficient length to contain all of the characters in your text string. If you need longer strings, use separate observations and POSITION='0' to continue the text.

Use a LENGTH statement to set the length of the TEXT variable if the length of a text string is longer than one character.

WHEN Variable

Specifies when the function is performed in relation to generating other graphics output for the procedure or in relation to generating other Annotate graphics.

Type: character

Length: 1

Default: B

Syntax

WHEN='B' | 'A ;

B | A
specifies whether to draw the annotation before (B) or after (A) the graph. These values are not case sensitive. A missing value is equivalent to specifying B.

Note: Some annotations coded with WHEN='B' that work on the server may not be visible with client-side rendering using Java or ActiveX because the annotations are drawn behind the backplane. The only solution is to code WHEN='A'. △

Functions

You can use the WHEN variable with these functions:

BAR

DRAW

DRAW2TXT

FRAME

LABEL

MOVE

PIE

PIECNTR

PIEXY

POINT

POLY

POLYCONT

SYMBOL

Details

Normally, observations in an Annotate data set are processed sequentially. If you use the WHEN variable, all those observations with a WHEN value of B are processed first, the procedure output is then processed (if one is to be produced), and finally the observations with a WHEN value of A are processed.

X Variable

Identifies the *x* coordinate of where a graphics element is to be drawn.

Type: numeric

Default: value of XLAST or XLSTT

Syntax

X=*horizontal-coordinate*;

Functions

You can use the X variable with these functions:

BAR

DRAW

IMAGE

LABEL

MOVE

PIE

PIECNTR

POINT

POLY

POLYCONT

SYMBOL

Note: The X or XC variable is required unless either the MIDPOINT, GROUP, or SUBGROUP variable provides the horizontal coordinate. △

Details

Specify a corresponding vertical coordinate when using the X variable. This vertical coordinate can be specified with the Y, YC, MIDPOINT, or SUBGROUP variables, depending on the type of graph that you are annotating.

The X variable uses the units that are specified in the XSYS variable. If you use XSYS='2' and the data axis is typed as character, use the XC variable instead of the X variable.

If the value of the X variable is missing for a function that requires it, the value of the XLAST variable is used with nontext functions and the value of the XLSTT variable is used with text functions.

XC Variable

Identifies the *x* coordinate of a graphics element when the coordinate value is character.

Type: character

Length: Should match that of the plot variable in the procedure.

Default: the value of XLAST or XLSTT

Restrictions: Used only with output from the GCHART and GPLOT procedures. Ignored if the axes are numeric.

Syntax

XC='*character-type-horizontal-coordinate*';

Functions

You can use the XC variable with these functions:

BAR

DRAW

LABEL

MOVE

PIE

PIECNTR

POINT

POLY

POLYCONT

SYMBOL

Details

The XC variable is the character equivalent of the X variable. Use XC when the axis values are character. You must also specify a value of 2 (absolute data values) for the XSYS variable. (See also "XSYS Variable" on page 670.) If you use a value other than 2 for the XSYS variable, the graphics output is not displayed properly.

Figure 25.23 on page 669 illustrates the XC variable.

Figure 25.23 Using the XC and YC Variables with Character Data

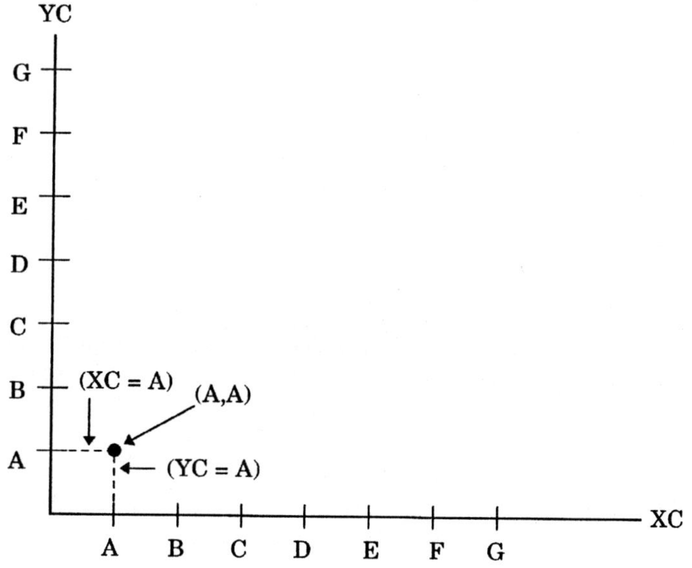

Note: The X or XC variable is required unless either the MIDPOINT, GROUP, or SUBGROUP variable provides the horizontal coordinate. △

CAUTION:
Do not use the X and XC variables in the same data set. Using both X and XC variables in the same data set can cause unpredictable results. △

XSYS Variable

Defines the coordinate system and area of the output used by the X and XC variables to display the Annotate graphics.

Type: character

Length: 1

Default: 4

Syntax

XSYS='*coordinate-system*';

coordinate-system
specifies a value that represents a coordinate system. Values can be 1 through 9 and A through C as shown in the following table:

Absolute Systems	Relative Systems	Coordinate System Units
1	7	percentage of data area
2	8	data values
3	9	percentage of graphics output area
4	A	cell in graphics output area
5	B	percentage of procedure output area
6	C	cell in procedure output area

These values are also used by the HSYS and YSYS variables. See "Coordinate Systems" on page 596 for a description of the areas and coordinate systems.

Functions

You can use the XSYS variable with these functions:

BAR

DRAW

FRAME

LABEL

MOVE

PIE

PIECNTR

POINT

POLY

POLYCONT

SYMBOL

The behavior of the XSYS variable is function-dependent for the following functions:.

BAR, DRAW The coordinate system that you specify with the XSYS variable affects how the function interprets the value of the X or XC variable. If XC is used, XSYS='2' must also be used.

FRAME The XSYS and YSYS variables define the area enclosed by the frame. To draw a frame that encloses the axis area, use XSYS='1' and YSYS='1', as shown in the following figure.

Figure 25.24 Frame Created When XSYS='1' and YSYS='1'

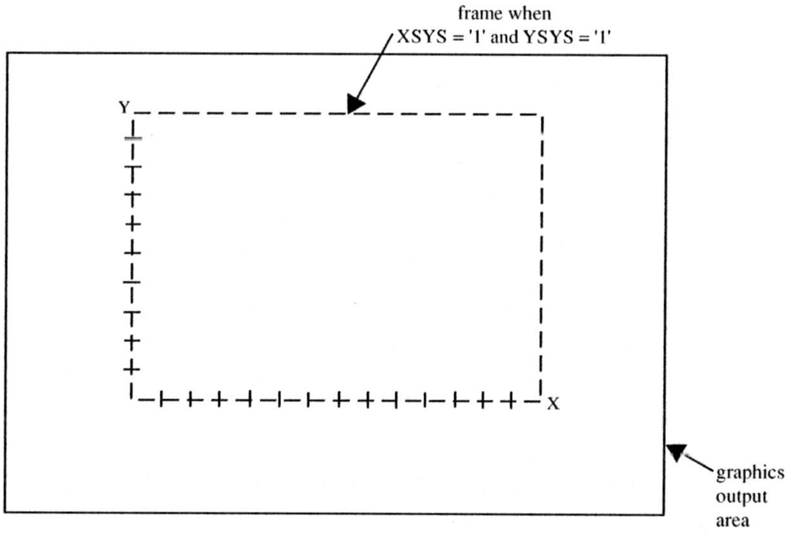

To draw a frame that encloses the entire graphics output area, specify XSYS='3' and YSYS='3', as shown in the following figure.

Figure 25.25 Frame Created When XSYS='3' and YSYS='3'

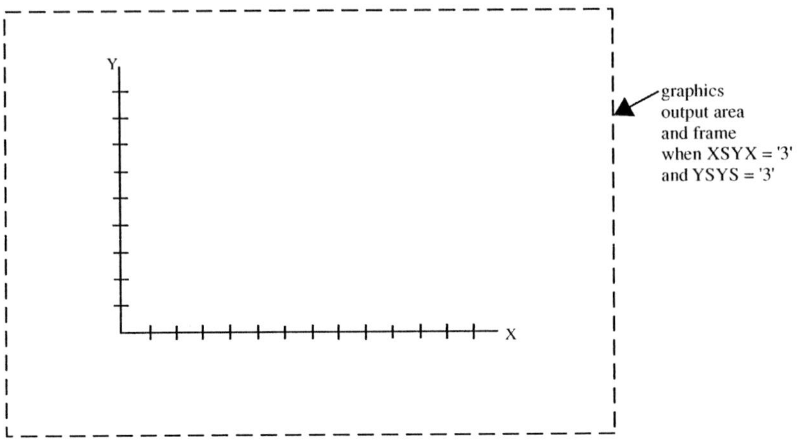

To limit the size of the frame to the size of the procedure output area, specify a value of 5 for XSYS and YSYS.

Note that the values of XSYS and YSYS can differ. You can specify a frame that occupies the entire width of the graphics output area and only the vertical width of the procedure output area by specifying XSYS='3' and YSYS='5', as shown in the following figure.

Figure 25.26 Frame Created When XSYS='3' and YSYS='5'

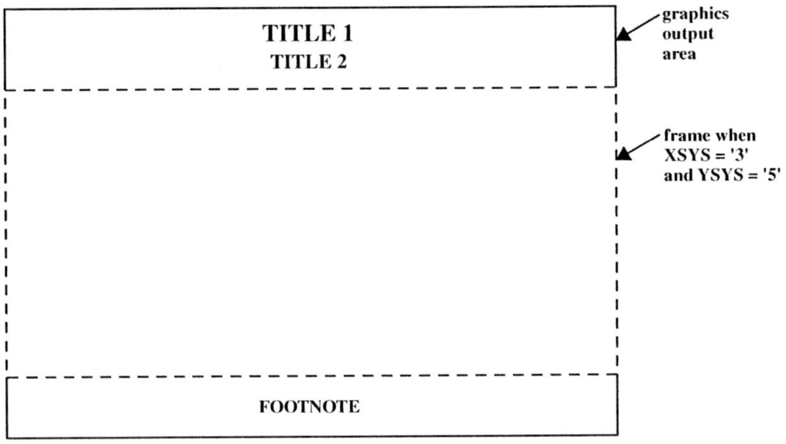

Details

The coordinate system that you specify with the XSYS variable affects how the function interprets the value of the X or XC variable.

Note: Not all coordinate systems can be used with all Annotate variables. For any restrictions, see the individual variables in this section. △

Y Variable

Identifies the *y* coordinate of where a graphics element is to be drawn.

Type: numeric

Default: value of YLAST or YLSTT

Syntax

Y=*vertical-coordinate*;

Functions

You can use the Y variable with these functions:

BAR

DRAW

IMAGE

LABEL

MOVE

PIE

PIECNTR

POINT

POLY

POLYCONT

SYMBOL

Note: The Y or YC variable is required unless either the MIDPOINT, GROUP, or SUBGROUP variable provides the vertical coordinate. △

Details

Specify a corresponding horizontal coordinate when using the Y variable. You can specify the horizontal coordinate with the X, XC, MIDPOINT, or SUBGROUP variable, depending on the type of graph you are annotating.

The Y variable uses the units specified in the YSYS variable. If you use YSYS='2' and the axis data is type character, use the YC variable instead of the Y variable.

If the value of the Y variable is missing for a function that requires it, the value YLAST is used for nontext functions and the value of YLSTT is used for text functions.

YC Variable

Identifies the *y* coordinate of a graphics element when the coordinate value is character.

Type: character

Length: Should match that of the plot variable in the procedure.

Default: YLAST | YLSTT

Restrictions: Used only with output from the GCHART and GPLOT procedures. Ignored if the axes are numeric.

Syntax

YC='*character-type-vertical-coordinate*';

Functions

You can use the YC variable with these functions:

- BAR
- DRAW
- LABEL
- MOVE
- PIE
- PIECNTR
- POINT
- POLY
- POLYCONT
- SYMBOL

Details

The YC variable is the character equivalent of the Y variable. Use YC when the axis values are character. You must also specify a value of 2 (absolute data values) for the YSYS variable. (See "YSYS Variable" on page 674.) If you use a value other than 2 for the YSYS variable, the graphics output is not displayed properly.

See Figure 25.23 on page 669 for an illustration of the YC variable.

Note: The X or XC variable is required unless either the MIDPOINT, GROUP, or SUBGROUP variable provides the horizontal coordinate. △

CAUTION:

Do not use Y and YC variables in the same data set. Using both Y and YC variables in the same data set can cause unpredictable results. △

YSYS Variable

Defines the coordinate system and area of the output used by Y and YC to display the Annotate graphics.

Type: character

Length: 1

Default: 4

Syntax

YSYS='*coordinate-system*';

coordinate-system

specifies a value that represents a coordinate system. Values can be 1 through 9 and A through C, as shown in the following table:

Absolute Systems	Relative Systems	Coordinate System Units
1	7	percentage of data area
2	8	data values
3	9	percentage of graphics output area
4	A	cell in graphics output area
5	B	percentage of procedure output area
6	C	cell in procedure output area

These values are also used by the HSYS and XSYS variables. See "Coordinate Systems" on page 596 for a description of the areas and coordinate systems.

Functions

The YSYS variable is function-dependent, as defined in the "XSYS Variable" on page 670 You can use the YSYS variable with these functions:

BAR

DRAW

FRAME

LABEL

MOVE

PIE

PIECNTR

POINT

POLY

POLYCONT

SYMBOL

Details

The coordinate system that you specify with the YSYS variable affects how the function interprets the value of the Y or YC variable.

Note: Not all coordinate systems can be used with all Annotate variables. For any restrictions, see the individual variables in this section. △

Z Variable

Identifies the *z* coordinate of where a graphics element is to be drawn.

Type: numeric

Length: 8

Default: none

Restrictions: On the server, is used only with output from the G3D procedure. For client-side annotation with Java or ActiveX, you can use the Z variable with GMAP, GCHART, GCONTOUR, GPLOT, and G3D, for example to add annotations above the plane of the map.

Syntax

Z=*depth-coordinate*;

Functions

You can use the Z variable with these functions:

BAR

DRAW

IMAGE

LABEL

MOVE

PIE

PIECNTR

POINT

POLY

POLYCONT

SYMBOL

Details

The Z variable uses the units that are specified in the ZSYS variable.

ZSYS Variable

Defines the coordinate system and area of the output used by Z variable to display the Annotate graphics.

Type: character

Length: 1

Default: 2

Syntax

ZSYS='*coordinate-system*';

coordinate-system
specifies a value that represents a coordinate system. Values can be 1, 2, 7, or 8 as shown in the following table:

Absolute Systems	Relative Systems	Coordinate System Units
1	7	percentage of data area
2	8	data values

See "Coordinate Systems" on page 596 for a description of the areas and coordinate systems.

Functions

You can use the ZSYS variable with these functions:

BAR

DRAW

IMAGE

LABEL

MOVE

PIE

PIECNTR

POINT

POLY

POLYCONT

SYMBOL

Details

The coordinate system that you specify with the ZSYS variable affects how the function interprets the value of the Z variable.

Note: Not all coordinate systems can be used with all Annotate variables. For any restrictions, see the individual variables in this section. △

Annotate Internal Coordinates

The Annotate facility maintains two sets of internal coordinates that are stored in the variable pairs (XLAST, YLAST) and (XLSTT, YLSTT). One set of variables (XLAST, YLAST) stores coordinate values that are generated by nontext functions and the other set (XLSTT, YLSTT) stores coordinates generated by text functions. These two variable pairs supply default values when the X or Y variable contains a missing value.

Both pairs are initially set to 0 and remain 0 until a function updates the values. You cannot assign explicit values to these variables, but you can manipulate their values with some of the Annotate functions.

XLAST, YLAST Variables

Track the last values specified for the X and Y variables when X and Y are used with nontext functions.

Details

The coordinate values that are stored in the (XLAST, YLAST) variables are automatically updated by these nontext functions: BAR, DRAW, MOVE, PIE, and POINT. These values are then available for use by other nontext functions that follow in the DATA step. (The DRAW2TXT graphics function uses XLAST and YLAST but does not update them.)

Because (XLAST, YLAST) are updated internally, you cannot specify values for them. However, their values can be manipulated by these programming functions:

CNTL2TXT

PIECNTR

PIEXY

POP

PUSH

SWAP

TXT2CNTL

XLSTT, YLSTT Variables

Track the last position for the X and Y variables when X and Y are used with text-handling functions.

Details

The coordinate values stored in the (XLSTT, YLSTT) variables are automatically updated by the LABEL and SYMBOL text functions. These values are then available for use by other text functions that follow in the DATA step.

Because (XLSTT, YLSTT) are updated internally, you cannot specify values for them. However, their values can be manipulated by these programming functions:

CNTL2TXT

DRAW2TXT

POP

PUSH

SWAP

TXT2CNTL

Annotate Macros

You can use Annotate macros within a SAS DATA step to simplify the process of creating Annotate observations. With a macro, you specify a function and assign variable values in one step without having to write explicit variable assignment statements. You can mix assignment statements and macro calls in the same DATA step.

This section describes all of the Annotate macros including the complete syntax and a description of the parameters. For more information on accessing and using macros, and for a summary of operations performed by the Annotate macros, see "Using Annotate Macros" on page 697.

%ANNOMAC Macro

Compiles Annotate macros and makes them available for use.

Variables written out: none directly

Syntax

%ANNOMAC;

Details

In a SAS session, you must submit the ANNOMAC macro before you can use the Annotate macros.

%BAR, %BAR2 Macros

Draws a rectangle using two sets of x/y coordinates, which specify diagonal corners. You can specify the rectangle's line type, line color, fill type, and fill color.

Variables written out: COLOR, FUNCTION, LINE, STYLE, X, Y

Internal variables updated: XLAST, YLAST

Prequisite: You must run the %ANNOMAC macro before using any other annotate macros. For more information, see “Making the Macros Available” on page 697.

Syntax

%BAR (*x1, y1, x2, y2, color, line, style*);

%BAR2(*x1, y1, x2, y2, color, line, style, width*);

x1, y1
specify the location of the first corner of the bar. Values can be numeric coordinates, numeric constants, or numeric variables. For details, see the Annotate “X Variable” on page 667.

x2, y2
specify the location of second corner of the bar, which is drawn diagonal to the first corner. Values can be numeric coordinates, numeric constants, or numeric variables.

color
specifies the outline color and optional fill color using a character string without quotation marks. For details, see the Annotate “COLOR Variable” on page 645.

line
specifies which of the outlines of the bar are to be drawn. The value can be a number, a numeric constant, or a numeric variable. For valid values, see the Annotate “LINE Variable” on page 652 for the BAR function.

style
specifies the fill pattern for the bar using a character string without quotation marks. For valid values, see the Annotate “STYLE Variable (Patterns)” on page 662 for the BAR function.

width
specifies the width of the outline and optional fill lines. The value can a number, a numeric constant, or a numeric variable. For details and valid values, see the Annotate “SIZE Variable” on page 660 for the DRAW function.

%CENTROID Macro

Retrieves the centroids of polygons

Variables written out: X, Y, id variables

Prequisite: You must run the %ANNOMAC macro before using any other annotate macros. For more information, see “Making the Macros Available” on page 697.

Syntax

%CENTROID (*input-data-set, output-data-set, list-of-id-variables*);

input-data-set

specifies a map data set.

output-data-set
contains the id variables and the X and Y variables.

list-of-id-variables
specifies the variables each of which is to be assigned the centroid coordinates of each observation in the input-data-set. There will be one observation for each unique set of ID values

%CIRCLE Macro

Draws an empty circle with the center at (*x*, *y*).

Variables written out: ANGLE, FUNCTION, ROTATE, SIZE, STYLE, X, Y

Internal variables updated: XLAST, YLAST

Prerequisite: You must run the %ANNOMAC macro before using any other annotate macros. For more information, see "Making the Macros Available" on page 697.

Syntax

%CIRCLE (*x*, *y*, *size*, *color*);

x, y
specify coordinates for the center of the circle. Values can be coordinate numbers, numeric constants, or numeric variables. For details, see the Annotate "X Variable" on page 667.

size
specifies the radius of the circle. The value can be a number, a numeric constant, or a numeric variable. For details and valid values, see the Annotate "SIZE Variable" on page 660.

color
specifies the color of the circle using a character string without quotation marks. For details, see the Annotate"COLOR Variable" on page 645. Use an asterisk (*) to specify the previous value of the *color* parameter.

See Also

"%SLICE Macro" on page 695 to draw a filled circle.

%CNTL2TXT Macro

Copies the values of the internal coordinates (XLAST, YLAST) to the text coordinate (XLSTT, YLSTT).

Variables written out: FUNCTION

Internal variables updated: XLSTT, YLSTT

Prequisite: You must run the %ANNOMAC macro before using any other annotate macros. For more information, see "Making the Macros Available" on page 697.

Syntax

%CNTL2TXT;

Details

The %CNTL2TXT macro is useful when you are calculating the position of labels on a graph. For an example, see "CNTL2TXT Function" on page 617.

%COMMENT Macro

Inserts a comment into an Annotate data set.

Variables written out: FUNCTION, TEXT

Prequisite: You must run the %ANNOMAC macro before using any other annotate macros. For more information, see "Making the Macros Available" on page 697.

Syntax

%COMMENT (*text-string*);

text-string
specifies the text to insert in the Annotate data set. The value can be a a character string enclosed in quotation marks or the name of a character variable. For details, see the Annotate"TEXT Variable" on page 666.

%DCLANNO Macro

Automatically sets the correct length and data type for all Annotate variables except the TEXT variable.

Prequisite: You must run the %ANNOMAC macro before using any other annotate macros. For more information, see "Making the Macros Available" on page 697.

Syntax

%DCLANNO;

%DRAW Macro

Draws a line from (XLAST, YLAST) to the specified coordinate.

Variables written out: COLOR, FUNCTION, LINE, SIZE, X, Y

Internal variables updated: XLAST, YLAST

Prequisite: You must run the %ANNOMAC macro before using any other annotate macros. For more information, see "Making the Macros Available" on page 697.

Syntax

%**DRAW** (*x*, *y*, *color*, *line*, *size*);

x*, *y
: specify coordinates for the end point of the line. Values can be coordinate numbers, numeric constants, or numeric variables. For details, see the Annotate "X Variable" on page 667.

color
: specifies the color of the line using a character string without quotation marks. For details, see the Annotate"COLOR Variable" on page 645. Use an asterisk (*) to specify the previous value of the *color* parameter.

line
: specifies the line type (continuous or segmented). The value can be a number, a numeric constant, or a numeric variable. For valid values, see the Annotate "LINE Variable" on page 652 for the DRAW function.

size
: specifies the width of the line. The value can be a number, a numeric constant, or a numeric variable. For valid numeric values, see the Annotate"SIZE Variable" on page 660 for the DRAW function.

Details

The point from which the line is drawn is usually set with the MOVE macro.

%DRAW2TXT Macro

Draws a line from the coordinate (XLAST, YLAST) to the text coordinate (XLSTT, YLSTT).

Variables written out: COLOR, FUNCTION, LINE, SIZE

Prequisite: You must run the %ANNOMAC macro before using any other annotate macros. For more information, see "Making the Macros Available" on page 697.

Syntax

%**DRAW2TXT** (*color*, *line*, *size*);

color
specifies the color of the line using a character string without quotation marks. For details, see the Annotate "COLOR Variable" on page 645. Use an asterisk (*) to specify the previous value of the *color* parameter.

line
specifies the line type (continuous or segmented). The value can be a number, a numeric constant, or a numeric variable. For valid values, see the Annotate "LINE Variable" on page 652 for the DRAW function.

size
specifies the width of the line. The value can be a number, a numeric constant, or a numeric variable. For valid values, see the Annotate "SIZE Variable" on page 660 for the DRAW function.

%FRAME Macro

Draws a border around the portion of the display area defined by the reference system and optionally fills the area.

Variables written out: COLOR, FUNCTION, LINE, SIZE, STYLE

Prequisite: You must run the %ANNOMAC macro before using any other annotate macros. For more information, see "Making the Macros Available" on page 697.

Syntax

%**FRAME** (*color*, *line*, *size*, *style*);

color
specifies the outline color and the optional fill color using a character string without quotation marks. For details, see the Annotate"COLOR Variable" on page 645. Use an asterisk (*) to specify the previous value of the *color* parameter.

line
specifies a line type (continuous or segmented) for the frame outline and fill lines. The value can be a number, a numeric constant, or a numeric variable. For valid numeric values, see the Annotate"LINE Variable" on page 652 for the DRAW function.

size
specifies the width of the frame outline and fill lines. The value can be a number, a numeric constant, or a numeric variable. For valid values, see the Annotate "SIZE Variable" on page 660 for the DRAW function.

style
specifies the fill pattern for the frame using a character string without quotation marks. For valid values, see the Annotate "STYLE Variable (Patterns)" on page 662 for the FRAME function.

Details

See "%SYSTEM Macro" on page 696for information on setting the reference system.

%LABEL Macro

Places a text label at the specified coordinates.

Variables written out: ANGLE, COLOR, FUNCTION, POSITION, ROTATE, SIZE, STYLE, TEXT, X, Y

Internal variables updated: XLSTT, YLSTT

Prequisite: You must run the %ANNOMAC macro before using any other annotate macros. For more information, see "Making the Macros Available" on page 697.

Syntax

%LABEL (*x*, *y*, *text-string*, *color*, *angle*, *rotate*, *size*, *style*, *position*);

x*, *y
: specifies the location of the text string. Values can be coordinate numbers, numeric constants, or numeric variables. The position of the text string relative to *x*, *y* is determined by the *position* parameter. For details, see the Annotate "X Variable" on page 667.

text-string
: specifies the text of the label. The value can be a character variable name or a character string enclosed in quotation marks. For details, see the Annotate "TEXT Variable" on page 666.

color
: specifies the color of the text string using a character string without quotation marks. For details, see the Annotate "COLOR Variable" on page 645. Use an asterisk (*) to specify the previous value of the *color* parameter.

angle
: specifies the angle of the text string with respect to the horizontal. The value can be a number, a numeric constant, or a numeric variable. For valid values, see the Annotate "ANGLE Variable" on page 642 for the LABEL function. The *x*, *y* coordinates specify the pivot point, and the *position* parameter positions the text relative to *x*, *y*.

rotate
: specifies the rotation angle of each character in the text string. The value can be a number, a numeric constant, or a numeric variable. For valid values, see the Annotate "ROTATE Variable" on page 659.

size
: specifies the size of the text string. The value can be a number, a numeric constant, or a numeric variable. For valid values, see the Annotate "SIZE Variable" on page 660 for the LABEL function.

style
: specifies the text font, using a character string without quotation marks. For valid values, see the Annotate "STYLE Variable (Fonts)" on page 661.

position
: specifies the placement and alignment of the text string relative to the *x*, *y* coordinates, using a text string without quotation marks. For valid values, see the Annotate "POSITION Variable" on page 656.

%LINE Macro

Draws a line between two sets of coordinates.

Variables written out: COLOR, FUNCTION, LINE, SIZE, X, Y

Internal variables updated: XLAST, YLAST

Prequisite: You must run the %ANNOMAC macro before using any other annotate macros. For more information, see “Making the Macros Available” on page 697.

Syntax

%LINE (*x1*, *y1*, *x2*, *y2*, *color*, *line*, *size*);

x1, y1
: specify the coordinates of the start of the line. Values can be numbers, numeric constants, or numeric variables. For details, see the Annotate “X Variable” on page 667 variable.

x1, y2
: specify the coordinates of the end of the line. Values can be numbers, numeric constants, or numeric variables.

color
: specifies the color of the line using a character string without quotation marks. For valid values, see the Annotate“COLOR Variable” on page 645. Use an asterisk (*) to specify the previous value of the *color* parameter.

line
: specifies the line type, which can be continuous or segmented. The value can be a number, a numeric constant, or a numeric variable. For valid values, see the Annotate“LINE Variable” on page 652 for the DRAW function.

size
: specifies the width of the line. The value can be a number, a numeric constant, or a numeric variable. For valid values, see the Annotate “SIZE Variable” on page 660 for the DRAW function.

%MAPLABEL Macro

Creates an output data set that can be used with the ANNO= option for PROC GMAP.

Variables written out: FUNCTION, STYLE, COLOR, SIZE, HSYS

Prequisite: You must run the %ANNOMAC macro before using any other annotate macros. For more information, see “Making the Macros Available” on page 697.

Syntax

%MAPLABEL (*map-dataset*,
attr-dataset,*output-dataset*,*label-var*,*id-list*,*font*=*font_name*,*color*=*n*,*size*=*n*,*hsys*=*n*);

map-dataset
the name of the map to be annotated.

attr-dataset
the name of the dataset containing the text to be shown on each ID value.

output-dataset
the name of the annotate data set created by the macro.

label-var
the name of the label variable to place on the map (the text for annotate).

id-list
the list of ID vars that you would issue in PROC GMAP to create the map. These values need to be on both the map and the attribute data sets. If you also supply the SEGMENT variable, then every polygon will get a value. Without the SEGMENT variable, only one label per ID set will be shown over the collection of polygons. For instance, Hawaii with SEGMENT gets a label on each island, whereas without SEGMENT, there is only one label centered on the entire set of islands.

font
specifies a font name for the "STYLE Variable (Fonts)" on page 661 variable.

color
specifies a value for the "COLOR Variable" on page 645 variable.

size
specifies a value for the "SIZE Variable" on page 660 variable. Defaults to 2.

hsys
specifies a value for the "HSYS Variable" on page 649 variable. Defaults to 3.

%MOVE Macro

Moves to the (*x*, *y*) coordinate.

Variables written out: FUNCTION, X, Y

Internal variables updated: XLAST, YLAST

Prequisite: You must run the %ANNOMAC macro before using any other annotate macros. For more information, see "Making the Macros Available" on page 697.

Syntax

%MOVE (*x*, *y*);

x*, *y
specify new coordinates for the next annotation. Values can be numeric coordinates, numeric constants, or numeric variables. For details, see the Annotate "X Variable" on page 667.

%PIEXY Macro

Calculates a point in relation to the latest pie slice.

Variables written out: ANGLE, FUNCTION, SIZE, X, Y

Internal variables updated: XLAST, YLAST

Prequisite: You must run the %ANNOMAC macro before using any other annotate macros. For more information, see "Making the Macros Available" on page 697.

Syntax

%PIEXY (*angle*, *size*);

angle
specifies the angle used to calculate the point, relative to the center of the latest pie slice. The value can be a number, a numeric constant, or a numeric variable. For details, see the Annotate "ANGLE Variable" on page 642 for the PIEXY function.

size
specifies the radius multiplier that works with the *angle* parameter to determine the location of the point. The value can be a number, a numeric constant, or a numeric variable. For details and valid values, see the Annotate "SIZE Variable" on page 660 for the PIEXY function.

Details

This macro is useful when you want to label a pie chart or a circle.

When you use this macro, the Annotate facility expects a slice to have been previously drawn. If a slice has not been drawn or if the "PIECNTR Function" on page 630 has not been processed, you can get erroneous results.

%POLY, %POLY2 Macro

Begins drawing a polygon at the specified coordinates and determines the color, fill pattern, and line type of the polygon.

Variables written out: FUNCTION, COLOR, LINE, STYLE, X, Y,

Prequisite: You must run the %ANNOMAC macro before using any other annotate macros. For more information, see "Making the Macros Available" on page 697.

Syntax

%POLY (*x*, *y*, *color*, *style*, *line*);

%POLY2(*x*, *y*, *color*, *style*, *line*, *width*);

x, y
specify the starting point for a new polygon. Values can be numeric coordinates, numeric constants, or numeric variables. For details, see the Annotate or the names of the Annotate variables "X Variable" on page 667.

color
specifies the optional polygon fill color using a character string without quotation marks. For valid values, see the Annotate"COLOR Variable" on page 645. Use an asterisk (*) to specify the previous value of the *color* parameter. To specify the color of the polygon outline, see the "%POLYCONT Macro" on page 689.

style
specifies the fill pattern for the polygon, using a character string without quotation marks. For valid values, see the Annotate "STYLE Variable (Patterns)" on page 662 for the POLY function.

line
specifies the polygon's line type, which can be continuous or segmented. The value can be a number, a numeric constant, or a numeric variable. For valid values, see the Annotate"LINE Variable" on page 652 for the POLY function.

width
specifies the width of the polygon's outline and optional fill lines. The value can be a number, a numeric constant, or a numeric variable. For details and valid values, see the Annotate "SIZE Variable" on page 660 for the POLY function.

See Also

"POLY Function" on page 634

%POLYCONT Macro

Continues drawing the polygon to the next specified coordinates.

Variables written out: COLOR, FUNCTION, X, Y

Prequisite: You must run the %ANNOMAC macro before using any other annotate macros. For more information, see "Making the Macros Available" on page 697.

Syntax

%POLYCONT (*x*, *y*, *color*);

x, y
specify the end point of the next line in the polygon. Values can be numeric coordinates, numeric constants, or numeric variables. For details, see the Annotate "X Variable" on page 667.

color
specifies the color of the polygon outline using a character string without quotation marks. For valid values, see the Annotate"COLOR Variable" on page 645. Use an asterisk (*) to specify the previous value of the *color* parameter.

Details

The first invocation of the %POLYCONT macro in the polygon-drawing sequence determines the outline color of that polygon. Subsequent color specifications for that polygon in later invocations of the %POLYCONT macro are ignored.

The polygon fill color and line type are specified in the initial "%POLY, %POLY2 Macro" on page 688 or %POLY2 macro.

%POP Macro

Removes the coordinates (XLAST, YLAST) and (XLSTT, YLSTT) from the LIFO system stack and updates the internal coordinate pairs with these retrieved values.

Variables written out: FUNCTION

Internal variables updated: XLAST, YLAST, XLSTT, YLSTT

Prequisite: You must run the %ANNOMAC macro before using any other annotate macros. For more information, see "Making the Macros Available" on page 697.

Syntax

%POP;

Details

Use the %POP macro when you want to access the values of the XLAST, YLAST, XLSTT, and YLSTT variables that you previously stored with the %PUSH macro. For more information, see "XLAST, YLAST Variables" on page 678, "XLSTT, YLSTT Variables" on page 678, and "%PUSH Macro" on page 690.

%PUSH Macro

Enters the coordinates (XLAST, YLAST) and (XLSTT, YLSTT) in a LIFO system stack.

Variables written out: FUNCTION, internal coordinates

Internal variables updated: XLAST, YLAST, XLSTT, YLSTT

Prequisite: You must run the %ANNOMAC macro before using any other annotate macros. For more information, see "Making the Macros Available" on page 697.

Syntax

%PUSH;

Details

The last-in, first-out (LIFO) stack provides a way to save previously calculated coordinates. It enables you to retain coordinate values for later use by utility functions without recalculating those values. In order to save coordinate values in the stack, you must explicitly push them onto the stack. See “Using the LIFO Stack” on page 603 for a description of the LIFO stack.

%RECT Macro

Draws a rectangle with diagonal corners at two specified points.

Variables written out: COLOR, FUNCTION, LINE, SIZE, X, Y

Internal variables updated: XLAST, YLAST

Prequisite: You must run the %ANNOMAC macro before using any other annotate macros. For more information, see “Making the Macros Available” on page 697.

Syntax

%RECT (*x1, y1, x2, y2, color, line, size*) ;

x1, y1
specify the coordinates of the first corner of the rectangle. Values can be numeric coordinates, numeric constants, or numeric variables. For details, see the Annotate “X Variable” on page 667.

x2, y2
specify the coordinates of the second corner of the rectangle, which is drawn diagonal to the first corner. Values can be numeric coordinates, numeric constants, or numeric variables.

color
specifies the color of the rectangular line using a character string without quotation marks. For valid values, see the Annotate“COLOR Variable” on page 645. Use an asterisk (*) to specify the previous value of the *color* parameter.

line
specifies the rectangle’s line type, which can be continuous or segmented. The value can be a number, a numeric constant, or a numeric variable. For details, see the Annotate “LINE Variable” on page 652 for the DRAW function.

size
specifies the width of the line. The value can be a number, a numeric constant, or a numeric variable. For valid values, see the “SIZE Variable” on page 660 for the DRAW function.

Details

The rectangle is drawn such that the first corner is diagonal to the second corner.
The %RECT macro produces rectangles that do not have fill patterns. Use the %BAR macro to generate filled rectangles. For more information, see “%BAR, %BAR2 Macros” on page 679.

%SCALE Macro

Scales input coordinates relative to the origin (0, 0) based on the relationship between two ranges of minima and maxima.

Variables written out: X, Y

Prequisite: You must run the %ANNOMAC macro before using any other annotate macros. For more information, see "Making the Macros Available" on page 697.

Syntax

%SCALE (*ptx, pty, x1, y1, x2, y2, vx1, vy1, vx2, vy2*);

ptx, pty
specifies the coordinates to scale. Values can be numbers, numeric constants, or numeric variables. For details, see the Annotate "X Variable" on page 667.

x1, y1
specifies the minima of the first range. Values can be numbers, numeric constants, or numeric variables.

x2, y2
specifies the maxima of the first range. Values can be numbers, numeric constants, or numeric variables.

vx1, vy1
specifies the minima of the second range. Values can be numbers, numeric constants, or numeric variables.

vx2, vy2
specifies the maxima of the second range. Values can be numbers, numeric constants, or numeric variables.

Details

The %SCALE macro reduces or enlarges Annotate graphics elements that use two-dimensional, numeric coordinates. The %SCALE macro does not affect graphics elements that are drawn with text functions.

The difference between the %SCALE and %SCALET macros is that the %SCALE macro always places the origin at (0, 0) and plots the new coordinates with respect to that origin. The %SCALET macro plots the new coordinates with respect to the minima of the second range. For details, see "%SCALET Macro" on page 693.

The following example uses the %SCALE macro to reduce *x* and *y* coordinates by 50 percent, as shown in Figure 25.27 on page 693:

```
%SCALE(x, y, 0, 0, 100, 100, 0, 0, 50, 50);
```

Figure 25.27 Using the %SCALE Macro to Reduce the Size of a Box

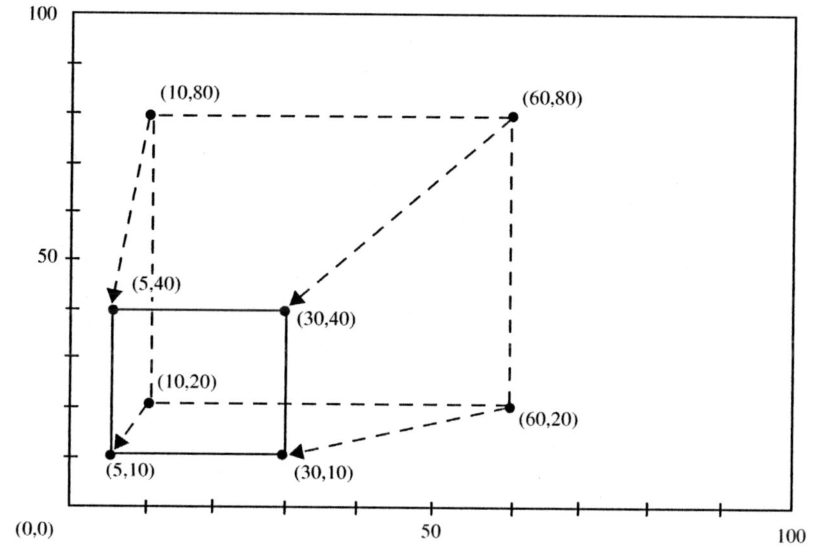

%SCALET Macro

Scales input coordinates based on the relationship between two ranges of minima and maxima. The scaled coordinates are plotted relative to the minima of the second range.

Variables written out: X, Y

Prequisite: You must run the %ANNOMAC macro before using any other annotate macros. For more information, see "Making the Macros Available" on page 697.

Syntax

%SCALET (*ptx*, *pty*, *x1*, *y1*, *x2*, *y2* , *vx1*, *vy1*, *vx2*, *vy2*);

ptx, pty
specifies the coordinates to scale. Values can be numbers, numeric constants, or numeric variables. For details, see the Annotate "X Variable" on page 667.

x1, y1
specifies the minima of the original range. Values can be numbers, numeric constants, or numeric variables.

x1, y2
specifies the maxima of the original range. Values can be numbers, numeric constants, or numeric variables.

vx1, vy1
specifies the minima of the second range using numeric values. Values can be numbers, numeric constants, or numeric variables. These coordinates are also used as the origin against which the scaled point is plotted.

vx2, vy2
specifies the maxima of the second range. Values can be numbers, numeric constants, or numeric variables.

Details

The %SCALET macro reduces or enlarges Annotate graphics elements that use two-dimensional numeric coordinates. The %SCALET macro does not affect graphics elements that are drawn with text functions.

The difference between the %SCALET and %SCALE macros is that the SCALET macro plots the new coordinates with respect to minima of the second range (*vx1, vy1*). The %SCALE macro plots the new coordinates with respect to the origin (0, 0).

The following example uses the %SCALET macro reduces *x* and *y* coordinates by 50 percent and plots the new coordinates with respect to (50, 0), as shown in Figure 25.28 on page 694:

```
%SCALET(x, y, 0, 0, 100, 100, 50, 0, 50, 100);
```

Figure 25.28 Using the %SCALET Macro to Reduce the Size of a Box

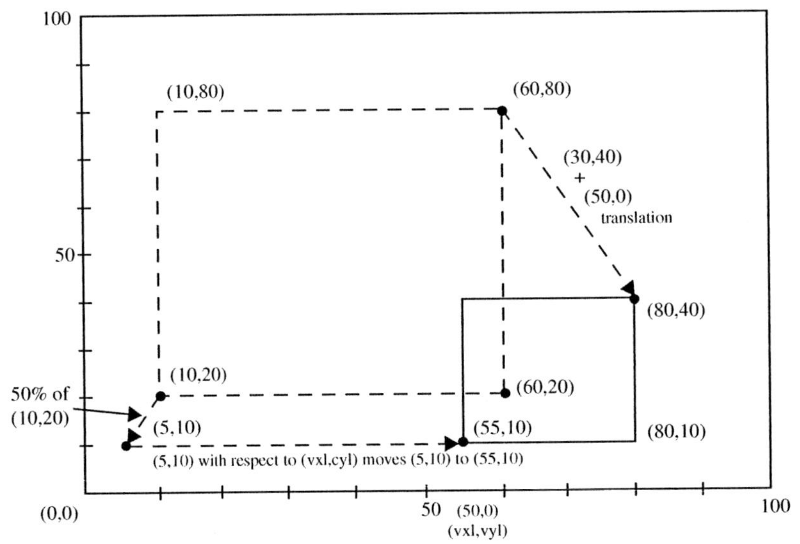

%SEQUENCE Macro

Specifies when to draw Annotate graphics elements, relative to the procedure's graphics output or relative to the other Annotate graphics drawn.

Variables written out: WHEN

Prequisite: You must run the %ANNOMAC macro before using any other annotate macros. For more information, see "Making the Macros Available" on page 697.

Syntax

%**SEQUENCE** (*when*);

when

Values can be BEFORE or AFTER, as defined for the Annotate "WHEN Variable" on page 666.

%SLICE Macro

Draws a arc, pie slice, or circle, with available line types, colors, and fill types.

Variables written out: ANGLE, COLOR, FUNCTION, LINE, ROTATE, SIZE, STYLE, X, Y

Internal variables updated: XLAST, YLAST

Prequisite: You must run the %ANNOMAC macro before using any other annotate macros. For more information, see "Making the Macros Available" on page 697.

Syntax

%**SLICE** (*x*, *y*, *angle*, *rotate*, *size*, *color*, *style*, *line*);

x*, *y

specify the center point of the arc. Values can be numbers, numeric constants, or numeric variables. For details, see the Annotate "X Variable" on page 667.

angle

specifies the starting point of the arc. The value can be a number, a numeric constant, or a numeric variable. For details and valid values, see the Annotate "ANGLE Variable" on page 642 for the PIE function.

rotate

specifies the sweep of the arc. The value can be a number, a numeric constant, or a numeric variable. For valid values, see the Annotate "ROTATE Variable" on page 659 for the PIE function.

size

specifies the radius of the arc. The value can be a number, a numeric constant, or a numeric variable. For details, see the Annotate "SIZE Variable" on page 660.

color

specifies the color of the arc outline and optional fill using a character string without quotation marks. For valid values, see the Annotate "COLOR Variable" on page 645. Use an asterisk (*) to specify the previous value of the *color* parameter.

style

specifies the fill pattern for the slice or circle, using a character string without quotation marks. For details and valid values, see the Annotate "STYLE Variable (Patterns)" on page 662 for the PIE function.

line
specifies which lines of a pie slice are to be drawn. The value can be a number, a numeric constant, or a numeric variable. For valid values and details, see the "LINE Variable" on page 652 for the PIE function.

%SWAP Macro

Exchanges control between (XLAST, YLAST) and text (XLSTT, YLSTT) coordinates.

Variables written out: FUNCTION

Internal variables updated: XLAST, YLAST, XLSTT, YLSTT

Prequisite: You must run the %ANNOMAC macro before using any other annotate macros. For more information, see "Making the Macros Available" on page 697.

Syntax

%SWAP;

%SYSTEM Macro

Defines the Annotate reference systems and the XSYS, YSYS, and HSYS variables.

Variables written out: HSYS, XSYS, YSYS

Prequisite: You must run the %ANNOMAC macro before using any other annotate macros. For more information, see "Making the Macros Available" on page 697.

Syntax

%SYSTEM (*xsys*, *ysys*, *hsys*);

xsys, ysys, hsys
specify values that represent a coordinate system and an area of the output, as defined for the Annotate "XSYS Variable" on page 670. The default is %SYSTEM (4, 4, 4).

Details

Note: Not all coordinate systems are valid with all Annotate variables or all SAS/GRAPH procedures. See "Annotate Functions" on page 615 for any restrictions that apply to the variable that you want to use. △

The ZSYS variable cannot be set through this macro. Use an explicit variable assignment instead:

```
zsys='value'; output;
```

See Coordinate Systems"Coordinate Systems" on page 596 for a description of the areas and coordinate systems.

%TXT2CNTL Macro

Assigns the values of the text (XLSTT, YLSTT) coordinates to the control (XLAST, YLAST) coordinates.

Variables written out: FUNCTION

Internal variables updated: XLAST, YLAST

Prequisite: You must run the %ANNOMAC macro before using any other annotate macros. For more information, see "Making the Macros Available" on page 697.

Syntax

%TXT2CNTL;

Details

Use the %TXT2CNTL macro when you want nontext functions to use the ending position of a text string as a starting or ending point.

Using Annotate Macros

Macro Structure

The general form of an Annotate macro is

```
%MACRO (parameters);
```

In general, the macro name represents a function and the parameters contain the values for the variables that can be used with the function. All macros except DCLANNO, SYSTEM, and SEQUENCE output an observation.

The parameters are either numeric or character. Numeric parameters can be numeric constants or numeric variable names that have been initialized to the appropriate value. Most character parameters must be expressed as literals, that is character strings without quotation marks. Exceptions are the text values that are used with the COMMENT and LABEL macros, which can be expressed as character strings enclosed in quotation marks or as character variable names.

The Annotate facility assigns the parameter values to the corresponding Annotate variables. Therefore, the observations in an Annotate data set that is created with macros that look the same as the ones that you created with assignment statements.

Making the Macros Available

To use Annotate macros, you must provide your program with access to the data set that contains the macros, and you must compile the macros before you use them. Check with your SAS Software Consultant to find out if the fileref for the data set that contains the Annotate macros that are supplied with SAS/GRAPH software is allocated automatically at your site. Then access the Annotate macros in one of these ways:

- If the fileref is not set automatically, find out where the Annotate macros are stored and allocate a fileref that points to the data set:

  ```
  filename fileref 'external-file';
  ```

  Then include the Annotate macros in your session:

  ```
  %include fileref (annomac);
  ```

- If the fileref is set automatically, compile the Annotate macros and make them available by simply submitting the ANNOMAC macro:

  ```
  %annomac;
  ```

Note: The ANNOMAC macro must be run before any other Annotate macros are used in a SAS session. You will see a message in the SAS log that indicates that the Annotate macros are now available. The message also shows you how to get help for using the macros. △

Annotate Macro Task Summary

The following table summarizes the tasks performed by the Annotate macros.

Table 25.1 Tasks with Annotate Macros

If you want to...	Use this macro...
assign values of (XLSTT,YLSTT) to (XLAST,YLAST)	%TXT2CNTL;
begin drawing a polygon	%POLY(*x, y, color, style, line*);
continue drawing a polygon	%POLYCONT(*x, y, color*);
copy (XLAST,YLAST) to (XLSTT,YLSTT)	%CNTL2TXT;
declare all variables	%DCLANNO;
draw a bar	%BAR(*x*1, *y*1, *x*2, *y*2, *color, line, style*);
draw a circle	%CIRCLE(*x, y, size, color*);
draw a frame	%FRAME(*color, line, size, style*);
draw a line from (XLAST,YLAST) to (XLSTT,YLSTT)	%DRAW2TXT(*color, line, size*);
draw a line from previous point	%DRAW(*x, y, color, line, size*);
draw a line	%LINE(*x*1, *y*1, *x*2, *y*2, *color, line, size*);
draw a pie slice or arc	%SLICE(*x, y, angle, rotate, size, color, style, line*);
draw a rectangle	%RECT(*x* 1,*y* 1,*x* 2,*y* 2, *color, line, size*);
draw text	%LABEL(*x, y, text, color, angle, rotate, size, style, position*);
exchange the values of (XLAST,YLAST) and (XLSTT,YLSTT)	%SWAP;
move to a point near a pie slice	%PIEXY(*angle, size*);

If you want to...	Use this macro...
move to a point without drawing	%MOVE(*x, y*);
put values into a stack	%PUSH;
retrieve values from a stack	%POP;
scale and move input	%SCALET(*ptx, pty, x*0, *y*0, *x*1, *y*1, *x*0, *vy*0, *vx*1, *vy*1);
scale input	%SCALE(*ptx, pty, x*0, *y*0, *x*1, *y*1, *x*0, *vy*0, *vx*1, *vy*1);
set the coordinate system for the observation	%SYSTEM(*xsys, ysys, hsys*);
set when to draw an observation	%SEQUENCE(*when*);
write a comment to the data set	%COMMENT(*text*);

Annotate Error Messages

If there is an error in your Annotate data set, one or more diagnostic messages are printed in the SAS log. A partial list of these messages is supplied here. Annotate data sets are checked for errors this way:

- If an error is found in preprocessing, this message appears:

  ```
  NOTE: ERROR DETECTED IN ANNOTATE= libref.dataset
  ```

- If an error is found as an observation is being read, this message appears:

  ```
  PROBLEM IN OBSERVATION number -- message
  ```

  where *message* is the text of the error message.

- If the error limit of 20 errors is reached at any point during processing of the data set, a termination message similar to this one appears:

  ```
  ERROR LIMIT REACHED IN ANNOTATE PROCESS

                 20 TOTAL ERRORS
  ```

Some common diagnostic messages are explained here.

A CALCULATED COORDINATE LIES OUTSIDE THE VISIBLE AREA
Explanation: The *x* or *y* coordinate is outside the display area (defined by HPOS= and VPOS= values).
User Action: Check for an invalid or misspecified coordinate system value, or *x* or *y* values outside displayed range.

A CALCULATED WINDOW COORDINATE LIES OUTSIDE THE WINDOW AREA
Explanation: the *x* or *y* coordinate is outside of the window area. This message may accompany the message for invalid coordinate system specification.
User Action: Check for an invalid or misspecified coordinate system value, or *x* or *y* values outside displayed range.

A PERCENTAGE VALUE LIES OUTSIDE 0 TO 100 BOUNDARIES
Explanation: The *x* or *y* value requested is negative or greater than 100 percent. This message is informational.
User Action: Check requested value for accuracy.

ANNOTATE MIDPOINT DATATYPE DOES NOT MATCH GCHART- INPUT WAS #
Explanation: The MIDPOINT variable in the Annotate data set is character, and the GCHART midpoint is numeric or vice versa.

User Action: Check for misspelling or wrong variable assignment, or check for quotes in the assignment statement.

ANNOTATE GROUP DATATYPE DOES NOT MATCH GCHART- INPUT WAS #

Explanation: The GROUP variable in the Annotate data set is character, and the GCHART group is numeric or vice versa.

User Action: Check for misspelling or wrong variable assignment, or check for quotes in the assignment statement.

ANNOTATE SUBGROUP DATATYPE DOES NOT MATCH GCHART- INPUT WAS #

Explanation: The SUBGROUP variable in the Annotate data set is character, and the GCHART subgroup is numeric or vice versa.

User Action: Check for misspelling or wrong variable assignment, or check for quotes in the assignment statement.

BOTH OLD AND NEW VARIABLE NAMES ENCOUNTERED IN ANNOTATE= DATA SET

Explanation: Variables named both MIDPOINT and MIDPNT or SUBGROUP and SUBGRP occur in the Annotate data set.

User Action: Determine which variable has the proper values for the Annotate data set and either delete the other variable or rename MIDPNT to MIDPOINT and SUBGRP to SUBGROUP.

CALCULATED COORDINATES LIE COMPLETELY OFF THE VISIBLE AREA

Explanation: Both the *x* and *y* coordinates supplied are outside the visible display area.

User Action: Check for improper or inappropriate coordinate system specification or coordinates out of range.

CANNOT HAVE MISSING GROUP VALUE IF GROUPS ARE PRESENT

Explanation: The GROUP variable in the Annotate data set contains a missing value.

User Action: If the GROUP= option is specified in the GCHART procedure, the Annotate GROUP variable cannot contain missing values. Remove the missing value from the request. Check reference system for data-dependent request.

CANNOT HAVE SUBGROUP AND X/Y MISSING IN GCHART STREAM

Explanation: Data coordinate system was requested and the X, Y and SUBGROUP variables contain missing values.

User Action: The X, Y or SUBGROUP variable must have a value if a data coordinate system is requested. Check stream for improper request.

CANNOT OMIT GROUP VARIABLE IF GCHART GROUPS ARE PRESENT

Explanation: You used a data coordinate system and specified GROUP= in the GCHART procedure, but the Annotate data set does not contain the GROUP variable.

User Action: Supply the GROUP variable in the Annotate data set.

CHARACTER VALUE SHOWN IS NOT ON THE HORIZONTAL AXIS

Explanation: The specified value of the XC variable is not on the *x* axis of the graph or chart. The observation is ignored.

User Action: Check for misspelling, for uppercase or lowercase conflict, or for exclusion in an axis specification.

CHARACTER VALUE SHOWN IS NOT ON THE VERTICAL AXIS

Explanation: The specified value of the YC variable does not occur on the *y* axis of the graph or chart. The observation is ignored.

User Action: Check for misspelling, for uppercase or lowercase conflict, or for exclusion in an axis specification.

CONFLICT BETWEEN PROCEDURE AXIS TYPE AND ANNOTATE DATA TYPE
Explanation: The axis type is character and the *x* and *y* coordinates are numeric or vice versa.
User Action: Check values for proper type matching.

DATA SYSTEM NOT SUPPORTED FOR THIS STATEMENT
Explanation: The data coordinate systems 1, 2, 7, 8 are not permitted for this statement.
User Action: Choose a different reference system for this observation.

DATA SYSTEM REQUESTED, BUT POINT IS NOT ON GRAPH
Explanation: The coordinate specified is not on displayed graph, and data coordinate system placement has been requested.
User Action: Check for improper specification of data value or graph axis parameters, or incorrect system specification. If this occurs, you may be able to use percent of the data area to position Annotate graphics.

G3D DATA SYSTEM REQUESTED, ALL SYSTEMS NOT DATA DEPENDENT
Explanation: Not all requested XSYS, YSYS, and ZSYS variable values are data values.
User Action: If one variable in G3D annotation is data-dependent, all variables must be data-dependent. Either specify all points in the data coordinate system or use another reference system value.

G3D DATA SYSTEM REQUESTED, VARIABLE CONTAINED MISSING VALUE
Explanation: The X, Y, or Z variable contained a missing value.
User Action: All values in G3D data placement requests must be specified. Remove the missing value from the request.

INTERNAL SYSTEM STACK OVERFLOW- TOO MANY PUSH FUNCTIONS
Explanation: The limit of stack positions has been exhausted. The maximum number of stack positions is system-dependent. Each PUSH operation uses one position; each POP frees one position for re-use.
User Action: Rewrite the program section to decrease the number of values stored in the stack.

INTERNAL SYSTEM STACK UNDERFLOW- TOO MANY POP FUNCTIONS
Explanation: The POP function has been issued with no values in the LIFO stack.
User Action: Check for unequal numbers of PUSH versus POP functions. They can be unequal, but you cannot have more values moved with the POP function than are stored with the PUSH function. At least one PUSH must occur (it before) a POP can be issued.

LABEL FUNCTION REQUESTED, BUT TEXT VARIABLE NOT ON DATA SET
Explanation: A TEXT variable has not been found for the LABEL function.
User Action: If FUNCTION='LABEL', the TEXT variable must contain the string to be placed in the display area. Check for misspelling of variable name or specification of the wrong Annotate data set.

LINE VALUE SPECIFIED IS NOT WITHIN LIMITS- 0<=L<=3
Explanation: An invalid special line value has been specified.
User Action: The LINE value specified was not acceptable for FUNCTION='BAR' or the RECT macro. Check function for definition of line values or previous value used in DATA step prior to this observation.

LINE VALUE SPECIFIED IS NOT WITHIN LIMITS- 1<=L<=46
Explanation: The LINE value specified is not in the range 1 through 46.
User Action: Check for improper specification of data value. Line styles represented by the LINE values can be found in the line-type table"Specifying Line Types" on page 207.

MINIMUM VARIABLES NOT MET–AMBIGUITY PREVENTS SELECTION.
Explanation: The combinations of available X, Y, XC, YC, GROUP, MIDPOINT, and SUBGROUP variables do not identify the data-dependent values uniquely.
User Action: Check variable requirements and respecify.

MINIMUM VARIABLES NOT MET- MUST HAVE X/XC,Y/YC IN DATA SET
Explanation: The X, XC, Y, or YC variables have not been found in the Annotate data set.
User Action: The X or XC and Y or YC variables must be in the data set. This message represents a minimum validity check of the supplied Annotate data set.

POLYCONT ENCOUNTERED BEFORE POLY
Explanation: The POLYCONT function was encountered with no POLY function specification.
User Action: Probable sequencing error. Check for missing POLY command, improper ordering of polygon points, or interruption of POLY type commands by other valued functions. Also, check the value of WHEN for a mismatch.

"POLYCONT" INTERRUPTED
Explanation: A POLYCONT definition has been interrupted and resumed in the Annotate data set. This usually accompanies the error message

```
POLYCONT ENCOUNTERED BEFORE POLY
```

User Action: Check data stream for proper order.

POSITION VALUE INVALID- MUST BE ONE OF "0123...9ABCDEF"
Explanation: The value of the POSITION variable is not in range ’0’ through ’9’ or ’A’ through ’F’ or ’<’, ’+’, or ’>’ in a LABEL command.
User Action: Check desired value in POSITION description and correct.

REQUESTED POLYGON CONTAINS TOO MANY VERTICES (OBSERVATIONS)
Explanation: The maximum allocation for polygon points is exhausted. The maximum number of vertices is limited by a device’s memory.
User Action: Define polygon with fewer points or break polygon into sections.

SYSTEM VALUE INVALID- MUST BE ONE OF "0123...9ABC"
Explanation: The value supplied for the XSYS, YSYS, or HSYS variable is not valid.
User Action: Check the desired value and correct the data set.

TEXT STRING EXTENDS BEYOND BOUNDARY OF SYSTEM DEFINED
Explanation: The text string is too long.
User Action: Check for excessive SIZE value or shorten the string. This error could be caused by HSYS=’4’ and a small value of the VPOS graphics option.

USE THE XC VARIABLE FOR DATA VALUES WHEN TYPE IS CHARACTER
Explanation: The X variable is character type in the Annotate data set when it should be numeric.
User Action: If character data are being plotted, use the XC variable to specify any data-related points pertaining to character values. If data are not character, omit quotes in X data value assignment.

USE THE YC VARIABLE FOR DATA VALUES WHEN TYPE IS CHARACTER
Explanation: The Y variable is character type in the Annotate data set when it should be numeric.
User Action: If character data are being plotted, use the YC variable to specify any data-related points pertaining to character values. If data are not character, omit quotes in Y data value assignment.

VALUE SHOWN IS NOT A VALID FONT OR PATTERN TYPE

Explanation: The value of the STYLE variable is not a valid font or pattern.

User Action: Check the value supplied for misspelling, truncation, and support in the FUNCTION description.

VALUE SHOWN IS NOT A VALID FUNCTION

Explanation: The value in the FUNCTION variable is not recognized as an available function.

User Action: Check for misspellings or truncation of value. Truncation can be corrected by specifying a length of 8 bytes in the LENGTH statement in the DATA step that generates the data set.

VALUE SHOWN IS NOT A VALID SIZE FACTOR

Explanation: The SIZE value of the variable is negative or excessive.

User Action: Check request or calculation for positive value result.

VARIABLE SHOWN HAS IMPROPER LENGTH IN ANNOTATE= DATA SET

Explanation: The length is incorrect for variable indicated. Either the length of the character string exceeds the length for the variable specified in a LENGTH statement, or the variable was not specified in a LENGTH statement.

User Action: Make sure the variable length is defined in a length statement and that the length specified adequately covers the length of the character strings that are used.

VARIABLE SHOWN IS NOT OF THE PROPER DATA TYPE

Explanation: The data type does not match required type for variable listed. Either variable type is character where a numeric is required, or numeric where a character is required.

User Action: Specify proper type for variable as described in "Annotate Variables" on page 642.

PART 4

SAS/GRAPH Procedures

CHAPTER 26

The GANNO Procedure

Overview

The GANNO procedure displays graphs created by Annotate data sets. The procedure can also be used to scale data-dependent graphics to fit the graphics output area. Note that the GANNO procedure ignores all currently defined title and footnote statements and some graphics option specifications, including BORDER=. To include titles, footnotes, and graphics options along with your Annotate data set, use the GSLIDE procedure instead of the GANNO procedure.

By default, both the GANNO and GSLIDE procedures scale graphics output from the data set to fill the entire graphics area. However, if you are using a data coordinate system and the data values are so large that some of the graphics elements do not fit in the graphics output area and are not displayed, you can use the GANNO procedure with the DATASYS option. This will cause the procedure to scale the output to fit the available space. The GSLIDE procedure does not have this capability.

Figure 26.1 on page 707 displays output from an Annotate data set.

Figure 26.1 Displaying Annotate Graphics with the GANNO Procedure

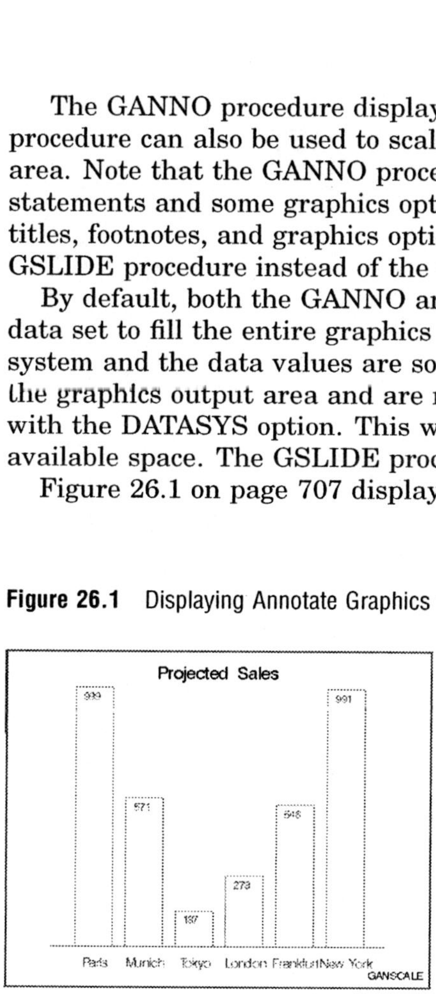

The program for this graph is in Example 1 on page 710.

Procedure Syntax

Requirements: An input Annotate data set is required.

Supports: Output Delivery System (ODS)

PROC GANNO ANNOTATE=*Annotate-data-set*
<DATASYS>
<DESCRIPTION='*entry-description*'>
<GOUT=<*libref.*>*output-catalog*>
<IMAGEMAP=*output-data-set*>
<NAME='*entry-name*' | *variable-name*>;

PROC GANNO Statement

Identifies the Annotate data set and draws the graphics output defined by that data set. Optionally, it scales the output to accommodate data-dependent coordinate values and specifies an output catalog.

Syntax

PROC GANNO ANNOTATE=*Annotate-data-set*
<DATASYS>
<DESCRIPTION='*entry-description*'>
<GOUT=<*libref.*>*output-catalog*>
<IMAGEMAP=*output-data-set*>
<NAME='*entry-name*' | *variable-name*>;

Required Arguments

ANNOTATE=*Annotate-data-set*
ANNO=*Annotate-data-set*
specifies a data set that includes Annotate variables that identify graphics commands and parameters.

See also: Chapter 24, "Using Annotate Data Sets," on page 587

Options

Options in the GANNO statement affect all graphs produced by that statement. You can specify as many options as you want and list them in any order.

DATASYS
indicates that absolute or relative data-dependent coordinates occur in the Annotate data set and scales the coordinates to fit the graphics output area. Use the DATASYS option only with Annotate data sets in which the coordinate system variables XSYS, YSYS, and HSYS specify the values 1, 2, 7, or 8.

Use the DATASYS option when graphics elements that were created with data-dependent variables do not fit in the graphics output area. This happens when the coordinate values generated by the data exceed a range of 0 to 100.

If you omit the DATASYS option, the GANNO procedure attempts to draw each graphics element according to the data values assigned to it, without scaling the values. If the range of data values is too large, some graphics elements will not display.

See also: "Using the DATASYS Option to Scale Graphs" on page 710

Featured in: Example 1 on page 710

DESCRIPTION='*entry-description*'
DES='*entry-description*'

specifies the description of the catalog entry for the chart. The maximum length is 256 characters. The description does not appear on the chart. By default, the GANNO procedure assigns the description OUTPUT FROM PROC GANNO.

Featured in: Example 2 on page 713

GOUT=<*libref.*>*output-catalog*

specifies the SAS catalog in which to save the graphics output produced by the GANNO procedure. If you omit the libref, the SAS/GRAPH software looks for the catalog in the temporary library called WORK and creates the catalog if it does not exist.

See also: "Storing Graphics Output in SAS Catalogs" on page 53

Featured in: Example 2 on page 713

IMAGEMAP=*output-data-set*

creates a temporary SAS data set that is used to generate an image map in an HTML output file. The information in the image map data set includes the shape and coordinates of the elements in the graph and drill-down URLs that have been associated with those elements. The drill-down URLs are provided by one or two variables in the input data set. These variables are identified to the GANNO procedure with the HTML= and/or HTML_LEGEND= options.

The %IMAGEMAP macro generates the image map in the HTML output file. The macro takes two arguments, the name of the image map data set and the name or fileref of the HTML output file, as shown in the following example:

```
%imagemap(imgmapds, myimgmap.html);
```

See also: Chapter 25, "Annotate Dictionary," on page 613 and "Adding Links with the HTML= and HTML_LEGEND= Options" on page 574.

Featured in: Example 4 on page 719

NAME='*entry-name*' | *variable-name*

specifies one of the following:

- the name of the catalog entry for the graph
- a variable name for each value for which a separate graph is produced.

If the value you assign to the NAME= option is enclosed in quotation marks, the procedure interprets it as a catalog entry name; if the value is not enclosed in quotes, the procedure interprets it as a variable name.

The value *entry-name* specifies the name of the catalog entry for the graph. The maximum length is 8 characters. The default name is GANNO. If the specified name duplicates the name of an existing entry, SAS/GRAPH software adds a number to the duplicate name to create a unique entry, for example, GANNO1.

If you specify *variable-name*, the GANNO procedure produces a separate graph for each different value of that variable. In addition, when you specify

NAME=*variable-name*, each value of the variable is used as the name of the catalog entry for that graph. A value that is longer than 8 characters is truncated. For example, if the value is **Frankfurt**, it is truncated to **Frankfur**. A second catalog entry would be **Frankful**. Consequently, you cannot use NAME='*entry-name*' at the same time.

Note: Specifying NAME=*variable-name* in the PROC GANNO statement produces results similar to those produced by the BY statement in a procedure that supports BY-group processing. See "BY Statement" on page 141 for details. △

Featured in: Example 2 on page 713Example 3 on page 715

Using the DATASYS Option to Scale Graphs

If your Annotate data set specifies a coordinate system that is based on data values (that is, XSYS, YSYS, and HSYS are assigned the values 1, 2, 7, or 8), the data values determine the size and location of the graphics elements on the output.

If the procedure that specifies the annotation generates axes (such as GPLOT or GCHART), by default the axes are scaled to accommodate the full range of data values and to fit in the procedure output area. Because all values are included in the axes, the graph displays all the Annotate output that is dependent on data values.

However, if the annotation displays with the GSLIDE or GANNO procedure, which do not generate axes, the data values may generate coordinate values that exceed the limits of the graphics output area.

In this case, you can use the DATASYS option to tell the procedure that the Annotate data set contains data-dependent coordinates and to scale the output accordingly. For an illustration of this process, see Example 1 on page 710.

When you use the DATASYS option, the GANNO procedure reads the entire input data set before drawing the graph and creates an output environment that is data dependent; that is, the environment is based on the minimum and maximum values that are contained in the data set. It then scales the data to fit this environment so that all graphics elements can be drawn.

Although the DATASYS option enables you to generate graphs using one of the data-dependent coordinate systems, it requires that the procedure scan the entire data set to determine the minimum and maximum data values. You can save this extra pass of the data set by using data-dependent values only in procedures that generate axes. Annotate coordinate system 5 (percent of the procedure output area) is recommended for use with the GANNO procedure. This coordinate system works equally well with the GSLIDE procedure if you decide to display the annotation with titles and footnotes.

Examples

Example 1: Scaling Data-Dependent Output

Procedure features:

PROC GANNO statement options:

ANNOTATE=
DATASYS

Sample library member: GANSCALE

Figure 26.2 Scaled GANNO Output

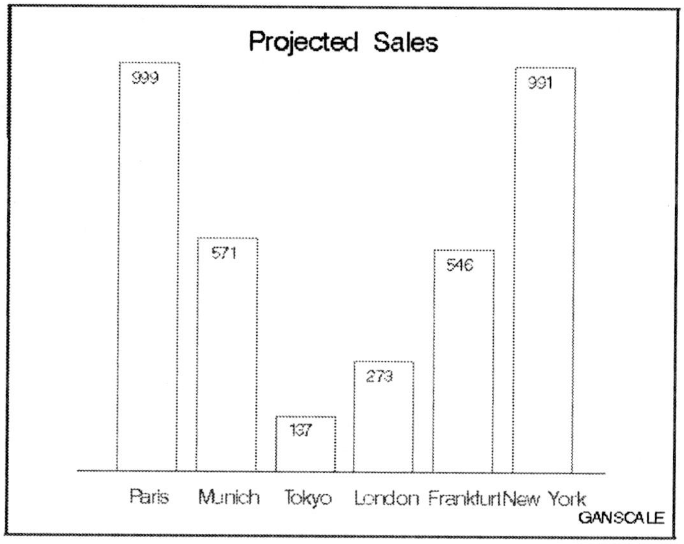

This example uses an Annotate data set to scale data-dependent output with the DATASYS option and create a vertical bar chart of sales for each of six sites. The values that determine the height of each bar range from 137 to 999. The range of values is so large that the GANNO procedure cannot fit all of the bars in the output area without scaling the output. This program uses the DATASYS option to scale the data values so that the bars fit in the graphics output area.

Set the graphics environment.

```
goptions reset=global gunit=pct cback=white
         colors=(black blue green red);
```

Create the data set WRLDTOTL. WRLDTOTL contains sales data for six sites. SITENAME contains the names of the sites. MEAN contains the average sales for each site.

```
data wrldtotl;
   length sitename $ 10;
   input sitename $ 1-10 mean 12-15;
   datalines;
Paris      999
Munich     571
Tokyo      137
London     273
Frankfurt  546
New York   991
;
run;
```

Create the Annotate data set, WRLDANNO. XSYS and YSYS specify coordinate system 2 (absolute data values) for X and Y. HSYS specifies coordinate system 3 (percent of the graphics output area) for SIZE. The SET statement processes every observation in WRLDTOTL.

```
data wrldanno;
   length function color $ 8 text $ 20;
   retain line 0 xsys ysys '2' hsys '3' x 8;
   set wrldtotl end=end;
```

Draw the bars. The MOVE function defines the lower left corner of the bar. The BAR function draws the bar. Bar height (Y) is controlled by MEAN.

```
   function='move'; x=x+8; y=20; output;
   function='bar'; y=y+(mean); x=x+9;
      style='empty'; color='red'; output;
```

Label the bar with the name of site.

```
   function='label'; y=0; x=x-4; size=3.5;
      position='E'; style='swiss';
      color='blue'; text=sitename; output;
```

Move to the top of the bar and write the value of MEAN.

```
   function='move'; y=y+(mean)-3; output;
   function='label'; x=x-1; text=left(put(mean,3.));
      position='5'; style='swiss'; size=3; output;
```

After all the observations are processed, add an axis line, title, footnote, and frame. The MOVE and DRAW functions draw the axis line. The LABEL function writes the title and the footnote. The FRAME function draws a border around the output.

```
   if end then do;
      function='move'; x=10; y=20; output;
      function='draw'; x=90; y=20; line=1;
         size=.5; color='blue'; output;
      function='label'; x=50; y=95; text='Projected Sales';
         xsys='3'; ysys='3'; position='5'; style='swissb';
         size=5; color=' '; output;
         x=92; y=5; size=3; style='swiss'; text='GANSCALE'; output;
      function='frame'; color='blue'; when='b';
         style='empty'; output;
   end;
run;
```

Display the annotate graphics. The ANNOTATE= identifies the data set that contains the graphics commands. DATASYS tells the procedure to use the maximum and minimum data values to construct the output environment. In addition, the values of X and Y are scaled to fit the environment and all of the bars display on the graph.

```
proc ganno annotate=wrldanno
   datasys;
run;
quit;
```

Example 2: Storing Annotate Graphics

Procedure features:

PROC GANNO statement options:

- DESCRIPTION=
- GOUT=
- NAME=

Sample library member: GANSQUAR

Figure 26.3 Four Squares

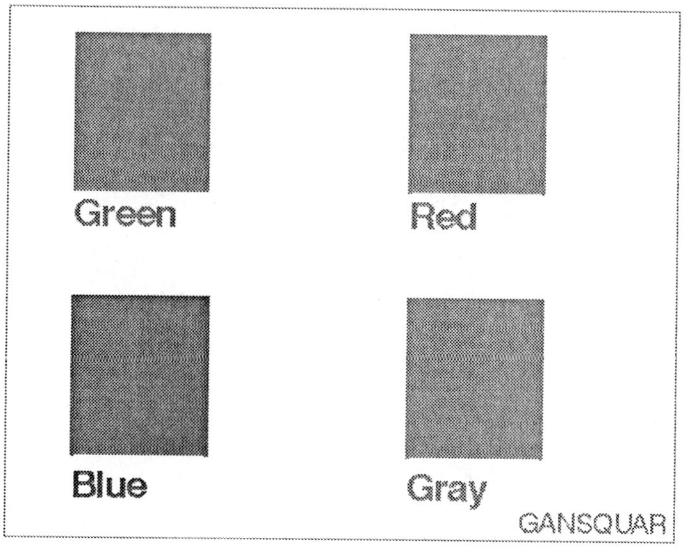

This example creates an Annotate data set that draws four colored squares, displays the data set as a single graphics output, and stores the output as a catalog entry in a permanent catalog. In this example, the NAME= option specifies a text string that identifies the name that is stored with the graphics output in the catalog.

Set the graphics environment.

```
goptions reset=global gunit=pct cback=white
   colors=(black blue green red);
```

Create the Annotate data set, SQUARES. XSYS and YSYS specify coordinate system 3 (percent of the graphics output area) for X and Y.

```
data squares;
   length function style color $ 8 text $ 15;
   xsys='3'; ysys='3';
```

Draw the first square. The COLOR variable assigns the color for the square. The FUNCTION variable selects the operation to be performed by the Annotate facility. The X and Y variables contain coordinate values. The BAR function draws the square. When the STYLE variable is used with the BAR function, it selects the fill pattern for the bar.

```
   color='green';
   function='move'; x=10; y=65; output;
   function='bar';  x=30; y=95; style='solid'; output;
```

Label the first square. The LABEL function creates the label. The POSITION value of 6 left-justifies the text with respect to X and Y. The TEXT variable specifies the text string to be written.

```
   function='label'; x=10; y=63; position='6';
      style='swissb'; size=2; text='Green'; output;
```

Draw and label the second square.

```
   color='red';
   function='move'; x=60; y=65; output;
   function='bar';  x=80; y=95; output;
   function='label'; x=60; y=63; position='6';
      style='swissb'; size=2; text='Red'; output;
```

Draw and label the third square.

```
   color='blue';
   function='move'; x=10; y=15; output;
   function='bar';  x=30; y=45; output;
   function='label'; x=10; y=12; position='6';
      style='swissb'; size=2; text='Blue'; output;
```

Draw and label the fourth square.

```
   color='gray';
   function='move'; x=60; y=15; output;
   function='bar';  x=80; y=45; output;
   function='label'; x=60; y=12; position='6';
      style='swissb'; size=2; text='Gray'; output;
```

Add a footnote.

```
x=88; y=5; position='5'; size=1.5; style='swiss';
   text='GANSQUAR'; output;
```

Draw a red frame.

```
   function='frame'; color='red'; when='b';
      style='empty'; output;
run;
```

Display the annotate graphics. GOUT= assigns the catalog in which the graphics output is stored. NAME= assigns a name to the entry stored in the WORK.EXCAT catalog. DESCRIPTION= assigns a description to the catalog entry.

```
proc ganno annotate=squares
   gout=excat
   name='GANSQUAR'
   description='Four squares';
run;
quit;
```

Example 3: Using the NAME= Option to Produce Multiple Graphs

Procedure features:

PROC GANNO statement option:

NAME=

Sample library member: GANMULTI

In this example, the GANNO procedure uses the NAME= option to generate multiple graphs from one Annotate data set. Since NAME= is assigned the variable COLOR, the GANNO procedure generates separate graphics output for each value of the COLOR, as shown in Figure 26.4 on page 717, Figure 26.5 on page 718, Figure 26.4 on page 717 and Figure 26.6 on page 718.

Each output is stored as a separate entry in the temporary output catalog WORK.EXCAT. The entries are named according to the values of COLOR: **BLUE, GRAY, GREEN**, and **RED**. Note that the output for **GRAY** includes the footnote shown in Example 2 on page 713. The output for **RED** shows the frame that is generated by the Annotate data set. The black borders in the other outputs are not generated by the code.

Set the graphics environment.

```
goptions reset=global gunit=pct cback=white
   colors=(black blue green red);
```

Create the Annotate data set, SQUARES. XSYS and YSYS specify coordinate system 3 (percent of the graphics output area) for X and Y.

```
data squares;
   length function style color $ 8 text $ 15;
   xsys='3'; ysys='3';
```

Draw the first square. The COLOR variable assigns the color for the square. The FUNCTION variable selects the operation to be performed by the Annotate facility. The X and Y variables contain coordinate values. The BAR function draws the square. When the STYLE variable is used with the BAR function, it selects the fill pattern for the bar.

```
   color='green';
   function='move'; x=10; y=65; output;
   function='bar';  x=30; y=95; style='solid'; output;
```

Label the first square. The LABEL function creates the label. The POSITION value of 6 left-justifies the text with respect to X and Y. The TEXT variable specifies the text string to be written.

```
   function='label'; x=10; y=63; position='6';
      style='swissb'; size=2; text='Green'; output;
```

Draw and label the second square.

```
   color='red';
   function='move'; x=60; y=65; output;
   function='bar';  x=80; y=95; output;
   function='label'; x=60; y=63; position='6';
      style='swissb'; size=2; text='Red'; output;
```

Draw and label the third square.

```
   color='blue';
   function='move'; x=10; y=15; output;
   function='bar';  x=30; y=45; output;
   function='label'; x=10; y=12; position='6';
      style='swissb'; size=2; text='Blue'; output;
```

Draw and label the fourth square.

```
   color='gray';
   function='move'; x=60; y=15; output;
   function='bar';  x=80; y=45; output;
   function='label'; x=60; y=12; position='6';
      style='swissb'; size=2; text='Gray'; output;
```

Add a footnote.

```
   x=88; y=5; position='5'; size=1.5; style='swiss';
      text='GANSQUAR'; output;
```

Draw a red frame.

```
   function='frame'; color='red'; when='b';
      style='empty'; output;
run;
```

Generate the annotate graphics, separating graphs by color. NAME= identifies the variable whose values PROC GANNO uses to generate the output. GANNO produces separate output for each value of COLOR. The COLOR value is the name of the catalog entry.

```
proc ganno annotate=squares
           name=color
           gout=excat
           description='Individual squares';
run;
```

Figure 26.4 Output for COLOR Value BLUE (WORK.EXCAT.BLUE.GRSEG)

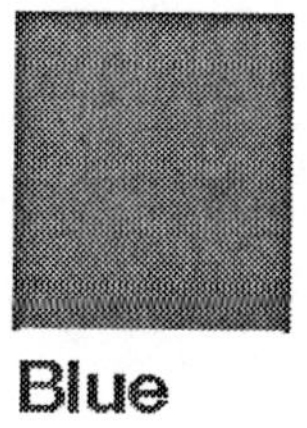

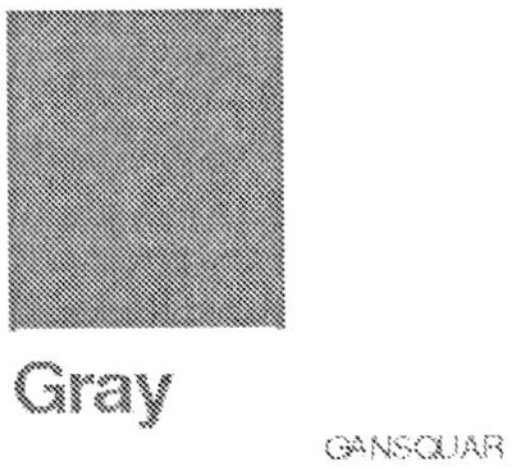

Figure 26.5 Output for COLOR Value GRAY (WORK.EXCAT.GRAY.GRSEG)

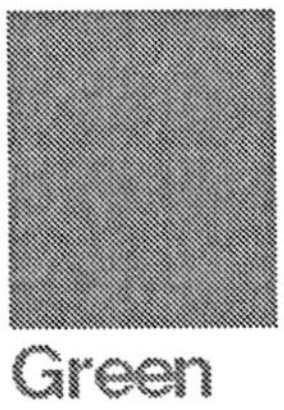

Figure 26.6 Output for COLOR Value GREEN (WORK.EXCAT.GREEN.GRSEG)

Figure 26.7 Output for COLOR Value RED (WORK.EXCAT.RED.GRSEG)

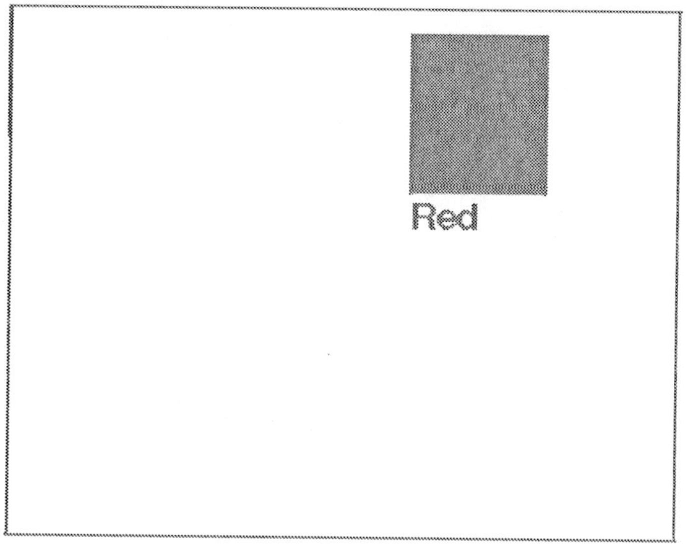

Example 4: Using Annotate Graphics in a Drill-Down Graph

Procedure features:
PROC GANNO statement option:
IMAGEMAP=

Sample library member: GANDRILL

This example creates essentially the same Annotate data set used in Example 2 on page 713. It draws four colored squares and displays the data set as a single graphics output.

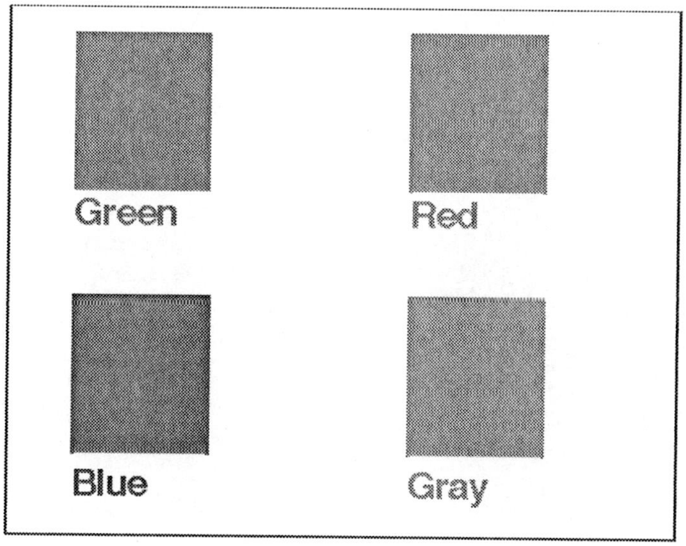

However, this time the example shows you how to use Annotate graphics to generate a drill-down graph. The example uses the HTML variable in the Annotate data set to specify linking information that defines each of the four squares as a hot zone. When the graph is viewed in a browser, you can click on a square to drill down to a related graph. For example, if you click on the green square, it drills down to a graph that confirms that you selected the green square.

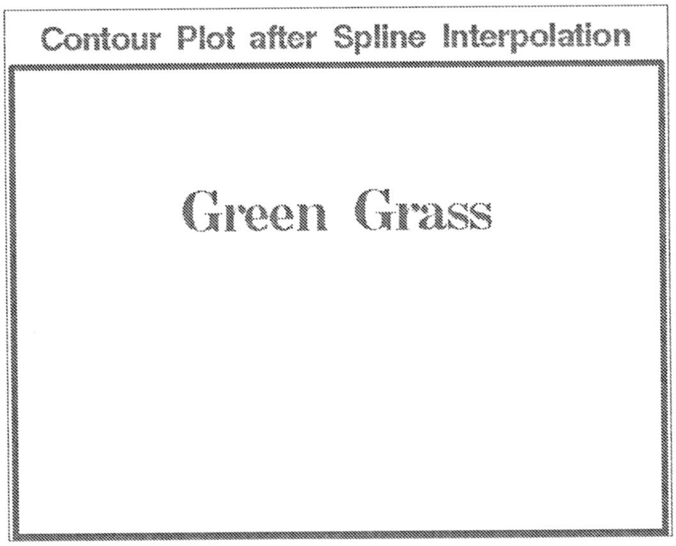

The example uses the HTML device driver to generate the drill-down graph. To implement the drill-down capability, the Annotate data set uses the HTML variable to provide the linking information (see "HTML Variable" on page 651), and the GANNO procedure uses the IMAGEMAP= option to create an Imagemap data set. The presence of the HTML variable in the Annotate data set and the IMAGEMAP= option on the GANNO procedure causes the HTML device driver to generate an image map for the graph. It writes the image map to the file index.html, which the HTML device driver creates for displaying Web output (see Chapter 17, "Generating Web Output with the Annotate Facility," on page 499).

To prevent the HTML device driver from writing over the contents of index.html after the drill-down graph has been generated, the example switches to the GIF device driver. It then runs four GSLIDE procedures to generate the target output. Each GSLIDE procedure uses the NAME= option to name the graph it produces, ensuring that the GIF driver creates files named green.gif, blue.gif, red.gif, and gray.gif. These are the files that are referenced as targets by the strings that are specified for the Annotate data set's HTML variable.

Allocate a storage location for all the output files, and set the graphics environment. The HTML device driver generates output that includes both HTML and GIF files, so the libref must point to an aggregate storage location. It cannot point to a file.

```
/* define the output location */
filename webout 'path-to-Web-server';
   /* set the graphics environment */
goptions reset=global gunit=pct
         colors=(black blue green red);
```

Create the Annotate data set. The HTML variable is used to define the linking information for each square. Because the GSLIDE procedures that generate the target output use NAME= to ensure the output files are named green.gif, red.gif, blue.gif, and gray.gif, strings that reference those names are assigned to the HTML variable for the appropriate observation in the data. For the final observation, the HTML variable's value is set to a null string; otherwise it would retain the last assigned value, which is **href=gray.gif**. In that case, the graph's background area would be defined as a hot zone that links to file gray.gif. For a description of the other functions and variables used in the Annotate data set, see Example 2 on page 713.

```
   /* create Annotate data set */
data squares;
     length function style color $ 8
            html text $ 15;
     xsys='3'; ysys='3';

        /* draw the green square */
     color='green';
     function='move'; x=10; y=65; output;
     function='bar';  x=30; y=95; style='solid';
        html='href=green.gif'; output;

        /* label green square */
     function='label'; x=10; y=63; position='6';
        style='swissb'; size=2; text='Green'; output;

        /* draw the red square */
     color='red';
     function='move'; x=60; y=65; output;
     function='bar';  x=80; y=95;
        html='href=red.gif'; output;

        /* label red square */
     function='label'; x=60; y=63; position='6';
        style='swissb'; size=2; text='Red'; output;

        /* draw the blue square */
     color='blue';
     function='move'; x=10; y=15; output;
     function='bar';  x=30; y=45;
        html='href=blue.gif'; output;

        /* label blue square */
     function='label'; x=10; y=12; position='6';
        style='swissb'; size=2; text='Blue'; output;

        /* draw the gray square */
     color='gray';
     function='move'; x=60; y=15; output;
     function='bar';  x=80; y=45;
        html='href=gray.gif'; output;

        /* label gray square and add a footnote */
     function='label'; x=60; y=12; position='6';
        style='swissb'; size=2; text='Gray'; output;
```

```
        /* draw a blue frame */
      function='frame'; color='blue'; style='empty';
        /* set null link for background area in frame */
        html=''; output;
run;
```

Set the graphics environment for the Web page. DEV= specifies the HTML device driver, which will create the HTML and GIF files needed for the Web page. GSFNAME= specifies the libref that points to the storage location that was allocated for the Web output. XPIXELS= and YPIXELS= define a size in pixels for the graphics area. TRANSPARENCY specifies that the background areas in all generated graphs should appear to be transparent when the images are displayed in a browser.

```
/* set the graphics options for the web page */
goptions dev=html gsfname=webout
         xpixels=450 ypixels=400
         transparency;
```

Generate the drill-down graph. IMAGEMAP= specifies ANNOMAP as the name for the Imagemap data set.

```
/* generate annotate graphics */
proc ganno annotate=squares
    imagemap=annomap
    description='Four squares';
run;
```

Change to the GIF driver and generate the target output. DEV= changes the device driver to GIF so that the target output files will be generated as GIF files. FTEXT= and CTEXT= specify a font and color for the text in graphics output. PROC GSLIDE is then run four times to generate the four graphs that will serve as target output for the links that are defined in the drill-down graph.

```
/* change to gif driver for target output */
goptions dev=gif ftext=centb ctext=green;

/* generate the target output */
proc gslide wframe=4
   cframe=green name='green';
   note height=20;
   note height=10
        justify=center
       'Green Grass';
run;

goptions ctext=blue;
proc gslide wframe=4
   cframe=blue name='blue';
   note height=20;
   note height=10
        justify=center
```

```
        'Blue Sky';
run;

goptions ctext=red;
proc gslide wframe=4
   cframe=red name='red';
   note height=20;
   note height=10
        justify=center
       'Red Wine';
run;

goptions ctext=gray;
proc gslide wframe=4
   cframe=gray name='gray';
   note height=20;
   note height=10
        justify=center
       'Gray Mare';
run;
quit;
```

CHAPTER

27

The GAREABAR Procedure

Overview

The GAREABAR procedure enables you to produce an area bar chart showing the magnitudes of *two* variables for each category of data. For example, the following area bar chart shows the sales total for each of three geographical sites. An additional dimension is graphed for the width variable, namely, the number of sales persons at each site. One can see from this chart that while the sales total of NY is the greatest, its number of sales people is also the greatest. In a plain bar chart, the width is the same for each bar. In an area bar chart, the width and height of each bar is determined by the value of variables.

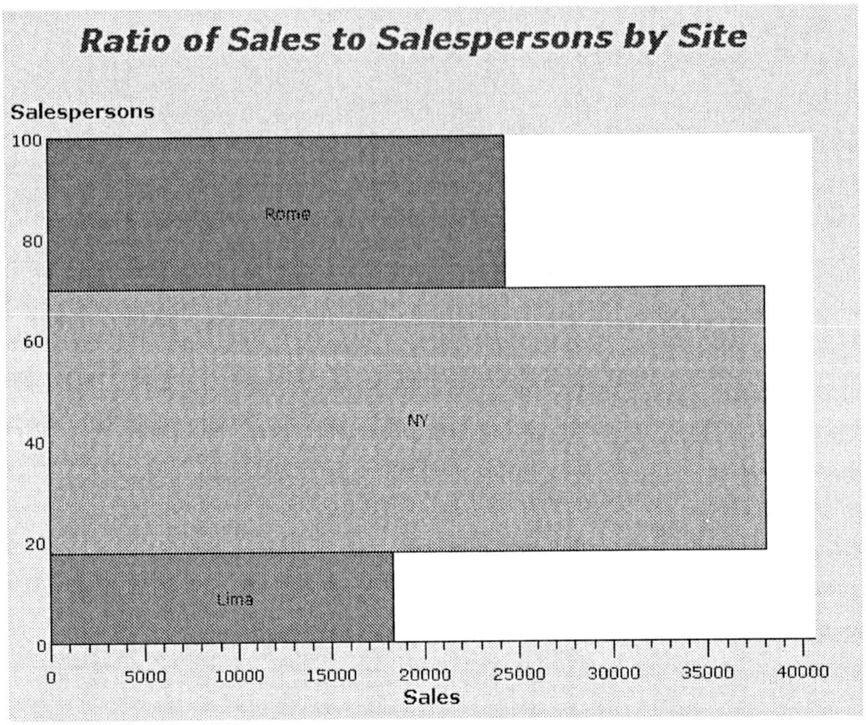

Note: The GAREABAR procedure requires the following:

- □ a prior GOPTIONS statement where DEV=ACTIVEX or DEV=ACTXIMG, because PROC GAREABAR only works with the ActiveX control on a Windows system
- □ a prior ODS HTML statement
- □ a closing ODS HTML CLOSE statement.

△

Concepts

The GAREABAR procedure produces a chart based on the values of a *category variable*. A category variable can be either character or numeric. The GAREABAR procedure treats all values of a numeric category variable as DISCRETE (such as quarters 1,2,3,4) even if the values are apparently continuous (such as 1.234 and 4.002). PROC GAREABAR does not calculate a midpoint.

Also, PROC GCHART, by default, sorts the values of the category variable either alphabetically or numerically. PROC GAREABAR displays the category variable in data order (the order in which its values occur in the data set).

For each category variable, PROC GAREABAR graphs the dimensions of two numeric variables. For the VBAR statement, the SUMVAR variable (response variable) is graphed along the vertical axis, and the width variable is graphed along the horizontal axis. Conversely, for the HBAR statement, the SUMVAR variable (response variable) determines the length of the bar on the horizontal axis, and the width variable determines the thickness of the bar on the vertical axis.

Both the width variable and the response variable can be displayed as either percentage or sum. Specify WSTAT=PERCENT or WSTAT=SUM for the width variable, and specify RSTAT=PERCENT or RSTAT=SUM for the response variable. The default for both is SUM.

In addition, you can use the SUBGROUP option to subgroup the response variable either by percentage or by sum. Examples of subgrouping are shown in Example 3 on page 733 and Example 4 on page 735.

Procedure Syntax

Requirements:
GOPTIONS statement with DEV=ACTIVEX | ACTXIMG
ODS HTML statement (before and after)
HBAR, HBAR3D, VBAR, or VBAR3D statement

Global statements: FOOTNOTE, GOPTIONS, TITLE

Supports: RUN-group processing

PROC GAREABAR< DATA=*input-data-set*>

VBAR *category-variable*width-variable* </ SUMVAR=*response-variable option(s)*>;

VBAR3D *category-variable*width-variable* </ SUMVAR=*response-variable option(s)*>;

HBAR *category-variable*width-variable*< / SUMVAR=*response-variable option(s)*>;

HBAR3D *category-variable*width-variable*< / SUMVAR=*response-variable option(s)*>;

PROC GAREABAR Statement

Identifies the data set containing the category variable, the response variable (SUMVAR), and the width variable.

Requirements: An input data set is required. If none is specified, the procedure uses the most recently created data set.

Syntax

PROC GAREABAR< DATA=*input-data-set;*>

Requirements

input-data-set
contains the data to be graphed.

GOPTIONS DEV=ACTIVEX|ACTXIMG
PROC GAREABAR requires a GOPTIONS statement where the value of DEV= is ACTIVEX or ACTXIMG (before the PROC).

ODS HTML
PROC GAREABAR requires an ODS HTML statement (both before and after the PROC).

HBAR, HBAR3D, VBAR, VBAR3D Statements

These statements create area bar charts where each bar shows two dimensions (a width variable and response variable) for each category variable.

Syntax

HBAR | HBAR3D | VBAR | VBAR3D *category-variable*width-variable*
</ SUMVAR=*response-variable option(s)*>;

Required Arguments

All arguments must be in the input data set.

category-variable
is either character or numeric. Defines the category of data to chart. Each category variable results in a separate bar. If the category-variable is numeric, all its values are treated as DISCRETE (such as the years 2000, 2001, 2002). No midpoint is calculated for a numeric category variable.

response-variable
is always numeric. For HBAR and HBAR3D, the length of the each bar along the horizontal axis represents the response variable. For VBAR and VBAR3D, the height of the each bar along the vertical axis measures the response variable.
Use the RSTAT option to specify whether the response variable is measured as a percentage or as a sum. The default is SUM.

width-variable
is always numeric. For HBAR and HBAR3D, the width variable is measured by the magnitude of each bar along the vertical axis. For VBAR and VBAR3D, the width variable is measured by the magnitude of each bar along the horizontal axis.
Use the WSTAT option to specify whether the width variable is measured as a percentage or as a sum. The default is SUM.

Options

CFR= | CFRAME=*background-color*
specifies a background color for the chart. The specified color must be a valid SAS/GRAPH color name, or a character variable of length eight whose value is the color. The default color is white.

CTEXT=*text-color*
specifies a color for all text on the chart. The specified color must be a valid SAS/GRAPH color name, or a character variable of length eight whose value is the color. The default color is black.

DISCRETE
causes the chart to show discrete width role values on the width axis rather than a continuous axis. If you do not specify DISCRETE, the continuous axis result is assumed. .

FRAME | NOFRAME
FRAME (the default) draws a frame around the procedure output area. The frame color is the first color in the colors list.

NOFRAME suppresses the frame that is drawn around the chart by default.

NAME=
when DEV=ACTXIMG, specifies the name of the graph (PNG file) produced by GAREABAR. The maximum length for entry-name is eight characters. If the specified name duplicates the name of an existing entry, then SAS/GRAPH software overwrites the existing entry.

Use the PATH or GPATH option of the ODS HTML statement or ODS MARKUP statement to specify the location for storing the .png file.

SUBGROUP=
used to subdivide the response-variable dimension (SUMVAR). A SUBGROUP variable can be either character or numeric. For example, if the category variable is company, and the response variable is revenue, then specifying a SUBGROUP of country will subdivide the revenue for each company according to country. A numeric example is subdividing revenue by quarters: 1, 2, 3, 4.

***WSTAT=* | *WIDTHSTAT*=SUM or PCT | PERCENT**
specifies whether the width variable is represented as a percentage or as a sum. The default is SUM.

***RSTAT=* | *RESPSTAT*=SUM or PCT | PERCENT**
If SUBGROUP is specified, then RSTAT specifies whether the subgrouping is represented as a percentage or as a sum. The default is SUM.

If SUBGROUP is *not* specified, then the response variable can only be SUM.

Examples

Example 1: A Simple Area Bar Chart

Procedure features:

SUMVAR=

Sample library member: GABSUMVR

This example graphs the total sales for each of three geographic sites (Rome, NY, Lima) along the X axis. Along the Y axis, the relative thickness of each bar shows the number of salespersons at each site. The chart shows that although NY had the highest sales (the longest bar), it also had the greatest number of salespersons (as shown by the thickness of the bar).

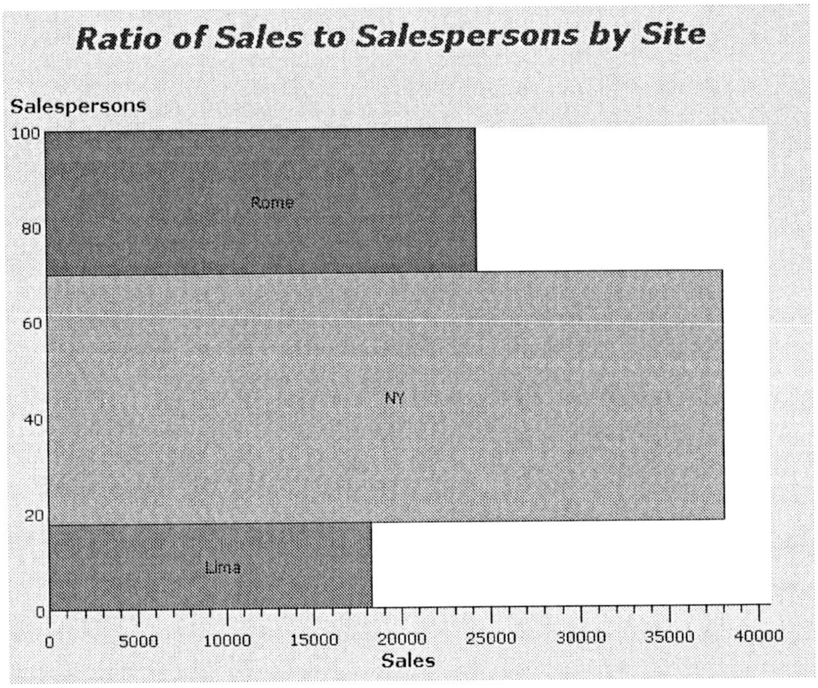

The procedure for this chart is:

Uncomment this line, and change the output destination to a directory and file name that makes sense for you.

```
*filename odsout 'c:\test\filename.htm';
```

PROC GAREABAR is only supported with device= ACTIVEX or ACTXIMG.

```
goptions reset=all dev=activex;
ods html file=odsout;


data totals;
 input Site $ Quarter Sales Salespersons;
 cards;
Lima    1 4043.97    4
NY      1 8225.26   12
Rome    1 3543.97    6
Lima    2 3723.44    5
NY      2 8595.07   18
Rome    2 5558.29   10
Lima    3 4437.96    8
NY      3 9847.91   24
Rome    3 6789.85   14
Lima    4 6065.57   10
NY      4 11388.51  26
Rome    4 8509.08   16
;
```

Because SUMVAR=SALES, the total sales are plotted along the horizontal axis (HBAR). Because SITE*SALESPERSONS and WSTAT=PERCENT, the percentage of salespersons at each site is shown by the relative thickness of each bar along the vertical axis.

```
proc gareabar data=totals;
   hbar site*salespersons /sumvar=sales wstat=PERCENT;
run;
```

ODS HTML CLOSE causes the HTML file to be written to disk.

```
ods html close;
```

The variables in this procedure are as follows:

site	the category variable: Lima, NY, Paris
salespersons	the width variable, in this case displayed as a percentage along the vertical axis
sales	the response variable (SUMVAR), displayed along the horizontal axis because, in this case, the statement is HBAR.

Example 2: Area Bar Chart with a Numeric Category Variable

Procedure features:

SUMVAR=

Sample library member: GABSUMVR

This example is similar to Example 1 and shows that the category variable can be numeric—in this case 1, 2, 3, 4 for the four quarters of a year. The GAREABAR procedure treats all values of a numeric category variable as DISCRETE and does not calculate a midpoint even if the values of the category variable are continuous.

This example graphs the total sales for each quarter of the year along the horizontal axis. The relative thickness of each bar along the vertical axis shows the total number of salespersons during that quarter. The chart shows that as the number of salespersons increased from quarter to quarter, the total sales also increased.

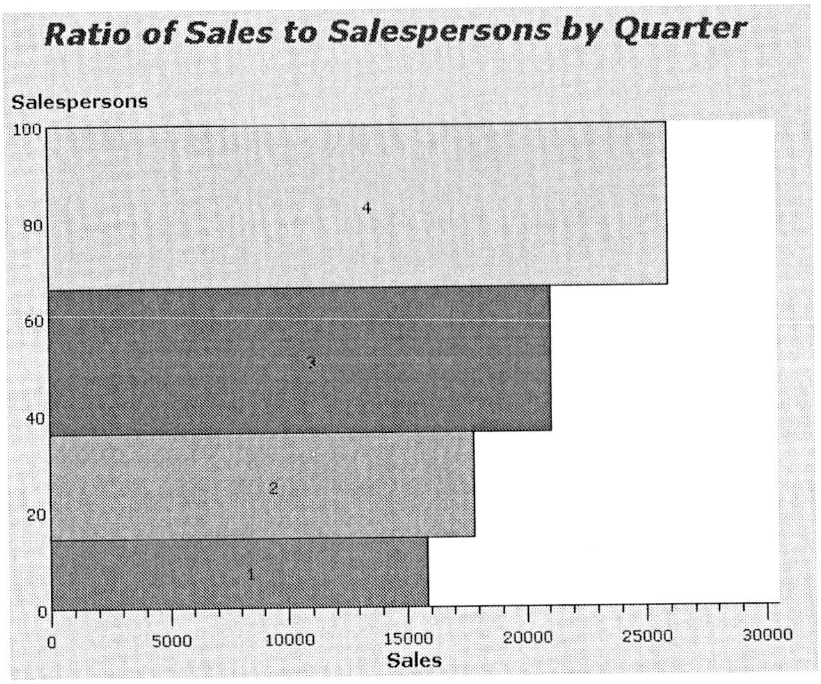

The procedure is as follows:

Uncomment this line, and change the output destination to a directory and file name that makes sense for you.

```
*filename odsout 'c:\test\filename.htm';
```

PROC GAREABAR is only supported with device= ACTIVEX or ACTXIMG.

```
goptions reset=all dev=activex;
ods html file=odsout;

data totals;
 input Site $ Quarter Sales Salespersons;
 cards;
Lima    1 4043.97    4
NY      1 8225.26   12
Rome    1 3543.97    6
Lima    2 3723.44    5
NY      2 8595.07   18
Rome    2 5558.29   10
Lima    3 4437.96    8
NY      3 9847.91   24
Rome    3 6789.85   14
Lima    4 6065.57   10
NY      4 11388.51  26
Rome    4 8509.08   16
;
```

Because SUMVAR=SALES, the total sales are plotted along the horizontal axis (HBAR).

Because QUARTER*SALESPERSONS and WSTAT=PERCENT, the percentage of salespersons for each quarter is shown by the relative thickness of each bar along the vertical axis.

```
proc gareabar data=totals;
   hbar quarter*salespersons / sumvar=sales wstat=PCT;
run;
```

ODS HTML CLOSE causes the HTML file to be written to disk.

```
ods html close;
```

The variables in the example are as follows:

quarter
: the category variable: quarters 1, 2, 3, and 4

salespersons
: the width variable, in this case displayed as a percentage along the vertical axis.

sales
: the response variable (SUMVAR), displayed along the horizontal axis.

Example 3: Area Bar Chart with a Subgrouping

Procedure features:

SUBGROUP=

Sample library member: GABSUBGR

This example uses the SUBGROUP= option to display the same magnitudes as displayed by Examples 1 and 2. Like Example 1, this example shows the total sales for each of three geographic sites along the horizontal axis. The relative thickness of each bar along the vertical axis shows the number of salespersons at each site.

In addition, by subgrouping the response variable by quarter, this example shows the relative percentage of sales for each quarter. Thus, one can see from this chart that NY (the middle bar) had most of its sales in the fourth quarter, whereas Rome (the topmost bar) had most of its sales in the first quarter.

The value of SUBGROUP= can be character or numeric.

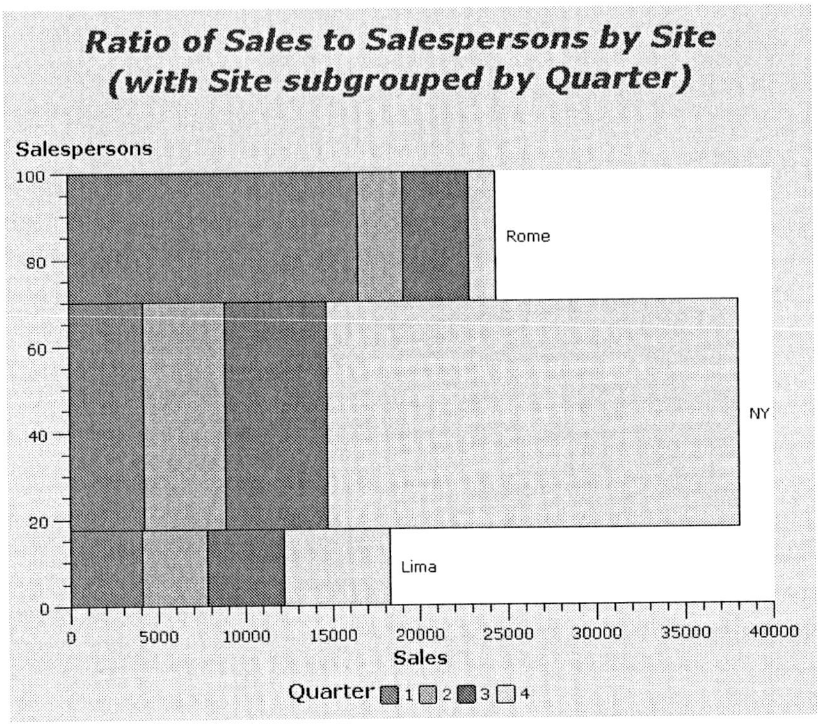

The procedure is as follows:

Uncomment this line, and change the output destination to a directory and file name that makes sense for you.

```
*filename odsout 'c:\test\filename.htm';
```

PROC GAREABAR is only supported with device= ACTIVEX or ACTXIMG.

```
goptions reset=all dev=activex;
ods html file=odsout;


data totals;
   input Site $ Quarter $ Sales Salespersons;
cards;
Lima     1 4043.97     4
NY       1 4225.26    12
Rome     1 16543.97    6
Lima     2 3723.44     5
NY       2 4595.07    18
Rome     2 2558.29    10
Lima     3 4437.96     8
NY       3 5847.91    24
Rome     3 3789.85    14
Lima     4 6065.57    10
NY       4 23388.51   26
Rome     4 1509.08    16
;
```

```
 /* define title */
title1 'Ratio of Sales to Salespersons by Site';
title2 '(with Site subgrouped by Quarter)';
```

Because SUMVAR=SALES, the total sales are plotted along the horizontal axis (HBAR).

Because SITE*SALESPERSONS and WSTAT=PERCENT, the percentage of salespersons for each quarter is shown by the relative thickness of each bar along the vertical axis.

Because SUBGROUP=QUARTER and RSTAT=SUM, the quarters are displayed as absolute numbers along the horizontal bar.

```
proc gareabar data=totals;
   hbar site*salespersons /sumvar=sales
                          subgroup=quarter
                          rstat=SUM
                          wstat=PCT;
run;
ods html close;
```

The variables in the example are as follows:

site	the category variable: Lima, NY, Rome.
salespersons	the width variable, in this case displayed as a percentage (wstat=PCT) along the vertical axis.
sales	the response variable (SUMVAR), displayed as a sum (rstat=SUM) along the horizontal axis because, in this case, the statement is HBAR.
quarter	quarters 1, 2, 3, and 4, displayed as absolute numbers (rstat=SUM) along the horizontal bar.

Example 4: Area Bar Chart with Subgrouping and RSTAT and WSTAT as Percentages

Procedure features:

SUBGROUP=, RSTAT=, WSTAT=

Sample library member: GABWSTAT

This example uses the RSTAT= option, in conjunction with the SUBGROUP= option, to display the response variable (medals won in the winter Olympics), subgrouped by the percentage (RSTAT=PCT) of each medal type (gold, silver, bronze). The width variable is the number of athletes, displayed (in this case along the vertical axis) as the percentage of athletes (WSTAT=PCT) of each of five different nationalities.

When the SUBGROUP= option is specified, you can use the RSTAT= option to specify whether the subgrouping is to be displayed as a percentage or as a sum.

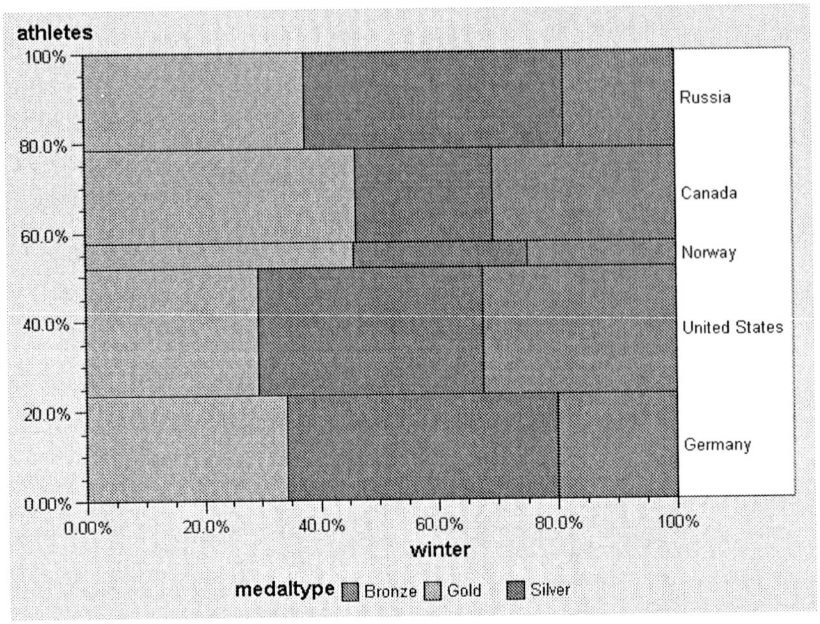

The procedure is as follows:

Uncomment this line, and change the output destination to a directory and file name that makes sense for you.

```
*filename odsout 'c:\test\filename.htm';
```

PROC GAREABAR is only supported with device= ACTIVEX or ACTXIMG.
ODS LISTING CLOSE prevents the output from going to the OUTPUT window in addition to disk.

```
ods listing close;
ods html file=odsout;
goptions dev=activex;


data medals;
input country $15. medaltype $ winter summer athletes;
datalines;
Germany        Gold    12 14 176
Germany        Silver  16 17   0
Germany        Bronze   7 26   0
United States  Gold    10 39 210
United States  Silver  13 25   0
United States  Bronze  11 33   0
Norway         Gold    11  4  42
Norway         Silver   7  3   0
Norway         Bronze   6  3   0
Canada         Gold     6  3 157
Canada         Silver   3  3   0
Canada         Bronze   4  8   0
Russia         Gold     6 32 160
Russia         Silver   7 28   0
```

```
Russia          Bronze  3 28   0
;
```

Because SUMVAR=WINTER, this proc displays the number medals won in the winter Olympics, subgrouped by the percentage (RSTAT=PCT) of each medal type (gold, silver, bronze). The width variable is the number of athletes, displayed (in this case along the vertical axis) as the percentage of athletes (WSTAT=PCT) of each of five different nationalities.

When the SUBGROUP= option is specified, you can use the RSTAT= option to specify whether the subgrouping is to be displayed as a percentage or as a sum.

```
PROC GAREABAR data=medals;
  hbar country*athletes /sumvar=winter
                         subgroup=medaltype
                         wstat=percent
                         rstat=percent;
run;
quit;
```

ODS HTML CLOSE causes the HTML file to be written to disk.

ODS LISTING restores subsequent output to the OUTPUT window.

```
ods html close;
ods listing;
```

The variables in the example are as follow:

country
: the category variable: Russia, Canada, Norway, United States, Germany.

athletes
: displayed as a percentage (WSTAT=PERCENT) along the vertical axis.

winter
: the value of SUMVAR, the number of medals won in the winter Olympics, displayed along the horizontal axis because, in this case, the statement is HBAR.

medaltype
: the value of SUBGROUP, displayed as a percentage (RSTAT=PERCENT) of each medal type (gold, silver, bronze).

CHAPTER

28

The GBARLINE Procedure

Overview

The GBARLINE procedure produces bar line charts. Bar line charts are vertical bar charts with a plot overlay. These charts graphically represent the value of a statistic calculated for one or more variables in an input SAS data set. The charted variables can be either numeric or character.

The procedure calculates these statistics:

- frequency or cumulative frequency counts
- percentages or cumulative percentages
- sums
- means.

Use the GBARLINE procedure to

- display and compare exact and relative magnitudes
- examine the contribution of parts to the whole
- analyze where data are out of balance
- display long series of data, showing trends and patterns.

In conjunction with the SYMBOL statement, the GBARLINE procedure can produce needle plot overlays, and overlay plots with stepped interpolation.

Note: PROC GBARLINE is not supported by Java. △

About Bar Line Charts

Bar line charts display the magnitude of data with bars, each of which represents a category of data (midpoint). The height of the bars represents the value of the bar statistic for the corresponding midpoint.

Figure 28.1 on page 740 shows the relationship between petal width and petal length for three species of flowers. The horizontal axis is the midpoint axis and the vertical axes are response axes. Each axis is labeled with the variable name. Each species is a midpoint, so each bar is labeled with the species identifier.

Figure 28.1 Bar Line Graph

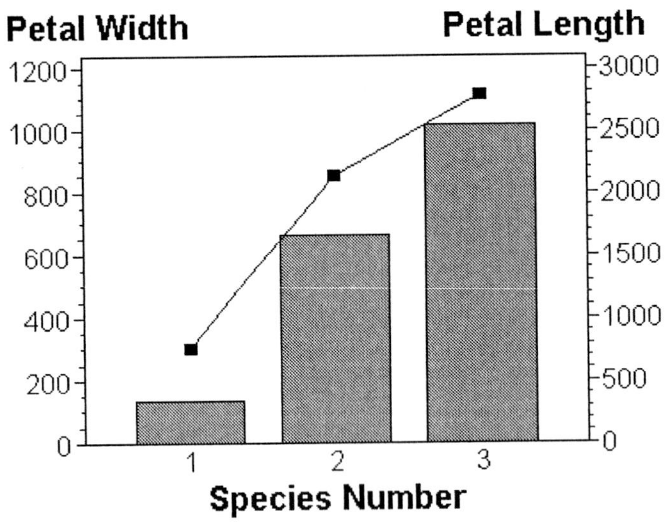

About Interpolation Methods

You can produce plot overlays such as needle plot overlays by specifying interpolation methods with the SYMBOL statement. For PROC GBARLINE, you can use the SYMBOL statement to

- connect the data points to the zero line on the vertical axis (NEEDLE)
- use a step function to connect the data points (STEP)
- produce overlay plots with unconnected data points (NONE)
- connect data points with straight lines (JOIN).

For bar line graphs, points on the plot overlay are automatically joined, which is equivalent to specifying the JOIN interpolation method.

"SYMBOL Statement" on page 183 describes the JOIN, NEEDLE, STEP, and NONE interpolation methods.

Concepts

The GBARLINE procedure produces bar charts based on the values of a *bar variable* with plot overlays based on the values of a *plot variable*. The values of the bar variable are represented by a set of *midpoints*. The graph itself displays information about the bar variable in the form of *bar statistics*.

Figure 28.2 on page 741 illustrates the parts of a bar line graph.

Figure 28.2 Parts of a Bar Line Graph

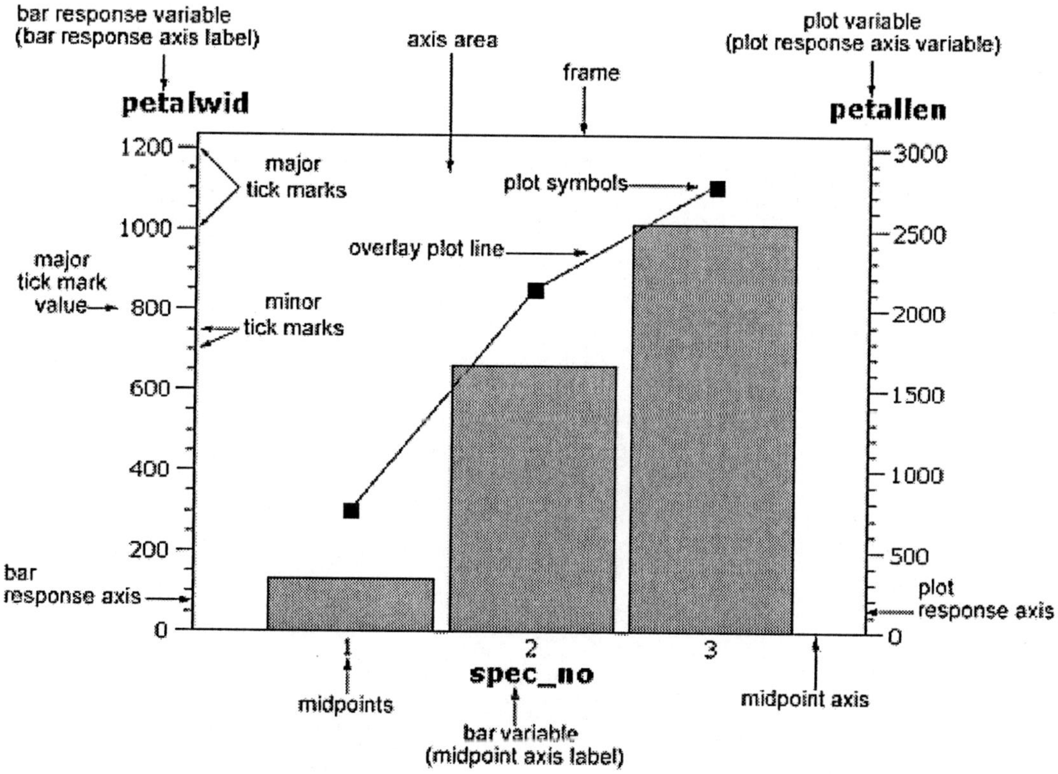

Bar line graphs have three axes:

- a midpoint axis that shows the categories of data, based on the bar variable
- a left response axis that displays the scale of values for the bar statistic (based on the summary variable, if specified)

- a right response axis that displays the scale of values for the plot statistic.

The response axes are divided into evenly spaced intervals identified with major tick marks that are labeled with the corresponding statistic value. Minor tick marks are evenly distributed between the major tick marks. Each axis is labeled with the variable name or label.

About the Bar Variable

The *bar variable* is the variable in the input data set whose value determines the categories of data represented by the bar. The bar variable generates the midpoints to which each observation in the data set contribute.

The bar variable can be either character or numeric. Character bar variables contain character values, which are always discrete. Numeric bar variables fall into two categories: discrete and continuous.

- *Discrete variables* contain a finite number of specific numeric values that are to be represented on the chart. For example, a variable that contains years, such as 1984 or 2002, is a discrete variable.
- *Continuous variables* contain a range of numeric values that are to be represented on the chart. For example, a variable of temperature data that contains real values between 0 and 212 is a continuous variable.

Numeric bar variables are always treated as continuous variables unless the DISCRETE option is used in the BAR statement.

About Midpoints

Midpoints are the values of the bar variable that identify categories of data. By default, midpoints are selected or calculated by the procedure. The way the procedure handles the midpoints depends on whether the values of the bar variable are character, discrete numeric, or continuous numeric.

Character Values

A character bar variable generates a midpoint for each unique value of the variable. In the following example, the bar variable CITY contains the names of three different cities, and each city is a midpoint, resulting in three midpoints for the chart:

Figure 28.3 Character Midpoints

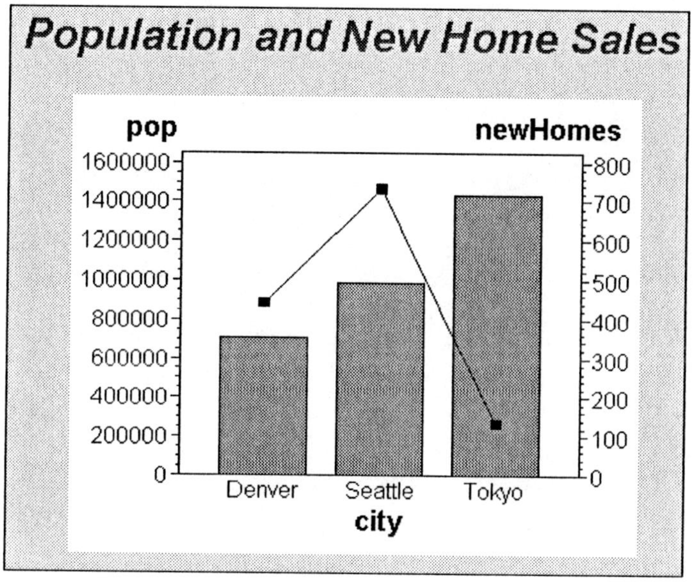

By default, character midpoints are arranged in alphabetic order. If a character variable has an associated format, then the values are arranged in order of the formatted values.

Discrete Numeric Values

A numeric bar variable used with the DISCRETE option generates a midpoint for each unique value of the bar variable. In the following example, the numeric variable YEAR used with the DISCRETE option produces one midpoint for each year:

Figure 28.4 Discrete Numeric Midpoints

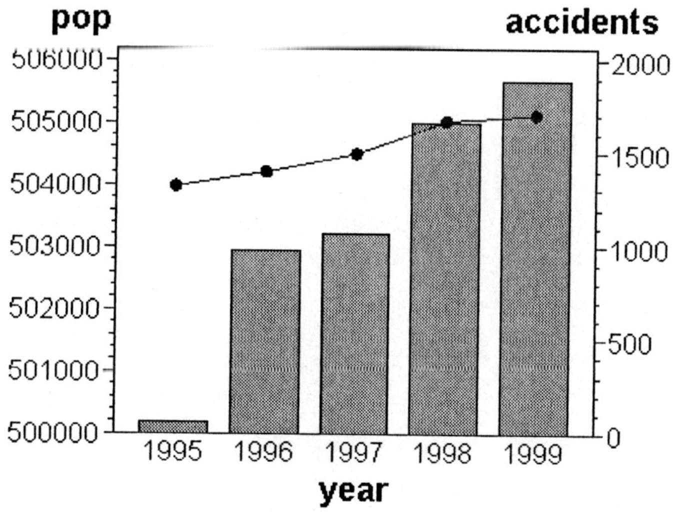

By default, numeric midpoints are arranged in ascending order. If the numeric variable has an associated format, then each formatted value generates a separate midpoint. Formatted numeric variables are arranged in ascending order according to their unformatted numeric values.

Continuous Numeric Values

A continuous numeric variable generates midpoints that represent ranges of values. By default, the GBARLINE procedure determines the ranges, calculates the median value of each range, and displays the appropriate median value at each midpoint on the chart. A value that falls exactly halfway between two midpoints is placed in the higher range.

In the following example, the numeric variable AGE produces five midpoints, each of which represents a six-year age range; the median value of the range is displayed at each midpoint:

Figure 28.5 Continuous Numeric Midpoints

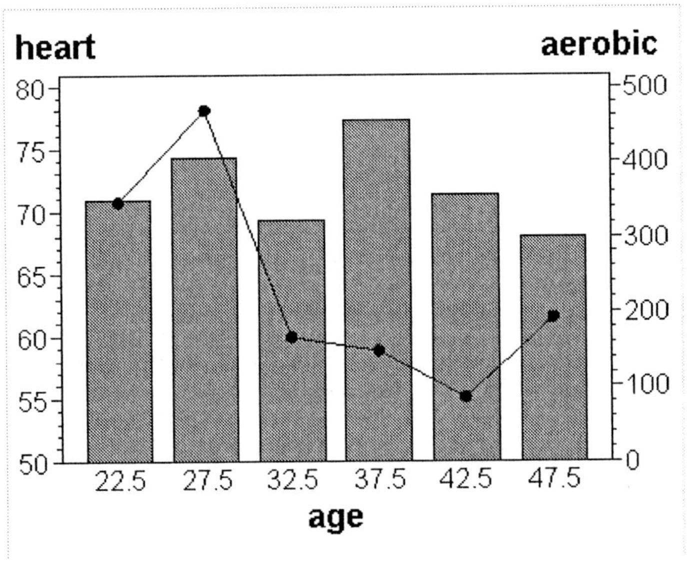

By default, midpoints of ranges are arranged in ascending order.

Selecting and Ordering Midpoints

For character or discrete numeric values, you can use the MIDPOINTS= option to rearrange the midpoints or to exclude midpoints from the chart. For example, to change the default alphabetic order of the midpoints in Figure 28.3 on page 743, specify

```
midpoints='Tokyo' 'Denver' 'Seattle'
```

To exclude the midpoint for Denver, specify

```
midpoints='Tokyo' 'Seattle'
```

In this case, values excluded by the option are not included in the calculation of the bar statistic.

You can order or select discrete numeric midpoint values just as you do character values, but you omit the quotation marks when specifying numeric values.

For continuous numeric variables, use the LEVELS= or MIDPOINTS= option to change the number of midpoints, to control the range of values each midpoint represents, or to change the order of the midpoints. To control the range of values each midpoint represents, use the MIDPOINTS= option to specify the median value of each range. For example, to select the ranges 20–29, 30–39, and 40–49, specify

```
midpoints=25 35 45
```

Alternatively, to select the number of midpoints that you want and let the procedure calculate the ranges and medians, use the LEVELS= option.

You can also use formats to control the ranges of continuous numeric variables, but in that case the values are no longer continuous but become discrete.

Note: You cannot use the MIDPOINTS= option to exclude continuous numeric values from the chart because values below or above the ranges specified by the option are automatically included in the first and last midpoints, respectively. To exclude continuous numeric values from a chart, use a WHERE statement in a DATA step or the WHERE= DATA set option. △

See also the description of the LEVELS= and MIDPOINTS= options.

About the Plot Variable

The *plot variable* is the variable in the input data set whose values are used to generate the overlay plot line. The plot variable is optional, but if specified, it must be a numeric variable.

To specify a plot variable, use the SUMVAR= option on the PLOT statement:

```
PLOT / SUMVAR=height;
```

When you specify a plot variable with the SUMVAR= option, the only statistics available for the plot are the sum or the mean. You can specify the statistic with the TYPE= option. SUM (TYPE=SUM) is the default.

If you do not specify a plot variable, then the bar variable is used as the plot variable. The only statistics available for the plot are percentage, cumulative percentage, frequency, or cumulative frequency. The default statistic is frequency (TYPE=FREQ).

For more information about these statistics, see "About Chart Statistics" on page 745. See also the descriptions of the SUMVAR= and TYPE= options for the PLOT statement.

About Chart Statistics

The *chart statistics* are the statistical values calculated for the bar variables and the plot variables. The GBARLINE procedure calculates six chart statistics. You can specify the chart statistics with the TYPE= option. For the bar, the default statistic is frequency. For the plot, the default statistic is sum.

The examples given in the descriptions of these statistics assume a data set with two variables, CITY and SALES. The values of CITY are `Denver`, `Seattle`, and `Tokyo`. There are 21 observations: seven for Denver, nine for Seattle, and five for Tokyo.

Frequency

The frequency statistic is the total number of observations in the data set for each midpoint. For example, seven observations of the bar variable, CITY, contain the value `Denver`, so the frequency for the `Denver` midpoint is 7.

Cumulative Frequency

The cumulative frequency statistic adds the frequency for the current midpoint to the frequency of all of the preceding midpoints. For example, the frequency for the `Denver` midpoint is 7, and the frequency for the next midpoint, **Seattle**, is 9, so the cumulative frequency for **Seattle** is 16.

Percentage

The percentage statistic is calculated by dividing the frequency for each midpoint by the total frequency count for all midpoints in the chart or group and multiplying it by 100. For example, the frequency count for the **Denver** midpoint is 7 and the total frequency count for the chart is 21, so the percentage statistic for **Denver** is 33.3%.

Cumulative Percentage

The cumulative percentage statistic adds the percentage for the current midpoint to the percentage for all of the preceding midpoints in the chart or group. For example, the percentage for the **Denver** midpoint is 33.3, and the percentage for the next midpoint, **Seattle**, is 42.9, so the cumulative percentage for **Seattle** is 76.2.

Sum

The sum statistic is the total of the values, for each midpoint, for the variable specified by the SUMVAR= option. For example, if you specify SUMVAR=SALES and the values of the SALES variable for the seven **Denver** observations are **8734**, **982**, **1504**, **3207**, **4502**, **624**, and **918**, the sum statistic for the **Denver** midpoint is 20,471.

You must use the SUMVAR= option to specify the variable for which you want the sum statistic.

Mean

The mean statistic is the average of the values, for each midpoint, for the variable specified by the SUMVAR= option. For example, if TYPE=MEAN and SUMVAR=SALES, the mean statistic for the **Denver** midpoint is 2924.42.

You must use the SUMVAR= option to specify the variable for which you want the mean statistic.

Calculating Weighted Statistics

By default, each observation is counted only once in the calculation of a chart statistic. To calculate weighted statistics in which an observation can be counted more than once, use the FREQ= option. This option identifies a variable whose values are used as a multiplier for the observation in the calculation of the statistic. If the value of the FREQ= variable is missing, 0, or negative, then the observation is excluded from the calculation.

If you use the SUMVAR= option, then the SUMVAR= variable value for an observation is multiplied by the FREQ= variable value for the observation for use in calculating the chart statistic.

For example, to use a variable called COUNT to produce weighted statistics, assign FREQ=COUNT. If you also assign the variable HEIGHT to the SUMVAR= option, then the following table shows how the values of COUNT and HEIGHT would affect the statistic calculation:

Value of COUNT	Value of HEIGHT	Number of times the observation is used	Value used for HEIGHT
1	55	1	55
5	65	5	325
.	63	0	-
-3	60	0	-

By default, the percentage and cumulative percentage statistics are calculated based on the frequency. If you want to graph a percentage or cumulative percentage based on a sum, then you can use the FREQ= option to specify a variable to use for the "sum" calculation and specify the PCT statistic, as shown in this example:

```
freq=count type=pct
```

Because the variable that is specified by the FREQ= option determines the number of times an observation is counted, the value of COUNT is the equivalent of the sum statistic.

See also the descriptions of the TYPE=, SUMVAR=, and FREQ= options.

Note: The FREQ= option is not supported by ActiveX or Java. △

Missing Values

By default, the GBARLINE procedure ignores missing midpoint values for the bar variable. If you specify the MISSING option, then missing values are treated as a valid midpoint and are included on the chart.

When the value of the variable that is specified in the FREQ= option is missing, 0, or negative, the observation is excluded from the calculation of the chart statistic.

When the value of the variable specified in the SUMVAR= option is missing, the observation is excluded from the calculation of the chart statistic.

If the value of the plot variable is missing, then the GBARLINE procedure does not include the observation in the plot overlay. If you specify interpolation with a SYMBOL definition, then the plot is not broken at the missing value.

Plot Variable Values Out of Range

Exclude data values from a plot overlay by restricting the range of axis values with the RAXIS= options or with the ORDER= option in an AXIS statement. When an observation contains a value outside of the specified axis range, the GBARLINE procedure excludes the observation from the plot and issues a message to the log.

If you specify interpolation with a SYMBOL definition, then by default values outside of the axis range are excluded from interpolation calculations and, as a result, can change interpolated values for the plot overlay.

To specify that values out of range are included in the interpolation calculations, use the MODE= option in a SYMBOL statement. When MODE=INCLUDE, values that fall outside of the axis range are included in interpolation calculations but excluded from the plot. The default (MODE=EXCLUDE) omits observations that are outside of the axis range from interpolation calculations. See the MODE= option of in "SYMBOL Statement" on page 183 for details.

About Patterns

When a chart needs one or more patterns, the procedure uses either default patterns and outlines that are automatically generated by SAS/GRAPH, or patterns, colors, outlines, and images that are defined by PATTERN statements, graphics options, and procedure options.

The following sections summarize pattern behavior for the GBARLINE procedure. For more information, see "PATTERN Statement" on page 169.

Default Patterns and Outlines

In general, the default pattern that the GBARLINE procedure uses is a solid fill that it rotates once through the colors list, skipping the color that is being used as the foreground color. The procedure also outlines all areas in the foreground color. (Typically, the foreground color is the first color in the device's colors list.)

Specifically, the GBARLINE procedure uses default patterns and outlines when you do not specify any of the following:

- *any* PATTERN statements
- the COLORS= graphics options (that is, you use the device's default colors list and it has more than one color)
- the COUTLINE= option in the BAR statement.

If you do not specify any of these statements or options, then the GBARLINE procedure

- selects the first default fill pattern, which is always solid, and rotates it through the colors list, generating one solid pattern for each color. If the first color in the device's colors list is black (or white), then the procedure skips that color and begins generating patterns with the next color.
- uses the foreground color to outline every patterned area.

If the procedure needs additional patterns, PROC GBARLINE selects the next default pattern fill (empty) and rotates it through the colors list, skipping the foreground color as before. The procedure continues in this fashion until it has generated enough patterns for the chart.

Changing any of these conditions may change or override the default behavior:

- If you specify a colors list with the COLORS= option in a GOPTIONS statement and the list contains more than one color, then the procedure rotates the default solid pattern through that list, using every color, even if the foreground color is black (or white). The default outline color remains the foreground color.
- Whenever there are PATTERN definitions in effect, whether or not the GBARLINE procedure can use them, the default outline color for all patterns changes from foreground to SAME, as described in "User-Defined Patterns, Outlines, and Images" on page 748.

For a description of these graphics options, see Chapter 8, "Graphics Options and Device Parameters Dictionary," on page 261.

User-Defined Patterns, Outlines, and Images

You can use PATTERN statements to explicitly specify patterns, including color or fill type or both. You can also specify images to fill the bars. For complete information on all patterns, see "PATTERN Statement" on page 169. See also the section on controlling patterns and colors for each chart type.

When you use PATTERN statements, the procedure uses the specified patterns until all of the PATTERN definitions they generate have been used. Then, if more patterns are required, the procedure returns to the default pattern rotation.

Whenever you specify *any* PATTERN statement, the default pattern outline changes. Instead of the foreground color, the outline color is the same as the fill color; for example, a blue bar has a blue outline. The effect is the same as specifying COUTLINE=SAME. Even when the procedure runs out of user-defined patterns and generates default patterns, the outlines continue to match the interior pattern color.

To change the outline color of any pattern, whether it's a default or user-defined pattern, use the COUTLINE= option in the BAR statement that generates the chart.

You can use the PATTERN statement to fill specified bars with specified images. For details, see "Placing Images on the Bars of Two-Dimensional Bar Charts" on page 116.

You can also add background images. The IBACK= goption (see "IBACK" on page 317) specifies image files that fill the background area. For further information, including a listing of recognized image file types, see "Image File Types Supported by SAS/GRAPH" on page 106 and "Placing a Background Image" on page 113.

Version 6 Patterns

If you specify the V6COMP graphics option, then the procedure generates patterns by rotating the appropriate Version 6 default patterns through all of the colors in the colors list. With V6COMP, all patterns are outlined in the same color as the fill.

Note: The V6COMP graphics option is not supported by ActiveX for graphs generated by the GBARLINE procedure. △

Procedure Syntax

Requirements:
One BAR statement

Global statements: AXIS, FOOTNOTE, GOPTIONS, PATTERN, TITLE

Reminder: The procedure can include the BY, FORMAT, LABEL, and WHERE statements also.

Supports:
RUN-group processing
Output Delivery System (ODS)

Not supported by: Java

PROC GBARLINE <DATA=*input-data-set*>
<ANNOTATE=*Annotate-data-set*>
<IMAGEMAP=*output-data-set*>;

BAR *bar-variable* </*option(s)*>;

<**PLOT** </*option(s)*>;>

PROC GBARLINE Statement

Identifies the data set containing the chart variables. Optionally specifies annotation.

Requirements: An input data set is required.

Not supported by: Java

Syntax

PROC GBARLINE <DATA=*input-data-set*>
<ANNOTATE=*Annotate-data-set*>
<IMAGEMAP=*output-data-set*>;

Options

PROC GBARLINE statement options affect all graphs produced by the procedure.

ANNOTATE=*Annotate-data-set*
ANNO=*Annotate-data-set*

specifies a data set to annotate all graphs that are produced by the GBARLINE procedure. To annotate individual graphs, use the ANNOTATE= option in the BAR statement.

See also: Chapter 24, "Using Annotate Data Sets," on page 587

DATA=*input-data-set*

specifies the SAS data set that contains the variable(s) to chart. By default, the procedure uses the most recently created SAS data set.

See also: "SAS Data Sets" on page 29 and "About the Bar Variable" on page 742

IMAGEMAP=*output-data-set*

creates a temporary SAS data set that is used to generate an image map in an HTML output file. The information in the image map data set includes the shape and coordinates of the elements in the graph and drill-down URLs that have been associated with those elements. The drill-down URLs are provided by one or two variables in the input data set. These variables are identified to the GBARLINE procedure with the HTML= option.

The %IMAGEMAP macro generates the image map in the HTML output file. The macro takes two arguments, the name of the image map data set and the name or fileref of the HTML output file, as shown in the following example:

```
%imagemap(imgmapds, myimgmap.html);
```

BAR Statement

Creates vertical bar charts in which the height of the bars represents the value of the bar statistic for each category of data.

Requirements: One bar variable is required.

Global statements: AXIS, FOOTNOTE, PATTERN, TITLE

Supports: Drill-down functionality

Not supported by: Java

Description

The BAR statement specifies the variable that defines the categories of data to chart. These statements automatically

- determine the midpoints
- calculate the bar statistic for each midpoint (the default is FREQ)
- scale the response axis and the bars according to the statistic value
- determine bar width and spacing
- assign patterns to the bars; the default bar pattern is SOLID
- draw a frame around the axis area using the first color in the colors list.

You can use statement options to select or order the midpoints (bars), to control the tick marks on the response axis, to change the type of bar statistic, to display specific statistics, and to modify the appearance of the chart. You can also specify additional variables by which to sum the data.

In addition, you can

- use global statements to modify the axes and the bar patterns. See Chapter 7, "SAS/GRAPH Statements," on page 121 for more information.
- add titles and footnotes to the chart. See "TITLE, FOOTNOTE, and NOTE Statements" on page 210 for more information.
- use an Annotate data set to enhance the chart. See Chapter 24, "Using Annotate Data Sets," on page 587 for more information.
- display an image in the background of the chart. See "IBACK" on page 317 for more information.
- display images in the bars of the chart. See the IMAGE= option on page 171 for the PATTERN statement.

Syntax

BAR *bar-variable* <*/option(s)*>;

option(s) can be one or more options from any or all of the following categories:

- appearance options

  ANNOTATE=*Annotate-data-set*

  CAUTOREF=*reference-line-color*

  CAXIS=*axis-color*

  CERROR=*error-bar-color*

  CFRAME=*background-color*

  COUTLINE=*bar-outline-color* | SAME

CREF=*reference-line-color* | (*reference-line-color*) | *reference-line-color-list*
CTEXT=*text-color*
FRAME | NOFRAME
FRONTREF
LAUTOREF=*reference-line-type*
LREF=*reference-line-type* | (*reference-line-type*) | *reference-line-type-list*
PATTERNID=BY | MIDPOINT
SPACE=*bar-spacing*
WIDTH=*bar-width*
WOUTLINE=*bar-outline-width*

- statistic options
  - CFREQ
  - CLM=*confidence-level*
  - CPERCENT
  - ERRORBARS=BARS | BOTH | TOP
  - FREQ
  - FREQ=*numeric-variable*
  - INSIDE=*statistic*
  - MEAN
  - OUTSIDE=*statistic*
  - PERCENT
  - SUM
  - SUMVAR=*summary-variable*
  - TYPE=*statistic*
- midpoint options
  - DISCRETE
  - LEVELS=*number-of-midpoints*
  - MIDPOINTS=*value-list*
  - MIDPOINTS=OLD
  - MISSING
- axes options
  - ASCENDING
  - AUTOREF
  - AXIS=AXIS<1...99>
  - CLIPREF
  - DESCENDING
  - MAXIS=AXIS<1...99>
  - MINOR=*number-of-minor-ticks*
  - NOAXIS
  - NOBASEREF
  - NOZERO
  - RANGE
  - RAXIS=*value-list* | AXIS<1...99>
  - REF=*value-list*
- catalog entry description options

DESCRIPTION='*entry-description*'

NAME='*string*'

- ODS options

  HTML=*variable*

Required Arguments

bar-variable

specifies the variable that defines the categories of data to chart. The variable must be in the input data set.

See also: "About the Bar Variable" on page 742

Options

Options in the BAR statement affect all graphs that are produced by that statement. You can specify as many options as you want and list them in any order. For details on specifying colors, see Chapter 6, "SAS/GRAPH Colors and Images," on page 91. For details on specifying images, see "Specifying Images in SAS/GRAPH Programs" on page 106. For a complete description of the graphics options, see Chapter 8, "Graphics Options and Device Parameters Dictionary," on page 261.

ANNOTATE=*Annotate-data-set*
ANNO=*Annotate-data-set*

specifies a data set to annotate charts produced by the BAR statement.

See also: Chapter 24, "Using Annotate Data Sets," on page 587

ASCENDING

arranges the bars in ascending order of the value of the bar statistic. By default, bars are arranged in ascending order of midpoint value, without regard to the lengths of the bars. ASCENDING reorders the bars from shortest to longest. The ordering is left to right.

ASCENDING overrides any midpoint order specified in the MIDPOINTS= option or specified in the ORDER= option in an AXIS statement assigned to the midpoint axis.

AUTOREF

draws a reference line at each major tick mark on the chart (left) response axis. To draw reference lines at specific points on the response axis, use the REF= option.

By default, reference lines are drawn in front of the bars. To draw reference lines behind the bars, use the CLIPREF option.

AXIS=AXIS<1...99>

See RAXIS= on page 761.

CAUTOREF=*reference-line-color*

specifies the color of reference lines drawn at major tick marks, as determined by the AUTOREF option. The default color is either the value of the CAXIS= option or the first color in the color list. To specify a line type for these reference lines, use the LAUTOREF= option.

CAXIS=*axis-color*

specifies a color for the response and midpoint axis lines and for the default axis area frame. If you omit the CAXIS= option, PROC GBARLINE searches for a color specification in this order:

1 the COLOR= option in AXIS definitions

2 the first color in the colors list (the default).

CERROR=*error-bar-color*
specifies the color of error bars. The default is the color of the response axis, which is controlled by the CAXIS= option.

CFRAME=*background-color*
CFR=*background-color*
specifies the color with which to fill the axis area.

The axis area color does not affect the frame color, which is always the same as the midpoint axis line color and controlled by the CAXIS= option. By default, the axis area is not filled.

The CFRAME= option is overridden by the NOFRAME option.

Note: If the background color, the bar color, and the outline color are the same, then you will not be able to distinguish the bars. △

CFREQ
displays the cumulative frequency statistic above the bars. A maximum of two statistics can be printed. This option is ignored if the bars are too narrow to avoid overlapping values or if the FREQ option is specified.

See also: "About Chart Statistics" on page 745 and "Displaying Statistics In Bar Line Charts" on page 763

CLIPREF
clips the reference lines at the bars. This makes the reference lines appear to be behind the bars.

CLM=*confidence-level*
specifies the confidence intervals to use when drawing error bars. Values for *confidence-level* must be greater than or equal to 50 and strictly less than 100. The default is 95. See ERRORBAR= for details on how error bars are computed and drawn.

COUTLINE=*bar-outline-color* | SAME
outlines all bars or bar segments using the specified color. SAME specifies that the outline color of a bar is the same as the interior pattern color.

The default outline color depends on the PATTERN statement:

- If you do not specify a PATTERN statement, the default outline color is black for the ActiveX device. Otherwise, the default outline color is the foreground color (the first color in the colors list).
- If you specify the PATTERN statement or the V6COMP graphics option, the default is COUTLINE=SAME.

The COUTLINE= option is not valid when SHAPE=CYLINDER.

See also: "Controlling Bar Line Chart Patterns, Colors, and Images" on page 764 and "About Patterns" on page 748

CPERCENT
CPCT
displays the cumulative percentage statistic above the bars. A maximum of two statistics can be printed. This option is ignored if the bars are too narrow to avoid overlapping values or if the FREQ, CFREQ, or PERCENT option is specified.

See also: "About Chart Statistics" on page 745 and "Displaying Statistics In Bar Line Charts" on page 763

CREF=*reference-line-color* | (*reference-line-color*) | *reference-line-color-list*
CR=*reference-line-color* | (*reference-line-color*) | *reference-line-color-list*

specifies colors for reference lines. Specifying a single color without parentheses applies that color to all reference lines, including lines drawn with the AUTOREF and REF= options. The CAUTOREF= option overrides the CREF= reference line color for reference lines drawn with the AUTOREF option. Specifying a single color in parentheses applies that color only to the first reference line drawn with the REF= option. Specifying a reference color list applies colors in sequence to successive lines drawn with the REF= option. The syntax of the color list is of the form (*color1* color2 ...*colorN*) or (*color1*, *color2* ..., *colorN*). The default color for reference lines is either the value of the CAXIS= option or the first color in the color list. To specify line types for these reference lines, use the LREF= option.

CTEXT=*text-color*

specifies the color of all text on the chart that is not otherwise assigned a color. Text includes axis values and axis labels in the response and midpoint axes; and the displayed statistics. For the ActiveX device, the default color is black. For other devices, if you omit the CTEXT= option, PROC GBARLINE searches for a color specification in this order:

1 the CTEXT= option in a GOPTIONS statement

2 the first color in the colors list (the default).

The CTEXT= option overrides the color specification for the axis label and the tick mark values in the COLOR= option in an AXIS definition assigned to an axis.

The CTEXT= option is overridden by the COLOR= suboption of a LABEL= or VALUE= option in an AXIS definition assigned to an axis. In this case the suboption determines the color of the axis label or the color of the tick mark values, respectively.

DESCENDING

arranges the bars in descending order of the value of the bar statistic. By default, bars are arranged in ascending order of midpoint value, without regard to the lengths of the bars. DESCENDING reorders the bars from longest to shortest. The ordering is left to right.

DESCENDING overrides any midpoint order that is specified with the MIDPOINTS= option or that is specified in the ORDER= option in an AXIS statement assigned to the midpoint axis.

DESCRIPTION='*entry-description*'
DES='*entry-description*'

specifies the description of the catalog entry for the chart. The maximum length for the *entry-description* is 256 characters. The description does not appear on the chart. By default, the GBARLINE procedure assigns a description of the form GBARLINE CHART OF *variable*, where *variable* is the name of the bar variable.

The *entry-description* can include the #BYLINE, #BYVAL, and #BYVAR substitution options, which work as they do when used on TITLE, FOOTNOTE, and NOTE statements. Refer to the description of the options on page 222 and to "Substituting BY Line Values in a Text String" on page 226. The 256-character limit applies before the substitution takes place for these options; thus, if in the SAS program the entry-description text exceeds 256 characters, it is truncated to 256 characters, and then the substitution is performed.

The descriptive text is shown in each of the following:

- the "description" portion of the Results window
- the catalog-entry properties that you can view from the Explorer window
- the Table of Contents that is generated when you use CONTENTS= on an ODS statement (see "Linking to Output through a Table of Contents" on page 495), assuming the GBARLINE output is generated while the contents page is open
- the Description field of the PROC GREPLAY window.

DISCRETE
treats a numeric bar variable as a discrete variable rather than as a continuous variable. The GBARLINE procedure creates a separate midpoint and, hence, a separate bar for each unique value of the bar variable. If the bar variable has a format associated with it, then each formatted value is treated as a midpoint.

The LEVELS= option is ignored when you use DISCRETE. The MIDPOINTS= option overrides DISCRETE. The ORDER= option in an AXIS statement that is assigned to the midpoint axis can rearrange or exclude discrete midpoint values.

ERRORBAR=BARS | BOTH | TOP
draws confidence intervals for either of the following:

- □ the mean of the SUMVAR= variable for each midpoint if you specify TYPE=MEAN
- □ the percentage of observations assigned to each midpoint if you specify TYPE=PCT with no SUMVAR= option.

The ERRORBAR= option cannot be used with values of the TYPE= option other than MEAN or PCT. Valid values for ERRORBAR= are:

BARS
draws error bars as bars half the width of the main bars.

BOTH
draws error bars as two ticks joined by a line (default).

TOP
draws the error bar as a tick for the upper confidence limit that is joined to the top of the bar by a line.

By default, ERRORBAR= uses a confidence level of 95 percent. You can specify different confidence levels with the CLM= option.

When you use ERRORBAR= with TYPE=PCT, the confidence interval is based on a normal approximation. Let TOTAL be the total number of observations, and PCT be the percentage assigned to a given midpoint. The standard error of the percentage is approximated as

```
APSTDERR=100 * SQRT((PCT/100) * (1--(PCT/100)) / TOTAL);
```

Let LEVEL be the confidence level specified using the CLM= option, with a default value of 95. The upper confidence limit for the percentage is computed as

```
UCLP = PCT + APSTDERR * PROBIT( 1-(1-LEVEL/100)/2 );
```

The lower confidence limit for the percentage is computed as

```
LCLP = PCT - APSTDERR * PROBIT( 1-(1-LEVEL/100)/2 );
```

When you use ERRORBAR= with TYPE=MEAN, the sum variable must have at least two non-missing values for each midpoint. Let N be the number of observations assigned to a midpoint, MEAN be the mean of those observations, and STD be the standard deviation of the observations. The standard error of the mean is computed as

```
STDERR = STD / SQRT(N);
```

Let LEVEL be the confidence level specified using the CLM= option, with a default value of 95. The upper confidence limit for the mean is computed as

```
UCLM = MEAN + STDERR * TINV( 1-(1-LEVEL/100)/2, N-1);
```

The lower confidence limit for the mean is computed as

```
LCLM = MEAN - STDERR * TINV( 1-(1-LEVEL/100)/2, N-1);
```

If you want the error bars to represent a given number C of standard errors instead of a confidence interval, and if the number of observations assigned to each midpoint is the same, then you can find the appropriate value for the CLM= option by running a DATA step. For example, if you want error bars that represent one standard error (C=1) with a sample size of N , you can run the following DATA step to compute the appropriate value for the CLM= option and assign that value to a macro variable &LEVEL:

```
data null;
c = 1;
n = 10;
level = 100 * (1 - 2 * (1 - probt( c, n-1)));
put all;
call symput('level',put(level,best12.));
run;
```

Then when you run the GBARLINE procedure, you can specify CLM=&LEVEL.

Note that this trick does not work precisely if different midpoints have different numbers of observations. However, choosing an average value for N may yield sufficiently accurate results for graphical purposes if the sample sizes are large or do not vary much.

FRAME | NOFRAME
FR | NOFR

specifies whether the axis area frame is drawn. The default is FRAME, which draws a frame around the axis area. Specifying NOFRAME removes the axis area frame, including any background color or image. To remove one or more axis elements, use either the AXIS statement or the NOAXIS option.

The NOFRAME option overrides the CFRAME= option and "IBACK" on page 317.

The color of the frame or backplane outline is the color of the midpoint axis, which is determined by the CAXIS= option.

If the V6COMP graphics option is in effect, the default value for GRSEGs is NOFRAME. See "Version 6 Patterns" on page 749 for more information.

FREQ

displays the frequency statistic above the bars. Non-integer values are rounded down to the nearest integer. A maximum of two statistics can be printed. This option is ignored if the bars are too narrow to avoid overlapping values. This option overrides the CFREQ, PERCENT, CPERCENT, SUM, and MEAN options.

See also: "About Chart Statistics" on page 745 and "Displaying Statistics In Bar Line Charts" on page 763

FREQ=*numeric-variable*

specifies a variable whose values weight the contribution of each observation in the computation of the bar statistic. Each observation is counted the number of times that is specified by the value of *numeric-variable* for that observation. If the value of *numeric-variable* is missing, 0, or negative, then the observation is not used in the statistic calculation. Non-integer values of *numeric-variable* are truncated to integers. The FREQ= option is valid with all bar statistics.

Because you cannot use TYPE=PERCENT, TYPE=CPERCENT, TYPE=FREQ, or TYPE=CFREQ with the SUMVAR= option, you must use the FREQ= option to calculate percentages, cumulative percentages, frequencies, or cumulative frequencies based on a sum.

The statistics will not be affected by applying a format to *numeric-variable*.

Not supported by: ActiveX, Java

See also: "Calculating Weighted Statistics" on page 746

FRONTREF
specifies that reference lines drawn by the AUTOREF or REF= options should be drawn in front of the bars.

HTML=*variable*
identifies the variable in the input data set whose values create links in the HTML file created by the ODS statement. These links are associated with the bars and point to the data or graph you wish to display when the user drills down on the area. The values of *variable* can be up to 1024 characters long. Characters after the 1024-character limit (including any closing quotes) are truncated.

INSIDE=*statistic*
displays the values of the specified statistic inside the bars. *Statistic* can be one of the following:

- FREQ
- CFREQ
- PERCENT | PCT
- CPERCENT | CPCT
- SUM
- MEAN

To display statistics with INSIDE=SUM or INSIDE=MEAN, you must also specify the SUMVAR= option.

See also: "About Chart Statistics" on page 745 and "Displaying Statistics In Bar Line Charts" on page 763

LAUTOREF=*reference-line-type*
specifies a line type for reference lines drawn at major tick marks, as specified by the AUTOREF option. The *reference-line-type* value can be a whole number from 1 to 46. A value of 1 specifies a solid line; values 2 through 46 specify dashed lines. The default value 1 draws a solid line. To specify colors for these reference lines, use the CAUTOREF= option.

LEVELS=*number-of-midpoints*
specifies the number of midpoints for a numeric bar variable. The range for each midpoint is calculated automatically, using the algorithm in Terrell and Scott (1985). The LEVELS= option is ignored if

- the bar variable is character type
- the DISCRETE option is used
- the MIDPOINTS= option is used.

Featured in: Example 1 on page 768

LREF=*reference-line-type* | (*reference-line-type* | *reference-line-type-list*)
LR=*reference-line-type* | (*reference-line-type* | *reference-line-type-list*)
specifies line types for reference lines. Line types are specified as whole numbers from 1 to 46, with 1 representing a solid line and the other values representing dashed lines. Specifying a line type without parentheses applies that type to all reference lines drawn with the AUTOREF and REF= options. Note that the LAUTOREF= option overrides LREF=*reference-line-type* for reference lines drawn with the AUTOREF option. Specifying a single line type in parentheses applies that line type to the first reference line drawn with the REF= option. Specifying a line type list applies line types in sequence to successive reference lines drawn with the REF= option. The syntax of the line-type list is of the form (*type1 type2 ...typeN*). The default line type is specified by the AXIS statement's STYLE= option. By default, STYLE=1, a solid line. To specify colors for these reference lines, use the CREF= option.

MAXIS=AXIS<1...99>
assigns the specified AXIS definition to the midpoint axis. The MAXIS= option is ignored if the specified AXIS definition does not exist.

See also: "AXIS Statement" on page 124 and "About Midpoints" on page 742

MEAN
displays the mean statistic above the bars. A maximum of two statistics can be printed. This option is ignored if the bars are too narrow to avoid overlapping values or if the FREQ, CFREQ, PERCENT, CPERCENT, or SUM option is specified. MEAN is ignored unless you also use the SUMVAR= option.

See also: "About Chart Statistics" on page 745 and "Displaying Statistics In Bar Line Charts" on page 763

MIDPOINTS=*value-list*
specifies the midpoint values for the bars. The way you specify *value-list* depends on the type of the bar variable.

- For numeric bar variables, *value-list* is either an explicit list of values, or a starting and an ending value with an interval increment, or a combination of both forms:

  n <...*n*>

  n TO *n* <BY *increment*>

  n<...*n*> TO *n* <BY *increment*> <*n* <...*n*>>

  If a numeric variable has an associated format, the specified values must be the *unformatted* values.

  By default, numeric variable values are treated as continuous (if you omit the DISCRETE option), and

  - the lowest midpoint consolidates all data points from negative infinity to the median of the first two midpoints
  - the highest midpoint consolidates all data points from the median of the last two midpoints up to infinity
  - all other values in *value-list* specify the median of a range of values, and the GBARLINE procedure calculates the midpoint values.

  If you include the DISCRETE option, then each value in *value-list* specifies a unique numeric value.

- For character bar variables, *value-list* is a list of unique character values enclosed in quotation marks and separated by blanks:

  'value-1' <...*'value-n'*>

  If a character variable has an associated format, the specified values must be the *formatted* values.

For a complete description of *value-list*, see ORDER= on page 130.

If the *value-list* for either type of variable specifies so many midpoints that the axis values overwrite each other, then the values may be unreadable. In this case the procedure writes a warning to the SAS log. On many devices, this problem can be corrected by either adjusting the size of the text with the HTEXT= graphics option or by increasing the number of cells in your graphics display using the HPOS= and VPOS= graphics options.

The ORDER= option in the AXIS statement overrides the order specified in the MIDPOINTS= option. The BAR statement options ASCENDING and DESCENDING also override both the MIDPOINTS= and ORDER= options in the AXIS statement.

See also: "About Midpoints" on page 742

MIDPOINTS=OLD
generates default midpoints using the Nelder algorithm (*Applied Statistics* 25:94–7, 1976). The MIDPOINTS=OLD option is ignored unless the bar variable is numeric.

MINOR=*number-of-minor-ticks*
specifies the number of minor tick marks between each major tick mark on the bar response axis.

The MINOR= option in a bar chart statement overrides the number of minor tick marks specified in the MINOR= option in an AXIS definition assigned to the response axis with the RAXIS= option.

MISSING
accepts a missing value as a valid midpoint for the bar variable. By default, observations with missing values are ignored.

NAME='*string*'
specifies the name of the catalog entry for the graph. The maximum length for entry-name is eight characters. The default name is GBARLIN. If the name duplicates an existing entry name, then SAS/GRAPH software uses a number to generate a unique name—for example, GBARLIN1.

NOAXIS
suppresses all axes, including axis lines, axis labels, axis values, and all major and minor tick marks. If you specify an axis definition with the MAXIS= or RAXIS= options, then the axes are generated as defined in the AXIS statement, but then all lines, labels, values, and tick marks are suppressed. Therefore, axis statement options such as ORDER=, LENGTH=, and OFFSET= will still be used.

To remove only selected axis elements such as lines, values, or labels, use specific AXIS statement options.

NOAXIS does not suppress either the default frame or an axis area fill requested by the CFRAME= option. To remove the axis frame, use the NOFRAME option in the procedure.

NOBASEREF
suppresses the zero reference line when the SUM or MEAN bar statistic has negative values.

NOZERO
suppresses any midpoints for which there are no corresponding values of the bar variable and, hence, no bar.

Note: If a bar is omitted and if you have also specified bar labels with the VALUE= option in an AXIS statement, then the labels can be shifted and not displayed with the correct bar. △

OUTSIDE=*statistic*
displays the values of the specified statistic above the bars. *Statistic* can be one of the following:

- FREQ
- CFREQ
- PERCENT | PCT
- CPERCENT | CPCT
- SUM
- MEAN

To display statistics with OUTSIDE=SUM or OUTSIDE=MEAN, you must also specify the SUMVAR= option.

See also: "About Chart Statistics" on page 745 and "Displaying Statistics In Bar Line Charts" on page 763

PATTERNID=BY | MIDPOINT

specifies the way fill patterns are assigned. By default, PATTERNID=MIDPOINT. Values for PATTERNID= are as follows:

BY

changes patterns each time the value of the BY variable changes. All bars use the same pattern if the GBARLINE procedure does not include a BY statement.

MIDPOINT

changes patterns every time the midpoint value changes.

See also: "Controlling Bar Line Chart Patterns, Colors, and Images" on page 764

PERCENT
PCT

displays the percentages of observations having a given value for the bar variable above the bars. A maximum of two statistics can be printed. This option is ignored if the bars are too narrow to avoid overlapping values or if the FREQ or CFREQ option is specified.

See also: "About Chart Statistics" on page 745 and "Displaying Statistics In Bar Line Charts" on page 763

RANGE

displays on the axis of the chart the range of numeric values represented by each bar. In the graphics output, the less-than symbol (<) and the less-than-or-equal-to symbol (<=) are used to accurately specify the starting and ending values of each range. The RANGE option has no affect on axes that represent character data. By default, the values shown on the axis are determined by the value of the MIDPOINTS= option on page 759. If specified, the DISCRETE option on page 756 overrides the RANGE option.

RAXIS=*value-list* | AXIS<1...99>
AXIS=*value-list* | AXIS<1...99>

specifies values for the major tick mark divisions on the response axis or assigns the specified AXIS definition to the axis. See the MIDPOINTS= option on page 759 for a description of *value-list*. By default, the GBARLINE procedure scales the response axis automatically and provides an appropriate number of tick marks.

You can specify negative values, but negative values are reasonable only when TYPE=SUM or TYPE=MEAN and one or more of the sums or means are less than 0. Frequency and percentage values are never less than 0.

For lists of values, a separate major tick mark is created for each individual value. A warning message is written to the SAS log if the values are not evenly spaced.

If the values represented by the bars are larger than the highest tick mark value, then the bars are truncated at the highest tick mark.

See also: "AXIS Statement" on page 124

REF=*value-list*

draws reference lines at the specified points on the bar response axis. See the MIDPOINTS= option on page 759 for a description of *value-list*.

Values can be listed in any order, but should be within the range of values represented by the response axis. A warning is written to the SAS log if any of the points are off of the axis, and no reference line is drawn for such points. You can use the AUTOREF option to draw reference lines automatically at all of the major tick marks.

SPACE=*bar-spacing*
specifies the amount of space between individual bars. *Bar-spacing* can be any non-negative number, including decimal values. Units are character cells. By default, the GBARLINE procedure calculates spacing based on the size of the axis area and the number of bars on the chart. Use SPACE=0 to leave no space between adjacent bars.

The SPACE= option is ignored if the specified spacing requests a chart that is too large to fit in the space available for the midpoint axis, and a warning message is issued.

SUM
displays the sum statistic above the bars. A maximum of two statistics can be printed. This option is ignored if the bars are too narrow to avoid overlapping values or if the FREQ, CFREQ, PERCENT, or CPERCENT option is specified. SUM is ignored unless you also use the SUMVAR= option.

See also: "About Chart Statistics" on page 745 and "Displaying Statistics In Bar Line Charts" on page 763

SUMVAR=*summary-variable*
specifies a numeric variable for sum or mean calculations. The GBARLINE procedure calculates the sum or, if requested, the mean of *summary-variable* for each midpoint. The resulting statistics are represented by the length of the bars along the response axis, and they are displayed at major tick marks.

When you use the SUMVAR= option, the TYPE= option must be either SUM or MEAN. With the SUMVAR= option, the default is TYPE=SUM.

Featured in: Example 1 on page 768

TYPE=*statistic*
specifies the bar statistic.

- If the SUMVAR= option is not used, *statistic* can be one of the following:

  FREQ
  frequency (the default)

  CFREQ
  cumulative frequency

  PERCENT PCT
  percentage

  CPERCENT CPCT
  cumulative percentage

- If the SUMVAR= option is used, *statistic* can be:

  SUM
  sum (the default)

  MEAN
  mean

Because you cannot use TYPE=FREQ, TYPE=CFREQ, TYPE=PERCENT, or TYPE=CPERCENT with the SUMVAR= option, you must use the FREQ= option to calculate percentages, cumulative percentages, frequencies, or cumulative frequencies based on a sum. See also "Calculating Weighted Statistics" on page 746.

See also: "About Chart Statistics" on page 745 for a complete description of statistic types

WIDTH=*bar-width*
specifies the width of the bars. By default, the GBARLINE procedure selects a bar width that accommodates the midpoint values displayed on the midpoint axis using a

hardware font and a height of one cell. Units for *bar-width* are character cells. The value for *bar-width* must be greater than 0, but it does not have to be an integer, for example,

```
bar site / width=1.5;
```

If the requested bar width results in a chart that is too large to fit in the space available for the midpoint axis, then the procedure issues a warning in the log and ignores the WIDTH= specification. If the specified width is too narrow, the procedure may display the midpoint values vertically.

WOUTLINE=*bar-outline-width*
specifies the width of the bar outline in pixels.

The Bar Statistic and the Response Axis

In bar line charts, the scale of values of the bar statistic is displayed on the left response axis. By default, the response axis is divided into evenly spaced intervals identified with major tick marks that are labeled with the corresponding statistic value. Minor tick marks are evenly distributed between the major tick marks unless a log axis has been requested. For sum and mean statistics, the major tick marks are labeled with values of the SUMVAR= variable (formatted if the variable has an associated format). The response axis is also labeled with the statistic type.

Displaying Statistics In Bar Line Charts

Statistic values on bar line charts are not printed by default, so you must explicitly request a statistic with the FREQ, CFREQ, PERCENT, CPERCENT, SUM, MEAN, INSIDE=, or OUTSIDE= option.

For graphs generated with the ActiveX device, you can display one statistic for each bar. For graphs generated with other devices, you can display up to two statistics for each bar. Statistics can be displayed either above the bars or inside the bars.

To specify a statistic that you want to display above the bars, specify the statistic option (FREQ, CFREQ, PERCENT, CPERCENT, SUM, or MEAN) or specify OUTSIDE=*statistic*. To specify a statistic that you want to display inside the bars, specify INSIDE=*statistic*.

For graphs generated with the ActiveX device, the OUTSIDE= option overrides INSIDE=, and INSIDE= overrides the FREQ, CFREQ, PERCENT, CPERCENT, SUM, and MEAN options. For graphs generated with other devices, the individual statistic options override the OUTSIDE= option.

If more than one statistic option is specified, only the highest priority statistic is displayed. The priority order, from highest to lowest, is as follows:

1 FREQ
2 CFREQ
3 PERCENT
4 CPERCENT
5 SUM
6 MEAN

The bars must be wide enough to accommodate the text. You can adjust the width of the bars with the WIDTH= option. To control the font and size of the text, use the HTEXT= and FTEXT= graphics options.

Ordering and Selecting Midpoints

To rearrange character or discrete numeric midpoint values or to select ranges for numeric values, use the MIDPOINTS= option. Remember that although changing the number of midpoints for numeric variables may change the range of values for individual midpoints, it does not change the range of values for the chart as a whole. For details, see "About Midpoints" on page 742.

Like the MIDPOINTS= option, the ORDER= option in the AXIS statement can rearrange the order of the midpoints or suppress the display of discrete numeric or character values. However, the ORDER= option cannot calculate the midpoints for a continuous numeric variable, or exclude values from the calculations. For details, see the description of the ORDER= option on page 130.

Controlling Bar Line Chart Patterns, Colors, and Images

Default Patterns and Outlines

Each bar in a bar line chart is filled with a pattern. By default, the procedure

- fills the bars with bar patterns, beginning with the default fill, SOLID, and rotating it through the colors list. When the solid patterns are exhausted, the procedure selects the next default bar pattern (empty) and rotates it through the colors list. It continues in this fashion until all of the required patterns have been assigned.

  If you use the device's default colors and the first color in the list is either black or white, then the procedure does not create a pattern in that color. If you specify a colors list with the COLORS= graphics option, then the procedure uses all the colors in the list to generate the patterns.
- outlines bars using the first color in the colors list.

See "About Patterns" on page 748 for more information on how the GBARLINE procedure assigns default patterns and outlines.

User-Defined Patterns

To override the default patterns and select fills and colors for the bars, use the PATTERN statement. Only solid and empty bar patterns are valid; all other pattern fills are ignored. For a complete description of all bar patterns, see the VALUE= option on page 171.

Whenever you use PATTERN statements, the default pattern outline color changes to SAME. That is, the outline color is the same as the fill color. To specify the outline color, use the COUTLINE= option (see COUTLINE= on page 754).

When Patterns Change

The PATTERNID= option controls when the pattern changes. By default, PATTERNID=MIDPOINT, which specifies that the pattern changes every time the midpoint value changes.

Instead of changing the pattern for each midpoint, you can change the pattern for each BY group by changing the value of the PATTERNID= option. See the PATTERNID= option on page 761 for details.

Axis Color

By default, axis elements use the first color in the colors list or the colors that are specified by AXIS statement color options. However, BAR statement options can also control the color of the axis lines, text, and frame.

To change the color of...	Use this option...
the axis text	CTEXT=
the axis lines	CAXIS=
the area within the frame	CFRAME=

Adding Images to Bar Line Charts

You can apply images to the bars and to the backplane frame of bar line charts developed with the BAR statement. For details, see "Specifying Images in SAS/GRAPH Programs" on page 106.

PLOT Statement

Creates a plot overlay on top of the bar line chart.

Requirements: If specified, the PLOT statement must be specified after the BAR statement.

Global statements: AXIS, FOOTNOTE, PATTERN, SYMBOL, TITLE

Supports: Drill-down functionality

Not supported by: Java

Description

The PLOT statement specifies one plot request. This statement automatically

- scales the plot response (right) axis to include the maximum and minimum data values
- plots data points within the axis
- labels the plot response axis with the name of its variable and displays each major tick mark value.

You can use statement options to specify a plot variable, manipulate the plot response axis, modify the appearance of your graph, and describe catalog entries. You can use SYMBOL definitions to modify plot symbols for the data points, join data points, or specify other types of interpolations. For more information on the SYMBOL statement, see "SYMBOL Statement" on page 183.

In addition, you can use global statements to modify the axis, or add titles, footnotes, and notes to the plot.

Syntax

PLOT *</options(s)>*;

The PLOT statement is optional, but if specified, it must follow the BAR statement. If you do not specify a PLOT statement, GBARLINE generates only a bar chart and duplicates the bar response axis (left axis) as the plot response axis (right axis).

To specify a variable to plot, use the SUMVAR= option. If you do not specify a plot variable, GBARLINE uses the bar variable as the plot variable. For more information, see "About the Plot Variable" on page 745 and the description of the SUMVAR= option.

option(s) can be one or more options from any or all of the following categories:

- appearance options:

  NOLINE

  NOMARKER

- statistic options:
  - CFREQ
  - CPERCENT
  - FREQ
  - FREQ=*numeric-variable*
  - MEAN
  - PERCENT
  - SUM
  - SUMVAR=*plot-variable*
  - TYPE=*statistic*
- axes options:
  - ASCENDING
  - AXIS=AXIS<1...99>
  - DESCENDING
  - RAXIS=*value-list* | AXIS<1...99>
  - MINOR=*number-of-minor-ticks*
- ODS options:
  - HTML=*variable*

Options

You can specify as many options as you want and list them in any order.

ASCENDING
joins the plot points in ascending order of the value of the plot statistic. By default, data points are joined in ascending order of the midpoint value.

AXIS=AXIS<1...99>
See RAXIS= on page 767.

DESCENDING
joins the plot points in descending order of the value of the plot statistic. By default, plot points are arranged in ascending order of the midpoint value.

FREQ=*numeric-variable*
specifies a variable whose values weight the contribution of each observation in the computation of the plot statistic. Each observation is counted the number of times that is specified by the value of *numeric-variable* for that observation. If the value of *numeric-variable* is missing, 0, or negative, then the observation is not used in the statistic calculation. Non-integer values of *numeric-variable* are truncated to integers. The FREQ= option is valid with all plot statistics.

Because you cannot use TYPE=PERCENT, TYPE=CPERCENT, TYPE=FREQ, or TYPE=CFREQ with the SUMVAR= option, you must use the FREQ= option to calculate percentages, cumulative percentages, frequencies, or cumulative frequencies based on a sum.

The statistics will not be affected by applying a format to *numeric-variable*.

Not supported by: ActiveX, Java

HTML=*variable*
identifies the variable in the input data set whose values create links in the HTML file created by the ODS statement. These links are associated with the plot points. The links point to the data or graph that you wish to display when the user drills down on the plot point or area. The values of *variable* can be up to 1024 characters

long. Characters after the 1024-character limit (including any closing quotes) are truncated.

Note: This option is supported only by the ActiveX device drivers. △

MINOR=*number-of-minor-ticks*
specifies the number of minor tick marks that are drawn between each major tick mark on the plot response axis. Minor tick marks are not labeled. The MINOR= option overrides the NUMBER= suboption of the MINOR= option in an AXIS definition. You must specify a positive number.

NOLINE
suppresses the drawing of the line plot overlay, regardless of what is specified in the SYMBOL statement.

NOMARKER
suppressed the drawing of the marker symbol, regardless of what is specified in the SYMBOL statement.

RAXIS=*value-list* | AXIS<1...99>
AXIS=*value-list* | AXIS<1...99>
specifies the major tick mark values for the plot (right) response axis or assigns an AXIS definition.

The way you specify *value-list* depends on the type of variable:

- *For numeric variables*, *value-list* is either an explicit list of values, or a starting and an ending value with an interval increment, or a combination of both forms:

  n <...*n*>

  n TO *n* <BY *increment*>

  n <...*n*> TO *n* <BY *increment* > <*n* <...*n*> >

  If a numeric variable has an associated format, the specified values must be the *unformatted* values.

- *For date-time values*, *value-list* includes any SAS date, time, or datetime value described for the SAS functions INTCK and INTNX, shown here as *SAS-value*:

  '*SAS-value*'i < ...'*SAS-value*'i>

  '*SAS-value*'i TO '*SAS-value*' i<BY *interval*>

SUMVAR=*plot-variable*
specifies the variable to plot. *Plot-variable*, if specified, must be numeric. The GBARLINE procedure calculates the sum or, if requested, the mean of *plot-variable* for each midpoint.

When you use the SUMVAR= option, the TYPE= option must be either SUM or MEAN. With the SUMVAR= option, the default is TYPE=SUM.

Featured in: Example 1 on page 768

See also: "About the Plot Variable" on page 745

TYPE=*statistic*
specifies the plot statistic.

- If the SUMVAR= option is not used, *statistic* can be one of the following:

  FREQ
  frequency (the default)

  CFREQ
  cumulative frequency

PERCENT PCT
: percentage

CPERCENT CPCT
: cumulative percentage

- If SUMVAR= is used, *statistic* can be one of the following:

SUM
: sum (the default)

MEAN
: mean

Because you cannot use TYPE=FREQ, TYPE=CFREQ, TYPE=PERCENT, or TYPE=CPERCENT with SUMVAR=, you must use FREQ= to calculate percentages or frequencies based on a sum.

See also: “About Chart Statistics” on page 745 and “Calculating Weighted Statistics” on page 746

About SYMBOL Definitions

SYMBOL statements control the appearance of plot symbols and lines, and define interpolation methods. They can specify

- the shape, size, and color of the plot symbols that mark the data points
- plot line style, color, and width
- an interpolation method for plotting data
- how missing values are treated in interpolation calculations.

SYMBOL definitions are assigned either by default by the GBARLINE procedure or explicitly with a plot request.

If no SYMBOL definition is currently in effect, the GBARLINE procedure produces a join interpolation using the default plot symbol. The default plot symbol for ActiveX device drivers is the square. For other devices, the default symbol is the plus sign (+).

See “SYMBOL Statement” on page 183 for a complete discussion of the features of the SYMBOL statement.

Examples

Example 1: Producing a Basic Bar Line Graph with Styles

Procedure Features:

BAR statement options:

SUMVAR=
DISCRETE

PLOT statement options:

SUMVAR=

Other Features:

INFORMAT statement

FORMAT statement

STYLE= option on the ODS statement

Sample library member: GBLSTOCK

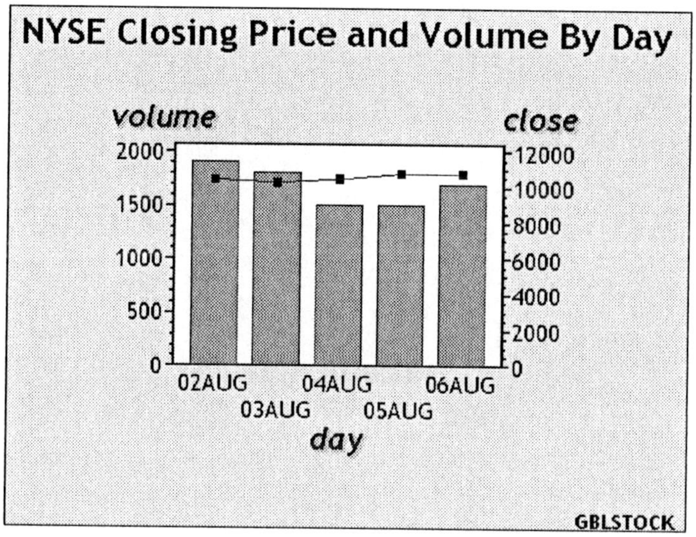

This example produces a basic bar line graph showing the volume and closing price for each of five days of trading activity on the New York Stock Exchange. The vertical bars indicate the volume, and the overlay plot graphs the closing price. It uses the ODS style ANALYSIS.

Set the graphics environment. Some graphics options may override style attributes, so if you are using a style, specify the minimum goptions needed by your graph.

```
goptions reset=all device=activex;
```

Define the odsout fileref. Specify the path of the HTML file where you want ODS to write the output.

```
filename odsout 'C:\your_web_path\';
```

Open the HTML output destination and specify the ANALYSIS style.

```
ods html file='gblstock.htm' path=odsout style=analysis;
```

Create the data set NYSE. NYSE contains one observation for each of five workdays. Each observation includes the date, closing price, and volume.

```
data nyse;
        informat day date9.;
        format day date5.;
        input day $ high low close volume;
```

```
        volume=volume/1000;
datalines;
02AUG2002 10478.76 10346.24 10426.91 1908809
03AUG2002 11042.92 10298.44 10274.65 1807543
04AUG2002 10498.22 10400.31 10456.43 1500656
05AUG2002 10694.47 10636.32 10762.98 1498403
06AUG2002 10801.12 10695.13 10759.48 1695602
;
run;
```

Define the title and footnote.

```
title1 "NYSE Closing Price and Volume By Day";
footnote j=r h=2 'GBLSTOCK';
```

Produce the bar line graph. The SUMVAR= option on the BAR statement specifies the variable whose values determine the height of the bars. The DISCRETE option creates a separate midpoint for each unique value of the bar variable. The SUMVAR= option on the PLOT statement specifies the variable whose values are used to calculate the overlay plot.

```
proc gbarline data=nyse;
        bar day / sumvar=volume discrete;
        plot / sumvar=close;
        run;
quit;
```

Close the ODS HTML destination. You must close the HTML destination before you can view the output with a browser.

```
ods html close;
```

Example 2: Calculating Weighted Statistics

Procedure Features:

BAR statement options:

- AXIS=
- DESCENDING
- SUMVAR=

PLOT statement options:

- ASCENDING
- AXIS=
- FREQ=
- SUMVAR=

Other Features:

AXIS statement

SYMBOL statement

Sample library member: GBLWTSTA

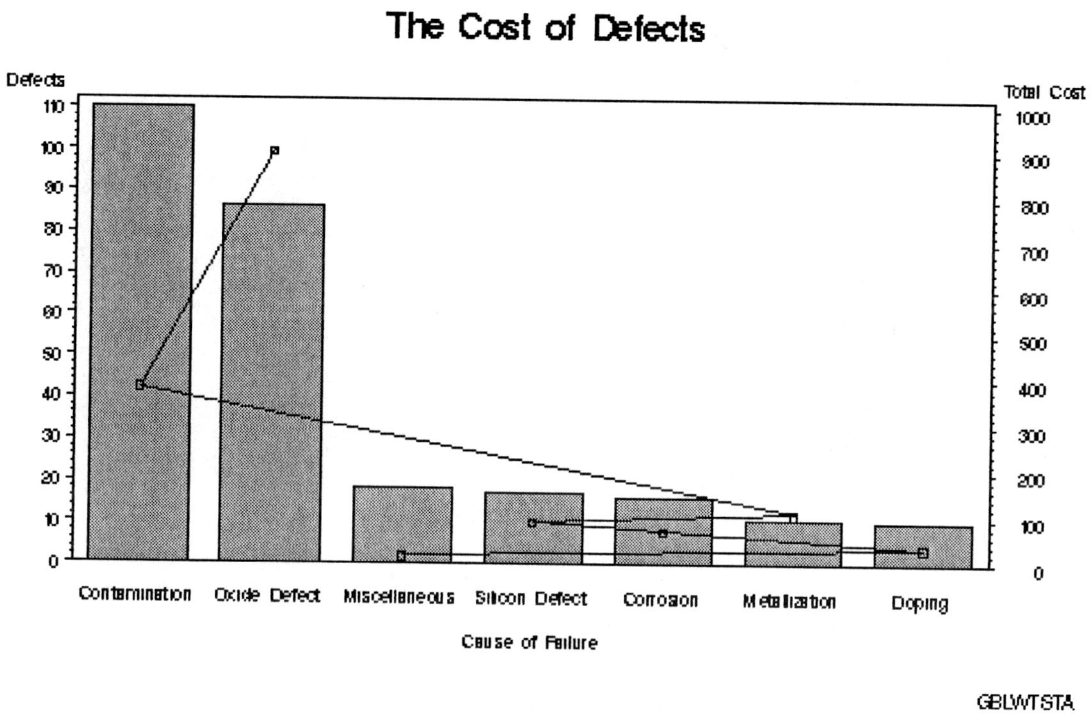

This example uses the FREQ= option to calculate weighted statistics for the overlay plot. During the manufacture of a metal-oxide semiconductor (MOS) capacitor, two different cleaning processes were used by two manufacturing systems that were operating in parallel. Process A used a standard cleaning solution, while Process B used a different cleaning mixture that contained less particulate matter. For five consecutive days, the causes of failure with each process were recorded.

Set the graphics environment.

```
goptions reset=all gunit=pct border cback=white
         ftitle=swissb ftext=swiss htitle=5
         htext=2;
```

Create the data set FAILURE. Each observation specifies the manufacturing process that resulted in the defect, the date, the cause of the defects, and the total number of defects for that date. Each observation also contains a variable, COST, that specifies the cost associated with that type of defect.

```
data failure;
   label  cause   = 'Cause of Failure' ;
   input  process $ 1-9 day $ 13-19 cause $ 23-36 count 40-41;
   datalines;
Process A   March 1   Contamination    15
Process A   March 1   Corrosion         2
Process A   March 1   Doping            1
Process A   March 1   Metallization     2
...more data lines...
Process B   March 5   Metallization     0
Process B   March 5   Miscellaneous     1
```

```
Process B   March 5   Oxide Defect       8
Process B   March 5   Silicon Defect     2
;
run;

data failure;
   set failure;
   if       cause='Contamination'  then cost=3.5;
   else if cause='Metallization'  then cost=10;
   else if cause='Oxide Defect'   then cost=10.5;
   else if cause='Corrosion'      then cost=4.5;
   else if cause='Doping'         then cost=3.6;
   else if cause='Silicon Defect' then cost=5.4;
   else                                cost=1.0;
   output;
run;
```

Define the title and footnote.

```
title1 "The Cost of Defects";
footnote j=r h=3 'GBLWTSTA ';
```

Define the labels for the axes.

```
AXIS1 label=("Defects");
AXIS2 label=("Total Cost");
```

Specify the symbol, color, and symbol size to use for the overlay plot.

```
symbol1 v=square c=black h=2;
```

Produce the bar line graph. The SUMVAR= option on the BAR statement specifies the variable that determines the height of the bars. The SUMVAR= option on the PLOT statement specifies the plot variable. GBARLINE multiplies the value of the FREQ= variable by the value of the COUNT variable, and uses the result to determine the plot points.

```
proc gbarline data=failure;
   bar cause / sumvar=count
               axis=axis1
               descending;
   plot / sumvar=count
          freq=cost
          axis=axis2
          ascending;
run;
quit;
```

CHAPTER 29

The GCHART Procedure

Overview

The GCHART procedure produces six types of charts: block charts, horizontal and vertical bar charts, pie and donut charts, and star charts. These charts graphically represent the value of a statistic calculated for one or more variables in an input SAS data set. The charted variables can be either numeric or character.

The procedure calculates these statistics:

- frequency or cumulative frequency counts
- percentages or cumulative percentages
- sums
- means.

Use the GCHART procedure to

- display and compare exact and relative magnitudes
- examine the contribution of parts to the whole
- analyze where data are out of balance.

About Block Charts

Block charts display the relative magnitude of data with blocks of varying height, each set in a square that represents a category of data (midpoint). Because block charts do not use axes, they are most useful when the relative magnitude of the blocks is more significant than the exact magnitude of any particular block.

Figure 29.1 on page 774 shows a simple block chart of total sales for three manufacturing sites. Each site is a midpoint and occupies one square. The name of the site (the midpoint value) is printed below the square. Midpoint values are, by default, arranged in ascending order from left to right. The label below the midpoint grid names the chart variable.

Sales for the site (the chart statistic) are represented by the height of the block; sales amount (the formatted statistic value) is printed below the block. The heading above the blocks describes the type of statistic, in this case SUM.

Figure 29.1 Block Chart (GCHBKSUM)

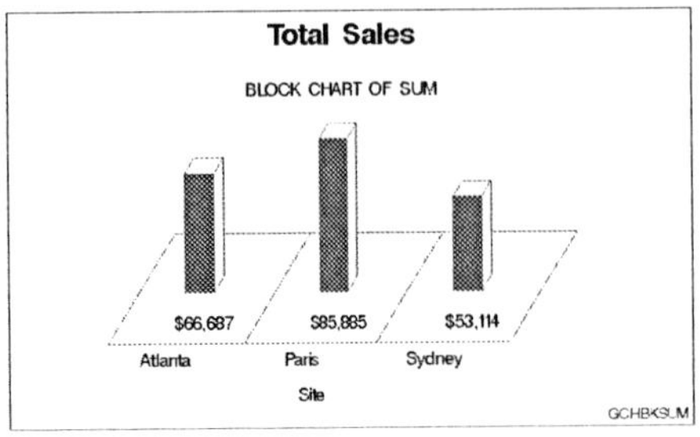

The program for this chart is in Example 1 on page 842. For more information on producing block charts, see "BLOCK Statement" on page 787.

About Bar Charts

Horizontal and vertical bar charts display the magnitude of data with bars, each of which represents a category of data (midpoint). The length (or height) of the bars represents the value of the chart statistic for the corresponding midpoint.

Figure 29.2 on page 775 shows a simple horizontal bar chart of total sales for three manufacturing sites. Each site is a midpoint and is displayed as a bar. The name of the site (the midpoint value) is printed on the midpoint axis beside the bar. Midpoint values are, by default, arranged in ascending order from top to bottom of the chart and labeled with the name of the chart variable.

The chart statistics, in this case total sales for each site, are represented by the length of the bars. The response axis displays the scale of values for the chart statistic. The table of statistics to the right of the bars displays the exact statistic for each bar. Both a column in the table and the response axis are labeled with the name of the summary variable and the type of statistic.

Figure 29.2 Horizontal Bar Chart (GCHBRSUM (a))

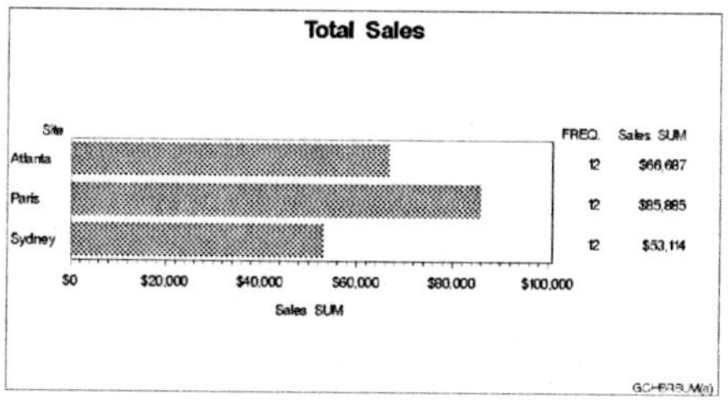

The program for this chart is Example 3 on page 846.

Figure 29.3 on page 775 shows the same data presented as a vertical bar chart. The two types of bar charts have essentially the same characteristics, except that horizontal bar charts by default display a table of statistic values to the right of the bars, while vertical bar charts can optionally display the statistic value above or inside of each bar.

Figure 29.3 Vertical Bar Chart (GCHBRSUM(b))

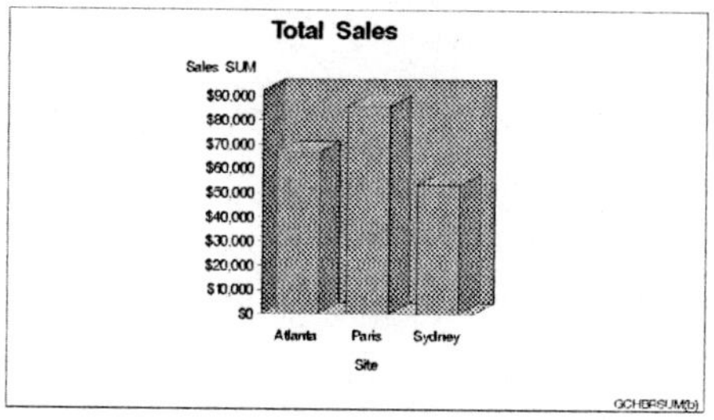

The program for this chart is Example 3 on page 846. For more information on producing horizontal and vertical bar charts, see "HBAR, HBAR3D, VBAR, and VBAR3D Statements" on page 796.

About Pie, Detail Pie, and Donut Charts

Pie and donut charts represent the relative contribution of parts to the whole by displaying data as wedge-shaped "slices" of a circle (either a "pie" or "donut"). Each slice represents a category of data (midpoint). The size of each slice (length of the arc) represents the contribution of the corresponding midpoint to the total chart statistic. Detail pie charts are pie charts with a second pie overlay that shows additional detail about the data that contributes to each of the outer pie's slices. Donut charts look like pie charts except that they have a hole in the middle in which you can place text.

Figure 29.4 on page 776 shows a pie chart of total sales for three manufacturing sites. Each site is a midpoint and is displayed as a slice. By default, the slices are ordered counterclockwise beginning at the 3 o'clock position.

Sales for the site (the chart statistic) are represented by the size of the slice. Both the sales amount (the formatted value of the chart statistic) and the name of the site (the midpoint value) are printed outside of the slice. You can also label pie slices with the percentage of the total statistic value that they represent. The heading above the pie describes the type of statistic (SUM), and names the summary variable (SALES) and the chart variable (SITE).

Figure 29.4 Pie Chart (GCHPISUM(a))

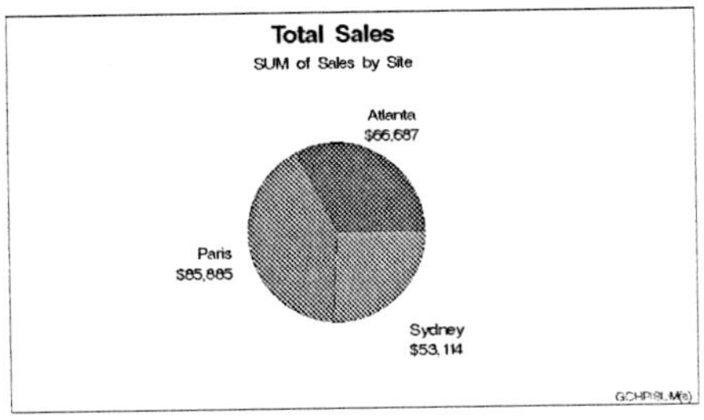

Figure 29.5 on page 776 show the three-dimensional version of the same pie chart.

Figure 29.5 3D Pie Chart (GCHPISUM(b))

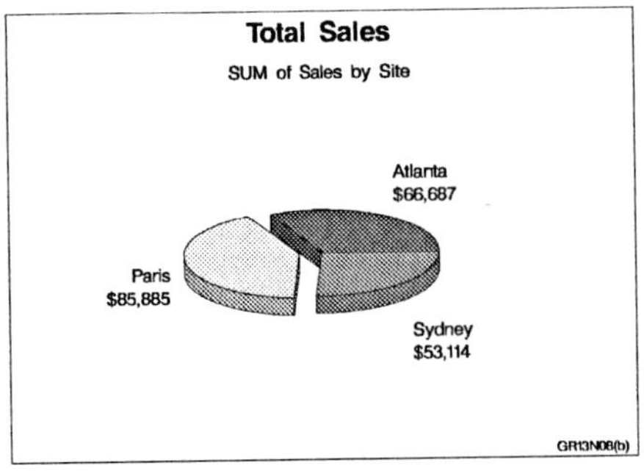

Figure 29.6 on page 777 shows a detail pie chart generated from the same data.

Figure 29.6 Detail Pie Chart (GCHDTPIE)

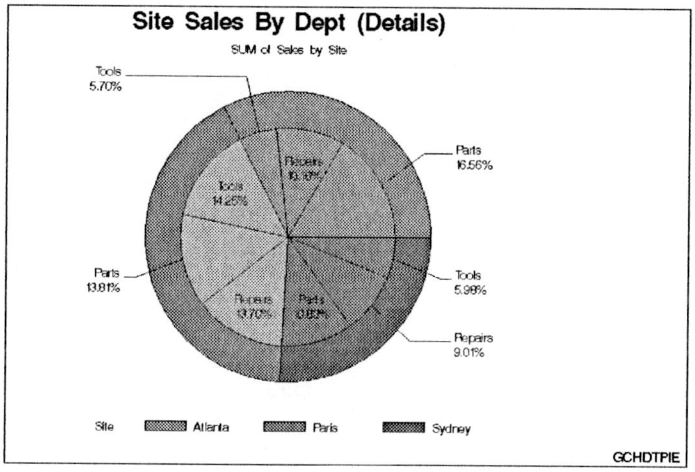

The programs for these charts are in Example 8 on page 869 and Example 15 on page 883. For more information on producing pie or donut charts, see "PIE, PIE3D, and DONUT Statements" on page 818.

About Star Charts

Star charts display data as lines ("spines") radiating from the center of a circle toward the perimeter. Each spine represents a category of data (midpoint). The length of a spine represents the magnitude of the chart statistic for that midpoint starting at the center of the circle, which by default represents 0. The radius of the circle is the length of the longest spine (greatest statistic value) in the chart. Instead of spines, star charts can also display the chart statistic as slices, which are enclosed areas formed by connecting the ends of the spines.

Figure 29.7 on page 777 shows the total sales for the three manufacturing sites as a star chart. Each site is a midpoint and is displayed as a spine. By default the ends of the spines are connected and they are ordered counterclockwise beginning at the 3 o'clock position.

Sales for the site (the chart statistic) are represented by the length of the spine. Both the sales amount (the formatted statistic value) and the name of the site (the midpoint value) are printed outside of the star chart. You can also label star charts with the percentage of the total statistic value that they represent. The heading above the chart describes the type of statistic (SUM), and names the summary variable (SALES) and the chart variable (SITE).

Figure 29.7 Star Chart (GCHSTSUM)

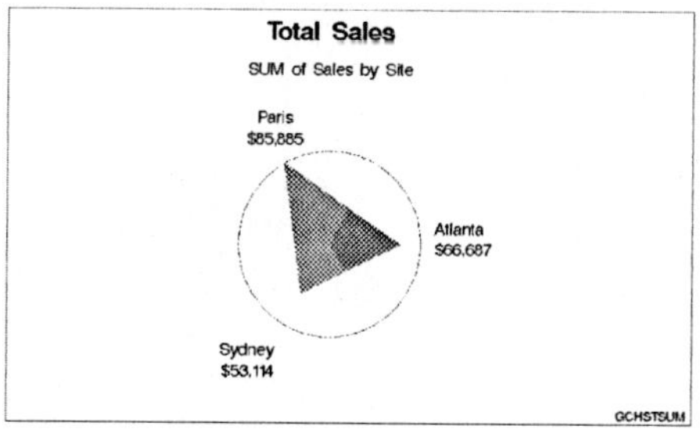

The program for this chart is Example 13 on page 879. For more information on producing star charts, see "STAR Statement" on page 833.

Concepts

The GCHART procedure produces charts based on the values of a *chart variable*. These values are represented by a set of *midpoints*. The chart itself displays information about the chart variable in the form of *chart statistics*.

Figure 29.8 on page 778 and Figure 29.9 on page 779 illustrate these terms as well as other terms used with the GCHART procedure.

Figure 29.8 Terms Used with Bar Charts

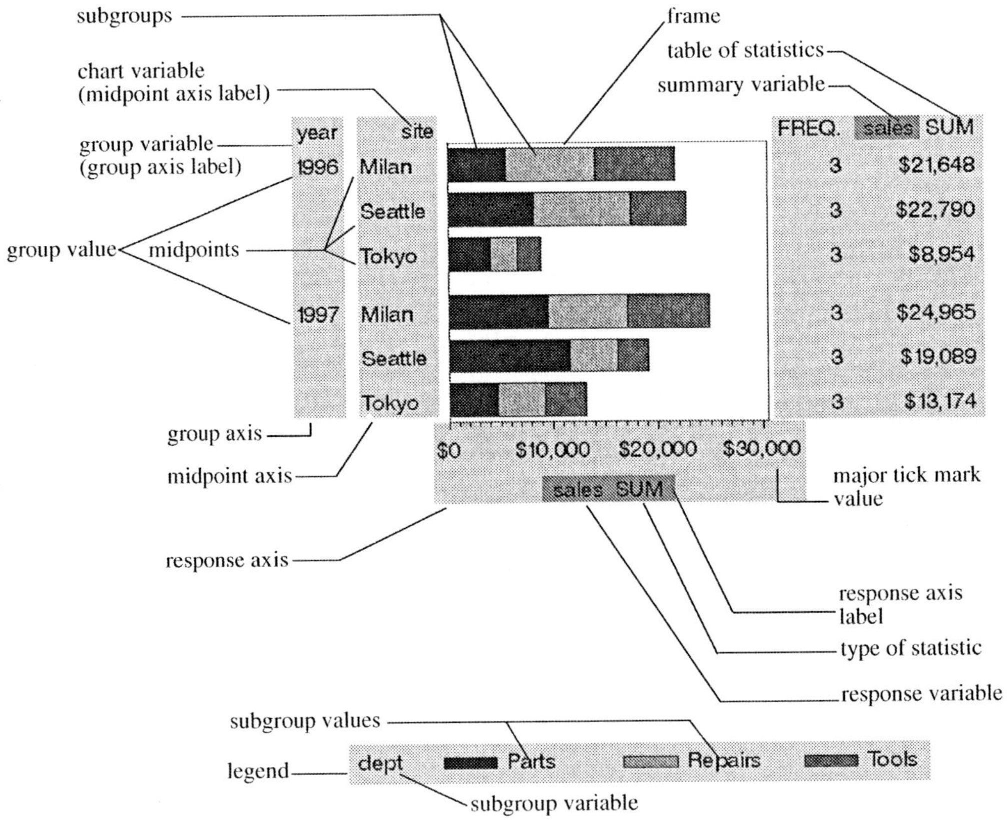

Bar charts have two axes: a midpoint axis that shows the categories of data, and a response axis that displays the scale of values for the chart statistic. The response axis is divided into evenly spaced intervals identified with major tick marks that are labeled with the corresponding statistic value. Minor tick marks are evenly distributed between the major tick marks. Each axis is labeled with the chart variable name or label. The response axis is also labeled with the statistic type.

Figure 29.9 Terms Used with Pie and Donut Charts

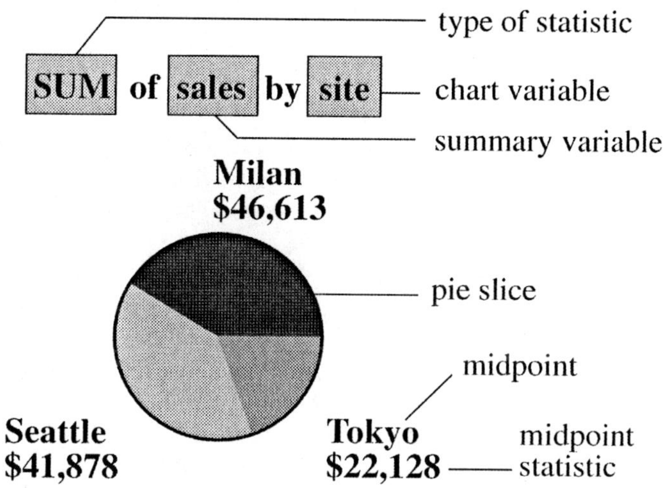

Pie charts show statistics based on values of a variable called the chart variable. Generally, the values of the chart variable are represented by the slices in the chart. Next to each pie slice a number (or character string) appears that identifies the value or range of values assigned to that slice by the GCHART procedure. This number (or character string) is known as the *midpoint* for that slice. The statistic value for each midpoint is displayed beneath the midpoint. The slices in the chart represent all the values of the chart variable included in the chart. The number of degrees included in each slice represents the statistic value for the midpoint.

About Chart Variables

The *chart variable* is the variable in the input data set whose values determine the categories of data represented by the bars, blocks, slices, or spines. The chart variable generates the midpoints to which each observation in the data set contribute.

The chart variable can be either character or numeric. Character chart variables contain character values, which are always discrete. Numeric chart variables fall into two categories: discrete and continuous.

- *Discrete variables* contain a finite number of specific numeric values that are to be represented on the chart. For example, a variable that contains years, such as 1984 or 2001, is a discrete variable.
- *Continuous variables* contain a range of numeric values that are to be represented on the chart. For example, a variable of temperature data that contains real values between 0 and 212 is a continuous variable.

Numeric chart variables are always treated as continuous variables unless the DISCRETE option is used in the action statement.

Missing Values

By default, the GCHART procedure ignores missing midpoint values for the chart variable. If you specify the MISSING option, then missing values are treated as a valid midpoint and are included on the chart. Missing values for the group and subgroup variables are always treated as valid groups and subgroups.

When the value of the variable that is specified in the FREQ= option is missing, 0, or negative, the observation is excluded from the calculation of the chart statistic.

When the value of the variable specified in the SUMVAR= option is missing, the observation is excluded from the calculation of the chart statistic.

About Midpoints

Midpoints are the values of the chart variable that identify categories of data. By default, midpoints are selected or calculated by the procedure. The way the procedure handles the midpoints depends on whether the values of the chart variable are character, discrete numeric, or continuous numeric.

Character Values

A character chart variable generates a midpoint for each unique value of the variable. For example, if the chart variable CITY contains the names of three different cities, each city is a midpoint, resulting in three midpoints for the chart:

Figure 29.10 Character Midpoints

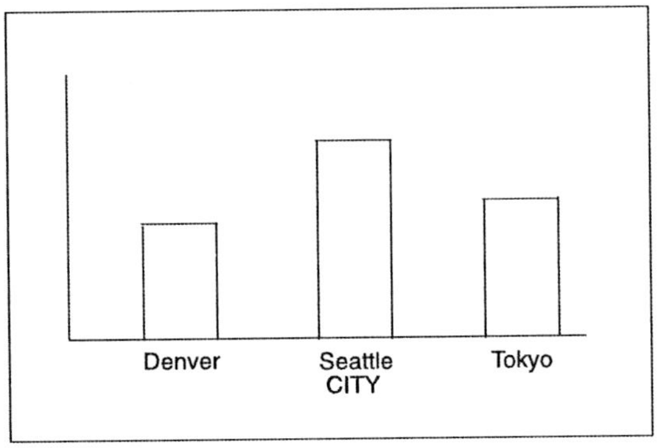

(In pie charts, midpoint values that compose a small percentage of the total for the chart may be placed in the OTHER slice and will not produce a separate midpoint.)

By default, character midpoints are arranged in alphabetic order. If a character variable has an associated format, the values are arranged in order of the formatted values.

Discrete Numeric Values

A numeric chart variable used with the DISCRETE option generates a midpoint for each unique value of the chart variable. For example, the numeric variable YEAR used with DISCRETE produces one midpoint for each year:

Figure 29.11 Discrete Numeric Midpoints

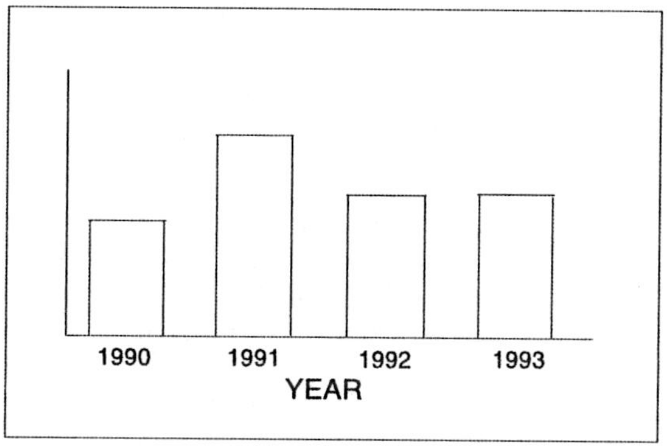

By default, numeric midpoints are arranged in ascending order. If the numeric variable has an associated format, each formatted value generates a separate midpoint. Formatted numeric variables are arranged in ascending order according to their unformatted numeric values.

Continuous Numeric Values

A continuous numeric variable generates midpoints that represent ranges of values. By default, the GCHART procedure determines the ranges, calculates the median value of each range, and displays the appropriate median value at each midpoint on the chart. A value that falls exactly halfway between two midpoints is placed in the higher range.

For example, the numeric variable AGE produces four midpoints, each of which represents a ten-year age range; the median value of the range is displayed at each midpoint:

Figure 29.12 Continuous Numeric Midpoints

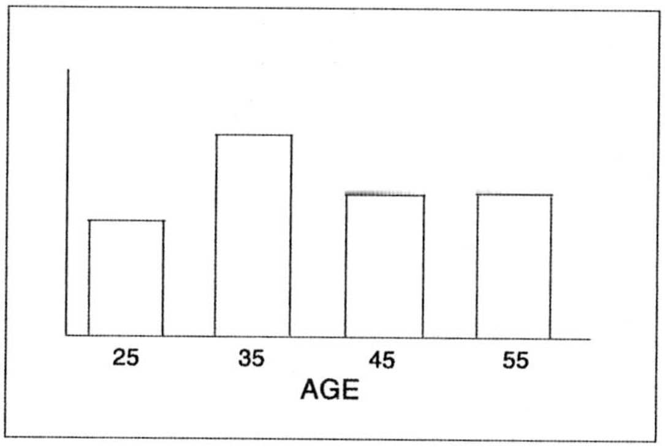

By default, midpoints of ranges are arranged in ascending order.

Selecting and Ordering Midpoints

For character or discrete numeric values, you can use the MIDPOINTS= option to rearrange the midpoints or to exclude midpoints from the chart. For example, to change the default alphabetic order of the midpoints in Figure 29.10 on page 780, specify

```
midpoints='Tokyo' 'Denver' 'Seattle'
```

To exclude the midpoint for Denver, specify

```
midpoints='Tokyo' 'Seattle'
```

In this case, values excluded by the option are not included in the calculation of the chart statistic.

You can order or select discrete numeric midpoint values just as you do character values, but you omit the quotation marks when specifying numeric values.

For continuous numeric variables, use the LEVELS= or MIDPOINTS= option to change the number of midpoints, to control the range of values each midpoint represents, or to change the order of the midpoints. To control the range of values each midpoint represents, use the MIDPOINTS= option to specify the median value of each range. For example, to select the ranges 20–29, 30–39, and 40–49, specify

```
midpoints=25 35 45
```

Alternatively, to select the number of midpoints that you want and let the procedure calculate the ranges and medians, use the LEVELS= option.

You can also use formats to control the ranges of continuous numeric variables, but in that case the values are no longer continuous but discrete.

Note: You cannot use the MIDPOINTS= option to exclude continuous numeric values from the chart because values below or above the ranges specified by the option are automatically included in the first and last midpoints, respectively. To exclude continuous numeric values from a chart, use a WHERE statement in a DATA step or the WHERE= DATA set option. △

See also the description of the LEVELS= and MIDPOINTS= options for the appropriate statement.

About Chart Statistics

The *chart statistic* is the statistical value calculated for the chart variable and represented by each block, bar, or slice. The GCHART procedure calculates six chart statistics; the default statistic is frequency.

The examples given in the descriptions of these statistics assume a data set with two variables, CITY and SALES. The values of CITY are **`Denver`**, **`Seattle`**, and **`Tokyo`**. There are 21 observations: seven for Denver, nine for Seattle, and five for Tokyo.

Frequency

The frequency statistic is the total number of observations in the data set for each midpoint. For example, seven observations of the chart variable, CITY, contain the value **`Denver`**, so the frequency for the **`Denver`** midpoint is 7.

Cumulative Frequency

The cumulative frequency statistic adds the frequency for the current midpoint to the frequency of all of the preceding midpoints. For example, the frequency for the **`Denver`** midpoint is 7, and the frequency for the next midpoint, **`Seattle`**, is 9, so the cumulative frequency for **`Seattle`** is 16.

You cannot request cumulative frequency with the DONUT, PIE, PIE3D, or STAR statements.

Percentage

The percentage statistic is calculated by dividing the frequency for each midpoint by the total frequency count for all midpoints in the chart or group and multiplying it by

100. For example, the frequency count for the `Denver` midpoint is 7 and the total frequency count for the chart is 21, so the percentage statistic for `Denver` is 33.3%.

Cumulative Percentage

The cumulative percentage statistic adds the percentage for the current midpoint to the percentage for all of the preceding midpoints in the chart or group. For example, the percentage for the `Denver` midpoint is 33.3, and the percentage for the next midpoint, `Seattle`, is 42.9, so the cumulative percentage for `Seattle` is 76.2.

You cannot request cumulative percentage with the DONUT, PIE, PIE3D, or STAR statements.

Sum

The sum statistic is the total of the values for the SUMVAR= variable for each midpoint. For example, if you specify SUMVAR=SALES and the values of the SALES variable for the seven `Denver` observations are `8734`, `982`, `1504`, `3207`, `4502`, `624`, and `918`, the sum statistic for the `Denver` midpoint is 20,471.

You must use the SUMVAR= option to specify the variable for which you want the sum statistic.

Mean

The mean statistic is the average of the values for the SUMVAR= variable for each midpoint. For example, if TYPE=MEAN and SUMVAR=SALES, the mean statistic for the `Denver` midpoint is 2924.42.

You must use the SUMVAR= option to specify the variable for which you want the mean statistic.

Calculating Weighted Statistics

By default, each observation is counted only once in the calculation of the chart statistic. To calculate weighted statistics in which an observation can be counted more than once, use the FREQ= option. This option identifies a variable whose values are used as a multiplier for the observation in the calculation of the statistic. If the value of the FREQ= variable is missing, 0, or negative, the observation is excluded from the calculation.

If you use the SUMVAR= option, then the SUMVAR= variable value for an observation is multiplied by the FREQ= variable value for the observation for use in calculating the chart statistic.

For example, to use a variable called COUNT to produce weighted statistics, assign FREQ=COUNT. If you also assign the variable HEIGHT to the SUMVAR= option, then the following table shows how the values of COUNT and HEIGHT would affect the statistic calculation:

Value of COUNT	Value of HEIGHT	Number of times the observation is used	Value used for HEIGHT
1	55	1	55
5	65	5	325
.	63	0	-
-3	60	0	-

By default, the percentage and cumulative percentage statistics are calculated based on the frequency. If you want to chart a percentage or cumulative percentage based on a sum, you can use the FREQ= option to specify a variable to use for the "sum" calculation and specify the PCT statistic, as shown in this example:

```
freq=count type=pct
```

Because the variable that is used by FREQ= determines the number of times an observation is counted, the value of COUNT is the equivalent of the sum statistic.

See also the descriptions of the TYPE=, SUMVAR=, and FREQ= options for the action statements.

About Patterns

When a chart needs one or more patterns, the procedure uses either

- □ default patterns and outlines that are automatically generated by SAS/GRAPH or
- □ patterns, colors, outlines, and images that are defined by PATTERN statements, graphics options, and procedure options.

The following sections summarize pattern behavior for the GCHART procedure. For more information, see "PATTERN Statement" on page 169.

Default Patterns and Outlines

In general, the default pattern that the GCHART procedure uses is a solid fill that it rotates once through the colors list, skipping the foreground color. The procedure also outlines all areas in the foreground color. (Typically, the foreground color is the first color in the device's colors list.)

Specifically, the GCHART procedure uses default patterns and outlines when you

- □ do not specify *any* PATTERN statements, and
- □ do not use the CPATTERN= graphics option, and
- □ do not use the COLORS= graphics options (that is, you use the device's default colors list and it has more than one color), and
- □ do not use the COUTLINE= option in the action statement.

If all of these conditions are true, then the GCHART procedure

- □ selects the first default fill pattern, which is always solid, and rotates it through the colors list, generating one solid pattern for each color. If the first color in the device's colors list is black (or white), the procedure skips that color and begins generating patterns with the next color.
- □ uses the foreground color to outline every patterned area.

If the procedure needs additional patterns, GCHART selects the next default pattern fill that is appropriate to the type of chart and rotates it through the colors list, skipping the foreground color as before. The procedure continues in this fashion until it has generated enough patterns for the chart.

Changing any of these conditions may change or override the default behavior:

- □ If you specify a colors list with the COLORS= option in a GOPTIONS statement and the list contains more than one color, the procedure rotates the default solid pattern through that list, using every color, even if the foreground color is black (or white). The default outline color remains the foreground color.
- □ If you specify either COLORS=(*one-color*) or the CPATTERN= graphics option, the default fill pattern changes from solid to the list of appropriate hatch patterns. The procedure uses the specified color to generate one pattern definition for each hatch pattern in the list. The default outline color remains the foreground color.

- Whenever there are PATTERN definitions in effect, whether or not the GCHART procedure can use them, the default outline color for all patterns changes from foreground to SAME, as described in the following section.

For a description of these graphics options, see Chapter 8, "Graphics Options and Device Parameters Dictionary," on page 261.

User-Defined Patterns, Outlines, and Images

You can use PATTERN statements to explicitly specify patterns, including color or fill type or both. You can also specify images to fill the bars of two-dimensional bar charts. For complete information on all patterns, see "PATTERN Statement" on page 169. See also the section on controlling patterns and colors for each chart type.

When you use PATTERN statements, the procedure uses the specified patterns until all of the PATTERN definitions they generate have been used. Then, if more patterns are required, it returns to the default pattern rotation.

Whenever you specify *any* PATTERN statement, the default pattern outline changes. Instead of the foreground color, the outline color is the same as the fill color; for example, a blue bar has a blue outline. The effect is the same as specifying COUTLINE=SAME. Even when the procedure runs out of user-defined patterns and generates default patterns, the outlines continue to match the interior pattern color.

To change the outline color of any pattern, whether it's a default or user-defined pattern, use the COUTLINE= option in the action statement that generates the chart.

Two-dimensional bar charts created with the HBAR and VBAR statements can use the PATTERN statement to fill specified bars with specified images. For details, see the IFRAME= option on page 806 and the IBACK= goption"Controlling Bar Chart Patterns, Colors, and Images" on page 816.

Other means of including images in charts include adding background images to two- and three-dimensional bar charts. For two-dimensional bar charts created with HBAR and VBAR statements, the IBACK= goption"IBACK" on page 317 specifies image files that fill the backplane frame. To fill the backplane frame of a three-dimensional image created with the HBAR3D or VBAR3D statements, use the IFRAME= option on page 806. For further information, including a listing of recognized image file types, see "Image File Types Supported by SAS/GRAPH" on page 106.

Version 6 Patterns

If you specify the V6COMP graphics option, then the procedure generates patterns by rotating the appropriate Version 6 default patterns through all of the colors in the colors list. With V6COMP, all patterns are outlined in the same color as the fill.

Procedure Syntax

Requirements: At least one BLOCK, HBAR, HBAR3D, VBAR, VBAR3D, PIE, PIE3D, DONUT, or STAR statement is required.

Global statements: AXIS, FOOTNOTE, GOPTIONS, LEGEND, PATTERN, TITLE

Reminder: The procedure can include the BY, FORMAT, LABEL, and WHERE statements as well as the SAS/GRAPHNOTE statement.

Supports:

RUN-group processing

Output Delivery System (ODS)

PROC GCHART<DATA=*input-data-set*>
<ANNOTATE=*Annotate-data-set*>
<GOUT=<*libref.*>*output-catalog*>
<IMAGEMAP=*output-data-set*>;

BLOCK *chart-variable(s)* </ *option(s)*>;

HBAR | HBAR3D | VBAR | VBAR3D*chart-variable(s)* </ *option(s)*>;

PIE | PIE3D | DONUT *chart-variable(s)* </ *option(s)*>;

STAR *chart-variable(s)* </ *option(s)*>;

PROC GCHART Statement

Identifies the data set containing the chart variables. Optionally specifies annotation and an output catalog.

Requirements: An input data set is required.

Syntax

PROC GCHART<DATA=*input-data-set*>
<ANNOTATE=*Annotate-data-set*>
<GOUT=<*libref.*>*output-catalog*>
<IMAGEMAP=*output-data-set*>;

Options

PROC GCHART statement options affect all graphs produced by the procedure.

ANNOTATE=*Annotate-data-set*
ANNO=*Annotate-data-set*
specifies a data set to annotate all graphs that are produced by the GCHART procedure. To annotate individual graphs, use ANNOTATE= in the action statement.

See also: Chapter 24, "Using Annotate Data Sets," on page 587

DATA=*input-data-set*
specifies the SAS data set that contains the variable(s) to chart. By default, the procedure uses the most recently created SAS data set.

See also: "SAS Data Sets" on page 29 and "About Chart Variables" on page 779

GOUT=<*libref.*>*output-catalog*
specifies the SAS catalog in which to save the graphics output that is produced by the GCHART procedure. If you omit the libref, SAS/GRAPH looks for the catalog in the temporary library called WORK and creates the catalog if it does not exist.

See also: "Storing Graphics Output in SAS Catalogs" on page 53

IMAGEMAP=*output-data-set*
creates a temporary SAS data set that is used to generate an image map in an HTML output file. The information in the image map data set includes the shape and coordinates of the elements in the graph and drill-down URLs that have been associated with those elements. The drill-down URLs are provided by one or two variables in the input data set. These variables are identified to the GCHART procedure with the HTML= and/or HTML_LEGEND= options.

The %IMAGEMAP macro generates the image map in the HTML output file. The macro takes two arguments, the name of the image map data set and the name or fileref of the HTML file, as shown in the following example:

```
%imagemap(imgmapds, myimgmap.html);
```

Not supported by: Java, ActiveX

BLOCK Statement

Creates block charts in which the height of the blocks represents the value of the chart statistic for each category of data.

Requirements: At least one chart variable is required.

Global statements: LEGEND, PATTERN, TITLE, FOOTNOTE

Supports: Drill-down functionality

Description

The BLOCK statement specifies the variable or variables that define the categories of data to chart. This statement automatically

- □ determines the midpoints
- □ calculates the chart statistic for each midpoint (the default is FREQ)
- □ scales the blocks according to the statistic value
- □ assigns patterns and colors to the block faces and the grid; the default block pattern is solid.

You can use statement options to select or order the midpoints (blocks), to change the type of chart statistic, and to modify the appearance of the chart. You can also specify additional variables by which to group, subgroup, or sum the data.

Block charts allow grouping, which organizes the blocks into rows based on the values of a group variable, and subgrouping, which subdivides the blocks into segments based on the values of a subgroup variable.

In addition, you can use global statements to modify the block patterns and the legend, as well as add titles, footnotes, and notes to the chart. You can also use an Annotate data set to enhance the chart.

Note: If you get a message that the chart is too large to display on your terminal or printer, try one or both of the following: △

- □ reduce the size of the character cells defined for the output device by specifying larger values for the HPOS= and VPOS= graphics options
- □ decrease the size of the chart text with the HTEXT= graphics option.

See "About the Graphics Output Area" on page 34 for details .

Syntax

BLOCK *chart-variable(s)* </ *option(s)*>;

option(s) can be one or more options from any or all of the following categories:

- □ appearance options

    ANNOTATE=*Annotate-data-set*

BLOCKMAX=*max-value*
CAXIS=*grid-color*
COUTLINE=*block-outline-color* | SAME
CTEXT=*text-color*
LEGEND=LEGEND<1...99>
NOHEADING
NOLEGEND
PATTERNID=BY |GROUP |MIDPOINT |SUBGROUP
WOUTLINE=*block-outline-width*

- midpoint options
  DISCRETE
  GROUP=*group-variable*
  LEVELS=*number-of-midpoints*
  MIDPOINTS=*value-list*
  MIDPOINTS=OLD
  MISSING
  SUBGROUP=*subgroup-variable*
- statistic options
  FREQ=*numeric-variable*
  G100
  SUMVAR=*summary-variable*
  TYPE=*statistic*
- catalog entry description options
  DESCRIPTION='*entry-description*'
  NAME='*entry-name*'
- ODS options
  HTML=*variable*
  HTML_LEGEND=*variable*

Required Arguments

chart-variable(s)

specifies one or more variables that define the categories of data to chart. Each chart variable draws a separate chart. All variables must be in the input data set. Separate multiple chart variables with blanks. The values of a chart variable used with the BLOCK statement have a maximum length of 13.

See also: "About Chart Variables" on page 779

Options

Options in a BLOCK statement affect all graphs produced by that statement. You can specify as many options as you want and list them in any order. For details on specifying colors, see Chapter 6, "SAS/GRAPH Colors and Images," on page 91. For a complete description of the graphics options, see Chapter 8, "Graphics Options and Device Parameters Dictionary," on page 261.

ANNOTATE=*Annotate-data-set*

ANNO=*Annotate-data-set*
specifies a data set to annotate charts produced by the BLOCK statement.

Note: Annotate coordinate systems 1, 2, 7, and 8 (data system coordinates) are not valid with block charts. △

See also: Chapter 24, "Using Annotate Data Sets," on page 587

BLOCKMAX=*max-value*
specifies the chart statistic value of the tallest block on the chart. This option lets you produce a series of block charts using the same scale. All blocks are rescaled as if *max-value* were the maximum value on the chart.

Not supported by: Java, ActiveX

CAXIS=*grid-color*
specifies the color for the midpoint grid. By default, the midpoint grid uses the foreground color (usually the first color in the colors list).

Featured in: Example 2 on page 844

COUTLINE=*block-outline-color* | SAME
outlines all blocks or all block segments and legend values in the subgroup legend (if it appears) using the specified color. SAME specifies that the outline color of a block or a block segment or a legend value is the same as the interior pattern color.

The default outline color depends on the PATTERN statement:

- If you do not specify a PATTERN statement, the default outline color is black for the Java or ActiveX devices. Otherwise, the default outline color is the foreground color (the first color in the colors list).
- If you specify the PATTERN statement or the V6COMP graphics option, the default is COUTLINE=SAME.

Note: If you specify empty patterns, (VALUE=EMPTY in a PATTERN statement) you should not change the outline color from the default value, SAME, to a single color. Otherwise all the outlines will be one color and you will not be able to distinguish between the empty areas. △

See also: "Controlling Block Chart Patterns and Colors" on page 794 and "About Patterns" on page 784

Featured in: Example 2 on page 844

Not supported by: Java (partial), ActiveX (partial)

CTEXT=*text-color*
specifies a color for all text on the chart. Text includes the values and labels for the midpoint grid, the subgroup legend, and the descriptive statistic values. For the Java and ActiveX devices, the default color is black. For other devices, if you omit CTEXT=, PROC GCHART searches for a color specification in this order:

1. the CTEXT= option in a GOPTIONS statement
2. the first color in the colors list (the default).

CTEXT= is overridden by the COLOR= suboption of the LABEL= or VALUE= option in a LEGEND definition assigned to the subgroup legend. The suboption determines the color of the legend label or the color of the legend value descriptions, respectively.

DESCRIPTION='*entry-description*'
DES='*entry-description*'
specifies the description of the catalog entry for the chart. The maximum length for *entry-description* is 256 characters. The description does not appear on the chart. By

default, the GCHART procedure assigns a description of the form BLOCK CHART OF *variable*, where *variable* is the name of the chart variable.

The *entry-description* can include the #BYLINE, #BYVAL, and #BYVAR substitution options, which work as they do when used on TITLE, FOOTNOTE, and NOTE statements. Refer to the description of the options on page 222, and "Substituting BY Line Values in a Text String" on page 226. The 256-character limit applies before the substitution takes place for these options; thus, if in the SAS program the entry-description text exceeds 256 characters, it is truncated to 256 characters, and then the substitution is performed.

The descriptive text is shown in each of the following:

- the "description" portion of the Results window
- the catalog-entry properties that you can view from the Explorer window
- the Table of Contents that is generated when you use CONTENTS= on an ODS statement (see "Linking to Output through a Table of Contents" on page 495), assuming the GCHART output is generated while the contents page is open
- the Description field of the PROC GREPLAY window
- the data tip text for web output (depending on the device driver you are using). See "Adding Data Tips to Web Presentations" on page 568 for details.

DISCRETE

treats a numeric chart variable as a discrete variable rather than as a continuous variable. The GCHART procedure creates a separate midpoint and, hence, a separate grid square and block for each unique value of the chart variable. If the chart variable has a format associated with it, each formatted value is treated as a midpoint.

The LEVELS= option is ignored when you use DISCRETE. The MIDPOINTS= option overrides DISCRETE.

FREQ=*numeric-variable*

specifies a variable whose values weight the contribution of each observation in the computation of the chart statistic. Each observation is counted the number of times specified by the value of *numeric-variable* for that observation. If the value of *numeric-variable* is missing, 0, or negative, the observation is not used in the statistic calculation. Non-integer values of *numeric-variable* are truncated to integers.

FREQ= is valid with all chart statistics.

Because you cannot use the PERCENT, CPERCENT, FREQ, or CFREQ statistics with the SUMVAR= option, you must use the FREQ= option to calculate percentages, cumulative percentages, frequencies, or cumulative frequencies based on a sum.

The statistics will not be affected by applying a format to *numeric-variable*.

See also: "Calculating Weighted Statistics" on page 783

G100

calculates the percentage and cumulative percentage statistics separately for each group. When you use G100, the individual percentages reflect the contribution of the midpoint to the group and total 100 percent for each group. G100 is ignored unless you also use the GROUP= option.

By default, the individual percentages reflect the contribution of the midpoint to the entire chart and total 100 percent for the entire chart.

GROUP=*group-variable*

organizes the data according to the values of *group-variable*. *Group-variable* can be either character or numeric and is always treated as a discrete variable. The group variable can have up to 12 different values.

GROUP= produces a group grid that contains a separate row of blocks for each unique value of the group variable. Each row contains a square for each midpoint. The groups are arranged from front to back in ascending order of the group variable values. These values are printed to the left of each row; the group variable name or label is printed above the list of group values.

By default, each group includes all midpoints, even if no observations for the group fall within the midpoint range. Missing values for *group-variable* are treated as a valid group.

Featured in: Example 2 on page 844

HTML=*variable*
identifies the variable in the input data set whose values create links in the HTML file that is created by the ODS statement. These links are associated with an area of the chart and point to the data or graph you wish to display when the user drills down on the area. The values of *variable* can be up to 1024 characters long. Characters after the 1024-character limit (including any closing quotes) are truncated.

HTML_LEGEND=*variable*
identifies the variable in the input data set whose values create links in the HTML file that is created by the ODS statement. These links are associated with a legend value and point to the data or graph that you wish to display when the user drills down on the value. The values of *variable* can be up to 1024 characters long. Characters after the 1024-character limit (including any closing quotes) are truncated.

Not supported by: Java, ActiveX

LEGEND=LEGEND<1...99>
assigns the specified LEGEND definition to the legend generated by the SUBGROUP= option. The LEGEND= option itself does *not* generate a legend.

LEGEND= is ignored if

- SUBGROUP= is not used.
- the specified LEGEND definition is not in effect.
- the NOLEGEND option is used.
- the PATTERNID= option is set to any value other than SUBGROUP; that is, the value of PATTERNID= is BY or GROUP or MIDPOINT.

To create a legend based on the chart midpoints instead of the subgroups, use the chart variable as the subgroup variable:

```
block city / subgroup=city;
```

The Java and ActiveX devices do not support all LEGEND statement options. See "LEGEND Statement" on page 151 for more information.

See also: SUBGROUP= on page 793 and "LEGEND Statement" on page 151

Featured in: Example 2 on page 844

Not supported by: Java (partial), ActiveX (partial)

LEVELS=*number-of-midpoints*
specifies the number of midpoints for the numeric chart variable. The range for each midpoint is calculated automatically using the algorithm described in Terrell and Scott (1985). LEVELS= is ignored if

- the chart variable is character type.
- the DISCRETE option is used.
- the MIDPOINTS= option is used.

MIDPOINTS=*value-list*
specifies the midpoint values for the blocks. The way you specify *value-list* depends on the type of variable:

- For numeric chart variables, *value-list* is either an explicit list of values, or a starting and an ending value with an interval increment, or a combination of both forms:

  n <...*n*>

  n TO *n* <BY *increment*>

  n <...*n*> TO *n* <BY *increment*> <*n* <...*n*>>

  If a numeric variable has an associated format, the specified values must be the *unformatted* values.

  By default, numeric variable values are treated as continuous (if you omit the DISCRETE option), and

  - the lowest midpoint consolidates all data points from negative infinity to the median of the first two midpoints
  - the highest midpoint consolidates all data points from the median of the last two midpoints up to infinity
  - all other values in *value-list* specify the median of a range of values, and the GCHART procedure calculates the midpoint values.

  If you include the DISCRETE option, each value in *value-list* specifies a unique numeric value.

- For character chart variables, *value-list* is a list of unique character values enclosed in quotation marks and separated by blanks:

  'value-1' <...*'value-n'*>

  If a character variable has an associated format, the specified values must be the *formatted* values.

For a complete description of *value-list*, see the ORDER= on page 130 option in the AXIS statement.

If *value-list* for either type of variable specifies so many midpoints that the axis values overwrite each other, the values may be unreadable. In this case the procedure writes a warning to the SAS log. On many devices, you can correct crowded values by increasing the number of cells in your graphics display using the HPOS= and VPOS= graphics options.

See also: "About Midpoints" on page 780

Featured in: Example 2 on page 844

MIDPOINTS=OLD

generates default midpoints using the Nelder algorithm (*Applied Statistics* 25:94–7, 1976). The MIDPOINTS=OLD option is ignored unless the chart variable is numeric.

MISSING

accepts a missing value as a valid midpoint for the chart variable. By default, observations with missing values are ignored. Missing values are always valid for the group and subgroup variables.

NAME=*'entry-name'*

specifies the name of the catalog entry for the graph. The maximum length for *entry-name* is eight characters. The default name is GCHART. If the name duplicates an existing entry name, thenSAS/GRAPH software adds a number to the duplicate name to create a unique name—for example, GCHART1.

NOHEADING

suppresses the heading describing the type of statistic. For the Java and ActiveX devices, NOHEADING is the default. For other devices, by default the heading is printed at the top of each block chart.

Featured in: Example 2 on page 844

Not supported by: Java, ActiveX

NOLEGEND

suppresses the legend automatically generated by the SUBGROUP= option. NOLEGEND is ignored if the SUBGROUP= option is not used.

PATTERNID=BY | GROUP | MIDPOINT | SUBGROUP

specifies the way fill patterns are assigned. By default, PATTERNID=SUBGROUP. Values for PATTERNID= are as follows:

BY

changes patterns each time the value of the BY variable changes. All blocks use the same pattern if the GCHART procedure does not include a BY statement.

GROUP

changes patterns every time the value of the group variable changes. All blocks in each group (row) use the same pattern, but a different pattern is used for each group.

MIDPOINT

changes patterns every time the midpoint value changes. If you use the GROUP= option, the respective midpoint patterns are repeated for each group.

SUBGROUP

changes patterns every time the value of the subgroup variable changes. The blocks must be subdivided by the SUBGROUP= option for the SUBGROUP value to have an effect. Without SUBGROUP=, all block faces have the same pattern.

Note: If you use the SUBGROUP= option and specify a PATTERNID= value other than SUBGROUP, the block segments use the same pattern and are indistinguishable. △

See also: "Controlling Block Chart Patterns and Colors" on page 794

Featured in: Example 7 on page 856

SUBGROUP=*subgroup-variable*

divides the blocks into segments according to the values of *subgroup-variable*. *Subgroup-variable* can be either character or numeric and is always treated as a discrete variable. SUBGROUP= creates a separate segment within each block for every unique value of the subgroup variable for that midpoint.

If PATTERNID=SUBGROUP (the default setting), each segment is filled with a different pattern, and a legend providing a key to the patterns is automatically generated. If the value of PATTERNID= is anything other than SUBGROUP, the segments are all the same color, the legend is suppressed, and the subgrouping effect is lost.

By default the legend appears at the bottom of the chart. To modify the legend, assign a LEGEND definition with the LEGEND= option. To suppress the legend, specify NOLEGEND.

See also: "LEGEND Statement" on page 151

Featured in: Example 2 on page 844

SUMVAR=*summary-variable*

specifies a numeric variable for sum or mean calculations. The GCHART procedure calculates the sum or, if requested, the mean of *numeric-variable* for each midpoint. The resulting statistics are represented by the height of the blocks in each square. The values of a summary variable used with the BLOCK statement have a maximum length of 8.

When you use SUMVAR=, the TYPE= option value must be either SUM or MEAN. With SUMVAR=, the default is TYPE=SUM.

Featured in: Example 1 on page 842

TYPE=*statistic*
specifies the chart statistic.

- If the SUMVAR= option is not used, *statistic* can be one of the following:

  FREQ
  frequency (the default)

  CFREQ
  cumulative frequency

  PERCENT PCT
  percentage

  CPERCENT CPCT
  cumulative percentage

- If SUMVAR= is used, *statistic* can be either:

  SUM
  sum (the default)

  MEAN
  mean

Because you cannot specify the statistics PERCENT, CPERCENT, FREQ, or CFREQ in conjunction with the SUMVAR= option, you must use FREQ= to calculate percentages, cumulative percentages, frequencies, or cumulative frequencies based on a sum. See also "Calculating Weighted Statistics" on page 783.

If you specify TYPE=MEAN and use the SUBGROUP= option, the height of the block represents the mean for the entire midpoint. The subgroup segments are proportional to the subgroup's contribution to the sum for the block.

See also: "About Chart Statistics" on page 782

Featured in: Example 2 on page 844

WOUTLINE=*block-outline-width*
specifies the width of the block outline in pixels.

Not supported by: Java

Controlling Block Chart Patterns and Colors

Default patterns and outlines

In a block chart, only the front faces of the blocks display patterns. By default, the procedure

- fills the block faces with bar/block patterns, beginning with the default fill, SOLID, and rotating it through the colors list. When the solid patterns are exhausted, the procedure selects the next default bar/block pattern and rotates it through the colors list. It continues in this fashion until all of the required patterns have been assigned.

  If you use the device's default colors and the first color in the list is either black or white, the procedure does not create a pattern in that color. If you specify a colors list with the COLORS= graphics option, the procedure uses all of the colors in the list to generate the patterns.
- outlines blocks and block segments using the first color in the colors list.
- colors the midpoint grid with the first color in the colors list.

See "About Patterns" on page 784 for more information on how the GCHART procedure assigns default patterns and outlines.

User-defined patterns

To override the default patterns and select fills and colors for the blocks or block segments, use the PATTERN statement. Only bar/block patterns are valid; all other pattern fills are ignored. For a complete description of all bar/block patterns, see the description of PATTERN statement option VALUE= on page 171.

Whenever you use PATTERN statements, the default pattern outline color changes to SAME. That is, the outline color is the same as the fill color. To specify the outline color, use the COUTLINE= on page 789 option.

When patterns change

The PATTERNID= option controls when the pattern changes. By default, PATTERNID=SUBGROUP. Therefore, when you use the SUBGROUP= option to subdivide the blocks, the pattern automatically changes each time the subgroup value changes, and each subdivision of the block displays a different pattern. As a result, the number of values for the SUBGROUP= variable determines the number of block patterns on the chart. If you do not subdivide the blocks, all blocks use the same pattern.

Instead of changing the pattern for each subgroup, you can change the pattern for each midpoint, each group, or each BY group, by changing the value of the PATTERNID= option. See the PATTERNID= on page 793 option for details.

Axis color

By default, axis elements use the first color in the colors list. To change the grid color, use the CAXIS= option. To change the axis text color, use the CTEXT= option.

Controlling Block Chart Text

To control the font and size of text on the chart, use the FTEXT= and HTEXT= graphics options. See Chapter 8, "Graphics Options and Device Parameters Dictionary," on page 261 for a description of these options.

Because block charts do not use AXIS statements, you must use a LABEL statement instead to suppress the label for the midpoint variable. See Example 2 on page 844.

Displaying Negative or Zero Values

The relative block heights in the chart represent the scaled value of the chart statistic value for the midpoint. If the statistic has a value of 0 or, in the case of sum and mean, a negative value, the base of the block is drawn in the square for the corresponding midpoint. Figure 29.13 on page 796 shows an example of a chart with 0 and negative statistic values.

Figure 29.13 Block Chart with 0 and Negative Statistic Values

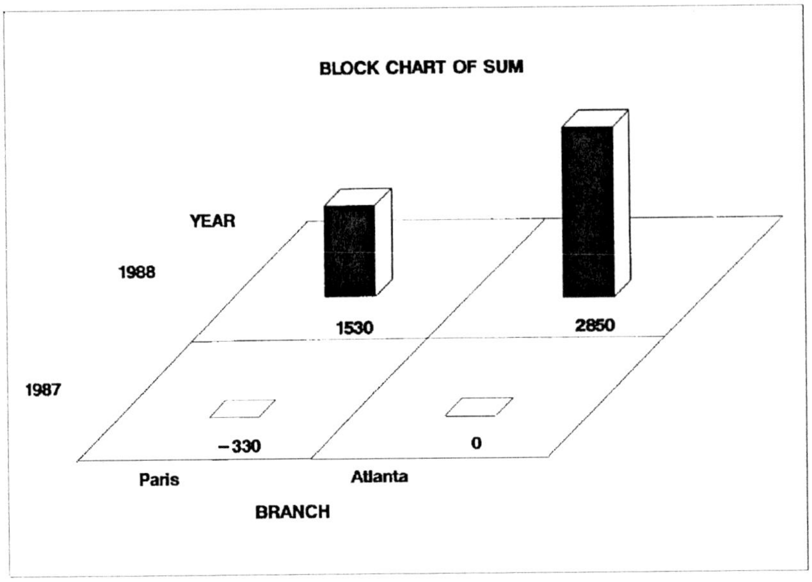

HBAR, HBAR3D, VBAR, and VBAR3D Statements

Create horizontal or vertical bar charts in which the length or height of the bars represents the value of the chart statistic for each category of data.

Requirements: At least one chart variable is required.

Global statements: AXIS, LEGEND, PATTERN, TITLE, FOOTNOTE

Supports: Drill-down functionality

Description

The HBAR, HBAR3D, VBAR, and VBAR3D statements specify the variable or variables that define the categories of data to chart. These statements automatically

- □ determine the midpoints
- □ calculate the chart statistic for each midpoint (the default is FREQ)
- □ scale the response axis and the bars according to the statistic value
- □ determine bar width and spacing
- □ assign patterns to the bars; the default bar/block pattern is SOLID.
- □ draw a frame around the axis area using the first color in the colors list.

You can use statement options to select or order the midpoints (bars), to control the tick marks on the response axis, to change the type of chart statistic, to display specific statistics, and to modify the appearance of the chart. You can also specify additional variables by which to group, subgroup, or sum the data.

All bar charts allow grouping, which uses an additional category to organize the bars into groups, and subgrouping, which divides the bars into segments.

In addition, you can:

- □ use global statements to modify the axes (including requesting a logarithmic axis), the bar patterns, and the legend. See Chapter 7, "SAS/GRAPH Statements," on page 121 for more information.

- add titles, footnotes, and notes to the chart. See "TITLE, FOOTNOTE, and NOTE Statements" on page 210 for more information.
- use an Annotate data set to enhance the chart. See Chapter 24, "Using Annotate Data Sets," on page 587 for more information.
- display an image in the background of the chart. For HBAR3D and VBAR3D charts, see the IFRAME= option on page 806. For HBAR and VBAR charts, see the IBACK= goption"IBACK" on page 317.
- display images in the bars of an HBAR or VBAR chart. See the PATTERN statement IMAGE= option on page 171.

Syntax

HBAR | **HBAR3D** | **VBAR** | **VBAR3D** *chart-variable(s)* </ *option(s)*>;

option(s) can be one or more options from any or all of the following categories:

- appearance options

  ANNOTATE=*Annotate-data-set*
  CAUTOREF=*reference-line-color*
  CAXIS=*axis-color*
  CERROR=*error-bar-color*
  CFRAME=*background-color*
  COUTLINE=*bar-outline-color* | SAME
  CREF=*reference-line-color* | (*reference-line-color*) | *reference-line-color-list*
  CTEXT=*text-color*
  FRAME | NOFRAME
  GSPACE= *group-spacing*
  IFRAME= *fileref* | *'external-file'*
  IMAGESTYLE = TILE | FIT
  LAUTOREF=*reference-line-type*
  LEGEND=LEGEND<1...99>
  LREF=*reference-line-type* | (*reference-line-type*) | *reference-line-type-list*
  NOLEGEND
  PATTERNID=BY | GROUP | MIDPOINT | SUBGROUP
  SHAPE=*3D-bar-shape* (HBAR3D and VBAR3D only)
  SPACE=*bar-spacing*
  WIDTH=*bar-width*
  WOUTLINE=*bar-outline-width*

- statistic options

  CFREQ
  CFREQLABEL=*'column-label'* | NONE (HBAR and HBAR3D only)
  CLM=*confidence-level*
  CPERCENT
  CPERCENTLABEL=*'column-label'* | NONE (HBAR and HBAR3D only)
  ERRORBAR=BARS | BOTH | TOP
  FREQ
  FREQLABEL=*'column-label'* | NONE (HBAR and HBAR3D only)
  FREQ=*numeric-variable*
  G100

  - INSIDE=*statistic*
  - MEAN
  - MEANLABEL='*column-label*' | NONE (HBAR and HBAR3D only)
  - NOSTATS (HBAR and HBAR3D only)
  - OUTSIDE=*statistic*
  - PERCENT
  - PERCENTLABEL='*column-label*' | NONE (HBAR and HBAR3D only)
  - SUM
  - SUMLABEL='*column-label*' | NONE (HBAR and HBAR3D only)
  - SUMVAR=*summary-variable*
  - TYPE=*statistic*
- □ midpoint options
  - DISCRETE
  - GROUP=*group-variable*
  - LEVELS=*number-of-midpoints* | ALL
  - MIDPOINTS=*value-list*
  - MIDPOINTS=OLD
  - MISSING
  - RANGE
  - SUBGROUP=*subgroup-variable*
- □ axes options
  - ASCENDING
  - AUTOREF
  - AXIS=AXIS<1...99>
  - CLIPREF
  - DESCENDING
  - FRONTREF (HBAR3D and VBAR3D only)
  - GAXIS=AXIS<1...99>
  - MAXIS=AXIS<1...99>
  - MINOR=*number-of-minor-ticks*
  - NOAXIS
  - NOBASEREF
  - NOZERO
  - RANGE
  - RAXIS=*value-list* | AXIS<1...99>
  - REF=*value-list*
- □ catalog entry description options
  - DESCRIPTION='*entry-description*'
  - NAME='*entry-name*'
- □ ODS options
  - HTML=*variable*
  - HTML_LEGEND=*variable*

Required Arguments

chart-variable(s)

specifies one or more variables that define the categories of data to chart. Each chart variable draws a separate chart. All variables must be in the input data set. Multiple chart variables must be separated with blanks.

See also: "About Chart Variables" on page 779

Options

Options in an HBAR, HBAR3D, VBAR, or VBAR3D statement affect all graphs that are produced by that statement. You can specify as many options as you want and list them in any order. For details on specifying colors, see Chapter 6, "SAS/GRAPH Colors and Images," on page 91. For details on specifying images, see "Specifying Images in SAS/GRAPH Programs" on page 106. For a complete description of the graphics options, see Chapter 8, "Graphics Options and Device Parameters Dictionary," on page 261.

ANNOTATE=*Annotate-data-set*
ANNO=*Annotate-data-set*

specifies a data set to annotate charts produced by the bar chart statement.

See also: Chapter 24, "Using Annotate Data Sets," on page 587

ASCENDING

arranges the bars in ascending order of the value of the chart statistic. By default, bars are arranged in ascending order of midpoint value, without regard to the lengths of the bars. ASCENDING reorders the bars from shortest to longest. In horizontal bar charts the ordering is top to bottom; in vertical bar charts the ordering is left to right.

If you also use the GROUP= option, the reordering is performed separately for each group, so the order of the midpoints may be different for each group.

ASCENDING overrides any midpoint order specified with the MIDPOINTS= option or specified in the ORDER= option in an AXIS statement assigned to the midpoint axis.

AUTOREF

draws a reference line at each major tick mark on the response axis. To draw reference lines at specific points on the response axis, use the REF= option.

By default, reference lines in 2D bar charts are drawn in front of the bars. To draw reference lines behind the bars, use the CLIPREF option.

By default, reference lines in 3D bar charts are drawn on the back plane of the axis. To draw reference lines in front of the bars, use the FRONTREF option.

Featured in: Example 5 on page 850

AXIS=AXIS<1...99>

See RAXIS= on page 812.

CAUTOREF=*reference-line-color*

specifies the color of reference lines drawn at major tick marks, as determined by the AUTOREF option. The default color is either the value of the CAXIS= option or the first color in the color list. To specify a line type for these reference lines, use the LAUTOREF= option.

CAXIS=*axis-color*

specifies a color for the response and midpoint axis lines and for the default axis area frame. If you omit the CAXIS= option, PROC GCHART searches for a color specification in this order:

1 the COLOR= option in AXIS definitions
2 the first color in the colors list (the default).

This option also specifies the default color for all reference lines.

CERROR=*error-bar-color*
specifies the color of error bars in bar charts. The default is the color of the response axis, which is controlled by the CAXIS= option.

CFRAME=*background-color*
CFR=*background-color*
specifies the color with which to fill the axis area in 2D bar charts or in the backplane in 3D bar charts.

The axis area color does not affect the frame color, which is always the same as the midpoint axis line color and controlled by the CAXIS= option. By default, the axis area in 2D bar charts is not filled.

CFRAME= is overridden by the NOFRAME and IFRAME= options.

Note: If the background color, the bar color, and the outline color are the same, you may not be able to distinguish the bars. △

Featured in: Example 4 on page 848

CFREQ
displays the cumulative frequency statistic in the table of statistics and above vertical bars. Default statistics are suppressed when you request specific statistics. For vertical bar charts, this option is ignored if the bars are too narrow to avoid overlapping values or if the FREQ option is specified.

See also: "About Chart Statistics" on page 782, "Displaying Statistics in Horizontal Bar Charts" on page 815, and "Displaying Statistics in Vertical Bar Charts" on page 815

CFREQLABEL='*column-label*' | NONE (HBAR and HBAR3D only)
specifies the text of the column label for the CFREQ statistic in the table of statistics. *Column-label* can be up to 32 characters long, but a single line of the label can be no more than 24 characters. By default, a label with more than one word will break as close to the center of the line as possible. A double space in the string forces a line break. To suppress the label, specify CFREQLABEL=NONE.

Not supported by: Java, ActiveX

CLIPREF
clips the reference lines at the bars. This makes the reference lines appear to be behind the bars. Because CLIPREF is the default for 3D bar charts, it affects only 2D charts.

Featured in: Example 5 on page 850

CLM=*confidence-level*
specifies the confidence intervals to use when drawing error bars on a bar chart. Values for *confidence-level* must be greater than or equal to 50 and strictly less than 100. The default is 95. See ERRORBAR= for details on how error bars are computed and drawn.

Featured in: Example 6 on page 854

COUTLINE=*bar-outline-color* | SAME
outlines all bars or bar segments and legend values in the subgroup legend (if it appears) using the specified color. SAME specifies that the outline color of a bar or a bar segment or a legend value is the same as the interior pattern color.

The default outline color depends on the PATTERN statement:

- If you do not specify a PATTERN statement, the default outline color is black for the Java or ActiveX devices. Otherwise, the default outline color is the foreground color (the first color in the colors list).
- If you specify the PATTERN statement or the V6COMP graphics option, the default is COUTLINE=SAME.

Note: For 2D bar charts, if you specify empty patterns, (VALUE=EMPTY in a PATTERN statement) you should not change the outline color from the default value, SAME, to a single color. Otherwise all the outlines will be one color and you will not be able to distinguish between the empty areas. △

COUTLINE= is not valid when SHAPE=CYLINDER.

See also: "Controlling Bar Chart Patterns, Colors, and Images" on page 816 and "About Patterns" on page 784

Featured in: Example 3 on page 846, Example 5 on page 850 and Example 6 on page 854

CPERCENT
CPCT

displays the cumulative percentage statistic in the table of statistics and above vertical bars. Default statistics are suppressed when you request specific statistics. For vertical bar charts, this option is ignored if the bars are too narrow to avoid overlapping values or if the FREQ, CFREQ, or PERCENT option is specified.

See also: "About Chart Statistics" on page 782, "Displaying Statistics in Horizontal Bar Charts" on page 815, and "Displaying Statistics in Vertical Bar Charts" on page 815

CREF=*reference-line-color* | (*reference-line-color*) | *reference-line-color-list*
CR=*reference-line-color* | (*reference-line-color*) | *reference-line-color-list*

specifies colors for reference lines. Specifying a single color without parentheses applies that color to all reference lines, including lines drawn with the AUTOREF and REF= options. Note that the CAUTOREF= option overrides CREF= reference color for reference lines drawn with the AUTOREF option. Specifying a single color in parentheses applies that color only to the first reference line drawn with the REF= option. Specifying a reference color list applies colors in sequence to successive lines drawn with the REF= option. The syntax of the color list is of the form (*color1 color2 ...colorN*) or (*color1, color2 ..., colorN*). The default color for reference lines is either the value of the CAXIS= option or the first color in the color list. To specify line types for these reference lines, use the LREF= option.

CPERCENTLABEL='*column-label*' | NONE (HBAR and HBAR3D only)

specifies the text of the column label for the CPERCENT statistic in the table of statistics. *Column-label* can be up to 32 characters long, but a single line of the label can be no more than 24 characters. By default, a label with more than one word will break as close to the center of the line as possible. A double space in the string forces a line break. To suppress the label, specify CPERCENTLABEL=NONE.

Not supported by: Java, ActiveX

CTEXT=*text-color*

specifies the color of all text on the chart that is not otherwise assigned a color. Text includes axis values and axis labels in the response, midpoint, and group axes; the subgroup legend; and the displayed statistics. For the Java and ActiveX devices, the default color is black. For other devices, if you omit CTEXT=, PROC GCHART searches for a color specification in this order:

1 the CTEXT= option in a GOPTIONS statement

2 the first color in the colors list (the default).

CTEXT= overrides the color specification for the axis label and the tick mark values in the COLOR= option in an AXIS definition assigned to an axis.

CTEXT= is overridden by

- the COLOR= suboption of the LABEL= or VALUE= option in a LEGEND definition assigned to the subgroup legend. In this case the suboption determines the color of the legend label or the color of the legend value descriptions, respectively.
- the COLOR= suboption of a LABEL= or VALUE= option in an AXIS definition assigned to an axis. In this case the suboption determines the color of the axis label or the color of the tick mark values, respectively.

DESCENDING

arranges the bars in descending order of the value of the chart statistic. By default, bars are arranged in ascending order of midpoint value, without regard to the lengths of the bars. DESCENDING reorders the bars from longest to shortest. In horizontal bar charts the ordering is top to bottom; in vertical bar charts the ordering is left to right. If you also use the GROUP= option, the reordering is performed separately for each group, so the order of the midpoints may be different for each group.

DESCENDING overrides any midpoint order that is specified with the MIDPOINTS= option or that is specified in the ORDER= option in an AXIS statement assigned to the midpoint axis.

DESCRIPTION='*entry-description*'
DES='*entry-description*'

specifies the description of the catalog entry for the chart. The maximum length for *entry-description* is 256 characters. The description does not appear on the chart. By default, the GCHART procedure assigns a description of the form HBAR CHART OF *variable*, where *variable* is the name of the chart variable.

The *entry-description* can include the #BYLINE, #BYVAL, and #BYVAR substitution options, which work as they do when used on TITLE, FOOTNOTE, and NOTE statements. Refer to the description of the options on page 222, and "Substituting BY Line Values in a Text String" on page 226. The 256-character limit applies before the substitution takes place for these options; thus, if in the SAS program the entry-description text exceeds 256 characters, it is truncated to 256 characters, and then the substitution is performed.

The descriptive text is shown in each of the following:

- the "description" portion of the Results window
- the catalog-entry properties that you can view from the Explorer window
- the Table of Contents that is generated when you use CONTENTS= on an ODS statement (see "Linking to Output through a Table of Contents" on page 495), assuming the GCHART output is generated while the contents page is open
- the Description field of the PROC GREPLAY window
- the data tip text for web output (depending on the device driver you are using). See "Adding Data Tips to Web Presentations" on page 568 for details.

Featured in: Example 7 on page 856

DISCRETE

treats a numeric chart variable as a discrete variable rather than as a continuous variable. The GCHART procedure creates a separate midpoint and, hence, a separate bar for each unique value of the chart variable. If the chart variable has a format associated with it, each formatted value is treated as a midpoint.

The LEVELS= option is ignored when you use DISCRETE. The MIDPOINTS= option overrides DISCRETE. The ORDER= option in an AXIS statement that is assigned to the midpoint axis can rearrange or exclude discrete midpoint values.

Featured in: Example 7 on page 856

ERRORBAR=BARS | BOTH | TOP

draws confidence intervals on a horizontal or vertical bar chart for either of the following:

- the mean of the SUMVAR= variable for each midpoint if you specify TYPE=MEAN
- the percentage of observations assigned to each midpoint if you specify TYPE=PCT with no SUMVAR= option.

The ERRORBAR= option cannot be used with values of the TYPE= option other than MEAN or PCT. Valid values for ERRORBAR= are:

BARS
draws error bars as bars half the width of the main bars.

BOTH
draws error bars as two ticks joined by a line (default).

TOP
draws the error bar as a tick for the upper confidence limit that is joined to the top of the bar by a line.

By default, ERRORBAR= uses a confidence level of 95 percent. You can specify different confidence levels with the CLM= option.

When you use ERRORBAR= with TYPE=PCT, the confidence interval is based on a normal approximation. Let TOTAL be the total number of observations, and PCT be the percentage assigned to a given midpoint. The standard error of the percentage is approximated as

```
APSTDERR=100 * SQRT((PCT/100) * (1--(PCT/100)) / TOTAL);
```

Let LEVEL be the confidence level specified using the CLM= option, with a default value of 95. The upper confidence limit for the percentage is computed as

```
UCLP = PCT + APSTDERR * PROBIT( 1-(1-LEVEL/100)/2 );
```

The lower confidence limit for the percentage is computed as

```
LCLP = PCT - APSTDERR * PROBIT( 1-(1-LEVEL/100)/2 );
```

When you use ERRORBAR= with TYPE=MEAN, the sum variable must have at least two non-missing values for each midpoint. If the GROUP= option is used, each midpoint within a group must also have two non-missing values. Let N be the number of observations assigned to a midpoint, MEAN be the mean of those observations, and STD be the standard deviation of the observations. The standard error of the mean is computed as

```
STDERR = STD / SQRT(N);
```

Let LEVEL be the confidence level specified using the CLM= option, with a default value of 95. The upper confidence limit for the mean is computed as

```
UCLM = MEAN + STDERR * TINV( 1-(1-LEVEL/100)/2, N-1);
```

The lower confidence limit for the mean is computed as

```
LCLM = MEAN - STDERR * TINV( 1-(1-LEVEL/100)/2, N-1);
```

If you want the error bars to represent a given number C of standard errors instead of a confidence interval, and if the number of observations assigned to each midpoint is the same, then you can find the appropriate value for the CLM= option by running a DATA step. For example, if you want error bars that represent one standard error (C=1) with a sample size of N , you can run the following DATA step to compute the appropriate value for the CLM= option and assign that value to a macro variable &LEVEL:

```
data null;
c = 1;
n = 10;
level = 100 * (1 - 2 * (1 - probt( c, n-1)));
put all;
call symput('level',put(level,best12.));
run;
```

Then when you run the GCHART procedure, you can specify CLM=&LEVEL.

Note that this trick does not work precisely if different midpoints have different numbers of observations. However, choosing an average value for N may yield sufficiently accurate results for graphical purposes if the sample sizes are large or do not vary much.

Featured in: Example 6 on page 854

FRAME | NOFRAME
FR | NOFR

specifies whether the 2D axis area frame or the 3D backplane is drawn. The default is FRAME, which draws a frame around the axis area (in 2D bar charts) or generates a colored 3D backplane (in 3D bar charts). Specifying NOFRAME removes the axis area frame from 2D charts, including any background color or image. For 3D charts, NOFRAME removes the backplane color or image, and leaves the vertical and horizontal axis planes and axes. To remove these planes, use the NOPLANE option in the AXIS statement. To remove one or more axis elements, use either the AXIS statement or the NOAXIS option.

The NOFRAME option overrides the CFRAME= and IFRAME= options and the IBACK= goption"IBACK" on page 317.

The color of the frame or backplane outline is the color of the midpoint axis, which is determined by the CAXIS= option.

If the V6COMP graphics option is in effect, the default is NOFRAME.

Featured in: Example 7 on page 856 and Example 6 on page 854

FREQ

displays the frequency statistic in the table of statistics and above vertical bars. Non-integer values are rounded down to the nearest integer. Default statistics are suppressed when you request specific statistics. For vertical bar charts, this option is ignored if the bars are too narrow to avoid overlapping values. This option overrides the CFREQ, PERCENT, CPERCENT, SUM, and MEAN options.

Featured in: Example 5 on page 850

See also: "About Chart Statistics" on page 782, "Displaying Statistics in Horizontal Bar Charts" on page 815, and "Displaying Statistics in Vertical Bar Charts" on page 815

FREQLABEL='*column-label*' | NONE (HBAR and HBAR3D only)

specifies the text of the column label for the FREQ statistic in the table of statistics. *column-label* can be up to 32 characters long, but a single line of the label can be no more than 24 characters. By default, a label with more than one word will break as close to the center of the line as possible. A double space in the string forces a line break. To suppress the label, specify FREQLABEL=NONE.

Featured in: Example 5 on page 850 and Example 6 on page 854

Not supported by: Java, ActiveX

FREQ=*numeric-variable*

specifies a variable whose values weight the contribution of each observation in the computation of the chart statistic. Each observation is counted the number of times that is specified by the value of *numeric-variable* for that observation. If the value of *numeric-variable* is missing, 0, or negative, the observation is not used in the statistic calculation. Non-integer values of *numeric-variable* are truncated to integers. FREQ= is valid with all chart statistics.

Because you cannot use TYPE=PERCENT, TYPE=CPERCENT, TYPE=FREQ, or TYPE=CFREQ with the SUMVAR= option, you must use FREQ= to calculate percentages, cumulative percentages, frequencies, or cumulative frequencies based on a sum.

The statistics will not be affected by applying a format to *numeric-variable.*

See also: "Calculating Weighted Statistics" on page 783

FRONTREF

specifies that reference lines drawn by the AUTOREF or REF= options should be drawn in front of the bars. By default, reference lines in 3D bar charts are drawn on the back plane of the axis.

G100

calculates the percentage and cumulative percentage statistics separately for each group. When you use G100, the individual percentages reflect the contribution of the midpoint to the group and total 100 percent for each group. G100 is ignored unless you also use the GROUP= option.

By default, the individual percentages reflect the contribution of the midpoint to the entire chart and total 100 percent for the entire chart.

GAXIS=AXIS<1...99>

assigns the specified AXIS definition to the group axis. (A group axis is created when you use the GROUP= option.) You can use the AXIS definition to modify the order of the groups, the text of the labels, and appearance of the axis. GAXIS= is ignored if the specified AXIS definition does not exist.

The AXIS statement options MAJOR= and MINOR= are ignored in AXIS definitions assigned to the group axis because the axis does not use tick marks. A warning message is written to the SAS log if these options appear in the AXIS definition.

The Java and ActiveX devices do not support all AXIS statement options. See "AXIS Statement" on page 124 for more information.

To remove groups from the chart, use the ORDER= option in the AXIS statement.

To suppress the brackets drawn around the values on the group axis in vertical bar charts, use the NOBRACKETS option in the AXIS statement.

See also: "AXIS Statement" on page 124

Featured in: Example 7 on page 856

Not supported by: Java (partial), ActiveX (partial)

GROUP=*group-variable*

organizes the data according to values of *group-variable. Group-variable* can be either character or numeric and is always treated as a discrete variable.

GROUP= produces a separate group of bars for each unique value of the group variable. Missing values for *group-variable* are treated as a valid group. The groups are arranged in ascending order of the group variable values.

By default, each group includes all midpoints, even if no observations for the group fall within the midpoint range, meaning that no bar is drawn at the midpoint. Use the NOZERO option to suppress midpoints with no observations.

GROUP= also produces a *group axis* that lists the values that distinguish the groups. The group axis has no axis line but displays the group variable name or label. To modify the group axis, assign an AXIS definition with the GAXIS= option.

In horizontal bar charts, the group axis is to the left of the midpoint axis and the groups are arranged from top to bottom, starting with the lowest value at the top.

In vertical bar charts, the group axis is below the midpoint axis and the groups are arranged from left to right starting with the lowest value at the left. If the group label in a vertical bar chart is narrower than all the bars in the group, brackets are added to the label to emphasize which bars belong in each group. Group brackets are not displayed if the space between the group values is less than one and one-half character cells. Use the NOBRACKETS option in the AXIS statement to suppress the group brackets.

Featured in: Example 7 on page 856

GSPACE=*group-spacing*

specifies the amount of extra space between groups of bars. *Group-space* can be any non-negative number. Units are character cells. Use GSPACE=0 to leave no extra space between adjacent groups of bars. In this case, the same space appears between groups of bars as between the bars in the same group.

GSPACE= is ignored unless you also use the GROUP= option. By default, the GCHART procedure calculates group spacing based on size of the axis area and the number of bars in the chart.

If the requested spacing results in a chart that is too large to fit in the space available for the midpoint axis, an error message is written to the SAS log and no chart is produced.

Featured in: Example 7 on page 856

HTML=*variable*

identifies the variable in the input data set whose values create links in the HTML file created by the ODS statement. These links are associated with an area of the chart and point to the data or graph you wish to display when the user drills down on the area. The values of *variable* can be up to 1024 characters long. Characters after the 1024-character limit (including any closing quotes) are truncated.

HTML_LEGEND=*variable*

identifies the variable in the input data set whose values create links in the HTML file created by the ODS statement. These links are associated with a legend value and point to the data or graph you wish to display when the user drills down on the value. The values of *variable* can be up to 1024 characters long. Characters after the 1024-character limit (including any closing quotes) are truncated.

Not supported by: Java, ActiveX

IFRAME=*fileref* | '*external-file*'

identifies the image file you wish to fill the backplane frame of your three-dimensional bar charts. See also the IMAGESTYLE= option and "Placing a Backplane Image on Graphs with Frames" on page 115.

This option is overridden by the NOIMAGEPRINT goption"IMAGEPRINT" on page 318 .

To fill the backplane frame of two-dimensional bar charts, see the IBACK= goption"IBACK" on page 317 .

Not supported by: Java

IMAGESTYLE= TILE | FIT

for three-dimensional bar charts, specifies whether to use multiple instances of an image to fill the backplane frame (TILE) or to stretch a single instance of an image to fill the backplane frame (FIT). The TILE value is the default. See also the IFRAME= option. Java supports only TILE.

Not supported by: Java (partial)

INSIDE=*statistic*

displays the values of the specified statistic inside the bars. For the Java and ActiveX devices, this option is valid for both horizontal and vertical bar charts. For other devices, this option is only valid for vertical bar charts.

Statistic can be one of the following:

- FREQ
- CFREQ
- CPERCENT | CPCT
- MEAN
- PERCENT | PCT
- SUM

If the bars are subgrouped, only the following statistics are valid:

- FREQ
- PERCENT | PCT
- SUBPCT
- SUM

With subgroups, PERCENT displays the percent contribution of each subgroup to the midpoint value of the bar, based on frequency. The PERCENT values for each subgroup total the percent contribution of the bar to the whole. For example, if the percent contribution of the whole bar is 60%, the PERCENT statistic for all the subgroups in that bar will total 60%. To calculate PERCENT based on the SUMVAR= variable, use the FREQ= and TYPE= options. For details, see "Calculating Weighted Statistics" on page 783.

SUBPCT displays the percent contribution of each subgroup to the total bar. The SUBPCT values for each subgroup total the percent contribution to the whole bar. Because of rounding, the total of the percents may not equal 100.

Featured in: Example 4 on page 848 Example 7 on page 856

See also: "About Chart Statistics" on page 782, "Displaying Statistics in Horizontal Bar Charts" on page 815, and "Displaying Statistics in Vertical Bar Charts" on page 815

LAUTOREF=*reference-line-type*

specifies the line type for reference lines at major tick marks, as determined by the AUTOREF option. Line types are specified as whole numbers from 1 to 46, with 1 representing a solid line and the other values representing dashed lines. The default value is 1. To specify a color for these reference lines, use the CAUTOREF= option.

LEGEND=LEGEND<1...99>

assigns the specified LEGEND definition to the legend generated by the SUBGROUP= option. The LEGEND= option itself does *not* generate a legend.

LEGEND= is ignored if

- SUBGROUP= is not used.
- the specified LEGEND definition is not in effect.
- the NOLEGEND option is used.
- the PATTERNID= option is set to any value other than SUBGROUP; that is, the value of PATTERNID= is BY or GROUP or MIDPOINT.

To create a legend based on the chart midpoints instead of the subgroups, use the chart variable as the subgroup variable:

```
hbar city / subgroup=city;
```

The Java and ActiveX devices do not support all LEGEND statement options. See "LEGEND Statement" on page 151 for more information.

See also: "LEGEND Statement" on page 151 and SUBGROUP= on page 813 option

Featured in: Example 4 on page 848

LEVELS=*number-of-midpoints* | ALL

specifies the number of midpoints for a numeric chart variable. The range for each midpoint is calculated automatically, using the algorithm in Terrell and Scott (1985).

If you specify LEVELS=ALL, then all unique midpoint values are graphed. If your data contains a large number of unique midpoint values (over 200), you can use the XPIXELS and YPIXELS GOPTIONS to allow the device driver to render a larger (and more readable) graph.

LEVELS= is ignored if

- the chart variable is character type
- the DISCRETE option is used
- the MIDPOINTS= option is used.

LREF=*reference-line-type* | (*reference-line-type* | *reference-line-type-list*)
LR=*reference-line-type* | (*reference-line-type* | *reference-line-type-list*)

specifies line types for reference lines. Line types are specified as whole numbers from 1 to 46, with 1 representing a solid line and the other values representing dashed lines. Specifying a line type without parentheses applies that type to all reference lines drawn with the AUTOREF and REF= options. Note that the LAUTOREF= option overrides LREF=*reference-line-type* for reference lines drawn with the AUTOREF option. Specifying a single line type in parentheses applies that line type to the first reference line drawn with the REF= option. Specifying a line type list applies line types in sequence to successive reference lines drawn with the REF= option. The syntax of the line-type list is of the form (*type1 type2 ...typeN*). The default line type is specified by the AXIS statement's STYLE= option. By default, STYLE=1, a solid line. To specify colors for these reference lines, use the CREF= option.

Not supported by: Java

MAXIS=AXIS<1...99>

assigns the specified AXIS definition to the midpoint axis. The MAXIS= option is ignored if the specified AXIS definition does not exist.

The Java and ActiveX devices do not support all AXIS statement options. See "AXIS Statement" on page 124 for more information.

See also: "AXIS Statement" on page 124 and "About Midpoints" on page 780

Featured in: Example 4 on page 848

Not supported by: Java (partial), ActiveX (partial)

MEAN

displays the mean statistic in the table of statistics and above vertical bars. By default, the column heading in the table includes the name of the variable for which the mean is calculated. Default statistics are suppressed when you request specific statistics. For vertical bar charts, this option is ignored if the bars are too narrow to avoid overlapping values or if the FREQ, CFREQ, PERCENT, CPERCENT, or SUM option is specified. MEAN is ignored unless you also use the SUMVAR= option.

See also: "About Chart Statistics" on page 782, "Displaying Statistics in Horizontal Bar Charts" on page 815, and "Displaying Statistics in Vertical Bar Charts" on page 815

MEANLABEL='*column-label*' | NONE (HBAR and HBAR3D only)

specifies the text of the column label for the MEAN statistic in the table of statistics. *column-label* can be up to 32 characters long, but a single line of the label can be no more than 24 characters. By default, a label with more than one word will break as close to the center of the line as possible. A double space in the string forces a line break. To suppress the label, specify MEANLABEL=NONE.

Featured in: Example 6 on page 854

Not supported by: Java, ActiveX

MIDPOINTS=*value-list*

specifies the midpoint values for the bars. The way you specify *value-list* depends on the type of the chart variable.

- For numeric chart variables, *value-list* is either an explicit list of values, or a starting and an ending value with an interval increment, or a combination of both forms:

  n <...*n*>

  n TO *n* <BY *increment*>

  n<...*n*> TO *n* <BY *increment*> <*n* <...*n*>>

  If a numeric variable has an associated format, the specified values must be the *unformatted* values.

  By default, numeric variable values are treated as continuous (if you omit the DISCRETE option), and

  - the lowest midpoint consolidates all data points from negative infinity to the median of the first two midpoints
  - the highest midpoint consolidates all data points from the median of the last two midpoints up to infinity
  - all other values in *value-list* specify the median of a range of values, and the GCHART procedure calculates the midpoint values.

  If you include the DISCRETE option, each value in *value-list* specifies a unique numeric value.

- For character chart variables, *value-list* is a list of unique character values enclosed in quotation marks and separated by blanks:

  'value-1' <...*'value-n'*>

  If a character variable has an associated format, the specified values must be the *formatted* values.

For a complete description of *value-list*, see the ORDER= on page 130 option in the AXIS statement.

If the *value-list* for either type of variable specifies so many midpoints that the axis values overwrite each other, the values may be unreadable. In this case the procedure writes a warning to the SAS log. On many devices, this problem can be corrected by either adjusting the size of the text with the HTEXT= graphics option or by increasing the number of cells in your graphics display using the HPOS= and VPOS= graphics options.

The ORDER= option in the AXIS statement overrides the order specified in the MIDPOINTS= option. The bar chart statement options ASCENDING and DESCENDING also override both MIDPOINTS= and ORDER= in the AXIS statement.

See also: "About Midpoints" on page 780

Featured in: Example 5 on page 850

MIDPOINTS=OLD

generates default midpoints using the Nelder algorithm (*Applied Statistics* 25:94–7, 1976). The MIDPOINTS=OLD option is ignored unless the chart variable is numeric.

MINOR=*number-of-minor-ticks*
specifies the number of minor tick marks between each major tick mark on the response axis.

MINOR= in a bar chart statement overrides the number of minor tick marks specified in the MINOR= option in an AXIS definition assigned to the response axis with the RAXIS= option.

MISSING
accepts a missing value as a valid midpoint for the chart variable. By default, observations with missing values are ignored. Missing values are always valid for group and subgroup variables.

NAME='*entry-name*'
specifies the name of the catalog entry for the graph. The maximum length for *entry-name* is eight characters. The default name is GCHART. If the name duplicates an existing entry name, thenSAS/GRAPH software adds a number to the duplicate name to create a unique name—for example, GCHART1.

Featured in: Example 7 on page 856

NOAXIS
suppresses all axes, including axis lines, axis labels, axis values, and all major and minor tick marks. If you specify an axis definition with the GAXIS, MAXIS=, or RAXIS= options, then the axes are generated as defined in the AXIS statement, but then all lines, labels, values, and tick marks are suppressed. Therefore, axis statement options such as ORDER=, LENGTH, and OFFSET= will still be used.

To remove only selected axis elements such as lines, values or labels, use specific AXIS statement options.

NOAXIS does not suppress either the default frame or an axis area fill requested by the CFRAME= option. To remove the axis frame or the 3D backplane, use the NOFRAME option in the procedure. To remove the horizontal or vertical axis planes, use the NOPLANE option in the AXIS statement.

NOBASEREF
suppresses the zero reference line when the SUM or MEAN chart statistic has negative values.

NOLEGEND
suppresses the legend that is automatically generated by the SUBGROUP= option. NOLEGEND is ignored if the SUBGROUP= option is not used.

NOSTATS (HBAR and HBAR3D only)
suppresses the table of statistics. NOSTATS suppresses both the default statistics and specific statistics requested by the FREQ, CFREQ, PERCENT, CPERCENT, SUM, and MEAN options.

Not supported by: Java

NOZERO
suppresses any midpoints for which there are no corresponding values of the chart variable and, hence, no bar. NOZERO usually is used with the GROUP= option to suppress midpoints when not all values of the chart variable are present for every group or if the chart statistic for the bar is 0.

Note: If a bar is omitted and if you have also specified bar labels with the VALUE= option in an AXIS statement, the labels may be shifted and not displayed with the correct bar. △

Featured in: Example 7 on page 856

Not supported by: Java

OUTSIDE=*statistic*

displays the values of the specified statistic above the bars. For the Java and ActiveX devices, this option is valid for both horizontal and vertical bar charts. For other devices, this option is only valid for vertical bar charts.

Statistic can be one of the following:

- FREQ
- CFREQ
- PERCENT | PCT
- CPERCENT | CPCT
- SUM
- MEAN

Featured in: Example 4 on page 848 and Example 7 on page 856

See also: "About Chart Statistics" on page 782, "Displaying Statistics in Horizontal Bar Charts" on page 815, and "Displaying Statistics in Vertical Bar Charts" on page 815

PATTERNID=BY | GROUP | MIDPOINT | SUBGROUP

specifies the way fill patterns are assigned. By default, PATTERNID=SUBGROUP. Values for PATTERNID= are as follows:

BY
: changes patterns each time the value of the BY variable changes. All bars use the same pattern if the GCHART procedure does not include a BY statement.

GROUP
: changes patterns every time the value of the group variable changes. All bars in each group use the same pattern, but a different pattern is used for each group.

MIDPOINT
: changes patterns every time the midpoint value changes. If you use the GROUP= option, the respective midpoint patterns are repeated for each group.

SUBGROUP
: changes patterns every time the value of the subgroup variable changes. The bars must be subdivided by the SUBGROUP= option for the SUBGROUP value to have an effect. Without SUBGROUP=, all bars have the same pattern.

Note: If you use the SUBGROUP= option and specify a PATTERNID= value other than SUBGROUP, the bar segments use the same pattern and are indistinguishable. △

See also: "Controlling Bar Chart Patterns, Colors, and Images" on page 816

Featured in: Example 4 on page 848 and Example 7 on page 856

PERCENT
PCT

prints the percentages of observations having a given value for the chart variable in the table of statistics and above vertical bars. Default statistics are suppressed when you request specific statistics. For vertical bar charts, this option is ignored if the bars are too narrow to avoid overlapping values or if the FREQ or CFREQ option is specified.

See also: "About Chart Statistics" on page 782, "Displaying Statistics in Horizontal Bar Charts" on page 815, and "Displaying Statistics in Vertical Bar Charts" on page 815

PERCENTLABEL='*column-label*' | NONE (HBAR and HBAR3D only)
specifies the text of the column label for the PERCENT statistic in the table of statistics. *column-label* can be up to 32 characters long, but a single line of the label can be no more than 24 characters. By default, a label with more than one word will break as close to the center of the line as possible. A double space in the string forces a line break. To suppress the label, specify PERCENTLABEL=NONE.

Not supported by: Java, ActiveX

RANGE
displays on the axis of the chart the range of numeric values represented by each bar. In the graphics output, the starting value of each range is indicated with the less-than symbol (<), and the ending value is indicated with the greater-than-or-equal-to symbol (>=). The RANGE option has no affect on axes that represent character data. By default, the values shown on the axis are determined by the value of the MIDPOINTS= option on page 809. If specified, the DISCRETE option on page 802 overrides the RANGE option.

RAXIS=*value-list* | AXIS<1...99>
AXIS=*value-list* | AXIS<1...99>
specifies values for the major tick mark divisions on the response axis or assigns the specified AXIS definition to the axis. See the MIDPOINTS= option on page 809 for a description of *value-list*. By default, the GCHART procedure scales the response axis automatically and provides an appropriate number of tick marks.

You can specify negative values, but negative values are reasonable only when TYPE=SUM or TYPE=MEAN and one or more of the sums or means are less than 0. Frequency and percentage values are never less than 0.

For lists of values, a separate major tick mark is created for each individual value. A warning message is written to the SAS log if the values are not evenly spaced.

If the values represented by the bars are larger than the highest tick mark value, the bars are truncated at the highest tick mark.

If you use a BY statement with the PROC GCHART statement, the same response axes are produced for each BY group when RAXIS=*value-list* is used or if there is an ORDER= list in the AXIS statement assigned to the response axis.

The Java and ActiveX devices do not support all AXIS statement options. See "AXIS Statement" on page 124 for more information.

See also: "AXIS Statement" on page 124

Featured in: Example 4 on page 848 and Example 7 on page 856

Not supported by: Java (partial), ActiveX (partial)

REF=*value-list*
draws reference lines at the specified points on the response axis. See the MIDPOINTS= option on page 809 for a description of *value-list*.

Values can be listed in any order, but should be within the range of values represented by the response axis. A warning is written to the SAS log if any of the points are off of the axis, and no reference line is drawn for such points. You can use the AUTOREF option to draw reference lines automatically at all of the major tick marks.

By default, reference lines in 3D bar charts are drawn on the back plane of the axis. To draw the reference lines in front of the bars, use the FRONTREF option.

SHAPE=*3D-bar-shape* (HBAR3D and VBAR3D only)
specifies the shape of the bars in charts that are produced with the HBAR3D and VBAR3D statements. *3D-bar-shape* can be one of the following:

- BLOCK | B (the default)
- CYLINDER | C

- HEXAGON | H
- PRISM | P
- STAR | S

The COUTLINE= option is not valid when SHAPE=CYLINDER.

Featured in: Example 7 on page 856

SPACE=*bar-spacing*

specifies the amount of space between individual bars or between the bars within each group if you also use the GROUP= option. *Bar-space* can be any non-negative number, including decimal values. Units are character cells. By default, the GCHART procedure calculates spacing based on the size of the axis area and the number of bars on the chart. Use SPACE=0 to leave no space between adjacent bars.

SPACE= is ignored if

- you specify the WIDTH= option and are using the Java or ActiveX devices.
- the specified spacing requests a chart that is too large to fit in the space available for the midpoint axis. In this case, a warning message is issued.

Featured in: Example 4 on page 848 and Example 7 on page 856

SUBGROUP=*subgroup-variable*

divides the bars into segments according to the values of *subgroup-variable*. *Subgroup-variable* can be either character or numeric and is always treated as a discrete variable. SUBGROUP= creates a separate segment within each bar for every unique value of the subgroup variable for that midpoint.

If PATTERNID=SUBGROUP (the default setting), each segment is filled with a different pattern and a legend that provides a key to the patterns is automatically generated. If the value of PATTERNID= is anything other than SUBGROUP, the segments are all the same color, the legend is suppressed, and the subgrouping effect is lost.

By default the legend appears at the bottom of the chart. To modify the legend, assign a LEGEND definition with the LEGEND= option. To suppress the legend, specify NOLEGEND.

See also: "LEGEND Statement" on page 151

Featured in: Example 4 on page 848, Example 7 on page 856 and Example 5 on page 850

SUM

displays the sum statistic in the table of statistics and above vertical bars. By default, the column heading in the table includes the name of the variable for which the sum is calculated. Default statistics are suppressed when you request specific statistics. For vertical bar charts, this option is ignored if the bars are too narrow to avoid overlapping values or if the FREQ, CFREQ, PERCENT, or CPERCENT option is specified. SUM is ignored unless you also use the SUMVAR= option.

See also: "About Chart Statistics" on page 782, "Displaying Statistics in Horizontal Bar Charts" on page 815, and "Displaying Statistics in Vertical Bar Charts" on page 815

SUMLABEL='*column-label*' | NONE (HBAR and HBAR3D only)

specifies the text of the column label for the SUM statistic in the table of statistics. *Column-label* can be up to 32 characters long, but a single line of the label can be no more than 24 characters. By default, a label with more than one word will break as close to the center of the line as possible. A double space in the string forces a line break. To suppress the label, specify SUMLABEL=NONE.

Not supported by: Java, ActiveX

SUMVAR=*summary-variable*
specifies a numeric variable for sum or mean calculations. The GCHART procedure calculates the sum or, if requested, the mean of *summary-variable* for each midpoint. The resulting statistics are represented by the length of the bars along the response axis, and they are displayed at major tick marks.

When you use SUMVAR=, the TYPE= option must be either SUM or MEAN. With SUMVAR=, the default is TYPE=SUM.

Featured in: Example 3 on page 846 and Example 6 on page 854

TYPE=*statistic*
specifies the chart statistic.

- If the SUMVAR= option is not used, *statistic* can be one of the following:

  FREQ
  frequency (the default)

  CFREQ
  cumulative frequency

  PERCENT PCT
  percentage

  CPERCENT CPCT
  cumulative percentage

- If SUMVAR= is used, *statistic* can be:

  SUM
  sum (the default)

  MEAN
  mean

Because you cannot use TYPE=FREQ, TYPE=CFREQ, TYPE=PERCENT, or TYPE=CPERCENT with the SUMVAR= option, you must use FREQ= to calculate percentages, cumulative percentages, frequencies, or cumulative frequencies based on a sum. See also "Calculating Weighted Statistics" on page 783.

If you specify TYPE=MEAN and use the SUBGROUP= option, the height or length of the bar represents the mean for the entire midpoint. The subgroup segments are proportional to the subgroup's contribution to the sum for the bar. See also SUBGROUP= on page 813.

See also: "About Chart Statistics" on page 782 for a complete description of statistic types

Featured in: Example 6 on page 854

WIDTH=*bar-width*
specifies the width of the bars. By default, the GCHART procedure selects a bar width that accommodates the midpoint values displayed on the midpoint axis using a hardware font and a height of one cell. Units for *bar-width* are character cells. The value for *bar-width* must be greater than 0, but it does not have to be an integer, for example,

```
vbar site / width=1.5;
```

If the requested bar width results in a chart that is too large to fit in the space available for the midpoint axis, the procedure issues a warning in the log and ignores the WIDTH= specification. If the specified width is too narrow, the procedure may display the midpoint values vertically.

Featured in: Example 4 on page 848

WOUTLINE=*bar-outline-width*

specifies the width of the outline in pixels. WOUTLINE= affects both the bar and the subgroup outlines.

Not supported by: Java

The Chart Statistic and the Response Axis

In bar charts, the scale of values of the chart statistic is displayed on the response axis. By default, the response axis is divided into evenly spaced intervals identified with major tick marks that are labeled with the corresponding statistic value. Minor tick marks are evenly distributed between the major tick marks unless a log axis has been requested. For sum and mean statistics, the major tick marks are labeled with values of the SUMVAR= variable (formatted if the variable has an associated format). The response axis is also labeled with the statistic type.

Specifying Logarithmic Axes

Logarithmic axes can be specified with the AXIS statement. See "AXIS Statement" on page 124 for a complete discussion.

Displaying Statistics in Horizontal Bar Charts

For graphs generated with the Java and ActiveX devices, default statistics are not generated, but you can display one statistic at the end of each bar. To specify the statistic, specify the FREQ, CFREQ, PERCENT, CPERCENT, SUM, or MEAN option.

For graphs generated with other devices, the HBAR and HBAR3D statements print a table of statistic values to the right of the bars. When the value of TYPE= is FREQ, CFREQ, PERCENT, or CPERCENT, the frequency, cumulative frequency, percentage, and cumulative percentage statistics are printed next to the bars by default. When TYPE=SUM, the frequency and sum statistic values are printed by default. When TYPE=MEAN, the frequency and mean statistic values are printed by default. However, if you use the FREQ, CFREQ, PERCENT, CPERCENT, SUM, or MEAN options to request specific statistics, the default statistics are not printed.

For sum and mean, the name of the SUMVAR= variable is added to the heading for the column of values.

Specifying the Table of Statistics

You can use the FREQ, CFREQ, PERCENT, CPERCENT, SUM, and MEAN options to select only certain statistics. Without the SUMVAR= option, only the frequency, cumulative frequency, percentage, and cumulative percentage statistics can be printed. With SUMVAR=, all statistics, including the sum and mean, can be printed. You can suppress all statistics with the NOSTATS option.

To change the column labels for any statistic in the table, use one or more of the statistic column label options: FREQLABEL=, CFREQLABEL=, PERCENTLABEL=, CPERCENTLABEL=, SUMLABEL=, and MEANLABEL=.

To control the font and size of the text in the table of statistics, use the HTEXT= and FTEXT= graphics options.

Displaying Statistics in Vertical Bar Charts

Statistic values on vertical bar charts are not printed by default, so you must explicitly request a statistic with the FREQ, CFREQ, PERCENT, CPERCENT, SUM, MEAN, INSIDE=, or OUTSIDE= option.

For graphs generated with the Java and ActiveX devices, you can display one statistic for each bar. For graphs generated with other devices, you can display up to two statistics. Statistics can be displayed either above the bars or inside the bars.

To specify a statistic that you want to display above the bars, specify the statistic option (FREQ, CFREQ, PERCENT, CPERCENT, SUM, or MEAN) or specify OUTSIDE=*statistic*. To specify a statistic that you want to display inside the bars, specify INSIDE=*statistic*.

For graphs generated with the Java and ActiveX devices, the OUTSIDE= option overrides INSIDE=, and INSIDE= overrides the FREQ, CFREQ, PERCENT, CPERCENT, SUM, and MEAN options. For graphs generated with other devices, the individual statistic options override the OUTSIDE= option.

If more than one statistic option is specified, only the highest priority statistic is displayed. The priority order, from highest to lowest, is as follows:

1 FREQ
2 CFREQ
3 PERCENT
4 CPERCENT
5 SUM
6 MEAN

The bars must be wide enough to accommodate the text. You can adjust the width of the bars with the WIDTH= option. To control the font and size of the text, use the HTEXT= and FTEXT= graphics options.

Ordering and Selecting Midpoints

To rearrange character or discrete numeric midpoint values or to select ranges for numeric values, use the MIDPOINTS= option. Remember that although changing the number of midpoints for numeric variables may change the range of values for individual midpoints, it does not change the range of values for the chart as a whole. For details, see "About Midpoints" on page 780.

Like MIDPOINTS=, the ORDER= option in the AXIS statement can rearrange the order of the midpoints or suppress the display of discrete numeric or character values. However, ORDER= cannot calculate the midpoints for a continuous numeric variable, or exclude values from the calculations. For details, see the description of the ORDER= on page 130 option.

Controlling Bar Chart Patterns, Colors, and Images

Default Patterns and Outlines

Each bar in a bar chart is filled with a pattern. By default, the procedure

- fills the bars with bar/block patterns, beginning with the default fill, SOLID, and rotating it through the colors list. When the solid patterns are exhausted, the procedure selects the next default bar/block pattern and rotates it through the colors list. It continues in this fashion until all of the required patterns have been assigned.

  Note: 3D bar charts always uses solid patterns. △

  If you use the device's default colors and the first color in the list is either black or white, the procedure does not create a pattern in that color. If you specify a colors list with the COLORS= graphics option, the procedure uses all the colors in the list to generate the patterns.
- outlines bars and bar segments using the first color in the colors list.

See "About Patterns" on page 784 for more information on how the GCHART procedure assigns default patterns and outlines.

User-Defined Patterns

To override the default patterns and select fills and colors for the bars or bar segments, use the PATTERN statement. Only bar/block patterns are valid; all other pattern fills are ignored. For a complete description of all bar/block patterns, see VALUE= on page 171 in "PATTERN Statement" on page 169.

Whenever you use PATTERN statements, the default pattern outline color changes to SAME. That is, the outline color is the same as the fill color. To specify the outline color, use the COUTLINE= option (see COUTLINE= on page 800).

When Patterns Change

The PATTERNID= option controls when the pattern changes. By default, PATTERNID=SUBGROUP. Therefore, when you use the SUBGROUP= option to subdivide the bars, the pattern automatically changes each time the subgroup value changes, and each subdivision of the bar displays a different pattern. As a result, the number of values for the SUBGROUP= variable determines the number of bar patterns on the chart. If you do not subdivide the bars, all bars use the same pattern.

Instead of changing the pattern for each subgroup, you can change the pattern for each midpoint, each group, or each BY group by changing the value of PATTERNID=. See the PATTERNID= on page 811 option for details.

Axis Color

By default, axis elements use the first color in the colors list or the colors that are specified by AXIS statement color options. However, action statement options can also control the color of the axis lines, text, and frame.

To change the color of...	Use this option...
the axis text	CTEXT=
the axis lines	CAXIS=
the area within the frame	CFRAME=

Adding Images to Bar Charts

You can apply images to the bars and to the backplane frame of two-dimensional bar charts developed with the HBAR and VBAR statements. In three–dimensional bar charts, you can apply images to the backplane frame. For details, see "Specifying Images in SAS/GRAPH Programs" on page 106.

PIE, PIE3D, and DONUT Statements

Create pie or donut charts in which the size of a pie slice represents the value of the chart statistic for that category of data in relation to the total chart statistic for all categories.

Requirements: At least one chart variable is required.

Global statements: LEGEND, PATTERN, TITLE, FOOTNOTE

Supports: Drill-down functionality

Description

The PIE, PIE3D, and DONUT statements specify the variable or variables that define the categories of data to chart. These statements automatically

- □ determine the midpoints.
- □ calculate the chart statistic for each midpoint (the default is FREQ).
- □ scale each slice to represent its chart statistic. No slice is drawn if the chart statistic for the midpoint is 0.
- □ order the slices by midpoint value in ascending order starting at the three o'clock position and proceeding counterclockwise around the pie.
- □ print the slice name (midpoint value) and slice value (chart statistic) beside each slice.
- □ assign patterns and colors to the slices. The default pie pattern is PSOLID.

You can use statement options to select or order the midpoints (slices), to change the type of chart statistic, and to modify the appearance of the chart, including the content and position of the slice labels, and patterns used by the slices. You can also specify additional variables by which to group, subgroup, or sum the data. Statement options can also produce special effects, such as exploded or invisible slices.

Donut and pie charts allow grouping and subgrouping. Grouping creates two or more separate pie or donut charts that display in rows or columns on one graph. Subgrouping creates a separate ring of slices within the circle for each value of the subgroup variable. The concentric rings of the subgrouped pie or donut chart make it easy to compare slice values between subgroups.

In addition, you can use global statements to modify patterns and legends, as well as add titles, footnotes, and notes to the chart. You can also use an Annotate data set to enhance the chart.

Syntax

PIE | PIE3D | DONUT *chart-variable(s)* </ *option(s)*>;

option(s) can be one or more options from any or all of the following categories:

- □ appearance options

  ANNOTATE=*Annotate-data-set*

  CFILL=*fill-color*

  COUTLINE=*slice-outline-color* | SAME

  DETAIL_RADIUS=*percent* (PIE and DONUT only)

  EXPLODE=*value-list*

  FILL=SOLID | X

  INVISIBLE=*value-list*

NOHEADING
WOUTLINE=*slice-outline-width*

- statistic options
  - FREQ=*numeric-variable*
  - SUMVAR=*summary-variable*
  - TYPE=*statistic*
- midpoint options
  - DISCRETE
  - LEVELS=*number-of-midpoints* | ALL
  - MIDPOINTS=*value-list*
  - MIDPOINTS=OLD
  - MISSING
  - OTHER=*percent-of-total*
- detail pie options (PIE and DONUT only)
  - DETAIL=*variable*
  - DETAIL_THRESHOLD=*percent*
- grouping and subgrouping options
  - ACROSS=*number-of-columns*
  - DOWN=*number-of-rows*
  - GROUP=*group-variable*
  - NOGROUPHEADING
  - SUBGROUP=*subgroup-variable*
- slice-ordering options
  - ANGLE=*degrees*
  - ASCENDING
  - CLOCKWISE
  - DESCENDING
  - JSTYLE
- slice-labeling options
  - CTEXT=*text-color*
  - LEGEND | LEGEND=LEGEND<1...99>
  - MATCHCOLOR
  - NOLEGEND
  - OTHERLABEL='*text-string*'
  - PERCENT=ARROW | INSIDE | NONE | OUTSIDE
  - SLICE=ARROW | INSIDE | NONE | OUTSIDE
  - VALUE=ARROW | INSIDE | NONE | OUTSIDE
- detail pie slice-labeling options (PIE and DONUT only)
  - DETAIL_PERCENT=BEST | NONE
  - DETAIL_SLICE=BEST | NONE
  - DETAIL_VALUE=BEST | NONE
- donut-labeling options (DONUT only):
  - DONUTPCT=*percent*
  - LABEL=(*text argument(s)*)
- catalog entry description options

DESCRIPTION='*entry-description*'

NAME='*entry-name*'

- ODS options

  HTML=*variable*

  HTML_LEGEND=*variable*

Required Arguments

chart-variable(s)
specifies one or more variables that define the categories of data to chart. Each chart variable draws a separate chart. All variables must be in the input data set. Separate multiple chart variables with blanks.

See also: "About Chart Variables" on page 779

Options

Options in a PIE, PIE3D, or DONUT statement affect all graphs that are produced by that statement. You can specify as many options as you want and list them in any order. For details on specifying colors, see Chapter 6, "SAS/GRAPH Colors and Images," on page 91. For a complete description of the graphics options, see Chapter 8, "Graphics Options and Device Parameters Dictionary," on page 261.

ACROSS=*number-of-columns*
draws *number-of-columns* pies across the procedure output area. ACROSS is ignored unless you also use the GROUP= option.

If *number-of-columns* calls for more pies than fit horizontally in the graphics output area, no pies are drawn and an error message is written to the SAS log.

If the DOWN= option also is used, the pies are drawn in left-to-right and top-to-bottom order.

Featured in: Example 11 on page 875

ANGLE=*degrees*
starts the first slice at the specified angle. A value of 0 for *degrees* corresponds to the 3 o'clock position. *Degrees* can be either positive or negative. Positive values move the starting position in the counterclockwise direction; negative values move the starting position clockwise. By default, ANGLE=0. Successive slices are drawn counterclockwise from the starting slice.

ANNOTATE=*Annotate-data-set*
ANNO=*Annotate-data-set*
specifies a data set to annotate charts produced by the PIE, PIE3D, or DONUT statement.

Note: Annotate coordinate systems 1, 2, 7, and 8 (data system coordinates) are not valid with pie or donut charts. △

See also: Chapter 24, "Using Annotate Data Sets," on page 587

ASCENDING
arranges the slices in ascending order of the value of the chart statistic. By default, slices are arranged in ascending order of midpoint value, without regard to size. ASCENDING reorders the slices from smallest to largest. The OTHER slice is still last regardless of its size.

If you also use the GROUP= option, the reordering is performed separately for each group, so the order of the midpoint values may be different for each pie or donut.

ASCENDING overrides any midpoint order that is specified with the MIDPOINTS= option.

CFILL=*fill-color*
specifies one color for all patterns in the chart, regardless of whether the fill is solid or hatch. For the PIE3D statement, the fill is always solid. For the PIE and DONUT statements, if no pattern is specified on the PATTERN statement or with the FILL= option, the procedure starts with the default solid fill and then, beginning with P2N0, uses each default pie hatch pattern with the specified color. For the outline color, the procedure uses the foreground color, which is the first color in the colors lists. Use COUTLINE= to specify a different outline color. CFILL= overrides any other pattern color specification and controls the color of all slices.

See also: "Controlling Bar Chart Patterns, Colors, and Images" on page 816 and "About Patterns" on page 784

Featured in: Example 10 on page 873

CLOCKWISE
draws the slices clockwise starting at the 12 o'clock position. Although this position implies ANGLE=90, you can use ANGLE= to specify a different starting angle.

Featured in: Example 11 on page 875

COUTLINE=*slice-outline-color* | SAME
outlines all slices, rings (subgroups), and legend values (if a legend appears) in the specified color. SAME specifies that the outline color of a slice or a slice segment or a legend value is the same as the interior pattern color.

The default outline color depends on the PATTERN statement:

- If you do not specify a PATTERN statement, the default outline color is black for the Java or ActiveX devices. Otherwise, the default outline color is the foreground color (the first color in the colors list).
- If a PATTERN statement or the V6COMP graphics options is specified, the default is COUTLINE=SAME.

Note: If you specify empty patterns (VALUE=PEMPTY in a PATTERN statement), you should not change the outline color from the default value, SAME, to a single color. Otherwise, all of the outlines will be one color and you will not be able to distinguish between the empty areas. △

See also: "Controlling Slice Patterns and Colors" on page 831 and "About Patterns" on page 784

Featured in: Example 8 on page 869, Example 9 on page 872 and Example 11 on page 875

CTEXT=*text-color*
specifies the color for all text on the chart that is not otherwise assigned a color. Text includes all slice labels, the chart heading, and group headings if grouping is used. CTEXT= also affects the color of the slice label arrows. See "Selecting and Positioning Slice Labels" on page 830.

For the Java and ActiveX devices, the default color is black. For other devices, if you omit CTEXT=, PROC GCHART searches for a color specification in this order:

1. the CTEXT= option in a GOPTIONS statement
2. the first color in the colors list (the default).

The MATCHCOLOR option overrides the CTEXT= option for slice labels.

Featured in: Example 9 on page 872 and Example 11 on page 875

DESCENDING

arranges the slices in descending order of the value of the chart statistic. By default, slices are arranged in ascending order of midpoint value, without regard to size. DESCENDING reorders the slices from largest to smallest. The OTHER slice is still last, regardless of its size.

If you also use the GROUP= option, the reordering is performed separately for each group, so the order of midpoint values may be different for each pie or donut.

DESCENDING overrides any midpoint order that is specified with the MIDPOINTS= option.

Featured in: Example 11 on page 875

DESCRIPTION='*entry-description*'

DES='*entry-description*'

specifies the description of the catalog entry for the chart. The maximum length for *entry-description* is 256 characters. The description does not appear on the chart. By default, the GCHART procedure assigns a description of the form PIE (or PIE3D or DONUT) CHART OF *variable*, where *variable* is the name of the chart variable.

The *entry-description* can include the #BYLINE, #BYVAL, and #BYVAR substitution options, which work as they do when used on TITLE, FOOTNOTE, and NOTE statements. Refer to the description of the options on page 222, and "Substituting BY Line Values in a Text String" on page 226. The 256-character limit applies before the substitution takes place for these options; thus, if in the SAS program the entry-description text exceeds 256 characters, it is truncated to 256 characters, and then the substitution is performed.

The descriptive text is shown in each of the following:

- the "description" portion of the Results window
- the catalog-entry properties that you can view from the Explorer window
- the Table of Contents that is generated when you use CONTENTS= on an ODS statement (see "Linking to Output through a Table of Contents" on page 495), assuming the GCHART output is generated while the contents page is open
- the Description field of the PROC GREPLAY window
- the data tip text for web output (depending on the device driver you are using). See "Adding Data Tips to Web Presentations" on page 568 for details.

DETAIL=*variable* (PIE and DONUT only)

produces a inner pie overlay whose slices show the major components that comprise the outer pie's slice. *Variable* is the variable whose values are used to construct the detail pie. If you specify the DETAIL= option and either GROUP= or SUBGROUP=, then the DETAIL= option is ignored.

DETAIL_PERCENT=BEST|NONE (PIE and DONUT only)

specifies the algorithm to use for displaying the percentage values for the detail pie slices. NONE turns off the display of the percentage values.

DETAIL_RADIUS=*percent* (PIE and DONUT only)

determines the size of the detail pie. *Percent* specifies the percent of the outer pie radius to use as the detail pie radius. The valid range is 25 to 90. The default is 75.

DETAIL_SLICE=BEST|NONE (PIE and DONUT only)

specifies the algorithm to use for displaying the detail variable labels for the inner pie slices. NONE turns off the display of the detail variable labels.

DETAIL_THRESHOLD=*percent* (PIE and DONUT only)

determines if a detail slice is included in the inner pie. Any detail slice comprising *percent* or more percent of the whole pie is included. The valid range for *percent* is 0 to 75. The default is 4.

DETAIL_VALUE=BEST|NONE (PIE and DONUT only)

specifies the algorithm to use for displaying the data values for the detail pie slices. NONE turns off the display of the data values.

DISCRETE

treats a numeric chart variable as a discrete variable rather than as a continuous variable. The GCHART procedure creates a separate midpoint and, hence, a separate slice for each unique value of the chart variable. If the chart variable has a format associated with it, each formatted value is treated as a midpoint.

The LEVELS= option is ignored when you use DISCRETE. The MIDPOINTS= option overrides DISCRETE.

DONUTPCT=*percent* (DONUT only)

specifies the size of the donut hole in percent of the radius of the whole chart. Values of *percent* range from 0 to 99. By default, DONUTPCT=25.

Featured in: Example 9 on page 872

DOWN=*number-of-rows*

draws *number-of-rows* pies vertically in the procedure output area. The DOWN= option is ignored unless you also use the GROUP= option.

If *number-of-rows* calls for more pies than fit vertically in the graphics area of the output device, no pies are drawn and an error message is written to the SAS log.

If you also use the ACROSS= option, the pies are drawn in left-to-right and top-to-bottom order.

EXPLODE=*value-list*

pulls the specified slices slightly out from the rest of the pie for added emphasis. *Value-list* is the list of midpoint values for the slices to be exploded. See the MIDPOINTS= on page 826 option for a description of *value-list*.

The values in the value list must match the existing midpoints exactly, including the case of character midpoints. Any values in the list that do not correspond to existing midpoints are ignored.

When you use EXPLODE=, the radius is reduced to allow room for exploded slices. EXPLODE= does not work with subgroups.

Featured in: Example 8 on page 869

FILL=SOLID | X

specifies the fill pattern for *all* slices in the chart:

SOLID S

rotates a solid fill through the colors list as many times as necessary. This is the default.

X

rotates a single hatch pattern through the colors list as many times as necessary. The Java and ActiveX devices and PIE3D do not support FILL=X.

If you use default device colors (the COLORS= option is omitted), the fill skips the first color in the colors list.

FILL= overrides any pattern that is specified in PATTERN statements.

By default, the outline color is the first color in the colors list. If PATTERN statements are used to specify colors, the slice outline color matches the slice fill color.

By default, the fill patterns take the colors from the current colors list in rotation. If any PATTERN statements have been defined, the colors in the PATTERN definitions are used, in order, before the default color rotation.

See also: "Controlling Bar Chart Patterns, Colors, and Images" on page 816 and "PATTERN Statement" on page 169

Not supported by: Java (partial), ActiveX (partial)

FREQ=*numeric-variable*

specifies a variable whose values weight the contribution of each observation in the computation of the chart statistic. Each observation is counted the number of times specified by the value of *numeric-variable* for that observation. If the value of *numeric-variable* is missing, 0, or negative, the observation is not used in the statistic calculation. Non-integer values of *numeric-variable* are truncated to integers.

FREQ= is valid with all chart statistics.

Because you cannot use TYPE=PERCENT or TYPE=FREQ with the SUMVAR= option, you must use FREQ= to calculate percentages and frequencies based on a sum.

The statistics will not be affected by applying a format to *numeric-variable*.

See also: "Calculating Weighted Statistics" on page 783

GROUP=*group-variable*

organizes the data according to values of *group-variable* and produces a separate pie (or donut) chart for each unique value of *group-variable*. *Group-variable* can be either character or numeric and is always treated as a discrete variable. Missing values for *group-variable* are treated as a valid group. By default, each group includes only those midpoints with nonzero chart statistic values.

By default, the charts are produced in ascending order of group variable value and each is drawn on a separate page or display. Therefore, the effect of GROUP= is essentially the same as using a BY statement except that GROUP= causes the midpoints with the same value to use the same color and fill pattern. To place more than one pie on a page or display, use the ACROSS= or DOWN= options, or both.

See also: "BY Statement" on page 141

Featured in: Example 12 on page 877

HTML=*variable*

identifies the variable in the input data set whose values create links in the HTML file that is created by the ODS statement. These links are associated with an area of the chart and point to the data or graph that you wish to display when the user drills down on the area. The values of *variable* can be up to 1024 characters long. Characters after the 1024-character limit (including any closing quotes) are truncated.

HTML_LEGEND=*variable*

identifies the variable in the input data set whose values create links in the HTML file created by the ODS statement. These links are associated with a legend value and point to the data or graph that you wish to display when the user drills down on the value. The values of *variable* can be up to 1024 characters long. Characters after the 1024-character limit (including any closing quotes) are truncated.

Not supported by: Java, ActiveX

INVISIBLE=*value-list*

makes the specified slices invisible, as if they had been removed from the pie. Labels are not printed for invisible slices. *Value-list* is the list of midpoint values for the invisible slices. See the MIDPOINTS= option on page 826 for a description of *value-list*.

The values in the value list must match the existing midpoints exactly, including the case of character midpoints. Any values in the list that do not correspond to existing midpoints are ignored.

JSTYLE

arranges the midpoints in descending order of the statistic value and draws the slices clockwise starting at the 12 o'clock position. The JSTYLE option has the same effect as specifying both the DESCENDING and CLOCKWISE options.

LABEL=(*text argument(s)*) (DONUT only)

defines the text that is displayed in the donut hole. *Text-argument(s)* defines the text or the appearance of the label, or both. *Text-argument(s)* can be one or more of the following:

'text-string'
: provides the text of the label. Enclose each string in quotation marks. Separate multiple strings with blanks.

text-description-suboption
: modifies a characteristic such as the font, color, or size of the text string(s) that follows it. *Text-description-suboption* can be

ANGLE=*degrees*

COLOR=*color*

FONT=*font*

HEIGHT=*text-height* <*units*>

JUSTIFY=LEFT | CENTER | RIGHT

ROTATE=*degrees*

The Java and ActiveX devices do not support all of the suboptions. See "Text Description Suboptions" on page 829 for a complete description.

Specify as many text strings and text description suboptions as you want, but enclose them all in one set of parentheses.

Featured in: Example 9 on page 872

Not supported by: Java (partial), ActiveX (partial)

LEGEND | LEGEND=LEGEND<1...99>

generates a legend for the slice names (midpoint values) instead of printing them beside the slices. The legend displays each slice name and its associated pattern. This option also suppresses the display of the chart statistic values. To display the chart statistics, use the VALUE= option.

If you use the SUBGROUP= option, the legend is automatically generated. However, because patterning is always by midpoint, the legend still describes the midpoint values, not the subgroups.

Note: If you request a legend and the slices use hatch patterns, the patterns in the slices are oriented to be visually equivalent to the legend. △

Specifying LEGEND=LEGEND*n* assigns the specified LEGEND statement to the legend. The Java and ActiveX devices do not support all LEGEND statement options. See "LEGEND Statement" on page 151 for more information.

See also: "LEGEND Statement" on page 151 and SUBGROUP= option on page 828

Featured in: Example 9 on page 872 Example 11 on page 875

Not supported by: Java (partial), ActiveX (partial)

LEVELS=*number-of-midpoints* | ALL

specifies the number of midpoints for a numeric chart variable. The range for each midpoint is calculated automatically.

If you specify LEVELS=ALL, then all unique midpoint values are graphed. If your data contains a large number of unique midpoint values (over 200), you can use the XPIXELS and YPIXELS GOPTIONS to allow the device driver to render a larger (and more readable) graph.

LEVELS= is ignored if

- □ the chart variable is character type
- □ the DISCRETE option is used
- □ the MIDPOINTS= option is used.

MATCHCOLOR

uses the slice pattern color for all slice labels. MATCHCOLOR overrides the color that is specified in the CTEXT= option.

MIDPOINTS=*value-list*
specifies the midpoint values for the slices. The way you specify *value-list* depends on the type of variable:

- For numeric chart variables, *value-list* is either an explicit list of values, or a starting and an ending value with an interval increment, or a combination of both forms:

  n <*...n*>

  n TO *n* <BY *increment*>

  <*n...*> *n* TO *n* <BY *increment*> <*n* <*...n*>>

  If a numeric variable has an associated format, the specified values must be the *unformatted* values.

  By default, numeric variable values are treated as continuous (if you omit the DISCRETE option), and

  - the lowest midpoint consolidates all data points from negative infinity to the median of the first two midpoints
  - the highest midpoint consolidates all data points from the median of the last two midpoints up to infinity
  - all other values in *value-list* specify the median of a range of values, and the GCHART procedure calculates the midpoint values.

  If you include the DISCRETE option, each value in *value-list* specifies a unique numeric value.

- For character chart variables, *value-list* is a list of unique character values enclosed in quotation marks and separated by blanks:

  'value-1' <*...'value-n'*>

  If a character variable has an associated format, the specified values must be the *formatted* values.

For a complete description of *value-list*, see the ORDER= option on page 130 in the AXIS statement.

Midpoints that represent small percentages are collected into a generic midpoint named OTHER. See the OTHER= option on page 827 and the OTHERLABEL= option on page 827 for more information.

See also: "About Midpoints" on page 780

Featured in: Example 10 on page 873

MIDPOINTS=OLD
generates default midpoints using the Nelder algorithm (*Applied Statistics* 25:94–7, 1976). The MIDPOINTS=OLD option is ignored unless the chart variable is numeric

MISSING
accepts a missing value as a valid midpoint for the chart variable. By default, observations with a missing value are ignored. Missing values are always valid for the group and subgroup variable.

NAME='*entry-name*'
specifies the name of the catalog entry for the graph. The maximum length for *entry-name* is eight characters. The default name is GCHART. If the name duplicates an existing entry name, thenSAS/GRAPH software adds a number to the duplicate name to create a unique name—for example, GCHART1.

NOGROUPHEADING

suppresses the headings that are normally printed above each pie when you use the GROUP= option.

NOHEADING

suppresses the heading that is normally printed at the top of each page or display of output for all devices except Java and ActiveX. For the Java and ActiveX devices, NOHEADING is the default.

Featured in: Example 9 on page 872

Not supported by: Java, ActiveX

NOLEGEND

suppresses the legend that is automatically generated by the SUBGROUP= option. NOLEGEND is ignored if the SUBGROUP= option is not used.

OTHER=*percent-of-total*

collects all midpoints with chart statistic values less than or equal to *percent-of-total* into a generic midpoint named OTHER. The value of *percent-of-total* can be 0 to 100; the default value is 4. Therefore, any slice that represents 4 percent or less of the total is put in the OTHER category.

Note: If you specify a small value for *percent-of-total*, the GCHART procedure may not be able to label all of the small slices. △

The OTHER slice is the last slice in the pie, regardless of the order of the slices. (In other words, it is the slice immediately before the starting slice.)

If only one midpoint falls into the OTHER category, its slice is displayed in its normal position in the pie and retains its original label. For example, suppose a pie has these slices and percent values: Coal 35%, Gas 15%, Hydro 5%, and Oil 45%. If you specify OTHER=5, Hydro remains the third slice instead of becoming the last slice.

Featured in: Example 11 on page 875 and Example 12 on page 877

OTHERCOLOR=*color*

specifies the color to use for the OTHER slice. If you omit the OTHERCOLOR= option, GCHART searches for a color specification in this order:

1 the CFILL= option

2 the COLOR= option in a PATTERN statement

3 the COLOR= in a GOPTIONS statement

4 the default color list.

For more information, see "Controlling Slice Patterns and Colors" on page 831.

OTHERLABEL='*text-string*'

specifies a text string up to 16 characters for the label for the OTHER slice. The default label is OTHER.

Featured in: Example 11 on page 875

PERCENT=ARROW | INSIDE | NONE | OUTSIDE

prints the percentage represented by each slice using the specified labeling method. For a description of the option values, see "Selecting and Positioning Slice Labels" on page 830. By default, PERCENT=NONE (percentage is not displayed).

Whether the slice percent displays with or without decimal places, depends on the range of values across the chart. The only way to control the appearance of these values is to calculate the percentage with a DATA step or statistical procedure and use the resulting data set as input to the GCHART procedure. Assign the variable that contains the calculated percentages to the SUMVAR= option.

Featured in: Example 10 on page 873 and Example 12 on page 877

SLICE=ARROW | INSIDE | NONE | OUTSIDE
controls the position and style of the slice name (midpoint value) for each slice. For a description of the option values, see "Selecting and Positioning Slice Labels" on page 830. By default, SLICE=OUTSIDE (the name is outside of the slice).

Featured in: Example 10 on page 873 and Example 12 on page 877

SUBGROUP=*subgroup-variable*
divides the chart into concentric rings according to the values of *subgroup-variable*. For DEVICE=JAVA, subgroups are implemented using drill-down functionality instead of concentric rings. In the resulting graph, you can select a pie slice to display subgroup information. *Subgroup-variable* can be either character or numeric and is always treated as a discrete variable.

The width of the rings, which is the same for each subgroup, is determined by the radius of the pie and the size of the donut hole, if any.

By default, the subgroup rings are ordered from the outside in, alphabetically (if character) or numerically (if numeric). If the JSTYLE option is also used, the order of the slices within the subgroups is determined by the outermost subgroup. Any inner subgroup that contains a value that is not in the outer subgroup, places the new slice for that value either last or just before the "other" slice, if one is present. That slice order is continued for any remaining subgroups.

Each ring is labeled with its subgroup value; labels are placed to the right of the chart. If the GROUP= option is also used and if all groups contain the same subgroups, then only the first (upper left) chart on each page is labeled. If any group differs in the number of subgroups it contains, then all charts are labeled.

By default the subgroups are outlined in the foreground color. To specify an outline color, use the COUTLINE= option.

SUBGROUP= automatically generates a legend for the midpoint values (not the subgroup values) and suppresses display of the chart statistic. By default the legend appears at the bottom of the chart. To modify the legend, assign a LEGEND definition. To suppress the legend, specify NOLEGEND. To display the chart statistic, use the VALUE= option.

If EXPLODE is also used, it is ignored.

See also: "Controlling Bar Chart Patterns, Colors, and Images" on page 816 and "LEGEND Statement" on page 151

Featured in: Example 9 on page 872 and Example 10 on page 873

SUMVAR=*summary-variable*
specifies a numeric variable for sum or mean calculations. The GCHART procedure calculates the sum or, if requested, the mean of *numeric-variable* for each midpoint. The resulting statistics are represented by the size of the slice and displayed beside of each slice.

When you use SUMVAR=, the TYPE= option must be either SUM or MEAN. With SUMVAR=, the default is TYPE=SUM.

Featured in: Example 8 on page 869

TYPE=*statistic*
specifies the chart statistic.

- If the SUMVAR= option is not used, *statistic* can be one of the following:

  FREQ
  frequency (the default)

  PERCENT PCT
  percentage

- If SUMVAR= is used, *statistic* can be one of the following:

  SUM

sum (the default)

MEAN
mean

Because you cannot use TYPE=FREQ or TYPE=PERCENT with the SUMVAR= option, you must use FREQ= to calculate percentages or frequencies based on a sum.

See also: "About Chart Statistics" on page 782 and "Calculating Weighted Statistics" on page 783

VALUE=ARROW | INSIDE | NONE | OUTSIDE
controls the position and style of the slice value (chart statistic) for each slice. For a description of the option values see "Selecting and Positioning Slice Labels" on page 830. By default, VALUE=OUTSIDE (the value is outside the slice).

Featured in: Example 10 on page 873 and Example 11 on page 875

WOUTLINE=*slice-outline-width*
specifies the width of the outline in pixels. WOUTLINE= affects both the slice and the subgroup outlines.

Not supported by: Java, ActiveX

Text Description Suboptions

The LABEL= option in the DONUT statement uses text description suboptions to change the color, height, justification, font, and angle of the following text string(s).

ANGLE=*degrees*
A=*degrees*
specifies the angle at which the baseline of the text string(s) is rotated with respect to the horizontal. A positive value for *degrees* moves the baseline counterclockwise; a negative value moves it clockwise. By default, ANGLE=0 (horizontal).

Not supported by: Java

COLOR=*color*
C=*color*
specifies the color for the text string(s). The COLOR= suboption stays in effect until another COLOR= specification is encountered. If you omit COLOR=, LABEL= uses the first color in the colors list. It ignores the CTEXT= graphics option. See Chapter 6, "SAS/GRAPH Colors and Images," on page 91 for details on specifying *color*.

FONT=*font*
F=*font*
specifies the font for the text string(s). If you omit FONT=, LABEL= uses the font that is specified by the FTEXT= graphics option. If no font is specified, it uses the default hardware font, NONE. See Chapter 5, "SAS/GRAPH Fonts," on page 75 for details on specifying *font*. The Java and ActiveX devices do not support all fonts.

Not supported by: Java (partial), ActiveX (partial)

HEIGHT=*text-height <units>*
H=*text-height <units>*
specifies the height of the text string(s). *Text-height* is the number of units. If you omit HEIGHT=, LABEL= uses the height that is specified by the HTEXT= graphics option. If no text height is specified and if the default text height is too large for the donut hole, the size of the label is reduced to fit. *Units* can be CELLS | CM | IN | PCT | PT. If you omit *units*, HEIGHT= uses the unit that is specified by the GUNIT= graphics option, or the default unit, CELLS.

JUSTIFY=LEFT | CENTER | RIGHT
J=L | C | R
specifies the alignment of the text string(s). By default, JUSTIFY=CENTER.

Not supported by: Java, ActiveX

ROTATE=*degrees*
specifies the angle at which each character is rotated with respect to the baseline of the text string. The angle is measured from the current text baseline angle specified by the ANGLE= suboption. A positive value for *degrees* rotates the character counterclockwise; a negative value rotates it clockwise. By default, ROTATE=0 (parallel to the baseline).

Not supported by: Java

Selecting and Positioning Slice Labels

By default, each slice is labeled with its midpoint value (slice name) and its chart statistic value (slice value), which are printed outside of the slice. You can control where and how these labels are displayed with the SLICE= and VALUE= options, respectively. In addition, each slice can display the percentage its midpoint contributes to the total chart statistic (slice percent). Use the PERCENT= option to request slice percent.

The SLICE=, VALUE=, and PERCENT= options use the same values:

ARROW
places the text outside the slice and connects the text to the slice with a line. This labeling method reduces the radius of the pie. The arrow uses the color that is specified by CTEXT= in the PIE, PIE3D, or DONUT statement. If CTEXT= is omitted, the arrow uses the first color in the colors list.

INSIDE
places the text inside the slice. The label overlays the slice fill patterns. This labeling method increases the radius of the pie.

NONE
suppresses the text.

OUTSIDE
places the text outside of the slice.

Figure 29.14 on page 831 illustrates these values.

Figure 29.14 Slice Labeling Methods

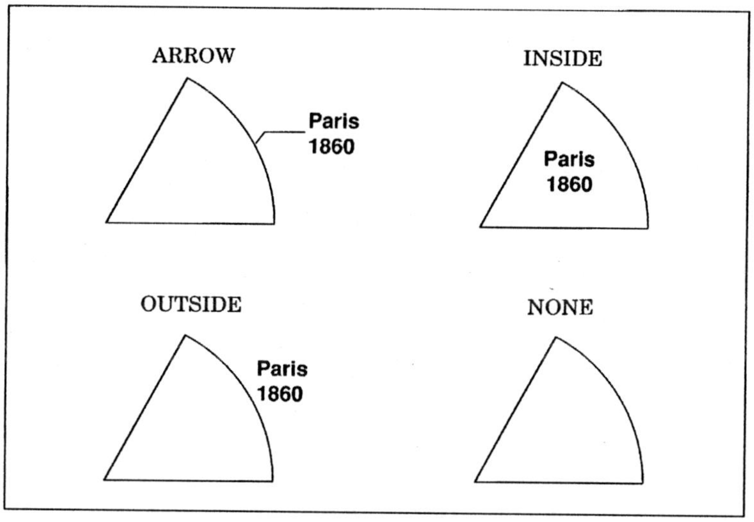

The SLICE= and VALUE= options are dependent on each other. If you specify only VALUE= or only SLICE=, the other option automatically uses the same labeling method. PERCENT= is independent of these two.

Be careful about the combinations that you specify. For example, if you specify PERCENT=ARROW and VALUE=OUTSIDE, the line that connects the percentage information to each slice may overlay the statistic value.

If your pie has many slices, the labels may overlap, particularly if there are several small slices together. You can correct the overlapping labels by using

- FTEXT= graphics option to decrease the size of the labels.
- the Graphics Editor to adjust the labels by moving or resizing the text.
- ANGLE= to change the orientation of the pie.
- MIDPOINTS= to rearrange slices so that small slices are not together.
- OTHER= to group more midpoints into the OTHER category.
- the HPOS= and VPOS= graphics options to increase the number of cells in your display. (See "About the Graphics Output Area" on page 34 for details.)

Controlling Slice Patterns and Colors

Pie and donut charts are always patterned by midpoint. Even when you specify subgrouping, the patterning method does not change from midpoint to subgroup.

Default patterns and outlines

Each slice in a pie or donut chart is filled with a pattern. By default, the procedure

- fills the slices with pie patterns, beginning with the default fill, PSOLID, and rotating through the colors in the colors list. When the solid patterns are exhausted, the procedure selects the next default pie pattern and rotates it through the colors list. It continues in this fashion until all of the required patterns have been assigned.

  Note: PIE3D always uses solid patterns. △

  If you use the device's default colors and the first color in the list is either black or white, the procedure does not create a pattern in that color. If you specify a colors list with the COLORS= graphics option, the procedure uses all the colors in the list to generate the patterns.

- outlines slices and subgroup segments using the first color in the colors list. To change the outline color, use the COUTLINE= option.

See "About Patterns" on page 784 for more information on how the GCHART procedure assigns default patterns and outlines.

Controlling patterns

You can control slice patterns and their outlines in several ways.

- To select a different fill for the slices, such as empty or hatched, you can
  - request a single hatched fill pattern for all slices by specifying the FILL=X option on the PIE or DONUT statement. The pattern specified by FILL=X rotates through the colors list as many times as needed to generate all of the patterns that are required by the chart. If you specify a single color with either CFILL= or the graphics option, CPATTERN=, all slices use the same color as well as the same pattern.
  - specify a pattern with the VALUE= option in the PATTERN statement. Only pie patterns are valid; all other pattern specifications are ignored. For a complete description of all pie patterns, see VALUE= on page 174 in "PATTERN Statement" on page 169.

    If no color options are specified, the procedure rotates each specified fill once through the colors list. Otherwise the PATTERN statement generates one pattern definition for the specified pattern and color. When all of the specified patterns are exhausted, the procedure starts rotating through the default pie patterns, beginning with PSOLID.
- To select colors for the slices, you can
  - specify a single pattern color with the CFILL= option, or with the CPATTERN= graphics option, or with a colors list of one color. For the PIE and DONUT statements, CFILL= starts with the default solid color and uses the foreground color for outlines, whereas CPATTERN= and a colors list of one color skip the solid pattern and, beginning with P2N0, use each pie hatch pattern with the specified color, and use the fill color for the outline color.
  - specify only COLOR= in one or more PATTERN statements. In this case, the procedure creates a solid pattern for each specified color. When it runs out of PATTERN statements, it returns to the default patterns, beginning with PSOLID, and rotates them each through the colors list. Whenever you specify a PATTERN statement, the default outline color is SAME.
- To define specific patterns and colors for the slices, use PATTERN statements and specify both the VALUE= and COLOR= options. If you provide fewer PATTERN definitions than the chart requires, the GCHART procedure uses the default pattern rotation for the slices that are drawn after all of the defined patterns are exhausted.

  Whenever you use PATTERN statements, the default outline color changes to SAME. That is, the outline color is the same as the fill color. To change the outline color, use the COUTLINE= option on page 821.

See "About Patterns" on page 784 for more information on how the GCHART procedure uses patterns and outlines. See "PATTERN Statement" on page 169 for a description of default pie patterns.

Modifying the Statistic Heading and the Group Heading

By default, the procedure prints a heading at the top of each pie (or donut) chart that indicates the type of statistic charted and the name of the chart variable– for example, *SUM of SALES by SITE*. You can suppress this heading with the NOHEADING option.

When you use the GROUP= option, a heading is printed above each pie indicating the name of the group variable and its value for the particular pie– for example, *SITE=Paris*. You can suppress these headings with the NOGROUPHEADING option. You can also suppress the variable name *SITE=* so that only the value *Paris* remains. To do this, use a LABEL statement and assign a null value to the variable name, for example,

```
label site='00'x;
```

Because the AXIS statement cannot be used by the PIE, PIE3D, and DONUT statements, you should use the FTEXT= and HTEXT= graphics options to control the font and height of text on the chart. Increasing the value of the HTEXT= graphics option decreases the size of the pie if any slice labels are positioned outside.

STAR Statement

Creates star charts in which the length of the spines represents the value of the chart statistic for each category of data or midpoint.

Requirements: At least one chart variable is required.

Global statements: FOOTNOTE, PATTERN, TITLE,

Supports: Drill-down functionality (slices only)

Not supported by: Java, ActiveX

Description

The STAR statement specifies the variable or variables that define the categories of data to chart. This statement automatically

- determines the midpoints.
- calculates the chart statistic for each midpoint (the default is FREQ).
- scales each spine or slice to represent the chart statistic. Slices or spines are drawn for all midpoints where the value of the chart statistic is greater than the value that is specified in the STARMIN= option.
- arranges the spines or slice counterclockwise around the star in ascending order of midpoint value, starting at the three o'clock position.
- prints the midpoint value and chart statistic beside each spine or slice.
- assigns patterns to the slices.

If all the data to be charted with the STAR statement are positive, the center of the star represents 0 and the outside circle represents the maximum value. If negative values are calculated for the chart statistic, the center represents the minimum value in the data. You can specify other values for the center and outside of the circle with the STARMIN= and STARMAX= options.

You can also use statement options to select or order the midpoints, to change the type of chart statistic, and to modify the appearance of the chart, including the content and position of the spine or slice labels, and patterns that fill the slice. You can specify additional variables by which to group or sum the data.

Star charts allow grouping, which creates two or more separate charts that display in rows or columns on one graph.

In addition, you can use global statements to modify patterns as well as add titles, footnotes, and notes to the chart. You can also use an Annotate data set to enhance the chart.

Syntax

STAR *chart-variable(s)* </ *option(s)*>;

option(s) can be one or more options from any or all of the following categories:

- appearance options
  - ANGLE=*degrees*
  - ANNOTATE=*Annotate-data-set*
  - CFILL=*fill-color*
  - COUTLINE=*star-outline-color* | SAME
  - FILL=SOLID | X
  - NOCONNECT
  - STARMAX=*max-value*
  - STARMIN=*min-value*
  - WOUTLINE=*slice-outline-width*
- statistic options
  - FREQ=*numeric-variable*
  - SUMVAR=*summary-variable*
  - TYPE=*statistic*
- midpoint options
  - DISCRETE
  - LEVELS=*number-of-midpoints*
  - MIDPOINTS=*value-list*
  - MIDPOINTS=OLD
  - MISSING
- grouping options
  - ACROSS=*number-of-columns*
  - DOWN=*number-of-rows*
  - GROUP=*group-variable*
- labeling options
  - CTEXT=*text-color*
  - MATCHCOLOR
  - NOGROUPHEADING
  - NOHEADING
  - PERCENT=ARROW | INSIDE | NONE | OUTSIDE
  - SLICE=ARROW | INSIDE | NONE | OUTSIDE
  - VALUE=ARROW | INSIDE | NONE | OUTSIDE
- catalog entry description options
  - DESCRIPTION='*entry-description*'
  - NAME='*entry-name*'
- ODS options
  - HTML=*variable*

Required Arguments

chart-variable(s)

specifies one or more variables that define the categories of data to chart. Each chart variable draws a separate chart. All variables must be in the input data set. Separate multiple chart variables with blanks.

See also: "About Chart Variables" on page 779

Options

Options in a STAR statement affect all of the graphs that are produced by that statement. You can specify as many options as you want and list them in any order. For details on specifying colors, see Chapter 6, "SAS/GRAPH Colors and Images," on page 91.

ACROSS=*number-of-columns*

draws *number-of-columns* stars across the procedure output area. ACROSS= is ignored unless you also use the GROUP= option. If *number-of-columns* calls for more stars than fit horizontally in the graphics area of the output device, no stars are drawn and an error message is written to the SAS log.

If you also use the DOWN= option, the star charts are drawn in left-to-right and top-to-bottom order.

ANGLE=*degrees*

starts the first slice at the specified angle. A value of 0 for *degrees* corresponds to the 3 o'clock position. *Degrees* can be either positive or negative. Positive values move the starting position counterclockwise; negative values move the starting position clockwise.

If the star chart uses spines instead of slices, *degrees* specifies the angle of the position halfway between the first spine and the last spine.

By default, ANGLE=0, which places the first spine or the center of the first slice of the star at the 0 degree position. Successive star spines or slices are drawn counterclockwise from the starting position.

ANNOTATE=*Annotate-data-set*
ANNO=*Annotate-data-set*

specifies a data set to annotate charts that are produced by the STAR statement.

Note: Annotate coordinate systems 1, 2, 7, and 8 (data system coordinates) are not valid with star charts. △

See also: Chapter 24, "Using Annotate Data Sets," on page 587

CFILL=*fill-color*

specifies one color for all slices in the chart, regardless of whether the fill is solid or hatch. If no pattern is specified on the PATTERN statement or with the FILL= option, the procedure starts with the default solid fill and then, beginning with P2N0, uses each default star hatch pattern with the specified color. For the outline color, the procedure uses the foreground color, which is the first color in the colors lists. Use COUTLINE= to specify a different outline color. CFILL= overrides any other pattern color specification and controls the color of all slices.

COUTLINE=*star-outline-color* | SAME

specifies the color for the circle that surrounds the star chart and for the slice outlines or spines.

SAME specifies that the outline color of a slice is the same as the interior pattern color. Specifying COUTLINE=SAME affects only slice outlines and has no effect on the color of the circle.

The default circle color is the first color in the colors list (the foreground color).

The default slice outline color depends on the PATTERN statement:

- If you do not specify the PATTERN statement, the default outline color is the foreground color (the first color in the colors list).
- If you do not specify the PATTERN statement or the V6COMP graphics options, the default is COUTLINE=SAME.

Note: If you specify empty patterns, (VALUE=PEMPTY in a PATTERN statement) you should not change the outline color from the default value, SAME, to a single color. Otherwise all the outlines will be one color and you will not be able to distinguish between the empty areas. △

See also: "Selecting Patterns for the Star Charts" on page 840 and "About Patterns" on page 784

Featured in: Example 14 on page 880

CTEXT=*text-color*
specifies a color for all text on the chart. Text includes all slice labels, the chart heading, and group headings if grouping is used.

If you omit CTEXT=, PROC GCHART searches for a color specification in this order:

1. the CTEXT= option in a GOPTIONS statement
2. the first color in the colors list (the default).

The MATCHCOLOR option overrides the CTEXT= option for star slice labels.

DESCRIPTION='*entry-description*'
DES='*entry-description*'
specifies the description of the catalog entry for the chart. The maximum length for *entry-description* is 256 characters. The description does not appear on the chart. By default, the GCHART procedure assigns a description of the form STAR CHART OF *variable*, where *variable* is the name of the chart variable.

The *entry-description* can include the #BYLINE, #BYVAL, and #BYVAR substitution options, which work as they do when used on TITLE, FOOTNOTE, and NOTE statements. Refer to the description of the options on page 222, and "Substituting BY Line Values in a Text String" on page 226. The 256-character limit applies before the substitution takes place for these options; thus, if in the SAS program the entry-description text exceeds 256 characters, it is truncated to 256 characters, and then the substitution is performed.

The descriptive text is shown in each of the following:

- the "description" portion of the Results window
- the catalog-entry properties that you can view from the Explorer window
- the Table of Contents that is generated when you use CONTENTS= on an ODS statement (see "Linking to Output through a Table of Contents" on page 495), assuming the GCHART output is generated while the contents page is open
- the Description field of the PROC GREPLAY window.

DISCRETE
treats a numeric chart variable as a discrete variable rather than as a continuous variable. The GCHART procedure creates a separate midpoint and, hence, a separate star slice for each unique value of the chart variable. If the variable has a format associated with it, each format value is treated as a separate value.

The LEVELS= option is ignored when you use the DISCRETE option. The MIDPOINTS= option overrides the DISCRETE option.

Featured in: Example 14 on page 880

DOWN=*number-of-rows*

draws *number-of-rows* stars vertically in the procedure output area. The DOWN= option is ignored unless you also use the GROUP= option. If *number-of-rows* calls for more stars than fit vertically in the graphics area of the output device, no stars are drawn and an error message is written to the SAS log.

If you also use the ACROSS= option, the stars are drawn in left-to-right and top-to-bottom order.

FILL=SOLID | X

specifies the fill pattern for *all* slices in the star chart:

SOLID
S

rotates a solid fill through the colors list as many times as necessary. This is the default.

X

rotates a single hatch pattern through the colors list as many times as necessary.

If you use default device colors (the COLORS= option is omitted), the fill skips the first color in the colors list.

FILL= overrides any patterns that are specified in PATTERN statements.

By default, the fill patterns take the colors from the current colors list in rotation. If any PATTERN statements have been defined, the colors in the PATTERN definitions are used, in order, before the default color rotation.

Featured in: Example 14 on page 880

FREQ=*numeric-variable*

specifies a variable whose values weight the contribution of each observation in the computation of the chart statistic. Each observation is counted the number of times that are specified by the value of *numeric-variable* for that observation. If the value of *numeric-variable* is missing, 0, or negative, the observation is not used in the statistic calculation. Non-integer values of *numeric-variable* are truncated to integers.

FREQ= is valid with all chart statistics.

Because you cannot use TYPE=PERCENT or TYPE=FREQ with the SUMVAR= option, you must use FREQ= to calculate percentages and frequencies based on a sum.

The statistics will not be affected by applying a format to *numeric-variable*.

See also: "Calculating Weighted Statistics" on page 783

GROUP=*variable*

organizes the data according to values of *group-variable* and produces a separate star chart for each unique value of *group-variable*. *Group-variable* can be either character or numeric and is always treated as a discrete variable. Missing values for *group-variable* are treated as a valid group.

By default, the charts are produced in ascending order of group variable value and each is drawn on a separate page or display. Therefore, the effect of GROUP= is essentially the same as using a BY statement except that GROUP= causes the midpoints with the same value to use the same color and fill pattern. To place more than one star chart on a page or display, use the ACROSS= or DOWN= options, or both.

HTML=*variable*

identifies the variable in the input data set whose values create links in the HTML file that is created by the ODS statement. These links are associated with an area of the chart and point to the data or graph that you wish to display when the user drills down on the area. Only star charts with slices support drill-down functionality. The values of *variable* can be up to 1024 characters long. Characters after the 1024-character limit (including any closing quotes) are truncated.

LEVELS=*number-of-midpoints*

specifies number of midpoints for a numeric chart variable. The range for each midpoint is calculated automatically using the algorithm described by Terrell and Scott (1985). LEVELS= is ignored if

- the chart variable is character type
- the DISCRETE option is used
- the MIDPOINTS= option is used.

MATCHCOLOR

uses the slice pattern color for all slice labels. MATCHCOLOR overrides the color that is specified in the CTEXT= option. If the chart uses spines instead of slices, the spine color is used for the slice label and value text.

MIDPOINTS=*value-list*

specifies the midpoint values for the slices. The way you specify *value-list* depends on the type of variable:

- For numeric chart variables, *value-list* is either an explicit list of values, or a starting and an ending value with an interval increment, or a combination of both forms:

  n <...*n*>

  n TO *n* <BY *increment*>

  n <...*n*> TO *n* <BY *increment*> <*n* <...*n*>>

  If a numeric variable has an associated format, the specified values must be the *unformatted* values.

  By default, numeric variable values are treated as continuous (if you omit the DISCRETE option), and

  - the lowest midpoint consolidates all data points from negative infinity to the median of the first two midpoints
  - the highest midpoint consolidates all data points from the median of the last two midpoints up to infinity
  - all other values in *value-list* specify the median of a range of values, and the GCHART procedure calculates the midpoint values.

  If you include the DISCRETE option, each value in *value-list* specifies a unique numeric value.

- For character chart variables, *value-list* is a list of unique character values enclosed in quotation marks and separated by blanks:

  'value-1' <...'value-n'>

  If a character variable has an associated format, the specified values must be the *formatted* values.

For a complete description of *value-list*, see the ORDER= option on page 130 in the AXIS statement.

See also: "About Midpoints" on page 780

MIDPOINTS=OLD

generates default midpoints using the Nelder algorithm (*Applied Statistics* 25:94–7, 1976). The MIDPOINTS=OLD option is ignored unless the chart variable is numeric

MISSING

accepts a missing value as a valid midpoint for the chart variable. By default, observations with a missing value are ignored. Missing values are always valid for the group variable.

NAME=*'entry-name'*

specifies the name of the catalog entry for the graph. The maximum length for *entry-name* is eight characters. The default name is GCHART. If the name duplicates an existing entry name, thenSAS/GRAPH software adds a number to the duplicate name to create a unique name—for example, GCHART1.

NOCONNECT
draws only star spines without connecting lines. By default, the spines are connected to form slices.

Featured in: Example 14 on page 880

NOGROUPHEADING
suppresses the headings normally printed above each star when you use the GROUP= option.

NOHEADING
suppresses the heading normally printed at the top of each page or display of star chart output.

Featured in: Example 14 on page 880

PERCENT=ARROW | INSIDE | NONE | OUTSIDE
prints the percentage represented by each slice using the specified labeling method. For a description of the option values see "Selecting and Positioning Spine and Slice Labels" on page 840. By default, PERCENT=NONE (percentage is not displayed).

SLICE=ARROW | INSIDE | NONE | OUTSIDE
controls the position and style of the slice name (midpoint value) for each slice. For a description of the option values, see "Selecting and Positioning Spine and Slice Labels" on page 840. By default, SLICE=OUTSIDE (the name is outside the slice).

STARMAX=*max-value*
scales the chart so that the outside (or edge) of the circle represents the value that is specified by *max-value*. By default, the value for STARMAX= is the maximum chart statistic value.

STARMIN=*min-value*
scales the chart so that the center of the circle represents the value that is specified by *min-value*. By default, STARMIN=0. If the chart statistic has negative values, by default the value for STARMIN= is the minimum chart statistic value.

SUMVAR=*summary-variable*
specifies a numeric variable for sum or mean calculations. The GCHART procedure calculates the sum or, if requested, the mean of the value of *numeric-variable* for each midpoint. The resulting statistics are represented by the size of the slice and displayed beside each slice.

When you use SUMVAR=, the TYPE= option must be either SUM or MEAN. With SUMVAR=, the default is TYPE=SUM.

Featured in: Example 13 on page 879

TYPE=*statistic*
specifies the chart statistic.

- If the SUMVAR= option is not used, *statistic* can be one of the following:

  FREQ
  frequency (the default)

  PERCENT PCT
  percentage

  If SUMVAR= is used, *statistic* can be one of the following:

  SUM

sum (the default)

MEAN
mean

Because you cannot use TYPE=FREQ or TYPE=PERCENT with the SUMVAR= option, you must use FREQ= to calculate percentages or frequencies based on a sum.

See also: "About Chart Statistics" on page 782 and "Calculating Weighted Statistics" on page 783

VALUE=ARROW | INSIDE | NONE | OUTSIDE
controls the position and style of the slice value (chart statistic) for each slice. For a description of the option values, see "Selecting and Positioning Spine and Slice Labels" on page 840. By default, VALUE=OUTSIDE (the value is outside of the slice).

WOUTLINE=*slice-outline-width*
specifies the width of the outline in pixels. WOUTLINE= affects the slice outlines.

Selecting and Positioning Spine and Slice Labels

By default, each spine or slice is labeled with its midpoint value and its chart statistic value, which are printed outside of the circle. You can control where and how these labels are displayed with the SLICE= and VALUE= options, respectively. In addition, each spine can display the percentage that its midpoint contributes to the total chart statistic (spine percent). Use the PERCENT= option to request spine percent.

The SLICE=, VALUE=, and PERCENT= options use the same values:

ARROW
places the text outside of the star circle and connects the text to the circle with a line. The line points to the spine or the center of the slice. The arrow uses the color that is specified by CTEXT= in the STAR statement. If you omit CTEXT=, the arrow uses the first color in the colors list.

INSIDE
places the text inside the star circle.

NONE
suppresses the text.

OUTSIDE
places the text outside the star circle.

Figure 29.14 on page 831 illustrates these values.

The SLICE= and VALUE= options are dependent on each other. If you specify only VALUE= or only SLICE=, the other option automatically uses the same labeling method. PERCENT= is independent of these two.

Be careful about the combinations that you specify. For example, if you specify PERCENT=ARROW and VALUE=OUTSIDE, the line that connects the percentage information to each spine may overlay the statistic value.

Selecting Patterns for the Star Charts

Star charts are always patterned by midpoint.

Default patterns and outlines

Each slice in a star chart is filled with a pattern. By default, the procedure

- fills the slices with star patterns, beginning with the default fill, PSOLID, and rotating through the colors in the colors list. When the solid patterns are exhausted, the procedure selects the next default star pattern and rotates it through the colors list. It continues in this fashion until all the required patterns have been assigned.

If you use the device's default colors and the first color in the list is either black or white, the procedure does not create a pattern in that color. If you specify a colors list with the COLORS= graphics option, the procedure uses all of the colors in the list to generate the patterns.

- outlines slices using the first color in the colors list. To change the outline color, use the COUTLINE= option.

See "About Patterns" on page 784 for more information on how the GCHART procedure assigns default patterns and outlines.

Controlling patterns

You can control slice patterns and their outlines in several ways.

- To select a different fill for the slices, such as empty or hatched, you can
  - request a single hatched fill pattern for all slices by specifying the FILL=X option on the STAR statement. The pattern that is specified by FILL=X rotates through the colors list as many times as needed to generate all the patterns required by the chart. If you specify a single color with either CFILL= or the graphics option, CPATTERN=, all slices use the same color as well as the same pattern.
  - specify a pattern with the VALUE= option in the PATTERN statement. Only star patterns are valid; all other pattern specifications are ignored. For a complete description of all star patterns, see VALUE= on page 174 in "PATTERN Statement" on page 169.

    If no color options are specified, the procedure rotates each specified fill once through the colors list. Otherwise the PATTERN statement generates one pattern definition for the specified pattern and color. When all of the specified patterns are exhausted, the procedure starts rotating through the default star patterns, beginning with PSOLID.
- To select colors for the slices, you can
  - specify a single pattern color with the CFILL= option, or with the CPATTERN= graphics option, or with a colors list of one color. If you use CFILL=, the procedure starts with the default solid color and uses the foreground color for outlines. If you use CPATTERN= or a colors list of one color, the procedure skips the default solid fill and, beginning with P2N0, uses each default star hatch pattern with the specified color, and uses the fill color for the outline color.
  - specify only COLOR= in one or more PATTERN statements. In this case, the procedure creates a solid pattern for each specified color. When it runs out of PATTERN statements, it returns to the default patterns, beginning with PSOLID, and rotates them each through the colors list. Whenever you specify a PATTERN statement, the default outline color is SAME.
- To define specific patterns and colors for the slices, use PATTERN statements and specify both the VALUE= and COLOR= options. If you provide fewer PATTERN definitions than the chart requires, the GCHART procedure uses the default pattern rotation for the slices that are drawn after all defined patterns are exhausted.

  Whenever you use PATTERN statements, the default outline color changes to SAME. That is, the outline color is the same as the fill color. To change the outline color, use the COUTLINE= option on page 821.

See “About Patterns” on page 784 for more information on how the GCHART procedure uses patterns and outlines. See “PATTERN Statement” on page 169 for a description of default star patterns.

Modifying the Statistic Heading and the Group Heading

By default, the procedure prints a heading at the top of each chart indicating the type of statistic charted and the name of the chart variable– for example, `SUM of SALES by SITE`. You can suppress this heading with the NOHEADING option.

When you use the GROUP= option, a heading is printed above each star indicating the name of the group variable and its value for the particular star– for example, `SITE=Paris`. You can suppress these headings with the NOGROUPHEADING option. You can also suppress the variable name *SITE=* so that only the value *Paris* remains. To do this, use a LABEL statement and assign a null value to the variable name, as shown in this example:

```
label site='00'x;
```

Because the AXIS statement cannot be used by the STAR statement, you should use the FTEXT= and HTEXT= graphics options to control the font and height of text on the chart. Increasing the value of HTEXT= decreases the size of the star if any slice labels are positioned outside. For a description of these graphics options, see Chapter 8, “Graphics Options and Device Parameters Dictionary,” on page 261.

Examples

Example 1: Specifying the Sum Statistic in a Block Chart

Procedure features:

BLOCK statement option:

SUMVAR=

Other features: FORMAT statement

Sample library member: GCHBKSUM

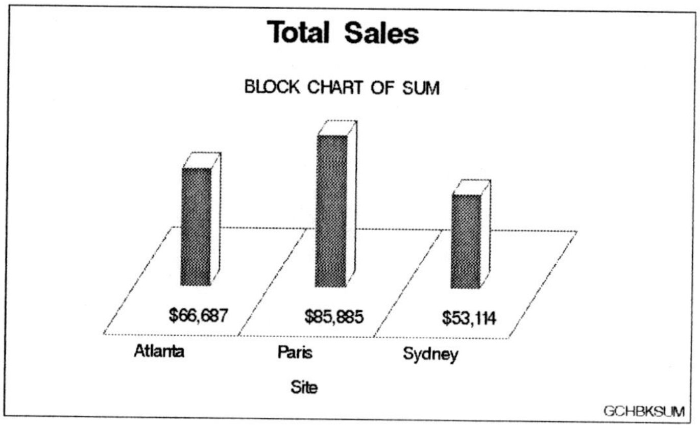

This example produces a block chart of total sales for three sites by charting the values of the character variable SITE and calculating the sum of the variable SALES for each site. It prints formatted values of the sales statistics below the blocks.

The chart uses default patterns and colors. The block faces use the default pattern fill, which is solid. Because a colors list is specified in the GOPTIONS statement, the default fill color is the first color in the list, blue. The midpoint grid and the block outlines also use the first color in the list.

All the blocks use the same pattern because by default patterns change for subgroups and in this chart subgroups are not specified.

Set the graphics environment. CTEXT= specifies the color for all text on the output. COLORS= specifies the colors list, which is used by the default patterns and outlines.

```
goptions reset=global gunit=pct border cback=white
         ctext=black colors=(blue green red)
         ftext=swiss ftitle=swissb
         htitle=6 htext=3.5;
```

Create data set TOTALS. TOTALS contains quarterly sales data for three manufacturing sites for one year. Sales figures are broken down by department.

```
data totals;
   length dept $ 7 site $ 8;
   input dept site quarter sales;
   datalines;
Parts    Sydney  1 7043.97
Parts    Atlanta 1 8225.26
Parts    Paris   1 5543.97
...more data lines...
Tools    Sydney  4 1775.74
Tools    Atlanta 4 3424.19
Tools    Paris   4 6914.25
;
```

Define title and footnote.

```
title 'Total Sales';
footnote j=r 'GCHBKSUM ';
```

Produce the block chart. The BLOCK statement produces a block chart. SUMVAR= calculates the sum of SALES for each value of the chart variable SITE. With SUMVAR= the default statistic is SUM. The summary variable SALES is assigned a dollar format.

```
proc gchart data=reflib.totals;
   format sales dollar8.;
   block site / sumvar=sales;
run;
quit;
```

Example 2: Grouping and Subgrouping a Block Chart

Procedure features:

BLOCK statement options:

- CAXIS=
- COUTLINE=
- GROUP=
- LEGEND=
- MIDPOINTS=
- NOHEADING
- SUBGROUP=
- TYPE=

Other features:

LABEL statement

LEGEND statement

Default pattern rotation

Data set: TOTALS

Sample library member: GCHBKGRP

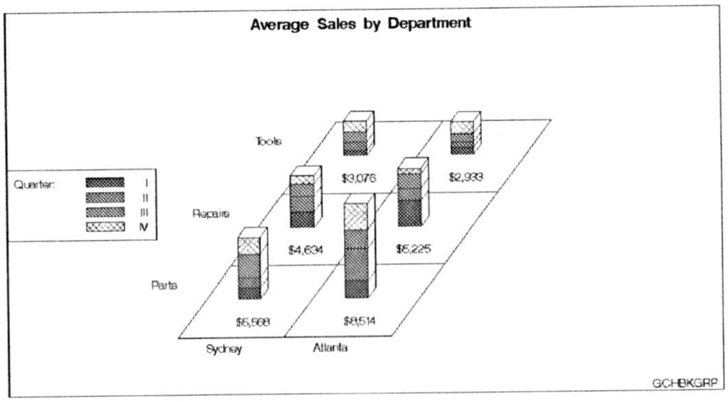

This example shows average quarterly sales for each department at two of the three manufacturing sites in the TOTALS data set; it excludes the Paris site from the chart.

The program groups the chart data (sites) by department, and subgroups department sales data by quarter. Each site is a midpoint. Because the sites are grouped by department, each midpoint has a separate square for each department and the height of the block represents total sales for that department.

The blocks are subgrouped to show how quarterly sales contribute to total sales; each segment represents sales for a quarter. A legend explaining the subgroup patterns appears below the midpoint grid.

The subgroups use four default patterns, The first three patterns are created by rotating the first default fill, solid, through the three colors in the colors list defined in the GOPTIONS statement. The fourth default pattern is created by using the second default pattern fill, X1, with the first color in the colors list, blue.

Because the first color in the colors list is also the default color for several other elements, the program includes several options that override the default: CTEXT= colors all text, CAXIS= colors the midpoint grid, COUTLINE= colors the pattern outline. For more information on patterns and colors, see "Controlling Block Chart Patterns and Colors" on page 794.

Assign the libref and set the graphics environment. COLORS= specifies a colors list that is used by the default patterns. CTEXT= specifies black for all text.

```
libname reflib 'SAS-data-library';
goptions reset=global gunit=pct border cback=white
         colors=(blue green red) ctext=black
         ftitle=swissb ftext=swiss htitle=4 htext=3;
```

Define title and footnote.

```
title 'Average Sales by Department';
footnote j=r 'GCHBKGRP  ';
```

Define legend characteristics. LABEL= assigns new text to the legend label. CBORDER= draws a black frame around the legend.

```
legend1 cborder=black
        label=('Quarter:')
        position=(middle left outside)
        mode=protect
        across=1;
```

Produce the block chart. The LABEL statement suppresses the midpoint and group labels by assigning a null hexadecimal string to each variable name.

```
proc gchart data=reflib.totals;
   format quarter roman.;
   format sales dollar8.;
   label site='00'x dept='00'x;
```

TYPE= specifies the chart statistic as the mean value of the summary variable SALES for each site. MIDPOINTS= selects the two sites and the order in which they appear. GROUP= creates a separate row of blocks for each different value of DEPT. SUBGROUP= divides each block into separate segments for the four quarters. LEGEND= assigns the LEGEND1 statement to the graph. NOHEADING suppresses the default heading that would otherwise appear above the chart. CAXIS= colors the grid black. COUTLINE= specifies the outline color for the blocks.

```
   block site / sumvar=sales
                type=mean
                midpoints='Sydney' 'Atlanta'
                group=dept
                subgroup=quarter
                legend=legend1
                noheading
                coutline=black
                caxis=black;
run;
quit;
```

Example 3: Specifying the Sum Statistic in Bar Charts

Procedure features:

HBAR statement options:

SUMVAR=

VBAR3D statement options:

SUMVAR=
COUTLINE=

Other features:

FORMAT statement

PATTERN statement

RUN-group processing

Data set: TOTALS

Sample library member: GCHBRSUM

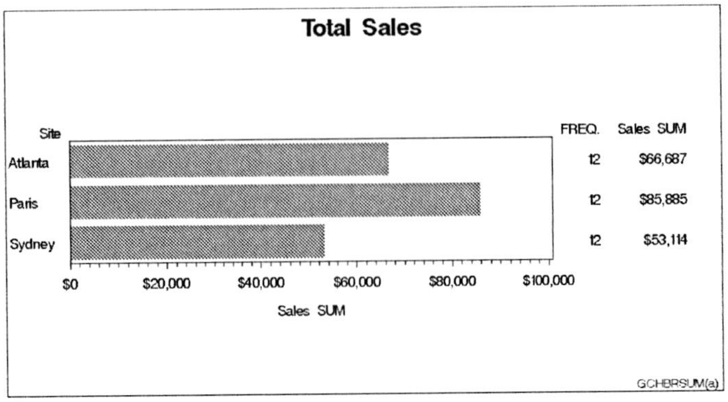

This example produces two bar charts that show total sales for three sites by charting the values of the character variable SITE and calculating the sum of the variable SALES for each site.

In the horizontal bar chart shown above, the summary statistics are printed by default to the right of the bars and display the formatted values of SALES.

The bars use the default pattern fill, which is solid. Because a colors list is specified in the GOPTIONS statement, the first default pattern color is the first color in the list. To avoid having black bars, the program uses a PATTERN statement to specify the pattern color. Using a PATTERN statement causes the default bar outline color to match the fill color. All the bars display the same pattern because by default patterns change for subgroups and in this chart subgroups are not specified.

The output also shows the frame that is drawn by default around the axis area.

The second bar chart is a 3D vertical bar chart, shown in the following output. Vertical bar charts do not generate a table of statistics and by default do not print any chart statistics. This chart uses the same pattern as the horizontal bar chart, but the VBAR3D statement specifies a black outline for the bars.

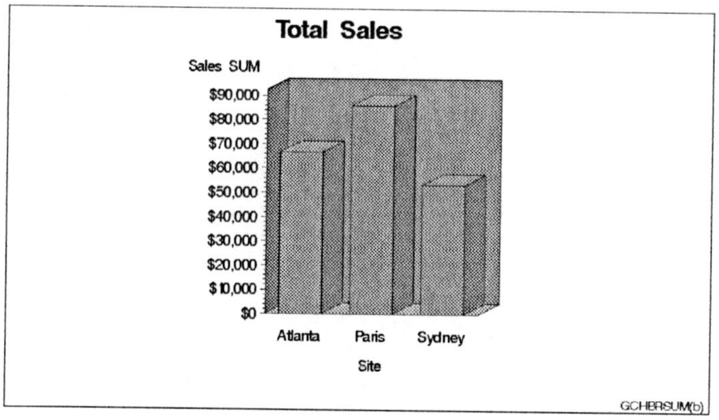

Assign the libref and set the graphics environment. COLORS= specifies the colors list, which is used by the default patterns and outlines.

```
libname reflib 'SAS-data-library';
goptions reset=global gunit=pct border
         colors=(black red blue green)
         cback=white ftitle=swissb ftext=swiss
         htitle=6 htext=3.5;
```

Define title and footnote for the first chart.

```
title1 'Total Sales';
footnote1 h=3 j=r 'GCHBRSUM(a) ';
```

Specify a color for the pattern. The PATTERN statement explicitly defines RED as the color for the first solid pattern.

```
pattern1 color=red;
```

Produce the horizontal bar chart. The HBAR statement produces a two-dimensional bar chart. SUMVAR= calculates the sum of SALES for each value of the chart variable SITE. The default statistic for SUMVAR= is SUM. The summary variable SALES is assigned a dollar format.

```
proc gchart data=reflib.totals;
   format sales dollar8.;
   hbar site / sumvar=sales;
run;
```

Produce the vertical bar chart. Because the procedure supports RUN-group processing, you do not have to repeat the PROC GCHART statement to generate the second chart. The VBAR3D statement produces a three-dimensional vertical bar chart. The FOOTNOTE1 statement replaces the previous footnote. COUTLINE= assigns a black outline to the bars.

```
   footnote1 h=3 j=r 'GCHBRSUM(b) ';
   vbar3d site / sumvar=sales
                 coutline=black;
run;
quit;
```

Example 4: Subgrouping a 3D Vertical Bar Chart

Procedure features:

VBAR statement options:

- CFRAME=
- INSIDE=SUBPCT
- LEGEND=
- MAXIS=
- OUTSIDE=SUM
- RAXIS=
- SPACE=
- SUBGROUP=
- WIDTH=

Other features:

AXIS statement

FORMAT statement

GOPTIONS statement

- OFFSHADOW=

LEGEND statement

PATTERN statement

Data set: TOTALS

Sample library member: GCHBRGRP

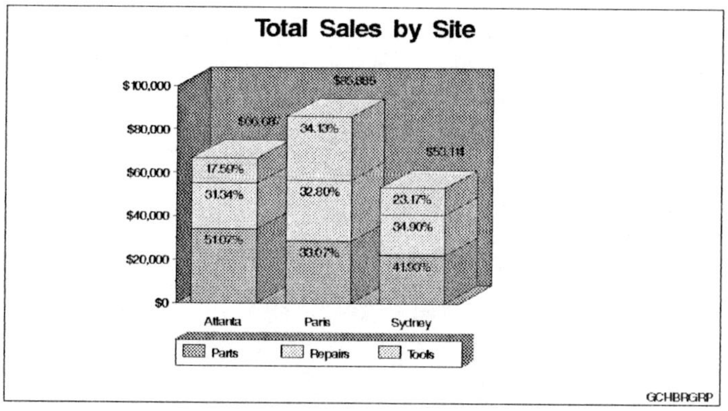

This example subgroups by department the 3D vertical bar chart of total sales for each site that is shown in Example 3 on page 846. In addition to subdividing the bars to show the amount of sales for each department for each site, the chart displays statistics both inside and outside of the bars. OUTSIDE=SUM prints the total sales for the site above each bar. INSIDE=SUBPCT prints the percent each department contributed to the total sales for its site inside of each subgroup segment.

The legend has a block-effect shadow whose color matches the backplane. The graphics option OFFSHADOW= defines the size and position of the block shadow. Both the LEGEND statement and the AXIS statement use the ORIGIN= option to line up the legend and the chart by explicitly positioning their lower left corners.

Assign the libref and set the graphics environment. OFFSHADOW= defines the depth of the block around the legend box. The positive values position the shadow above and to the right of the legend.

```
libname reflib 'SAS-data-library';
goptions reset=global gunit=pct border cback=white
         colors=(black red green blue) ftitle=swissb
         ftext=swiss htitle=6 htext=4
         offshadow=(1.5,1.5);
```

Define title and footnote.

```
title1 'Total Sales by Site';
footnote1 h=3 j=r 'GCHBRGRP ';
```

Modify the midpoint axis. LABEL= suppresses the axis label. ORIGIN= positions the left end of the horizontal axis at a point that is 25% of the width of the graphics output area.

```
axis1 label=none
      origin=(24,);
```

Modify the response axis. ORDER= specifies the major tick values for the response axis. OFFSET= moves the top tick mark to the end of the axis line.

```
axis2 label=none
      order=(0 to 100000 by 20000)
      minor=(number=1)
```

```
      offset=(,0);
```

Modify the legend. LABEL= suppresses the legend label. SHAPE= defines the size of the legend values. CBORDER= draws a black frame around the legend. CBLOCK= specifies a gray block that matches the 3D planes. ORIGIN= specifies the same position as in the AXIS1 statement.

```
legend1 label=none
        shape=bar(3,3)
        cborder=black
        cblock=gray
        origin=(24,);
```

Define pattern characteristics. PATTERN statements define the colors that are assigned to subgroups. Light colors allow the black labels to show up. Default pattern fill is solid.

```
pattern1 color=lipk;
pattern2 color=cyan;
pattern3 color=lime;
```

Produce the vertical bar chart. SUBGROUP= creates a separate bar segment for each department. INSIDE= prints the subgroup percent statistic inside each bar segment. OUTSIDE= prints the sum statistic above each bar. WIDTH= makes the bars wide enough to display the statistics. SPACE= controls the space between the bars. MAXIS= assigns the AXIS1 statement to the midpoint axis. RAXIS= assigns the AXIS2 statement to the response axis. LEGEND= assigns the LEGEND1 statement to the subgroup legend. CFRAME= specifies the color for the 3D planes.

```
proc gchart data=reflib.totals;
   format quarter roman.;
   format sales dollar8.;
   vbar3d site / sumvar=sales
                 subgroup=dept
                 inside=subpct
                 outside=sum
                 width=9
                 space=4
                 maxis=axis1
                 raxis=axis2
                 cframe=gray
                 coutline=black
                 legend=legend1;
run;
quit;
```

Example 5: Controlling Midpoints and Statistics in a Horizontal Bar Chart

Procedure features:

HBAR statement options:

- AUTOREF
- COUTLINE=
- CLIPREF
- SUBGROUP=

HBAR3D statement options:

- FREQ
- FREQLABEL=
- MIDPOINTS=

Other features:

- AXIS statement
- LEGEND statement
- PATTERN statement
- RUN-group processing

Sample library member: GCHBRMID

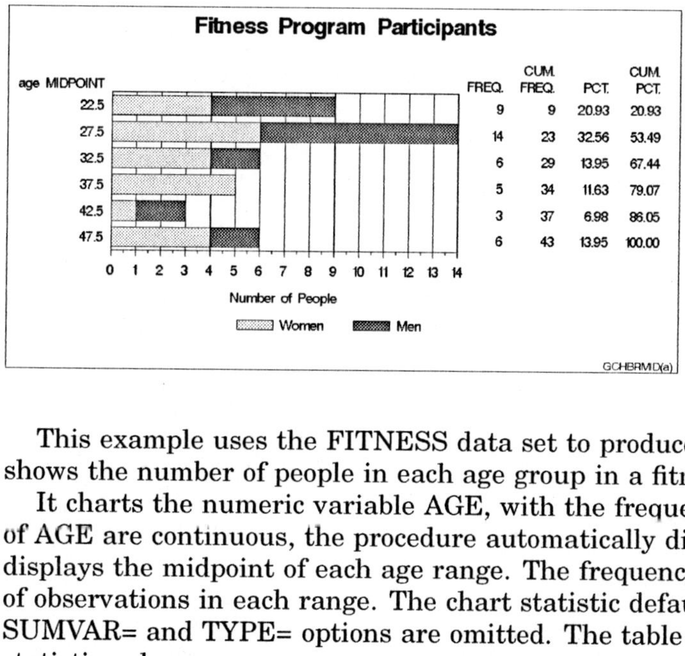

This example uses the FITNESS data set to produce a horizontal bar chart that shows the number of people in each age group in a fitness program.

It charts the numeric variable AGE, with the frequency statistic. Because the values of AGE are continuous, the procedure automatically divides the ages into ranges and displays the midpoint of each age range. The frequency statistic calculates the number of observations in each range. The chart statistic defaults to FREQ because the SUMVAR= and TYPE= options are omitted. The table of statistics displays all the statistic values.

The program also subgroups each age group bar to show the number of men and women in the group. Because the default value for the PATTERNID= option is SUBGROUP, the procedure automatically assigns a different pattern to each subgroup and the PATTERNID= option is unnecessary.

PATTERN statements specify the colors for the subgroups. Whenever the GCHART procedure uses PATTERN statements, the default outline color of the bars changes from black to the color of the bar. Because this program uses PATTERN statements, it also uses COUTLINE= to specify a black outline for the bars.

The second part of this example modifies the midpoint axis and the table of statistics, and uses RUN-group processing to produce the following chart. This part of the program specifies the midpoint value for each bar and requests only the FREQ statistic for the table.

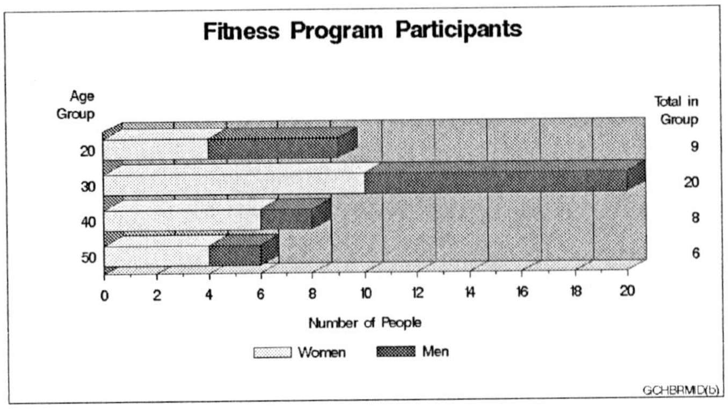

Assign the libref and set the graphics environment. Black is the first color in the colors list and, by default, is used for all text and for the axis lines and frame. Therefore, it is not necessary to use CTEXT= (GOPTIONS statement) and CAXIS= (HBAR statement) to specify a color.

```
libname reflib 'SAS-data-library';
goptions reset=global gunit=pct border cback=white
         colors=(black blue green red) ftext=swiss
         ftitle=swissb htitle=6 htext=3.5;
```

Create the data set FITNESS. FITNESS contains age and sex of participants, as well as the number of times they exercise each week and their resting heart rate and aerobic power.

```
data reflib.fitness;
   input age sex $ heart exer aero;
   datalines;
28  M  86  2   36.6
41  M  76  3   26.7
30  M  78  2   33.8
...more data lines...
29  M  54  3   44.8
48  F  66  2   28.9
36  F  66  2   33.2
;
```

Define the title and footnote.

```
title1 'Fitness Program Participants';
footnote h=3 j=r 'GCHBRMID(a) ';
```

Modify the response axis. OFFSET= moves the first and last tick marks to the ends of the axis line.

```
axis1 label=('Number of People')
      minor=(number=1)
      offset=(0,0);
```

Modify the legend. VALUE= specifies the text that describes the values.

```
legend1 label=none
        value=('Women' 'Men');
```

Define pattern colors for the subgroups. The procedure automatically assigns a pattern to each subgroup, using the default fill, SOLID, with the specified color.

```
pattern1 color=cyan;
pattern2 color=blue;
```

Produce the first horizontal bar chart. Because neither MIDPOINTS= nor DISCRETE is used, the procedure automatically selects the midpoints. SUBGROUP= divides the bars according to the values of SEX and automatically generates a legend. AUTOREF adds reference lines to the chart at each major tick mark. CLIPREF positions the reference lines behind the bars. COUTLINE= specifies the outline color for the bars.

```
proc gchart data=reflib.fitness;
   hbar age / subgroup=sex
              legend=legend1
              autoref
              clipref
              coutline=black
              raxis=axis1;
run;
```

Define the footnote for the second chart.

```
footnote h=3 j=r 'GCHBRMID(b) ';
```

Modify the response axis for the second chart. ORDER= places major tick marks on the response axis at intervals of 2.

```
axis1 order=(0 to 20 by 2)
      label=('Number of People')
      minor=(number=1)
      offset=(0,0);
```

Modify the midpoint axis label for the second chart.

```
axis2 label=('Age ' j=r 'Group');
```

Produce the second horizontal bar chart with modified midpoints. MIDPOINTS= specifies the middle value of the range of values represented by each bar. FREQ requests that only the frequency statistic appears in the table. FREQLABEL= specifies the text for the column header in the table of statistics.

```
   hbar3d age / midpoints=(20 30 40 50)
                freq
                freqlabel='Total in Group'
                subgroup=sex
                autoref
                maxis=axis2
                raxis=axis1
                legend=legend1
                coutline=black;
run;
quit;
```

Example 6: Generating Error Bars in a Horizontal Bar Chart

Procedure features:

HBAR statement options:

- CLM=
- COUTLINE=
- ERRORBAR=
- FREQLABEL=
- MEANLABEL=
- NOFRAME
- SUMVAR=
- TYPE=

Other features:

AXIS statement

PATTERN statement

Data set: FITNESS

Sample library member: GCHERRBR

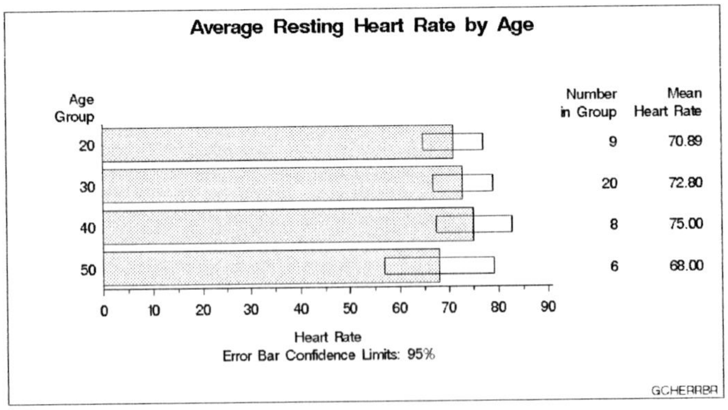

This example uses the FITNESS data set to chart the mean heart rate for each age group with error bars showing the confidence limits for the average. The response axis label describes the confidence limit for the error bars. To make the error bars easier to read, the program suppresses the frame that the procedure draws around the axis area.

Descriptive column head labels in the table of statistics replace the statistic names that appear by default.

Assign the libref and set the graphics environment.

```
libname reflib 'SAS-data-library';
goptions reset=global gunit=pct border cback=white
         colors=(black blue green red) ftext=swiss
         ftitle=swissb htitle=5 htext=3.5;
```

Define the title and footnote.

```
title1 'Average Resting Heart Rate by Age';
footnote h=3 j=r 'GCHERRBR ';
```

Modify the axis labels. AXIS1 is assigned to the response axis and AXIS2 is assigned to the midpoint axis.

```
axis1 label=('Heart Rate' j=c
             'Error Bar Confidence Limits: 95%')
      minor=(number=1);
axis2 label=('Age' j=r 'Group');
```

Define a color for the bars. The PATTERN statement uses the default fill, SOLID, with the specified color to create a pattern for the bars. Using a PATTERN statement causes the default bar outline color to be the same as the fill color. COUTLINE= in the HBAR statement assigns a black outline.

```
pattern1 color=cyan;
```

Produce the horizontal bar chart. SUMVAR= calculates the mean of the variable HEART for all the observations in each midpoint group. TYPE= specifies the mean statistic for the summary variable, HEART. FREQLABEL= and MEANLABEL= specify new column labels for the frequency and mean statistics. ERRORBAR= draws the error bars as empty bars and CLM= specifies the confidence level. COUTLINE= outlines the bars in black. NOFRAME suppresses the axis area frame.

```
proc gchart data=reflib.fitness;
   hbar age / type=mean
              sumvar=heart
              freqlabel='Number in Group'
              meanlabel='Mean  Heart Rate'
              errorbar=bars
              clm=95
              midpoints=(20 30 40 50)
              raxis=axis1
              maxis=axis2
              noframe
              coutline=black;
run;
```

```
quit;
```

Example 7: Creating Bar Charts with Drill-down for the Web

Procedure Features:
VBAR3D statement

ODS Features:
ODS HTML statement:
- ANCHOR=
- BODY=
- CONTENTS=
- FRAME=
- NEWFILE
- NOGTITLE
- PATH=

Other Features:
- AXIS statement
- BY statement
- FORMAT statement
- GOPTIONS statement
- LEGEND statement
- PATTERN statement
- RUN-group processing
- TITLE statement
- WHERE statement

Sample library member: GCHDDOWN

This example shows how to create 3D bar charts with drill-down functionality for the Web. In addition to showing how to use the ODS HTML statement and the HTML options to create the drill-down, the example also illustrates other VBAR3D statement options.

For creating output with drill-down for the Web, the example shows how to

- □ explicitly name the HTML files and open and close them throughout the program
- □ specify names and destination for the GIF files created by the ODS HTML statement and the GIF device driver
- □ assign anchor names to the graphics output
- □ use the HTML= and HTML_LEGEND= procedure options to assign link targets
- □ use BY-group processing to store multiple graphs in one file or in individual files
- □ use incremented anchor names and incremented file names.

For more information, see "ODS HTML Statement" on page 164 in Chapter 7, "SAS/GRAPH Statements," on page 121.

For creating 3D bar charts, the example shows how to

- □ group the midpoints, including patterning bars by group, modifying the group axis, adjusting the space between groups of bars
- □ identify midpoint values with a legend instead of labeling each bar

- □ subgroup bars
- □ remove an axis and its axis plane
- □ add reference lines.

The introduction to each part lists the VBAR3D options that it features.

The program generates twelve linked bar charts that display data about the world's leading grain producers. The data contain the amount of grain produced by five countries in 1995 and 1996. Each of these countries is one of the three leading producers of wheat, rice, or corn, worldwide.

The first chart, shown in Figure 29.15 on page 857 as it appears in a browser, is an overview of the data that shows the total grain production for the five countries for both years.

Figure 29.15 Browser View of Overview Graph

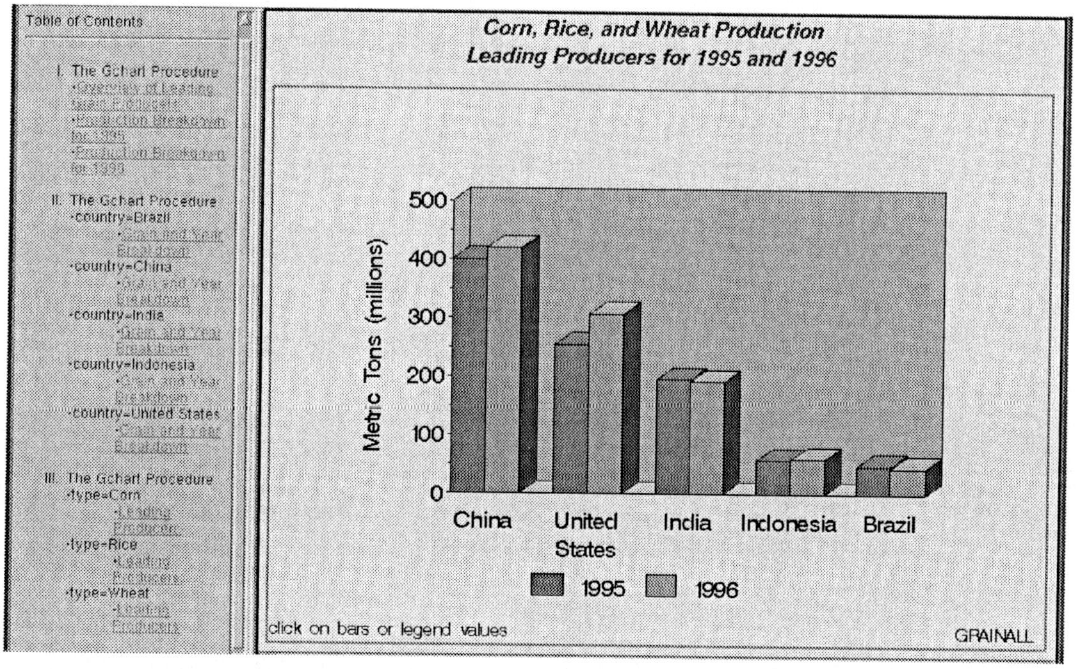

The next two charts break down grain production by year. These charts are linked to the legend values in Figure 29.15 on page 857. For example, when you select the legend value for 1995, the graph in Figure 29.16 on page 858 appears.

Figure 29.16 Browser View of Year Breakdown for 1995

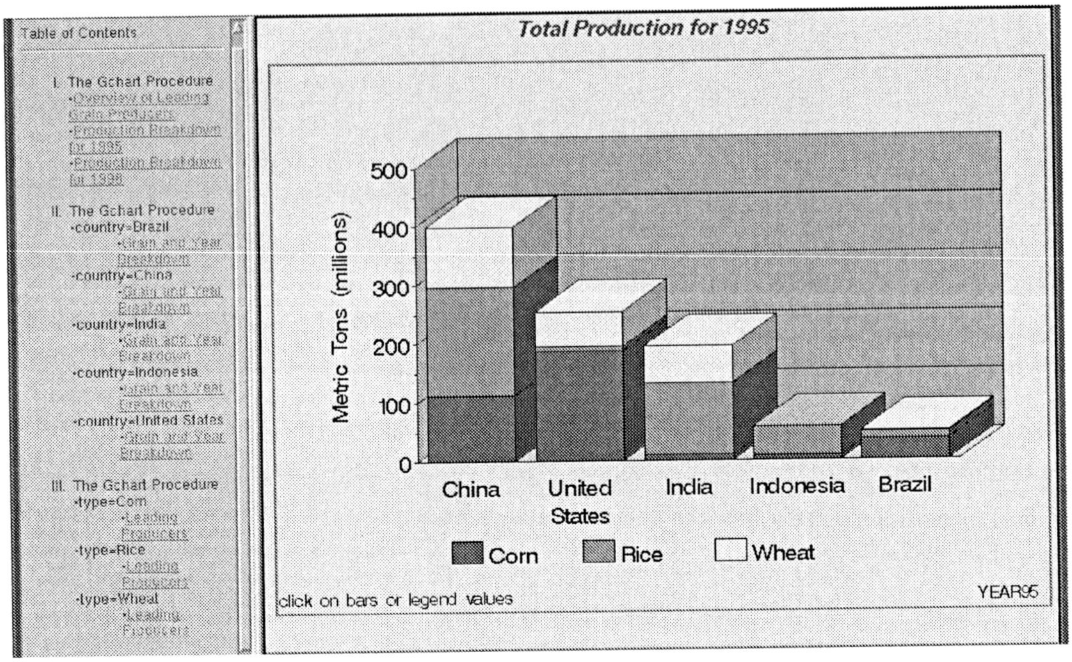

Another group of charts breaks down the data by country. These charts are linked to the bars. For example, when you drill down on the bar for China in either Figure 29.15 on page 857 or Figure 29.16 on page 858, the graph in Figure 29.17 on page 858 appears.

Figure 29.17 Browser View of Breakdown for China

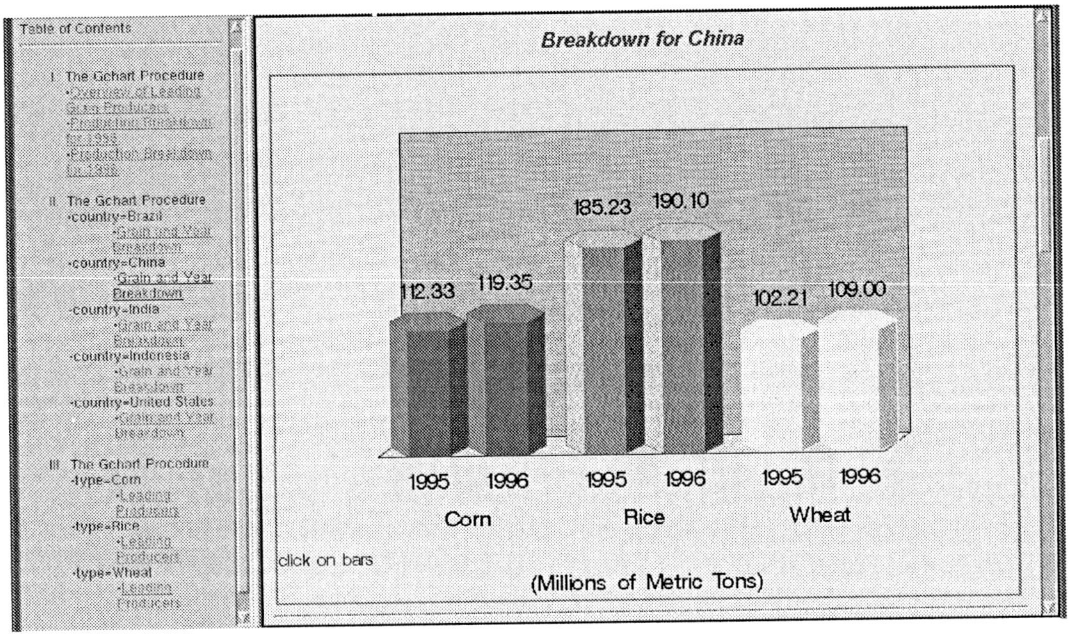

Finally the data is charted by grain type. These graphs are linked to the bars in Figure 29.17 on page 858. If you select the legend value or bar for `Rice`, Figure 29.18 on page 859 appears.

Figure 29.18 Browser View of Breakdown for Rice

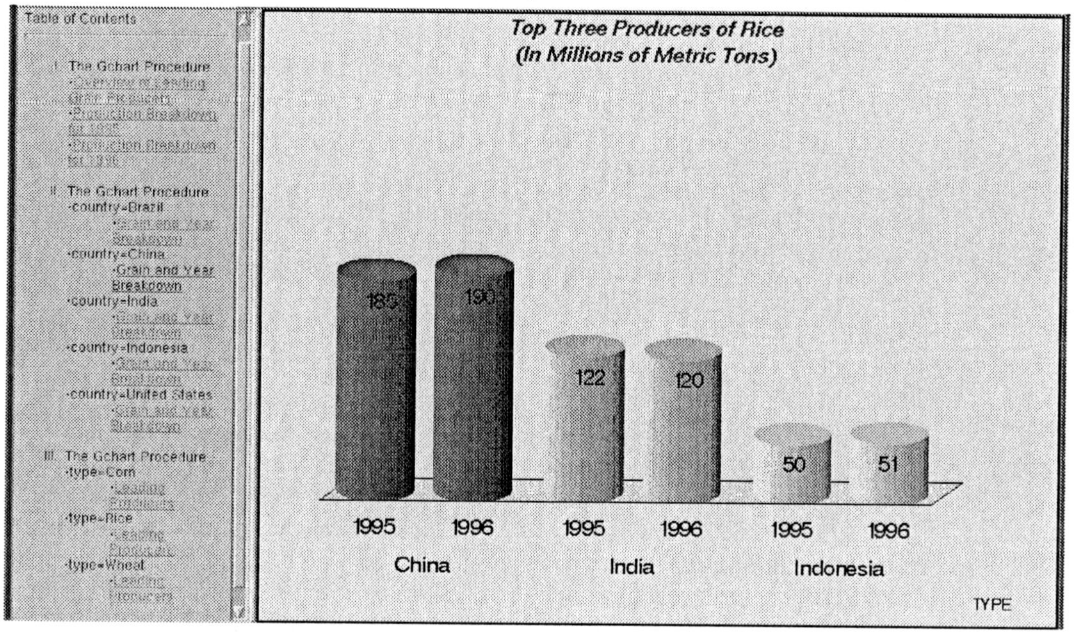

This program is divided into four parts:

- □ "Example 7, Part A" on page 859 generates the graph shown in Figure 29.15 on page 857.
- □ "Example 7, Part B" on page 864 generates the pair of graphs represented by Figure 29.16 on page 858.
- □ "Example 7, Part C" on page 866 generates the five graphs represented by Figure 29.17 on page 858.
- □ "Example 7, Part D" on page 868 generates the three graphs represented by Figure 29.18 on page 859.

Example 7, Part A

Features:

VBAR3D options:

- DES=
- DISCRETE
- GROUP=
- GSPACE=
- HTML=
- HTML_LEGEND=
- NAME=
- SUBGROUP=

ODS HTML options:

- BODY=
- CONTENTS=
- FRAME=
- GPATH=
- NOGTITLE

The first part of the program, which includes setting the graphics environment and creating the data set, does the following:

- □ Adds three HTML variables to the data set. The variables contain the link targets for all of the graphs that support drill-down functionality. The HREF values for the HTML variables in the data set contain this information about the link targets:
  - □ the name of the body file that is the target. BODY= in the ODS HTML statement names the body file.
  - □ the anchor name of the output if the target file contains more than one graph. By default, all output is assigned a unique anchor name unless you specify a name with ANCHOR= in the ODS HTML statement.
- □ Opens the HTML destination for the frame and contents files and the first body file.
- □ Creates one grouped 3D vertical bar chart (shown in Figure 29.15 on page 857) with drill-down on the bars and legend values. The bars, which represent total production for each year for each country, are grouped and labeled by COUNTRY. Instead of displaying the year below each bar, the program suppresses the midpoint values with an AXIS statement and creates a legend that associates bar color and year. To create the legend, the chart variable YEAR is assigned to the SUBGROUP= option. Because the chart variable and the subgroup variable are the same, each bar contains only one "subgroup." As a result, the subgroup legend has an entry for each value of YEAR, thereby creating a legend for the midpoints. The values of COUNTRY label each group of bars.
- □ Assigns the HTML variables that contain link information for the bars and for the legend values to the HTML= and HTML_LEGEND= options, respectively.

Assign the Web-server path. FILENAME assigns the fileref ODSOUT, which specifies a destination for the HTML and GIF files produced by the example program. To assign that location as the HTML destination for program output, ODSOUT is specified later in the program on the ODS HTML statement's PATH= option. ODSOUT must point to a Web-server location if procedure output is to be viewed on the Web.

```
filename odsout 'path-to-Web-server-space';
```

Close the ODS listing destination for procedure output, and set the graphics environment. To conserve system resources, the graphics output is not displayed in the GRAPH window, although it is written to the graphics catalog and to the GIF files.

```
ods listing close;
goptions reset=global gunit=pct
         htitle=6 htext=4 ftitle=zapfb ftext=swiss;
```

Create the data set GRAINLDR. GRAINLDR contains data about grain production in five countries for 1995 and 1996. The quantities in AMOUNT are in thousands of metric tons. MEGTONS converts these quantities to millions of metric tons.

```
data grainldr;
   length country $ 3 type $ 5;
   input year country $ type $ amount;
   megtons=amount/1000;
```

```
   datalines;
1995 BRZ  Wheat    1516
1995 BRZ  Rice     11236
1995 BRZ  Corn     36276
1995 CHN  Wheat    102207
1995 CHN  Rice     185226
1995 CHN  Corn     112331
1995 IND  Wheat    63007
1995 IND  Rice     122372
1995 IND  Corn     9800
1995 INS  Wheat    .
1995 INS  Rice     49860
1995 INS  Corn     8223
1995 USA  Wheat    59494
1995 USA  Rice     7888
1995 USA  Corn     187300
1996 BRZ  Wheat    3302
1996 BRZ  Rice     10035
1996 BRZ  Corn     31975
1996 CHN  Wheat    109000
1996 CHN  Rice     190100
1996 CHN  Corn     119350
1996 IND  Wheat    62620
1996 IND  Rice     120012
1996 IND  Corn     8660
1996 INS  Wheat    .
1996 INS  Rice     51165
1996 INS  Corn     8925
1996 USA  Wheat    62099
1996 USA  Rice     7771
1996 USA  Corn     236064
;
```

Add three HTML variables to GRAINLDR to create the NEWGRAIN data set. Each HTML variable is assigned the targets for a certain variable value. These targets are specified by the HREF attribute within an AREA element in the HTML file. Each HREF value specifies the HTML body file and, optionally, the name of the anchor within the body file that identifies the target graph. The HTML variable YEARDRILL contains the targets for the values of the variable YEAR.

```
data newgrain;
     set grainldr;
     length yeardrill typedrill countrydrill $ 40;
     if year=1995 then
        yeardrill='HREF="year95_body.html"';
     else if year=1996 then
        yeardrill='HREF="year96_body.html"';
```

The HTML variable COUNTRYDRILL contains the targets for the values of the variable COUNTRY. Because the graphs of COUNTRY are in one file, the targets must include the anchor name.

```
   if country='BRZ' then
      countrydrill='HREF="country_body.html#country"';
   else if country='CHN' then
      countrydrill='HREF="country_body.html#country1"';
   else if country='IND' then
      countrydrill='HREF="country_body.html#country2"';
   else if country='INS' then
      countrydrill='HREF="country_body.html#country3"';
   else if country='USA' then
      countrydrill='HREF="country_body.html#country4"';
```

The HTML variable TYPEDRILL contains the names of the files that are the targets for the values of the variable TYPE.

```
   if type='Corn' then
      typedrill='HREF="type1_body.html"';
   else if type='Rice' then
      typedrill='HREF="type2_body.html"';
   else if type='Wheat' then
      typedrill='HREF="type3_body.html"';
run;
```

Create a format for the values of COUNTRY.

```
proc format;
     value $country 'BRZ' = 'Brazil'
                    'CHN' = 'China'
                    'IND' = 'India'
                    'INS' = 'Indonesia'
                    'USA' = 'United States';
run;
```

Define pattern colors for all graphs. To avoid solid black patterns (BLACK is the first color in the colors list), explicitly assign the pattern colors.

```
pattern1 color=blue;
pattern2 color=green;
pattern3 color=cyan;
```

Define legend characteristics for all legends. OFFSET= moves the legend down.

```
legend1 label=none
        shape=bar(4,4)
        position=(bottom center)
        offset=(-3);
```

Assign the GOPTIONS for ODS HTML destination. DEVICE= generates the SAS/GRAPH output as GIF files. TRANSPARENCY makes the background of the graphs the same as the Web-page background. NOBORDER turns off the border around the graphics output area.

```
goptions transparency device=gif noborder;
```

Open the ODS HTML destination for the ODS graphics output. BODY= names the file for storing the HTML output. CONTENTS= names the HTML file that contains the table of contents to the HTML procedure output. The contents file links to each of the body files written to the HTML destination. FRAME= names the HTML file that integrates the contents and body files. PATH= specifies the ODSOUT fileref as the HTML destination for all the HTML and GIF files. NOGTITLE suppress the graph titles from the SAS/GRAPH output and displays them through the HTML page.

```
ods html body='grain_body.html'
         frame='grain_frame.html'
         contents='grain_contents.html'
         path=odsout
         nogtitle;
```

Suppress the label and values for the midpoint axis. The midpoint values 1995 and 1996 do not appear below each bar.

```
axis1 label=none value=none;
```

Modify the response axis. ANGLE=90 prints the axis label vertically.

```
axis2 label=(angle=90 'Metric Tons (millions)')
      minor=(n=1)
      order=(0 to 500 by 100)
      offset=(0,0);
```

Suppress the label and order the values for the group axis. Because the values of COUNTRY are formatted, ORDER= must specify their formatted value.

```
axis3 label=none
      order=('China' 'United States' 'India'
             'Indonesia' 'Brazil')
      split=' ';
```

Define titles and footnote. The footnote uses the catalog entry name to identify the graph.

```
title1 'Corn, Rice, and Wheat Production';
title2 h=2 'Leading Producers for 1995 and 1996';
footnote1 j=l h=3 'click on bars or legend values' j=r h=3 'GRAINALL ';
```

Generate the vertical bar chart that summarizes all grain production for all countries for both years. DISCRETE creates a separate bar for each unique value of YEAR. GROUP= groups the bars by country. To create a legend for midpoint values, SUBGROUP= is assigned the chart variable. GSPACE= controls the space between the groups of bars.

```
proc gchart data=newgrain;
     format country $country.;
     vbar3d year / discrete
                   sumvar=megtons
                   group=country
                   subgroup=year
                   legend=legend1
                   space=0
                   width=4
                   gspace=5
                   maxis=axis1
                   raxis=axis2
                   gaxis=axis3
                   cframe=grayaa
                   coutline=black
```

HTML= specifies COUNTRYDRILL as the variable that contains the targets for the bars. HTML_LEGEND= specifies YEARDRILL as the variable that contains the targets for the legend values. Specifying HTML variables causes SAS/GRAPH to add an image map to the HTML body file. NAME= specifies the name of the catalog entry. Because the PATH= destination is a file storage location and not a specific file name, the catalog entry name GRAINALL is automatically assigned to the GIF file. DES= specifies the description that is stored in the graphics catalog and used in the Table of Contents.

```
                   html=countrydrill
                   html_legend=yeardrill
                   name='grainall'
                   des='Overview of leading grain producers';
run;
```

Example 7, Part B

Features: VBAR3D options:
- AUTOREF
- HTML=
- HTML_LEGEND=
- SUBGROUP=
- SPACE=
- NAME=

ODS HTML options:
- BODY=

In the second part, the PROC GCHART step continues, using RUN-group processing and WHERE statements to produce two graphs of grain production for each year, one of which is shown in Figure 29.16 on page 858. Each bar represents a country and is subgrouped by grain type. As before, both the bars and the legend values are links to other graphs. The bars link to targets stored in COUNTRYDRILL and the legend values link to targets in TYPEDRILL. These two graphs not only *contain* links, they *are* the link targets for the legend values in Figure 29.15 on page 857. Before each graph is generated, the ODS HTML statement opens a new body file in which to store the output. Because each of these graphs is stored in a separate file, the HREF attributes that are stored in the variable YEARDRILL point only to the file. The name of the file is specified by the BODY= option in the ODS HTML statement. For example, this is the HREF attribute that points to the graph of 1995 and is stored in the variable YEARDRILL:

```
HREF=year95_body.html
```

YEARDRILL is assigned to the HTML_LEGEND= option in Part A.

Open a new body file for the graph of 1995 production. Assigning a new body file closes GRAIN_BODY.HTML. The contents and frame files, which remain open, will provide links to all body files.

```
ods html body='year95_body.html' path=odsout;
```

Define the title and footnote for the chart.

```
title1 'Total Production for 1995';
footnote1 j=l h=3 'click on bars or legend values' j=r h=3 'YEAR95 ';
```

Subset the data for 1995 and generate the vertical bar chart for 1995. AUTOREF draws a reference line on the backplane for every major tick mark value. SUBGROUP= creates a separate bar segment for each department. SPACE= controls the space between the bars. HTML= names the variable that contains the targets for the bars. HTML_LEGEND= names the variable that contains the targets for the legend values. The GIF files use the catalog entry name specified by NAME=.

```
where year=1995;
vbar3d country / sumvar=megtons
                 subgroup=type
                 autoref
                 html=countrydrill
                 html_legend=typedrill
                 legend=legend1
                 cframe=grayaa
                 space=3
                 coutline=black
                 maxis=axis3
                 raxis=axis2
                 name='year95'
                 des='Production Breakdown for 1995';
run;
```

Open a new body file for the graph of 1996 production. Assigning a new body file closes YEAR95_BODY.HTML.

```
ods html body='year96_body.html' path=odsout;
```

Define title and footnote for the second graph.

```
title1 'Total Production for 1996';
footnote1 j=l h=3 'click on bars or legend values' j=r h=3 'YEAR96 ';
```

Subset the data for 1996 and generate the vertical bar chart for 1996.

```
where year=1996;
vbar3d country / sumvar=megtons
                 subgroup=type
```

```
                autoref
                html=countrydrill
                html_legend=typedrill
                legend=legend1
                cframe=grayaa
                space=3
                coutline=black
                maxis=axis3
                raxis=axis2
                name='year96'
                des='Production Breakdown for 1996';
run;
quit;
```

Example 7, Part C

Features:

VBAR3D options:

- DES=
- GAXIS=
- GROUP=
- HTML=
- NAME=
- OUTSIDE=
- PATTERNID=
- RAXIS=
- SHAPE=

ODS HTML options:

- BODY=
- ANCHOR=

The third part produces the five graphs that show the breakdowns by country. These graphs are generated with BY-group processing and are all stored in one body file. When the file is displayed in the browser, all the graphs appear in one frame that can be scrolled. Because the graphs are stored in one file, the links to them must explicitly point to the location of each graph in the file, not just to the file. This location is defined by an anchor. ODS HTML assigns anchor names by default, but you can specify anchor names with the ANCHOR= option. When the procedure uses BY-group processing to generate multiple pieces of output, ODS automatically increments the anchor name to produce a unique name for each graph. This example assigns the base name {mono country} to ANCHOR=. The graphs created by this part are referenced by the COUNTRYDRILL variable. With BY-group processing the catalog entry name also increments automatically. NAME= specifies COUNTRY as the base name for the graphics output. Because you cannot specify a different description for each graph, DES= specifies a generic description for the HTML Table of Contents.

Sort the data set for the graphs of production by country. The data must be sorted in order of the BY variable before running PROC GCHART with BY-group processing.

```
proc sort data=newgrain out=country;
by country;
run;
```

Open a new body file and specify the base anchor name for the graphs of individual countries. Assigning a new body file closes YEAR96_BODY.HTML. Because all the graphs generated by the BY-group processing are stored in one file, each one is automatically assigned an anchor name. ANCHOR= specifies a base name for these anchors.

```
ods html body='country_body.html'
         anchor='country'
         gfootnote
         path=odsout;
```

Redefine AXIS2 to change the range of values and suppress all axis elements. Setting all the label and tick mark options to NONE and assigning a line style of 0 removes the response axis. NOPLANE removes the 3D axis plane. Specifying ORDER= makes all the graphs use the same range of values.

```
axis2 order=(0 to 250 by 50)
      label=none
      value=none
      style=0
      major=none
      minor=none
      noplane;
```

Suppress the axis label for the midpoint axis.

```
axis4 label=none;
```

Suppress the default BY-line and define a title that includes the BY-value. #BYVAL inserts the value of the BY variable COUNTRY into the title of each report.

```
options nobyline;
title1 'Breakdown for #byval(country)';
footnote1 j=l h=3 'click on bars';
footnote2 j=c '(Millions of Metric Tons)';
```

Generate the vertical bar chart of production for each country. GROUP= groups the bars by country. PATTERNID= assigns patterns by group value. SHAPE= assigns the bar shape. OUTSIDE= displays the SUM statistic above the bars. RAXIS= assigns the AXIS statement that removes all exis elements. GAXIS= assigns the AXIS statement that removes the label. HTML= specifies TYPEDRILL as the variable that contains the targets for the bars. NAME= specifies the name of the catalog entry. The graphics catalog entry name increments so the GIF files are named sequentially from COUNTRY to COUNTRY4. The DES= option specifies a general description that appears in the table of contents for all five graphs.

```
proc gchart data=country;
     format country $country.;
     by country;
     vbar3d year / discrete
                   sumvar=megtons
                   patternid=group
```

```
                    group=type
                    shape=hexagon
                    outside=sum
                    html=typedrill
                    width=9
                    gspace=3
                    space=0
                    cframe=grayaa
                    raxis=axis2
                    gaxis=axis4
                    maxis=axis4
                    name='country'
                    des='Grain and Year Breakdown';
run;
```

Example 7, Part D

Features: VBAR3D options:
INSIDE=
NOZERO

ODS HTML options:
BODY=
NEWFILE=TABLE

Like Part C, this part uses BY-group processing to generate three graphs that show the three leading producers for each type of grain. The program subsets the data and suppresses midpoints with no observations. Instead of storing all of the output in one body file, it stores each graph in a separate file. To do this, the program uses the ODS HTML option NEWFILE=TABLE. When NEWFILE=TABLE is used with BY-group processing, each new piece of output automatically generates a new body file and simply increments the name of the file that is specified by BODY=. Because each graph is stored in a separate file, the links to these graphs reference only the file name and do not require an anchor name. The graphs created by this part are referenced by the TYPEDRILL variable.

Sort the data set for the graphs of leading producers of each grain type.

```
proc sort data=grainldr out=type;
by type;
run;
```

Open a new body file. Assigning a new body file closes COUNTRY_BODY.HTML. NEWFILE=TABLE opens a new body file for each piece of output generated by the procedure. Each new file increments the name specified by BODY= using the number within the body file name as the starting number.

```
ods html body='type1_body.html'
         newfile=table
         path=odsout;
```

Modify the group axis. Because SPLIT= assigns a blank as the split character, the value **United States** automatically prints on two lines.

```
axis5 label=none
      split=' ';
```

Define title and footnote. #BYVAL inserts the value of the BY variable TYPE into the title of each report.

```
title1 'Top Three Producers of #byval(type)';
title2 '(In Millions of Metric Tons)';
footnote j=r h=3 'TYPE ';
```

Generate the vertical bar chart of leading producers for each grain type.BY-group processing generates a separate graph for each value TYPE. Each new graph generates a new body file. NOZERO suppresses the midpoints that do not have any observations. INSIDE= displays the SUM statistic inside the bars.

```
proc gchart data=type (where=(megtons gt 31));
     format country $country.;
     by type;
     vbar3d year / discrete
                   sumvar=megtons
                   group=country
                   nozero
                   shape=cylinder
                   noframe
                   patternid=group
                   inside=sum
                   width=8
                   maxis=axis4
                   raxis=axis2
                   gaxis=axis5
                   cframe=grayaa
                   name='type'
                   des='Leading Producers';
run;
quit;
```

Close the ODS HTML destination, and open the ODS Listing destination. You must close the HTML destination before you can view the output with a browser.

```
ods html close;
ods listing;
```

Example 8: Specifying the Sum Statistic for a Pie Chart

Procedure features:

PIE statement options:

COUTLINE=

SUMVAR=

PIE3D statement options:

COUTLINE=
EXPLODE=
SUMVAR=

Other features:

FORMAT statement

RUN-group processing

Data set: TOTALS

Sample library member: GCHPISUM

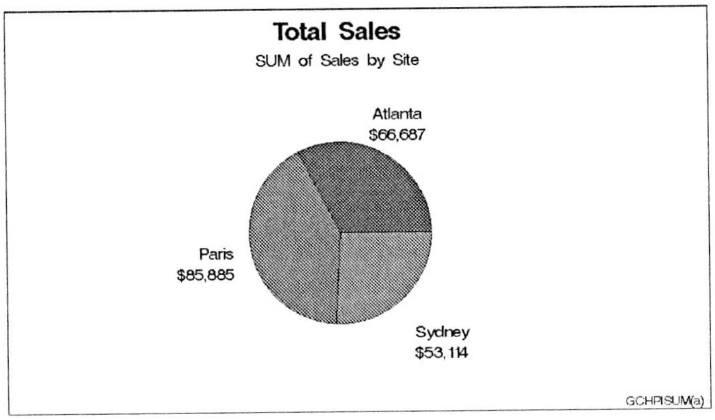

This example produces two pie charts that show total sales for three sites by charting the values of the character variable SITE and calculating the sum of the variable SALES for each site. It represents the statistics as slices of the pie. By default, the midpoint value and the summary statistic are printed beside each slice.

The pie slices use the default pattern fill, which is solid. Because a colors list is specified in the GOPTIONS statement, the default solid patterns rotate through the colors in the list, beginning with the first color, blue. Each slice displays a different color because, by default, pie charts are patterned by midpoint. Because the default outline color is also the first color in the list, the example uses the COUTLINE= option to assign black to the outlines.

The second pie chart is a 3D pie chart with an exploded slice, as shown in the following output.

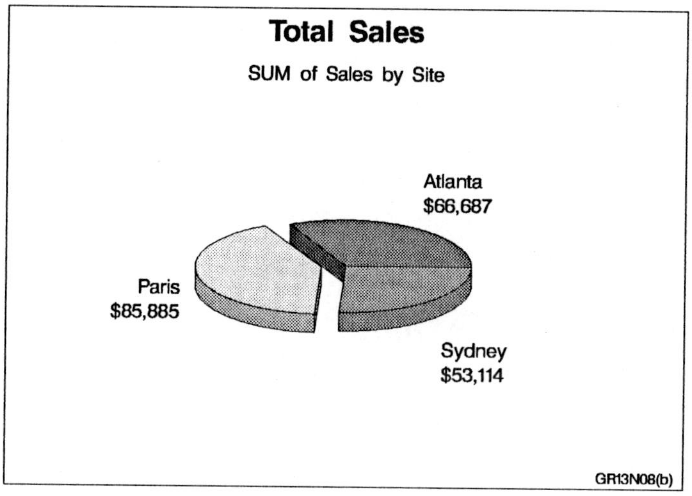

Assign the libref and set the graphics environment. CTEXT= specifies the color for all text on the output. COLORS= specifies the colors list, which is used by the default patterns and outlines.

```
libname reflib 'SAS-data-library';
goptions reset=global gunit=pct border cback=white
         colors=(blue green red) ctext=black
         ftitle=swissb ftext=swiss htitle=6 htext=4;
```

Define title and footnote.

```
title 'Total Sales';
footnote j=r 'GCHPISUM(a) ';
```

Produce the first pie chart. The PIE statement produces a two-dimensional pie chart. SUMVAR= calculates the sum of SALES for each value of the chart variable SITE. The default statistic for SUMVAR= is SUM. The summary variable SALES is assigned a dollar format. COUTLINE= specifies the outline color for the slices.

```
proc gchart data=reflib.totals;
   format sales dollar8.;
   pie site / sumvar=sales
              coutline=black;
run;
```

Define footnote for second pie chart.

```
   footnote j=r 'GCHPISUM(b) ';
```

Produce the second pie chart. The PIE3D statement produces a three-dimensional pie chart. EXPLODE= separates the slice for Paris from the rest of the pie.

```
   pie3d site / sumvar=sales
                coutline=black
                explode='Paris';
run;
quit;
```

Example 9: Subgrouping a Donut or Pie Chart

Procedure features:

DONUT statement options:

- COUTLINE=
- CTEXT=
- DONUTPCT=
- LABEL=
- LEGEND=
- NOHEADING
- SUBGROUP=

Other features: LEGEND statement

Data set: TOTALS

Sample library member: GCHSBGRP

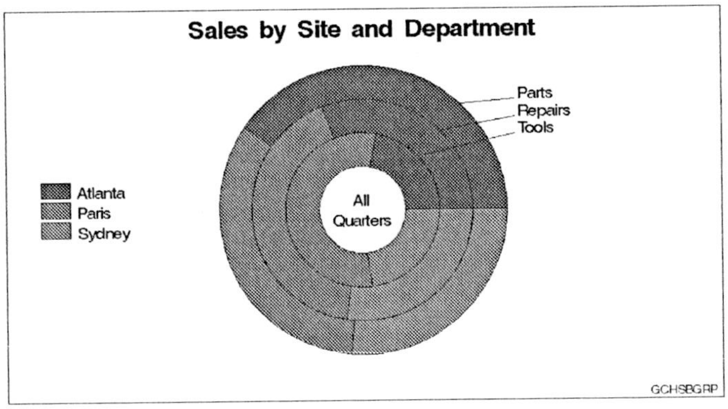

This example produces a donut chart that is similar to the pie chart in Example 8 on page 869 in that each slice represents total sales for a site and each slice is a different color. However, in this donut chart the sites are subgrouped by department, so that each department is represented as a concentric ring with slices.

Subgrouping suppresses the chart statistic and the midpoint labels. Instead it automatically labels the rings with the subgroup values and generates a legend that shows how the patterns are associated with the midpoint values. Subgrouping a pie chart produces the same results but without the hole in the center.

To allow the donut chart to be as large as possible, the program suppresses the default heading and moves the legend into the space at the left of the chart.

Assign the libref and set the graphics environment.

```
libname reflib 'SAS-data-library';
goptions reset=global gunit=pct border cback=white
         colors=(blue green red) ctext=black
         ftext=swissb ftext=swiss htitle=6 htext=4;
```

Define title and footnote.

```
title 'Sales by Site and Department';
footnote h=3 j=r 'GCHSBGRP ';
```

Modify the subgroup legend. LABEL= suppresses the legend label. SHAPE= defines the shape of the legend values. POSITION=, OFFSET=, and ACROSS= arrange the legend entries in a column to the left of the pie chart. MODE= allows the legend to occupy the procedure output area.

```
legend1 label=none
        shape=bar(4,4)
        position=(middle left)
        offset=(5,)
        across=1
        mode=share;
```

Produce the donut chart. SUBGROUP= divides the donut into rings. Each ring represents a value of the subgroup variable, DEPT. The DONUTPCT= option controls the size of the donut hole, which contains the text specified by LABEL=. The NOHEADING option suppresses the default heading that contains the name of the chart variable and the type of statistic. LEGEND= assigns the LEGEND1 statement to the chart COUTLINE= specifies the outline color for the slices and subgroup rings. CTEXT= specifies the color used by the donut label and by the subgroup arrows.

```
proc gchart data=reflib.totals;
   format sales dollar8.;
   donut site / sumvar=sales
                subgroup=dept
                donutpct=30
                label=('All' justify=center 'Quarters')
                noheading
                legend=legend1
                coutline=black
                ctext=black;
run;
quit;
```

Example 10: Ordering and Labeling Slices in a Pie Chart

Procedure features:

PIE statement options:

CFILL=

MIDPOINTS=
PERCENT=ARROW
SLICE=ARROW
SUBGROUP=
VALUE=NONE

Sample library member: GCHLABEL

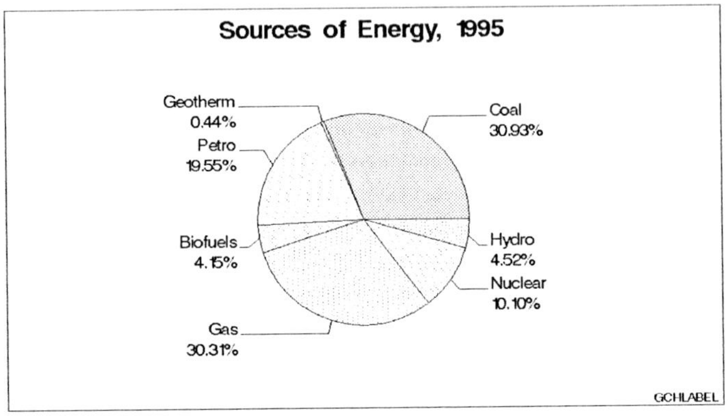

This example produces a pie chart of sources of energy production for 1995. The labeled slices represent the percent of total production for each source. Instead of the sum statistic, each slice displays the percent each midpoint contributes to the whole pie. Arrows connect the midpoint labels to the slices, which are arranged by the MIDPOINTS= option so that the small slices are not next to each other and their labels do not overlap.

Assign the libref and set the graphics environment.

```
libname reflib 'SAS-data-library';
goptions reset=global gunit=pct border cback=white
         colors=(black blue green red cyan lime gray)
         ftext=swiss ftitle=swissb htitle=6 htext=4;
```

Create the data set ENPROD.

ENPROD contains the amount of energy produced (PRODUCED) for seven sources (ENGYTYPE) for two years (YEAR). The amounts of energy produced are in quadrillion btu.

```
data reflib.enprod;
   input @1  year 4. @6 engytype $8. @16 produced 5.2;
   datalines;
1985 Coal      19.33
1985 Gas       19.22
1985 Petro     18.99
...more data lines...
1995 Hydro      3.21
1995 Geotherm    .31
1995 Biofuels   2.95
;
```

Define title and footnote.

```
title 'Sources of Energy, 1995';
footnote h=3 j=r 'GCHLABEL ';
```

Produce the pie chart. The WHERE data set option subsets the data for 1995. OTHER=0 specifies that all midpoints, no matter how small, display a slice. MIDPOINTS= assigns the order of the slices. Each slice displays the percent contribution to total production and the slice name. VALUE=NONE suppresses the chart statistic. Both SLICE= and PERCENT= are assigned the ARROW labeling method to point to the slice, but only one arrow line is displayed. CFILL= specifies a color for the fill used by all slices.

```
proc gchart data=reflib.enprod (where=(year=1995));
     pie engytype / sumvar=produced
                    other=0
                    midpoints='Coal' 'Geotherm' 'Petro'
                              'Biofuels' 'Gas' 'Nuclear'
                              'Hydro'
                    value=none
                    percent=arrow
                    slice=arrow
                    cfill=cyan
                    noheading;
run;
quit;
```

Example 11: Assigning Patterns and Identifying Midpoints with a Legend

Procedure features:

PIE statement options:

- COUTLINE=
- CTEXT=
- DESCENDING
- LEGEND=
- OTHER=
- OTHERLABEL=
- VALUE=INSIDE

Other features:

LEGEND statement

PATTERN statement

Data set: ENPROD

Sample library member: GCHLEGND

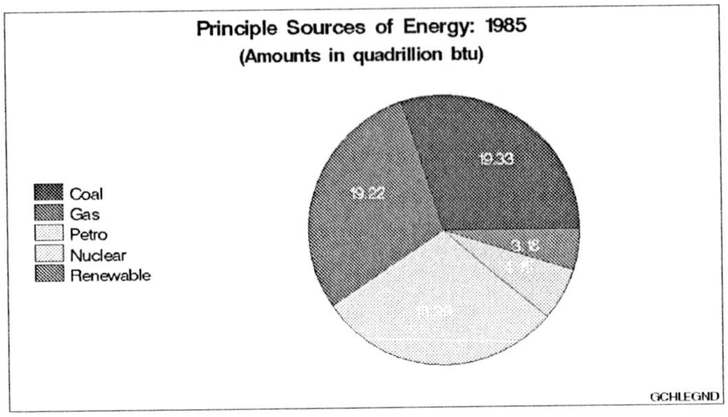

This example shows the actual amount of energy that is produced by each source for 1985. It displays the chart statistic inside each slice and uses a legend instead of slice labels to identify the slices. Pattern colors are assigned explicitly to each energy source.

All of the variables with midpoint values less than or equal to 5 percent of the total (in this case, *biofuels*, *geotherm*, and *hydro*) are grouped into one slice labeled "Other." The slices are ordered from largest to smallest based on the statistic value. Although the "Other" slice is always last, it is in this case also the smallest.

Assign the libref and set the graphics environment.

```
libname reflib 'SAS-data-library';
goptions reset=global gunit=pct border cback=white
         colors=(black blue green red) ftitle=swissb
         ftext=swiss htitle=5 htext=4;
```

Define a title and footnote.

```
title1 'Principle Sources of Energy: 1985';
title2 font=swissb h=4.5 '(Amounts in quadrillion btu)';
footnote h=3 j=r 'GCHLEGND ';
```

Define pattern colors. Each value of the chart variable ENGYTYPE is assigned a pattern whether or not it is displayed as a separate slice. Patterns are assigned to midpoints in the order the values appear in the data set. Because ENGYTYPE is character, the patterns are assigned alphabetically. The eighth pattern is for the "other" slice, which is always last.

```
pattern1 color=black;       /* biofuels      */
pattern2 color=blue;        /* coal          */
pattern3 color=green;       /* gas           */
pattern4 color=gray;        /* geothermal    */
pattern5 color=lipk;        /* hydroelectric */
pattern6 color=lime;        /* nuclear       */
pattern7 color=cyan;        /* petro         */
pattern8 color=red;         /* other         */
```

Modify the legend. LABEL= removes the legend label. VALUE= defines the color for the value labels; by default legend value color is determined by the CTEXT= option in the procedure statement. In this case, CTEXT=WHITE, so the legend statement uses the VALUE= option to override that color specification. ORDER= orders the legend values to match the slice order in the pie chart.

```
legend1 label=none
        position=(left middle)
        offset=(4,)
        across=1
        order=('Coal' 'Gas' 'Petro'
               'Nuclear' 'Renewable')
        value=(color=black)
        shape=bar(4,4);
```

Create the pie chart. OTHER= collects all the midpoints with statistic values less than or equal to 5 percent of the total into one slice. OTHERLABEL= specifies the label for the "other" slice. DESCENDING arranges the slices in descending order of the statistic value. LEGEND= displays the customized legend created in the LEGEND statement and suppresses the slice labels. VALUE= places the chart statistics inside the slices. CTEXT= specifies white for the statistic text. Because CTEXT= also affects the color of the legend text, the LEGEND statement specifies black text so that the values can be seen. Because the PATTERN statement is used, the default slice outline matches the fill color; COUTLINE= changes the outline color to black.

```
proc gchart data=reflib.enprod(where=(year=1985));
   pie engytype / sumvar=produced
                  other=5
                  otherlabel='Renewable'
                  descending
                  legend=legend1
                  value=inside
                  ctext=white
                  coutline=black
                  noheading;
run;
quit;
```

Example 12: Grouping and Arranging Pie Charts

Procedure features:

PIE statement options:

- ACROSS=
- CLOCKWISE
- GROUP=
- OTHER=
- PERCENT=OUTSIDE
- SLICE=OUTSIDE

Other features: PATTERN statement

Data set: ENPROD

Sample library member: GCHPIGRP

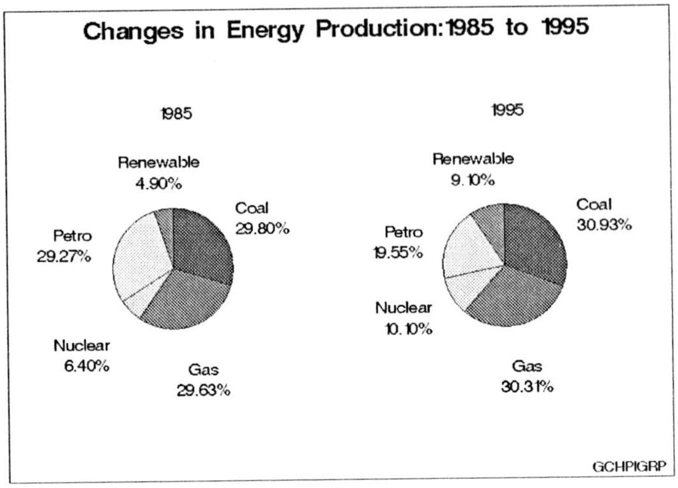

This example produces two pie charts that shows energy sources by year. Both charts are displayed on one page and are arranged two across. The program uses the CLOCKWISE option to arrange the slices, which begin at the 12 o'clock position and proceed clockwise in alphabetic order of the midpoint.

The chart statistic is suppressed and the midpoint label and the percent of the chart statistic are displayed outside of the slice.

A different color is defined for each energy type. The patterns are assigned in order of midpoint value. Some colors do not appear because the slices they represent are grouped into the OTHER slice, which is assigned the eighth color, red.

Set the graphics environment.

```
goptions reset=global gunit=pct border cback=white
         colors=(black blue green red) ftext=swiss
         ftext=swissb htitle=5 htext=3.5;
```

Define title and footnote.

```
title 'Changes in Energy Production:1985 to 1995';
footnote j=r 'GCHPIGRP ';
```

Define patterns for the pie slices. PATTERN statements define a different solid color for each midpoint value.

```
pattern1 color=black;        /* biofuels      */
pattern2 color=blue;         /* coal          */
pattern3 color=green;        /* gas           */
pattern4 color=gray;         /* geothermal    */
pattern5 color=lipk;         /* hydroelectric */
pattern6 color=lime;         /* nuclear       */
pattern7 color=cyan;         /* petro         */
pattern8 color=red;          /* other         */
```

Produce the pie charts. The WHERE= data set option selects the data for only two years. The LABEL statement suppresses the variable name, so only the YEAR value is displayed.

```
proc gchart data=reflib.enprod gout=reflib.excat;
     label year='00'x;
```

GROUP= creates a separate pie for each year. In combination with GROUP=, ACROSS= draws two charts across one page. OTHER= collects all the midpoints with statistic values less than or equal to 5 percent of the total into one slice. CLOCKWISE begins drawing the slices at the 12 o'clock position in alphabetic order of the midpoint. PERCENT=OUTSIDE and SLICE=OUTSIDE display the labels outside the slices.

```
     pie engytype / sumvar=produced
                    group=year
                    across=2
                    other=5
                    otherlabel='Renewable'
                    clockwise
                    value=none
                    slice=outside
                    percent=outside
                    coutline=black
                    noheading;
run;
quit;
```

Example 13: Specifying the Sum Statistic in a Star Chart

Procedure features:

STAR statement options:

SUMVAR=

Other features: FORMAT statement

Data set: TOTALS

Sample library member: GCHSTSUM

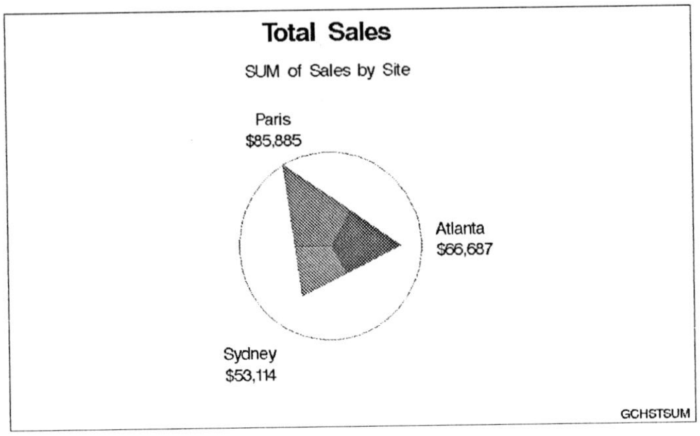

This example produces a star chart of total sales for three sites by charting the values of the character variable SITE and calculating the sum of the variable SALES for each site. It represents the statistics as slices of the star. The center of the circle represents 0 and the edge of the circle represents the largest value, in this case Paris sales. By default, the spines are joined and filled with a solid pattern to form slices, and the midpoint value and the formatted values of the sales statistics are printed beside each slice.

By default, the circle and the slice outlines use the first color in the colors list, in this case, BLUE.

Assign the libref and set the graphics environment.

```
libname reflib 'SAS-data-library';
goptions reset=global gunit=pct border cback=white
         colors=(blue green red) ctext=black
         ftitle=swissb ftext=swiss htitle=6 htext=4;
```

Define title and footnote.

```
title 'Total Sales';
footnote h=3 j=r 'GCHSTSUM ';
```

Produce the star chart. SUMVAR= calculates the sum of SALES for each value of the chart variable SITE. Because the TYPE= option is omitted, the default statistic is sum. The FORMAT statement assigns a format to the summary variable SALES.

```
proc gchart data=reflib.totals;
   format sales dollar8.;
   star site  / sumvar=sales;
run;
quit;
```

Example 14: Charting a Discrete Numeric Variable in a Star Chart

Procedure features:

STAR statement options:

- COUTLINE=
- DISCRETE
- FILL=
- NOCONNECT
- NOHEADING
- SUMVAR=

Sample library member: GCHDSCRT

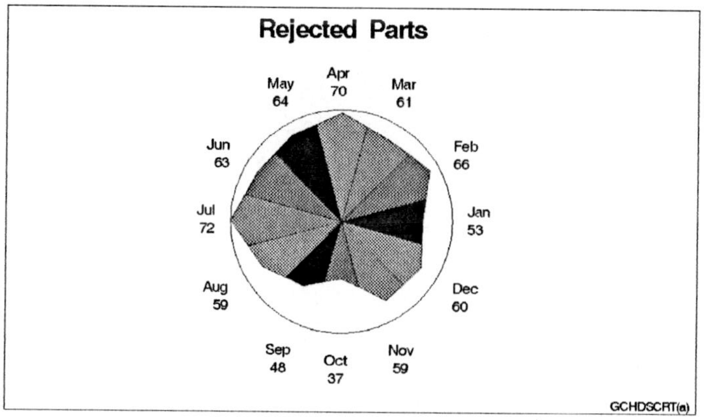

This example produces two star charts that show the total number of parts that were rejected each month for a year. The STAR statement uses the DISCRETE option so that each unique value of the numeric variable DATE is a separate midpoint and has a separate spine. Each slice displays the formatted midpoint value and the chart statistic. Specifying FILL=S rotates the solid pattern through all the colors in the colors list as many times as necessary to provide patterns for all the slices.

The second chart uses the NOCONNECT option so that the chart uses spines instead of slices.

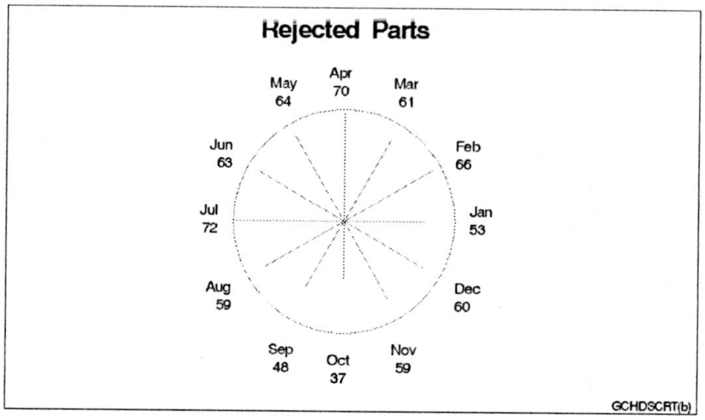

Set the graphics environment. COLORS= specifies the colors list, which is used by the default patterns and outlines.

```
goptions reset=global gunit=pct border cback=white
         colors=(black blue green red) ftext=swiss
         ftitle=swissb htext=3.5 htitle=6;
```

Create the data set REJECTS. REJECTS contains data on the number of defective parts produced at each of three sites for 12 months. BADPARTS is the number of parts that were rejected at each site for each month.

```
data rejects;
   informat date date9.;
   input site $ date badparts;
   datalines;
Sydney  01JAN1997 22
Sydney  01FEB1997 26
...more data lines...
Paris   01NOV1997 12
Paris   01DEC1997 19
;
```

Define title and footnote.

```
title 'Rejected Parts';
footnote j=r 'GCHDSCRT(a)   ';
```

Produce the first star chart. DISCRETE must be specified because the numeric chart variable, DATE is assigned the WORDDATE3. Using FILL=S fills all the slices with solid patterns.

```
proc gchart data=rejects;
   format date worddate3.;
   star date / discrete
               sumvar=badparts
               noheading
               fill=s;
run;
```

Define footnote for the second chart.

```
footnote j=r 'GCHDSCRT(b) ';
```

Produce the second star chart with slices and a solid fill. NOHEADING suppresses the default heading for the star chart. NOCONNECT suppresses the lines that by default join the ends of the spines. COUTLINE= colors the spines and the circle.

```
   star date / discrete
               sumvar=badparts
               noheading
               noconnect
```

```
                          coutline=red;
run;
quit;
```

Example 15: Creating a Detail Pie Chart

Procedure Features:

PIE statement options:

- DETAIL=
- DETAIL_PERCENT=
- DETAIL_SLICE=
- DETAIL_VALUE=
- LEGEND
- SUMVAR=

Sample library member: GCHDTPIE

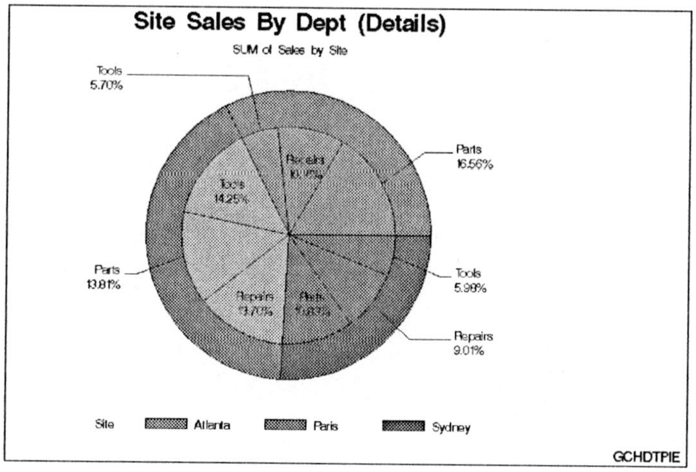

This example produces a normal pie chart with a detail pie overlay. The pie chart shows percentages of sales for three sites by charting the values of the character variable SITE and calculating the percentage of the variable SALES for each site. The detail pie overlay shows the percentages of sales for each DEPT at each SITE. The pie slices use the colors in the default color list and the default fill, which is solid.

Set the graphics environment. The CBACK= option sets the background color. The FTITLE= and HTITLE= options set the font and size of the title text. The FTEXT and HTEXT= options set the font and size of other text, such as slice labels.

```
goptions reset=all gunit=pct border cback=white
         ftitle=swissb ftext=swiss htitle=5
         htext=2.5;
```

Create the data set TOTALS. TOTALS contains quarterly sales data for three manufacturing sites for one year. Sales figures are broken down by department.

```
data totals;
   length Dept $ 7 Site $ 8;
   input Dept Site Quarter Sales;
   datalines;
Parts   Sydney  1 4043.97
Parts   Atlanta 1 6225.26
Parts   Paris   1 3543.97
...more data lines
Tools   Sydney  4 3817.36
Tools   Atlanta 4 4354.18
Tools   Paris   4 6511.70
;
```

Define the title and footnote.

```
title1 'Site Sales By Dept (Details)';
footnote1 h=3 j=r 'GCHDTPIE ';
```

Produce the detail pie chart. SUMVAR= calculates the sum of SALES for each value of the chart variable SITE. DETAIL= produces a inner pie overlay showing the percentage that each DEPT contributes toward each site's sales. DETAIL_PERCENT= and DETAIL_SLICE= control the positioning of the detail slice labels. DETAIL_VALUE= turns off the display of the sales values for each detail slice.

```
proc gchart data=totals;
   pie site / sumvar=sales
              detail=dept
              detail_percent=best
              detail_value=none
              detail_slice=best
              legend;
run;
quit;
```

References

Nelder, J. A. (1976), "A Simple Algorithm for Scaling Graphs," *Applied Statistics, Volume 25, Number 1,* London: The Royal Statistical Society.

Terrell, G. R. and Scott, D. W. (1985), "Oversmoothed Nonparametric Density Estimates," *Journal of the American Statistical Association*, 80.

CHAPTER

30

The GCONTOUR Procedure

Overview

The GCONTOUR procedure produces plots that represent three-dimensional relationships. The colors, contours, or surface areas of a contour plot represent the values of a contour variable at each point in a plane that is formed by a dependent and an independent variable. The contour variable is applied to the Z axis of the plot, the dependent variable is applied to the X axis of the plot, and the independent variable is applied to the Y axis of the plot.

Concepts

About Contour Plots

Contour plots represent the levels of magnitude of a variable z, called the *contour variable*, for a position on a plane given by the values of two variables x and y. Contour lines of different colors and line types show different levels of magnitude of z for locations of x and y.

Display 30.1 on page 886 shows a simple contour plot that illustrates the percentage of clay found in soil samples at various locations of a testing site. The x and y axes on the plot represent a graph of surface height at various x-y locations. The contour lines within the plot represent the locations on the plane that have the clay percentages specified in the legend. The program for this plot is in Example 1 on page 904.

By default, the GCONTOUR procedure automatically scales the axes to include the maximum and minimum data values, labels each axis with the name of its variable or an associated label, and draws a frame around the plot. In addition, it plots values using seven contour levels of the contour variable, representing those levels with default colors and line types. Finally, it generates a legend that is labeled with the contour variable's name.

Display 30.1 Sample Contour Plot

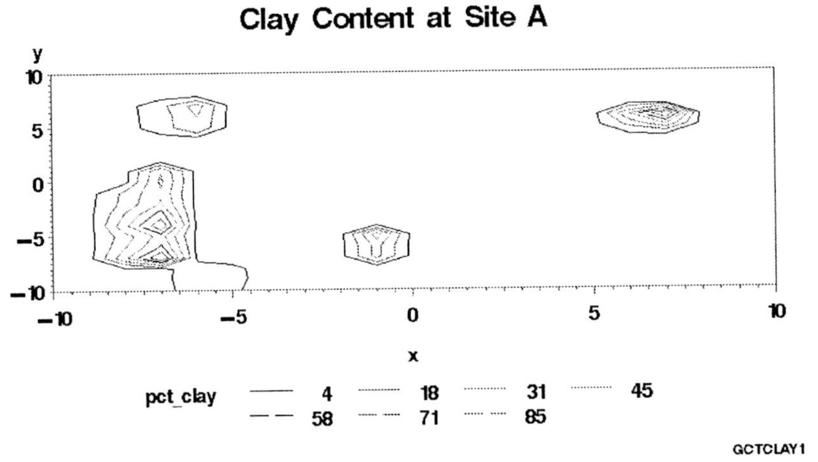

Parts of a Contour Plot

Some of the terms used in the discussion of the GCONTOUR procedure are illustrated in Figure 30.1 on page 887.

Figure 30.1 GCONTOUR Procedure Terms

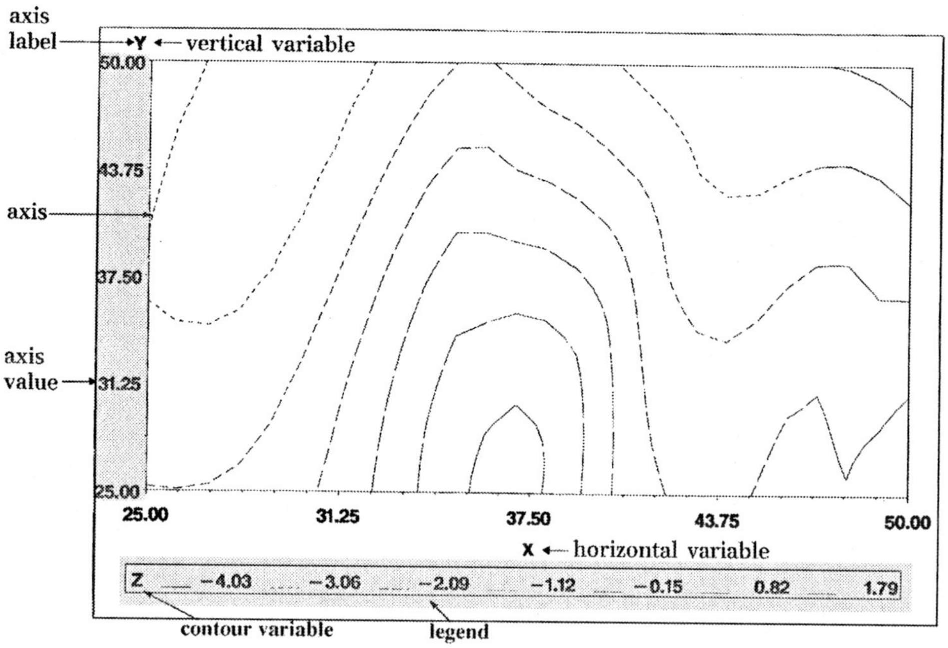

About the Input Data Set

The GCONTOUR procedure requires data sets that include three numeric variables: *x*, *y*, and *z*. The observations in the input data set should form a rectangular grid of *x* and *y* values and exactly one *z* value for each (*x*, *y*) combination. For example, data that contain 5 distinct values of *x* and 10 distinct values for *y* should be part of a data set that contains 50 observations with values for *x*, *y*, and *z*. If a single (*x*, *y*) grid location has more than one associated *z* value, only the last such observation appears in the plot.

Interpolating Additional Values

By default, the data set must contain values for the *z* variable for at least 50 percent of the grid in order for the GCONTOUR procedure to produce a satisfactory plot. If your data are clustered in relatively small patches over a larger study area, you can use the PROC GCONTOUR statement's INCOMPLETE option, which allows plotting of data when you have values for the *z* variable for less than 50 percent of the plot grid.

When the GCONTOUR procedure cannot produce a satisfactory contour plot because of missing values, the SAS/GRAPH software issues an error message, and no graph is produced. To correct this problem, you can use the G3GRID procedure to process data sets to be used by the GCONTOUR procedure. The G3GRID procedure interpolates the necessary values to produce a data set with nonmissing values of the *z* variable values for every combination of the *x* and *y* variables. The G3GRID procedure can also smooth data for use with the GCONTOUR procedure. For details, see Chapter 47, "The G3GRID Procedure," on page 1327.

You can use the output data set from the G3GRID procedure as the input data set for the GCONTOUR procedure. For an example of using PROC G3GRID to interpolate values, see Example 1 on page 904.

Procedure Syntax

Requirements: At least one PLOT statement is required.

Global statements: AXIS, FOOTNOTE, GOPTIONS, LEGEND, PATTERN, SYMBOL, TITLE

Reminder: The procedure can include the BY, FORMAT, LABEL, NOTE, and WHERE statements.

Supports: Output Delivery System (ODS)

PROC GCONTOUR <DATA=*input-data-set*>
<ANNOTATE=*Annotate-data-set*>
<GOUT=<*libref.*>*output-catalog*>
<INCOMPLETE>;

PLOT *plot-request* </*option(s)*>;

PROC GCONTOUR Statement

Identifies the data set that contains the plot variables. Optionally specifies annotation and an output catalog.

Requirements: An input data set is required.

PROC GCONTOUR <DATA=*input-data-set*>
<ANNOTATE=*Annotate-data-set*>
<GOUT=<*libref.*>*output-catalog*>
<INCOMPLETE>;

ANNOTATE=*Annotate-data-set*
ANNO=*Annotate-data-set*
specifies a data set to annotate all graphs produced by the GCONTOUR procedure. To annotate individual graphs, use ANNOTATE= in the action statement.

See also: Chapter 24, "Using Annotate Data Sets," on page 587

DATA=*input-data-set*
identifies the SAS data set that contains the variables to plot. By default, the procedure uses the most recently created SAS data set.

See also: "SAS Data Sets" on page 29 and "About the Input Data Set" on page 887.

GOUT=< *libref.* >*output-catalog*
specifies the SAS catalog in which to save the graphics output produced by the GCONTOUR procedure. If you omit the libref, the SAS/GRAPH software looks for the catalog in the temporary library called WORK and creates the WORK catalog if it does not exist.

See also: "Creating and Specifying Catalogs" on page 54

Not supported by: Java, ActiveX

INCOMPLETE
allows plotting of data when values are missing for more than half of the variables in the data set.

Not supported by: Java, ActiveX

PLOT Statement

Creates contour plots using values of three numeric variables from the input data set as the source of the contour coordinates.

Requirements: A plot request is required.

Global statements: AXIS, FOOTNOTE, LEGEND, PATTERN, SYMBOL, TITLE

Description

The PLOT statement specifies the three variables to plot. Optionally, it controls the contour levels, labels the plot lines, and modifies axes as well as the general appearance of the graph. Only one plot request can be specified in a PLOT statement. To specify multiple plots for a single PROC GCONTOUR statement, use multiple PLOT statements.

The PLOT statement automatically

- plots the values using seven contour levels of the *z* variable
- scales the axes to include the maximum and minimum data values
- labels the *x* and *y* axes and displays the contour levels in the plot's legend
- draws a frame around the plot.

You can use global statements to modify the axes, the legend, the contour lines and contour line labels, and the fill patterns and pattern colors for contour areas. You can also add titles, footnotes, and notes to the chart, and you can use an Annotate data set to enhance the appearance of the chart.

PLOT *plot-request </option(s)>*;

Required Arguments

y*x=z
specifies three numeric variables from the input data set:

y	is the variable that is plotted on the vertical axis.
x	is the variable that is plotted on the horizontal axis.
z	is the variable that is plotted as contour lines, on the Z axis, which is perpendicular to the plane formed by the X and Y axes.

Options by Category

option(s) can be one or more options in the following categories:

- appearance options:
  - ANNOTATE=*Annotate-data-set*
  - CAXIS=*axis-color*
  - CFRAME=*background-color*
  - COUTLINE=*outline-color*
  - CTEXT=*text-color*
  - GRID
  - NOAXIS | NOAXES
  - NOFRAME
- horizontal axis options:
  - AUTOHREF
  - CAUTOHREF=*reference-line-color*
  - LAUTOHREF=*reference-line-type*
  - CHREF=*reference-line-color* | (*reference-line-color*) | *reference-line-color-list*
  - HAXIS=AXIS<1...99>
  - HMINOR=*number-of-minor-ticks*
  - HREF=*value-list*
  - HREVERSE
  - LHREF=*reference-line-type* | (*reference-line-type*) | *reference-line-type-list*
  - XTICKNUM=*number-of-ticks*
- vertical axis options:
  - AUTOVREF
  - CAUTOVREF=*reference-line-color*
  - CVREF=*reference-line-color* | (*reference-line-color*) | *reference-line-color-list*
  - LAUTOVREF=*reference-line-type*
  - LVREF=*reference-line-type* | (*reference-line-type*) | *reference-line-type-list*
  - VAXIS=AXIS<1...99>
  - VMINOR=*number-of-minor-ticks*
  - VREF=*value-list*
  - VREVERSE
  - YTICKNUM=*number-of-ticks*
- contour options:
  - CLEVELS=*color(s)*
  - JOIN
  - LEGEND=LEGEND<1...99>
  - LEVELS=*value-list*
  - LLEVELS=*line-type-list*
  - NLEVELS=*number-of-levels*
  - NOLEGEND
  - PATTERN
- labeling options:
  - AUTOLABEL | AUTOLABEL=(*autolabel-suboptions*)

where *autolabel-suboptions* can be one or more of these:

CHECK=*checking-factor* | NONE

MAXHIDE=*amount<units>*

REVEAL

TOLANGLE=*angle*

- ☐ catalog entry description options:

  DESCRIPTION=*'entry-description'*

  NAME=*'entry-name'*

Options

You can specify any of the following options in your PLOT statement, in any order. If you use a BY statement on the procedure, the options in each PLOT statement affect all graphs produced by that BY statement.

ANNOTATE=*Annotate-data-set*
ANNO=*Annotate-data-set*

specifies an Annotate data set to enhance the charts produced by the PLOT statement.

See also: Chapter 26, "The GANNO Procedure," on page 707 and Chapter 25, "Annotate Dictionary," on page 613.

AUTOHREF

displays reference lines at major tick marks on the horizontal axis. The positions of the major tick marks are determined by the HAXIS= or XTICKNUM= option. To specify colors and line types for these reference lines, use the CAUTOHREF= and LAUTOHREF= options. To specify labels for these reference lines, use the HAXIS= option.

Not supported by: Java

AUTOLABEL | AUTOLABEL=(*autolabel_suboptions*)

automatically labels the contour lines. Autolabel-suboptions"Autolabel Suboptions" on page 898 allow you to control the appearance of these labels.

The label for each contour line is the value of the *z* variable for that contour level. By default, labels are displayed in BEST format. To change the format, use a FORMAT statement.

When AUTOLABEL is used, the LLEVELS= and CLEVELS= options are ignored and the SYMBOL"SYMBOL Statement" on page 183 statement controls label text and contour-line attributes.

Even though AUTOLABEL labels the contour lines, a default legend is still generated. To suppress the legend, use the NOLEGEND option.

Featured in: Example 2 on page 906

Not supported by: Java, ActiveX

AUTOVREF

displays reference lines at major tick marks on the vertical axis. The number of major tick marks is determined by the VAXIS= or YTICKNUM= option. To specify colors and line types for these reference lines, use the CAUTOVREF= and LAUTOVREF= options. To specify labels for these reference lines, use the VAXIS= option.

Not supported by: Java.

CAUTOHREF=*reference-line-color*

specifies a color for reference lines drawn at major tick marks on the horizontal axis, as specified by the AUTOHREF option. The default color for reference lines is determined by the CAXIS= option or by the first color in the color list. To specify line types for these reference lines, use the LAUTOHREF= option. To specify labels for these reference lines, use the HAXIS= option.

CAUTOVREF=*reference-line-color*
specifies a color for reference lines drawn at major tick marks on the vertical axis, as specified by the AUTOVREF option. The default color for reference lines is determined by the CAXIS= option or by the first color in the color list. To specify line types for these reference lines, use the LAUTOVREF= option. To specify labels for these reference lines, use the VAXIS= option.

Not supported by: Java

CAXIS=*axis-color*
specifies a color for axis lines, tick marks, and reference lines. By default, axes are displayed in the second color in the colors list.

If you use the CAXIS= option, it may be overridden by the COLOR= suboption of the MAJOR= or MINOR= option in an AXIS definition.

CFRAME=*background-color*
CFR=*background-color*
fills the axis area with the specified color and draws a frame around the axis area.

CHREF=*reference-line-color* | (*reference-line-color*) | *reference-line-color-list*
CH=*reference-line-color* | (*reference-line-color*) | *reference-line-color-list*
specifies the color of reference lines drawn perpendicular to the horizontal axis. Specifying a single color without parentheses applies that color to all reference lines drawn with the AUTOHREF and HREF= options. Note that the CAUTOHREF= option overrides the CHREF= option for lines drawn with the AUTOHREF option. Specifying a single color in parentheses applies that color only to the first reference line drawn with the HREF= option. Specifying a color list applies colors sequentially to successive reference lines drawn with the HREF= option. The syntax of the color list is of the form (*color1 color2... colorN*) or (*color1, color2..., colorN*). Default colors for reference lines are determined by the CAXIS= option or by the first color in the color list. To specify line types for these reference lines, use the LHREF= option. To specify labels for these reference lines, use the HAXIS= option.

Not supported by: Java

CLEVELS=*color(s)*
specifies a list of colors for plot contour levels. The number of specified colors should correspond to the number of contour levels since one color represents each level of contour. If fewer colors are specified than the number of levels in the plot, the procedure provides default colors from the current colors list. The procedure default is to rotate through the current colors list for each line type.

This option is ignored if AUTOLABEL is used.

COUTLINE=*outline-color*
specifies a color for outlining filled areas. This option is ignored unless the PATTERN option is also used. By default, the outline color is the same as the color of the filled area.

The default outline color depends on the PATTERN statement. If you do not specify a PATTERN statement, the default outline color is black for the Java or ActiveX devices. Otherwise, the default outline color is the foreground color (the first color in the colors list). If you specify the PATTERN statement or the V6COMP graphics option, the default is COUTLINE=SAME.

Note: The outline color is the only distinction between empty patterns. Use of this option makes the patterns look the same when VALUE=EMPTY in PATTERN definitions. △

Featured in: Example 4 on page 910

Not supported by: ActiveX (partial)

CTEXT=*text-color*

specifies a color for all text on the axes and legend, including axis labels, tick mark values, legend labels, and legend value descriptions.

For the Java and ActiveX device drivers, the default text color is black. Otherwise, the default text color is determined in the following order:

1 specified colors on assigned AXIS and LEGEND statements

2 the CTEXT= option in a GOPTIONS statement

3 the first color in the colors list.

For legend text, colors that you specify on an assigned LEGEND statement override CTEXT=. Thus, a LEGEND statement's VALUE= color is used for legend values, and its LABEL= color is used for legend labels.

For axes text, colors that you explicitly specify for values and labels on an assigned AXIS statement override CTEXT=. Thus, an AXIS statement's VALUE= color is used for axis values, and its LABEL= color is used for axis labels. However, if the AXIS statement specifies only general axis colors with its COLOR= option, the CTEXT= color overrides that general specification and is used for axis labels and values; the COLOR= color is still used for all other axis colors, such as tick marks.

If you use a BY statement in the procedure, the color of the BY variable labels is controlled by the CBY= option in the GOPTIONS statement.

Featured in: Example 4 on page 910

CVREF=*reference-line-color* | (*reference-line-color*) | *reference-line-color-list*
CV=*reference-line-color* | (*reference-line-color*) | *reference-line-color-list*

specifies the color of reference lines drawn perpendicular to the vertical axis. Specifying a single color without parentheses applies that color to all reference lines drawn with the AUTOVREF and VREF= options. Note that the CAUTOVREF= option overrides CVREF= option for lines drawn with the AUTOVREF option. Specifying a single color in parentheses applies that color only to the first reference line. Specifying a color list applies colors sequentially to successive reference lines. The syntax of the color list is of the form (*color1 color2... colorN*) or (*color1, color2..., colorN*). Default colors for reference lines are determined by the CAXIS= option or by the first color in the color list. To specify line types for these reference lines, use the LVREF= option. To specify labels for these reference lines, use the VAXIS= option.

Not supported by: Java

DESCRIPTION='*entry-description*'
DES='*entry-description*'

specifies the description of the catalog entry for the chart. The maximum length for *entry-description* is 256 characters. The description does not appear on the chart. By default, the GCONTOUR procedure assigns a description of the form PLOT OF *y*x=z*, where *y*x=z* is the request specified in the PLOT statement.

GRID

draws reference lines at all major tick marks on both axes and outlines the axis area. This is the same as specifying both AUTOHREF and AUTOVREF.

Not supported by: ActiveX

HAXIS=AXIS<1...99>

assigns axis characteristics from the corresponding axis definition to the horizontal (X) axis. If the AXIS statement specifies the REFLABEL= option, labels will be applied in sequence to all reference lines generated with the AUTOHREF and HREF= options.

For Web output that is generated with a Java or ActiveX device driver, certain options of the AXIS statement are not supported. For details, see “AXIS Statement” on page 124.

See also: “AXIS Statement” on page 124

Featured in: Example 2 on page 906

Not supported by: Java (partial), ActiveX (partial)

HMINOR=*number-of-minor-ticks*
HM=*number-of-minor-ticks*
specifies the number of minor tick marks to draw between each major tick mark on the horizontal (X) axis. The HMINOR= option overrides the MINOR= option in an AXIS definition assigned to the horizontal axis.

HREF=*value-list*
draws one or more reference lines perpendicular to the horizontal axis at points specified by *value-list*. See the LEVELS= option for a description of *value-list*. To specify colors for these reference lines, use the CHREF= option. To specify line types for these reference lines, use the LHREF= option. To specify labels for these reference lines, use the HAXIS= option.

Not supported by: Java

HREVERSE
specifies that the order of the values on the horizontal (X) axis be reversed.

Not supported by: Java

JOIN
combines adjacent grid cells with the same pattern to form a single pattern area. This option is ignored unless the PATTERN option is also used.

Featured in: Example 4 on page 910

LAUTOHREF=*reference-line-type*
specifies a line type for reference lines drawn at major tick marks on the horizontal axis, as specified by the AUTOHREF option. The *reference-line-type* value can be a whole number from 1 to 46. A value of 1 specifies a solid line; values 2 through 46 specify dashed lines. The default value 1 draws a solid line. To specify colors for these reference lines, use the CAUTOHREF= option. To specify labels for these reference lines, use the HAXIS= option.

Not supported by: Java

LAUTOVREF=*reference-line-type*
specifies a line type for reference lines drawn at major tick marks on the vertical axis, as specified by the AUTOVREF option. The *reference-line-type* value can be a whole number in the range of 1 to 46. A value of 1 specifies a solid line; values 2 through 46 specify dashed lines. The default value 1 draws a solid line. To specify colors for these reference lines, use the CAUTOVREF= option. To specify labels for these reference lines, use the VAXIS= option.

Not supported by: Java

LEGEND=LEGEND<1...99>
assigns a legend definition that specifies the location, text, and appearance of axes on the plots. To suppress the legend, use the NOLEGEND option. The LEGEND= option is ignored if the specified LEGEND definition is not currently in effect.

If you use the SHAPE= option in a LEGEND statement, the value LINE is valid. If you use the PATTERN option, SHAPE=BAR is also valid.

In Web output that uses a Java or ActiveX device driver, the legend will always appear on the right side of the plot.

See also: "LEGEND Statement" on page 151

Featured in: Example 2 on page 906

Not supported by: Java (partial), ActiveX (partial)

LEVELS=*value-list*

specifies values for the *z* variable for plot contour levels and therefore changes the number of contour levels. You can specify up to 100 values. This option is ignored if you use the AUTOLABEL option.

By default, the GCONTOUR procedure plots seven contour levels for the *z* variable. These levels occur at every 15th percent of the range between the 5th and 95th percentiles.

For numeric variables, *value-list* can be an explicit list of values, a starting and an ending value with an interval increment, or a combination of both forms:

- *n* <...*n*>
- *n* TO *n* <BY *increment*>
- *n* <...*n*> TO *n* <BY *increment*> *n* <...*n*>

If a numeric variable has an associated format, the specified values must be the *unformatted* values.

By default, the GCONTOUR procedure selects colors and line types for the contour levels by rotating through the colors list for each line type (1 through 46) until all the levels have been represented. The level lines on the plot represent the intersection of a plane, parallel to the X/Y plane, and the surface that is formed by the values of the *z* variable. See "Selecting Contour Levels" on page 899 for more information.

You can specify the colors and line types for contour levels. The way to do this depends on whether AUTOLABEL is used:

- If AUTOLABEL is used, the "SYMBOL Statement" on page 183 controls colors and line types for contour levels.
- If AUTOLABEL is not used, the CLEVELS= and LLEVELS= options control colors and line types for contour levels.

As an alternative to representing contour levels with contour lines, you can use the PATTERN option to fill each level with a solid pattern or with the colors and patterns specified in PATTERN statements.

Featured in: Example 2 on page 906 and Example 3 on page 908

LHREF=*reference-line-type* | *(reference-line-type)* | *reference-line-type-list*
LH=*reference-line-type* | *(reference-line-type)* | *reference-line-type-list*

specifies line types for reference lines drawn perpendicular to the horizontal axis. The *reference-line-type* value can be a whole number from 1 to 46. A value of 1 specifies a solid line; values 2 through 46 specify dashed lines. Specifiying a single line type without parentheses applies that line type to all reference lines drawn with the AUTOHREF and HREF= options. Note that the CAUTOHREF= option overrides LHREF=*reference-line-type* for lines drawn with the AUTOHREF option. Specifying a single line type in parentheses applies that line type only to the first reference line drawn by the HREF= option. Specifying a line-type list applies line types in sequence to successive reference lines drawn with the HREF= option. The syntax of the line type list is of the form (*type1 type2... type3*). The default value of 1 draws a solid line. To specify colors for these references lines, use the CHREF= option. To specify labels for these reference lines, use the HAXIS= option.

Not supported by: Java (partial), ActiveX (partial)

LLEVELS=*line-type-list*

lists line type numbers for plot contour lines. Each line type represents one contour level, so the number of line types listed should correspond to the number of contour levels. Thus, for a contour plot that uses the default seven levels, specify seven line types.

If fewer line types are specified than the number of levels in the plot, the procedure provides default line types. With the default, contour levels rotate through line types 1 through 46, displaying each line type in all of the colors in the colors list before moving to the next line type. Line type 1 is a solid line and the others are dashed line. See "Specifying Line Types" on page 207 for available line types.

For colors and lines specified with both the CLEVELS= and LLEVELS= options, the first contour level is displayed in the first color in the CLEVELS= color list and in the first line type specified with the LLEVELS= option. The second level is displayed in the second color and the second line type, and so on.

This option is ignored if AUTOLABEL is used.

Featured in: Example 3 on page 908

Not supported by: Java

LVREF=*reference-line-type* | (*reference-line-type*) | *reference-line-type-list*
LV=*reference-line-type* | (*reference-line-type*) | *reference-line-type-list*

specifies line types for reference lines drawn perpendicular to the vertical axis. The *reference-line-type* value can be a whole number from 1 to 46. A value of 1 specifies a solid line; values 2 through 46 specify dashed lines. Specifying a single line type without parentheses applies that line type to all reference lines drawn with the AUTOVREF and VREF= options. Note that the CAUTOVREF= option overrides LVREF=*reference-line-type* for lines drawn with the AUTOVREF option. Specifying a single line type in parentheses applies that line type only to the first reference line drawn by the VREF= option. Specifying a line-type list applies line types in sequence to successive reference lines drawn with the VREF= option. The syntax of the line type list is of the form (*type1 type2... type3*). The default value 1 draws a solid line. To specify colors for these references lines, use the CVREF= option. To specify labels for these reference lines, use the VAXIS= option.

Not supported by: Java (partial), ActiveX (partial)

NAME='*entry-name*'

specifies the name of the catalog entry for the graph. The maximum length for *entry-name* is 8 characters. The default name is GCONTOUR. If you specify DEVICE=ACTIXIMG or DEVICE=JAVAIMG, then the name that you specify will be used for the client image output even in the file exists. For all other devices, if the name duplicates an existing entry name, SAS/GRAPH adds a number to the duplicate name to create a unique entry, for example, GCONTOU1.

NLEVELS=*number-of-levels*

specifies the number of contour levels to plot. Values can be integers from 1 to 100. The default is NLEVELS=7. The contour levels are computed as follows, where `L` represents an array of levels:

- If the value of NLEVELS= is less than 7, then

```
D = (Zmax - Zmin) / NLEVELS
d = 0.5 * D
L[0] = Zmin + d, L[i] = L[i-1] + D
```

  In this case, each level is the midpoint of a number of ranges equal to the value of the NLEVELS= option. These ranges exactly cover the range of the *z* variable.

- If the value of NLEVELS= is greater than or equal to 7, then

```
e = 0.05 * (100 - NLEVELS) / 93
d = (Zmax - Zmin) * e
D = ((Zmax - Zmin - 2*d) / (NLEVELS - 1)
```

```
L[0]  = Zmin + d, L[i]  = L[i-1]  + D
```

In this case, the first and last midpoints are set closer to the minimum and maximum values of the *z* variable as the values of NLEVELS= gets closer to 100, and the remaining midpoints are equally spaced between them.

NOAXIS
NOAXES
specifies that a plot have no axes, axis values, or axis labels. The frame is displayed around the plot unless you use the NOFRAME option.

NOFRAME
suppresses the frame that is drawn by default around the plot area.

NOLEGEND
suppresses the plot legend that describes contour levels and their line types or fill patterns and colors.

PATTERN
specifies the fill pattern and pattern colors for contour areas. The plot contour levels are represented by rectangles filled with patterns. The pattern for each rectangle is determined by calculating the mean of the values of the *z* variable for the four corners of the rectangle and assigning the pattern for the level closest to the mean.

By default, the procedure uses a solid pattern for the levels and rotates the pattern through the colors list. If the V6COMP option is in effect for the GOPTIONS statement, cross-hatch patterns are used instead of solid patterns. To explicitly define patterns, use PATTERN definitions for map/plot patterns.

For information on PATTERN statement that are enabled for Web output, see "PATTERN Statement" on page 169.

See also: "Selecting Contour Levels" on page 899

Featured in: Example 4 on page 910

Featured in: Example 3 on page 908

Not supported by: Java (partial), ActiveX (partial)

VAXIS=AXIS<1...99>
assigns axis characteristics from the corresponding axis definition to the vertical (Y) axis. If the AXIS statement specifies the REFLABEL= option, labels will be applied in sequence to all reference lines generated with the AUTOVREF and VREF= options.

For Web output that is generated with a Java or ActiveX device driver, certain options of the AXIS statement are not supported. For details, see "AXIS Statement" on page 124.

See also: "AXIS Statement" on page 124

Featured in: Example 2 on page 906

Not supported by: Java (partial), ActiveX (partial)

VMINOR=*number-of-minor-ticks*
VM=*number-of-minor-ticks*
specifies the number of minor tick marks located between each major tick mark on the vertical (Y) axis. No values are displayed for minor tick marks. The VMINOR= option overrides the MINOR= option in an AXIS definition that is assigned to the vertical axis.

VREF=*value-list*
draws one or more reference lines perpendicular to the vertical axis at points specified by *value-list*. See the LEVELS= option for a description of *value-list*. To specify colors for these reference lines, use the CVREF= option. To specify line types for these reference lines, use the LVREF= option. To specify labels for these reference lines, use the VAXIS= option.

Not supported by: Java

VREVERSE
specifies that the order of the values on the vertical axis be reversed.

Not supported by: Java

XTICKNUM=*number-of-ticks*
YTICKNUM=*number-of-ticks*
specify the number of major tick marks located on a plot's X or Y axis, respectively. The value of *number-of-ticks* must be 2 or greater. The defaults are XTICKNUM=5 and YTICKNUM=5.

The MAJOR= or ORDER= option in an AXIS definition that is assigned to the X axis overrides the XTICKNUM= option. The MAJOR= or ORDER= option in an AXIS definition that is assigned to the Y axis overrides the YTICKNUM= option.

Autolabel Suboptions

The AUTOLABEL= option accepts the following autolabel suboptions.

CHECK=*checking-factor* | NONE
specifies a collision checking factor that controls collisions between contour label text and other contour lines or other labels. Values can be integers from 0 to 100, inclusive, where 0 provides minimal collision checking and 100 provides maximal collision checking. Fractional values are permitted. The default is CHECK=75.

CHECK=NONE suppresses contour label collision checking and may lessen the time needed to compute the contour graph.

MAXHIDE=*amount* <*units*>
specifies the maximum amount of contour line that can be hidden by contour labels. The value of *amount* must be greater than zero.

Valid *units* are CELLS (horizontal character cell positions), CM (centimeters), IN (inches), or PCT (percentage of the width of the graphics output area). The default is MAXHIDE=100PCT. If you omit *units*, a unit specification is searched for in this order:

1 the GUNIT= option in a GOPTIONS statement

2 the default unit, CELLS.

If you specify units of PCT or CELLS, the MAXHIDE= suboption calculates the amount of contour line that can be hidden based on the width of the graphics output area. For example, if you specify MAXHIDE=50PCT and if the graphics output area is 9 inches wide, the maximum amount of the contour line that can be hidden by labels is 4.5 inches.

This option maintains data integrity. It provides a check for overly small increments in the STEP= option in the SYMBOL statement. Additionally, it can prevent small contours from being significantly hidden even when the value of STEP= is sufficiently large.

REVEAL
specifies that the contour lines are visible through the label text as dashed lines. Line style 33 is used. This option provides a simple way to see all portions of labeled contours and can be used to inspect the label positions with respect to the contour lines. It is primarily used for debugging. Occasionally, single-character contour labels can be placed off center from the clipped portion of the contour line when the contour line is irregular or jagged.

TOLANGLE=*angle*

specifies the maximum angle (the tolerance angle) between any two adjacent characters of a contour label. The value of *angle* must be between 1 and 85 degrees. The default is TOLANGLE=30. To force contour labels to fall on very smooth sections, specify a small tolerance angle.

Selecting Contour Levels

You can use the LEVELS= option to select the contour levels for your plot. You use LEVELS= values differently, depending on whether you specify the PATTERN option in the PLOT statement.

When you do not use the PATTERN option, the levels represent the intersection of a plane (parallel to the X/Yplane at the value of the *z* variable) and the surface formed by the data. That is, if you use the data to create a surface plot with the G3D procedure, the contour lines in a GCONTOUR procedure plot represent the intersection of the plane and the surface.

For example, suppose that you use the G3D procedure, and your data produces a surface plot like the one shown in Figure 30.2 on page 899. The same data used with the following PLOT statement in the GCONTOUR procedure produces a similar contour plot:

```
plot y*x=z / levels=-7.5 to 7.5 by 2.5;
```

The contour lines in Figure 30.3 on page 900 represent the intersection of the surface in Figure 30.2 on page 899 with planes parallel to the plane formed by the variables *x* and *y* and located at *z* values of –7.5, –5.0, –2.5, and so on.

Figure 30.2 Surface Plot

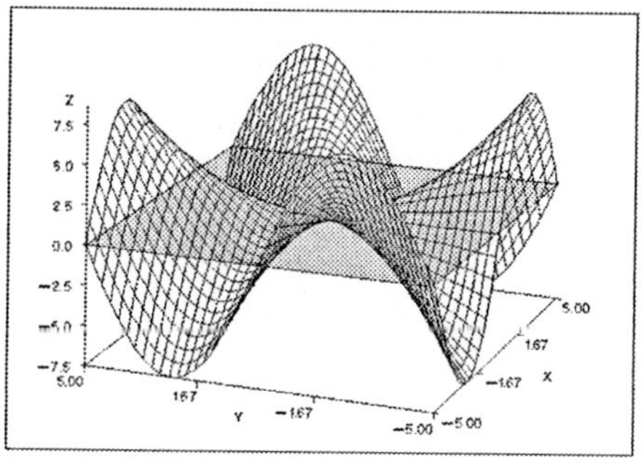

Figure 30.3 Line Contour Levels

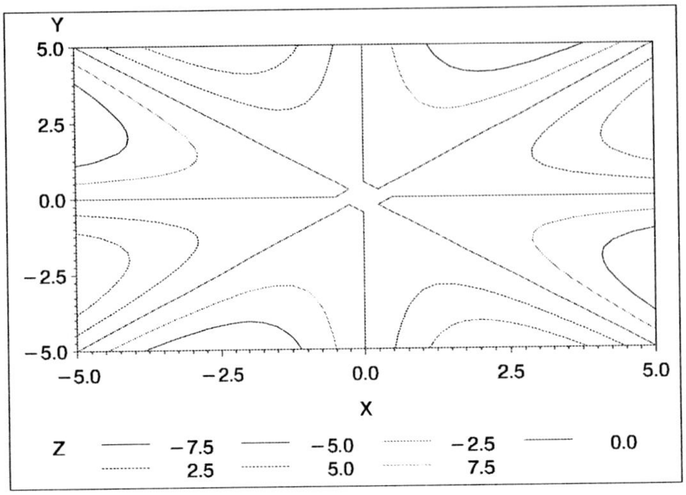

When you use the PATTERN option, contour levels are represented by rectangles filled with patterns. The rectangles are formed by points in the *x-y* grid. The contour pattern of a rectangle, or grid cell, is determined by the mean or average value of the *z* variable for the four corners of the rectangle. The grid cell is assigned the pattern for the level closest to the calculated mean. For example, if you have specified contour levels of 0, 5, and 10, and the plot contains a grid cell with a mean of 100, it is assigned the pattern for the nearest level: 10. A grid cell with a mean of 7.6 will also be assigned the pattern for the 10 level.

Figure 30.4 on page 900 shows a contour plot with the PATTERN option that uses the same data and contour levels as Figure 30.3 on page 900. The pattern for the rectangle is assigned depending on the mean of the grid values at the four corners. As a result, two contour plots using the same contour levels can present your data differently if one plot uses a pattern and the other does not. The contour pattern boundaries do not correspond to the contour lines shown in Figure 30.3 on page 900.

Figure 30.4 Pattern Contour Levels

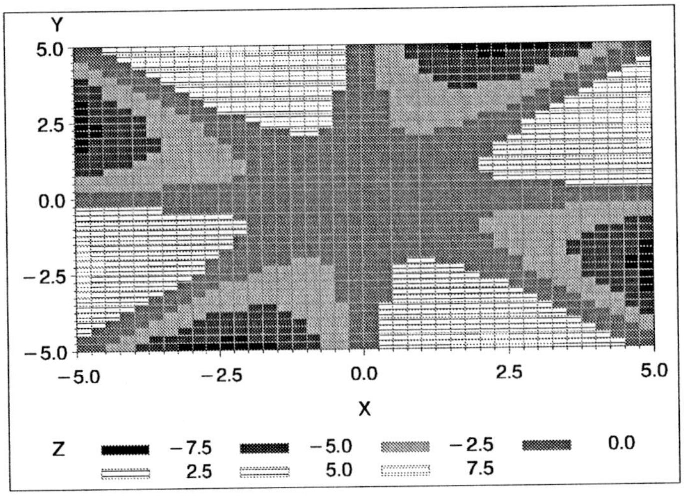

Specifying Axis Order

You can use AXIS statements to modify the text and appearance of plot axes, and then you can assign the axes to the contour plot with the PLOT statement's HAXIS= and VAXIS= options. If the AXIS statement uses an ORDER= option, there are special considerations for using that AXIS definition with the GCONTOUR procedure.

A list of variable values that are specified with the AXIS statement's ORDER= option must contain numbers listed in ascending or descending order; these numbers are treated as a continuous data range for an axis. Thus, for a contour line or pattern to span the entire specified range, it is not necessary for the maximum and minimum values of the list to match exactly with the maximum and minimum data values of the corresponding x or y variable. For example, suppose that you assign this AXIS definition to the horizontal (x) axis:

```
axis1 order=-2.5 to 2.5 by .5
```

Suppose also that the horizontal axis variable has these values: –5, –4, –3, –2, –1, 0, 1, 2, 3, 4, 5. Depending on the data, contours could extend through the full range of the ORDER= list rather than from –2 to 2, which are the actual values of the variable assigned to the horizontal (x) axis. In this case, values are interpolated for the x variable at any point where the y variable intersects the minimum axis value (–2.5) or the maximum axis value (2.5). Data values that are outside of the axis range (in this case, –5, –4, –3, 3, 4, and 5) are clipped from the plot.

When ORDER= lists cause data clipping, internal plotting grids are modified according to these rules:

- If an ORDER= list causes data clipping on a single axis, linear interpolation generates the z values of the starting and/or ending column of the plotting grid. For example, in the previous example, the value of z is interpolated for –2.5 and 2.5 on the horizontal (x) axis.
- If ORDER= lists cause data clipping on both axes, the response variable values of the new corners are derived by fitting the new x, y location on a plane formed by three of the original four points of the corresponding grid square.

In addition, if you assign the following AXIS definition to a plot of the same data, the contour levels on the plot will not extend beyond the range of the data:

```
axis1 order=-10 to 10 by 1;
```

To see the effects of the ORDER= option:

- Figure 30.5 on page 902 shows the effects when the range of ORDER= values matches the range of values for the variables assigned to the horizontal (x) and vertical (y) axes.
- Figure 30.6 on page 902 shows the effects when the range of ORDER= values is smaller than the range of data values.
- Figure 30.7 on page 903 shows the effects when the range of ORDER= values is larger than the range of data values.

Figure 30.5 AXIS Statement's ORDER= Option, where Option Values Match Variable Values

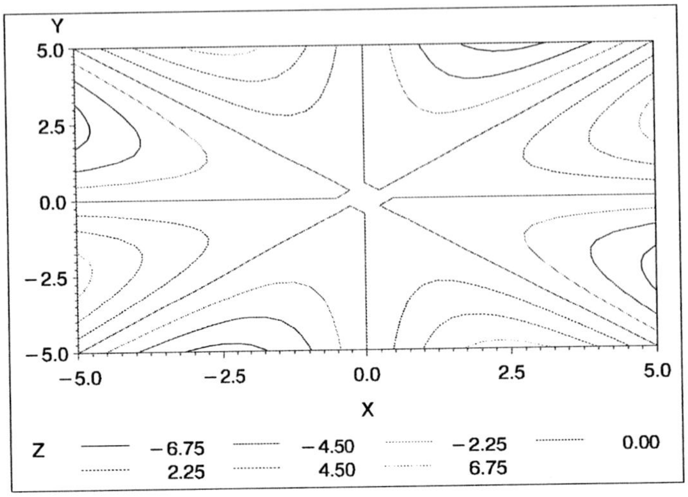

Figure 30.6 ORDER= Option, where the Option Range is Smaller than the Variable Range

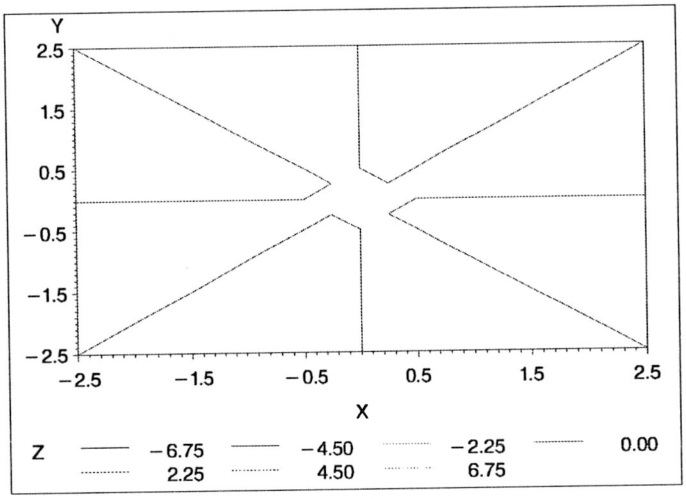

Figure 30.7 ORDER= Option, where the Option Range is Larger than Variable Range

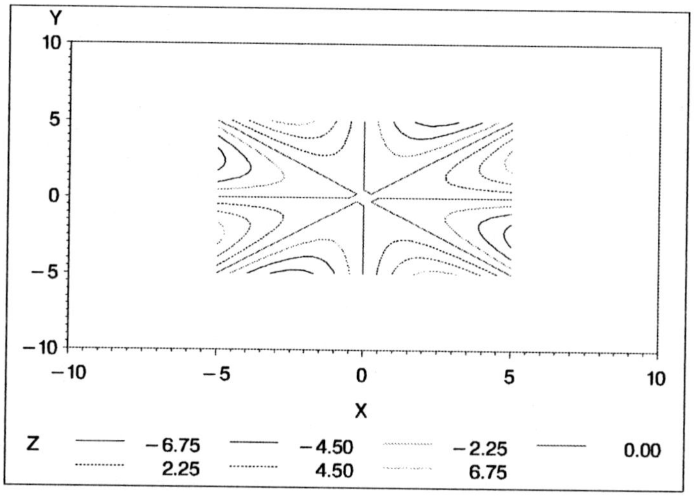

Modifying Contour Lines and Labels with the SYMBOL Statement

When you use the AUTOLABEL option, the LLEVELS= and CLEVELS= options are ignored, and contour-line and label attributes are controlled by the SYMBOL statement. Defaults are used if not enough SYMBOL statements are specified to match the number of contour levels.

If a SYMBOL statement does not include a color option, that statement may be applied to more than one contour level. In this case, the SYMBOL statement is used once with every color in the colors list and generates more than one SYMBOL definition. See "SYMBOL Statement" on page 183 for details.

Table 30.1 on page 903 describes how SYMBOL statement options affect contour plot lines and labels.

Table 30.1 The Effect of SYMBOL Statement Options on Contour Lines and Labels

SYMBOL Statement Option	Contour Line or Label Element Affected
LINE=*line-type*	Contour line style
WIDTH=*n*	Contour line thickness
CI=*line-color* or COLOR=*color*	Contour line color
FONT=*font*	Contour label font
HEIGHT=*height*	Contour label height
CV=*color* or COLOR=*color*	Contour label color
STEP=*distance<units>*	Minimum distance between labels on the same contour line
VALUE='*text*'	Contour label text
VALUE=NONE	Suppresses the contour label text

The SYMBOL statement option INTERPOL= is not supported by the GCONTOUR procedure.

The STEP= option specifies the minimum distance between contour labels. The lower the value, the more labels the procedure uses. A STEP= value of less than 10 percent is ignored by the GCONTOUR procedure and a value of 10 percent is substituted.

For more information, see "SYMBOL Statement" on page 183.

Specifying Text for Contour Labels

To override the default labels that are displayed by the AUTOLABEL option, you can specify label text for one or more contour lines. To do so, use both the FONT= and VALUE= options on the SYMBOL statement that is assigned to the contour level. Default labels are used for contour levels that you do not label.

For example, this SYMBOL1 statement displays the text string **Highest** in the Swiss font on the contour line that it modifies:

```
symbol1 font=swiss value='Highest';
```

You must specify both FONT= and VALUE= or the text is not used. For an example, see Example 2 on page 906.

Examples

Example 1: Generating a Simple Contour Plot

Procedure features:
PLOT statement

Other features:
FORMAT statement
G3GRID procedure

Sample library member: GCTCLAY1

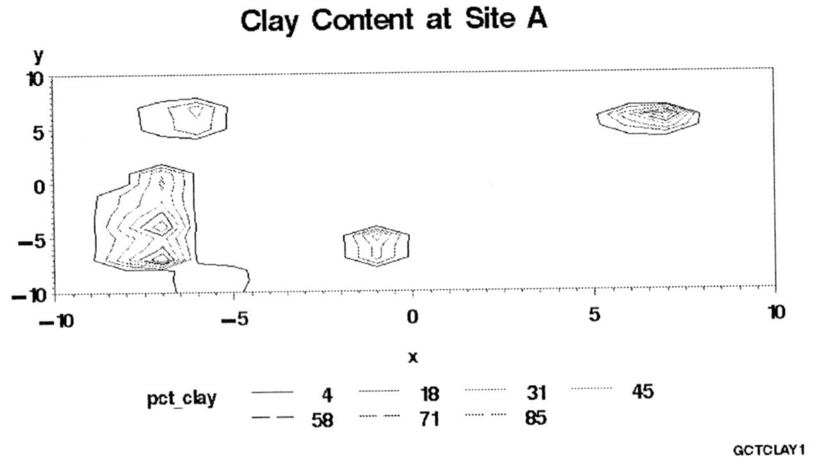

This example shows a simple contour plot that describes the percentage of clay found in soil samples at various locations of a testing site. By default, the axes are scaled to include all data values and are labeled with the names of the axes variables. Values are plotted with seven contour levels, which are represented by contour lines with default colors and line types. The default contour levels occur at every 15th percent of the range between the contour variable's 5th and 95th percentile. The legend is labeled with the contour variable's name and identifies the contour levels that are included in the plot.

This example uses the G3GRID procedure to interpolate clay percentages for grid cells that do not have percentages in the data. Without the G3GRID procedure, there are too many missing values for the percentages, and the GCONTOUR procedure cannot produce a satisfactory contour plot.

Assign the libref and set the graphics environment.

```
libname reflib 'SAS-data-library';
goptions reset=global gunit=pct border cback=white
         colors=(black blue green red)
         ftext=swiss ftitle=swissb htitle=6 htext=4;
```

Create the data set. REFLIB.CLAY contains the percent of clay at various locations of a test site.

```
data reflib.clay;
   input x y pct_clay;
   datalines;
-10    -10       2.316
-10     -9       1.816
-10     -8       2.427
...more data lines...
 10      8        .
 10      9        .
 10     10        .
;
```

Interpolate values for the contour plot. The interpolated data set is stored in REFLIB.CLAY2.

```
proc g3grid data=reflib.clay out=reflib.clay2;
   grid y*x=pct_clay / naxis1=21
                       naxis2=21
                       join;
run;
```

Define title and footnote.

```
title1 'Clay Content at Site A';
footnote1 j=r ' GCTCLAY1 ';
```

Generate a simple contour plot. The procedure uses REFLIB.CLAY2, the output data set from PROC G3GRID. To simplify the legend labels, clay percentages are formatted with no decimal positions.

```
proc gcontour data=reflib.clay2;
   format pct_clay 2.0;
   plot y*x=pct_clay;
run;
quit;
```

Example 2: Labeling Contour Lines

Procedure features:

PLOT statement options:

AUTOLABEL=
HAXIS=
LEGEND=
LEVELS=
VAXIS=

Other features:

AXIS statement

LEGEND statement

SYMBOL statement

Data set: REFLIB.CLAY2

Sample library member: GCTCLAY2

Display 30.2 A Simple Contour Plot with Labelled Contour Levels

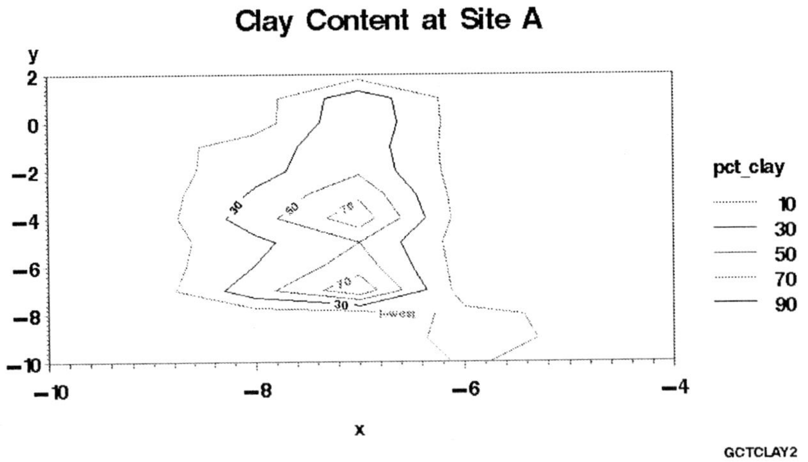

This example modifies Example 1 on page 904 to label contour levels with the AUTOLABEL option. When AUTOLABEL is used, the SYMBOL statement controls the labels and attributes of contour lines. In this example, SYMBOL1 defines a text label for the lowest contour level. Each remaining contour line gets the default label, which is the contour variable's value at that contour level. All the contour lines are solid, which is the default line type for the SYMBOL statement.

This example also uses AXIS statements to limit the plot to one of the contour areas from the output of Example 1 on page 904, and it uses a LEGEND statement to move the legend so the procedure has more room for displaying the *y* axis.

Assign the libref and set the graphics environment.

```
libname reflib 'SAS-data-library';
goptions reset=global gunit=pct border cback=white
         colors=(black blue green red)
         ftext=swiss ftitle=swissb htitle=6 htext=4;
```

Define title and footnote.

```
title1 'Clay Content at Site A';
footnote1 j=r 'GCTCLAY2';
```

Define axes characteristics. AXIS1 uses ORDER= to set major tick marks at 2-unit intervals from -10 to -4. AXIS2 uses ORDER= to specify 2-unit intervals from -10 to 2. These axes ranges effectively zoom in on one of the contour areas from Example 1 on page 904.

```
axis1 order=(-10 to -4 by 2);
axis2 order=(-10 to 2 by 2);
```

Define legend characteristics. POSITION= centers the legend to the right of the graphics area, and LABEL= positions the legend label above the legend entries. ACROSS= places legend entries in rows 1 entry wide.

```
legend1 position=(right middle)
        label=(position=top)
        across=1;
```

Define symbol characteristics. SYMBOL1 specifies a font and text string to label the lowest-level contour lines. COLOR= ensures that each SYMBOL definition is used only once. In SYMBOL2, STEP= increases the number of contour labels by placing the labels closer together than the default distance of 65 percent.

```
symbol1 height=2.5
        font=swissb
        value='lowest'
        color=red;
symbol2 height=2.5
        step=25pct
        color=black;
symbol3 height=2.5
        color=blue;
symbol4 height=2.5
        color=green;
```

Generate the contour plot. LEVELS= specifies contour levels from 10 to 90 at 20-unit intervals. AUTOLABEL= turns on labeling, and CHECK=NONE turns off collision checking so the maximum number of contour labels can be displayed. HAXIS= and VAXIS= assign AXIS definitions to the plot. LEGEND= assigns the LEGEND1 definition to the plot.

```
proc gcontour data=reflib.clay2;
   plot y*x=pct_clay / levels=10 to 90 by 20
                       autolabel=(check=none)
                       haxis=axis1
                       vaxis=axis2
                       legend=legend1;
run;
quit;
```

Example 3: Specifying Contour Levels

Procedure features:
PLOT statement options:
LEVELS=
LLEVELS=

Sample library member: GCTPOND

Display 30.3 A Contour Plot Generated with Specific Contour Levels

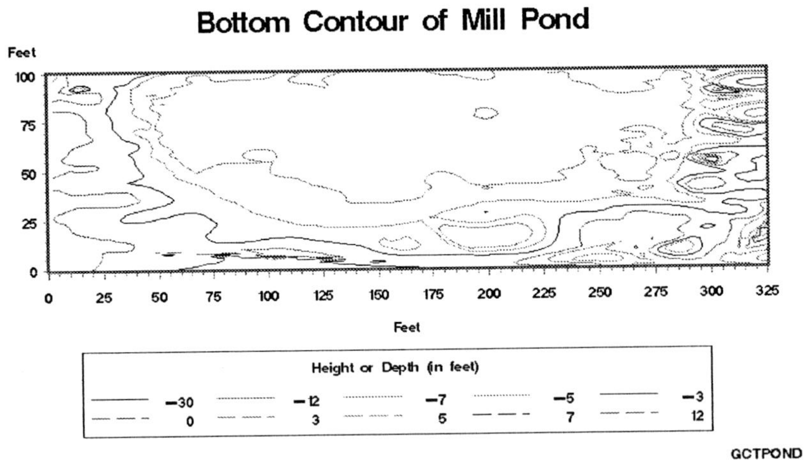

This example generates a contour plot that shows the height or depth of a pond and its surrounding land. In the example, the PLOT statement uses the LEVELS= and LLEVELS= options to specify explicit contour levels and line types for the contour plot. It also uses a LEGEND statement to modify the plot's default legend.

This example uses the G3GRID procedure to interpolate points for grid cells that do not have a needed dimension in the data. Without the G3GRID procedure, there are too many missing values for the point locations, and the GCONTOUR procedure cannot produce a satisfactory contour plot.

Assign the libref and set the graphics environment.

```
libname reflib 'SAS-data-library';
goptions reset=global gunit=pct border cback=white
         colors=(black blue green red)
         ftext=swiss ftitle=swissb htitle=6 htext=3;
```

Create the data set. REFLIB.POND contains the raw data for a pond floor and surrounding land.

```
data reflib.pond;
   input vdist hdist height;
   datalines;
10     88        0
18     55       -1
24     22.5     -1.67
...more data lines...
64     272.5   -6.25
60     277.5   -6.5
62     277.5   -6.5
;
```

Define title and footnote.

```
title 'Bottom Contour of Mill Pond';
footnote j=r ' GCTPOND ';
```

Define axis characteristics.

```
axis1 order=(0 to 325 by 25) width=3 minor=(n=4)
      label=('Feet');
axis2 order=(0 to 100 by 25) width=3 minor=(n=4)
      label=(' Feet');
```

Define legend characteristics.

```
legend1 frame shape=line(7)
        label=(position=top j=c 'Height or Depth (in feet)');
```

Interpolate points for the contour plot.

```
proc g3grid data=reflib.pond out=reflib.pondgrid;
   grid vdist*hdist=height / naxis1=100 naxis2=100;
run;
```

Generate the contour plot. LEVELS= specifies the values of the contour levels. LLEVELS= sets the line types for the contour lines. Solid lines identify negative contour levels, and dashed lines identify positive contour levels.

```
proc gcontour data=reflib.pondgrid;
   plot vdist*hdist=height /levels= -30 -12 -7  -3 0 3 5 7 12
                            llevels= 1   1  1  1  1 2 2 2 2  2
                            legend=legend1
                            haxis=axis1
                            vaxis=axis2;
run;
quit;
```

Example 4: Using Patterns and Joins

Procedure features:
PLOT statement options:

COUTLINE=
CTEXT=
JOIN
PATTERN

Sample library member: GCTPATRN

Display 30.4 A Contour Plot that uses Contour Lines

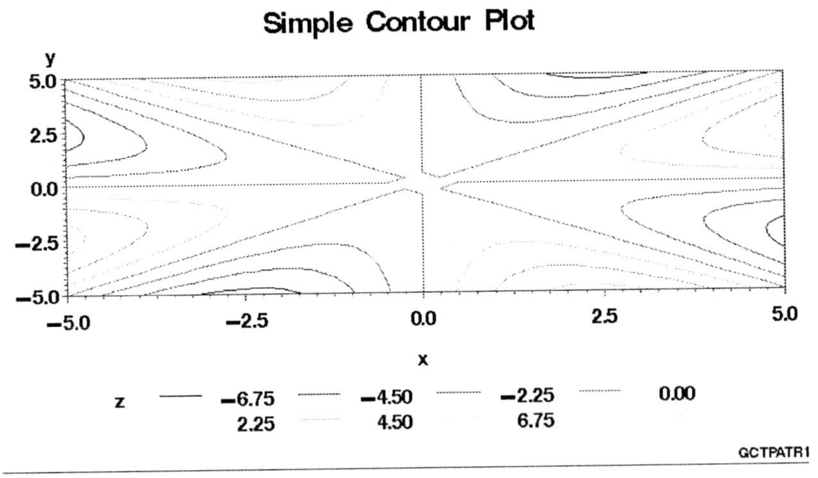

This example demonstrates the differences between using lines and patterns to represent contour levels. It first uses a simple PLOT statement to generate the default output, which uses lines to represent contour levels.

As shown in the following output, the example then modifies the PLOT statement by specifying the PATTERN option, which uses patterns to distinguish between contour levels. Additional PLOT statement options outline filled areas in gray and specify green text for all text on the axes and in the legend.

Display 30.5 A Contour Plot that uses Patterns

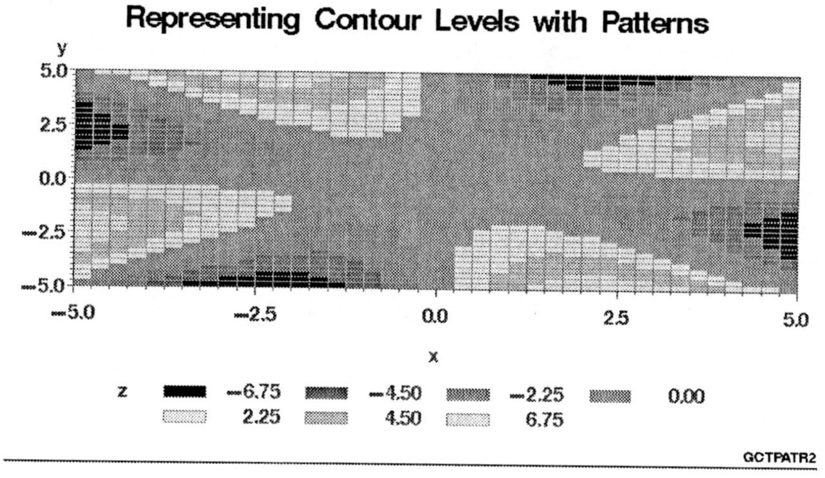

Finally, as shown by the following output, the example uses the JOIN option to combine the patterns in grid cells for the same contour level. Additional options enhance the plot by modifying the axes and framing the legend.

Display 30.6 A Contour Plot with Joined Cells

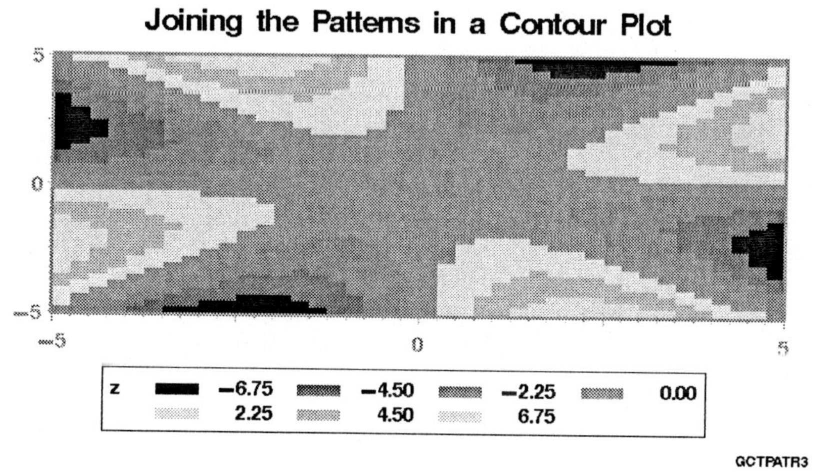

Assign the libref and set the graphics environment.

```
libname reflib 'SAS-data-library';
goptions reset=global gunit=pct border cback=white
         colors=(black blue green red)
         ftext=swiss ftitle=swissb htitle=6 htext=4;
```

Create the data set. REFLIB.SWIRL is generated data that produces a symmetric contour pattern, which is useful for illustrating the PATTERN option.

```
data reflib.swirl;
   do x= -5 to 5 by 0.25;
      do y= -5 to 5 by 0.25;
         if x+y=0 then z=0;
         else z=(x*y)*((x*x-y*y)/(x*x+y*y));
         output;
      end;
   end;
run;
```

Define title and footnote for the default output.

```
title 'Simple Contour Plot';
footnote j=r 'GCTPATR1 ';
```

Generate a simple contour plot.

```
proc gcontour data=reflib.swirl;
   plot y*x=z;
run;
```

Define title and footnote for second plot.

```
title 'Representing Contour Levels with Patterns';
footnote j=r 'GCTPATR2 ';
```

Generate the contour plot. PATTERN fills the contour levels with solid patterns. COUTLINE= names the color that outlines the grid cells. CTEXT= names a color for axes and legend text.

```
proc gcontour data=reflib.swirl;
   plot y*x=z / pattern
                coutline=gray
                ctext=green;
run;
```

Define title and footnote for last plot.

```
title 'Joining the Patterns in a Contour Plot';
footnote j=r 'GCTPATR3 ';
```

Define axis and legend characteristics for last plot. Blanks are used to suppress tick labels at positions -2.5 and 2.5.

```
axis1 label=none value=('' ' ' '0' ' ' '5')
      color=red width=3;
axis2 label=none value=('' ' ' '0' ' ' '5')
```

```
      color=red width=3;

legend frame;
```

Generate the last contour plot. JOIN combines grid cells for the same contour levels.

```
proc gcontour data=reflib.swirl;
   plot y*x=z / pattern
                join
                haxis=axis1
                vaxis=axis2
                legend=legend1;
run;
quit;
```

References

Snyder, W.V. (1978), "Contour Plotting [J6] ," *ACM Transactions on Mathematical Software*, 4, 290–294.

CHAPTER

31

The GDEVICE Procedure

Overview

The GDEVICE procedure is a tool for examining and changing the parameters of the graphics device driver catalog entries used with SAS/GRAPH software. With the GDEVICE procedure, you can use either the GDEVICE windows or GDEVICE procedure statements to

- □ list the device entries stored in any DEVICES catalog
- □ view the parameters for any device entry
- □ create and modify new device entries
- □ copy, modify, rename, or delete existing device entries.

See Chapter 3, "Device Drivers," on page 41 for a discussion of device drivers and device entries, as well directions for selecting device drivers and changing the settings of device parameters.

For a complete list of Institute-supplied device entries supported by your operating environment, see the SASHELP.DEVICES catalog that is supplied with SAS/GRAPH software.

Concepts

About Device Catalogs

Device entries are stored in SAS catalogs that are named *libref*.DEVICES. Device entries for your operating environment that are supplied with SAS/GRAPH software are stored in the Institute-supplied catalog, SASHELP.DEVICES.

Custom device entries are typically stored in a catalog named GDEVICE*n*.DEVICES (where *n* can be any number from 0 to 9). However, device entries that have been created or modified by a system administrator specifically for your site also may be stored in SASHELP.DEVICES. (On multi-user systems, the SAS Support Consultant is usually the person who has write access to the SASHELP.DEVICES catalog and makes any changes.)

About the Current Catalog

When the GDEVICE procedure determines which catalog it should use, it searches for the catalog in the following order:

1. the catalog name specified in the CATALOG= option in the PROC GDEVICE statement
2. the catalog associated with the GDEVICE0 libref, if the libref has been assigned
3. the Institute-supplied catalog, SASHELP.DEVICES. (SASHELP.DEVICES is usually write-protected and is opened in browse mode.)

The first catalog it finds becomes the current catalog.

You can specify the current catalog by

- □ using the CATALOG= option in the PROC GDEVICE statement (this is required to open a driver entry in update mode)
- □ assigning the GDEVICE0 libref to the appropriate catalog.

Search Order of Device Catalogs

When you specify a device driver, SAS/GRAPH software looks only into catalogs with certain librefs and names to find a device entry for that driver. It searches these catalogs sequentially in the following order:

1. If the libref GDEVICE0 has been assigned to a SAS library, SAS/GRAPH software looks in that library for a catalog named DEVICES. If the GDEVICE0.DEVICES catalog exists, it is checked for the specified device entry. If the device entry is not there, SAS/GRAPH software looks next for a library with the libref GDEVICE1 and for a catalog named DEVICES in that library. The search is repeated for the sequence of librefs through GDEVICE9.
2. If SAS/GRAPH fails to find the specified device entry in any DEVICES catalog in the libraries GDEVICE0 through GDEVICE9, or if before locating the specified device entry it encounters in that sequence an undefined libref or a library that does not contain a DEVICES catalog, it jumps to SASHELP.DEVICES to search for the device entry. For example, if a GDEVICE0 libref is allocated but this library does not contain a DEVICES catalog, SAS/GRAPH software jumps to the SASHELP.DEVICES catalog, without searching for a GDEVICE1.DEVICES catalog, even if it exists. (SASHELP.DEVICES is the device catalog supplied with SAS/GRAPH software. SASHELP is one of the standard librefs defined automatically whenever you start your SAS session; you do not need to issue a LIBNAME statement to define it.)
3. If the specified device entry is not found in the SASHELP.DEVICES catalog, you receive an error message.

Since the GDEVICE0.DEVICES catalog is the first place that SAS/GRAPH software looks, you always should assign that libref to the library containing your personal catalog of device entries, if you have one. If for some reason you have personal device catalogs in more than one SAS data library, assign them librefs in the sequence GDEVICE0, GDEVICE1, GDEVICE2, and so on.

Note: As stated above, the search for entries terminates if there is a break in the sequence; the catalog GDEVICE1.DEVICES is not checked if the libref GDEVICE0 is undefined, or if GDEVICE0 does not contain a catalog named DEVICES. △

To cancel or redefine the libref GDEVICE*n*, first clear the current graphics options:

```
goptions reset=all;
```

You can then redefine the libref with another LIBNAME statement. To cancel a libref, use a null LIBNAME statement.

Ways to Use the GDEVICE Procedure

There are two ways to use the GDEVICE procedure:

- browse or edit the fields in the GDEVICE procedure windows (windowing mode)
- submit GDEVICE procedure statements in a SAS program (program mode).

If you run SAS software in a windowing environment (the SAS Display Manager System, for example), you can use either the GDEVICE procedure windows or the GDEVICE procedure statements. In a windowing environment, the GDEVICE procedure automatically opens the GDEVICE procedure windows.

If you run SAS software in a non-windowing environment (such as line-mode or batch), you can use only GDEVICE procedure statements. In a non-windowing environment, the GDEVICE procedure automatically uses program mode.

Both methods provide identical functionality and allow you to display or modify device parameters, or create new device entries.

Windowing Mode

In a windowing environment, open the GDEVICE windows by submitting the PROC GDEVICE statement without the NOFS option:

```
proc gdevice;
```

This opens the DIRECTORY window in browse mode. This window lists all of the device entries in the current catalog. (See "About the Current Catalog" on page 916.)

To open the DIRECTORY window in edit mode, or to specify a different catalog, include the CATALOG= option in the PROC GDEVICE statement.

From the DIRECTORY window you can select the device entry you want to work with and open other GDEVICE windows in which you can view or modify device parameters. For more information, see "Using the GDEVICE Windows" on page 928.

In a windowing environment, you can switch between the GDEVICE windows and program statements while you are running the procedure. See the "FS Statement" on page 925 and the NOFS window command in the SAS Help facility for SAS/GRAPH.

To exit the GDEVICE windows, submit the End command or close the window.

Program Mode

If you are in a non-windowing or batch environment, the GDEVICE procedure automatically starts in program mode. If you are in a windowing environment, specify the NOFS option to start the GDEVICE procedure in program mode:

```
proc gdevice nofs;
```

By default, the GDEVICE procedure accesses the current catalog in browse mode and prompts you in the LOG to enter additional program statements. (See "About the Current Catalog" on page 916.) To specify the current catalog, include the CATALOG= option in the PROC GDEVICE statement.

Once you start the GDEVICE procedure, you can enter and run additional statements without re-entering the PROC GDEVICE statement. For example, the following statement generates a listing of the device parameters for the PSCOLOR device entry that is stored in the Institute-supplied catalog, SASHELP.DEVICES:

```
list pscolor;
```

PROC GDEVICE procedure output is displayed in the Output window. Output 31.1 shows the listing generated by the LIST statement.

Output 31.1 Sample Device Entry Listing Generated in Program Mode

```
                        GDEVICE procedure
              Listing from SASHELP.DEVICES - Entry PSCOLOR

 Orig Driver: PSCOLOR              Module:   SASGDPSL  Model:     1251
 Description: PostScript color--RGB color defs             Type: PRINTER
 *** Institute-supplied ***
 Lrows:    0  Xmax:    8.500 IN    Hsize:    8.000 IN  Xpixels:       2550
 Lcols:    0  Ymax:   11.000 IN    Vsize:    8.500 IN  Ypixels:       3300
 Prows:   68                       Horigin:  0.218 IN
 Pcols:   80                       Vorigin:  1.496 IN
 Aspect:    0.000                  Rotate:
 Driver query: Y                   Queued messages: N
                                   Paperfeed:   0.000 IN

 OPTIONS

 Erase:                    Autofeed:      Y          Chartype:    1
 Swap:                     Cell:                     Maxcolors: 256
 Autocopy:                 Characters:               Repaint:     0
 Handshake:      XONXOFF   Circlearc:                Gcopies:     0
                           Dash:                     Gsize:       0
 Prompt - startup:         Fill:                     Speed:       0
        end graph:         Piefill:                  Fillinc:     0
        mount pen:         Polyfill:                 Maxpoly:  1450
        chg paper:         Symbol:                   Lfactor:     0
                           Pensort:       N
 Promptchars:  '000A010D05000000'X
 Devopts:        'FD9230402C130000'X
 UCC:       '0001'X

 Cback:       WHITE
 Color list:

   BLACK      RED        GREEN      BLUE       CYAN
   MAGENTA    YELLOW     GRAY

 CHARTYPE RECORDS

 Chartype  Rows  Cols                Font Name                 Scalable
      1     89    85    Courier                                    Y
      2     89    85    Courier-Oblique                            Y
      .
     {ob ...more hardware fonts...}
      .
     34     89    85    Bookman-LightItalic                        Y
     35     89    85    Bookman-DemiItalic                         Y
 Gend:      '0A'X

 FILE INFORMATION

 Gaccess:     sasgastd>sasgraph.ps
 Gsfname:                           Gsfmode:   PORT      Gsflen:       0
 Trantab:                           Devmap:
 Devtype:     DISK
 Gprotocol:
 Fileclose:   DRIVERTERM
 Hostspec:

 HOST INFORMATION
```

You can exit the GDEVICE procedure in these three ways:

- Submit the END, QUIT, or STOP statement.
- Submit another PROC statement or DATA step.
- Exit your SAS session.

Procedure Syntax

Requirements: Statements other than the PROC GDEVICE statement can be used only in a non-windowing or batch environment. In these environments, at least one statement is required to give GDEVICE an action to perform. In a windowing environment, only the PROC GDEVICE statement is required. In program mode, at least one additional statement is required, and you can submit as many of each statement as you want.

Note: You must have write access to the device catalog in order to modify, add, or delete entries.

Supports: Output Delivery System (ODS LISTING).

PROC GDEVICE <CATALOG=<*libref.*>*SAS-catalog*>
<BROWSE>
<NOFS>;

ADD*new-device-entry*
required-parameters
<*optional-parameters*>;

COPY*device-entry*
<FROM=<*libref.*>*SAS-catalog*>
<NEWNAME=*new-device-entry*>;

DELETE *device-entry*;

FS;

LIST *device-entry* | _ALL_ | _NEXT_ | _PREV_ | DUMP>;

MODIFY *device-entry*
parameter(s)

QUIT | *END* | *STOP*;

RENAME *device-entry* NEWNAME=*new-entry-name*;

PROC GDEVICE Statement

Starts the procedure and determines whether it runs in windowing mode or program mode. Optionally identifies a device catalog and determines how that catalog is opened.

PROC GDEVICE <CATALOG=<*libref.*>*SAS-catalog*>
<BROWSE>
<NOFS>;

Options

Options used in the PROC GDEVICE statement affect the way you use the procedure.

BROWSE
opens a catalog in browse mode. You cannot modify a catalog when you open it with the BROWSE option. If you are running in program mode when you use BROWSE, you can use only the FS, LIST, QUIT, END, or STOP statements.

CATALOG=<*libref.*>*SAS-catalog*
CAT=<*libref.*>*SAS-catalog*
C=<*libref.*>*SAS-catalog*

specifies the catalog containing device information. If you do not specify a catalog, the procedure opens the first catalog found in the search order of catalogs in browse mode. (See "About the Current Catalog" on page 916. for information on how the GDEVICE procedure determines which catalog to use.)

To edit the device entries in a catalog, you must use the CATALOG= option.

NOFS

specifies that you are using program mode. In windowing environments, the GDEVICE windows are the default and you must specify NOFS to start GDEVICE in program mode.

ADD Statement

Adds a new device entry to the catalog selected by the CATALOG= option in the PROC GDEVICE statement. The device entry is initialized with NULL values for most parameters.

Requirements: You must have write access to the device catalog in order to add entries, and use CATALOG= in the PROC GDEVICE statement.

Restriction: Not valid in browse mode.

ADD *new-device-entry*
required-parameters
<*optional-parameters*>;

required-parameters are all of the following:

MODULE=*driver-module*

XMAX=*width* <IN | CM>

YMAX=*height* <IN | CM>

XPIXELS=*width-in-pixels*

YPIXELS=*height-in-pixels*

plus one or both of the following parameter pairs:

LCOLS=*landscape-columns*

LROWS=*landscape-rows*

or

PCOLS=*portrait-columns*

PROWS=*portrait-rows*

optional-parameters can be one or more of the following:

ASPECT=*scaling-factor*

AUTOCOPY=Y | N

AUTOFEED=Y | N

CBACK=*background-color*

CELL=Y | N

CHARACTERS=Y | N
CHARREC=(*charrec-list(s)*)
CHARTYPE=*hardware-font-chartype*
CIRCLEARC=Y | N
CMAP=('*from-color* : *to-color*' <...,'*from-color-n* : *to-color-n*'>)
COLORS=(<*colors-list*>)
COLORTYPE=NAME | RGB | HLS | GRAY | CMY | CMYK | HSV | HSB
DASH=Y | N
DASHLINE='*dashed-line-hex-string*'X
DESCRIPTION='*text-string*'
DEVMAP=*device-map-name* | NONE
DEVOPTS='*hardware-capabilities-hex-string*'X
DEVTYPE=*device-type*
DRVINIT1='*system-command(s)*'
DRVINIT2='*system-command(s)*'
DRVQRY | NODRVQRY
DRVTERM1='*system-command(s)*'
DRVTERM2='*system-command(s)*'
ERASE=Y | N
FILECLOSE=DRIVERTERM | GRAPHEND
FILL=Y | N
FILLINC=0...9999
FORMAT=CHARACTER | BINARY
GACCESS=*output-format* | '*output-format* > *destination*'
GCOPIES=*current-copies*
GEND='*string*' <...'*string-n*'>
GEPILOG='*string*' <...'*string-n*'>
GPROLOG='*string*' <...'*string-n*'>
GPROTOCOL=*module-name*
GSFLEN=*record-length*
GSFMODE=APPEND | REPLACE | PORT
SFNAME=*fileref*
GSIZE=*lines*
GSTART='*string*' <...'*string-n*'>
HANDSHAKE=HARDWARE | NONE | SOFTWARE | XONXOFF
HEADER='*command*'
HEADERFILE=*fileref*
ORIGIN=*horizontal-offset* <IN | CM>
HOSTSPEC='*text string*'
HSIZE=*horizontal-size* <IN | CM>
ID='*description*'
INTERACTIVE=USER | GRAPH | PROC
LFACTOR=*line-thickness-factor*
MAXCOLORS=*number-of-colors*
MAXPOLY=*number-of-vertices*

MODEL=*model-number*

NAK='*negative-handshake-response*'X

PAPERFEED=*feed-increment* <IN | CM>

PATH=*angle-increment*

PENSORT=Y | N

PIEFILL=Y | N

POLYGONFILL=Y | N

POSTGRAPH1='*system-command(s)*'

POSTGRAPH2='*system-command(s)*'

PREGRAPH1='*system-command(s)*'

PREGRAPH2='*system-command(s)*'

PROCESS='*command*'

PROCESSINPUT=*fileref*

PROCESSOUTPUT=*fileref*

PROMPT=0...7

PROMPTCHARS='*prompt-chars-hex-string*'X

QMSG | NOQMSG

RECTFILL='*rectangle-fill-hex-string*'X

REPAINT=*redraw-factor*

ROTATE=LANDSCAPE | PORTRAIT

ROTATION=*angle-increment*

SPEED=*pen-speed*

SWAP=Y | N

SYMBOL=Y | N

SYMBOLS='*hardware-symbols-hex-string*'X

TRAILER='*command*'

TRAILERFILE=*fileref*

TRANTAB=*table* | *user-defined-table*

TYPE= CAMERA | CRT | EXPORT | PLOTTER | PRINTER

UCC='*control-characters-hex-string*'X

VORIGIN=*vertical-offset* <IN | CM>

VSIZE=*vertical-size* <IN | CM>

Required Arguments

new-device-entry

specifies the one-level name of the new device entry. *New-device-entry* must be a valid name for a SAS catalog entry for your operating environment and cannot already exist in the current catalog.

required-parameters

all required parameters for the ADD statement correspond to device parameters of the same name. Refer to Chapter 8, "Graphics Options and Device Parameters Dictionary," on page 261 for a description of each parameter.

Options

All optional parameters for the ADD statement correspond to device parameters of the same name. Refer to Chapter 8, "Graphics Options and Device Parameters Dictionary," on page 261 for a description of each parameter.

Note: The COLORS= device parameter is not required; the device entry will be created if you do not use it. However, the GDEVICE procedure issues an error message if you do not specify at least one color for COLORS=. △

Details

The ADD statement is rarely used because it initializes parameter values to NULL and you have to set values for all the parameters. The best way to add a new driver is to copy an existing driver and modify it.

COPY Statement

Copies a device entry and places the copy in the current catalog. The original device entry can be either in the current catalog or in a different catalog.

Requirements: You must have write access to the catalog to which the device entry is being copied.

Restriction: Not valid in browse mode.

See also: "Creating or Modifying Device Entries" on page 934

Featured in: Example 1 on page 936

COPY *device-entry where*;

Where *where* must be one or both of the following:

FROM=<*libref.*>*SAS-catalog*

NEWNAME=*new-device-entry*

Required Arguments

device-entry
specifies the one-level name of the device entry to copy. The entry must exist in either the current catalog (the default) or the catalog specified by FROM=.

FROM=<*libref.*>*SAS-catalog*
names the catalog from which to copy *device-entry*.

NEWNAME=*new-device-entry*
specifies a name for the copy of the device entry that is placed in the current catalog. *New-device-entry* must be a valid name for a SAS catalog entry and cannot already exist in the current catalog.

If you copy device entries across catalogs and you do not specify a new name, the GDEVICE procedure uses the original name for the new device entry.

DELETE Statement

Deletes the device entry from the current catalog.

Requirements: You must have write access to the current catalog to delete a device entry from it, and use CATALOG= in the PROC GDEVICE statement.

Restriction: Not valid in browse mode.

Caution: A device entry cannot be restored once it has been deleted. Depending on the environment in which you are using the GDEVICE procedure, you may be asked to verify that you really want to delete the entry.

DELETE *device-entry*;

Required Arguments

device-entry
specifies the one-level name of device entry to delete. The entry must exist in the current catalog.

FS Statement

Switches from program mode to the GDEVICE windows.

Requirements: You must be running SAS software in a windowing environment.

FS;

Options

No options.

LIST Statement

Lists all of the parameters of the specified device entry in the Output window.

Default: _ALL_

See also: "Program Mode" on page 918

LIST <*device-entry*>
<_ALL_>
<_NEXT_>

<_PREV_>
<DUMP>;

Options

device-entry
specifies the one-level name of the device entry whose contents you want to list. The entry must exist in the current catalog.

ALL
lists only the name, description, and creation date of all device entries in the current catalog. This is the default. If no entries exist in the catalog, the GDEVICE procedure issues a message.

NEXT
lists the contents of the next device entry. The GDEVICE procedure lists the first entry in the catalog if no entries have been previously listed.

PREV
lists the contents of the previous device entry. If you have not previously listed the contents of a device entry, the GDEVICE procedure issues the following message:

```
No objects preceding current object.
```

DUMP
lists detailed information on *all* device entries in the current catalog. Depending on the number of device entries in the catalog, the DUMP option can create a *large* amount of output.

MODIFY Statement

Changes the values in a device entry.

Requirements: You must have write access to the current catalog to modify a device entry, and use CATALOG= in the PROC GDEVICE statement.

Restriction: Not valid in browse mode.

See also: "Creating or Modifying Device Entries" on page 934

Featured in: Example 1 on page 936

MODIFY *device-entry*
parameter(s);

Required Arguments

device-entry
specifies the one-level name of the device entry that you want to modify. The entry must exist in the current catalog.

parameter(s)
are the parameters you want to modify. These can be any of the parameters listed in the ADD statement, whether listed as required or optional for ADD. See "ADD Statement" on page 921 for a complete list. Refer to Chapter 8, "Graphics Options and Device Parameters Dictionary," on page 261 for a description of each parameter.

Details

To modify a device entry, create your own catalog and then copy the device entries you need into it. You can then change your personal copies of the device entries without affecting the original drivers in SASHELP.DEVICES. (To copy device entries, use the COPY statement, the COPY command available after you choose Import Device Entry from the DIRECTORY window's File menu, or the CATALOG procedure, which is part of base SAS.

CAUTION:
Be careful when modifying device entries in program mode. In program mode, you cannot cancel any modifications you have just made. To change a value you have modified, you must use another MODIFY statement to replace the original value or reset it to its default. (In the GDEVICE windows, you can type the CANCEL command in the command line to cancel changes you have made to the fields.) △

QUIT Statement

Saves all modifications made to device entries during the procedure and exits the GDEVICE procedure.

QUIT | *END* | *STOP*;

Options

No options.

RENAME Statement

Changes the name of the device entry to the name specified in the statement.

Requirements: You must have write access to the current catalog to rename a device entry, and use CATALOG= in the PROC GDEVICE statement.

Restriction: Not valid in browse mode.

RENAME *device-entry*
NEWNAME=*new-entry-name*;

Required Arguments

device-entry
specifies the one-level name of the device entry that you want to rename. The entry must exist in the current catalog.

NEWNAME=*new-entry-name*
specifies the new entry name. *New-entry-name* must be a valid name for a SAS catalog entry and cannot already exist in the current catalog. If the name already exists, the GDEVICE procedure issues an error message.

Using the GDEVICE Procedure

Using the GDEVICE Windows

You can use the GDEVICE windows instead of program mode to view, modify, copy, create, or delete device entries. You perform tasks in the GDEVICE windows by entering values in the fields, by using the pulldown menus, and by issuing commands from the command line.

These are the thirteen GDEVICE windows in order of appearance:

- Directory Window
- Detail Window
- Parameters Window
- Gcolors Window
- Chartype Window
- Colormap Window
- Metagraphics Window
- Gprolog Window
- Gepilog Window
- Gstart Window
- Gend Window
- Host File Options Window
- Host Commands Window

The fields in these windows represent device entry parameters. The GDEVICE windows group the device parameters by topic, to make it easy for you to review or modify the entry. If you open the device entry in edit mode, you can modify the fields directly. For a description of each field, see the corresponding parameter in Chapter 8, "Graphics Options and Device Parameters Dictionary," on page 261 or refer to the SAS Help facility. For a complete list of device parameters, see "ADD Statement" on page 921.

Note: The parameters are sometimes an abbreviation of the field names, but the correspondence should be clear. For example, in the Detail window, the "Driver query" field corresponds to the DRVQRY parameter, and the "Queued messages" field corresponds to the QMSG parameter. △

This section briefly describes the GDEVICE windows; for a complete description of each window and its fields, refer to the SAS Help facility.

GDEVICE Window Commands

You can navigate and manipulate the GDEVICE windows by entering commands on the command line or selecting them from the menus. For a complete description of all the GDEVICE window commands, refer to the SAS Help facility.

Note: In a Windows environment, the GDEVICE commands are presented on pop-up menus rather than on the menubar. Right-click a GDEVICE window to access a pop-up menu. △

GDEVICE Window Descriptions

DIRECTORY Window

This window appears when you start the GDEVICE procedure in window mode. It lists all the device entries in the default catalog or the catalog you specified in the PROC GDEVICE statement. You can use it to

- copy, rename, or delete device entries in the catalog
- select a device entry whose parameters you want to browse or edit.

You can enter these commands in the Directory window selection field:

B | S
: open the Detail window and browse (B) or, if you are in edit mode, edit (S) the selected device entry.

D
: delete the selected device entry. You cannot restore a device entry once it has been deleted.

E
: open the Detail window and edit the selected device entry.

R
: rename the device entry and/or description.

You cannot edit the TYPE and UPDATED fields in the Directory Window.

Figure 31.1 The DIRECTORY Window

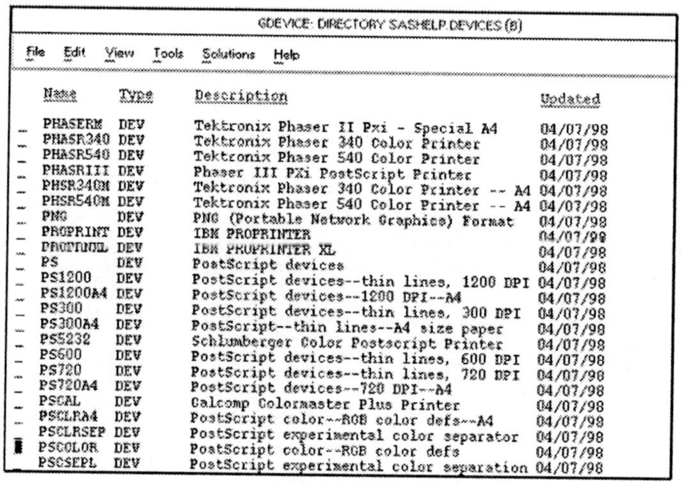

Detail window

This window contains device parameters that control basic characteristics of the device, for example, the size of the graphics output area.

Figure 31.2 The Detail Window

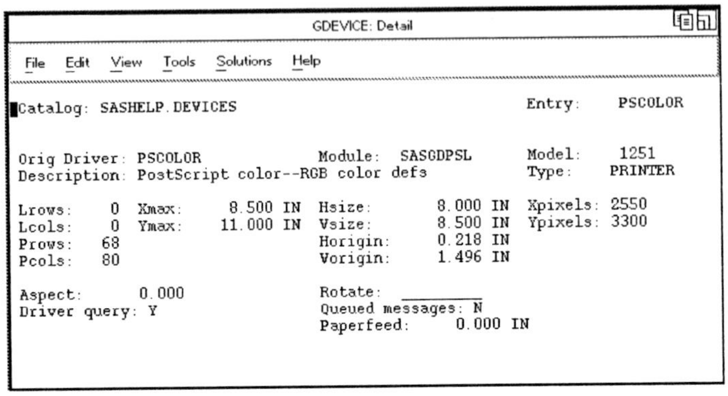

From this window you can access any of the subsidiary GDEVICE windows by

- entering the name of the window on the command line
- selecting the window from the Tools pulldown
- opening the subsidiary windows in order of appearance by using the View pulldown and choosing Next Screen, or using the NEXTSCR command on the command line.

Parameters window

This window includes additional device parameters that affect the way graphs are drawn. For example, you choose whether certain graphics primitives are drawn by your hardware or by SAS/GRAPH software, whether to feed paper to printers or plotters automatically, and whether to have SAS/GRAPH software prompt you with messages under certain conditions.

Note: If the device does not support a hardware characteristic, the catalog entry cannot enable the support. △

Figure 31.3 The Parameters Window

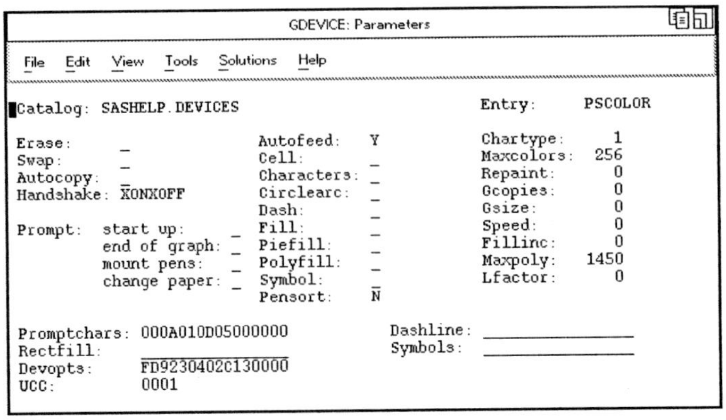

Gcolors window

This window lists the colors that the device driver uses by default. When you do not explicitly specify the color of a graphics feature in your program or in a GOPTIONS statement, SAS/GRAPH software uses this list to determine what color to use.

Figure 31.4 The Gcolors Window (partial view)

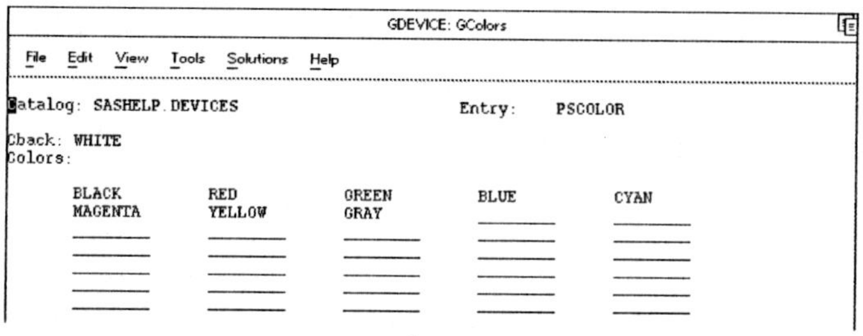

Chartype window

This window lists the hardware fonts that the device can use, along with information about the size of the characters. The Chartype value is the value you can use to reference a font in another window. For example, you would enter a Chartype number in the Parameters window's Chartype field.

Figure 31.5 The Chartype Window (partial view)

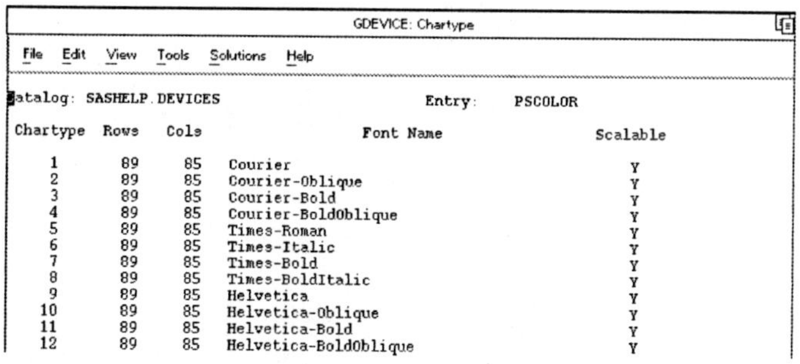

Colormap window

This window allows you to specify a color map for the device. The FROM field specifies the name to assign to the color designated by the *color* value, and the TO field specifies a SAS/GRAPH color name up to eight characters long. Once you have defined the color mapping, you can use the new color name in any color option. For example, if your device entry maps the color name DAFFODIL to the SAS color value PAOY, you can specify COLOR=DAFFODIL on any statement that supports a COLOR= option, and the driver will map this to the color value PAOY.

Figure 31.6 The Colormap Window (partial view)

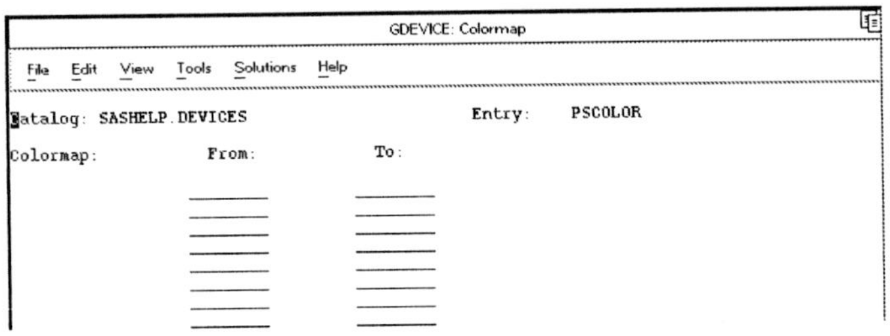

Metagraphics window

This window is used by all drivers that support multiple color spaces, for example, RGB or CMYK. It is also used if the device entry is a Metagraphics (user-written) driver. Metagraphics drivers are created when an Institute-supplied device entry cannot be adapted to support your graphics device. For information about Metagraphics drivers, contact Technical Support.

Do not alter the fields in the Metagraphics window unless you are changing the color scheme (colortype), or building a Metagraphics driver.

Figure 31.7 The Metagraphics Window

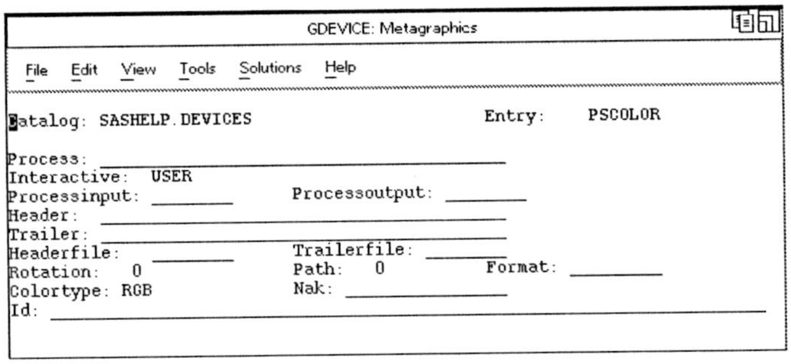

Gprolog window

This window enables you to specify one or more hexadecimal strings that are sent to the device just before graphics commands are sent. Additional commands can be sent with the PREGPROLOG= and POSTGPROLOG= graphics options. See Chapter 8, "Graphics Options and Device Parameters Dictionary," on page 261 for details.

Figure 31.8 The Gprolog Window (partial view)

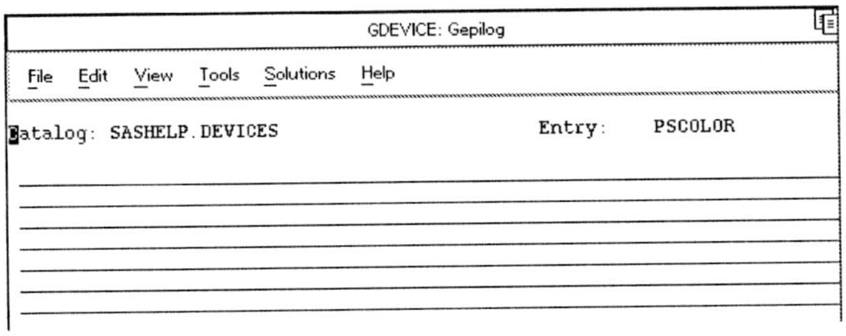

Gepilog window

This window enables you to specify one or more hexadecimal strings that are sent to the device just after graphics commands are sent. Additional commands can be sent with the PREGEPILOG= and POSTGEPILOG= graphics options. See Chapter 8, "Graphics Options and Device Parameters Dictionary," on page 261 for details.

Figure 31.9 The Gepilog Window (partial view)

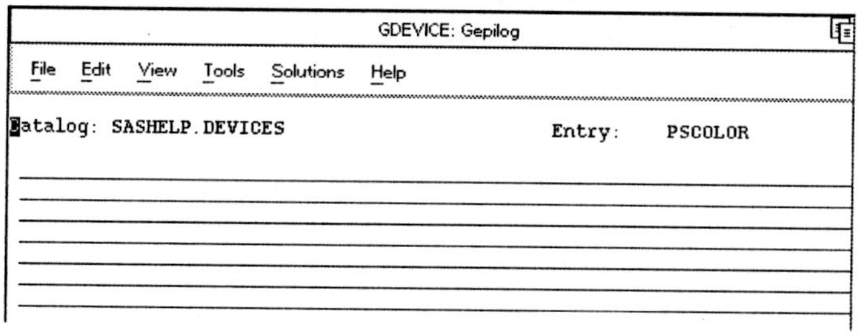

Gstart window

This window enables you to specify one or more hexadecimal strings that are placed at the beginning of each record of graphics data.

Figure 31.10 The Gstart Window (partial view)

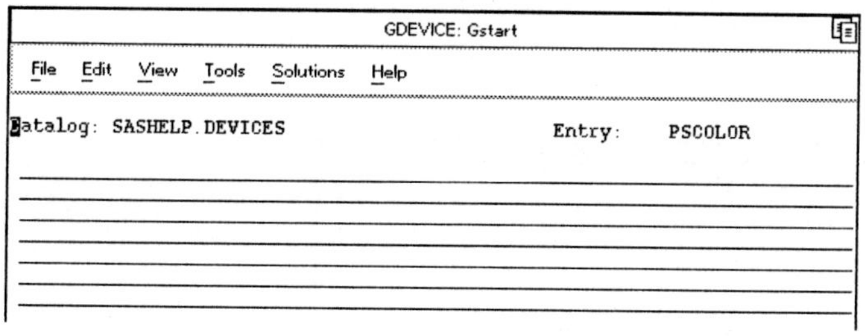

Gend window

This window enables you to specify one or more hexadecimal strings that are placed at the end of each record of graphics data.

Figure 31.11 The Gend Window (partial view)

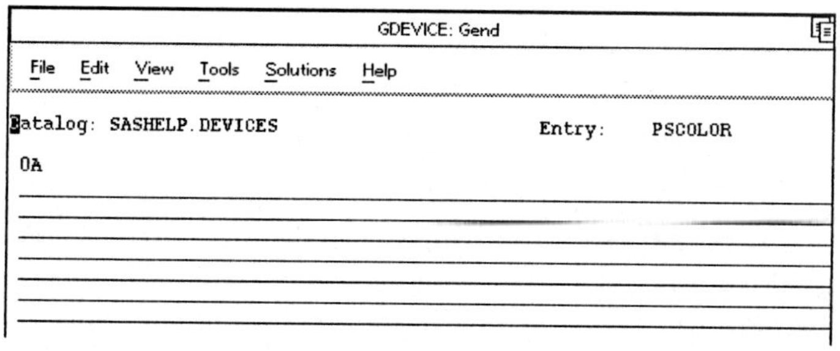

Host File Options window

This window controls the output destination and formatting of the data stream produced by the driver. (Most of these values can also be specified with the GOPTIONS statement and with the FILENAME statement. See also “Exporting SAS/GRAPH Output with Program Statements” on page 62.)

Figure 31.12 The Host File Options Window

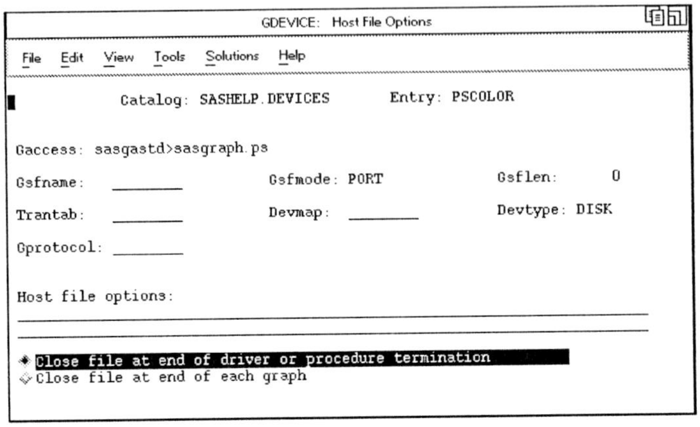

Host Commands window

This window stores the host commands issued at driver initialization, before and after each graph is produced, and at driver termination. These commands are typically used to send graphics output to a hardcopy device such as a printer or a plotter.

Figure 31.13 The Host Commands Window

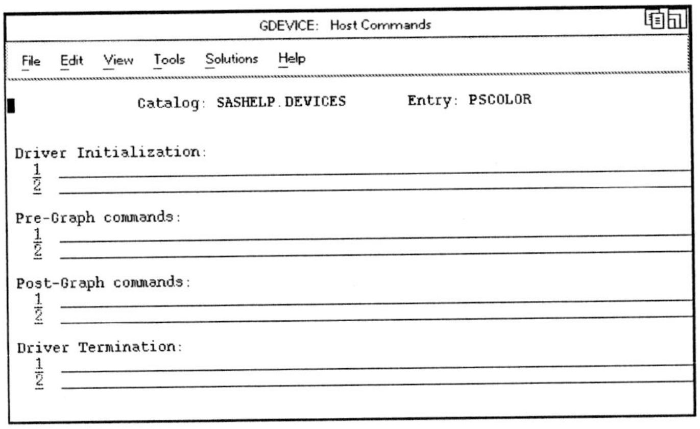

Creating or Modifying Device Entries

In order to add, modify, or delete device entries, you must have write access to the catalog. On multi-user systems, the SAS support consultant is usually the only person who has write access to the SASHELP.DEVICES catalog and can make any changes. Therefore, when creating new entries or modifying existing ones, individual users usually work in a personal catalog. Be sure the catalog in which you store new or modified device entries is named DEVICES.

To use a device entry stored in a personal catalog, you must assign the GDEVICE*n* libref to the library that contains the device catalog. See “About Device Catalogs” on page 916.

It is a good idea to give a new or modified device entry a name that is different from the original. Then, if you want to use the original device, SAS/GRAPH can find that device when it searches the device catalogs. Remember that SAS/GRAPH searches the GDEVICE*n* libraries *before* it searches SASHELP.DEVICES and uses the first device it finds whose name matches the one you have specified. (See "Search Order of Device Catalogs" on page 917.)

For example, suppose there is a customized copy of PSCOLOR in your GDEVICE0.DEVICES catalog as well as the original in SASHELP.DEVICES. If you specify DEV=PSCOLOR and if the libref GDEVICE0 is assigned, SAS/GRAPH will search GDEVICE0.DEVICES first and use the copy of PSCOLOR stored there. Unless you cancel the GDEVICE0 libref, SAS/GRAPH will never find the original in SASHELP.DEVICES.

Creating a New Device Entry

Typically you create a new device entry by copying an existing device and modifying its parameters to suit your needs. You can copy and modify a device entry in two ways:

- Use the DIR command on the command line to open the DIRECTORY window, and then use the COPY command to make a copy of an existing device entry. Then edit the new entry and modify its parameters. The existing device entry can be from any catalog. (See the SAS Help facility for information on using GDEVICE windows and commands.)
- In program mode, use the COPY statement to make a copy of the device entry and use the MODIFY statement to change the parameters (see Example 1 on page 936).

If you want to start with a blank device entry and fill in values for the parameters, use the EDIT command from the DIRECTORY window or use the ADD statement with program mode PROC GDEVICE.

With either method, you must provide values for the parameters listed in "Required Arguments" on page 923. If you copy and modify an existing entry, all the required parameters will already have values. If you create a new entry with GDEVICE windows, you are prompted to fill in the appropriate fields.

Note: When you change a field in an Institute-supplied device entry (either the original device entry in SASHELP.DEVICES or a copy), SAS/GRAPH software asks whether you really want to change the entry. Answer Y to change the entry or N to cancel the operation. △

Modifying an Existing Device Entry

Typically, you modify an existing device entry when you want to change the device parameters permanently in order to customize a device entry. The process is similar to creating a new entry in that you usually begin by copying the entry you want to modify into your personal catalog and making the changes there. See Example 1 on page 936 for an example of creating a custom device entry.

Changing Device Parameters Temporarily

You can change some device parameters temporarily by overriding their settings with graphics options in a GOPTIONS statement. In this case, the settings remain in effect until you change them or end your SAS session. For details, see "Overriding Device Parameters Temporarily" on page 46.

Examples

The following examples illustrate major features of the GDEVICE procedure.

Example 1: Creating a Custom Device Entry with Program Statements

Procedure features:
COPY statement
MODIFY statement

Other features:
PROC GTESTIT

Sample library member: GDVCSTOM

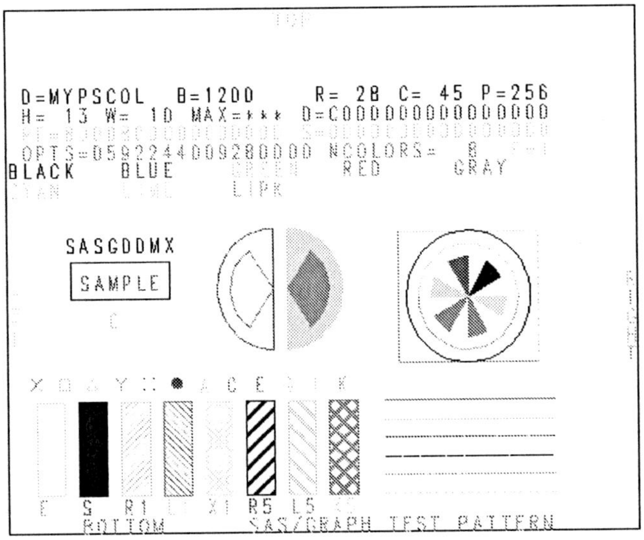

This example shows how to use GDEVICE procedure statements to modify a device entry by copying the original entry into a personal catalog and changing the device parameters. You can submit these statements one at a time or together.

This example permanently changes the default colors list for the PSCOLOR device entry. The contents of the original PSCOLOR entry are shown in Output 31.1. The new device entry is illustrated in the PROC GTESTIT output above.

Assign the libref GDEVICE0. The LIBNAME statement assigns the libref to the aggregate file storage location that contains (or will contain) the DEVICES catalog.

```
libname gdevice0 'SAS-data-library';
```

Start the GDEVICE procedure. NOFS causes GDEVICE to use program mode. CATALOG= assigns GDEVICE0.DEVICES as the current catalog. If the DEVICES catalog does not already exist in the library, it is automatically created.

```
proc gdevice nofs catalog=gdevice0.devices;
```

Copy the original device entry from SASHELP.DEVICES to the current catalog. NEWNAME= specifies a name for the copy of PSCOLOR that is placed in GDEVICE0.DEVICES. The name of a catalog entry cannot exceed eight characters.

```
copy pscolor from=sashelp.devices newname=mypscol;
```

Modify the new entry. DESCRIPTION= specifies a new device description that appears in the catalog listing. COLORS= defines a new colors list.

```
   modify mypscol
     description='PSCOLOR with new colors list'
     colors=(black blue green red gray cyan
            lime lipk);
```

Exit the procedure.

```
quit;
```

Test the new device entry. The TARGET= graphics option specifies the new device. Since GDEVICE0 is already defined, SAS/GRAPH looks first in that catalog for the specified device entry. The GTESTIT procedure produces a test picture that show the new colors list and a listing in the LOG.

```
goptions target=mypscol;
proc gtestit pic=1;
run;
```

CHAPTER 32

The GFONT Procedure

Overview

The GFONT procedure displays new or existing fonts and creates user-generated fonts for use in SAS/GRAPH programs. These fonts can contain standard Roman alphabet characters, foreign language characters, symbols, logos, or figures.

The GFONT procedure

- displays SAS/GRAPH software fonts
- displays fonts that were previously generated with the GFONT procedure (user-generated fonts)
- displays hardware font that are available on your device and have a corresponding Chartype value
- displays the character codes or hexadecimal values that are associated with the characters in a font
- creates stroked fonts or polygon fonts.

Each of these activities has its own requirements, its own process, and its own options (although some options are valid for either process). In this chapter, each topic to which this distinction applies is divided into two sections: "Displaying Fonts" and "Creating Fonts."

About Displaying Fonts

You can use the GFONT procedure to display a font when you want to do one of the following:

- review the characters that are available in Institute-supplied fonts, hardware fonts, or user-generated fonts
- see the character codes or the hexadecimal values that are associated with the characters in a font.

When you display a font, you can modify the color and height of displayed font characters, draw reference lines around the characters, or display the associated character codes or hexadecimal values. See Example 1 on page 962.

About Creating Fonts

You can use the GFONT procedure to create and store fonts of your own design. The GFONT procedure is not limited to creating alphabet fonts. You can use it to create and store any series of figures that you can draw using X and Y coordinates or that you can digitize. The characters or figures in a font can be displayed with any SAS/GRAPH statement or option that allows for font specification and a text string (for example, a TITLE statement). See “Creating a Font” on page 951 for details.

Concepts

About Fonts

Some specialized terms are associated with font characteristics. The *capline* of a font is the highest point of a normal uppercase letter. The *baseline* is the line upon which the characters rest. The *font maximum* is the highest vertical coordinate in a font. The *font minimum* is the lowest vertical coordinate in a font. Figure 32.1 on page 940 illustrates these GFONT procedure terms:

Figure 32.1 Parts of a Font

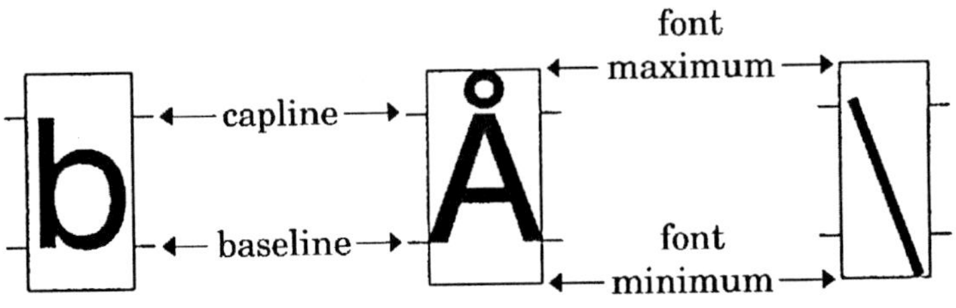

Specialized terms also exist for types of fonts. The term *uniform font* refers to a font in which all of the characters occupy exactly the same amount of space, even though the characters themselves are different sizes. Each character in a uniform font is placed in the center of its space, and a fixed amount of space is added between characters. A *proportional font* is a font in which each character occupies a space that is proportional to its actual width (for example, m occupies more space than i). The characters in a *stroked font* are drawn with discrete line segments or circular arcs. Figure 32.2 on page 941 illustrates a stroked font with several characters from the Simplex font.

Figure 32.2 Characters from a Stroked Font

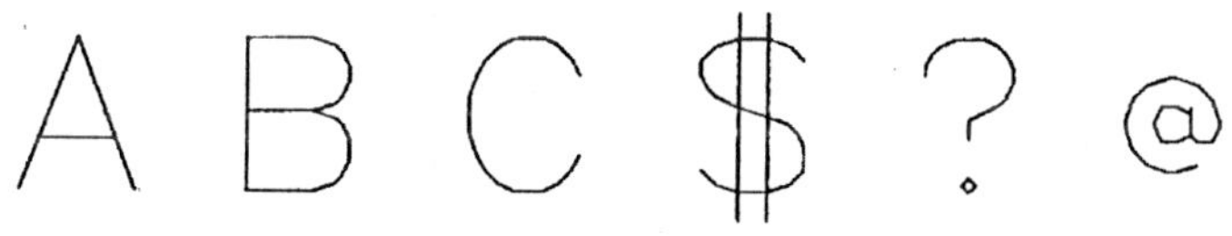

Figure 32.3 on page 941 illustrates two types of *polygon fonts*: filled (CENTBI) and outline (CENTBIE). A *filled font* is a polygon font in which the areas between the lines are solid. An *outline font* is a polygon font in which the areas are empty.

Figure 32.3 Filled and Outline Characters from Polygon Fonts

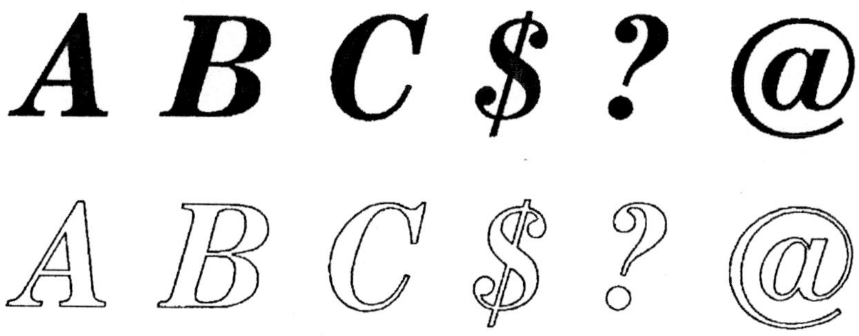

All font characters, regardless of whether they are stroked or polygon, are drawn with line segments. In the GFONT procedure, the term *line segment* means a continuous line that can change direction. For example, the letter C in Figure 32.2 on page 941 is drawn with one line segment, while the letter A can be drawn with two.

Polygon characters can also be drawn with one or more line segments. In a polygon font, one character can be made up of a single polygon, multiple polygons, or polygons with holes. For example, the letter C in Figure 32.3 on page 941 is a single polygon with one line segment. The question mark (?) is made up of two polygons, each drawn with a separate line segment. The letter A is one polygon with a hole in it. It is drawn with one line segment that is broken to form the outer boundary of the figure and the boundary of the hole.

About the Libref GFONTO

The GFONT procedure stores user-generated fonts in the location that is associated with the libref GFONTO. Therefore, before you create a font or display a user-generated font, you must submit a LIBNAME statement that associates the libref GFONTO with the location where the font is to be stored, as follows:

```
libname gfont0 'SAS-data-library';
```

Since the GFONT0 library is the first place that SAS/GRAPH software looks for fonts, you should always assign that libref to the library that contains your personal fonts. If for some reason you have personal fonts in more than one SAS data library, assign them librefs in the sequence GFONT0, GFONT1, GFONT2, and so forth. The search for entries terminates if there is a break in the sequence; the catalog GFONT1.FONTS is not checked if the libref GFONT0 is undefined. If the libref GFONT0 is not defined, by default SAS/GRAPH software begins searching for fonts in SASHELP.FONTS.

To cancel or redefine the libref GFONT*n*, submit the following statement:

```
goptions reset=all fcache=0;
```

Note that when you specify RESET=ALL, all graphics options are reset to their default values. Once you have cleared the font cache, you can redefine the libref with another LIBNAME statement.

Procedure Syntax

Requirements: A font name is required. To display a font, include NOBUILD. To create a font, include DATA=.

Global statements: FOOTNOTE, TITLE

Reminder: The procedure can include the SAS/GRAPH NOTE statement.

Supports: Output Delivery System (ODS)

PROC GFONT NAME=*font-name* | *hardware-font-name*
mode
<*display-option(s)*>
<*creation-option(s)*>;

PROC GFONT Statement

The PROC GFONT statement can either create user-defined fonts or display existing software fonts. Therefore, it names the font to be created or displayed. If the procedure creates a font it names the input data set. Optionally, the procedure modifies the design and appearance of the fonts that you create or display, and specifies a destination catalog for graphics output.

Syntax

PROC GFONT NAME=*font-namehardware-font-name*
mode
<*display-option(s)*>
<*creation-option(s)*>;

- *mode* must be one of the following:

  DATA=*font-data-sethardware-font-name*

  NOBUILD

- *display-option(s)* can be one or more of the following:

  CTEXT=*text-color*
  GOUT=*<libref.>output-catalog*
  HEIGHT=*character-height<units>*
  NOKEYMAP
  NOROMAN
  NOROMHEX
  REFCOL=*reference-line-color*
  REFLINES
  ROMCOL=*code-color*
  ROMFONT=*font*
  ROMHEX
  ROMHT=*height<units>*
  SHOWALL
  SHOWROMAN

- *creation-option(s)* can be one or more of the following:

  BASELINE=*y*
  CAPLINE=*y*
  CHARSPACETYPE=DATA | FIXED | NONE | UNIFORM
  CODELEN=1 | 2
  FILLED
  KERNDATA=*kern-data-set*
  MWIDTH=*character-width*
  NODISPLAY
  NOKEYMAP
  RESOL=1...4
  ROMHEX
  SHOWROMAN
  SPACEDATA=*space-data-set*
  UNIFORM

For more detail on using the GFONT syntax, see "Displaying Fonts: Required Arguments, Options" on page 943 and "Creating Fonts: Required Arguments, Options "on page 946.

Displaying Fonts: Required Arguments, Options

Required Arguments for Displaying Fonts

NAME=*font-name* | *hardware-font-name*
N=*font-name* | *hardware-font-name*

specifies the font to be displayed. *Font-name* can be the name of a SAS software font or a font you previously created. Any hardware font that is available on your device and has a corresponding Chartype value may be used. The *hardware-font-name* must be enclosed in quotes.

See also: "Specifying Alternative Hardware Fonts" on page 80 , "Chartype window" on page 931, and Chapter 5, "SAS/GRAPH Fonts," on page 75.

NOBUILD
NB
specifies that the GFONT procedure is to display an existing font. The NOBUILD argument tells the procedure that no font is being generated and not to look for an input data set.

Featured in: Example 1 on page 962.

To display a user-generated font, you must define libref GFONT0. See "About the Libref GFONT0" on page 941.

Options for Displaying Fonts

Options that can be used for either font display or font creation are described here and in "Options for Creating Fonts" on page 947.

Options that display a font can be used when you create a font if you also display it (that is, the NODISPLAY option is not used in the PROC GFONT statement). However, none of the display options affect the design and appearance of the stored font except the NOKEYMAP, SHOWROMAN, and ROMHEX options.

When the syntax of an option includes *units*, use one of these:

CELLS	character cells
CM	centimeters
IN	inches
PCT	percentage of the graphics output area
PT	points

If you omit *units*, a unit specification is searched for in this order:

1 the value of GUNIT= in a GOPTIONS statement

2 the default unit, CELLS.

CTEXT=*text-color*
CT=*text-color*
specifies a color for the body of the characters. If you do not use the CTEXT= option, a color specification is searched for in the following order:

1 the CTEXT= option in a GOPTIONS statement

2 the default, the first color in the colors list.

The CTEXT= value is not stored as part of the font.

Featured in: Example 2 on page 964.

GOUT=*<libref.>output-catalog*
specifies the SAS catalog in which to save the graphics output produced by the display of the font. The GOUT option is ignored if you use the NODISPLAY option in the PROC GFONT statement. You can use the GREPLAY procedure to view the output that is stored in the catalog. If you omit the libref, SAS/GRAPH looks for the catalog in the temporary library called WORK and creates the catalog if it does not exist.

See also: "Storing Graphics Output in SAS Catalogs" on page 53.

HEIGHT=*character-height<units>*

H=*character-height<units>*

specifies the height of the font characters in number of units, *n*. Height is measured from the minimum font measurement to the capline. By default, HEIGHT=2.

Featured in: Example 1 on page 962.

NOKEYMAP

specifies that the current key map is ignored when displaying the font and its character codes or hexadecimal values. If you do not use the NOKEYMAP option when you display a font, the current key map remains in effect. If any characters in the font are not available through the current key map, they are not displayed and a warning is issued in the SAS log. This happens when the key map is asymmetrical, that is, not all characters in the font are mapped into the current key map.

Displaying a font using the NOKEYMAP option enables you to see all of the characters in the font, including those that are not mapped into your current key map. Note that only those characters that are mapped into your current key map are available (that is, those that are displayed when you display the font without the NOKEYMAP option).

See also: Chapter 5, "SAS/GRAPH Fonts," on page 75, Chapter 34, "The GKEYMAP Procedure," on page 983, and theNOKEYMAP option on page 949 for Creating Fonts.

NOROMAN
NR

turns off the automatic display of character codes that are produced when you use the SHOWROMAN option during font creation.

NOROMHEX
NOHEX

turns off the automatic display of hexadecimal values that are produced when you use the ROMHEX option during font creation.

REFCOL=*reference-line-color*

specifies a color for reference lines. By default, the first color in the colors list is used.

REFLINES

draws reference lines around each displayed character. Vertical reference lines show the width of the character. Horizontal reference lines show the font maximum and the font minimum, as well as the baseline and the capline. See Figure 32.1 on page 940 for an illustration of the placement of reference lines.

ROMCOL=*code-color*
RC=*code-color*

specifies the color of the character codes or hexadecimal values that are displayed with the SHOWROMAN and ROMHEX options. If you do not use the ROMCOL= option, a color specification is searched for in the following order:

1 the CTEXT= option in a GOPTIONS statement

2 the default, the first color in the colors list.

The ROMCOL= value is not stored as part of the font.

Featured in: Example 1 on page 962.

ROMFONT=*font*
RF=*font*

specifies the font for character codes and hexadecimal values that are displayed by the SHOWROMAN and ROMHEX options. If you do not use the ROMFONT= option, a font specification is searched for in the following order:

1 the FTEXT= option in a GOPTIONS statement

2 the default hardware font, NONE.

Featured in: Example 1 on page 962.

ROMHEX
HEX
displays hexadecimal values below the font characters. If you use both the ROMHEX and SHOWROMAN options, both the character codes and the hexadecimal values are displayed. You also can use the ROMHEX option when you create a font.

See also: the ROMHEX option on page 950.

ROMHT=*height<units>*
RH=*height<units >*
specifies the height of the character codes and the hexadecimal values that are displayed with the SHOWROMAN and ROMHEX options in number of units, *n*. If you do not use the ROMHT= option, a height specification is searched for in the following order:

1 the HTEXT= option in a GOPTIONS statement

2 the default, ROMHT=1.

Featured in: Example 1 on page 962.

SHOWALL
displays the font with a space for every possible character position whether or not a font character exists for that position. The characters that are displayed are those available under your current key map, unless you use the NOKEYMAP option. The SHOWALL option usually is used in conjunction with the ROMHEX option, in which case all possible hexadecimal values are displayed. If, under your current key map, a font character is available for a position, it displays above the hexadecimal value. If no character is available for a position, the space above the hexadecimal value is blank. You can use the SHOWALL option to show where undefined character positions fall in the font.

SHOWROMAN
SR
displays character codes below the font characters even if they are not displayed automatically with the font. If you use both the SHOWROMAN and ROMHEX options, both the character codes and the hexadecimal values are displayed. You can also use the SHOWROMAN option when you create a font.

See also: "About Creating Fonts" on page 940

Featured in: Example 1 on page 962.

Details

To display a font, you must specify the name of the font with the NAME= argument and include the NOBUILD argument. For example, to display the Weather font with character codes that are displayed in the Swiss font, use the following statement:

```
proc gfont name=weather nobuild romfont=swiss;
```

Creating Fonts: Required Arguments, Options

Required Arguments for Creating Fonts

NAME=*font-name*
N=*font-name*

assigns a name to the font that you create. *Font-name* is the name of a catalog entry and must be a valid SAS name of no more than eight characters. Do not use the name of an Institute-supplied font or NONE for the name of a font.

Featured in: Example 2 on page 964.

DATA=*font-data-set*

specifies the SAS data set that the GFONT procedure uses to build the font. The data set must be sorted by the variables CHAR and SEGMENT. By default, the procedure uses the most recently created data set as the font data set.

See also: "SAS Data Sets" on page 29.

Featured in: Example 2 on page 964.

When you create a font, you must define the libref GFONT0. See "About the Libref GFONT0" on page 941 for details.

Note: If a user-generated font has the same name as an Institute-supplied font and if the libref GFONT0 has been defined, the user-generated font is used because GFONT0 is searched first. △

Options for Creating Fonts

Options that can be used for either font display or font creation are described here and in "Options for Displaying Fonts" on page 944.

Options that display a font can be used when you create a font if you also display it (that is, the NODISPLAY option is not used in the PROC GFONT statement). However, none of the display options affect the design and appearance of the stored font except the NOKEYMAP, SHOWROMAN, and ROMHEX options.

When the syntax of an option includes *units*, use one of these:

CELLS	character cells
CM	centimeters
IN	inches
PCT	percentage of the graphics output area
PT	points

If you omit *units*, a unit specification is searched for in this order:

1 the value of GUNIT= in a GOPTIONS statement

2 the default unit, CELLS.

BASELINE=*y*
B=*y*

specifies the vertical coordinate in the font data set that is the baseline of the characters. The baseline is the line upon which the letters rest. If you do not use the BASELINE= option, the GFONT procedure uses the lowest vertical coordinate of the first character in the font data set.

CAPLINE=*y*
C=*y*

specifies the vertical coordinate in the font data set that is the capline of the characters. The capline is the highest point of normal Roman capitals. If you do not use the CAPLINE= option, the GFONT procedure uses the highest vertical coordinate in the font data set, in which case the capline and the font maximum are the same. See Figure 32.1 on page 940 for an illustration of capline and font maximum.

If you use the CAPLINE= option, then when the GFONT procedure calculates the height of a character, any parts of the character that project above the capline are ignored in the calculation.

You can use this option to prevent an accented capital like A from being shortened to accommodate the accent. For example, if you do not use the CAPLINE= option, the capline and the font maximum are the same and the A is shortened to make room for the accent below the capline. However, if CAPLINE= is used, the top of the letter A is at the capline, and the accent is drawn above the capline and below the font maximum.

CHARSPACETYPE=DATA | FIXED | NONE | UNIFORM
CSP=DATA | FIXED | NONE | UNIFORM

specifies the type of intercharacter spacing. The following are valid values:

DATA

specifies that the first observation for each character sets the width of that character. When CHARSPACETYPE=DATA, the PTYPE variable is required, and the observation that specifies the width of the character must have a PTYPE value of W. See "The Font Data Set" on page 951 for details on the PTYPE variable.

Intercharacter spacing is included in the character's width. For example, if the first observation for the letter A specifies a character width of 10 units and the A itself occupies only 8 units, the remaining 2 units serve as intercharacter spacing.

Note: The character can extend beyond the width that you specified in the first observation if desired. △

FIXED

adds a fixed amount of space between characters based on the font size. The width of the individual character is determined by the data that generate the character.

NONE

specifies that no space is added between characters. The width of the individual character is determined by the data that generate the character. This type of spacing is useful for script fonts in which the characters should appear connected.

UNIFORM

specifies that the amount of space that is used for each character is uniform rather than proportional. This means that each character occupies the same amount of space. For example, in uniform spacing the letters m and i occupy the same amount of space, whereas in proportional spacing m occupies more space than i. In uniform spacing, the character is always centered in the space and a fixed space is added between characters.

When UNIFORM is specified, the amount of space that is used for each character is one of the following:

- by default, the width of the widest character in the font.
- the width specified by the MWIDTH= option. See the MIDWIDTH= option on page 949 for details.

Specifying CHARSPACETYPE=UNIFORM is the same as using the UNIFORM option.

Note: By default, CHARSPACETYPE=FIXED. △

CODELEN=1 | 2

specifies the length in bytes of the CHAR variable. By default, CODELEN=1. To specify double-byte character sets for languages such as Chinese, Japanese, or Korean, use CODELEN=2. If you specify a double-byte character set, you cannot specify kerning or space adjustment with the KERNDATA= or SPACEDATA= options.

FILLED
F

specifies that the characters in a user-generated polygon font are filled.

Featured in: Example 2 on page 964.

KERNDATA=*kern-data-set*
KERN=*kern-data-set*

specifies the SAS data set that contains kerning information. When the KERNDATA= option is used during font creation, the data that are contained in the kern data set are applied to the font and stored with it. You cannot specify kerning for a double-byte character set that is created by using the option CODELEN=2.

See also: "The Kern Data Set" on page 958.

MWIDTH=*character-width*

specifies the width of a character in a uniform font, where *character-width* is the number of font units. The MWIDTH= option is only valid when you specify uniform spacing by using the UNIFORM option or when you specify CHARSPACETYPE=UNIFORM. If you do not use MWIDTH=, the default is the width of the widest character in the font (usually the letter m).

Typically, you use the MWIDTH= option to tighten the spacing between characters. To do this, specify a smaller value (narrower width) for *character-width*. Figure 32.4 on page 949 shows the effect of decreasing the space that is allowed for uniformly spaced characters.

Figure 32.4 Using the MWIDTH= Option to Modify Spacing

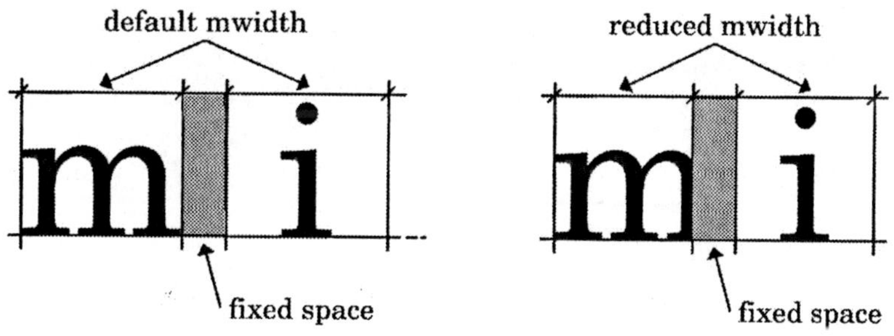

See also: the CHARSPACETYPE= option on page 948 and the UNIFORM option on page 951.

NODISPLAY
ND

specifies that the GFONT procedure is not to display the font that it is creating.

NOKEYMAP

specifies that the current key map is ignored when you generate and use the font that is being created, and that the character codes you enter are not mapped in any way before being displayed. As a result, the generated font is *never* affected by any setting of the KEYMAP= graphics option.

CAUTION:

Fonts generated with the NOKEYMAP option are never affected by any setting of the KEYMAP= graphics option. △

By default, the NOKEYMAP option is *not* used; in which case, when you build a font, the current key map is applied to the values in the CHAR variable.

However, your current key map may not be symmetrical; that is, two or more input character codes may be mapped to the same output character. For example, if A is mapped to B, then both A and B map to B, but nothing maps to A. In this case, more than one code in your input data set can map to the same character in the resulting font. For example, if A and B are values of CHAR, both map to B. If this happens, a message that indicates the problem characters is displayed in the SAS log. To solve this problem, you can do one of the following:

- change the character code of one of the characters
- eliminate one of the characters
- use the NOKEYMAP option.

When you use the NOKEYMAP option, your font works correctly only if the end user's host or controller encoding is the same as the encoding used to create the input data set.

See also: the NOKEYMAP option on page 945 for Displaying Fonts and Chapter 34, "The GKEYMAP Procedure," on page 983.

RESOL=1...4
R=1...4

controls the resolution of the fonts by specifying the number of bytes (1 through 4) for storing coordinates in the font. The GFONT procedure provides three resolution levels (RESOL=3 produces the same resolution level as RESOL=4). By default, RESOL=1.

The higher the number, the closer together the points that define the character can be spaced. A high value specifies a denser set of points for each character so that the characters approximate smooth curved lines at very large sizes. RESOL=2 works well for most applications; RESOL=3 or 4 may be too dense to be practical.

The table below shows the resolution number and the maximum number of distinct points that can be defined horizontally or vertically.

Resolution	Number of Distinct Points
2	32,766
3	2,147,483,646
4	2,147,483,646

Featured in: Example 2 on page 964.

ROMHEX
HEX

specifies that hexadecimal values display automatically below the font characters when the GFONT procedure displays the font. If you use the ROMHEX option for a font that you create, you can later use the NOROMHEX option to suppress display of the hexadecimal values.

See also: the SHOWROMAN option on page 950, the ROMHEX option on page 946 for Displaying Fonts, and the NOROMHEX option on page 945.

SHOWROMAN
SR

specifies that character codes display automatically below the font characters when the GFONT procedure displays the font. If you use the SHOWROMAN option for a font you create, you can later use the NOROMAN option to suppress display of the character codes.

See also: the ROMHEX option on page 946, the SHOWROMAN option for Displaying Fonts, and the NOROMAN option on page 945.

SPACEDATA=*space-data-set*
SPACE=*space-data-set*

specifies the SAS data set that contains font spacing information. When you use the SPACEDATA= option during font creation, the data contained in the space data set are applied to the font and stored with it. You cannot specify space adjustment for a double-byte character set that is created by using the option CODELEN=2.

See also: "The Space Data Set" on page 960.

UNIFORM
U

specifies that characters are spaced uniformly rather than proportionately. Using the UNIFORM option is the same as specifying CHARSPACETYPE=UNIFORM.

See also: the CHARSPACETYPE= option on page 948 and the MWIDTH= option on page 949.

Creating a Font

To create a font, you must create a data set that contains font information. Typically, you use a DATA step to create a SAS data set from which the GFONT procedure generates the font. The data set is referred to as the *font data set* and you can specify it with the DATA= argument.

To produce the font, invoke the GFONT procedure and specify the data set that contains the font information. In addition you can include options to modify the design and appearance of the font. For example, the following statement uses the data set FONTDATA to generate the font MYLOGO:

```
proc gfont data=fontdata name=mylogo;
```

For a demonstration of the font creation process, see Example 2 on page 964.

The GFONT procedure uses three types of data sets: the font data set, the kern data set, and the space data set. Each type of data set must contain certain variables and meet certain requirements. The following sections explain what each data set contains, how it is built, and what the requirements of the variables are.

The Font Data Set

The font data set consists of a series of observations that include the horizontal and vertical coordinate values and line segment numbers that the GFONT procedure uses to generate each character. In addition, each observation must include a character code that is associated with the font character and is used to specify the font character in a text string. The font data set also determines whether the font is stroked or polygon. A font data set that generates a polygon font produces an outline font by default. You can use the FILLED option with the same data set to generate a filled font.

The variables in the font data set must be assigned certain names and types. The table below summarizes the characteristics of the variables which are described further in "Font Data Set Variables" on page 952.

Table 32.1 Font Data Set Variables

Variable	Description	Type	Length	Valid Values	With Stroked Fonts	With Polygon Fonts
CHAR	the character code associated with the font character	character	1 or 2	keyboard characters or hexadecimal values	required	required
LP	the type of line segment being drawn, either a line or a polygon	character	1	L or P	optional	required
PTYPE	the type of data in the observation	character	1	V or C or W	optional	optional
SEGMENT	the number of the line segment or polygon being drawn	numeric		number	required	required
X	the horizontal coordinate	numeric		number	required	required
Y	the vertical coordinate	numeric		number	required	required

Font Data Set Variables

CHAR
provides a code for the character or figure that you are creating. CHAR is a character variable with a length of 1 or 2 and is required for all fonts.

CAUTION:
Using reserved or undefined hexadecimal codes as CHAR values may require the use of the NOKEYMAP option. △

The CHAR variable takes any character as its value, including characters that you can enter from your keyboard and hexadecimal values from '00'x to 'FF'x. (If you use hexadecimal values as CHAR values, your font may not work correctly under a key map that is different from the one under which the font was created because positions that are not defined in one key map may be defined in another.)

When you specify the code character in a text string, the associated font character is drawn. For example, if you create a Roman alphabet font, typically the characters you specify for CHAR are keyboard characters that match the character in the font. All of the observations that build the letter A have a CHAR value of A. When you specify 'A' in a text string this produces A in the output.

However, if you build a symbol font, the symbols may not have corresponding keyboard characters. In that case, you select a character or hexadecimal value to represent each symbol in the font and assign it to CHAR. For example, in the Special font, the letter G is assigned as the code for the fleur-de-lis symbol. When you specify the code in a text string, the associated symbol displays.

If the CODELEN= option is set to 2, the values for CHAR represent two characters, such as AA, or a four-digit hexadecimal value, such as '00A5'x.

LP

tells the GFONT procedure whether the coordinates of each segment form a line or a polygon. LP is a character variable with a length of 1. It is required for polygon fonts but optional for stroked fonts. You can assign the LP variable either of the following values:

L lines

P polygons.

Every group of line segments with an LP value of P is designated as a polygon; if the observations do not draw a completely closed figure, the program closes the figure automatically. For example, the following observations do not contain an LP variable. They produce a shape like the one in Figure 32.5 on page 953.

OBS	CHAR	SEG	X	Y
1	b	1	1	1
2	b	1	1	3
3	b	1	3	3
4	b	1	3	1

Figure 32.5 Using a LP Value of Line

LP (continued)

An LP variable with a value of P for all observations added to the data set produces a complete box like the one in Figure 32.6 on page 954.

OBS	CHAR	SEG	X	Y	LP
1	b	1	1	1	P
2	b	1	1	3	P
3	b	1	3	3	P
4	b	1	3	1	P

Figure 32.6 Using a LP Value of Polygon

LP (continued)

The LP variable allows you to mix lines and polygons when you create characters in a font. For example, the following observations produce the single figure that is composed of a polygon and a line segment, as shown in Figure 32.7 on page 954:

OBS	CHAR	SEG	X	Y	LP
1	b	1	1	1	P
2	b	1	1	3	P
3	b	1	3	3	P
4	b	1	3	1	P
5	b	2	0	0	L
6	b	2	2	4	L
7	b	2	4	0	L

Figure 32.7 Mixing LP Values of Line and Polygon

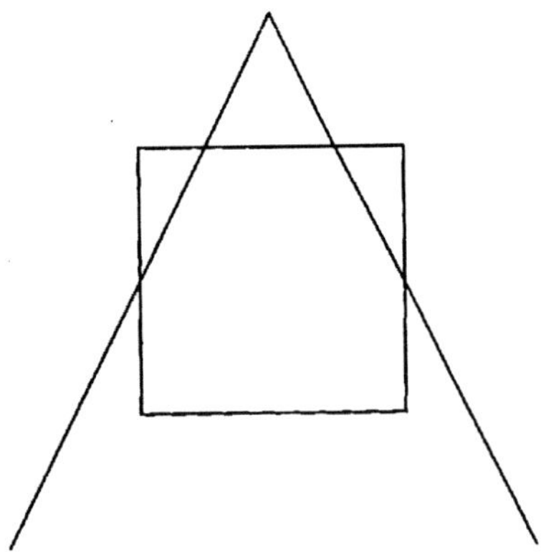

PTYPE

tells the GFONT procedure what type of data are in the observation. PTYPE is a character variable of length 1 that is optional for both stroked and polygon fonts. For each observation, the PTYPE variable assigns a characteristic to the point that is determined by the X and Y values. You can assign the PTYPE variable any of the following values:

V
: normal point in the line segment

C
: center of a circular arc joining two V points

W
: width value for CHARSPACETYPE=DATA.

If the GFONT procedure encounters the sequence V-C-V in consecutive observations, it draws an arc that connects the two V points and has its center at the C point. If a circle cannot be centered at C and pass through both V points, the results are unpredictable. Arcs are limited to 106 degrees or less.

If you specify an observation with a PTYPE value of W, it must always be the first observation for a character. Instead of providing digitizing data to the procedure, the observation gives the minimum and maximum X values for the character. Note that in this case, the Y variable observation actually contains the maximum X value. Usually, these values include a little extra space for intercharacter spacing. Use a PTYPE of W only if you have specified CHARSPACETYPE=DATA; otherwise, the points are ignored. For more information on intercharacter spacing, see the description of the CHARSPACETYPE= option.

If you do not specify a PTYPE variable in the font data set, all points are assumed to be V-type points.

The following observations illustrate how the PTYPE variable is used to draw an arc similar to Figure 32.8 on page 956. (After the figure was generated, a grid was overlaid on it to show the location of the points.) A comment following each observation explains its function.

OBS	CHAR	SEG	X	Y	LP	PTYPE	Comment
1	a	1	40	60	P	W	define width of character as 20 font units, which is the number of units from left margin, 40, to right margin, 60
2	a	1	45	40	P	V	start line segment at position 45,40
3	a	1	45	50	P	V	draw a line to position 45,50, which is start point of arc

OBS	CHAR	SEG	X	Y	LP	PTYPE	Comment
4	a	1	45	40	P	C	draw an arc whose center is at 45,40
5	a	1	55	40	P	V	finish drawing the arc at 55,40

Figure 32.8 Using the PTYPE Variable to Create an Arc

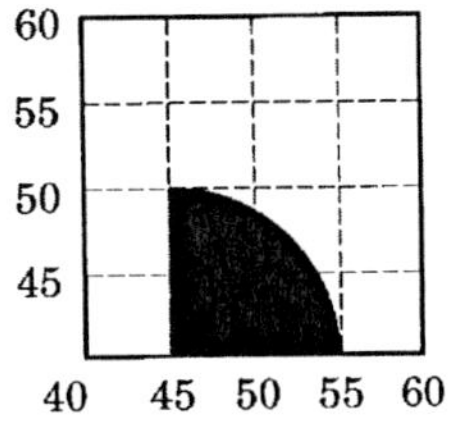

PTYPE (continued)

Note the following:

- Three observations are required to draw the arc: observation 3 and observation 5 denote the start point and endpoint of the arc, respectively, and observation 4 locates the center of the arc.
- The figure is closed because the line segments have an LP value of P (polygon).
- The font that contains the figure of the arc was generated with a PROC GFONT statement like the following:

```
proc gfont data=arc name=arcfig charspacetype=data filled ;
```

  Note that the GFONT procedure uses the CHARSPACETYPE= option with a value of DATA to specify that the first observation sets the width of the character. The FILLED option fills the area of the arc.

SEGMENT

numbers the line segments that compose a character or symbol. SEGMENT is a numeric variable that is required for both polygon and stroked fonts. All the observations for a given line segment have the same segment number. The segment number changes when a new line segment starts.

When the GFONT procedure draws a stroked character with more than one line segment (for example, the letter E), or a polygon character with a hole (for example, the letter A), it needs to know when one line stops and where the next line begins. There are two ways to do this, as follows:

1. Change the segment number when a new line segment starts. If the value of LP is L (line), a change in segment numbers tells the GFONT procedure not to connect the last point in line segment 1 and the first point in line segment 2. If the value of LP is P (polygon), a change in segment numbers causes both of the following:

- □ The last point in line segment 1 is joined to the first point in line segment 1, thus closing the polygon.
- □ The program starts a new polygon. If the value of CHAR has not changed, the new polygon is part of the same character.

Use this method for characters that are composed of two polygons, such as a question mark (?). If you draw a polygon with a hole in it, such as the letter A, use the second method.

2 Keep the same segment number for all lines, but insert an observation with missing values for X and Y between the observation that marks the end of the first line and the observation that begins the next line. For example, if you are drawing the letter O, insert an observation with a missing value between the line that draws the outer circle and the beginning of the line that draws the inner circle.

The first method is preferred, unless you are creating a polygon character with a hole in it. In this case, you should separate the lines with a missing value and keep the same segment numbers. (Note that if you use separate line segments when you create a polygon with a hole, the results may be unpredictable.) For example, observations such as the following from a data set called BOXES were used to draw the hollow square in Figure 32.9 on page 958. The data points that form the figure are laid out on a grid shown next to the square.

OBS	CHAR	SEG	X	Y	LP
1	b	1	1	1	P
2	b	1	1	3	P
3	b	1	3	3	P
4	b	1	3	1	P
5	b	1	.	.	P
6	b	1	0	0	P
7	b	1	0	4	P
8	b	1	4	4	P
9	b	1	4	0	P

Note that observation 5, which has missing values for X and Y, separates the observations that draw the inner box from those that draw the outer box and that the segment number is the same for all the observations. Figure 32.9 on page 958 was generated with a GFONT statement like the following:

```
proc gfont data=boxes name=boxes filled;
```

Note that the FILLED option is included and that only the space between the two squares is filled.

Figure 32.9 Drawing Nested Polygons

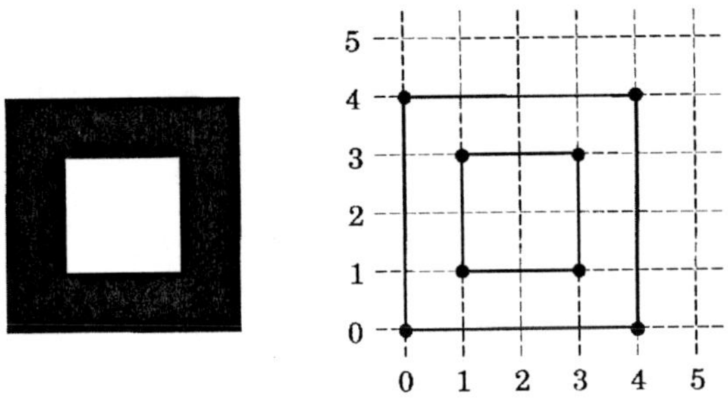

a. b.

X and Y

specify the horizontal and vertical coordinates of the points for each character. These variables must be numeric, and they must be named X and Y for the horizontal and vertical coordinates, respectively. Their values describe the position of the points on the character. These values can be in any range that you choose, but both variables must describe the character in the same scale or font units. In other words, 10 horizontal units must be the same distance as 10 vertical units. You should define vertical coordinates for all characters on the same baseline.

Note: When you specify PTYPE=W, both X and Y contain horizontal coordinate values. △

Creating a Font Data Set

You can create a font data set by digitizing the shape of the characters or figures either manually or with special digitizing equipment. To create a font data set by digitizing the characters manually, follow these steps:

1. Determine the coordinate points for each line segment by drawing the characters on a grid.
2. Lay out the observations for each character. Each observation describes a move from one point to another along a line segment. For each line segment, enter the coordinate points in the order in which they are drawn. For a stroked font, when you start a new line segment, change the segment number. For a polygon font, when you start a new polygon, change the line segment number.

   If the polygon has a hole in it, as in the letter O, keep the line segment number and separate the lines with a missing value. Use the same value for CHAR for all of the observations that describe one character.
3. Create a SAS data set that contains the variables CHAR, SEGMENT, X, and Y, and read in the data for each observation. Include the variables LP and PTYPE if necessary.
4. Sort the data set by CHAR and SEGMENT.
5. Assign the font data set with the DATA= argument.

This process is illustrated in Example 2 on page 964.

The Kern Data Set

The kern data set consists of observations that specify how much space to add or remove between any two characters when they appear in combination. This process, called *kerning*, increases or decreases space between the characters. Kerning usually is applied to certain pairs of characters that, because of their shape, have too much space between them. Reducing the space between characters may allow part of one character to extend over the body of the next. Examples of some combinations that should be kerned are AT, AV, AW, TA, VA, and WA.

You can apply kerning to the intercharacter spacing that you specify with the CHARSPACETYPE= option (except for uniform fonts). You can refine the kerning of your characters as little or as much as you like. You assign the kern data set with the KERNDATA= option.

Kern Data Set Variables

The kern data set must contain these variables:

CHAR1
: specifies the first character in the pair to be kerned. CHAR1 is a character variable with a length of 1.

CHAR2
: specifies the second character in the pair to be kerned. CHAR2 is a character variable with a length of 1.

XADJ
: specifies the amount of space to add or remove between the two characters. XADJ is a numeric variable that uses the same font units as the font data set. The value of XADJ specifies the horizontal adjustment to be applied to CHAR2 whenever CHAR1 is followed immediately by CHAR2. Negative numbers decrease the spacing, and positive numbers increase the spacing.

Creating a Kern Data Set

Each observation in a kern data set names the pair of characters to be kerned and the amount of space to be added or deleted between them. To create a kern data set, follow these steps:

1 Select the pairs of characters to be kerned, and specify the space adjustment (in font units) for each pair as a positive number (more space) or negative number (less space).

2 Create a SAS data set that contains the variables CHAR1, CHAR2, and XADJ; produce one observation for each pair of characters and the corresponding space adjustment.

```
data kern1;
   input char1 $ char2 $ xadj;
   datalines;
A T -4
D A -3
T A -4
;
```

3 Assign the kern data set with the KERNDATA= option.

```
proc gfont data=fontdata
           name=font2
           charspacetype=data
           kerndata=kern1
           nodisplay;
run;
```

Figure 32.10 on page 960 illustrates how you can use the KERNDATA= option to create a font in which the space between specified pairs of letters is reduced. The characters A, D, and T are shown as the word DATA. The first line uses the unkerned font, FONT1, and the second line uses the kerned font, FONT2. Note that the characters in FONT2 are spaced more closely than the characters in FONT1.

The following title statements specify the kerned and unkerned fonts and are used with the GSLIDE procedure to produce Figure 32.10 on page 960:

```
title2 lspace=6 f=font1 h=10 j=l 'DATA';
title3 lspace=4 f=font2 h=10 j=l 'DATA';
```

Figure 32.10 Comparison of Kerned and Unkerned Text

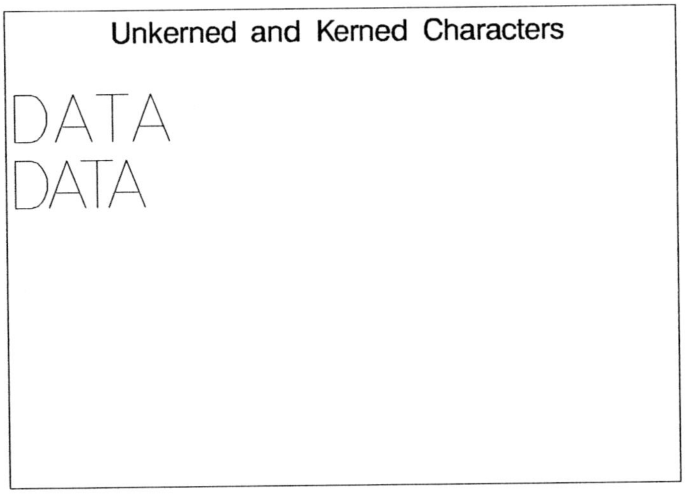

The Space Data Set

As the height (point size) of a font increases, less space is required between letters in relation to their height. If the point size decreases, more space may be needed. The space data set tells the GFONT procedure how much to increase or decrease the intercharacter spacing for a given point size. Like kerning, spacing is added to or subtracted from the intercharacter spacing that is specified by the CHARSPACETYPE= option. However, kerning applies the adjustment to specified pairs of characters, while spacing is applied uniformly to all characters.

Values that are specified in the space data set are added to the normal intercharacter spacing and any kerning data. Normal intercharacter spacing is determined by the CHARSPACETYPE= option.

Space Data Set Variables

The space data set must contain these variables:

SIZE
: specifies the point size of the font. SIZE is a numeric variable.

ADJ
: specifies the spacing adjustment for the point size in hundredths (1/100) of a point. (A point is equal to 1/72 of an inch.) ADJ is a numeric variable. Positive values for

the ADJ variable increase the spacing between characters; negative values reduce the space.

Creating a Space Data Set

Each observation in a space data set specifies a point size (SIZE) and the amount of space (ADJ) to be added or subtracted between characters when a font of that point size is requested. When you specify a point size that is not in the space data set, the adjustment for the next smaller size is used. To create a space data set, follow these steps:

1. Determine the amount of adjustment that is required for typical point sizes; positive numbers increase spacing, and negative numbers decrease spacing.
2. Create a SAS data set that contains the variables SIZE and ADJ; produce one observation for each point size and corresponding space adjustment.

```
data space1;
   input size adj;
   datalines;
 6   40
12    0
18  -40
24  -90
30 -150
36 -300
42 -620
;
```

3. Assign the space data set with the SPACEDATA= option.

```
proc gfont data=fontdata
           name=font3
           charspacetype=data
           spacedata=space1
           nodisplay;
run;
```

Figure 32.11 on page 962 illustrates how to use the SPACEDATA= option to generate a font in which intercharacter spacing is adjusted according to the height of the characters. The characters A, D, and T are shown as the word DATA. Each pair of lines displays the word DATA and at the same size uses first the font with spacing adjustment (FONT3) and then the original font (FONT1). Note that as the size of the characters increases, the space between them decreases.

The following title statements are used with the GSLIDE procedure to produce Figure 32.11 on page 962:

```
title2;
title3 f=font3 h=.25in j=l 'DATA'; /* 18 points */
title4 f=font1 h=.25in j=l 'DATA';
title5;
title6 f=font3 h=.50in j=l 'DATA'; /* 36 points */
title7 f=font1 h=.50in j=l 'DATA';
title8;
title9 f=font3 h=1.0in j=l 'DATA'; /* 72 points */
title10 f=font1 h=1.0in j=l 'DATA';
```

Figure 32.11 Comparison of Text with and without Spacing Adjustments

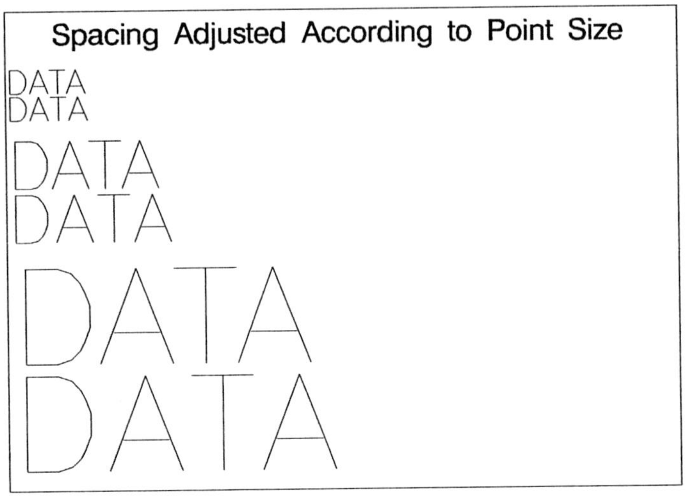

Examples

The following examples illustrate major features of the GFONT procedure.

Example 1: Displaying Fonts and Character Codes

Procedure features:

GFONT statement options:

- HEIGHT=
- NOBUILD
- ROMCOL=
- ROMFONT=
- ROMHT=
- SHOWROMAN

Sample library member: GFODISFO

Figure 32.12 Display of the Greek Font with Character Codes (GFODISFO)

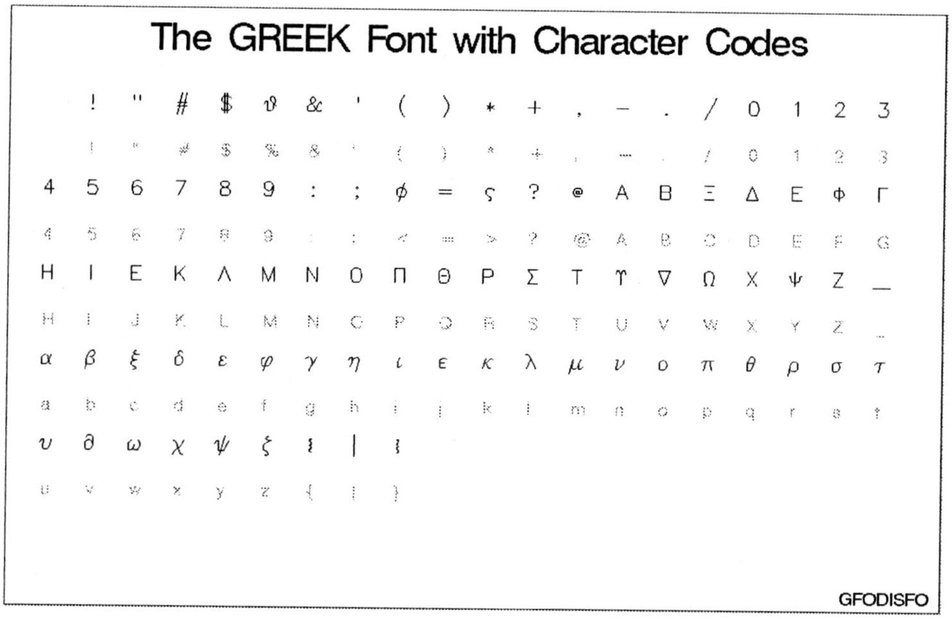

This example illustrates the SHOWROMAN option, which displays the character codes that are associated with the font characters that are being displayed. A display such as this one shows which keyboard character you enter to produce the Greek character you want. In addition, this example shows how to modify the appearance of both the font characters and the character codes when they are displayed.

Set the graphics environment.

```
goptions reset=global gunit=pct border cback=white
         colors=(black blue green red)
         ftext=swiss htitle=6 htext=3;
```

Define title and footnote.

```
title 'The GREEK Font with Character Codes';
footnote j=r 'GFODISFO ';
```

Display the GREEK font with character codes. NOBUILD indicates that the font specified in the NAME= argument is an existing font. HEIGHT= specifies the height of the Greek characters. ROMCOL=, ROMFONT=, and ROMHT= assign the color, type style, and height of the character codes. SHOWROMAN displays the character codes.

```
proc gfont name=greek
           nobuild
           height=3.7
           romcol=red
           romfont=swissl
           romht=2.7
           showroman;
run;
```

```
quit;
```

Example 2: Creating Figures for a Symbol Font

Procedure features:
GFONT statement options:
- CTEXT=
- DATA=
- FILLED
- NAME=
- RESOL=

Other features:
LIBNAME statement

Sample library member: GFOCRFIG

Figure 32.13 Display of Symbols For Characters

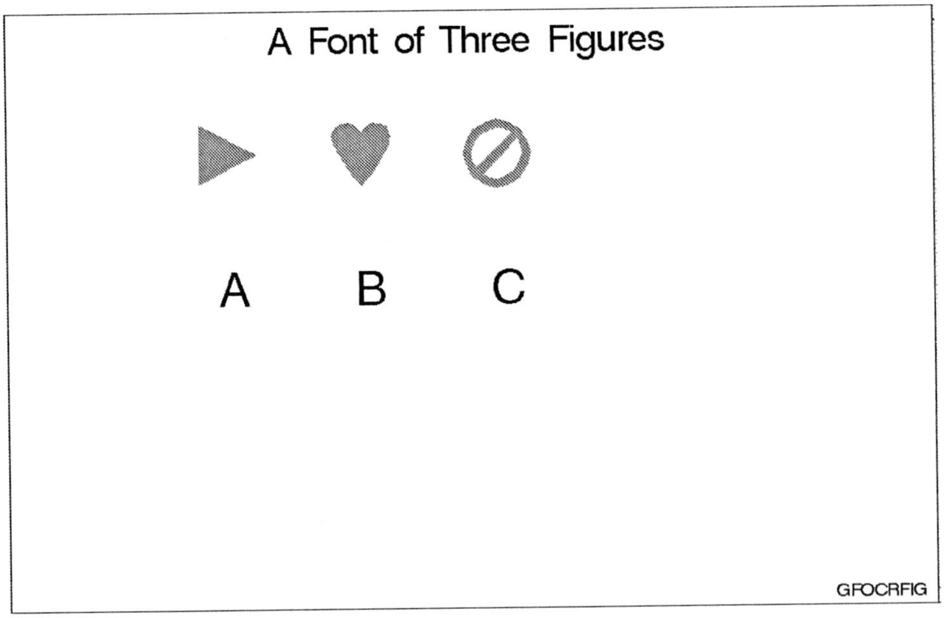

This example shows how to create three simple figures for a symbol font. Each figure is laid out on a grid that is 64 font units square. The third figure is a circle with a slash through it. Figure 32.14 on page 965 shows the figure and some of its coordinate points laid out on a grid.

Figure 32.14 Diagram of Circle with Slash Figure

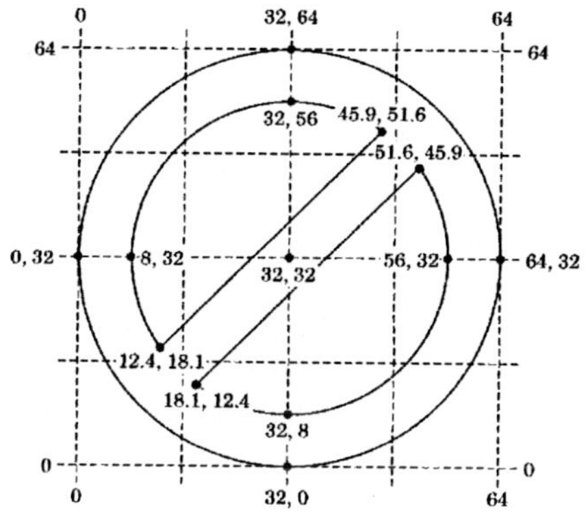

Assign the librefs and set the graphics environment. The LIBNAME statement associates the libref GFONT0 with the SAS data library in which the font catalog is stored.

```
libname gfont0 'SAS-data-library';
goptions reset=global gunit=pct border cback=white
         colors=(black blue green red)
         ftext=swiss htitle=6 htext=3;
```

Create the font data set FIGURES for a triangle, a heart, and a circle with slash. The first figure, a right-pointing triangle that is assigned the character code A, is a polygon drawn with three straight lines.

```
data figures;
   input char $ ptype $ x y segment lp $;
   datalines;
A   W    0    64   0    P   /* triangle pointing right */
A   V    4     4   1    P
A   V   60    32   1    P
A   V    4    60   1    P
A   V    4     4   1    P
```

The second figure, a heart that is assigned the character code B, uses the PTYPE variable combination V-C-V to draw the arcs that make up the top of the heart. Each side requires two arcs. Since the arcs are continuous, the observation that marks the end of one arc is also the beginning of the next arc. The heart drawing begins at the bottom point and continues counterclockwise.

```
B   W    0    64   0    P   /* heart */
B   V   32     2   1    P
B   V   44    17   1    P
B   V   58    40   1    P
B   C   46    47   1    P
B   V   56    58   1    P
B   C   46    47   1    P
```

```
B    V    32    52    1    P
B    C    18    47    1    P
B    V     8    58    1    P
B    C    18    47    1    P
B    V     6    40    1    P
B    V    20    17    1    P
B    V    32     2    1    P
```

The third figure, a circle with a slash through it that is assigned the character code C, is composed of three polygons: a circle and two empty arcs. An observation with missing values separates the observations defining each of the three polygons. The outer circle is defined by the first group of observations. The empty arcs are drawn with three continuous arcs using the PTYPE variable pattern V-C-V-C-V-C-V. The straight line that closes the arc is drawn automatically by the GFONT procedure in order to complete the polygon. Because all the polygons are part of one character, the continuous space they define is filled.

```
C    W     0     64    0    P   /* circle with slash */
C    V    32     64    1    P
C    C    32     32    1    P
C    V    64     32    1    P
C    C    32     32    1    P
C    V    32      0    1    P
C    C    32     32    1    P
C    V     0     32    1    P
C    C    32     32    1    P
C    V    32     64    1    P
C    V     .      .    1    P
C    V    12.4   18.1  1    P
C    C    32     32    1    P
C    V     8     32    1    P
C    C    32     32    1    P
C    V    32     56    1    P
C    C    32     32    1    P
C    V    45.9   51.6  1    P
C    V     .      .    1    P
C    V    51.6   45.9  1    P
C    C    32     32    1    P
C    V    56     32    1    P
C    C    32     32    1    P
C    V    32      8    1    P
C    C    32     32    1    P
C    V    18.1   12.4  1    P
;
```

Define the title and footnote.

```
title 'A Font of Three Figures';
footnote j=r 'GFOCRFIG ';
```

Generate and display the font FIGURES. The DATA= argument names the input data set that is used to generate the font. The NAME= argument names the font that the procedure generates and automatically stores it in the GFONT0 catalog. (Note that you do not need to specify GFONT0.) FILLED specifies a filled polygon font. CTEXT= specifies the color of the figures in the font display. The color specification is not stored with the font. RESOL= is set to 2 to improve the resolution of the lines. By default, the newly generated font is displayed (the NODISPLAY option is not used).

```
proc gfont data=figures
           name=figures
           filled
           height=.75in
           ctext=red
           showroman
           romht=.5in
           resol=2;
run;
quit;
```

CHAPTER 33

The GIMPORT Procedure

Overview

The GIMPORT procedure enables you to import into SAS/GRAPH software graphics output that is produced with other software applications, graphics output that is produced by SAS/GRAPH software, or graphics output that is produced on other machines. The GIMPORT procedure takes as its input a computer graphics metafile (CGM) and produces graphics output that can be displayed in your SAS/GRAPH session and stored in a SAS catalog. This graphics output can be reviewed and played like any other SAS/GRAPH output using the GREPLAY procedure. The GIMPORT procedure may also write any of the following information to the log:

- □ any elements used in the CGM that the procedure cannot process
- □ color mapping information when a color in a CGM is not available on the destination device
- □ a list of fonts that are used by the application that produced the CGM.

Note: In addition to the GIMPORT procedure, you can use commands in the File pull-down menu in the Image Editor, Graph Editor, and Graph window to import other graphic formats such as GIF, TIFF, and WMF. △

Concepts

About Importing Graphics

A computer graphics metafile (CGM) is a graphics output file that is created according to a standard (ANSI X3.122). Since many graphics applications, including SAS/GRAPH software, can generate and import CGMs, these files can be read by different applications programs or used on different machines.

The GIMPORT procedure imports a CGM with which a fileref has been associated. Using the CGM as input, the procedure displays the graphics output and creates a catalog entry. The following sections address how to assign the fileref to the external file (CGM) and how to import the file.

Specifying a Fileref

You must assign a fileref to the external file that contains the CGM that you want to use as input so that the GIMPORT procedure can locate it. You can do this with a FILENAME statement that has the following form:

```
FILENAMEcgm-fileref'external-file';
```

Replace *cgm-fileref* with any fileref name that you want. Replace *'external-file'* with the complete file name of the CGM. You can omit the FILENAME statement if you have already defined the fileref. You can also specify a fileref with a host command in some operating environments. See "FILENAME Statement" on page 28 for additional information.

Importing the File

The PROC GIMPORT statement reads the input CGM and displays the graphics output. When the CGM is displayed using only the PROC GIMPORT statement, the resulting graphics output may not be sized or positioned correctly for the device on which it is displayed. In these cases, you can use the SCALE and TRANSLATE statements to adjust the size and location of the new graphics output.

In addition, if the CGM contains the FONT LIST element, the procedure lists in the log the fonts used in the CGM. You can change these fonts to SAS software fonts using the MAP statement. If you do not change these fonts to SAS software fonts, the GIMPORT procedure uses a default font.

Because it is easier to determine what adjustments the graphics output needs after it has been displayed, you may want to follow these steps:

1. Import the CGM and display the graphics output using only the PROC GIMPORT statement.
2. Decide what adjustments you want to make to the size and position of the graphics output.
3. If the procedure lists the fonts that are used by the CGM, decide what font substitutions you want to make.
4. Run the procedure again with the appropriate MAP, SCALE, or TRANSLATE statements.

Note: Once you have determined the correct values for the SCALE and TRANSLATE statements for the graphics output produced by a particular CGM, you can use the same values for all other graphics output that is generated by the same software application. △

CGM Elements Not Supported

The GIMPORT procedure does not support certain CGM elements. If the input CGM contains any of the following elements, the GIMPORT procedure writes a message to the log noting that the procedure cannot process them:

- the CELL ARRAY primitive element (a bitmap CGM file)
- the CHARACTER SPACING attribute element
- the APPLICATION DATA element
- the ESCAPE element.

These elements are rarely used and their absence should not affect the graphics output produced by the GIMPORT procedure.

About Color Mapping

If the CGM specifies colors for the graphics elements that it generates, you may or may not be able to map them to the color that you want in your SAS/GRAPH output, depending on the way these colors are specified in the CGM.

You cannot change the color mapping if, in the CGM, the COLOUR SELECTION MODE element is set to DIRECT. In this case, the colors are explicitly defined by the CGM and you cannot change them. However, if the CGM was created with a SAS/GRAPH CGM device driver, you can control the colors by specifying the appropriate colors when you create the graphics output or by changing the colors in the CGM device entry and re-creating the CGM. See Chapter 31, "The GDEVICE Procedure," on page 915 for details. In addition, you can use a color map with the GREPLAY procedure to remap the colors. In the color map, the FROM color must be specified in RGB format, but the TO color can be any valid color name. See Chapter 43, "The GREPLAY Procedure," on page 1237 for details on color maps.

You can change the color mapping if the COLOUR SELECTION MODE element is set to INDEXED and there is no color table defined in the CGM file. In this case, you can map the colors from the CGM to the colors of your choice by using the COLORS= graphics option when you run the GIMPORT procedure. The CGM colors are mapped to match the order of the colors in the colors list. If the procedure cannot reproduce the colors specified in the CGM, the following message is written to the log:

```
WARNING: Invalid color index n encountered.
         It has been mapped to color-name.
```

Note: The color name from the CGM is converted to the RGB format for SAS/GRAPH color names; that is, WHITE is converted to CXFFFFFF, and so on. See Chapter 6, "SAS/GRAPH Colors and Images," on page 91 for details. △

About Pattern Mapping

If the CGM contains pattern specifications, you may be able to map them to patterns of your choice using SAS/GRAPH PATTERN definitions.

If the CGM defines a PATTERN TABLE, then the patterns defined by this table are the patterns that are used and you cannot change them.

If a PATTERN TABLE is not defined in the CGM, under certain conditions you may be able to use SAS/GRAPH PATTERN definitions to control the patterns that are used. If INTERIOR STYLE is set to PATTERN and if a PATTERN TABLE INDEX has been specified, then the GIMPORT procedure uses the PATTERN TABLE INDEX to look up SAS/GRAPH PATTERN definitions. If patterns are defined, the procedure uses the first available pattern. For example, if the PATTERN TABLE INDEX *n* has been defined, the procedure uses SAS/GRAPH PATTERN definition *n*. If the SAS/GRAPH PATTERN definition is not the correct pattern type, the procedure modifies the pattern as necessary. If no PATTERN definitions are currently in effect, an INVALID PATTERN TABLE INDEX warning is issued and no pattern is used.

About Font Mapping

By default, the GIMPORT procedure maps all of the fonts in the CGM to the font that is specified by the FTEXT= graphics option. If the FTEXT= graphics option is not used, the default is the hardware font NONE. However, you may be able to specify a different font either by mapping the fonts or by using a graphics option.

When the CGM is imported, a numbered list of the fonts that are used in the CGM may be displayed in the LOG window. These are the fonts that were available to the application that originally generated the CGM. Depending on how the fonts are represented in the CGM, you may be able to map these fonts to fonts of your choice.

If the font and text in the imported graphics output are produced with move and draw commands that are included in the CGM, then no font name appears in the LOG window and the font cannot be mapped to a different one.

If the fonts used in the imported graphics output are represented in the CGM as a font name accompanied by a text string, they can be mapped to SAS/GRAPH fonts using the MAP statement. You can use the MAP statement if the message "WARNING: Invalid font index *n*. Font has been mapped to *font-name*" appears in the LOG window after the list of fonts. This means that font *n* in the list could not be reproduced and was mapped to the font specified in the FTEXT= graphics option or to the hardware font. You can map this font to a SAS/GRAPH software font of your choice using the MAP statement. See "MAP Statement" on page 974 for more information on mapping fonts.

You can also specify a font with the FTEXT= or CHARTYPE= graphics options if both of the following conditions are true:

- The font has not been mapped with a MAP statement.
- The CGM font contains a font name and text rather than the move and draw commands that draw the text in the specified font. In the latter case, the font name is not included in FONT LIST.

However, using a graphics option causes all fonts to be mapped to the one that is specified. See Chapter 5, "SAS/GRAPH Fonts," on page 75 for details of font specification and Example 2 on page 979.

Procedure Syntax

Supports: Output Delivery System (ODS)

PROC GIMPORT FILEREF=*cgm-fileref* | *'external-file'*
FILETYPE=CGM
FORMAT=BINARY | CHARACTER | CLEARTEXT
<GOUT=<*libref.*>*output-catalog*>;

MAP *'cgm-font'* TO *font* ;

SCALE X=*factor* | Y=*factor* | X=*factor* Y=*factor*;

TRANSLATE X=*offset* | Y=*offset* | X=*offset* Y=*offset*;

PROC GIMPORT Statement

Identifies the input file to be processed, and specifies its file type and format. Optionally specifies an output catalog.

Syntax

PROC GIMPORT FILEREF=*cgm-fileref* | *'external-file'*
FILETYPE=CGM
FORMAT=BINARY | CHARACTER | CLEARTEXT
<GOUT=<*libref.*>*output-catalog*>;

Required Arguments

FILEREF=*cgm-fileref* | *'external-file'*
specifies the computer graphics metafile (CGM) that is input for PROC GIMPORT. Following are the possible values for FILEREF=:

cgm-fileref
a fileref that is associated with the CGM and that has been previously defined using a FILENAME statement or host command.

'external-file'
the complete file name of the CGM that you want to import. See the operating system companion for your system for valid values for *external-file*.

Featured in: Example 2 on page 979.

FILETYPE=CGM
specifies the type of the input file, that is, the graphics standard to which the file conforms. CGM is the only valid value for the FILETYPE= argument. If the FILETYPE= argument is omitted, an error is issued and the procedure stops.

Featured in: Example 2 on page 979.

FORMAT=BINARY | CHARACTER | CLEARTEXT
specifies the format of the input file. CGMs can be encoded in one of the following three formats:

BINARY
specifies binary encoding. It is not printable.

CHARACTER
specifies an encoding suitable for transfer through networks that cannot support binary transfers. It is printable but not readable.

CLEARTEXT
specifies a text format that can be read using a standard text editor.

Most graphics packages use BINARY format. If you specify the wrong format, an "ERROR: Unable to interpret the CGM file" message is issued and the procedure stops. If this occurs, try a different format.

Featured in: Example 2 on page 979.

Options

GOUT=*<libref.>output-catalog*
specifies the SAS catalog in which to save the graphics output produced by the GIMPORT procedure. If you omit the libref, SAS/GRAPH looks for the catalog in the temporary library called WORK and creates the catalog if it does not exist.

See also: "Storing Graphics Output in SAS Catalogs" on page 53.

MAP Statement

Substitutes a SAS/GRAPH software font for a font in the CGM.

Requirements: Submit a separate MAP statement for each CGM font that you want to map.

Tip: You can submit multiple MAP statements with the procedure.

Featured in: Example 2 on page 979.

Syntax

MAP *'cgm-font'* TO *font*;

Required Arguments

'cgm-font'
identifies a font in the CGM. The name of the font must be enclosed in single quotation marks and written exactly as it appears in the font list; *cgm-font* is case sensitive. Do not include the font list number in *cgm-font*.

font
specifies the SAS/GRAPH font to which the CGM font is mapped. You can specify software fonts or hardware fonts for the destination device. You can also use fonts that are created by the GFONT procedure.

Note: Remember to specify the libref GFONT0 with a LIBNAME statement if *font* is a user-generated font. △

By default, the GIMPORT procedure maps all of the CGM fonts to the font specified by the FTEXT= graphics option or, if the FTEXT= graphics option is not used, to the default hardware font, NONE.

Details

If the CGM includes the FONT LIST element, the GIMPORT procedure automatically lists the CGM font names in the log. Use this list to select the fonts for mapping. For example, suppose the font list includes the following entry:

3. Times Roman

If the LOG window displays the message "WARNING: Invalid font index *n*," you can map the Times Roman font to the SAS/GRAPH font CENTX with the following statement:

```
map 'Times Roman' to centx;
```

SCALE Statement

Enlarges or reduces the graphics output by increasing or decreasing the values of the *x* and *y* coordinates.

Requirements: You can submit only one SCALE statement.

Tip: You can submit the SCALE statement alone or in conjunction with the TRANSLATE statement, but the SCALE statement is always processed first.

Featured in: Example 2 on page 979.

Syntax

SCALE X=*factor* | Y=*factor* | X=*factor* Y=*factor*;

Required Arguments

At least one of the following arguments is required; both may be used and can be listed in either order:

X=*factor*
: specifies the enlargement or reduction of the values of the *x* coordinates. *Factor* is the number by which these values are multiplied and cannot be less than or equal to 0. By default, X=1. Values less than 1 reduce the size of the graphics output while values greater than 1 increase the size of the graphics output. There is no limit on the size of *factor*.

Y=*factor*
: specifies the enlargement or reduction of the values of the *y* coordinates. *Factor* is the number by which these values are multiplied and cannot be less than or equal to 0. By default, Y=1. Values less than 1 reduce the size of the graphics output while values greater than 1 increase the size of the graphics output. There is no limit on the size of *factor*.

Details

If the shapes in the imported graphics output are too narrow, you can make them wider by increasing the values of the *x* coordinate. To make the elements in the graphics output twice as wide, specify X=2. To make them half as high, specify Y=.5.

For example, if the values of the *x* coordinates range from 5 to 50 and if in the SCALE statement the factor for X= is specified as 2, then the values of all of the *x* coordinates are multiplied by 2 and the range of these values increases. The new range is 10 to 100. And if the values of the *y* coordinates range from 0 to 25 and if in the SCALE statement the factor for Y= is specified as .5, then the values of all of the *y* coordinates are multiplied by .5 and the range of these values decreases. The new range is 0 to 12.5.

If you specify a factor that causes the graphics output to exceed the size of the graphics output area, the procedure draws as much of the graphics output as will fit in the available space.

TRANSLATE Statement

Adjusts the location on the display of the graphics output imported by the procedure. Graphics output can be shifted left or right by offsetting the *x* values or shifted up or down by offsetting the *y* values.

Requirements: You can submit only one TRANSLATE statement.

Tip: You can submit the TRANSLATE statement alone or in conjunction with the SCALE statement but the SCALE statement is always processed first.

Featured in: Example 2 on page 979.

Syntax

TRANSLATE X=*offset* | Y=*offset* | X=*offset* Y=*offset* ;

Required Arguments

At least one of the following arguments is required; both may be used and can be listed in either order:

X=*offset*
specifies the number of units in percent of the display area to move the graphics output right (positive numbers) or left (negative numbers). The value of *offset* is added to the value of the x coordinate. By default, X=0.

Y=*offset*
specifies the number of units in percent of the display area to move the graphics output up (positive numbers) or down (negative numbers). The value of *offset* is added to the value of the y coordinate. By default, Y=0.

Details

The TRANSLATE statement adjusts the position of the graphics output without changing its size. The amount of the *offset* that is specified for X= or Y= in the TRANSLATE statement is the amount that the graphics output is moved.

For example, suppose your imported graphics output is positioned in the upper-left corner of the display. To move it right 10% and down 5%, use the following statement:

```
translate x=10 y=-5;
```

Examples

The following examples illustrate major features of the GIMPORT procedure. For illustration purposes, these examples create a CGM using SAS/GRAPH software and import the resulting CGM by using the GIMPORT procedure. Ordinarily, you would use the GIMPORT procedure to import graphics output that is generated by another software package.

Note: Because this example uses a CGM device driver to produce a graphics stream file, you may need to respecify a device driver for your output device. In addition, these examples use the HSIZE= and VSIZE= graphics options to set a specific size for the graphics output area for the CGM so that the second example can illustrate the use of the SCALE and TRANSLATE statements. Depending on the output device that you are using, you may need to adjust the HSIZE= and VSIZE= values in this example and the values in the SCALE and TRANSLATE statements in the second example. △

Example 1: Creating and Importing a CGM

Procedure features:

GIMPORT statement options:

FILEREF=
FILETYPE=
FORMAT=

Other features:

FILENAME statement

GOPTIONS stratement

Sample library member: GIPCRCGM

This example creates a CGM in binary format by directing SAS/GRAPH output to a graphics stream file (GSF) and using a CGM device driver. It uses the GIMPORT procedure to import the resulting CGM into SAS/GRAPH where it can be viewed and stored in a catalog. (See Chapter 2, "SAS/GRAPH Programs," on page 25 for additional information on catalog entries and graphics stream files.) The output shows the imported version of the graphic. Note that the output uses the default font because the specified fonts are unavailable. Example 2 on page 979 shows how to map these fonts to get the output that you want. Also see "About Font Mapping" on page 972 for additional information.

Assign the fileref for a graphics stream file and set the graphics environment. Set graphics stream file characteristics, and select the CGM device driver for binary CGM.

```
filename gsasfile 'external-file';
goptions reset=global gunit=pct border cback=white
         colors=(black)
         gaccess=gsasfile gsfmode=replace
         noprompt device=cgm
         hsize=5 in vsize=5 in
         vpos=60 hpos=150;
```

Define titles and footnote for slide.

```
title1 f=script h=7 'Title One is SCRIPT Font';
title2 f=centb h=5 'Title Two is CENTB Font';
title3 f=zapf h=5 'Title Three is ZAPF Font';
footnote h=3 f=swiss j=r 'GIPCRCGM ';
```

Generate a slide. The graphics output is stored in the GSF file that was specified with the fileref and in the GOPTIONS statement.

```
proc gslide;
run;
quit;
```

Reset the graphics environment.

```
goptions reset=goptions border cback=white
         colors=(black);
```

Import the GSF file created by the CGM device driver. FILEREF= specifies the fileref where the CGM is located. FILETYPE= specifies the type of file to be imported. FORMAT= specifies the format of the CGM being imported.

```
proc gimport fileref=gsasfile
             filetype=cgm
             format=binary;
run;
```

Output 33.1 shows the font list that is displayed in the log file. The font list contains all of the fonts that are used by the CGM. The warning messages following the font list indicate which fonts can be remapped using the MAP statement.

Output 33.1 Font List

```
 .
 .
 .

 NOTE: These fonts are used in this CGM file. You may use the MAP statement
       to map these fonts to  SAS/GRAPH
fonts.
 1. SIMPLEX
 2. BRUSH
 3. CENTB
 4. CENTBE
 5. CENTBI
 6. CENTBIE
 7. CENTX
 8. CENTXE
 9. CENTXI
 10. CENTXIE
 11. GERMAN
 12. GITALIC
 13. DUPLEX
 14. COMPLEX
 15. TRIPLEX
 16. TITALIC
 17. ITALIC
 18. OLDENG
 19. SCRIPT
 20. CSCRIPT
 21. SWISS
 22. SWISSE
 23. SWISSB
 24. SWISSBE
 25. SWISSBI
 26. SWISSBIE
 27. SWISSX
 28. SWISSXE
 29. SWISSXB
 30. SWISSXB
 31. SWISSXBE
 32. SWISSI
 33. SWISSIE
 34. SWISSL
 35. SWISSLE
 36. ZAPF
 37. ZAPFE
 38. ZAPFB
 39. ZAPFBE
 40. ZAPFBI
 41. ZAPFBIE
 42. ZAPFI
 43. ZAPFIE
WARNING: Unspecified font index 19. Font has been mapped to the default font.
WARNING: Unspecified font index 3. Font has been mapped to the default font.
WARNING: Unspecified font index 36. Font has been mapped to the default font.
WARNING: Unspecified font index 21. Font has been mapped to the default font.
 .
 .
 .
```

Example 2: Adjusting the Graphics Output

Procedure features:

SCALE statement

TRANSLATE statement

MAP statement

Sample library member: GIPGROUT

This example imports the CGM file that was created in the earlier example and modifies the output. This example uses the SCALE and TRANSLATE statements to correct the size and position of the imported CGM. The MAP statement is also used to substitute a SAS/GRAPH software font for a font in the CGM.

Assign the fileref for a GSF file and set the graphics environment.

```
filename gsasfile 'external-file';
goptions reset=goptions gunit=pct border cback=white
         colors=(black) htitle=6 htext=3
         vpos=60 hpos=150;
```

Import the GSF file created by the CGM device driver. The SCALE statement specifies the scale factor for the values of the x and y coordinates. The TRANSLATE statement specifies the amount that the imported graphics output should be moved horizontally and vertically. The MAP statements remap the fonts shown in the first example.

```
proc gimport fileref=gsasfile filetype=cgm format=binary;
   scale x=.7 y=.8;
   translate x=3.5 y=10;
   map 'SCRIPT' to script;
   map 'CENTB' to centb;
   map 'ZAPF' to zapf;
   map 'SWISS' to swiss;
run;
```

Output 33.2 shows the font list that is displayed in the log file. Note that no warning messages follow the font list because all of the fonts that are used in the CGM have been remapped.

Output 33.2 Font List

```
 .
 .
 .

 NOTE: These fonts are used in this CGM file. You may use the MAP statement
       to map these fonts to  SAS/GRAPH
fonts.
 1. SIMPLEX
 2. BRUSH
 3. CENTB
 4. CENTBE
 5. CENTBI
 6. CENTBIE
 7. CENTX
 8. CENTXE
 9. CENTXI
 10. CENTXIE
 11. GERMAN
 12. GITALIC
 13. DUPLEX
 14. COMPLEX
 15. TRIPLEX
 16. TITALIC
 17. ITALIC
 18. OLDENG
 19. SCRIPT
 20. CSCRIPT
 21. SWISS
 22. SWISSE
 23. SWISSB
 24. SWISSBE
 25. SWISSBI
 26. SWISSBIE
 27. SWISSX
 28. SWISSXE
 29. SWISSXB
 30. SWISSXB
 31. SWISSXBE
 32. SWISSI
 33. SWISSIE
 34. SWISSL
 35. SWISSLE
 36. ZAPF
 37. ZAPFE
 38. ZAPFB
 39. ZAPFBE
 40. ZAPFBI
 41. ZAPFBIE
 42. ZAPFI
 43. ZAPFIE
 .
 .
 .
```

References

ANSI X3.122–1986, *Computer Graphics Metafile for the Storage and Transfer of Picture Description Information.*

Arnold, D.B. and Bono, P.R. (1988), *CGM and CGI: Metafile Interface Standards for Computer Graphics*, New York: Springer-Verlag.

CHAPTER 34

The GKEYMAP Procedure

Overview

The GKEYMAP procedure creates key maps and device maps that compensate for differences between the way that characters are encoded internally by SAS/GRAPH software and the way that they are encoded by different operating environments and output devices. In addition, the GKEYMAP procedure can create SAS data sets from existing key maps and device maps, either Institute-supplied or user-generated. This capability is useful when you want to make minor alterations in a large key map or device map and you do not want to or cannot re-create the original data set with a DATA step.

The Institute supplies key maps for many keyboard configurations and operating-environment character representations. Your SAS Software Consultant should have selected the appropriate key map for your site. If the Institute-supplied device maps and key maps do not meet your needs, you can use this procedure to modify an existing map or create a new one.

Concepts

About Key Maps and Device Maps

The characters A through Z (upper- and lowercase), 0 through 9, and many symbols and national characters are represented by a set of hexadecimal codes. However, a character may be represented by one code for the keyboard, another code for the operating environment, and yet another for the output device. To resolve these differences, SAS/GRAPH software stores all characters using its own internal encoding scheme, which is a set of hexadecimal values that are associated with all supported characters. Figure 34.1 on page 985 shows these internal character encoding (ICE) codes. To view such a table for yourself, run the following code, which uses the Swiss font:

```
goptions keymap=none;
proc gfont nb name=swiss hex;
run;
quit;
```

To accommodate differences in the encoding of characters, you must be able to translate the hexadecimal codes generated by your keyboard or operating environment into the corresponding SAS/GRAPH internal encoding. A key map gives you this ability.

You also must be able to convert the internal encoding that is used by SAS/GRAPHsoftware to the codes required to produce the corresponding hardware characters on your output device. A device map gives you this ability.

Key maps and device maps are SAS catalog entries. Institute-supplied key maps and device maps are stored in the catalog SASHELP.FONTS. User-generated key maps and device maps are stored in the catalog GFONT0.FONTS. Key maps are stored with the extension KEYMAP (for example, GERMAN.KEYMAP), and device maps are stored with the extension DEVMAP (for example, DEFAULT.DEVMAP).

Figure 34.1 SAS/GRAPH Internal Character Encoding

Note: Positions 00-1F are reserved.
Note: SAS Institute reserves the right to change, at any time, the character displayed and the hexadecimal code returned for all undefined codes.

Note: Positions 00-1F are reserved. SAS Institute reserves the right to change, at any time, the character displayed and the hexidecimal code returned for all undefined codes. △

What Key Maps Do

A key map changes the code generated by a keyboard key to the value corresponding to the SAS/GRAPH internal character encoding. Otherwise, a different character (or no character) may be drawn when the character is requested in a SAS/GRAPH software font.

Key maps are required when the code that is sent to the operating environment does not match the SAS/GRAPH internal encoding for the character corresponding to the key that is pressed. They are useful for generating a character in a software font that is not available on your keyboard or when the same key on different keyboards sends a different character to the operating environment. They are also useful for creating new characters by combining existing characters with accent characters (called *diacritics*).

Note: In Figure 34.1 on page 985, the diacritic characters specified by the codes D2 through DB are backspaced before being drawn and can be used to create new characters (characters resulting from codes B0 through B7, B9, and BA are not backspaced before being drawn). See Example 1 on page 990 for an example of using a diacritic character as an accent. Two commonly used characters have already been created for you: the character located in position F0 of the ICE table could be created by combining DA with an uppercase C, and the character located in position BC could be created by combining DB with an uppercase G. △

What Device Maps Do

A device map maps the code stored in the SAS/GRAPH internal encoding to the code required to reproduce the character on the output device when a particular hardware character is requested in a SAS/GRAPH program.

You usually use device maps in these two situations:

- reversing the translation performed by key maps (if needed). To display the proper hardware character, you must use a device map to convert the SAS/GRAPH internal encoding of the character back to the encoding that the device expects.
- accounting for differences between the code that represents a character on the operating environment and the code or codes required to generate the same character as a hardware character on an output device. The problem can be further complicated if you have multiple output devices, each with its own way of generating a particular character using hardware text.

Using Key Maps and Device Maps

You use key maps and device maps by specifying them with the KEYMAP= or DEVMAP= options in a GOPTIONS statement. You also can specify a device map by filling in the DEVMAP field in the Detail window of the device entry for the device driver that you are using.

For example, if you use the GKEYMAP procedure to generate a key map called MYKEYMAP, you can specify it with a statement like this:

```
goptions keymap=mykeymap;
```

Once you specify MYKEYMAP as your current key map, you can press a key and the code it generates is translated by MYKEYMAP into the ICE code that is specified by the key map.

When you specify a device map with the DEVMAP= graphics option and you use a hardware character set, mapped characters are converted from their SAS/GRAPH internal encoding to the codes required to display the corresponding characters on your device. See Chapter 8, "Graphics Options and Device Parameters Dictionary," on page 261 for more information on the KEYMAP= and DEVMAP= graphics options.

Asymmetrical Maps

It is possible, and sometimes necessary, to define a key map or device map that is not symmetrical (that is, two or more input character codes map to the same output character code). For example, if you define a key map to map the keyed character A to the internal encoding for B, the keyed characters A and B both map to the internal encoding for B, but no code maps to A. This situation may make it impossible for you to display certain characters defined in software fonts.

Seeing What Characters in a Font are Available

To see what characters in a font can be displayed if a particular key map is used, do the following:

1. Use the KEYMAP= option in a GOPTIONS statement to specify the key map that you are interested in.
2. Then, use the GFONT procedure with the ROMHEX option to display the font that you want to use.

The hexadecimal values and corresponding font characters that are displayed are the ones available under the specified map. If the map is not symmetrical, a warning is issued. See Chapter 32, "The GFONT Procedure," on page 939 for more information on using hexadecimal values to display special characters.

About the GKEYMAP Data Set

To generate a key map or device map, you must create a data set that contains the mapping information and use that data set as input for the GKEYMAP procedure. The mapping information is specified as values for the variables in the data set, which should contain one observation for each character or key to be mapped. Any characters not specified in the data set are passed through the map unchanged.

GKEYMAP Data Set Variables

To provide information on the character mapping that is to be performed for a key map or a device map, you must use a variable named FROM to specify the character that you are mapping from, and a variable named TO to specify the character to map to. For key maps, these are the only variables in the data set. For device maps, you may also need variables named CHARTYPE and TOLEN.

Here are definitions for these variables:

CHARTYPE

specifies which hardware character set to use when a device requires that you select an alternate character set in order to display certain characters. CHARTYPE is a numeric variable.

All of the characters in the TO string for a particular FROM value must use the same character set. The CHARTYPE variable is required if you use the MULTFONT option in the PROC GKEYMAP statement; otherwise, it is ignored. (The CHARTYPE variable is always ignored when you are creating a key map.) The CHARTYPE value must match a value listed in the Chartype field in the Chartype window of the device entry for the device to which the map is applied. However, you can set the CHARTYPE variable to a missing value to specify that the character can be drawn in any hardware character set.

FROM

specifies the character you are mapping from. FROM is a character variable. For each observation, the FROM variable should contain a single character value. Any characters after the first are ignored. The data set must be sorted by the FROM variable.

Featured in: Example 1 on page 990

TO

specifies the string that the character in the FROM variable is mapped to. TO is a character variable.

For device maps, if the TO variable contains more than one character, you must also specify TYPE=MAP1N in the PROC GKEYMAP statement to indicate that a single FROM character is being mapped to multiple TO characters. In addition, you must include the TOLEN variable in the data set to specify the length of each TO string. If you specify TYPE=MAP11 in the PROC GKEYMAP statement or if you do not use the TYPE= option, only the first byte of the TO string is recognized.

Featured in: Example 1 on page 990

TOLEN
specifies the length of the string in the TO variable. TOLEN is a numeric variable. The TOLEN variable is used only with device maps and is required if you specify TYPE=MAP1N in the PROC GKEYMAP statement; otherwise, it is ignored.

Procedure Syntax

Requirements: The NAME= argument is always required. To create a key map or device map, the DATA= argument is required. To output a data set, the OUT= argument is required.

PROC GKEYMAP NAME=*map-name*
data-set-argument
<*option(s)*>;

PROC GKEYMAP Statement

The PROC GKEYMAP Statement names the key map or device map to be created or output as a data set. If the procedure creates a key map or a device map, it identifies the data set that is used as input. If it outputs a map, it identifies the data set to which the map is written.

Syntax

PROC GKEYMAP NAME=*map-name*
data-set-argument
<*option(s)*>;

data-set-argument must be one or more of the following:

DATA=*keymap-data-set*

OUT=*output-data-set*

option(s) can be one or more of the following:

DEVICE=*device-name*

DEVMAP | KEYMAP

TYPE=MAP11 | MAP1N

MULTFONT

Required Arguments

NAME=*map-name*
identifies the map that is to be created or converted to a SAS data set. Key maps are stored as *map-name*. KEYMAP, and device maps are stored as *map-name*. DEVMAP. The value of the KEYMAP or DEVMAP option determines the type of map and the extension added to *map-name*. It is possible to use the same *map-name* value for both a key map and a device map.

If you create a key map or device map, the map is stored as an entry in the catalog GFONT*n*.FONTS where *n* is a number from 1 to 9, and you must use a LIBNAME statement to specify a libref for GFONT*n*. See “About the Libref GFONT0” on page 941 for details.

If you specify an existing key map or device map, SAS/GRAPH software searches for the map using the same search path that it uses to search for fonts. See “Font Locations” on page 77 for details .

Featured in: Example 1 on page 990.

DATA=*keymap-data-set*
identifies the input data set for the GKEYMAP procedure. Used only when you are creating a key map or device map.

See also: “SAS Data Sets” on page 29 and “About the GKEYMAP Data Set” on page 987.

Featured in: Example 1 on page 990.

OUT=*output-data-set*
identifies the output data set to which the data from a key map or device map are to be written. Used only when you output an existing key map or device map as a SAS data set.

Featured in: Example 1 on page 990.

Options

You can specify as many options as you want and list them in any order.

DEVICE=*device-name*
specifies the device driver that a device map is associated with, where *device-name* is the name of an entry in a device catalog. DEVICE= is not required when creating a device map, but it can be used if you want to limit the use of the device map to one particular driver. If you do not use DEVICE=, the device map can be used with any device. DEVICE= is valid only if you are creating a device map.

DEVMAP | KEYMAP
specifies whether you are working with a device map or a key map. The default is KEYMAP unless you use an option that can be used only with DEVMAP. This option also specifies the type of map you are outputting as a data set.

Featured in: Example 1 on page 990.

TYPE=MAP11 | MAP1N
specifies whether you are mapping characters in a device map one-to-one or one-to-many. If you specify TYPE=MAP11 (the default), each character in a graphics text string is mapped to only one character on the output device. If you specify TYPE=MAP1N, a single character in a graphics text string can be mapped to multiple characters on the output device. For example, if two characters have to be sent to the graphics output device to display a single hardware character, specify TYPE=MAP1N. Specify TYPE=MAP1N only when you create a device map.

MULTFONT
specifies that an alternate hardware character set is required to display one or more characters in the device map. Specify the MULTFONT option only when you create a device map.

Creating a Data Set from an Existing Key Map or Device Map

To generate a data set from an existing key map or device map, follow these steps:

1. Specify the name of the key map or device map with the NAME= argument. If the map is user generated, you must first submit a LIBNAME statement to associate the libref GFONT0 with the location where the map is stored, and NAME= must specify the name that was specified for the key map or device map when it was created. If the map is an Institute-supplied map, it is located in the catalog SASHELP.FONTS, and you do not need to submit a LIBNAME statement to access it.
2. In the OUT= argument, specify the name of the data set to which the data are to be written. By default, the data set is written to the temporary library WORK.
3. Use the DEVMAP option if a device map is selected.
4. Optionally, use the PRINT procedure to display the newly created data set (most values will be unprintable, so you should use a $HEX2. format for the FROM and TO variables).

Creating and Using Key Maps and Device Maps

To create and use a key map or device map, follow these steps:

1. Submit a LIBNAME statement that associates the libref GFONT0 with the location where your map is to be stored.
2. Create a data set that contains the mapping information you need. You can use a DATA step to create all of the mapping information for the key map or device map, or you can create a data set from an existing key map or device map, then update that data set with the mappings that you need. This process is illustrated in Example 1 on page 990.
3. Use the GKEYMAP procedure to create the key map or device map, using as input the data set that contains the mapping information. The GKEYMAP procedure stores the map in the catalog GFONT0.FONTS.
4. Use the KEYMAP= or DEVMAP= option in a GOPTIONS statement to assign the key map or device map in your SAS session. The specified map is used automatically in your SAS/GRAPH programs. (The device map is used only when you use a hardware character set.)

Examples

Example 1: Modifying a Key Map

Procedure features:
GKEYMAP options:
DATA=

KEYMAP
NAME=
OUT=

Other features:

DATA step
GOPTIONS procedure
GOPTIONS statement
LIBNAME statement
SORT procedure

Sample library member: GKYMODIF

This example shows how to change multiple characters in an existing key map. It assumes that the national characters ß and ã are not on your keyboard, so you want to create a key map that provides them.

To provide the ß character, this example's key map converts the @ character into the SAS/GRAPH internal encoding for ('B8'x). Whenever the @ character is typed in text that is displayed with a software font, the character ß is drawn instead. In this case, the replacement character uses the text position that would have been used by the typed character.

Note: Once you have modified your key map so that @ is mapped to ß, you can no longer generate @ in a software font from your keyboard when the key map is in effect. △

To provide the ã character, which is not on the keyboard or in the ICE table, this example's key map converts the asterisk (*) into the SAS/GRAPH internal encoding for the accent character 'D5'x (a tilde). In this case, when the character * is typed, the resulting tilde does not take up a text position but is backspaced and used as an accent over the character preceding it in the text. To create the ã character, therefore, the text must contain the two characters a*.

Note: The example updates the current key map rather than creating a new key map so that all of the other character mapping in the key map remains in effect. △

Assign the libref and set the graphics environment. LIBNAME associates the libref GFONT0 with the location of the SAS data library where your device maps and key maps are stored.

```
libname gfont0 'SAS-data-library';
goptions reset=global gunit=pct border cback=white
         colors=(black blue green red)
         ftext=swiss ftitle=swissb htext=6;
```

Determine the name of the current key map. The SAS log in Output 34.1 shows that the keymap name is DEFAULT.

```
proc goptions
   option=keymap;
run;
```

Copy the DEFAULT key map to a temporary SAS data set. NAME= specifies the DEFAULT key map as input to the procedure. OUT= specifies the data set TEMP, which is created from the specified key map.

```
proc gkeymap name=default
   out=temp;
run;
```

Create data set NEW. NEW will be used to create the key map for the character conversions. Values for the FROM variable are the keyboard characters to be converted. Values for the TO variable are hexadecimal codes from the SAS ICE table. OUTPUT is required to write a separate observation for each character to be mapped.

```
data new;
   from='@';
   to='b8'x;
   output;
   from='*';
   to='d5'x;
   output;
run;
```

Sort data set NEW and update data set TEMP with the mapping information. The data set NEW must be sorted by the FROM variable before its observations can be used to update data set TEMP.

```
proc sort data=new;
   by from;
data temp;
   update temp new;
   by from;
run;
```

Create a new key map from the modified data set. NAME= assigns a name to the new key map. DATA= specifies the data set TEMP as input to the procedure. KEYMAP specifies that the map being generated is a key map (the default).

```
proc gkeymap name=mykeymap
             data=temp
             keymap;
run;
```

Specify the new key map in a GOPTIONS statement. KEYMAP= specifies the name of the new key map so that when the characters @ and a* are specified in TITLE statements, the characters ß and ã are displayed in the output.

```
goptions keymap=mykeymap;
```

Print two titles with the special characters. The character @ is typed where the character ß should print, and the character * is typed after the character it will accent.

```
title1 'Kaiserstra@e';
title2 'Sa*o Paulo';
footnote j=r 'GKYMODIF ';
proc gslide;
run;
quit;.
'
```

Output 34.1 Log from GOPTIONS Procedure

```
                 SAS/GRAPH software options and parameters
                   (executing in DMS Process environment)
KEYMAP=DEFAULT                        Input character map for hardware and software
                                      text
```

CHAPTER

35

The GMAP Procedure

Overview

The GMAP procedure produces two-dimensional (choropleth) or three-dimensional (block, prism, and surface) color maps that show variations of a variable value with respect to an area. A wide assortment of map data sets are available with SAS/GRAPH software.

Use the GMAP procedure to

- produce maps
- summarize data that vary by physical area
- show trends and variations of data between geographic areas
- highlight regional differences or extremes.

About Block Maps

Block maps display a block at the approximate center of each map area to convey information about response variable values. The height of each block represents a response level. The height is not directly proportional to the value of the response variable. Instead, the block heights increase in order of the response levels.

Figure 35.1 on page 997 shows a simple block map of hazardous waste sites that are installed in each state. The number of sites in each state (the response value) is represented by the height of the block.

Figure 35.1 Block Map

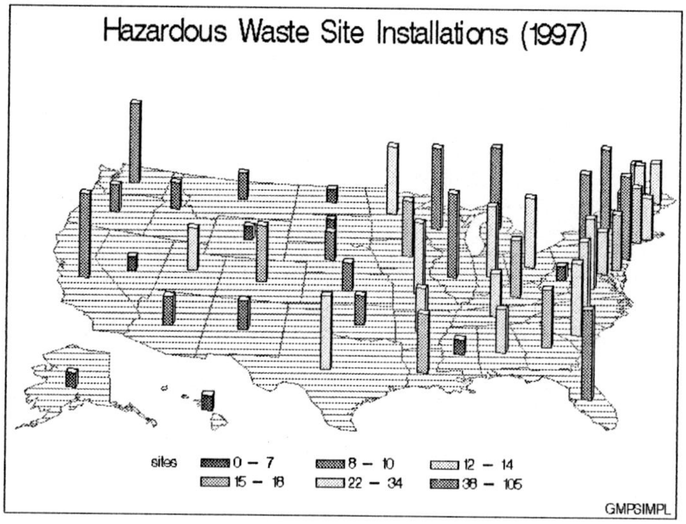

The program for this map is in Example 1 on page 1045. For more information on producing block maps, see "BLOCK Statement" on page 1009.

About Choropleth Maps

Two-dimensional (choropleth) maps indicate levels of magnitude or response levels of the corresponding response variable by filling map areas with different colors and patterns.

Figure 35.2 on page 997 shows a choropleth map of hazardous waste sites that are installed in each state. The number of sites in each state (the response value) is represented by the pattern that is assigned to the state.

Figure 35.2 Two-dimensional (Choropleth) Map

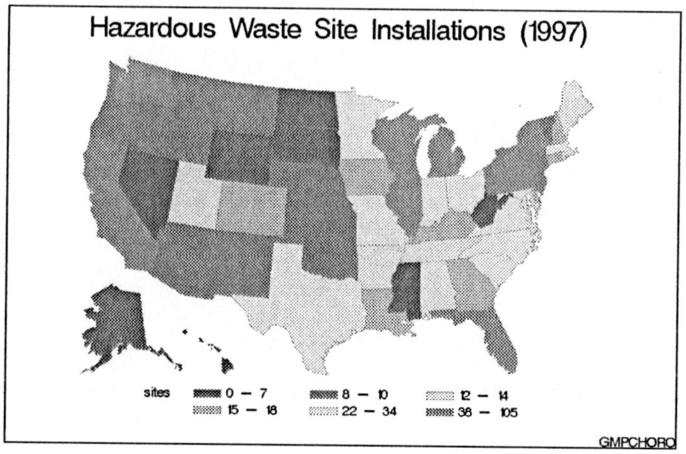

The program for this map is in Example 4 on page 1052.

You can also produce a simple choropleth map that shows an outline of a map's areas by specifying your map data set as both the map data set and the response data set in a GMAP statement and adding a PATTERN statement with VALUE=EMPTY. For more information on the PATTERN statement, see “PATTERN Statement” on page 169. For more information on producing choropleth maps, see “CHORO Statement” on page 1017.

About Prism Maps

Prism maps use polyhedrons (raised polygons) in the shape of each map area to convey information about response variable values. The height of each polyhedron, or prism, represents an ordinal level of the response variable. Prism heights increase in order of response levels. That is, the lowest prisms correspond to the first level, and the tallest prisms correspond to the last level.

You can alter the perspective of the map by selecting a viewing position (the point in space from which you view the map). You can also change the position of the light source so that the shadowing on the prisms enhances the illusion of height.

Figure 35.3 on page 998 shows a prism map of hazardous waste sites installed in each state. The number of sites in each state (the response value) is represented by the height of the state.

Figure 35.3 Prism Map

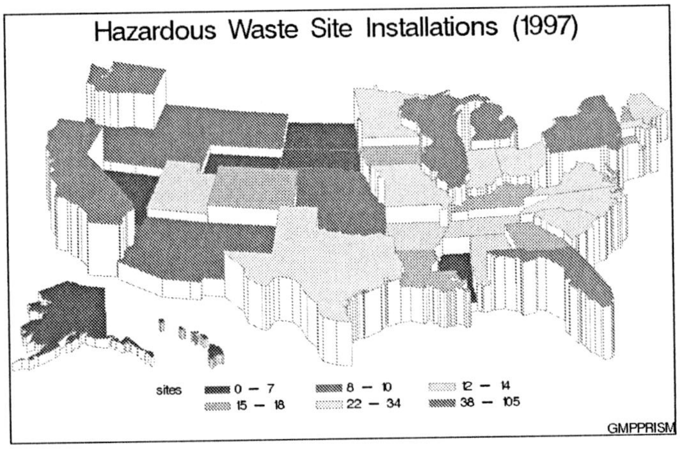

The program for this map is in Example 7 on page 1063. For more information on producing prism maps, see “PRISM Statement” on page 1022.

About Surface Maps

Surface maps display a spike at the approximate center of each map area to convey information about response variable values. The height of the spike corresponds to the relative value of the response variable, not to the actual value of the response variable. Thus, a spike that represents a value of 100 may not be exactly 10 times higher than a spike that represents a value of 10. Map area boundaries are not drawn.

Surface maps provide no clear map area boundaries and no legend. Thus, surface maps provide a simple way to judge relative trends in the response data but are an inappropriate way to represent specific response values.

Figure 35.4 on page 999 shows a surface map of hazardous waste sites that are installed in each state. The number of sites in each state (the response value) is represented by the height of the spike.

Figure 35.4 Surface Map

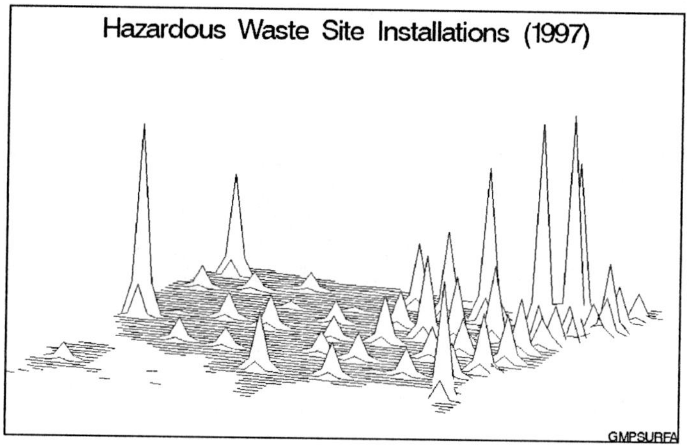

The program for this map is in Example 9 on page 1066. For more information on producing surface maps, see "SURFACE Statement" on page 1030.

Concepts

Map data sets and response data sets are used in the GMAP procedure. These data sets must contain the required variables or the procedure stops and you get an error message. Depending on the type of map data set used, the map and response data sets can be used individually in the GMAP procedure or merged into a single data set to be used in the GMAP procedure. Each data set must contain the same identification variable.

About Map Data Sets

There are two types of map data sets: traditional map data sets and feature tables. Each uses a different data arrangement to store the spatial information needed to create maps. All of the map data delivered with SAS/GRAPH is available in both the traditional map data set and feature table format.

About Traditional Data Sets

A *traditional map data set* is a SAS data set that contains coordinates that define the boundaries of map areas, such as states or counties.

Required Variables

A traditional map data set must contain at least these variables:

- □ a numeric variable named X that contains the horizontal coordinates of the boundary points. The value of this variable could be either projected or unprojected. If unprojected, X represents longitude.
- □ a numeric variable named Y that contains the vertical coordinates of the boundary points. The value of this variable could be either projected or unprojected. If unprojected, Y represents latitude.

- one or more variables that uniquely identify the areas in the map. Map area identification variables can be either character or numeric and are indicated in the ID statement.

The X and Y variable values in the traditional map data set do not have to be in any specific units because they are rescaled by the GMAP procedure based on the minimum and maximum values in the data set. The minimum X and Y values are in the lower-left corner of the map, and the maximum X and Y values are in the upper-right corner.

Traditional map data sets in which the X and Y variables contain longitude and latitude should be projected before you use them with PROC GMAP. See Chapter 39, "The GPROJECT Procedure," on page 1161 for details.

Segment Variable

Optionally, the traditional map data set also can contain a variable named SEGMENT to identify map areas that comprise noncontagious polygons. Each unique value of the SEGMENT variable within a single map area defines a distinct polygon. If the SEGMENT variable is not present, each map area is drawn as a separate closed polygon that indicates a single segment.

The observations for each segment of a map area in the map data set must occur in the order in which the points are to be joined. The GMAP procedure forms map area outlines by connecting the boundary points of each segment in the order in which they appear in the data set, eventually joining the last point to the first point to complete the polygon.

LONG and LAT Variables

In addition to the variables described in "Required Variables" on page 999, the SAS/GRAPH map data sets can also contain the following variables:

- a numeric variable named LONG containing the unprojected longitude (in radians or degrees) of the boundary points
- a numeric variable named LAT containing the unprojected latitude (in radians or degrees) of the boundary points.

The GMAP procedure uses the values of the X and Y variables to draw the map. Therefore, if you want to produce an unprojected map by using the values in LONG and LAT, you would have to rename LONG and LAT to X and Y first.

SAS/GRAPH software includes a number of predefined map data sets. These data sets are described in "Viewing Map Data Sets" on page 1001.

Traditional Map Data Sets Containing X, Y, LONG, and LAT

Most of the traditional map data sets that are provided with SAS/GRAPH software contain four coordinate variables (X, Y, LONG, and LAT). In this case, X and Y are always projected values that will be used by the SAS/GRAPH procedures (by default). If you need to use the unprojected values that are contained in the LONG and LAT variables, then you must

1 drop the existing X and Y variables

2 rename the LONG and LAT variables to X and Y.

The MAP= value in the GMAP procedure automatically uses X and Y. See "Input Map Data Sets that Contain Both Projected and Unprojected Values" on page 1164 for more details.

Traditional Map Data Sets Containing Only X and Y

The traditional map data sets that contain X and Y variables (and no LONG and LAT variables), are usually projected maps. However, there are a few traditional map data sets for the US and Canada that contain X and Y values that are unprojected longitude and latitude. In this case, you will need to use the GPROJECT procedure to project the map (see Chapter 39, "The GPROJECT Procedure," on page 1161).

Note: You can determine whether a SAS traditional map data set is projected or unprojected by looking at the description of each variable that is displayed when you use the CONTENTS procedure or by browsing the MAPS.METAMAPS data set. △

About Feature Tables

An alternative to using the traditional map data set is the feature table. While the traditional map data set stores the spatial information across multiple observations, the feature table uses a data arrangement to store all of the spatial information in a single variable value. The feature table's data arrangement uses the $GEOREF SAS/GRAPH format.

$GEOREF format

The $GEOREF format stores spatial information in binary data streams, making it possible to store as a single variable value all the information needed to draw a map area. Thus, the feature tables use only a single observation for each map area, and they treat a field of spatial information just like any other information that can be added to a data set. Each $GEOREF value points to a corresponding traditional map data set to retrieve the coordinate values. The traditional map data set associated with the feature table must be located in the SAS library with the feature table for GMAP to proceed correctly.

To locate the variable that contains the spatial information, run PROC CONTENTS on a feature table. In the Output window, the variable containing the spatial information will have $GEOREF as the value in the column labelled Format.

Note: Some feature tables, like MAPS.NAMES, have more than one $GEOREF format variable. △

Merging Feature Tables with Response Data Sets

To display response data with a feature table, the feature table must be merged with a response data set. The merged data set is then specified by the DATA= option in the PROC GMAP statement. The combined data set can be used repeatedly for generating maps, without having to merge the map and response data again.

First, a PROC SORT must be used to sort the response and feature tables by a variable that is present within both the data sets. Once sorted, the data sets can then be merged with a SQL or DATA step MERGE with the BY variable being the variable used to sort the data sets. Once the data set is merged, the $GEOREF formatted variable from the feature table becomes the new data set's identification variable to be used in the GMAP procedure. See Example 11 on page 1069 for more details.

Viewing Map Data Sets

When viewed in SAS, a data set is displayed as a table, with the variable names or labels displayed as column headings and the variable values arranged in columns and rows. The data sets that contain geometry objects describe a map by its spatial features, so their data tables are referred to as *feature tables*. Because feature tables store the spatial information in a single variable value, the spatial data and response data is viewed as a 1:1 ratio. The traditional MAP data sets define map areas using geometric coordinates, so their data tables are also referred to as *geometry tables*. Traditional map data sets store the geometric coordinates across multiple observations.

In the MAPS library, there is a data set named METAMAPS, which contains meta data about all of the data sets that are delivered in the library. Among the meta data in MAPS.METAMAPS are the following four variables, which you can use to determine which feature table corresponds to a particular geometry table:

Table 35.1

Variable	Description
MEMNAME	Identifies the names of all of the data sets that are delivered in the MAPS library.
MEMCODE	Indicates whether a data set represents a feature table (F) or a geometry table (G).
F_TABLE	Indicates the corresponding feature table for a geometry table. This variable is blank for rows that contain meta data about a feature table.
F_GEOCOL	Indicates the variable, in the feature table, whose values encapsulate the geometry object.

For example, consider the data sets MAPS.ASIA, MAPS.STATES, and MAPS.US. Each of these represents a geometry table, and to locate the corresponding feature tables, you would look in MAPS.METAMAPS to find the MEMNAME values ASIA, STATES, and US. Here are the relevant values on those rows:

Table 35.2

MEMNAME	MEMCODE	F_TABLE	F_GEOCOL
Asia	G	NAMES	CONT95_GEO
STATES	G	US2	GEO_STATE
US	G	US2	_MAP_GEOMETRY_

From these values, you can see that the data sets that are named ASIA, STATES, and US all represent geometry tables because their MEMCODE values are G. The feature table corresponding to the ASIA data set is the data set NAMES, which stores the spatial information in the variable CONT95_GEO. The feature tables corresponding to STATES and US are both in the data set US2. The spatial information corresponding to STATES is stored in the variable GEO_STATE, and the spatial information corresponding to US is stored in the variable _MAP_GEOMETRY_.

Speciality Map Data Sets

There are several map data sets available with SAS/GRAPH software that allow you to easily label maps:

MAPS.USCENTER
: contains the coordinates of the visual center of each state in the U.S. and Washington, D.C., as well as coordinates in the ocean for states that are too small to contain a label. There are two pairs of variables for locating labels using Annotate data sets. The X and Y variables are projected and can be used with the MAPS.US and MAPS.USCOUNTY data sets. The LONG and LAT variables are unprojected longitude and latitude in degrees and can be used with the MAPS.STATES, MAPS.COUNTIES, and MAPS.COUNTY data sets.

MAPS.USCITY
: contains the locations of selected cities in the U.S. Many city names occur in more than one state, so you may have to subset by state to avoid duplication. There are two pairs of variables for locating labels using Annotate data sets. The X and Y variables contain projected coordinates and can be used with the MAPS.US and MAPS.COUNTY data sets. The LONG and LAT variables contain the unprojected longitude and latitude in degrees. These can be used to place labels on the MAPS.STATES, MAPS.COUNTIES, or MAPS.COUNTIES data sets.

MAPS.CANCENS
: contains the names of the Canadian census divisions. You can use MAPS.CANCENS with the MAPS.CANADA and MAPS.CANADA3 data sets.

For details on each of these data sets, see the MAPS.METAMAPS data set.

About Response Data Sets

A *response data set* is a SAS data set that contains

- one or more response variables that contain data values that are associated with map areas. Each value of the response variable is associated with a map area in the map data set.
- identification variables that identify the map area to which a response value belongs. These variables must be the same as those that are contained in the map data set.

The response data set can contain other variables in addition to these required variables.

Using the Response Data Set with the Map Data Sets

The traditional map data set and the response data set must be used independently in the PROC GMAP statement, where the response data set is specified by the DATA= option and the traditional map data set is specified by the MAP= option. The values of the map area ID variables in the response data set determine the map areas to be included on the map. Unless the ALL option is used in the PROC GMAP statement, only the map areas with response values are shown on the map. As a result, you do not need to subset your map data set if you are mapping only a small section of the map. However, if you map the same small section frequently, then create a subset of the map data set for efficiency.

If you have a response data set named WORK.SITES, then the syntax for using GMAP might resemble the following:

```
/* if necessary, define a libref pointing to the SAS maps library */
libname maps 'SAS-data-library';
/* generate a map */
proc gmap map=maps.us data=work.sites;
   id state;
   choro region/discrete;
run;
quit;
```

A feature table and response data set are merged using a variable contained in both data sets. The new combined data set becomes the DATA= value in the PROC GMAP statement. When the response data set and the feature table are merged into one, do not use MAP=*map-data-set* in the PROC GMAP statement. The $GEOREF formatted variable is the ID variable for the combined data set. See Example 11 on page 1069 for more details.

Note: Response data that does not correspond to a map feature will be included in the legend. △

About Response Variables

The GMAP procedure can produce block, choropleth, prism, and surface maps for both numeric and character response variables. Numeric variables fall into two categories: discrete and continuous.

- *Discrete variables* contain a finite number of specific numeric values that are to be represented on the map. For example, a variable that contains only the values 1989 or 1990 is a discrete variable.
- *Continuous variables* contain a range of numeric values that are to be represented on the map. For example, a variable that contains any real value between 0 and 100 is a continuous variable.

Numeric response variables are always treated as continuous variables unless the DISCRETE option is used in the action statement.

About Response Levels

Response levels are the values that identify categories of data on the graph. The categories that are shown on the graph are based on the values of the response variable. Based on the type of the response variable, a response level can be determined by any of the following:

- a character value
- the MIDPOINTS= option
- a range of numeric values
- a specific numeric value.

When response levels are determined by a character value, the GMAP procedure treats each unique value as a response level. For example, if the response variable contains the names of ten regions, each region will be a response level, resulting in ten response levels.

When character response levels are determined by the MIDPOINTS= option, any response variable values that do not match one of the specified response level values are ignored.

When response levels are determined by a range of numeric values, each response level has the same number of observations. These options are exceptions to this:

- The LEVELS= option specifies the number of response levels to be used on the map.
- The DISCRETE option causes the numeric variable to be treated as a discrete variable.
- The MIDPOINTS= option chooses specific response level values as medians of the value ranges.

If the response variable values are continuous, then the GMAP procedure assigns response level intervals automatically unless you specify otherwise. The response levels represent a range of values rather than a single value.

When response levels are determined by specific numeric values, and the DISCRETE option is specified, one level is created for each value. If the response variable has an associated format, then each formatted value is represented by a different response level. Formatted values are truncated to 16 characters.

The BLOCK, CHORO, and PRISM statements assign patterns to response levels. In CHORO and PRISM maps, response levels are shown as map areas. However, in BLOCK maps, response levels are shown as blocks. The default fill pattern for the response level is solid.

PATTERN statements can define the fill patterns and colors for both blocks and map areas. PATTERN definitions that define valid block patterns are applied to the blocks (response levels), and PATTERN definitions that define valid map patterns are applied to map areas.

See "PATTERN Statement" on page 169 for more information on fill pattern values and default pattern rotation.

About Identification Variables

For traditional map data sets and response data sets, *id-variable(s)* identify the map areas (for example, counties, states, or provinces) that make up the map. A *unit area* or *map area* is a group of observations with the same ID value. The GMAP procedure matches the value of the response variables for each map area in the response data set to the corresponding map area in the traditional map data set in order to create the output graphs.

With feature tables, the *geo-variable*, or $GEOREF formatted variable containing the spatial information, is the identification variable. Each observation in a feature table has a unique $GEOREF formatted variable value. When merging the feature table with the response data set using a SQL or DATA step statement, the identification variable can be any variable that is contained within both data sets. Once the merged data set has been created, the *geo-variable* is used in the PROC GMAP ID statement for the merged feature table and response data set. See Example 11 on page 1069 for more details.

Displaying Map Areas and Response Data

Whether the GMAP procedure draws a map area and whether it displays patterns for response values depends on the contents of the response data set and on the ALL and MISSING options. The following table describes the conditions under which the procedure does or does not display map areas and response data.

If the response data set...	*And if...*	*Then the procedure...*
includes the map area	the map area has a response value	draws the map area and displays the response data
includes the map area	the map area has no response value (that is, the value is missing)	draws the map area but leaves it empty
includes the map area	the map area has no response value and the MISSING option is used in the map statement	draws the map area and displays a response level for the missing value
does not include the map area	the ALL option is used in the PROC GMAP statement	draws the map area but leaves it empty
does not include the map area	the ALL option is not used	does not draw the map area

Summary of Use

To use the GMAP procedure, you must do the following:

1 If necessary, issue a LIBNAME statement for the SAS data library that contains the map data set that you want to display.

2 If using a traditional map data set, determine what processing needs to be done to the map data set before it is displayed. Use the GPROJECT, GREDUCE, and GREMOVE procedures or a DATA step to perform the necessary processing.

3 Issue a LIBNAME statement for the SAS data set that contains the response data set, or use a DATA step to create a response data set.

4 If using a traditional map data set, use the PROC GMAP statement to identify the map data set as the MAP= value and response data set as the DATA= value.

5 If using a feature table, use PROC SORT to individually sort the feature table and response data set by a variable common to both data sets. Next, use SQL or the DATA step MERGE to merge the feature table with the response data set by using a variable common to both data sets. Use the combined data set as the DATA= value in the PROC GMAP statement (do not include MAP= in the PROC GMAP statement).

6 Use the ID statement to name the *id-variable(s)* or the *geo-variable*.

7 Use a BLOCK, CHORO, PRISM, or SURFACE statement to identify the response variable and generate the map.

Accessing SAS Maps Online

Visit SAS Maps Online to download data updates, sample SAS/GRAPH programs that use the map data sets delivered with SAS/GRAPH, and GIF images of maps. SAS Maps Online is located at the following URL:

http://support.sas.com/rnd/datavisualization/mapsonline/html/

Procedure Syntax

Requirements: One ID statement (see "ID Statement" on page 1009)and at least one CHORO (see "CHORO Statement" on page 1017), BLOCK (see "BLOCK Statement" on page 1009), PRISM (see "PRISM Statement" on page 1022), or SURFACE (see "SURFACE Statement" on page 1030)statement is required.

Global statements: FOOTNOTE, LEGEND, PATTERN, TITLE

Reminder: The GMAP procedure can include the BY (see "BY Statement" on page 141), FORMAT, LABEL, and WHERE statements as well as the "TITLE, FOOTNOTE, and NOTE Statements" on page 210.

Supports: RUN-group processing, Output Delivery System (ODS)

PROC GMAP <MAP=*map-data-set*>
DATA=*response-data-set* | *feature-table*
<ALL>
<ANNOTATE=*Annotate-data-set*>
<GOUT=<*libref.*>*output-catalog*>
<IMAGEMAP=*output-data-set*>;
ID *id-variable(s)* | *geo-variable*;
BLOCK *response-variable(s)* </ *option(s)*>;
CHORO *response-variable(s)* </ *option(s)*>;
PRISM *response-variable(s)*</ *option(s)*>;
SURFACE *response-variable(s)* </ *option(s)*>;

PROC GMAP Statement

Identifies the map data set and the response data set that contain the variables associated with the map. If the response data set and the feature table have been merged, the statement identifies the merged map data set. The statement optionally causes the procedure to display all map areas and specifies annotation and an output catalog.

Requirements: Both a map data set and a response data set are required. This can include a traditional map data set and response data set or a merged response data set and feature table.

PROC GMAP <MAP=*map-data-set*>
DATA=*response-data-set* | *feature-table*
<ALL>
<ANNOTATE=*Annotate-data-set*>
<GOUT=<*libref.*>*output-catalog*>
<IMAGEMAP=*output-data-set*>;

Required Argument

DATA=*response-data-set* | *feature-table*
identifies the SAS data set that contains the response values or the response values and the spatial information that are evaluated and represented on the map. If a

response data set is specified, it must contain the same identification variable or variables as the map data set, along with the values of the response variable. If a feature table is specified, it must contain response data information and spatial geometry information. By default, the GMAP procedure uses the most recently created SAS data set.

See Also: "Concepts" on page 999, "SAS Data Sets" on page 29, and "About Feature Tables" on page 1001.

Options

PROC GMAP statement options affect all of the graphs that are produced by the procedure.

ALL

specifies that all maps generated by the procedure should include every map area from the map data set, even if the response data set does not include an observation for the map area.

When you use the ALL option and a BY statement in a RUN group, the maps generated for each BY group include every map area from the map data set.

See also: "Displaying Map Areas and Response Data" on page 1005, CEMPTY= and the MISSING options.

ANNOTATE=*Annotate-data-set*
ANNO=*Annotate-data-set*

specifies a data set to annotate all of the maps that are produced by the GMAP procedure. To annotate individual maps, use the ANNOTATE= option in the action statement.

Note: You can use the %MAPLABEL Macro to create the *Annotate-data-set*. See "%MAPLABEL Macro" on page 686 for more information. △

See also: Chapter 24, "Using Annotate Data Sets," on page 587.

GOUT=*<libref.>output-catalog*

specifies the SAS catalog in which to save the graphics output that is produced by the GMAP procedure for later replay. You can use the GREPLAY procedure to view the graphs stored in the catalog. If you do not use the GOUT= option, catalog entries are written to the default catalog WORK.GSEG, which is erased at the end of your session.

Not supported by: Java, ActiveX

See also: "Storing Graphics Output in SAS Catalogs" on page 53.

IMAGEMAP=*output-data-set*

creates a temporary SAS data set that contains information about the graph that is replayed from the graphics catalog. The information in the image map data set includes the shape and coordinates of the elements in the graph, along with values that were associated with those elements in variables that were identified for that purpose in the HTML= and/or HTML_LEGEND= options. The image map data set can be used to generate an HTML image map in an HTML output file using the IMAGEMAP macro. The IMAGEMAP macro takes two arguments, the name of the image map data set and the name or fileref of an HTML output file, as shown in the following example:

```
%imagemap(imgmapds, myimgmap.html);
```

Not supported by: Java, ActiveX

MAP=*map-data-set*
names a SAS traditional map data set that contains the Cartesian coordinates for the boundary points of each map area. The traditional map data set must contain the same identification variable or variables as the response data set being used. This statement is required if a feature table is not being used.

See also: "About Traditional Data Sets" on page 999.

ID Statement

Identifies the variable or variables in the input data set(s) that define map areas.

Requirements: At least one *id-variable* or *geo-variable* is required.

ID *id-variable(s)* | *geo-variable*;

Required Arguments

id-variable(s)
identifies one or more variables in the map and response data sets that define map area. This argument is used only when map and response data sets are specified. If a feature table is specified, then specify the *geo-variable* argument.

Every variable that is listed in the ID statement must appear in both the map and response data sets. The variable identified by the *id-variable(s)* argument can be of type numeric or character and should have the same name, type, and length in both the response and map data sets.

See also: "About Identification Variables" on page 1005.

Featured in: Example 1 on page 1045, Example 3 on page 1049, and Example 4 on page 1052.

geo-variable
identifies the $GEOREF formatted variable in the feature table containing the spatial geometry information for the map. The variable identified by the *geo-variable* argument must be of character type.

See also: "About Identification Variables" on page 1005.

Featured in: Example 11 on page 1069.

BLOCK Statement

Creates three-dimensional block maps on which levels of magnitude of the specified response variables are represented by blocks of varying height, pattern, and color.

Requirements: At least one response variable is required. The ID statement must be used in conjunction with the BLOCK statement.

Global statements: FOOTNOTE, LEGEND, PATTERN, TITLE

Description

The BLOCK statement specifies the variable or variables that contain the data that are represented on the map by blocks of varying height, pattern, and color. This statement automatically

- □ determines the midpoints ranges
- □ scales the blocks
- □ assigns patterns to the block faces and map areas. (See "About Block Maps and Patterns" on page 1016 for more information.)

You can use statement options to enhance the appearance of the map. For example, you can specify the width and shape of the blocks, the outline colors for the blocks and the map areas, and the angle of view. Other statement options control the response levels.

In addition, you can use global statements to modify the block patterns, the map patterns, and the legend, as well as to add titles and footnotes to the map. You can also use an Annotate data set to enhance the map.

BLOCK *response-variable(s)* </ *option(s)*>;

The *option(s)* argument can be one or more of the following:

- □ appearance options:
  - ANNOTATE=*Annotate-data-set*
  - BLOCKSIZE=*size*
  - CBLKOUT=*block-outline-color* | SAME
  - CEMPTY=*empty-area-outline-color*
  - COUTLINE=*area-outline-color* | SAME
  - SHAPE=*3D-block-shape*
  - WOUTLINE=*block-outline-width*
  - XSIZE=*map-width* <*units*>
  - YSIZE=*map-height* <*units*>
  - XVIEW=*x*
  - YVIEW=*y*
  - ZVIEW=*z*
- □ mapping options:
  - AREA=*n* | *response-variable-name*
  - DISCRETE
  - LEVELS=*number-of-response-levels* | ALL
  - MIDPOINTS=*value-list* | OLD
  - MISSING
- □ legend options:
  - CTEXT=*text-color*
  - LEGEND=LEGEND<1...99>
  - NOLEGEND
- □ description options:
  - DESCRIPTION='*entry-description*'
  - NAME='*entry-name*'
- □ ODS options
  - HTML=*variable*

HTML_LEGEND=*variable*

Required Arguments

response-variable(s)

specifies one or more variables in the response data set, or in the merged response and feature table, that contain response values that are to be represented on the map. Each response variable produces a separate map. All variables must be in the input data set. Multiple response variables are separated with blanks. Blocks are not drawn for missing values for the response variable unless you use the MISSING option in the BLOCK statement.

See also: "About Response Variables" on page 1004.

Options

Options in a BLOCK statement affect all of the maps that are produced by that statement. You can specify as many options as you want and list them in any order.

ANNOTATE=*Annotate-data-set*
ANNO=*Annotate-data-set*

specifies a data set to annotate onto maps that are produced by the BLOCK statement. Annotate coordinate systems 1, 2, 7, and 8 are not valid with block maps.

Note: You can use the %MAPLABEL Macro to create the *Annotate-data-set*. See "%MAPLABEL Macro" on page 686 for more information. △

See also: Chapter 24, "Using Annotate Data Sets," on page 587.

AREA=*n* | *response-variable-name*

specifies that a different map pattern be used for the surface of each map area or group of map areas on the map.

The value of *n* indicates which variable in the ID statement determines the groups that are distinguished by a surface pattern. By default, all map unit areas are drawn using the same surface fill pattern. If your ID statement has only one map area identification variable, then use AREA=1 to indicate that each map area surface uses a different pattern. If you have more than one variable in your ID statement, then use *n* to indicate the position of the variable that defines groups that will share a pattern. When you use the AREA= option, the map data set should be sorted in order of the variables in the ID statement.

A column name defined in either the MAP= or DATA= data sets may be indicated with the *column-name* value. If the column name exists in both the MAP= and DATA= data sets, the column in the map= data set will be used. When *column-name* is used, the areas will be colored based on the AREA= value. Duplicate AREA= values may have different patterns assigned

By default, using the AREA= option fills map areas by rotating the default hatch patterns through the colors list, beginning with the M2N0 pattern. The default outline color depends on the PATTERN statement:

- If you do not specify a PATTERN statement, the default outline color is black for the Java or ActiveX devices. Otherwise, the default outline color is the foreground color (the first color in the colors list).
- If you specify the PATTERN statement or the V6COMP graphics option, the default is COUTLINE=SAME.

You can specify pattern fills or colors or both with PATTERN statements that specify map/plot patterns. A separate PATTERN definition is needed for each specified area.

See also: "PATTERN Statement" on page 169.

Featured in: Example 3 on page 1049.

BLOCKSIZE=*size*
specifies the width of the blocks. The unit of *size* is the character cell width for the selected output device. By default, BLOCKSIZE=2.

Featured in: Example 5 on page 1054.

CBLKOUT=*block-outline-color* | SAME
outlines all blocks in the specified color. The SAME value specifies that the outline color of a block, a block segment, or a legend is the same as the interior pattern color.

The default outline color depends on the PATTERN statement:

- If no PATTERN statements are specified, then the default outline color is the foreground color (the first color in the colors list).
- If a PATTERN statement or the V6COMP graphics option is specified, then the default is CBLKOUT=SAME.

CBLKOUT= is not valid when SHAPE=CYLINDER.

Note: If you specify empty block patterns (VALUE=EMPTY in a PATTERN statement), you should not change the outline color from the default value, SAME, to a single color. Otherwise all the outlines will be one color and you will only be able to distinguish between empty areas by their size. Empty block patterns (VALUE=EMPTY in a PATTERN statement) are not supported by DEVICE=ACTIVEX. △

Featured in: Example 1 on page 1045 and Example 3 on page 1049.

CEMPTY=*empty-area-outline-color*
outlines empty map areas in the specified color. This option affects only map areas that are empty. Empty map areas are generated in block maps only when a map area is omitted from the response data set and the ALL option is included in the PROC GMAP statement.

The default outline color is the same as the default COUTLINE= color.

Not supported by: Java

See also: ALL on page 1008 and "Displaying Map Areas and Response Data" on page 1005.

COUTLINE=*area-outline-color* | SAME
outlines non-empty map areas in the specified color. When COUTLINE=*area-outline-color* and DEVICE=JAVA or ACTIVEX, both empty and non-empty map areas are outlined. The SAME value specifies that the outline color of a map area is the same as the interior pattern color.

The default outline color depends on the PATTERN statement:

- If you do not specify a PATTERN statement, the default outline color is black for the Java or ActiveX devices. Otherwise, the default outline color is the foreground color (the first color in the colors list).
- If you specify the PATTERN statement or the V6COMP graphics option, the default is COUTLINE=SAME.

Note: If you specify empty map patterns (VALUE=EMPTY in a PATTERN statement), then you should not change the outline color from the default value

SAME. Otherwise all the outlines will be one color and you will not be able to distinguish between the empty areas. Empty block patterns (VALUE=EMPTY in a PATTERN statement) are not supported by DEVICE=ACTIVEX. △

Featured in: Example 3 on page 1049.

CTEXT=*text-color*

specifies a color for the text in the legend. If you omit the CTEXT= option, a color specification is searched for in this order:

1 the CTEXT= option in a GOPTIONS statement

2 the default, the first color in the colors list.

The CTEXT= color specification is overridden if you also use the COLOR= suboption of a LABEL= or VALUE= option in a LEGEND definition that is assigned to the map legend. The COLOR= suboption determines the color of the legend label or the color of the legend value descriptions, respectively.

For the Java and ActiveX devices, the default color is black.

DESCRIPTION='*entry-description*'

DES='*entry-description*'

specifies a descriptive string up to 256 characters long, that appears in the description field of the catalog entry for the map. The description does not appear on the map. By default, the GMAP procedure assigns a description of the form BLOCK MAP OF *variable*, where *variable* is the name of the map variable.

Featured in: Example 5 on page 1054.

DISCRETE

treats a numeric, formatted response variable as though it has discrete values rather than continuous values. When you use DISCRETE, the response variable values are not grouped into ranges; instead, the GMAP procedure uses a separate response level (block height, pattern, and color) for each value of the formatted response variable.

The LEVELS= option is ignored when you use the DISCRETE option.

Use this option only if your numeric response variable is assigned a user-written format.

Note: If the data does not contain a value in a particular range of the format, that formatted range is not displayed in the legend. △

Featured in: Example 3 on page 1049 .

HTML=*variable*

identifies the variable in the input data set whose values create links in the HTML file created by the ODS HTML statement. These links are associated with an area of the map and point to the data or graph you wish to display when the user drills down on the area.

HTML_LEGEND=*variable*

identifies the variable in the input data set whose values create links in the HTML file created by the ODS HTML statement. These links are associated with a legend value and point to the data or graph you want to display in response to drill-down input from the user.

Not supported by: Java, ActiveX

LEGEND=LEGEND<1...99>

specifies the LEGEND statement to associate with the map. The LEGEND= option is ignored if the specified LEGEND definition is not currently in effect. In the GMAP procedure, the BLOCK statement produces a legend unless you use the NOLEGEND option. If you use the SHAPE= option in a LEGEND statement, only the value BAR is valid. Most of the LEGEND options described in "LEGEND Statement" on page

151 are supported by both Java and ActiveX. If a LEGEND option is not supported by Java or ActiveX, it is noted in the LEGEND option definition.

Not supported by: Java (partial), ActiveX (partial)

See also: "LEGEND Statement" on page 151.

Featured in: Example 2 on page 1047 and Example 5 on page 1054.

LEVELS=*number-of-response-levels* | ALL

number-of-response-levels specifies the number of response levels that are to be graphed when the response variables are continuous. Each level is assigned a different block height, pattern, and color combination.

If you specify DEVICE=ACTIVEX or DEVICE=ACTXIMG, and if you specify LEVELS=ALL, then a color ramp is used to assign each response value a continuous color scheme. The response values are assigned lighter and darker values of a color scheme to express lower and higher response values. When used with all other devices, the LEVELS=ALL and DISCRETE options behave exactly the same. For more information, see the DISCRETE option on page 1013.

If you do not use the LEVELS= option or the DISCRETE option, the GMAP procedure determines the number of response levels by using the formula FLOOR(1 + 3.3 log(n)), where n is the number of unique identification variable values for map areas.

The LEVELS= option is ignored when you use the DISCRETE or MIDPOINTS=*value-list* option. When MIDPOINTS=OLD is used with the LEVELS= option, default midpoints are generated using the Nelder algorithm (*Applied Statistics* 25:94–7, 1976).

Note: LEVELS=ALL is a . △

MIDPOINTS=*value-list* | OLD

specifies the response levels for the range of response values that are represented by each level (block height, pattern, and color combination).

For numeric response variables, value-list is either an explicit list of values or a starting and an ending value with an interval increment, or a combination of both forms:

n <...*n*>

n TO *n* <BY *increment*>

n <...*n* > TO *n* <BY *increment*> <*n*<...*n*>>

By default, the increment value is 1. You can specify discrete numeric values in any order. In all forms, *n* can be separated by blanks or commas. For example,

```
midpoints=(2 4 6)
midpoints=(2,4,6)
midpoints=(2 to 10 by 2)
```

If a numeric variable has an associated format, the specified values must be the *unformatted* values. With numeric response values, DEVICE=JAVA only uses midpoints that fall in the range of the data being used. Thus, if your data ranged from 30-80, but midpoints were specified at 25, 50, 75,and 100, only 50 and 75 are used.

For character response variables, value-list is a list of unique character values enclosed in quotes and separated by blanks:

'value-1' <...*'value-n'*>

```
midpoints='Midwest' 'Northeast' 'Northwest'
```

Specify the values in any order. If a character variable has an associated format, the specified values must be the *formatted* values. Character response values specified with the MIDPOINTS= option are not supported by DEVICE=JAVA.

You can selectively exclude some response variable values from the map, as shown here:

```
midpoints='Midwest'
```

Only those observations for which the response variable exactly matches one of the values listed in the MIDPOINTS= option are shown on the map. As a result, observations may be excluded inadvertently if values in the list are misspelled or if the case does not match exactly.

Specifying MIDPOINTS=OLD generates default midpoints using the Nelder algorithm (*Applied Statistics* 25:94–7, 1976). Specifying GOPTIONS V6COMP serves the same purpose.

Not supported by: Java (partial)

Featured in: Example 5 on page 1054.

MISSING

accepts a missing value as a valid level for the response variable.

See also: "Displaying Map Areas and Response Data" on page 1005.

NAME='*entry-name*'

If you specify DEVICE=ACTXIMG or DEVICE=JAVAIMG, then the name that you specify will be used for the client image output even in the file exists. For all other devices, if the name duplicates an existing entry name, SAS/GRAPH specifies the name of the catalog entry for the map. The maximum length for *entry-name* is 8 characters. The default name is GMAP. If the specified name duplicates the name of an existing entry, SAS/GRAPH appends a number to the duplicate name to create a unique name, for example, GMAP1.

Featured in: Example 5 on page 1054.

NOLEGEND

suppresses the legend.

SHAPE=*3D-block-shape*

specifies the shape of the blocks. Use this option to enhance the look of the block shape, or to specify a different shape. When using the SHAPE= option, only solid fill patterns will be used. The value of *3D-block-shape* can be one of the following:

- BLOCK | B
- CYLINDER | C
- HEXAGON | H
- PRISM | P
- STAR | S

The CBLKOUT= option is not valid when SHAPE=CYLINDER.

WOUTLINE=*block-outline-width*

specifies the width, in pixels, of the outline for all outlined blocks and for the outline of the map areas.

Not supported by: Java

XSIZE=*map-width <units>*
YSIZE=*map-height <units>*

specify the physical dimensions of the map to be drawn. By default, the map uses the entire procedure output area.

Valid *units* are CELLS (character cells), CM (centimeters), IN (inches), or PCT (percentage of the graphics output area). The default unit is CELLS.

If you specify values for *map-width* or *map-height* that are greater than the dimensions of the procedure output area, the map is drawn using the default size.

Not supported by: Java, ActiveX

XVIEW=*x*
YVIEW=*y*
ZVIEW=*z*

specify coordinates of the viewing position in the reference coordinate system. In this system, the four corners of the map lie on the X-Y plane at coordinates (0,0,0), (0,1,0), (1,1,0), and (1,0,0). No axes are actually drawn on the maps that are produced by PROC GMAP. Your viewing position cannot coincide with the viewing reference point at coordinates (0.5,0.5,0), the center of the map. The value for *z* cannot be negative.

If you omit the XVIEW=, YVIEW=, and ZVIEW= options, the default coordinates are (0.5, –2, 3). This viewing position is well above and to the south of the center of the map. You can specify one, two, or all three of the view coordinates; any that you do not specify are assigned the default values. While you can use the XVIEW= and YVIEW= options with DEVICE=JAVA, ZVIEW= can not be used with DEVICE=JAVA.

Not supported by: Java (partial)

Featured in: Example 2 on page 1047.

Figure 35.5 on page 1016 shows the position of the viewing reference point, as well as the default viewing position.

Figure 35.5 Viewing Position and Viewing Reference Point

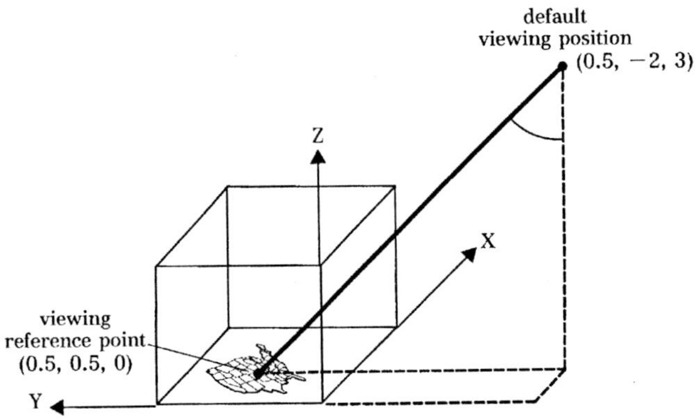

About Block Maps and Patterns

Block maps are different from other maps in that they display two different types of areas that use patterns:

- the blocks themselves, which represent the response levels
- the map areas from which the blocks rise.

By default, the blocks use solid pattern fills and the map areas use a hatch pattern of slanting lines. The map areas in block maps are the *only* map areas that by default do not use solid fills. The map areas and their outlines use the first color in the colors list regardless of whether the list is the device's default colors list or one specified with the COLORS= option in a GOPTIONS statement.

The BLOCK statement has the following options that explicitly control the outline colors used by the blocks and the map areas.

- CBLKOUT=
- CEMPTY=

□ COUTLINE=

In addition the AREA= option controls how the map areas are patterned.

When you use PATTERN statements to define the patterns for the map, you must be sure to specify the correct type of pattern for the area. The blocks use bar/block patterns and the map areas use map/plot patterns. See "PATTERN Statement" on page 169 for more information on specifying patterns.

Note: If you specify only one PATTERN statement and include only the COLOR= option, that color will be used for both the blocks and the map areas. For example, this statement makes the blocks solid blue and the map areas blue hatch. △

```
pattern1 color=blue;
```

Note: Empty block patterns (VALUE=EMPTY in a PATTERN statement) are not supported by DEVICE=ACTIVEX. △

CHORO Statement

Creates two-dimensional maps in which values of the specified response variables are represented by varying patterns and colors.

Requirements: At least one response variable is required. The ID statement must be used in conjunction with the CHORO statement

Global statements: FOOTNOTE, LEGEND, PATTERN, TITLE

Description

The CHORO statement specifies the variable or variables that contain the data represented on the map by patterns that fill the map areas. This statement automatically

- □ determines the midpoints
- □ assigns patterns to the map areas.

You can use statement options to enhance the appearance of the map, for example, by selecting the colors and patterns that fill the map areas. Other statement options control the selection of ranges for the response variable.

In addition, you can use global statements to modify the map area patterns and legend, as well as add titles and footnotes to the map. You can also use an Annotate data set to enhance the map.

CHORO *response-variable(s)* </ *option(s)*>;

option(s) can be one or more from any of the following categories:

□ appearance options:

ANNOTATE=*Annotate-data-set*

CEMPTY=*empty-area-outline-color*

COUTLINE=*area-outline-color* | SAME

WOUTLINE=*area-outline-width*

XSIZE=*map-width*<*units*>

YSIZE=*map-height <units>*
XVIEW=*x*
YVIEW=*y*
ZVIEW=*z*

- mapping options:
  - DISCRETE
  - LEVELS=*number-of-response-levels* | ALL
  - MIDPOINTS=*value-list* | OLD
  - MISSING
- legend options:
  - CTEXT=*text-color*
  - LEGEND=LEGEND<1...99>
  - NOLEGEND
- description options:
  - DESCRIPTION='*entry-description*'
  - NAME='*entry-name*'
- ODS options
  - HTML=*variable*
  - HTML_LEGEND=*variable*

Required Arguments

response-variable(s)
specifies one or more variables in the response data set, or in the merged response and feature table, that contain response values that are to be represented on the map. Each response variable produces a separate map. All variables must be in the input data set. Multiple response variables are separated with blanks.

Missing values for the response variable are not considered valid response values unless you use the MISSING option on the CHORO statement.

Response variables can be either numeric or character in type. Numeric response variables are normally grouped into ranges, or response levels, as determined by the MIDPOINTS= or LEVELS= options. Each response level is assigned a different combination of pattern and color. Character response variables are assigned unique response levels, as are numeric variables when the DISCRETE option is specified.

See also: "About Response Variables" on page 1004.

Options

Options in a CHORO statement affect all graphs that are produced by that statement. You can specify as many options as you want and list them in any order.

ANNOTATE=*Annotate-data-set*
ANNO=*Annotate-data-set*
specifies a data set to annotate onto maps that are produced by the CHORO statement.

Note: You can use the %MAPLABEL Macro to create the *Annotate-data-set*. See "%MAPLABEL Macro" on page 686 for more information. △

See also: Chapter 24, "Using Annotate Data Sets," on page 587.

Featured in: Example 6 on page 1061.

CEMPTY=*empty-area-outline-color*

outlines empty map areas in the specified color. This option affects only the empty map areas, which are generated in choro maps either

- □ when there is no response value for a map area and the MISSING option is not used, or
- □ when a map area is omitted from the response data set and the ALL option is included in the PROC GMAP statement.

The default outline color is the same as the default COUTLINE= color.

Not supported by: Java

See also: ALL on page 1008 and "Displaying Map Areas and Response Data" on page 1005.

COUTLINE=*area-outline-color* | SAME

outlines non-empty map areas in the specified color. When COUTLINE=*area-outline-color* and DEVICE=JAVA or ACTIVEX, both empty and non-empty map areas are outlined. The value SAME specifies that the outline color of a map area is the same as the interior pattern color.

The default outline color depends on the PATTERN statement:

- □ If no PATTERN statement is specified, the default outline color is the foreground color (the first color in the colors list).
- □ If a PATTERN statement or the V6COMP graphics option is specified, the default is COUTLINE=SAME.

Note: If you specify empty map patterns (VALUE=EMPTY in a PATTERN statement), then you should not change the outline color from the default value SAME to a single color. Otherwise all the outlines will be one color and you will not be able to distinguish between the empty areas. △

Featured in: Example 4 on page 1052.

CTEXT=*text-color*

specifies a color for the text in the legend. If you omit the CTEXT= option, a color specification is searched for in this order:

1. the CTEXT= option in a GOPTIONS statement
2. the default, the first color in the colors list.

The CTEXT= color specification is overridden if you also use the COLOR= suboption of a LABEL= or VALUE= option in a LEGEND definition that is assigned to the map legend. The COLOR= suboption determines the color of the legend label or the color of the legend value descriptions, respectively.

For the Java and ActiveX devices, the default color is black.

DESCRIPTION='*entry-description*'

DES='*entry-description*'

specifies a descriptive string up to 256 characters long that appears in the description field of the catalog entry for the map. The description does not appear on the map. By default, the GMAP procedure assigns a description of the form CHOROPLETH MAP OF *map_variable*.

Featured in: Example 5 on page 1054.

DISCRETE

generates a unique response value (pattern and color combination) for each numeric response variable.

The LEVELS= option is ignored when you use the DISCRETE option.

Be sure to use this option if your numeric response variable is assigned a user-written format.

Note: If the data does not contain a value in a particular range of the format, that formatted range is not displayed in the legend. △

Featured in: Example 5 on page 1054 and Example 11 on page 1069.

HTML=*variable*

identifies the variable in the input data set whose values create links in the HTML file created by the ODS HTML statement. These links are associated with an area of the map and point to the data or graph you wish to display when you drill down on the area.

Featured in: Example 5 on page 1054.

HTML_LEGEND=*variable*

identifies the variable in the input data set whose values create links in the HTML file created by the ODS HTML statement. These links are associated with a legend value and point to the data or graph you wish to display when you drill down on the value.

Not supported by: Java, ActiveX

Featured in: Example 5 on page 1054.

LEGEND=LEGEND<1...99>

assigns the specified LEGEND statement that is to be applied to the map. The LEGEND= option is ignored if the specified LEGEND definition is not currently in effect. In the GMAP procedure, the CHORO statement produces a legend by default unless you specify the NOLEGEND option. If you use the SHAPE= option in a LEGEND statement, then only the value BAR is valid. Most of the LEGEND options described in "LEGEND Statement" on page 151 are supported by both Java and ActiveX. If a LEGEND option is not supported by Java or ActiveX, it is noted in the LEGEND option definition.

Not supported by: Java (partial), ActiveX (partial)

See also: "LEGEND Statement" on page 151.

Featured in: Example 2 on page 1047.

LEVELS=*number-of-response-levels* | ALL

specifies the number of response levels to be graphed for numeric response variables, when the DISCRETE or MIDPOINTS= options are not specified. Each response level is assigned a different combination of color and fill pattern.

If you specify DEVICE=ACTIVEX or DEVICE=ACTXIMG, and if you specify LEVELS=ALL, then a color ramp is used to assign each response value a continuous color scheme. The response values are assigned lighter and darker values of a color scheme to express lower and higher response values. When used with all other devices, the LEVELS=ALL and DISCRETE options behave exactly the same. For more information, see the DISCRETE option on page 1019.

If the LEVELS= option is not used, the GMAP procedure determines the number of response levels by using the formula FLOOR(1+3.3 log(*n*)), where *n* is the number of unique map area identification variable values.

The LEVELS= option is ignored when you use the DISCRETE or MIDPOINTS=*value-list* option. When MIDPOINTS=OLD is used with the LEVELS= option, default midpoints are generated using the Nelder algorithm (*Applied Statistics* 25:94–7, 1976).

Note: LEVELS=ALL is a . △

Featured in: Example 2 on page 1047.

MIDPOINTS=*value-list* | OLD

specifies the response levels for the range of response values that are represented by each level (pattern and color combination).

For numeric response variables, the *value-list* argument is either an explicit list of values, a starting and an ending value with an interval increment, or a combination of both forms:

n <...*n*>

n TO *n* <BY *increment* >

n <...*n*> TO *n* <BY *increment* > *n* <...*n*>

By default the increment value is 1. You can specify discrete numeric values in any order. In all forms, *n* can be separated by blanks or commas. For example,

```
midpoints=(2 4 6)
midpoints=(2,4,6)
midpoints=(2 to 10 by 2)
```

If a numeric variable has an associated format, the specified values must be the *unformatted* values. With numeric response values, DEVICE=JAVA only uses midpoints that fall in the range of the data being used. Thus, if your data ranged from 30-80, but midpoints were specified at 25, 50, 75,and 100, only 50 and 75 are used.

For character response variables, *value-list* is a list of unique character values enclosed in quotation marks and separated by blanks:

'value-1' <...*'value-n'*>

The values are character strings enclosed in single quotation marks and separated by blanks. For example,

```
midpoints='Midwest' 'Northeast' 'Northwest'
```

Specify the values in any order. If a character variable has an associated format, the specified values must be the *formatted* values. Character response values specified with the MIDPOINTS= option are not supported by DEVICE=JAVA.

You can selectively exclude some response variable values from the map, as shown here:

```
midpoints='Midwest'
```

The only observations that are shown on the map are those observations for which the response variable exactly matches one of the values that are listed in the MIDPOINTS= option. As a result, observations may be excluded inadvertently if values in the list are misspelled or if the case does not match exactly.

Specifying MIDPOINTS=OLD generates default midpoints using the Nelder algorithm (*Applied Statistics* 25:94–7, 1976). Specifying GOPTIONS V6COMP serves the same purpose.

Not supported by: Java (partial)

Featured in: Example 8 on page 1065.

MISSING

accepts a missing value as a valid level for the response variable.

See also: "Displaying Map Areas and Response Data" on page 1005.

NAME=*'entry-name'*

If you specify DEVICE=ACTXIMG or DEVICE=JAVAIMG, then the name that you specify will be used for the client image output even in the file exists. For all other devices, if the name duplicates an existing entry name, SAS/GRAPH specifies the name of the catalog entry for the map. The maximum length of the *entry-name* value is eight characters. The default name is GMAP. If the specified name duplicates the name of an existing entry, SAS/GRAPH appends a number to the duplicate name to create a unique entry, for example, GMAP1.

Featured in: Example 5 on page 1054.

NOLEGEND
suppresses the legend.

Featured in: Example 6 on page 1061.

WOUTLINE=*area-outline-width*
specifies the width of all map area outlines, in pixels.

Not supported by: Java

XSIZE=*map-width <units>*
YSIZE=*map-height <units>*
specify the physical dimensions of the map. By default, the map uses the entire procedure output area.

Valid *units* are CELLS (character cells), CM (centimeters), IN (inches), or PCT (percentage of the graphics output area). The default unit is CELLS.

If you specify values for *units* that are greater than the dimensions of the procedure output area, the map is drawn using the default size.

If you specify either the XSIZE= or YSIZE= option without specifying the other option, the GMAP procedure scales the dimension for the option that was not specified to retain the original shape of the map.

Not supported by: Java, ActiveX

XVIEW=*x*
YVIEW=*y*
ZVIEW=*y*
specify coordinates of the viewing position in the reference coordinate system. In this system, the four corners of the map lie on the X-Y plane at coordinates (0,0,0), (0,1,0), (1,1,0), and (1,0,0). No axes are actually drawn on the maps that are produced by PROC GMAP. Your viewing position cannot coincide with the viewing reference point at coordinates (0.5,0.5,0), the center of the map. The value for *z* cannot be negative.

If you omit the XVIEW=, YVIEW=, and ZVIEW= options, the default coordinates are (0.5, –2, 3). This viewing position is well above and to the south of the center of the map. You can specify one, two, or all three of the view coordinates; any that you do not specify are assigned the default values. While you can use the XVIEW= and YVIEW= options with DEVICE=JAVA, ZVIEW= can not be used with DEVICE=JAVA.

Figure 35.5 on page 1016 shows the position of the viewing reference point, as well as the default viewing position.

Not supported by: Java (partial)

PRISM Statement

Creates three-dimensional prism maps in which levels of magnitude of the specified response variables are represented by polyhedrons (raised polygons) of varying height, pattern, and color.

Requirements: At least one response variable is required. You must use the ID statement in conjunction with the PRISM statement.

Global statements: FOOTNOTE, LEGEND, PATTERN, TITLE

Description

The PRISM statement specifies the variable or variables that contain the data that are represented on the map by raised map areas. This statement automatically

- determines the midpoints ranges or midpoints
- assigns patterns to the map areas.

You can use statement options to control the ranges of the response values, specify the angle of view, and enhance the appearance of the map.

In addition, you can use global statements to modify the map area patterns and the legend, as well as add titles and footnotes to the map. You can also use an Annotate data set to enhance the map.

Note: For maps that contain intersecting polygons or polygons within polygons, extremely complicated maps, or maps that contain line segments that cross, use the GREDUCE procedure to reduce and simplify the map if necessary. △

PRISM *response-variable(s)* </ *option(s)*>;

The *option(s)* can be one or more options from any or all of the following categories:

- appearance options:

  ANNOTATE=*Annotate-data-set*

  CEMPTY=*empty-area-outline-color*

  COUTLINE=*area-outline-color* | SAME

  WOUTLINE=*area-outline-width*

  XLIGHT=*x*

  YLIGHT=*y*

  XSIZE=*map-width* <*units*>

  YSIZE=*map-height* <*units*>

  XVIEW=*x*

  YVIEW=*y*

  ZVIEW=*x*

- mapping options:

  AREA=*n* | *response-variable-name*

  DISCRETE

  LEVELS=*number-of-response-levels* | ALL

  MIDPOINTS=*value-list* | OLD

  MISSING

- legend options:

  CTEXT=*text-color*

  LEGEND=LEGEND<1...99>

  NOLEGEND

- description options:

  DESCRIPTION='*entry-description*'

  NAME='*entry-name*'

- ODS options

  HTML=*variable*

  HTML_LEGEND=*variable*

Required Arguments

response-variable(s)

specifies one or more variables in the response data set, or in the merged response and feature table, that contain response values that are to be represented on the map. Each response variable produces a separate map. All variables must be in the input data set. Multiple response variables are separated with blanks.

Missing values for the response variable are not considered valid unless you use the MISSING option.

Response variables can be either numeric or character. By default, and as determined by the LEVELS= or MIDPOINTS= values, numeric response variables are grouped into ranges, or response levels. Each response level is assigned a different prism height and a different pattern and color combination.

Character variables and numeric variables (when you use the DISCRETE option) have a unique response level for each unique response variable value.

See also: "About Response Variables" on page 1004.

Options

Options in a PRISM statement affect all of the graphs that are produced by that statement. You can specify as many options as you want and list them in any order.

ANNOTATE=*Annotate-data-set*
ANNO=*Annotate-data-set*

specifies a data set to annotate onto the maps that are produced by the PRISM statement. Annotate coordinate systems 1, 2, 7, and 8 are not valid with Prism maps.

Note: You can use the %MAPLABEL Macro to create the *Annotate-data-set*. See "%MAPLABEL Macro" on page 686 for more information. △

See also: Chapter 24, "Using Annotate Data Sets," on page 587.

AREA=*n* | *response-variable-name*

specifies that a different map pattern be used for the surface of each map area or group of map areas on the map.

The value of *n* indicates which variable in the ID statement determines the groups that are distinguished by a surface pattern. By default, all map unit areas are drawn using the same surface fill pattern. If your ID statement has only one map area identification variable, then use AREA=1 to indicate that each map area surface uses a different pattern. If you have more than one variable in your ID statement, then use *n* to indicate the position of the variable that defines groups that will share a pattern. When you use the AREA= option, the map data set should be sorted in order of the variables in the ID statement.

A column name defined in either the MAP= or DATA= data sets may be indicated with the *response-variable-name* value. If the column name exists in both the MAP= and DATA= data sets, then the column in the MAP= data set will be used. When *column-name* is used, the areas will be colored based on the AREA= value. Duplicate AREA= values may have different patterns assigned.

By default, the AREA= option fills map areas by rotating the default hatch patterns through the colors list, beginning with the M2N0 pattern. The default outline color depends on the PATTERN statement:

- If no PATTERN statement is specified, the default outline color is the foreground color (the first color in the colors list).
- If a PATTERN statement or the V6COMP graphics option is specified, the default is COUTLINE=SAME.

You can specify pattern fills or colors or both with PATTERN statements that specify map/plot patterns. A separate PATTERN definition is needed for each specified area.

See also: "PATTERN Statement" on page 169.

Featured in: Example 3 on page 1049.

CEMPTY=*empty-area-outline-color*
outlines empty map areas in the specified color. Empty map areas are generated in prism maps either

- when there is no response value for a map area and the MISSING option is not used, or
- when a map area is omitted from the response data set and the ALL option is included in the PROC GMAP statement.

The default outline color is the same as the default COUTLINE= color.

Not supported by: Java

See also: ALL on page 1008 and "Displaying Map Areas and Response Data" on page 1005.

COUTLINE=*area-outline-color* | SAME
outlines non-empty map areas in the specified color. When COUTLINE=*area-outline-color* and DEVICE=JAVA or ACTIVEX, both empty and non-empty map areas are outlined. SAME specifies that the outline color of a map area is the same as the interior pattern color.

The default outline color depends on the PATTERN statement:

- If no PATTERN statement is specified, the default outline color is the foreground color (the first color in the colors list).
- If a PATTERN statement or the V6COMP graphics option is specified, the default is COUTLINE=SAME.

Note: If you specify empty map patterns (VALUE=EMPTY in a PATTERN statement), you should not change the outline color from the default value SAME to a single color. Otherwise, all the outlines will be one color and you will not be able to distinguish between the empty areas. Empty block patterns (VALUE=EMPTY in a PATTERN statement) are not supported by DEVICE=ACTIVEX. △

Featured in: Example 7 on page 1063.

CTEXT=*text-color*
specifies a color for the text in the legend. If you omit the CTEXT= option, a color specification is searched for in this order:

1. the CTEXT= option in a GOPTIONS statement
2. the default, the first color in the colors list.

The CTEXT= color specification is overridden if you also use the COLOR= suboption of a LABEL= or VALUE= option in a LEGEND definition assigned to the map legend. The COLOR= suboption determines the color of the legend label or the color of the legend value descriptions, respectively.

For the Java and ActiveX devices, the default color is black.

DESCRIPTION='*entry-description*'
DES='*entry-description*'
specifies the description of the catalog entry for the map. The maximum length for *entry-description* is 256 characters. By default, the GMAP procedure assigns a description of the form PRISM MAP OF *map_variable*.

DISCRETE
generates a separate response level (prism height, color, and surface pattern) for each different value of the formatted response variable. The LEVELS= option is ignored when you use the DISCRETE option.

Use this option if your numeric response variable is assigned a user-written format.

Note: If the data does not contain a value in a particular range of the format, that formatted range is not displayed in the legend. △

Featured in: Example 5 on page 1054 and Example 11 on page 1069 (with the CHORO statements).

HTML=*variable*
identifies the variable in the input data set whose values create links in the HTML file created by the ODS HTML statement. These links are associated with an area of the map and point to the data or graph that are displayed in response to drill-down input.

HTML_LEGEND=*variable*
identifies the variable in the input data set whose values create links in the HTML file created by the ODS HTML statement. These links are associated with legend values and point to the data or graphs that are displayed in response to drill-down input.

Not supported by: Java, ActiveX

LEGEND=LEGEND<1...99>
specifies the LEGEND definition to associate with the map. LEGEND= is ignored if the specified LEGEND definition is not currently in effect. In the GMAP procedure, the PRISM statement produces a legend unless you use the NOLEGEND option. If you use the SHAPE= option in a LEGEND statement, only the value BAR is valid. Most of the LEGEND options described in "LEGEND Statement" on page 151 are supported by both Java and ActiveX. If a LEGEND option is not supported by Java or ActiveX, it is noted in the LEGEND option definition.

Not supported by: Java (partial), ActiveX (partial)

See also: "LEGEND Statement" on page 151

Featured in: Example 8 on page 1065.

LEVELS=*number-of-response-levels* | ALL
specifies the number of response levels to be graphed when the response variables are numeric and the DISCRETE and MIDPOINTS= options are not specified. Each response level is assigned a different prism height, surface pattern, and color combination.

If you specify DEVICE=ACTIVEX or DEVICE=ACTXIMG, and if you specify LEVELS=ALL, then a color ramp is used to assign each response value a continuous color scheme. The response values are assigned lighter and darker values of a color scheme to express lower and higher response values. When used with all other devices, the LEVELS=ALL and DISCRETE options behave exactly the same. For more information, see the DISCRETE option on page 1026.

If neither the LEVELS= option nor the DISCRETE option is used, then the GMAP procedure determines the number of response levels by using the formula FLOOR(1+3.3 log(n)), where n is the number of unique map area identification variable values.

The LEVELS= option is ignored when you use the DISCRETE or MIDPOINTS=*value-list* option. When MIDPOINTS=OLD is used with the LEVELS= option, default midpoints are generated using the Nelder algorithm (*Applied Statistics* 25:94–7, 1976).

Note: LEVELS=ALL is a . △

Featured in: Example 2 on page 1047.

MIDPOINTS=*value-list* | OLD
specifies the response levels for the range of response values that are represented by each level (prism height, pattern, and color combination).

For numeric response variables, *value-list* is either an explicit list of values, or a starting and an ending value with an interval increment, or an combination of both forms:

n <...*n*>

n TO *n* <BY *increment*>

n <...*n*> TO *n* <BY *increment* > *n* <...*n*>

By default the increment value is 1. You can specify discrete numeric values in any order. In all forms, *n* can be separated by blanks or commas. For example,

```
midpoints=(2 4 6)
midpoints=(2,4,6)
midpoints=(2 to 10 by 2)
```

If a numeric variable has an associated format, the specified values must be the *unformatted* values. With numeric response values, DEVICE=JAVA only uses midpoints that fall in the range of the data being used. Thus, if your data ranged from 30-80, but midpoints were specified at 25, 50, 75,and 100, only 50 and 75 are used.

For character response variables, *value-list* has this form:

'value-1' <...*'value-n'*>

The values are character strings enclosed in single quotation marks and separated by blanks. For example,

```
midpoints='Midwest' 'Northeast' 'Northwest'
```

Specify the values in any order. If a character variable has an associated format, the specified values must be the *formatted* values. Character response values specified with the MIDPOINTS= option are not supported by DEVICE=JAVA.

You can selectively exclude some response variable values from the map, as shown here:

```
midpoints='Midwest'
```

Only those observations for which the response variable exactly matches one of the values listed in the MIDPOINTS= option are shown on the map. As a result, observations may be inadvertently excluded if values in the list are misspelled or if the case does not match exactly.

Specifying MIDPOINTS=OLD generates default midpoints using the Nelder algorithm (*Applied Statistics* 25:94–7, 1976). Specifying GOPTIONS V6COMP serves the same purpose.

Not supported by: Java (partial)

Featured in: Example 8 on page 1065.

MISSING
accepts a missing value as a valid level for the response variable.

See also: "Displaying Map Areas and Response Data" on page 1005.

NAME=*'entry-name'*
When you specify DEVICE=ACTXIMG or DEVICE=JAVAIMG, specifies the name that will be used for the client image output even in the file exists. For all other devices, if the name duplicates an existing entry name, then SAS/GRAPH specifies the name of the catalog entry for the map. The maximum length for *entry-name* is eight characters. The default name is GMAP. If the specified name duplicates an

existing name, then SAS/GRAPH software appends a number to the duplicate name to create a unique entry, for example, GMAP1.

NOLEGEND
suppresses the legend.

WOUTLINE=*area-outline-width*
specifies the width, in pixels, of all map area outlines.

Not supported by: Java, ActiveX

XLIGHT=*x*
YLIGHT=*y*
specify the coordinates of the imaginary light source in the map coordinate system. The position of the light source affects the way the sides of the map polygons are shaded. Although you can specify any point for the light source using the XLIGHT= and YLIGHT= options, the light source is actually placed in one of only four positions.

Table 35.3 on page 1028 shows how the point you specify is positioned.

Table 35.3 Light Source Coordinates

Specified Light Source	Light Source Position
in quadrants I or II, or on the X or +Y axis	behind the map (point A), and all side polygons are shadowed
on or within approximately 10 degrees of the Y axis	the viewing position (point D), and none of the side polygons are shadowed
in quadrant III (except within 10 degrees of the Y axis)	to the left of the map (point B), and the right-facing sides of polygons are shadowed
in quadrant IV (except within 10 degrees of the Y axis)	to the right of the map (point C), and the left-facing side polygons are shadowed

Figure 35.6 on page 1029 illustrates the light source positions. Assume that your viewing position, selected by the XVIEW=, YVIEW=, and ZVIEW= options, is point D.

Figure 35.6 Coordinates of Imagined Light Source in a Map Coordinate System

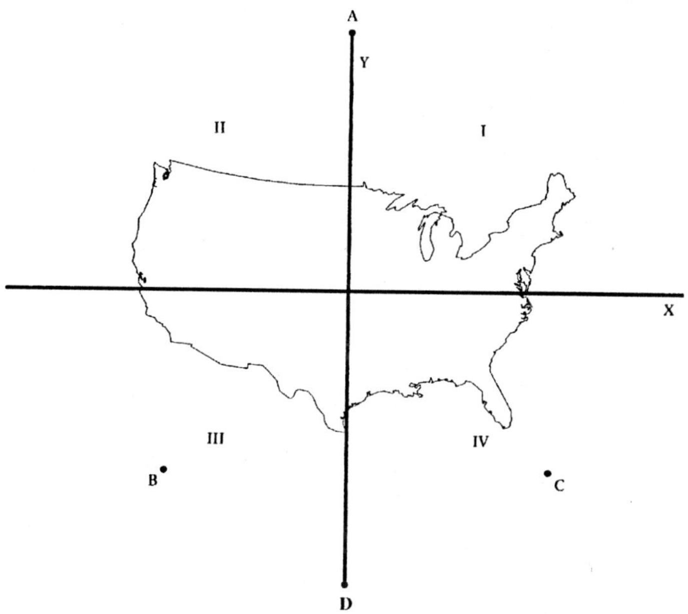

By default, the light source position is the same as the viewing position specified by the XVIEW=, YVIEW=, and ZVIEW= options. The light source position cannot coincide with the viewing reference point (0.5,0.5), which corresponds with the position directly above the center of the map.

Not supported by: Java, ActiveX

See also: XVIEW= on page 1029.

Featured in: Example 8 on page 1065.

XSIZE=*map-width* *<units>*
YSIZE=*map-height* *<units>*

specify the dimensions of the map that you are drawing. By default, the map uses the entire procedure output area.

Valid *units* are CELLS (character cells), CM (centimeters), IN (inches), or PCT (percentage of the graphics output area). The default unit is CELLS.

If you specify values for *map-width* and *map height* that are greater than the dimensions of the procedure output area, the map is drawn using the default size. If you specify one value and not the other, the dimension is adjusted to maintain the correct aspect ratio.

Not supported by: Java, ActiveX

XVIEW=*x*
YVIEW=*y*
ZVIEW=*z*

specify the viewing position coordinates for the map. In this system, the four corners of the map lie on the X-Y plane at coordinates (0, 0, 0), (0, 1, 0), (1, 1, 0), and (1, 0, 0).

The viewing position cannot coincide with the viewing reference point at coordinates (0.5, 0.5, 0).

The value for *z* cannot be negative.

If you omit the XVIEW=, YVIEW=, and ZVIEW= options, the default coordinates are (0.5, –2,3). This viewing position is well above and to the south of the center of the map. One, two, or all three view coordinates can be specified; any that are not specified are assigned the default values.

Figure 35.5 on page 1016 shows the position of the viewing reference point, as well as the default viewing position.

To ensure that the polygon edges are distinguishable, the angle from vertical must be less than or equal to 45 degrees. If you specify a ZVIEW= value such that this condition cannot be satisfied (that is, a very small value), PROC GMAP increases the ZVIEW= value automatically so that the angle is 45 degrees or less. While you can use the XVIEW= and YVIEW= options with DEVICE=JAVA, ZVIEW= can not be used with DEVICE=JAVA.

Not supported by: Java (partial)

Featured in: Example 8 on page 1065.

SURFACE Statement

Creates three-dimensional surface maps in which levels of magnitude of the specified response variables are represented by spikes of varying height.

Requirements: At least one response variable is required and must be numeric. The ID statement must be used in conjunction with the SURFACE statement.

Global statements: FOOTNOTE, TITLE

Not supported by: Java, ActiveX

Description

The SURFACE statement specifies the variable or variables that contain the data that are represented on the map by raised map areas. This statement automatically determines the midpoints. You can use statement options to control spike proportions, specify the angle of view, and modify the general appearance of the map. For example, you can select the color and number of lines for the representation of the surface area. You can control the selection of spike heights and base widths.

In addition, you can use global statements to add titles and footnotes to the map. You can also enhance the map with an Annotate data set.

SURFACE *response-variable(s)* </ *option(s)*>;

option(s) can be one or more of the following:

- appearance options:
  - ANNOTATE=*Annotate-data-set*
  - CBODY=*surface-map-color*
  - CONSTANT=*n*
  - NLINES=*number-of-lines*
  - ROTATE=*degrees*
  - TILT=*degrees*
  - XSIZE=*map-width* <*units*>
  - YSIZE=*map-height* <*units*>
- description options:
  - DESCRIPTION='*entry-description*'
  - NAME='*entry-name*'

Required Arguments

response-variable(s)

specifies one or more variables in the response data set, or in the merged response and feature table, that contain response values that are to be represented on the map. The *response-variable* must be numeric and must contain only positive values. Each response variable produces a separate map. All variables must be in the input data set. Multiple response variables are separated with blanks.

The GMAP procedure scales response variables for presentation on the map. The height of the spikes on the map correspond to the relative value of the response variable, not to the actual value of the response variable. However, when the viewing angle is changed, the spikes may not appear this way. The spikes in the front may appear to be higher than the spikes in the back, which represent greater values.

See also: "About Response Variables" on page 1004.

Options

SURFACE statement options affect all maps that are produced by that statement.

ANNOTATE=*Annotate-data-set*
ANNO=*Annotate-data-set*

specifies a data set to annotate onto maps that are produced by the SURFACE statement. Annotate coordinate systems 1, 2, 7, and 8 are not valid with surface maps.

Note: You can use the %MAPLABEL Macro to create the *Annotate-data-set*. See "%MAPLABEL Macro" on page 686 for more information. △

See also: Chapter 24, "Using Annotate Data Sets," on page 587.

CBODY=*surface-map-color*

specifies the color that is used to draw the surface map. By default, the first color in the current colors list is used.

CONSTANT=*n*

specifies a denominator to use in the distance decay function. This function determines the base width of the spike that is drawn at each map area center.

By default, CONSTANT=10. Values greater than 10 yield spikes that are wider at the base. Values less than 10 yield spikes that are narrower at the base.

Let x_k and y_k represent the coordinates, and z_k represent the function value at the center of each map area. The z_k values are scaled from 1 to 11. A square grid of x by y points (where the size of the grid is the NLINES= option value) and the associated function value *f(x,y)* are generated from the map area center value using this formula:

$$f(x, y) = \sum^{k} \left(1 - 1.5^{k} + .5\mathrm{D}^{3k}\right) \Delta^{kzk}$$

where

$$\mathrm{D}^{k} = \left(x - x^{k}\right)^{2} + \left(y - y^{k}\right)^{k}$$

and

$$\triangle^k = \left[\mathrm{martix\,cdelim} = \mathrm{XXXXXXXXXXXXXXX1\,if\,D}^k < 1,\ 0\,\mathrm{otherwise.}\right]$$

Featured in: Example 10 on page 1068.

DESCRIPTION=*'entry-description'*
DES=*'entry-description'*
specifies the description of the catalog entry for the map. The maximum length for *entry-description* is 256 characters. By default, the GMAP procedure assigns a description of the form SURFACE MAP OF *variable*, where *variable* is the name of the map variable.

NAME=*'entry-name'*
When you specify DEVICE=ACTXIMG or DEVICE=JAVAIMG, specifies the name that will be used for the client image output even in the file exists. For all other devices, if the name duplicates an existing entry name, then SAS/GRAPH specifies the name of the catalog entry for the map. The maximum length for *entry-name* is eight characters. The default name is GMAP. If the specified name duplicates the name of an existing entry, then SAS/GRAPH software appends a number to the duplicate name to create a unique entry, for example, GMAP1.

NLINES=*number-of-lines*
N=*number-of-lines*
specifies the number of lines used to draw the surface map. Values can range from 50 to 100; the higher the value, the more solid the map appears and the more resources used. By default, NLINES=50.

Featured in: Example 10 on page 1068.

ROTATE=*degrees*
specifies the degrees of the angle at which to rotate the map about the Z axis in the map coordinate system. The *degrees* argument can be any angle. Positive values indicate rotation in the counterclockwise direction. By default, ROTATE=70. The ROTATE= option also affects the direction of the lines that are used to draw the surface map.

Featured in: Example 10 on page 1068.

TILT=*degrees*
specifies the degrees of the angle at which to tilt the map about the X axis in the map coordinate system. The value of *degrees* can be 0 to 90. Increasing values cause the map to tilt backward and makes the spikes more prominent. Decreasing values make the map shape more distinguishable and the spikes less prominent. TILT=90 corresponds to viewing the map edge-on, while TILT=0 corresponds to viewing the map from directly overhead. By default, TILT=70.

Featured in: Example 10 on page 1068.

XSIZE=*map-width <units>*
YSIZE=*map-height <units>*
specify the physical dimensions of the map. By default, the map uses the entire procedure output area.

Valid *units* are CELLS (character cells), CM (centimeters), IN (inches), or PCT (percentage of the graphics output area). The default unit is CELLS.

If you specify values for *map-width* and *map-height* that are greater than the dimensions of the procedure output area, the map is drawn using the default size. And if you specify only one dimension, the other is scaled to maintain the aspect ratio.

Using FIPS Codes and Province Codes

The map area identification variable in some SAS/GRAPH map data sets contain standardized numeric codes. The data sets for the United States contain a variable whose values are FIPS (Federal Information Processing Standards) codes. The data sets for Canada contain standard province codes or census division codes. When you use the GMAP procedure with a traditional map data set, the variables that identify map areas in your response data set must have the same values as the map area identification variables in the traditional map data set.

If both a feature table and a response data set contain FIPS Codes or Province Codes, then once both data sets have been sorted, a SQL or DATA step MERGE can be used to merge the two data sets using the variable containing the codes. However, with the merged response and feature table, the identification variable used in the GMAP procedure must be the $GEOREF formatted variable that contains the spatial information. See "$GEOREF format" on page 1001 for more information.

If the map area identification variables in your response data set are state or province names or abbreviations, convert them to FIPS codes or province codes before using the response data set with one of the map data sets supplied by SAS. Table 35.4 on page 1033 lists the FIPS codes for the United States and Table 35.5 on page 1034 lists the standard codes for Canadian provinces.

Table 35.4 U.S. FIPS Codes

FIPS Code	State	FIPS Code	State
01	Alabama	30	Montana
02	Alaska	31	Nebraska
04	Arizona	32	Nevada
05	Arkansas	33	New Hampshire
06	California	34	New Jersey
08	Colorado	35	New Mexico
09	Connecticut	36	New York
10	Delaware	37	North Carolina
11	District of Columbia	38	North Dakota
12	Florida	39	Ohio
13	Georgia	40	Oklahoma
15	Hawaii	41	Oregon
16	Idaho	42	Pennsylvania
17	Illinois	44	Rhode Island
18	Indiana	45	South Carolina
19	Iowa	46	South Dakota
20	Kansas	47	Tennessee
21	Kentucky	48	Texas
22	Louisiana	49	Utah
23	Maine	50	Vermont

FIPS Code	State	FIPS Code	State
24	Maryland	51	Virginia
25	Massachusetts	53	Washington
26	Michigan	54	West Virginia
27	Minnesota	55	Wisconsin
28	Mississippi	56	Wyoming
29	Missouri	72	Puerto Rico

Table 35.5 Canadian Province Codes

Province Code	Province
10	Newfoundland
11	Prince Edward Island
12	Nova Scotia
13	New Brunswick
24	Quebec
35	Ontario
46	Manitoba
47	Saskatchewan
48	Alberta
59	British Columbia
60	Yukon
61	Northwest Territories

Note: The ID variables in Canadian maps are character. △

The CNTYNAME data set contains a cross-reference of names and FIPS codes for all counties in the United States. The CANCENS data set contains a cross-reference of census district names and codes for Canadian provinces.

Base SAS software provides several functions that convert state names to FIPS codes and vice versa. The following table lists these functions and a brief description of each. See *SAS Language Reference: Dictionary* for more information.

Table 35.6 FIPS and Postal Code Functions

Function	Description
STFIPS	converts state postal code to FIPS state code
STNAME	converts state postal code to state name in upper case
STNAMEL	converts state postal code to state name in mixed case
FIPNAME	converts FIPS code to state name in upper case

FIPNAMEL	converts FIPS code to state name in mixed case
FIPSTATE	converts FIPS code to state postal code

Using Formats for Maps

You can specify an output map area name or numeric value using one of the predefined formats for maps. The following prefixes are used in the names of the formats for maps:

CONT	Continent
CNTRY	Country
GLC	Geographic Location Code, distributed by Government Services Administration. USA
ISO	International Standard Organization

The formats for maps are located in the SASHELP.MAPFMTS catalog. See the MAPS.NAMES table to view all the continent and country names and corresponding GLC, ISO, and numeric representation for the continent values.

To use one of the formats for maps, you must specify the SASHELP.MAPFMTS catalog on the FMTSEARCH= option on a SAS OPTIONS statement:

```
options fmtsearch=(sashelp.mapfmts);
```

In addition to using the PUT statement (as shown in the examples in the following table), the formats can also be invoked using a FORMAT statement.

FORMAT	DESCRIPTION	EXAMPLE	OUTPUT
contfmt	use a continent's numeric value to output the continent's name	cont= 91 **put(cont,contfmt.);**	North America
$cntrysl	use a country's short name in uppercase to output the country's long name in uppercase	name='IRAN' **put(name,cntrysl.);**	IRAN, ISLAMIC REPUBLIC OF
glcnlu	use the GLC numeric code to output the country's long name in uppercase	id=460 **put(id,glclu.);**	IRAN, ISLAMIC REPUBLIC OF
glcnsu	use the GLC numeric code to output the country's short name in uppercase	id=460 **put(id,glcnsu.);**	IRAN
glcnsm	use the GLC numeric code to output the country's name in mixed case	id=460 **put(id,glcnsm.);**	Iran

FORMAT	DESCRIPTION	EXAMPLE	OUTPUT
$glcalu	use the GLC alpha code to output the country's long name in uppercase	country='IR' **put(country,glcalu.);**	IRAN, ISLAMIC REPUBLIC OF
$glcsua	use the country's short name in uppercase to output the GLC alpha code name	name='IRAN' **put(name,glcsua.);**	IR
glcna	use the country's GLC numeric code to output the country's GLC alpha code	id=460 **put(id,glcna.);**	IR
$glcsun	use the country's short name in uppercase to output the country's GLC numeric code	name='IRAN' **put(name,glcsun.);**	460
$glcan	use the country's GLC alpha code to output the country's GLC numeric code	country='IR' **put(country,glcan.);**	460
$glcsma	use the country's short name in mixed-case to output the country's GLC alpha code	mixname='Iran' **put(mixname,glcsma.);**	IR
$glcsmn	use the country's short name in mixed-case to output the country's GLC numeric code	mixname='Iran' **put(mixname,glcsmn.);**	460
$glcprov	use a province/city name appended by || as a delimiter, followed by the country's GLC alpha code to output a province||country code, the province/city code, and the country's GLC alpha numeric code	provname='TEHRAN||IR' **put(provname,glcprov.);**	8250460 8250 — province/ city code 460 — country GLC numeric code
$isosu2a	use the country's short name in uppercase to output the country's ISO alpha2 code	name='IRAN' **put(name,$isosu2a.);**	IR
$isosu3a	use the country's name in uppercase to output the country's ISO alpha3 code	name='IRAN' **put(name,$isosu3a.);**	IRN
$isosun	use the country's short name in uppercase to output the country's ISO numeric code	name='IRAN' **put(name,isosun.);**	364

FORMAT	DESCRIPTION	EXAMPLE	OUTPUT
ison2a	use the country's ISO numeric code to output the country's ISO alpha2 code	iso=364 **put(iso,ison2a.);**	IR
ison3a	use the country's ISO numeric code to output the country's ISO alpha3 code	iso=364 **put(iso,ison3a.);**	IRN
isonlu	use the country's ISO numeric code to output the country's long name in uppercase	iso=364 **put(iso,isonlu.);**	IRAN, ISLAMIC REPUBLIC OF
isonsu	use the country's ISO numeric code to output the country's short name in uppercase	iso=364 **put(iso,isonsu.);**	IRAN
isoa2lu	use the country's ISO alpha2 code to output the country's long name in uppercase	alpha2='IR' **put(alpha2,isoa2lu.);**	IRAN, ISLAMIC REPUBLIC OF
isoa2su	use the country's ISO alpha2 code to output the country's short name in uppercase	alpha2='IR' **put(alpha2,isoa2lu.);**	IRAN
isoa3lu	use the country's ISO alpha3 code to output the country's long name uppercase	alpha3='IRN' **put(alpha3,isoa3lu.);**	IRAN, ISLAMIC REPUBLIC OF
isoa3su	use the country's ISO alpha3 code to output the country's short name in uppercase	alpha3='IRN' **put(alpha3,isoa3su.);**	IRAN
$isoa2n	use the country's ISO alpha2 code to output the country's ISO numeric code	alpha2='IR' **put(alpha2,$isoa2n.);**	364
$isoa3n	use the country's ISO alpha3 code to output the country's ISO numeric code	alpha3='IRN' **put(alpha3,$isoa3n.);**	364
$isosm2a	use the country's short name in mixed-case to output the country's ISO alpha2 code	mixname='Iran' **put(mixname,$isosn2a.);**	IR

FORMAT	DESCRIPTION	EXAMPLE	OUTPUT
$isosm3a	use the country's short name in mixed-case to output the country's ISO alpha3 code	mixname='Iran' **put(mixname,$isosn3a.);**	IRN
$isosmn	use the country's short name in mixed-case to output the country's ISO numeric code	mixname='Iran' **put(mixname,$isosmn.);**	364

SAS/GRAPH Map Data Sets Reference Information

Before using your map data sets, contact your SAS Support Consultant to verify the name and location of the SAS data library that contains the map data sets at your site. Many sites automatically assign a libref of MAPS to the SAS data library that contains the SAS-supplied map data sets. However, if you use the map data sets regularly and your site does not automatically assign a libref to the data library that contains the map data sets, you can add a LIBNAME statement to your AUTOEXEC file that defines the location of the map data set library. If you do this, the libref for the maps is established automatically whenever you begin a SAS session.

Accessing Detailed Descriptions of Map Data Sets

You may need detailed information on the map data sets in order to determine their type, size, the variables they contain, or, in the case of traditional data sets, whether they are projected or unprojected. You can get this information by using the CONTENTS or DATASETS procedure, or browsing the MAPS.METAMAPS (see "Viewing Map Data Sets" on page 1001) data set in the MAPS library (or the library where your SAS-supplied map data sets reside). If the libref MAPS has automatically been assigned, you can see a complete list of map data sets by viewing the MAPS.METAMAPS data set. See

These statements list the map data sets in the SAS data library that is assigned to the libref MAPS:

```
libname maps 'SAS-data-library';

proc datasets lib=maps;
run;
```

Note: Be sure to replace *SAS-data-library* with the location of the SAS data library that contains map data sets at your site. △

The following statements provide detailed information on a traditional map data set, including the number of observations, the variables in each data set, and a description of each variable:

```
libname maps 'SAS-data-library';

proc contents data=maps.canada3;
```

```
run;
```

To see the contents and descriptions of all of the SAS-supplied map data sets you can specify DATA=MAPS._ALL_ in the CONTENTS procedure. See the *Base SAS Procedures Guide* for more information on the CONTENTS and DATASETS procedures.

Customizing SAS/GRAPH Map Data Sets

You can customize the area that is displayed on your map by using only part of a particular map data set. There are several ways to accomplish this. You can use WHERE processing or a DATA step to subset the map data to be used by the GMAP procedure.

With the traditional map data set, you can also use the GPROJECT procedure to create a rectangular subset of a map data set by using minimum and maximum longitude and latitude values.

You can combine traditional map data sets in either of these situations:

- The map data sets to be combined were originally projected together.
- The map data sets all contain the same type of coordinates. That is, all are in radians or all are in degrees.

SAS-supplied traditional map data sets that have coordinates expressed only as longitude and latitude, with variable names LONG and LAT, must be renamed X and Y and should be projected before displaying.

Subsetting Traditional Map Data Sets

Some of the SAS/GRAPH map data sets contain a large number of observations. Programs that use only a few states or provinces will run faster if you exclude the unused portion of the map data set or use an already reduced map data set. SAS provides several ways to accomplish this. One is to use the WHERE statement or WHERE= data set option within the GMAP procedure to select only the states or provinces you want.

The WHERE statement and WHERE= data set option are most useful when you produce a simple map and do not need to make any other changes to the data set. For example, to use only the observations for Quebec in the CANADA traditional map data set, begin the GMAP procedure with this statement:

```
proc gmap map=maps.canada(where=(province=24));
```

To use only North Carolina in US2MERGED, a data set created by using SQL or DATA step MERGE on the feature table US2 and a response data set also containing the variable STATE, the GMAP procedure would begin with the following statement:

```
proc gmap data=work.us2merged(where=(STATE=37));
```

The WHERE= data set option applies only to the data set that you specify in the argument in which the WHERE= option appears. If you use the WHERE statement, the WHERE condition applies to the traditional map data set and the response data sets or the merged response and feature table.

Another approach is to use a DATA step to create a subset of the larger data set. This code illustrates another way to extract the observations for Quebec from the CANADA traditional map data set:

```
data quebec;
   set maps.canada(where=(province=24));
```

This code illustrates another way to extract North Carolina data from the US2 feature table:

```
data ncarolina;
   set maps.us2(where=(STATE=37));
```

This approach is most useful when you want to create a permanent subset of a map data set or when you need to make additional changes to the map data set.

Also see Chapter 42, "The GREMOVE Procedure," on page 1223 for an example how to use GREMOVE to create a regional map from one of the traditional map data sets that are supplied with SAS/GRAPH.

Reducing Traditional Map Data Sets

A *reduced map data set* is one that can be used to draw a map that retains the overall appearance of the original map but that contains fewer points, requires considerably less storage space, and can be drawn much more quickly. You can improve performance by plotting fewer observations for each map area. You reduce a traditional map data set when you subset it on the variable DENSITY. You can add the variable DENSITY to a map data set by using the GREDUCE procedure. For more information, see Chapter 41, "The GREDUCE Procedure," on page 1213.

An *unreduced map data set* contains all of the coordinates that were produced when the map was digitized. This type of map data set has more observations than most graphics output devices can accurately plot. Some unreduced map data sets already contain a DENSITY variable like the one calculated by the GREDUCE procedure, so it is not necessary to use the GREDUCE procedure to process these data sets. Values for DENSITY range from 0 through 6 (the lower the density, the coarser the boundary line).

A statement of this form excludes all points with a density level of 2 or greater:

```
proc gmap map=maps.states(where=(density<2));
```

The resulting map is much coarser than one drawn by using all of the observations in the data set, but it is drawn much faster.

Another way to create a reduced map data set is to use a DATA step to exclude observations with larger density values:

```
data states;
   set maps.states(where=(density<2));
```

Projecting Traditional Map Data Sets

Map data can be stored as unprojected or projected coordinates. Unprojected map data contains spherical coordinates, that is, longitude and latitude values usually expressed in radians.*

Each of the feature tables in the MAPS library are projected. A few traditional map data sets that are provided with SAS/GRAPH contain only unprojected coordinates and should be projected before you use them. They are

CANADA3
CANADA4
COUNTIES
COUNTY
STATES

Projected map data contains Cartesian coordinates. The GMAP procedure is designed to plot maps by using projected map data sets. Feature tables store the

* If your data is in degrees, then it can be converted to radians by multiplying by the degree-to-radian constant [atan(1)/45].

projected data in the $GEOREF formatted variable (see "$GEOREF format" on page 1001). Most SAS/GRAPH traditional map data sets contain projected coordinates that are stored as X and Y.

If the projection supplied with the traditional map data set does not meet your needs, then you can use the GPROJECT procedure (on unprojected map coordinates) to create a different projection. For more information on traditional map data sets with unprojected coordinates, see "Traditional Map Data Sets Containing X, Y, LONG, and LAT" on page 1000. You should select a projection method that least distorts the regions that you are mapping. (All projection methods inherently distort map regions.) See Chapter 39, "The GPROJECT Procedure," on page 1161 for more information.

Note: Using an unprojected traditional map data set with the GMAP procedure can cause your map to be reversed and distorted. △

Controlling the Display of Lakes

Some countries contain a lake that is located completely within a single unit area. Occasionally these lakes can be a problem when mapping traditional map data sets. In addition, displaying lakes may not be appropriate for some applications. In these cases, you may want to remove the lakes from the map data set before you proceed.

Traditional map data sets that contain coordinates for a lake that is located within a single internal division are identified by the presence of the numeric variable LAKE. The value of LAKE is 1 for points that correspond to lakes and 0 otherwise. The following statements illustrate how to delete the lakes from your traditional map data sets using WHERE processing:

```
proc gmap map=maps.chile(where=(lake=0))
          data=maps.chile;
   id id;
   choro id / levels=1 nolegend;
   title box=1 f=none h=4
         'Chile with Lakes Removed';
run;
```

You can also create a new traditional map data set that is a subset of the traditional map data set:

```
data nolake;
   set maps.chile;
   if lake=0;
run;
```

Creating Traditional Map Data Sets

In addition to using map data sets that are supplied with SAS/GRAPH software, you can also create your own map data sets. Map data sets are not limited to geographic data; you use them to define other spaces such as floor plans or street diagrams.

A unit area is defined by observations in the map data set that have the same identification (ID) variable value. A unit area may be composed of a single polygon or a collection of polygons. A polygon is defined by all of the observations that have the same SEGMENT variable value within the same unit area.

- If the unit area is a single polygon, then all values of SEGMENT are the same.
- If the unit area contains multiple polygons, such as islands, then the SEGMENT variable has multiple values. For example, in the MAPS.US data set, the state of Hawaii (a unit area) contains six different values in the SEGMENT variable, one for each island in the state.

- If the unit area contains enclosed polygons, such as lakes, then the SEGMENT variable has one value but the interior polygon is defined by separate boundaries. To separate boundaries, a missing X and Y value must be inserted at the separation point. For example, in the CANADA2 data set supplied with SAS/GRAPH, the map data for the Northwest Territories (a unit area) use enclosed polygons for two lakes.

Creating a Unit Area that is a Single Polygon

This DATA step creates a SAS data set that contains coordinates for a unit area with a single polygon, a square:

```
data square;
   input id x y;
   datalines;
1 0 0
1 0 40
1 40 40
1 40 0
;
```

This data set does not have a SEGMENT variable.

Creating a Unit Area that Contains Multiple Polygons

Use different values of the SEGMENT variable to create separate polygons within a single unit area. For example, this DATA step assigns two values to the SEGMENT variable. The resulting data set produces a single unit area that contains two polygons, as shown in Figure 35.7 on page 1043:

```
data map;
   input id $ 1-8 segment x y;
   datalines;
square   1 0 0
square   1 0 4
square   1 4 4
square   1 4 0
square   2 5 5
square   2 5 7
square   2 7 7
square   2 7 5
;
```

Figure 35.7 Single Unit Area with Two Segments (Polygons)

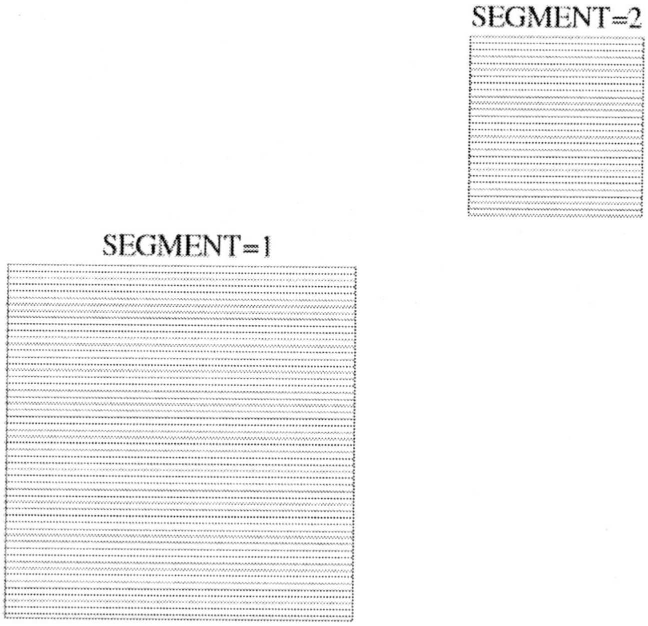

Creating a Unit Area that Contains Enclosed Polygons as Holes

Use separate boundaries to create an enclosed polygon (that is, a polygon that falls within the primary polygon for a single segment). The separate boundaries are separated from the primary polygon boundary by missing values for X and Y. For example, the data set that is created by this DATA step produces the map shown in Figure 35.8 on page 1044:

```
data map;
   input id $ 1-8 segment x y;
   datalines;
square   1 0 0
square   1 0 4
square   1 4 4
square   1 4 0
square   1 . .
square   1 1 1
square   1 2 2
square   1 3 1
;
```

Figure 35.8 Single Unit Area with Hole

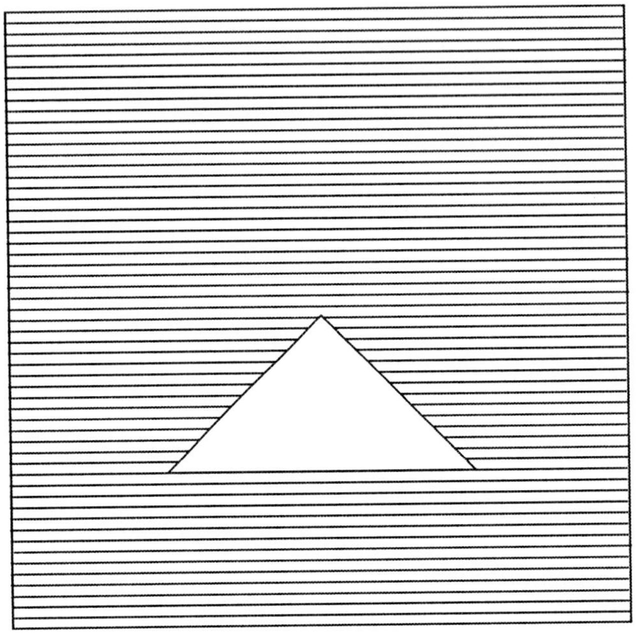

Creating a Unit Area that Contains Enclosed Polygons as Cities

Ordinarily, if one unit area is surrounded by another, the pattern of the external unit area is drawn over the pattern for the internal one, instead of around it. Avoid this problem by adding an observation to the map data for the external unit area with missing values for X and Y, followed by the coordinates of the internal unit area, but using the ID values for the external unit area. For example, this DATA step creates a data set that produces the map shown in Figure 35.9 on page 1045:

```
data map;
   input id $ 1-8 segment x y;
   datalines;
square   1 0 0
square   1 0 4
square   1 4 4
square   1 4 0
square   1 . .
square   1 1 1
square   1 2 2
square   1 3 1
triangle 1 1 1
triangle 1 2 2
triangle 1 3 1
;
```

Figure 35.9 Unit Area within a Unit Area

Note: A single map segment (a section of a unit area with a single value of the SEGMENT variable) cannot contain multiple polygons without at least one observation with missing values for X and Y. All segments within the map data sets that are supplied by SAS/GRAPH contain a single polygon that can have one or more separate boundaries, each separated by an observation with missing values for X and Y. △

Examples

The following examples include features from one or more of the GMAP statements.

Example 1: Producing a Simple Block Map

Procedure features:

ID statement

BLOCK statement option:

CBLKOUT=

Sample library member: GMPSIMPL

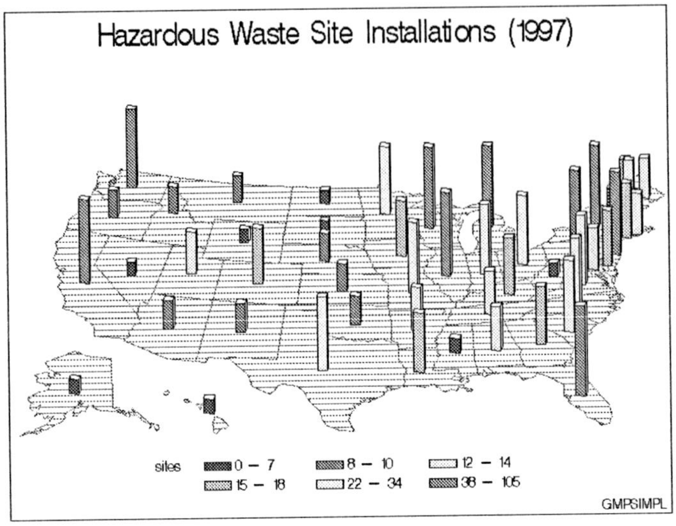

This example produces a block map that shows the total number of hazardous waste sites in each state in 1997. Since the DISCRETE option is not used, the response variable is assumed to have a continuous range of values. Because neither the LEVELS= nor MIDPOINTS= option is used, the GMAP procedure selects a number of levels based on the number of map areas and then calculates the appropriate response levels.

The blocks use the default pattern, which is a solid fill that rotates through the colors list. Because the colors list is specified in the GOPTIONS statement, all colors are used in the rotation. CBLKOUT= outlines the blocks in black, instead of using the default outline color, which is the first color in the list– in this case, BLUE.

The map areas use the default pattern for map areas in a block map. This is the first hatch pattern for maps, M2N0. By default, both the fill and the outline use the first color in the colors list.

Assign the libref and set the graphics environment. COLORS= specifies the colors list, which is used by the default patterns and outlines. CTEXT= specifies the color for all text on the output.

```
libname maps 'SAS-data-library';
goptions reset=global gunit=pct border cback=white
         colors=(blue green lime lipk cyan red)
         ctext=black ftext=swiss htitle=6 htext=3;
```

Create response data set SITES. This data set contains a map area identification variable, STATE, and a response variable, SITES. The STFIPS function is used to convert the state postal codes to FIPS state codes. STATE contains the FIPS codes for each state and matches the values of STATE in the MAPS.US data set. SITES contains the total number of waste sites installed in the state.

```
data sites;
   length stcode $ 2;
   input region stcode $ sites;
   state=stfips(stcode);
   datalines;
6   AR  12
10  AK  7...moredata lines...
```

```
3   WV  6
8   WY  3
;
```

Define title and footnote for map.

```
title1 'Hazardous Waste Site Installations (1997)';
footnote1 j=r 'GMPSIMPL';
```

Produce the block map. The ID statement specifies the variable that is in both the map data set and the response data set and defines map areas. The BLOCK statement specifies the variable in the response data set that contains the response values for each of the map areas. CBLKOUT= specifies the color for the block outlines.

```
proc gmap map=maps.us data=sites;
   id state;
   block sites / cblkout=black;
run;
quit;
```

Example 2: Specifying Response Levels in a Block Map

Procedure features:

BLOCK statement options:

- LEGEND=
- LEVELS=
- SHAPE=
- XVIEW=
- ZVIEW=

Other features:

LEGEND statement

PATTERN statement

Sample library member: GMPLEVEL

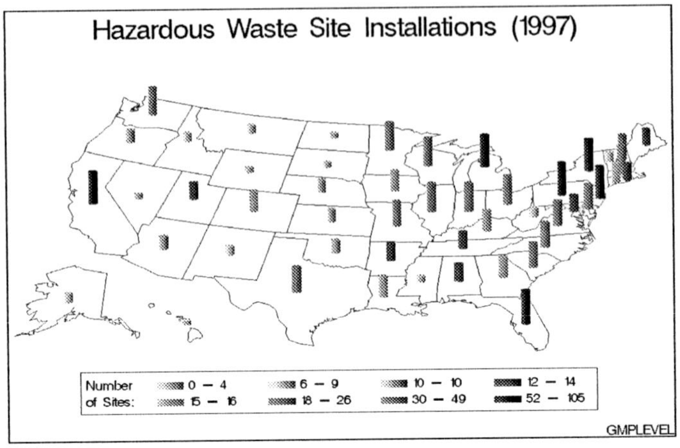

This example uses LEVELS= to specify the number of response levels for the blocks. LEVELS= tells GMAP how many response levels and GMAP calculates the quantiles. Eight PATTERN statements explicitly define a color for each of these response levels.

A single PATTERN statement uses the REPEAT= option to define an empty map/plot pattern outlined in black for all the map areas.

The example also changes the viewpoint by rotating the map to provide a better view of the northeast states. As a result, the blocks appear shorter.

Assign the libref and set the graphics environment.

```
libname maps 'SAS-data-library';
goptions reset=global gunit=pct border cback=white
         colors=(black blue green red)
         ctext=black ftext=swiss htitle=6 htext=3;
```

Create response data set SITES. This data set contains a map area identification variable, STATE, and a response variable, SITES. The STFIPS function is used to convert the state postal codes to FIPS state codes. STATE contains the FIPS codes for each state and matches the values of STATE in the MAPS.US data set. SITES contains the total number of waste sites installed in the state.

```
data sites;
   length stcode $ 2;
   input region stcode $ sites;
   state=stfips(stcode);
   datalines;
6   AR  12
10  AK  7...moredata lines...
3   WV  6
8   WY  3
;
```

Define title and footnote for map.

```
title1 'Hazardous Waste Site Installations (1997)';
footnote1 j=r 'GMPLEVEL';
```

Define the patterns for the blocks. PATTERN statements 1-8 specify bar/block patterns and cannot be used by the map areas. They are applied to the blocks in order of the response level.

```
pattern1 value=solid color=lime;
pattern2 value=solid color=cyan;
pattern3 value=solid color=green;
pattern4 value=solid color=blue;
pattern5 value=solid color=lipk;
pattern6 value=solid color=red;
pattern7 value=solid color=gray;
pattern8 value=solid color=black;
```

Define a pattern for the map areas. PATTERN9 defines a single map pattern that is repeated for each of the 50 map areas (states). The pattern is an empty fill with a black border. VALUE= defines a map/plot pattern, which cannot be used by the blocks. Specifying a color causes PATTERN9 to generate only one pattern definition. REPEAT= specifies the number of times to repeat the pattern definition.

```
pattern9 value=empty color=black repeat=50;
```

Define legend characteristics. LABEL= produces a two line label and places it to the left of the legend values. FRAME draws a border around the legend using the first color in the colors list.

```
legend1 value=(justify=left)
        label=('Number' justify=left 'of Sites:'
               position=(middle left))
        frame;
```

Produce the block map. LEVELS= specifies the number of response levels for the graph. SHAPE= draws the blocks as 3D cylinders. XVIEW= changes the viewpoint for the map so that the map appears to be slightly rotated. ZVIEW= raises the height of the viewpoint. LEGEND= assigns the LEGEND1 statement to the map legend.

```
proc gmap map=maps.us data=sites;
   id state;
   block sites / levels=8
                 shape=cylinder
                 xview=0.75
                 zview=5
                 legend=legend1;
run;
quit;
```

Example 3: Assigning a Format to the Response Variable

Procedure features:

BLOCK statement options:

AREA=
CBLKOUT=
COUTLINE=
DISCRETE
WOUTLINE=

Other features:

FORMAT statement

LEGEND statement

PATTERN statement

Sample library member: GMPFORMT

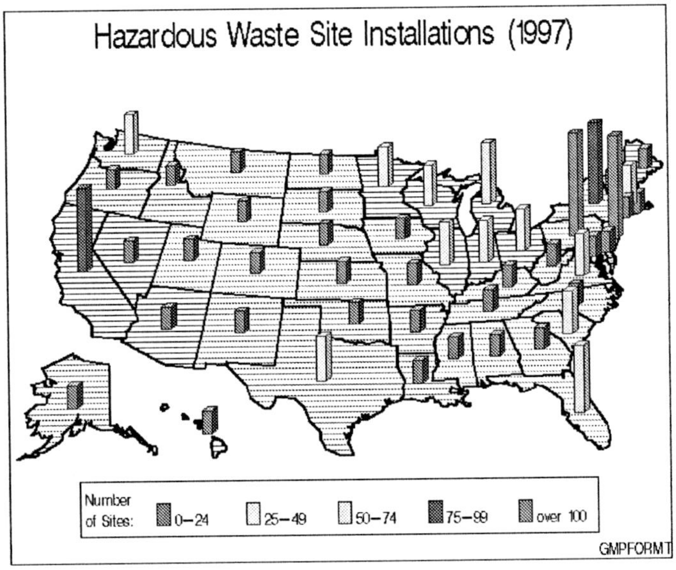

This example creates a format that defines the ranges of values for the response values and assigns this format to the response variable. These ranges appear in the legend and make the map easier to understand. When a format is assigned to a numeric response variable, the DISCRETE option must be used so that each formatted value is treated as a separate response level.

The example also patterns the map areas by region. To do this, both data sets must contain the ID variable, REGION. The response data set, SITES, already contains REGION, so the program only needs to add it to the map data set. Then the map data set is sorted by both the ID variables, REGION and STATE. Finally, the AREA= option specifies that the ID variable REGION is the one by which the map areas are patterned.

Assign the libref and set the graphics environment.

```
libname maps 'SAS-data-library';
goptions reset=global gunit=pct border cback=white
         colors=(black blue green red)
         ftext=swiss htitle=6 htext=3;
```

Create map data set STATES1 by adding REGION to the MAPS.US map data set.

```
data states1;
   set maps.us;
   select;
      when (state in (9,23,25,33,44,50))         region=1;
      when (state in (34,36))                    region=2;
      when (state in (10,11,24,42,51,54))        region=3;
      when (state in (1,12,13,21,28,37,45,47)) region=4;
      when (state in (17,18,26,27,39,55))        region=5;
      when (state in (5,22,35,40,48))            region=6;
      when (state in (19,20,29,31))              region=7;
      when (state in (8,30,38,46,49,56))         region=8;
      when (state in (4,6,15,32))                region=9;
      otherwise                                  region=10;
   end;
run;
```

Sort the new map data set. The map data must be sorted in the order of the ID variables.

```
proc sort data=states1 out=states2;
   by region state;
run;
```

Create response data set SITES. This data set contains a map area identification variable, STATE, and a response variable, SITES. The STFIPS function is used to convert the state postal codes to FIPS state codes. STATE contains the FIPS codes for each state and matches the values of STATE in the MAPS.US data set. SITES contains the total number of waste sites installed in the state.

```
data sites;
   length stcode $ 2;
   input region stcode $ sites;
   state=stfips(stcode);
   datalines;
6   AR  12
10  AK  7...moredata lines...
3   WV  6
8   WY  3
;
```

Create a format for SITES. SITESFMT. defines and labels the ranges of values for SITES.

```
proc format;
   value sitesfmt low-24='0-24'
                  25-49='25-49'
                  50-74='50-74'
                  75-99='75-99'
                  100-high='over 100';
run;
```

Define title and footnote for map.

```
title1 'Hazardous Waste Site Installations (1997)';
footnote j=r 'GMPFORMT';
```

Define a hatch pattern for the map areas. PATTERN1 defines a dense hatch pattern for the map areas. Because there are four colors in the colors list, the pattern rotation must be repeated three times to create enough patterns for the ten regions.

```
pattern1 value=m3n0 r=3;
```

Define a solid pattern for the blocks. PATTERN2 through PATTERN6 define the patterns for the block surfaces.

```
pattern2 value=solid color=green;
pattern3 value=solid color=cyan;
pattern4 value=solid color=lime;
pattern5 value=solid color=blue;
pattern6 value=solid color=red;
```

Define legend characteristics.

```
legend1 shape=bar(2,4)
        value=(j=l)
        label=('Number' j=l 'of Sites:')
        frame;
```

Produce the block maps. The FORMAT statement assigns SITESFMT. to the response variable. DISCRETE specifies that each formatted value is a separate response level. AREA= specifies that the map surface should be patterned by the first variable in the ID statement, REGION. CBLKOUT= and COUTLINE= specify the color that outlines the blocks and the regions, respectively. WOUTLINE= specifies the width of the block outline in pixels.

```
proc gmap map=states2 data=sites;
   format sites sitesfmt.;
   id region state;
   block sites / discrete
                 area=1
                 legend=legend1
                 shape=block
                 cblkout=black
                 coutline=black
                 woutline=3;
run;
quit;
```

Example 4: Producing a Simple Choropleth Map

Procedure features:

ID statement
CHORO statement option:
COUTLINE=

Sample library member: GMPCHORO

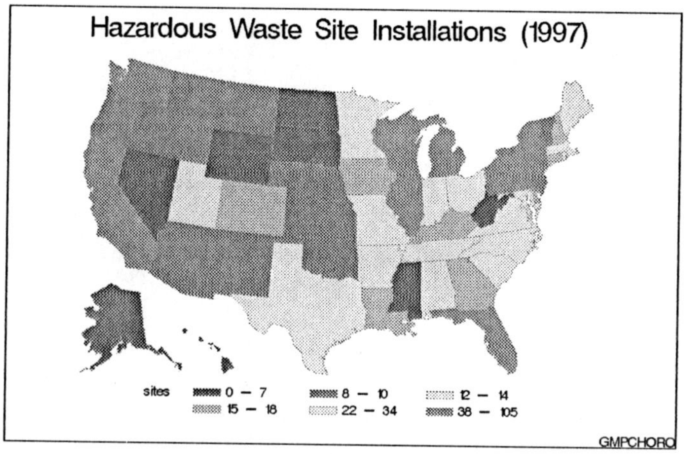

This example produces a choropleth (2D) map that shows the total number of hazardous waste sites in each state in 1997. Since the DISCRETE option is not used, the response variable is assumed to have a continuous range of values. Because neither the LEVELS= nor MIDPOINTS= option is used, the GMAP procedure selects a number of levels based on the number of map areas and then calculates the appropriate response levels. The legend shows the midpoint value of each level.

The map areas use the default pattern, which is a solid fill that rotates through the colors list. Because the colors list is specified in the GOPTIONS statement, all colors are used in the rotation. COUTLINE= outlines the map areas in gray, instead of the default outline color, which is the first color in the list, in this case, BLUE.

Assign the libref and set the graphics environment. COLORS= specifies the colors list, which is used by the default patterns and outlines. CTEXT= specifies the color for all text on the output.

```
libname maps 'SAS-data-library';
goptions reset=global gunit=pct border cback=white
         colors=(blue green lime lipk cyan red)
         ctext=black ftext=swiss htitle=6 htext=3;
```

Create response data set SITES. This data set contains a map area identification variable, STATE, and a response variable, SITES. The STFIPS function is used to convert the state postal codes to FIPS state codes. STATE contains the FIPS codes for each state and matches the values of STATE in the MAPS.US data set. SITES contains the total number of waste sites installed in the state.

```
data sites;
   length stcode $ 2;
   input region stcode $ sites;
```

```
   state=stfips(stcode);
   datalines;
6   AR  12
10  AK  7...moredata lines...
3   WV  6
8   WY  3
;
```

Define title and footnote for map.

```
title1 'Hazardous Waste Site Installations (1997)';
footnote1 j=r 'GMPCHORO';
```

Produce the choropleth map. The ID statement specifies the variable that is in both the map data set and the response data set that defines map areas. COUTLINE= specifies the color for the map area outlines.

```
proc gmap map=maps.us data=sites;
   id state;
  choro sites / coutline=gray;
run;
quit;
```

Example 5: Creating Maps with Drill-down for the Web

Procedure Features:

CHORO statement options:

- DES=
- DISCRETE
- HTML=
- NAME=

BLOCK statement options:

- BLOCKSIZE=
- DES=
- MIDPOINTS=
- NAME=

ODS Features:

ODS HTML statement :

- BODY=
- CONTENTS=
- FRAME=
- NOGTITLE
- PATH=

Other Features:

BY statement

GOPTIONS statement

LEGEND statement

PATTERN statement

TITLE statement

Sample library member: GMPDRILL

This example shows how to create a 2D choropleth map with simple drill-down functionality for the Web. When this map is displayed in a browser, you can select an area of the map and display additional information about the data.

The example explains how to use the ODS HTML statement and the HTML procedure options to create the drill-down. It shows how to

- □ explicitly name the HTML files and open and close them throughout the program
- □ use BY-group processing with ODS HTML, including storing multiple graphs in one file and incrementing anchor names, catalog entry names, and graphics file names
- □ use the PATH= option to specify the destination for the HTML and GIF files created by the ODS HTML statement
- □ use the NAME= option to name the graphics catalog entries
- □ assign anchor names to the graphics output with the ANCHOR= option in the ODS HTML statement
- □ add an HTML HREF string to a data set to define a link target
- □ assign link targets with the HTML= procedure option
- □ use DES= to control the text of the table of contents entry
- □ suppress the titles in the GIF files and display them in the HTML file.

For more information, see "ODS HTML Statement" on page 164.

The example also illustrates other CHORO and BLOCK statement options.

The program produces one choro map that shows Environmental Protection Agency (EPA) regions and block maps of the states in each region. Each block map shows the number of hazardous waste sites for each state in the selected region. Figure 35.10 on page 1055 shows the map of the EPA regions.

Figure 35.10 Browser View of Regional Map

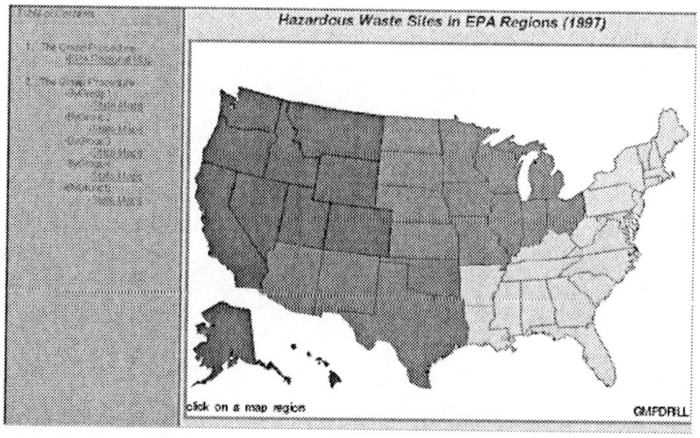

Figure 35.11 on page 1056 shows the block map that appears when you select Region 5 in the map.

Figure 35.11 Browser View of Region 5 Block Map

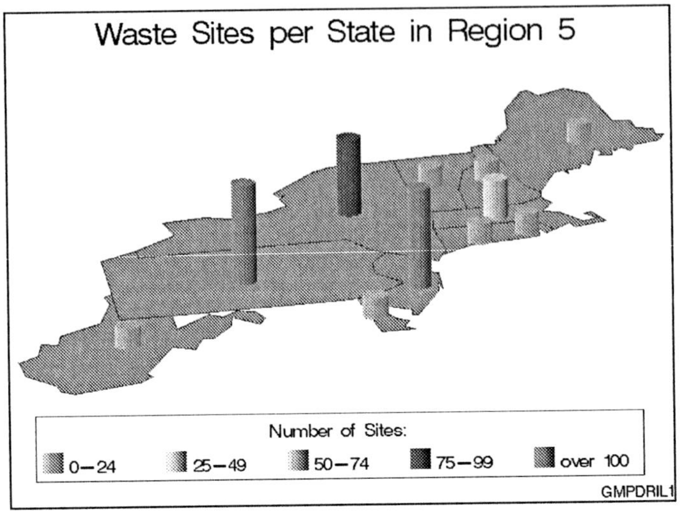

Assign the libref and the Web-server path. FILENAME assigns the fileref ODSOUT, which specifies a destination for the HTML and GIF files produced by the example program. To assign that location as the HTML destination for program output, ODSOUT is specified later in the program on the ODS HTML statement's PATH= option. ODSOUT must point to a Web-server location if procedure output is to be viewed on the Web.

```
libname maps 'SAS-MAPS-library';
filename odsout 'path-to-Web-server-space';
```

Close the ODS Listing destination for procedure output, and set the graphics environment. To conserve system resources, ODS LISTING CLOSE closes the Listing destination for procedure output. Thus, the graphics output is not displayed in the GRAPH window, although it is written to the catalog.

```
ods listing close;
goptions reset=global gunit=pct cback=white
         colors=(black blue green red)
         ftext=swiss htitle=6 htext=3.5;
```

Create the data set SITES. SITES contains the FIPS codes for each state and the total number of hazardous waste sites installed in each state. The STFIPS function converts state postal codes to FIPS state codes.

```
data sites;
   length stcode $ 2;
   input region stcode $ sites;
   state=stfips(stcode);
   datalines;
1  AK  12
4  AL  7
4  AR  12
```

```
2   AZ  10
1   CA  90
1   CO  15
5   CT  15
5   DE  18
4   FL  52
4   GA  15
1   HI  4
3   IA  16
1   ID  8
3   IL  38
3   IN  30
3   KS  10
4   KY  16
4   LA  15
5   MA  30
4   MD  13
5   ME  12
3   MI  72
3   MN  30
3   MO  22
4   MS  1
1   MT  8
4   NC  22
3   ND  0
3   NE  10
5   NH  18
5   NJ  105
2   NM  9
1   NV  1
5   NY  78
3   OH  34
2   OK  10
1   OR  10
5   PA  100
5   RI  12
4   SC  26
3   SD  2
4   TN  14
2   TX  26
1   UT  12
4   VA  25
5   VT  8
1   WA  49
3   WI  40
5   WV  6
1   WY  3
;
```

Add the HTML variable to SITES and create the NEWSITES data set. The HTML variable REGIONDRILL contains the targets for the values of the variable REGION.

```
data newsites;
   length regiondrill $40;
   set sites;
   if region=1 then
      regiondrill='HREF="hazsite_statebody.html#Region1"';
   if region=2 then
      regiondrill='HREF="hazsite_statebody.html#Region2"';
   if region=3 then
      regiondrill='HREF="hazsite_statebody.html#Region3"';
   if region=4 then
      regiondrill='HREF="hazsite_statebody.html#Region4"';
   if region=5 then
      regiondrill='HREF="hazsite_statebody.html#Region5"';
run;
```

Assign graphics options for producing the ODS HTML output. DEVICE=GIF causes the ODS HTML statement to generate the graphics output as GIF files. TRANSPARENCY causes the graphics output to use the Web-page background as the background of the graph.

```
goptions device=gif transparency;
```

Open the ODS HTML destination. BODY= names the file for storing HTML output. CONTENTS= names the HTML file that contains the table of contents to the HTML procedure output. The contents file links to each of the body files written to the HTML destination. FRAME= names the HTML file that integrates the contents and body files. NOGTITLE suppress the graph titles from the SAS/GRAPH output and displays them through the HTML page. PATH= specifies the ODSOUT fileref as the HTML destination for all the HTML and GIF files.

```
ods html body='hazsite_mapbody.html'
         contents='hazsite_contents.html'
         frame='hazsite_frame.html'
         nogtitle
         path=odsout;
```

Define the title and footnote for the map of the EPA regions.

```
title1 'Hazardous Waste Sites in EPA Regions (1997)';
footnote1 h=3 j=l 'click on a map region' j=r 'GMPDRIL1';
```

Define a map pattern for each region. Each PATTERN statement defines one map/plot pattern. The patterns are assigned to the map areas that represent the EPA regions

```
pattern1 value=msolid color=blue;
pattern2 value=msolid color=green;
pattern3 value=msolid color=red;
pattern4 value=msolid color=lime;
pattern5 value=msolid color=cyan;
```

Generate the regional map. The ID statement specifies the variable that defines the map areas and is in both the map data set and the response data set. DISCRETE specifies that each value of the numeric response variable, STATE, be treated as a separate response level. HTML= specifies REGIONDRILL as the variable that contains the targets for the map regions. Specifying HTML variables causes SAS/GRAPH to add an image map to the HTML body file. DES= specifies the description that is stored in the catalog and used in the Table of Contents. NAME= specifies the name of the graphics catalog entry. Because the PATH= destination is a file storage location and not a specific file name, the catalog entry name EPAMAP is automatically assigned to the GIF file.

```
proc gmap map=maps.us data=newsites;
   id state;
   choro region / discrete
                  html=regiondrill
                  coutline=black
                  nolegend
                  des='EPA Regional Map'
                  name='epamap';
run;
quit;
```

Open a new body file for the state maps. Assigning a new body file closes HAZSITE_MAPBODY.HTML. The contents and frame files, which remain open, will provide links to all body files. ANCHOR= specifies the name of the anchor that identifies the link target. This name is automatically incremented when the graphics output is generated. GTITLE uses titles in the GIF files.

```
ods html body='hazsite_statebody.html'
         anchor='Region1'
         gtitle
         path=odsout;
```

Assign new graphics options for ODS HTML output. The active device is still GIF.

```
goptions notransparency
         border;
```

Sort the response data set NEWSITES in order of the BY variable. The data must be in sorted order before running the GMAP procedure with BY-group processing.

```
proc sort data=newsites;
   by region;
run;
```

Define legend characteristics for the state maps. VALUE= specifies text for the legend values that describes the ranges specified by MIDPOINTS= in the BLOCK statement.

```
legend1 shape=bar(3,4)
        label=('Number of Sites'
               position=(top center))
```

```
      value=(j=l '0-24' '25-49' '50-74' '75-99' 'over 100')
      frame;
```

Define a pattern for the map areas. Because the procedure uses BY-group processing to generate the maps, all map areas use the same map pattern.

```
pattern1 value=ms color=gray;
```

Define the patterns for the blocks.

```
pattern2 value=solid color=lipk;
pattern3 value=solid color=cyan;
pattern4 value=solid color=green;
pattern5 value=solid color=blue;
pattern6 value=solid color=red;
```

Suppress the default BY-line and define a title that includes the BY-values. #BYVAL inserts the value of the BY variable into the title of each block map.

```
options nobyline;
title1 'Wastes Sites per State in Region #byval(region)';
footnote1 h=3 j=r 'GMPDRIL2';
```

Generate the block maps for each region. MIDPOINTS= defines the midpoints of the ranges described in the legend. NAME= is a full 8 characters ending in `1` so the incremented names match the regions. NAME= specifies the name of the first catalog entry. Because BY-group processing generates multiple graphs from one BLOCK statement, the name assigned by NAME= is incremented to provide a unique name for each piece of output. These names are automatically assigned to the GIF files. DES= specifies the description that is stored in the catalog and used in the Table of Contents. Because BY-group processing is used, the same description is assigned to all the output.

```
proc gmap map=maps.us data=newsites;
   by region;
   id state;
   block sites / midpoints=(12 37 62 87 112)
                 legend=legend1
                 shape=cylinder
                 blocksize=4
                 coutline=black
                 des='State Maps'
                 name='states01';
run;
quit;
```

Close the ODS HTML destination, and open the ODS Listing destination. You must close the HTML destination before you can view the output with a browser.

```
ods html close;
ods listing;
```

Example 6: Labeling the States on a U.S. Map

Procedure features:
CHORO statement options:
- ANNOTATE=
- NOLEGEND

Other features:
Annotate Facility

Sample library member: GMPLABEL

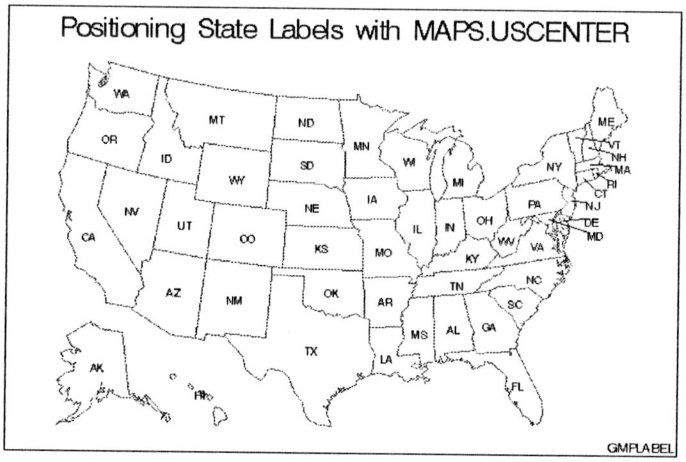

This example uses the MAPS.USCENTER data set and the Annotate facility to add postal code labels to each state. The program first builds an Annotate data set that contains the instructions for drawing the labels. Some of the labels are in the center of the state and others use external labeling with leader lines. The CHORO statement assigns the Annotate data set to the map.

Note: The coordinates in MAPS.USCENTER have been projected to match coordinates in the MAPS.US data set. △

Assign the libref and set the graphics environment.

```
libname maps 'SAS-data-library';
goptions reset=global gunit=pct border cback=white
         colors=(black blue green red)
         ftext=swiss htitle=6 htext=3;
```

Create annotate data set, CENTER, from MAPS.USCENTER. The annotate data set labels each state with a two-letter abbreviation. MAPS.USCENTER provides the x and y coordinates for the labels. FLAG, which is initially turned off, signals when external labeling is in effect. The labels are drawn after the map because the value of WHEN is **a** (after). The FIPSTATE function converts the FIPS codes to state postal codes.

```
data center;
   length function $ 8;
   retain flag 0 xsys ysys '2' hsys '3' when 'a'
          style 'swiss';
   set maps.uscenter
       (where=(fipstate(state) ne 'DC')
       drop=long lat);
```

The FIPSTATE function creates the label text by converting the FIPS codes from MAPS.USCENTER to two-letter postal codes.

```
   function='label';
   text=fipstate(state);
   size=2.5;
   position='5';
```

If the labeling coordinates are outside the state (`OCEAN='Y'`), Annotate adds the label and prepares to draw the leader line. **Note:** OCEAN is a character variable and is, therefore, case sensitive. `OCEAN='Y'` must specify an uppercase Y.

```
   if ocean='Y' then
      do;
         position='6';
         output;
         function='move';
         flag=1;
      end;
```

When external labeling is in effect, Annotate draws the leader line and resets the flag.

```
   else if flag=1 then
      do;
         function='draw';
         size=.25;
         flag=0;
      end;
   output;
run;
```

Define title and footnote for map.

```
title 'Positioning State Labels with MAPS.USCENTER';
footnote j=r 'GMPLABEL';
```

Define pattern characteristics. PATTERN1 defines a single map pattern that is repeated for each of the 50 map areas (states). The pattern is an empty fill with a blue border. VALUE= defines a map/plot pattern, which cannot be used by the blocks. Specifying a color causes PATTERN1 to generate only one pattern definition. REPEAT= specifies the number of times to repeat the pattern definition.

```
pattern1 value=mempty color=blue repeat=50;
```

Produce the choropleth map. NOLEGEND suppresses the legend. ANNOTATE= specifies the data set to annotate the map.

```
proc gmap data=maps.us map=maps.us;
   id state;
   choro state / nolegend
                 annotate=center;
run;
quit;
```

Example 7: Producing a Simple Prism Map

Procedure features:

ID statement

PRISM statement option:

COUTLINE=

Sample library member: GMPPRISM

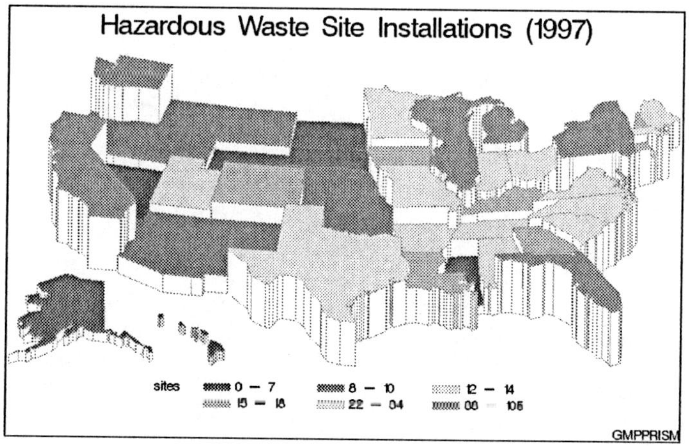

This example produces a prism map of the hazardous waste sites. Since the DISCRETE option is not used, the response variable is assumed to have a continuous range of values. Because neither the LEVELS= nor MIDPOINTS= option is used, the GMAP procedure selects a number of levels based on the number of map areas and then calculates the appropriate response levels.

The map areas use the default pattern, which is a solid fill that rotates through the colors list. Because the colors list is specified in the GOPTIONS statement, all colors are used in the rotation. COUTLINE= outlines the map areas in gray, instead of the default outline color, which is the first color in the list, in this case, BLUE.

Since the XVIEW=, YVIEW=, and ZVIEW= options are not used, the default viewing position, above and to the east and south of the center of the map, is used. Since the XLIGHT= and YLIGHT= options are not used, none of the side polygons of the prisms are shadowed. The light source is the same as the viewing position.

Assign the libref and set the graphics environment. COLORS= specifies the colors list, which is used by the default patterns and outlines. CTEXT= specifies the color for all text.

```
libname maps 'SAS-data-library';
goptions reset=global gunit=pct border cback=white
         colors=(blue green lime lipk cyan red)
         ctext=black ftext=swiss htitle=6 htext=3;
```

Create response data set SITES. This data set contains a map area identification variable, STATE, and a response variable, SITES. The STFIPS function is used to convert the state postal codes to FIPS state codes. STATE contains the FIPS codes for each state and matches the values of STATE in the MAPS.US data set. SITES contains the total number of waste sites installed in the state.

```
data sites;
   length stcode $ 2;
   input region stcode $ sites;
   state=stfips(stcode);
   datalines;
6   AR  12
10  AK  7...moredata lines...
3   WV  6
8   WY  3
;
```

Define title and footnote for the map.

```
title1 'Hazardous Waste Site Installations (1997)';
footnote1 j=r 'GMPPRISM';
```

Produce the prism map. The ID statement specifies the variable in the map data set and the response data set that defines map areas. COUTLINE= specifies the map area outline color.

```
proc gmap map=maps.us data=sites;
   id state;
   prism sites / coutline=gray;
run;
quit;
```

Example 8: Specifying Midpoints in a Prism Map

Procedure features:

PRISM statement options:

- LEGEND=
- MIDPOINTS=
- XLIGHT=
- XVIEW=
- ZVIEW=

Other features:

LEGEND statement

Sample library member: GMPMIDPT

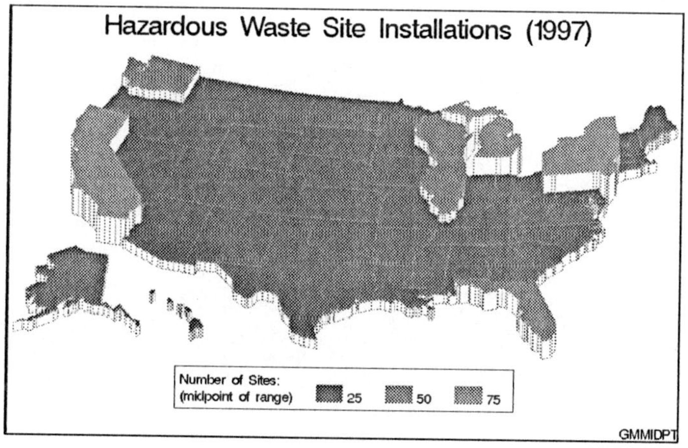

This example explicitly specifies the midpoints for three response levels. Each response level uses the default solid pattern and a color from the colors list.

The example also changes the map viewpoint and light source.

Assign the libref and set the graphics environment. COLORS= specifies the colors list, which is used by the default patterns and outlines. CTEXT= specifies the color for all text.

```
libname maps 'SAS-data-library';
goptions reset=global gunit=pct border cback=white
         colors=(blue green red) ctext=black
         ftext=swiss htitle=6 htext=3;
```

Create response data set SITES. This data set contains a map area identification variable, STATE, and a response variable, SITES. The STFIPS function is used to convert the state postal codes to FIPS state codes. STATE contains the FIPS codes for each state and matches the values of STATE in the MAPS.US data set. SITES contains the total number of waste sites installed in the state.

```
data sites;
   length stcode $ 2;
```

```
   input region stcode $ sites;
   state=stfips(stcode);
   datalines;
6   AR  12
10  AK  7...moredata lines...
3   WV  6
8   WY  3
;
```

Define title and footnote for map.

```
title1 'Hazardous Waste Site Installations (1997)';
footnote1 j=r 'GMPMIDPT';
```

Define legend characteristics. CBORDER= draws a black frame around the legend. If FRAME were specified, it would be BLUE, the first color in the colors list.

```
legend shape=bar(4,4)
       value=(j=l)
       label=('Number of Sites:'
              j=l '(midpoint of range)')
       cborder=black;
```

Produce the prism map. MIDPOINTS= specifies three response levels for the map. XLIGHT= moves the light source to the right and adds shadows to the left-side polygons of the prisms. XVIEW= and ZVIEW= shift the viewing point to the right and upward, respectively. This reduces the number of prisms that are partially hidden by taller neighbors.

```
proc gmap map=maps.us data=sites;
   id state;
   prism sites / midpoints=25 50 75
                 xlight=5
                 xview=.75
                 zview=5
                 legend=legend
                 coutline=gray;
run;
quit;
```

Example 9: Producing a Simple Surface Map

Procedure features:
SURFACE statement

Sample library member: GMPSURFA

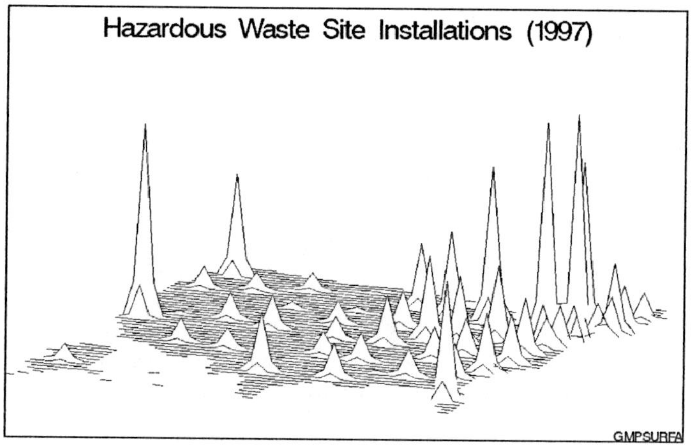

This example produces a surface map that shows the total number of hazardous waste sites in each state in 1997. Because the CONSTANT= and NLINES= options are not used, the GMAP procedure draws a surface that consists of 50 lines and uses the default decay function to calculate spike height and base width. And because the ROTATE= and TILT= options are not used, the map is rotated 70 degrees around the Z axis and tilted 70 degrees with respect to the X axis.

Assign the libref and set the graphics environment. COLORS= specifies the colors list. By default the map uses the first color in the list.

```
libname maps 'SAS-data-library';
goptions reset=global gunit=pct border cback=white
         colors=(black blue green red)
         ftext=swiss htitle=6 htext=3;
```

Create response data set SITES. This data set contains a map area identification variable, STATE, and a response variable, SITES. The STFIPS function is used to convert the state postal codes to FIPS state codes. STATE contains the FIPS codes for each state and matches the values of STATE in the MAPS.US data set. SITES contains the total number of waste sites installed in the state.

```
data sites;
   length stcode $ 2;
   input region stcode $ sites;
   state=stfips(stcode);
   datalines;
6   AR  12
10  AK  7...moredata lines...
3   WV  6
8   WY  3
;
```

Define title and footnote for the map.

```
title1 'Hazardous Waste Site Installations (1997)';
footnote1 j=r 'GMPSURFA';
```

Produce the surface map. The ID statement specifies the variable in the map data set and the response data set that defines the map areas.

```
proc gmap map=maps.us data=sites;
   id state;
   surface sites;
run;
quit;
```

Example 10: Rotating and Tilting a Surface Map

Procedure features:

SURFACE statement options:

- CONSTANT=
- NLINES=
- ROTATE=
- TILT=

Sample library member: GMPROSUR

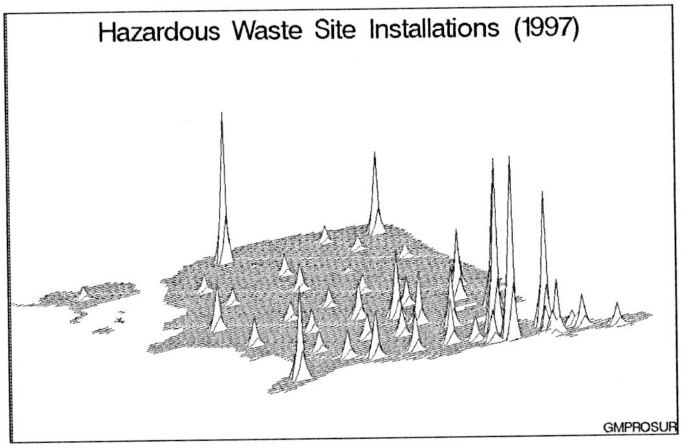

This example tilts and rotates the surface map and uses more lines to draw the surface.

Assign the libref and set the graphics environment.

```
libname maps 'SAS-data-library';
goptions reset=global gunit=pct border cback=white
         colors=(black blue green red)
         ftext=swiss htitle=6 htext=3;
```

Create response data set SITES. This data set contains a map area identification variable, STATE, and a response variable, SITES. The STFIPS function is used to convert the state postal codes to FIPS state codes. STATE contains the FIPS codes for each state and matches the values of STATE in the MAPS.US data set. SITES contains the total number of waste sites installed in the state.

```
data sites;
   length stcode $ 2;
   input region stcode $ sites;
   state=stfips(stcode);
   datalines;
6   AR  12
10  AK  7...moredata lines...
3   WV  6
8   WY  3
;
```

Define title and footnote for the map.

```
title1 'Hazardous Waste Site Installations (1997)';
footnote1 j=r 'GMPROSUR';
```

Produce the surface map. CONSTANT= specifies a value that is less than the default value so the spikes are narrower at the base. NLINES= specifies the maximum number of map lines, which gives the best map shape resolution. ROTATE= and TILT= adjust the map orientation to make the crowded spikes in the northeast portion of the map easier to distinguish.

```
proc gmap map=maps.us data=sites;
   id state;
   surface sites / constant=4
                   nlines=100
                   rotate=40
                   tilt=60;
run;
quit;
```

Example 11: Creating a Map Using the Feature Table

Procedure Features:

ID statement

CHORO statement option:

DISCRETE

ODS Features:

ODS HTML statement:

BODY=

Other Features:

MERGE statement

GOPTIONS statement

Sample library member: GMPSPATL

When you use a feature table on PROC GMAP, you merge the feature table with your response data set before generating a map, storing the combined data in a new data set.

On PROC GMAP, you use the DATA= option to name the combined data set, and you use the ID statement to identify the variable that contains the spatial information.

To illustrate the use of a feature table, assume you want to generate a map of the United States. Rather than using the traditional map data set MAPS.US, you want to use its corresponding feature table. To determine which feature table corresponds to a traditional map data set, look in the MAPS.METAMAPS data set:

- □ The feature table MAPS.US2 corresponds to the traditional map data set MAPS.US.
- □ In MAPS.US2, the values of the variable _MAP_GEOMETRY_ encapsulate the geometry object.

The sample program uses the following procedures and statements:

- □ PROC SORT sorts the current data set, WORK.SITES, by the values of variable STATE. This prepares SITES for a merge with the feature table MAPS.US2, which is delivered with SAS/GRAPH. The variable STATE identifies the map areas in both SITES and MAPS.US2.
- □ PROC SORT sorts the feature table MAPS.US2. The OUT= option specifies that the sorted data be written to a new data set WORK.MAPS.
- □ In the DATA step, the MERGE statement merges the feature table with the response data. The combined data set is saved to a new data set named BOTH. The data set BOTH is stored in WORK, a temporary library. To use the combined data set in other SAS/GRAPH programs, you would need to save the merged data set to a permanent library.
- □ On the PROC GMAP statement, the DATA= option points to the combined data set, BOTH. The ID statement specifies _MAP_GEOMETRY_ as the variable that contains the spatial data. Because both the map and response data are stored in a single data set, the MAP= option is not required on the PROC GMAP statement.

The following example creates the response data set SITES and merges it with the feature table US2. It then uses the combined data set to generate a map as a SAS/GRAPH Control for ActiveX.

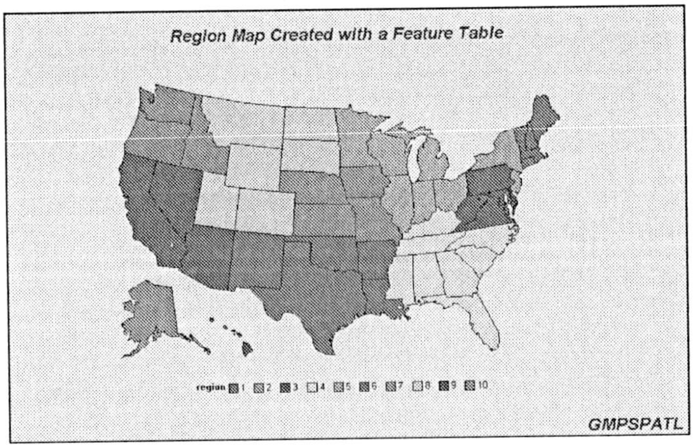

Specify a valid file name and assign the libref for the SAS Maps library. This program generates one HTML file. FILENAME assigns the fileref ODSOUT, which specifies a destination for the HTML file that is produced by the sample program. 'External-html-file' needs to be replaced with the complete path specifying where the files will be located. The following two lines are the only lines that need to be changed to run the program.

```
filename odsout 'external-html-file' ;
libname maps 'SAS-data-library';
```

Create the data set SITES with regional data. Sites contains a region number for each state and the total number of hazardous waste sites in each state. The STFIPS function converts the state postal codes to FIPS state codes.

```
data sites;
   length stcode $ 2;
   input region stcode $ sites;
   state=stfips(stcode);
   datalines;
6   AR  12
10  AK  7
4   AL  12
9   AZ  10
9   CA  90
8   CO  15
1   CT  15
3   DE  18
4   FL  52
4   GA  15
9   HI  4
7   IA  16
10  ID  8
5   IL  38
5   IN  30
7   KS  10
4   KY  16
6   LA  15
1   MA  30
3   MD  13
1   ME  12
5   MI  72
5   MN  30
7   MO  22
4   MS  1
8   MT  8
4   NC  22
8   ND  0
7   NE  10
1   NH  18
2   NJ  105
6   NM  9
9   NV  1
2   NY  78
5   OH  34
6   OK  10
10  OR  10
3   PA  100
1   RI  12
4   SC  26
8   SD  2
4   TN  14
6   TX  26
```

```
8   UT   12
3   VA   25
1   VT   8
10  WA   49
5   WI   40
3   WV   6
8   WY   3
;
```

Sort the response and the feature tables in the order of the BY variable. By default, the first PROC SORT sorts the response data set created in the code above. Both sorted data sets are stored in the SAS temporary library WORK. To allow the data sets to be merged, the same BY variable is used to sort both the response and feature tables.

```
proc sort;
   by state;
run;

proc sort data=maps.us2 out=maps;
   by state;
run;
```

Merge the data sets.

```
data both;
   merge maps sites;
   by state;
run;
```

Specify the ACTIVEX driver and HTML output. To conserve system resources, ODS LISTING CLOSE closes the Listing destination for procedure output. In the program's ODS HTML statement, the BODY= option names the file for storing HTML output. ODSOUT is defined in the beginning of the code in the FILENAME statement.

```
goptions reset=all device=activex;
ods listing close;
ods html body='odsout.html'
path=odsout;
```

Define title and footnote for the map.

```
title1 'Region Map Created with a Feature Table';
footnote1 j=r 'GMPSPATL';
```

Generate the choropleth map using the merged response data set and feature table. The ID variable is the $GEOREF formatted variable containing the spatial information. DISCRETE specifies that each level of REGION is a separate response level.